Marie Syrkin

HBI Series on Jewish Women

Shulamit Reinharz, General Editor
Joyce Antler, Associate Editor
Sylvia Barack Fishman, Associate Editor

The HBI Series on Jewish Women is an innovative book series created by the Hadassah-Brandeis Institute. The series publishes a wide range of books by and about Jewish women in diverse contexts and time periods, of interest to scholars, and for the educated public. The series fills a major gap in Jewish learning by focusing on the lives of Jewish women and Jewish gender studies.

For the complete list of books that are available in this series, please see www.upne.com

Brandeis Series in American Jewish History, Culture, and Life

Jonathan D. Sarna, Editor
Sylvia Barack Fishman, Associate Editor

For a complete list of books that are available in the series, visit www.upne.com

Carole S. Kessner
Marie Syrkin: Values Beyond the Self

Leonard Saxe and Barry Chazan
Ten Days of Birthright Israel: A Journey in Young Adult Identity

Jack Wertheimer, editor
Imagining the American Jewish Community

Murray Zimiles
Gilded Lions and Jeweled Horses: The Synagogue to the Carousel

Marianne R. Sanua
Be of Good Courage: The American Jewish Committee, 1945–2006

Hollace Ava Weiner and Kenneth D. Roseman, editors
Lone Stars of David: The Jews of Texas

Jack Wertheimer, editor
Jewish Education in an Age of Choice

Edward S. Shapiro
Crown Heights: Blacks, Jews, and the 1991 Brooklyn Riot

Marcie Cohen Ferris and Mark I. Greenberg, editors
Jewish Roots in Southern Soil: A New History

Kirsten Fermaglich
American Dreams and Nazi Nightmares: Early Holocaust Consciousness and Liberal America, 1957–1965

Andrea Greenbaum, editor
Jews of South Florida

Sylvia Barack Fishman
Double or Nothing? Jewish Families and Mixed Marriage

George M. Goodwin and Ellen Smith, editors
The Jews of Rhode Island

Marie Syrkin
Values Beyond the Self

❦

Carole S. Kessner

Brandeis University Press
Waltham, Massachusetts

PUBLISHED BY UNIVERSITY PRESS OF NEW ENGLAND
HANOVER AND LONDON

Brandeis University Press
Published by University Press of New England,
One Court Street, Lebanon, NH 03766
www.upne.com
© 2008 by Brandeis University Press
Printed in the United States of America
5   4   3   2   1

This book was published with the generous support of the Lucius N. Littauer Foundation, Inc., and Martin Peretz.

Library of Congress Cataloging-in-Publication Data

Kessner, Carole S., 1932–
Marie Syrkin : values beyond the self / Carole S. Kessner. — 1st ed.
    p.   cm. — (HBI series on Jewish women) (Brandeis series in American Jewish history, culture, and life)
Includes bibliographical references and index.
ISBN 978-1-58465-451-3 (cloth : alk paper)
1. Syrkin, Marie, 1899–1989.   2. Jews—New York (State)—New York—Biography.
3. Jews—New York (State)—New York—Intellectual life.   4. Intellectuals—New York (State)—New York—Biography.   5. Zionists—New York (State)—New York—Biography.
6. Jewish scholars—New York (State)—New York—Biography.   7. Jewish authors—New York (State)—New York—Biography.   8. New York (N.Y.)—Biography.   I. Title.
F128.9.J5S975 2008
974.7'10049240092—dc22
[B]   2008015100

University Press of New England is a member of the Green Press Initiative. The paper used in this book meets their minimum requirement for recycled paper.

For Stephanie, Adam, and Jared Garland;

Zachary and Nathan Landau

Contents

Illustrations follow page 242

Acknowledgments

First of all, I wish to thank Marie Syrkin for being who she was. In her role as mentor and friend, as a public idealist-activist and exemplar of humane values, she taught me much about the quest for meaning in difficult times. This book is my attempt to repay the debt. I thank David Bodansky, Marie Syrkin's son, and Zivia Syrkin Wurtele, her sister, for their generosity of spirit and time, for their encouragement and cooperation in this venture. They are proof of the possibility of transmission of values from one generation to the next.

I am grateful for this opportunity to thank publicly the research institutions and people who made this book possible. I am grateful to the American Jewish Archives in Cincinnati for providing me with two research fellowships, and I thank its Executive Director Gary Zola and the helpful staff, especially Camille Servizzi. I am grateful to the Hadassah-Brandeis Institute and its Director, Shulamit Reinharz, who provided me with two grants; I thank the Lucius N. Littauer Foundation for help with the publication of the book; with enormous gratitude, I thank Martin Peretz whose long commitment to this biography of Marie Syrkin began with awarding me the Marie Syrkin Fellowship at Mishkenot Sha'ananim in Jerusalem as well as generous support for the final publication.

I owe more than the conventional thanks to Phyllis Deutsch, Editor in Chief of University Press of New England, who played the major role in seeing this book through from chapter to chapter. I am grateful for the friends and colleagues who encouraged me during the many years of research and writing, but I especially thank Janet Burstein and Norma Rosen for reading much of the manuscript and giving me their incisive critical insights and Ellen Schiff, Ann Shapiro, and Lorraine Forman for lending a patient ear to my many tales of Marie Syrkin.

Above all, I am lovingly indebted to my husband Thomas Kranidas for his encouragement, patience, and wisdom that have sustained me throughout all the stages of this work.

Marie Syrkin

Introduction

WHEN MARIE SYRKIN died, she left behind a collection of unpublished poems written in the last decade of her life. Her poem, "Second Chance," was composed when she was eighty-seven years old.

SECOND CHANCE

(Haley's Comet returns in 1986)

Only the very old will see Haley's Comet twice.
In 1910 I heard, "Look child, one chance!"
Eager, I saw light streaking.
Now another chance looms in the heavens:
Haley's Comet will keep its date with the sun.

On this sad planet
I have had my fill of seeing.
I do not want to see Haley's Comet again.[1]

Marie Syrkin lived just seven weeks short of ninety years. And what years they were. How fully she lived them. Born on March 23, 1899, she died on February 1, 1989, her life virtually spanning the entire twentieth century. Easily she could have said, "Been there, done that." Her late-life poem belies a lifelong natural optimism; but she had been there and had done that and had seen much. By 1986, perhaps too much.

At this writing we are in the second half of the first decade of the twenty-first century. That long stretch of time since Syrkin's death may account for my own astonishment when I say her name and the response is "Marie who?" That is too bad. What those who have never heard of Marie Syrkin do not know is that she led a life that is the quin-

tessence of the romantic novel, the adventure tale, the report from a
war zone, letters from the home front, letters between lovers, collected
poems, the scholars' research, all these and more; and everything, despite mistakes, with an uncommon humanity, with an unshakeable
sense of justice, with values beyond the self. More astonishing is the
infinite variety of roles she played in her own self-created story: immigrant child, adolescent dreamer, daughter of a famous father, lover,
wife, mother, divorcée, muse, friend, teacher, journalist, polemicist, editor, professor, intellectual, poet, and finally, doyenne of the American
Labor Zionist movement. Her life was both exemplary and unique.

Marie Syrkin, daughter of Nachman Syrkin, the theoretician of
Socialist Zionism, emigrated to the United States at the age of nine. She
was a very beautiful child with an extraordinary intellect who at this
tender age could speak four languages. Within a year of coming to
America, she added English. Marie was an outstanding student in elementary school, but became a mediocre student, except for English, in
high school. She seemed afloat, drifting, dreaming, a voracious reader
of nineteenth-century novels and poetry. There is nothing at this stage
to suggest that Marie Syrkin was to become a leader of Labor Zionism.
If anything, her adolescent diary shows that she might become a woman
of *belles lettres;* and this is what she really always wanted and what would
have happened, had she not chosen at a certain point in her life to
use her literary gifts in the service of Zionism and the Jewish people.
Though she wrote poetry and published it throughout her life, that is
not why she is remembered — or at least should be — today.

In some ways, Marie's life follows the psycho-social model described
by Erik Erikson in his study of gifted men (and there is no reason why
his paradigm cannot be applied to gifted women as well). Erikson describes a period in such a young person's life that he calls a "moratorium"; among the gifted, this takes place between the years twenty and
thirty. During this period, the subject appears to be unfocussed, experiments with different roles, rebels, has feelings of self-doubt, drifts, with
no clear goals. It is, however, a period of preparation for the time when
some event or some act, whether deliberate or unconscious, galvanizes
the individual into self-awareness and she/he begins to achieve goals.
This is a fair description of the trajectory of Marie Syrkin's chosen
course. After the death of her mother when she was sixteen, after an
elopement at the age of eighteen followed by an annulment, a failed second marriage, the death of her first child, the death of her father, and

the abandonment of her hope to earn a Ph.D., at the age of thirty Syrkin emerged from these years with a new sense of purpose and a determination to steer her life on a course she had deliberately chosen. Erikson calls the successful negotiation of the "moratorium" period, "the virtue of fidelity" — that is, the ability to accept society with all its imperfections, to find a place in society to which one can contribute and commit one's self.

With Zionism, Syrkin put her skills to use in written and oral debate, but she also took the practical step of obtaining a teaching license and teaching in a New York City high school in order to care for her son. After marrying the poet Charles Reznikoff in 1930, she continued to teach, to do on-the-spot reporting that took her to Palestine, to Europe, and around America. Under an unusual divorce agreement (even for the present time), Marie's son lived alternate years with his mother and with his father, making it possible for Marie to fulfill her own aspirations without neglecting the care of the child. She would even insist, late in life, that though she lived her life convinced that sexism cannot be condoned, she also agreed with Freud that biology *is* destiny. Here, as in so many of her intellectual encounters, Marie did not hew to a doctrinaire line; her arguments were constructed out of a combination of intellect, experience, and straight-talk.

Often Marie was accused of being too liberal; but just as often she was accused of being a conservative. Willing to take on the formidable adversaries of her time, she sharply rebutted such eminences as Hannah Arendt and Arnold Toynbee, and she publicly rebuked Ben-Gurion, a man she venerated, in the pages of the *Jerusalem Post*. She gave Philip Roth's *Portnoy's Complaint* a bad review. She signed public declarations for the first Peace Now statement and against the Begin government for its Lebanon operation; she signed on to the supporters of the new *Tikkun* magazine, but removed her name after the first issue. Because Marie Syrkin was never afraid of taking risks, her writing is often challenging, frequently controversial, and usually witty. Moreover, it is always readable, never indulging in circumlocution, political euphemism, or academic jargon.

Finally, Marie Syrkin is one of the few American Jewish women intellectuals to have played an active role for over fifty years in the unfolding of events in Europe, Israel, and America, not only as a reporter, but as an actor in the tragic drama of the Holocaust and its aftermath, in the creation of the State of Israel, and at home in America, as well.

At the age of fifty, Marie Syrkin achieved her lifelong dream of becoming an academic. She was hired by Dr. Abram L. Sachar to be a professor of literature at the newly formed Brandeis University. That was a felicitous move for Professor Syrkin as well as for me, for this is where we first met. I had enrolled in Syrkin's course, "Survey of British Literature." I loved literature — but even more, I welcomed the chance to have a female professor. There were no other such role models for women at Brandeis in those years. In the aftermath of a dashed-off paper on *King Lear*, written over a very busy December vacation (and partially derived from a cousin's paper on the same subject), I awaited the return of my work. But there was to be no grade — only the words, "see me." I did. I was given a chance to rewrite without hope of a grade better than B+; but I was also invited to a home-cooked dinner to discuss *King Lear*. That was the inauspicious beginning of a lifelong friendship.

After I left the Boston area, Marie and I kept in touch by handwritten letter, by telephone, and sometimes in person during her periodic visits to New York or my visits to Boston. We saw more of each other once she retired to Manhattan. But after she moved to Santa Monica, we had to return to our telephone and mail connection — no e-mail then. But I did visit Marie in California a number of times — she had given me an open invitation to make use of the sleep sofa in her living room, and over the years, I did so.

In mid-January of 1989, I went once more to spend a week with my friend and mentor at her Santa Monica apartment, this time to gather material for an article in *Midstream* that was to be a celebration of her ninetieth birthday on March 23. A few days after my visit, Marie fell into a coma, and blessedly within a week, on February 1, she died. I say "blessedly" because when I arrived at her apartment she immediately asked me, "What would you do if I collapsed while you were here? Would you revive me?" Seriously taken aback, I responded, "What would you want me to do?" "If my mind is gone, don't," was her peremptory reply.

I soon noted that Marie's mind certainly was not gone! The week was filled with her acute answers to my questions, sometimes with her sharp and sometimes less than gentle retorts to my own pronouncements, sometimes with gossip and sometimes with memories. I recalled how a few years before in New York we had gone together to see a play about Emily Dickinson, *The Belle of Amherst*. Upon leaving the theater, Marie had commented that she liked Julie Harris, but the play left out "the dark side" of the poet. This memory led to our decision to go to the movies the next day to see *The Dead*, based on the James Joyce story; she loved it and was especially moved by the two elderly sisters, especially the one who sang "Arrayed for the Bridal." That night she proposed that we watch one of her favorite TV programs: *Murder, She Wrote*, starring Angela Lansbury as a woman writer-detective. Surprised as I was by this pop-culture choice, it was not hard to see the connection among play, story, and TV serial. It was feminism. Marie was drawn to the portrayal of women's experience in the arts and in all stages of life. Hadn't she herself chosen to write the biography of her friend Golda Meir, a woman she held up as a model of feminism? And hadn't she recently written the foreword to the second edition of the 1932 volume of *The Plough Woman*, memoirs of young women Zionists who had emigrated to Palestine during the first years of the twentieth century?

For all her adult life, Marie considered herself to be a feminist with feminist concerns, but she could not be called ideological. Her feminism was complex and idiosyncratic and must be interpreted in the context of its historical moment. After all, she was born into feminism, her mother having been a socialist revolutionary activist. In a 1983 interview in *Moment* magazine, Marie remarked, "You don't have to tell me to keep my family name; I kept my name long before I knew that was the thing to do. I've always used my name, through several marriages, strange as that may appear. And you don't have to tell me that a woman has to be independent. I was always independent, and very energetically so."[2]

By the 1960s and 1970s in the early years of the contemporary women's movement, Syrkin, then in her post-retirement years, took some positions that appeared to be in opposition to more radical feminist programs. When the movement adopted the anti-Freudian slogan that "biology is *not* destiny," Marie Syrkin demurred. After participating in a conference on Jewish feminism held in Jerusalem in 1984, in which leading feminists took part, Marie wrote a piece in *Midstream* titled "Does Feminism Clash with Jewish National Need?" Much of the agenda was predictable, she wrote, but a number of intriguing questions arose. Obviously, one was the question posed in the title. This was surprising because it came from religious feminists who suggested that there may be a conflict not only between feminism and Orthodox Judaism, but also between feminism and the national survival of the Jewish people. "Insofar as feminism liberates women from traditional roles and encourages life-styles antithetical to procreation and the fostering of the family," she points out, "feminist ideology affects the Jewish future. How reconcile a Jewish agenda aimed at preserving a threatened national entity and the feminist platform?"

Syrkin does not answer the question. She simply states that

freedom of choice is a right, not a privilege. Freedom demands that it be exercised honestly in response to genuine individual needs, not out of deference to fashion. Whatever the choice, a price will be paid by men as well as women. Only the most fortunate, energetic, and gifted can have the best of both worlds. And, as has already been mentioned, Jewish feminists, religious and secular, are troubled by the conflict between feminist and national agenda, in addition to the conflict women face between deep emotional impulses and compelling desires for intellectual and professional growth. Catch-phrases like "anatomy is not destiny" cast no light. Anatomy obviously affects destiny, though it need not determine the outcome.

During our last week together, Marie showed no signs of intellectual impairment, though she had deteriorated physically. She was visibly frail, and, though uncomplaining, in constant pain from the cancer she refused to reveal to me. Nonetheless, her voice was vigorous, her words straightforward, with the timbre of a much younger and stronger woman, and with the assurance and lucidity that marked the seventy years of her extraordinary career. I had come to interview Marie for an essay that was to have been a celebration of the marvel of her still acute mind; but, unfortunately, it became instead a memorial essay. I choose to repeat some of that *Midstream* memorial here, because it had been written with the clarity of immediate recall:

In these last days before her death, she took final stock of her lifelong work as a Labor Zionist. Aware of the current trend among many historians of revisiting the events and devaluing the accomplishments of Zionism, she asserted in her still strong and contentious voice, "something tremendous has been achieved!" Yes, she recognized the present difficulties and failures of Labor Zionism, but she insisted that those who now proclaim that the "myth" of Israel is dead are mistaken. It was no fable. Israel, she maintained, is an exemplar of what *can* be done. "Even if it lasts only forty, fifty years, what that state achieved can never be erased because it shows the potential of idealism. It achieved something in the political structure of the world. The phrase 'next year in Jerusalem' became clothed in flesh as the vision became reality to a greater extent than could have been imagined." Not one to gloss over even the most lamentable of facts, Marie admitted to regret over the present state of affairs — the re-election of Yizhak Shamir — but she went on to explain that the adaptation of the dream to realities is "merely the price of survival. I regret," she said sadly, "the failure of Labor to increase its hold over the population — because of the errors of Labor and the megalomania of Likud, but still Israel has lived, it suffered, it flourished. It is not lost and there is no telling how history will unfold. Study the record," she advised, "and you will see that it was done with blood, sweat, and tears; the so-called 'myth' was created by people who did not participate."

My last days with Marie were a gift. She would sit curled in a large wing chair that accentuated her frail small frame, her back against one arm, her legs incongruously draped over the other arm as we sipped tea, recalled past events, and argued current affairs. She was preparing a rebuttal to Benny Morris' book *The Birth of the Palestinian Refugee Problem*. "He's Jacob Morris' son, you know. His father's turning in his grave," she muttered. Had she lived to see Morris' revision of the book, she would have raised an eyebrow and smiled in smug satisfaction. She was, however, delighted with my gift to her — Yehoshefat Harkabi's then-new book, *Israel's Fateful Hour*. It was, she said, exactly what she wanted. In our last encounter, Marie's wit had been sharp, and so, often, was her tongue. Yet she had not lost the capacity for tenderness and friendship. Her clear dark eyes retained their glint, and her celebrated beauty was still apparent. The opening lines of a poem by John Donne, one of her favorite poets, came to me as we sat talking for the last time.

Nor Spring nor Summer beauty hath such grace
As I have seen in one Autumnal face.

PART I

Chapter 1

Marie's Birthright

MARIE SYRKIN'S LIFE reads like a gripping novel, full of romance, history, poetry, and action, all quickened by intellect, conviction, and most of all, wit. Born the only child of Nachman Syrkin and Bassya Osnos, hers was a blessed event that assured an impressive but daunting birthright. Marie's arrival on March 22, 1899, in Bern, Switzerland, two years after the First Zionist Congress and six years before the 1905 Russian Revolution, was exactly nine months after her parents' marriage. But as Marie Syrkin was to write, with clarity of hindsight some sixty years later, "No doubt it would have been more prudent, in view of my mother's ambitions and my father's finances, if they had waited before having a child." She was quick to add, however, that it was clear to her that her father took pleasure in her prompt arrival and that her birth was not unplanned. "My father," she explains, "was serious about love; marriage was a consecration, not a sexual convenience and only by an immediate readiness for its true fulfillment could love be honored."[1] This sentiment was to bear heavily on the course of his daughter's own life.

Bassya Osnos and Nachman Syrkin had met at the first Zionist Congress—Nachman, the erudite, moralistic theoretician of Socialist Zionism, Bassya a headstrong political activist who smuggled revolutionary pamphlets into Russia in the false bottom of her trunk. Marie's personality undoubtedly was shaped by both of these professional idealists, but Bassya, a true feminist who had been studying medicine before her marriage, suffered from tuberculosis for most of her married life and died when her daughter was only fifteen. Because of the death of her mother, psychobiography must take into account Marie's love-hatred for her father, who was an erudite ethical idealist, yet possessed of a blazing temperament that vented itself publicly in scathing argument and privately (as Marie Syrkin herself has described it) in a zealous "dedicated hardship" (*Memoir* 153).

Bassya and Nachman had gone to Bern to study medicine, but for quite a number of reasons — financial, philosophical, political, emotional, and medical — neither one completed the course to become a physician. In 1898, at the age of thirty, Nachman Syrkin had enrolled as a second-year medical student at the University of Bern, having already completed his first year at the *Königliche Friedrich-Wilhelms Universität* in Berlin. Perhaps for the first time in his life he tried to make a completely practical choice. At the age of thirty, Syrkin was virtually penniless; he had not completed his earlier studies in philosophy in Berlin, but he had published his first book in 1896 entitled *Geschichts-Philosophische Betrachtungen* [Observations on the Philosophy of History] (*Memoir* 58). The thesis of this work, like so much of his later thinking and writing, swam against the prevailing tide — this time against the pervasive Marxist interpretation of history as essentially determined by economic and social forces. Though he was a committed lifelong socialist, Syrkin opposed orthodox Marxist ideology, which envisioned a classless society as a necessary and desired consequence of class struggle. Syrkin also opposed the Marxist belief that its goal could be hastened by activist revolutionary organizations — in particular, the Communist Party.

Syrkin's opposition to Marxist orthodoxy was rooted in his commitment to the Jewish people. He feared not only that Jewish bourgeois liberalism would lead to assimilation, but also that socialist internationalism would result in the abandonment of Jewishness. Moreover, he could not accept the idea that history is determined solely by socioeconomic forces or, by its corollary, that man, being fundamentally passive, is merely swept along by the force of the current. Syrkin could not endorse a theory that so reduced the role of the individual in the shaping of history; rather, he argued for the power and significance of voluntarism, the exercise of human will. In a latter-day amalgam of Biblical morality, prophecy, and history, Nachman Syrkin conceived the seemingly paradoxical theory of socialist Zionism: the synthesis of Jewish nationalism and socialism. Paradoxical as socialist Zionism might appear, for Nachman Syrkin it was a logical conclusion. Far from being a contradiction in terms, Syrkin arrived at his theory of socialist Zionism through inductive reasoning, from the theoretical and practical consequence of Jewish life lived in Russia under the autocratic and antisemitic rule of the Czars.

Syrkin was born in 1868 in Mogilev, Belorussia, during the reign of

Czar Alexander II. For the Jews of Russia, this was a period of political contradictions, economic deprivation, social restriction, intellectual ferment, and rising revolutionary activity. In the year of Nachman's birth, Czar Alexander II had been on the throne for thirteen years following a period of brutal measures against the Jews that had been enacted by his father Nicholas I. Nicholas was notorious in the Jewish community of Russia for countless draconian measures against the liberals in the country, against religious and ethnic minorities, and against any alien group that resisted assimilation. To implement his goal of national unity, Nicholas began his rule with a decree announcing compulsory military service for Jewish boys between the ages of twelve and twenty-five, a measure that would remain in the memory of the Jewish community as one of the most ruthless edicts in their history.[2] Nicholas' reign had been so oppressive that it took nothing more than his death in 1855 to encourage the Jews to hold optimistic expectations for life under the new Czar (Sachar). Indeed, Alexander II appeared at first to promise an enlightened regime; he quickly became known as the Czar-Liberator and was hailed by jubilant throngs. But it would not be long before reaction set in, for Alexander II was committed to a policy of Russification. Moreover, unfortunately for the Jews, there remained a legacy from Czar Nicholas: the legally authorized territories of residence for Jews known as the restrictive Pale of Settlement, which under the new Czar persisted and was to remain in force until it finally was abolished in one of the first acts of the Soviet regime (Sachar 202–210).

Such was the legacy of the reigns of Nicholas I and Alexander II in the province of Mogilev, Belorussia, in the year of Nachman Syrkin's birth. The town of Mogilev had been founded in the sixteenth century by wealthy Jewish merchants who had leased the collection of customs duties. A poll tax list of 1766 showed a Jewish population of about 650 registered Jews who thereafter prospered, and grew in number and commercial success despite harsh governmental restrictions as well as brutal local hostilities. By 1847, almost 8,000 Jews were registered in Mogilev.[3]

As for the religious life of the Jewish community, the Mogilev Jews had early on been very much influenced by Habad Hasidism, a form of Hasidism that stressed intellectuality. But perhaps because of the success of a few wealthy industrialists whose commercial activities extended from Riga to Danzig and from Koenigsberg to the Crimea, the breezes of *Haskalah* (enlightenment) slowly began to waft over the Pale, dropping seeds of modernization and secular studies onto fertile soil. It

should be understood, however, that the goal of the *maskilim* (enlight-
eners) was acculturation, not assimilation — a program summed up in
the oft-quoted advice of a later proponent of *Haskalah,* Judah Leib
Gordon: "Be a Jew at home and a man in the street." In most towns and
villages, enlightenment was a slow process, and throughout the nineteenth century, the Jews in the Pale of Settlement suffered from a morass
of conditions that included stifling residential and travel restrictions,
political oppression, relentless economic pressures, social exclusion, and
periodic pogroms. In the face of a historically hostile and dangerous
world, they sought their escape in the insularity of the ghetto with its
infrangible religious faith, in the consoling bulwark of *Halakhah* (law)
and *minhag* (custom), though these all too often degenerated into
cramped piety and distorted lives. Some towns and cities, however,
were better than others at providing a fecund ground for the new ideas
of enlightenment. Mogilev was one of them. By the 1860s and into the
1870s, the brilliant intellectual, Paul (Pavel) Axelrod, who was to become a pioneer of early Marxist socialism and a mentor to Lenin and
Trotsky, lived and was educated in Mogilev. Here, Axelrod actively
spread *Haskalah* ideas among the youth (*Judaica* Mogilev). Almost certainly, Nachman Syrkin heard his tidings of new possibilities.

In this mix of governmental edicts, religious devotion, and intellectual awakening, Nachman Syrkin grew up. His daughter Marie describes the ambience of Mogilev as the young boy matured.

Any intellectually eager, sensitive youth, fascinated by the riches of European
culture seething with dangerous, "new," revolutionary ideas, impatient of the
ancient shelter of the synagogue, would soon find himself, literally and symbol-
ically, houseless on a Western Street, trying to construct a new home, fashioned
of ideologies and dreams. That such a lad would be a rebel goes without saying. It is easy enough to perceive what he would discard. More perplexing is the
question of what he would keep. In the welter of conflicts Nachman Syrkin,
born in Mo[g]ilev within the Pale, on February 12, 1868, was to make a singular choice and affirm a dual allegiance. (*Memoir* 13)

Nachman Syrkin was brilliant, but he also was lucky: he was born
into a comfortable middle-class mercantile family. Notwithstanding the
Russian restrictions on Jewish life, the Syrkins were able to provide their
son with whatever advantages money could buy — and in the context of
Czarist Russia, money could buy physical comforts, a moderate amount

of privileges, but most importantly, it could buy secular education. The distribution of labor in the Syrkin menage was not unusual for Jewish life in Eastern Europe. Zivia Syrkin, Nachman's mother, was the main provider, an energetic and exceptionally shrewd businesswoman. Nachman's father Eliezer Syrkin, a direct descendant of Rabbi Joel Sirkes (1561–1640), one of the greatest Talmudic scholars of Poland whose grave in Cracow remained a shrine for pilgrimage until 1917, continued in the family tradition of serious scholarship and pious devotion. As Eliezer's grandaughter, Marie, reports, he was "a gentle, retiring scholar, more at home in the study poring over a *blatt Gemora* than in examining ledgers" (*Memoir* 13). Perhaps that famous forefather, Joel Sirkes, was to have a greater influence on Nachman than his actual father had. Famous for independent judgement, Sirkes had ruled in favor of allowing rabbis to accept fees for services rendered and had broadened the practice of selling *Chametz* (leavened grain) to a Gentile by allowing the sale of the room in which it was found. He performed a marriage on the Sabbath to protect the life of an orphan; he could find no logic in the prohibition against listening to a woman's voice; and he permitted church melodies that were universal in appeal to be sung in the synagogue. Though Sirkes was completely devoted to *halakha* (law), he feared that its codification, along with an increasing dependence on the *Shulhan Arukh* (Joseph Caro's code of Jewish Law) would thwart interpretation (*Judaica* Sirkes, Joel). Sirkes' heterodox cast of mind seems to have traveled two centuries down the genetic path to take up residence in the mind of his descendant, Nachman Syrkin.

Curiously, however, only one generation later, Nachman's daughter Marie failed to make the right connection. She saw her father's pride of ancestry as merely holding fast to tradition. "In my youth" she recalls,

my father's obvious pride in his *Yichus-brief,* a long parchment on which the family tree of the Syrkins, beginning with the famous Rabbi Joel, was delineated seemed to me a shocking bourgeois deviation. A true radical, I thought, should be less conscious of genealogy. But my father, though he early broke away from his orthodox moorings, never concealed his appreciation of the long line of rabbis and scholars from which he sprang—the only aristocracy, that of intellectual merit, which he was ever to respect. (*Memoir* 14)

Marie herself was so detached from Judaism as a religion that she seems to have little understanding of the "intellectual merit" of her famous

forebear and less inclination to research it. She can only conclude that
"one gets a vivid sense of the iconoclast's obstinate sense of tradition
from the yellowing, crumbling, documents which Syrkin reverently preserved through a turbulent lifetime. Amid the exiles and uprootings of
his existence the rigid, ordered world from which he sprang remained
deeply precious to the man who, on the surface, became its foe" (*Memoir* 14). Nachman Syrkin's daughter could not grasp how cleverly Joel
Sirkes' great intellectual creativity operated within the apparently narrow margins of tradition and law. Presumably, her father could.

If Nachman Syrkin and his equally secularly educated siblings would
no longer follow in their father's religious footsteps, if after Eliezer died
in 1902 they readily could sell their patrimonial shares of five prayer-
stalls in five different synagogues in Minsk to strangers, this did not dis-
courage their mother's last exhortation to them. Zivia Syrkin was a superb businesswoman, she was unusually literate in spoken and written
Yiddish and Russian, and according to her grandaughter Marie, she was
rumored to have known French as well; but she also was a pious Jew.
Zivia's grief over her children's loss of faith is poignantly revealed in a
letter in Yiddish she wrote to her favored son Nachman shortly before
she died. In what Marie describes as "a kind of informal will directed to
all her children," Zivia first specifies the arrangements for her personal
possessions and then expresses her personal concerns. "Keep your father's *Yahrzeit* (anniversary of death); my own *Yahrzeit* you will know
yourselves. I will ask you nothing more; I know it won't help." The pain
in those last three words is unmistakable. She knows only too well that
the secular education she had provided for her children—one son became a doctor and a daughter became a dentist—led them to abandon
their religious heritage. Especially bitter was the path that her son Nachman was following. To this child she writes,

And you, dear Nachke, I want to remind you of the time when you stood at
your father's deathbed and he told you that there was a greater world than the
one we see. . . . Remember this, children, in this epoch we are living through,
strive to remain warm Jews, and let your children know they are Jews. Struggle
for the Jewish people and may the Jewish people not perish because of you.
This, children, is my wish and I hope that you will all fulfill it. (*Memoir* 16)

And indeed, her beloved Nachke did fulfill her last wish, as did his
daughter Marie, both having devoted their entire lives to the cause of

the Jewish people. Yet Zivia's grandaughter, seemingly unaware of the fact that the document is quite traditional, describes it as "a kind of informal will." Just such a letter derives from the medieval literary genre popularly known among Jews as an "ethical will," in which a dying father instructs his children in ethical teachings and leaves them a personal moral legacy. Ethical wills became customary in a great many families and Zivia Syrkin surely was familiar with this centuries-old Jewish literary form; two secularized generations later Marie Syrkin appears to be completely unacquainted with the tradition.

The Syrkin family lived in Mogilev until Nachman was sixteen. His early education was provided by a *rebbe* who tutored him at home, but when he was fortunate enough to be admitted to the local gymnasium, his Hebrew education was not terminated and private teachers continued to come to the house. When he was about sixteen, his family moved to Minsk. Here, he completed his education at the local Russian high school. In the city of Mogilev, where Nachman Syrkin spent his childhood, there had been a few *maskilim* among the well-to-do merchants as early as the late eighteenth century. But the major force in Mogilev was religious — *Habad Hasidism*. In Minsk, however, the city that the Syrkins moved to in 1884, the situation was quite different. Here the *mitnaggedim* (opponents of *Hasidism*) were far more prominent than the *Hasidim*. The *mitnaggedim* were followers of the Vilna *Gaon* (genius), Elijah ben Solomon Zalman (1720–1797), and were opposed to the charismatic, wonder-worker Hasidic rabbis, as well as to the Hasidic emphasis on the emotional and nonrational aspects of Judaism. The *mitnaggedim* instead stressed intellectuality, rationality, and skepticism. It might be said that the *Hasidim* were the party of Kabbalist mysticism and ritualism, whereas the *mitnaggedim* were the party of the preeminence of Talmudic study, though quite opposed to Talmudic *pilpul* (hairsplitting argument).

One of the most important communities in Russia, Minsk was a bustling city packed with opportunities for restless developing minds — a rich medium for young Nachman Syrkin's intellectual development. Jews had been in Minsk since the fifteenth century, and by the last decade of the nineteenth century, the Jewish population of the city was over 50 percent of the total. It is hardly surprising, then, that several of the Jewish schools had been including secular studies since the 1840s, and by midcentury, a group of *maskilim* had formed. Despite the fact that these *maskilim* were primarily interested in the war against religious

obscurantism, economic impotence, and cultural insularity, they nonetheless have been credited with a major role in the rise of the Jewish socialist movement because they had "secularized the outlook of tens of
thousands of their fellow Jews" (Sachar 337).

Plainly, by the time the Syrkin family moved to Minsk, the false hopes
held by the Jews during the reign of Alexander II had been completely
crushed. During his thirty years on the throne, Alexander actually had
enacted a number of edicts that improved the lives of the Russian Jews,
such as lifting some residential restrictions and easing admission into
governmental service. With motives less than altruistic, the Czar's hidden agenda was to make use of Jewish money, tap Jewish brains, and
take advantage of their skills. At first, he believed that the oppressive
actions of his predecessors were counterproductive to his dream of
amalgamation and that reform would be a better tactic. A natural Slavo-
phile, he abandoned his early accession to "Western liberalism" to openly
embrace Russian Orthodoxy in religion and nationalism in politics.
"Russification" — the fusion of the ethnic minorities with the Russian
people — was his true ideal (*Judaica,* Alexander II). But by the 1870s,
Alexander's reforms had come to a full stop. The long and bloody Polish revolt against Russian rule liberated his natural predilection for
reactionary ideas. Moreover, in the hinterland, the Russian population
increasingly resented the rising Jewish middle class and envied their apparent success, despising the famous railroad and banking barons, such
as the Frankels, Gunzbergs, Kronenbergs, among the small but elite
group of influential and wealthy Jews. In the face of complaints from
Russian tradesmen as well as the Jews' refusal to fuse with the Russians,
Alexander abruptly canceled his early liberal policies and began a program of intense reaction. Employing a combination of paid informers
and secret service police, the Czar ordered a hunt for liberals and subversive minorities — especially the Jews — throughout the empire. The
government's hostile attitudes could not help but spill over to the native
population, and inevitably there were sporadic flare-ups against the Jews,
including occasional charges of ritual murder. It became patently clear
that under this Czar, there would be no deliverance for the Jews of Russia. If any illusions still remained, they were eradicated on March 13,
1881, when Alexander II was assassinated by a bomb planted by revolutionaries; his son, Alexander III, who succeeded him, immediately
placed the blame on the Jews, whom he regarded as subversive liberals
and revolutionaries.

In the spring, a surge of government-inspired pogroms spread through southern Russia, ravaging over one hundred Jewish communities. Blamed for the Czar's death, the whole Jewish population was considered guilty of regicide because of their espousal of "liberal ideas." The official government position was to condone the pogroms — even to incite them — because Alexander's infamous Minister of the Interior, Count Ignatiev, a rabid antisemite, reported to Alexander that the pogroms were, in fact, the fault of the Jews themselves who had gained control of commerce and industry, acquired too much land, and "by means of their unity have succeeded in exploiting the main body of the population, particularly the poor, hence arousing them to protest, which has found distressing expression in acts of violence."[4]

Immediately, Czar Alexander ordered a government inquiry. His inquiry resulted in the so-called "temporary laws," not to be repealed until the Russian revolution in March 1917. As persecution was creatively escalated and the restrictions ruthlessly interpreted, the Jews of Russia were driven further and further along the road to hopeless destitution. These "temporary" laws were ever after to be remembered as the infamous May Laws of 1882.[5] These were the laws that changed the course of modern Jewish history, and they were the laws that were in place in 1884 when Nachman Syrkin and his family moved from Mogilev to Minsk.

In Minsk, Nachman completed his high school education. Exposed to the political and religious ferment of the city's intelligentsia, Syrkin soon began to develop his own analyses and solutions. The bustling city of Minsk had to have been exciting for a youth with a streak of rebellious independence, a sharp intellect, and a keen awareness of the severity of the "Jewish problem." Jewish Minsk of Syrkin's youth reflected every facet of the response to the death of illusion and the reality of dead-end. The blandishments of Russification had ended in disillusionment, for there could be no fusion with Russia without forfeit of Jewish particularity; the attraction of socialism required a similar surrender of self to internationalism; the resort to communism and revolution too often carried the price of blood and violence in addition to renunciation of religion; Zionism as a political movement was yet to be born; and emigration to America was a more popular escape than *aliyah* to *Eretz Israel*, for immediate opportunity offered the masses greater inducement than pipe dreams of the future.

If the majority of the able Jews of Russia soon would choose to respond to Emma Lazarus' gracious invitation of 1883, there were those intellectuals challenged by Leo Pinsker's call for auto-emancipation. A physician by profession, Pinsker and other well-known figures of the *Haskalah,* such as Moses Lilienblum and Peretz Smolenskin, realized that the Jewish Enlightenment had failed to live up to their expectations; emancipation was not at hand. In 1882, Pinsker published his famous work *Auto-Emancipation,* in which he analyzed the psychological and social roots of antisemitism and called for Jewish nationalism as a solution to the increasing antisemitic malevolence and brutality. His call for self-liberation hardly arose out of the blue; nor was it simply an immediate response to the wave of pogroms that had erupted in Russia in 1881. The idea emerged out of Pinsker's awareness of the rise of nineteenth-century European nationalism, his despair that *Haskalah* could never result in emancipation and that emancipation itself would not solve the Jewish problem. Hence, his participation in the *Hibbat Zion* (Love of Zion) movement, a forerunner of Zionism that advocated emigration to *Eretz Israel* and the establishment of Jewish agricultural settlements rather than European political activity.

In 1882, the year that Pinsker published his stunning call for auto-emancipation, Nachman Syrkin, a bright, spirited fourteen-year-old boy living in relative comfort in Mogilev, was probably not terribly concerned with the various political movements. This is not to say that there were no early signals. The brilliant Zionist leader, Shmarya Levin, reports in his autobiography that he had met Nachman in Minsk in 1888. Levin writes that by this time, the twenty-year-old Nachman already "had an interesting past. First, he had been expelled from the gymnasium in Mohilev, not for lack of ability but for impudence against a principal. But this was not a personal clash. The principal made a remark that was directed against the Jewishness of Syrkin, and Syrkin's reply was haughty and defiant. Second, Syrkin had already passed some time in London with a group of Jewish actors. He had even manufactured some dramas for the Yiddish theater."[6] But four years earlier in 1884, when the family moved to Minsk, sixteen-year-old Nachman was a boy without worldly experience. Much would happen in the next few years. Indeed, four years later, when Levin first met Syrkin, Levin recalls that at the age of twenty, Syrkin already was "seeking the synthesis of his two ideals — Jewish nationalism and socialism" (Levin 253).

Nachman Syrkin was fully committed to his unique hybrid philosophy when he arrived in Berlin in 1888 to study at the *Königlichen Friedrich-*

Wilhelms Universität in the Faculty of Philosophy. Because it was almost impossible for a Jew to be admitted to a Russian university, large numbers of Jewish students went abroad to Germany or Switzerland in pursuit of education. Berlin was a favored venue where there was "a large colony of Russian Jewish students . . . with an intense life of its own and with almost no contact with either the German Jewish or German students. The ideological currents that ran hot in this group were peculiar to it. The intellectual caliber was high as is seen from the number of future leaders to be found concentrated in the colony" (*Memoir* 28). Nachman Syrkin's circle included Chaim Weizmann, Leo Motzkin, and Leib Wilensky, among other distinguished Zionists. It was Syrkin, Motzkin, and Wilensky who founded the Russian Jewish Scientific Society, which provided an electrically charged platform for the fierce ideological disagreements between the socialists and the nationalists. The debates were heated and often vitriolic, but Syrkin's position remained *sui generis,* for he was both a socialist and a nationalist. Speaking of his Berlin student days, his daughter Marie writes, "'Crazy Nachman,' they called him without even paying him the compliment of taking him seriously" (*Memoir* 33). But if his peers dismissed his ideas as idiosyncratic absurdity, they did admire his debating gifts, particularly his sharp satiric lunges, his ironic retorts, and his impulsive vitriolic outbursts. These always added spice to the boiling brew. One other situation that astonished Syrkin's friends was the austere level of his material comfort. He had only minimal financial help from his parents, who had five more sons and daughters to be educated. Perhaps because he was so public about his break with religion and his attacks on the synagogue — despite his wide Hebrew scholarship and devotion to the Jewish people — and perhaps because he was something of a worry and a disappointment, more help was not forthcoming (*Memoir* 31). Syrkin tried to get by with lessons, translations, and a few articles by borrowing from Shmarya to pay Chaim, but his subsistence was so Spartan that his roommate, Shmarya Levin, was moved to write:

His personal needs were so modest that he could be said to be living on the absolute minimum possible to civilized man. . . . But, as against this, I have seldom met a Jew with the same national daring and the same vast national appetite as Syrkin. The man who lived cheaply on the absolute human minimum was in his nationalism content with nothing less than the maximum. (as qtd. in *Memoir* 29, 30)

Despite his unusually creative ways to stave off hunger, such as writing for trial offers of sausage, new cheeses, herring, cereal, these food samples were not enough to maintain even minimal nutrition. Subsisting below the poverty level, Syrkin decided to try practicality, and thus, in 1898, he left Berlin and philosophy for Bern and medical studies.

The decision must have been very difficult because the eight years in Berlin had not been without academic success. In 1896, his first book, *Geschichts-Philosophishe Betrachtungen* (Observations on the Philosophy of History) had been published in German, and now he was a second year medical student at the University of Bern. This move could not fail to fail, for Syrkin was a born philosopher, a lover of words and ideas, not of science. Ultimately, he gave up medicine and returned to philosophy, receiving his Ph.D. in 1903 for a dissertation entitled *Empfindung und Vorstellung* (Sensation and Idea). It had taken Nachman Syrkin fifteen years to complete his degree.

That it took fifteen years is not so surprising. Not only were the odds heavily against him financially, but also he was as immersed in political action as he was in academic studies. Perhaps, even more so. Then again, not long after his arrival in Bern he met a fellow medical student, a girl of twenty named Bassya Osnos. He must have spent much of his time as a second-year medical student wooing the charming Bassya, for it took only a few months before he proposed to her. Nachman was then thirty years old, Bassya, twenty-one. Bassya had been born in Russia into a large family, "not as distinguished or well-to-do as the Syrkins" comments Marie Syrkin, "but richly endowed with ability, as the various careers of the sons and daughters were to show" (*Memoir* 60).

It is easy to see the attraction Nachman and Bassya had to one another physically and intellectually. Both were good looking. Marie describes her mother as she appears in a few period photographs: Bassya, dressed

in the high-necked dress with puffed sleeves of the nineties, show a very pretty girl with delicate features and soft, dreamy brown eyes. Her expression meditative, tender, is very different from that of Nachman on a companion picture. He is handsome as she is pretty and his features are as fine, but his intense gray eyes blaze and his face is taut, as though he were holding some energy in check even while the photographer cries, "one moment please." For each it is a characteristic expression retained beyond youth. (*Memoir* 60)

Beyond physical attraction, Bassya was a fitting partner for Nachman. She was actually a better student. As independent as he, she had shown her own version of courageous initiative in leaving not only her home but her country as well to gain admission to a university where, as a Jew and as a woman, she could pursue an independent career in medicine. In 1897, this required much more than simple desire and belief. It required a sense of mission. "Of course she was a feminist," Bassya's daughter later would declare. "That is to say she believed that women should have independent careers, that they should not be 'shackled' by men or society — in short, they should be 'free'" (*Memoir* 60). Six months after they met, on June 20, 1898, Nachman Syrkin and Bassya Osnos were married. They took up residence in a room in the old section of Bern to await the arrival of their child, who would be born exactly nine months later.

A Zionist Legacy

Nachman Syrkin once told his daughter Marie that when her mother Bassya was pregnant, she would gaze longingly each day at a photograph of Theodore Herzl hoping that she would have a boy who would look like Herzl. More likely, Bassya gazed at the great Zionist leader in admiration for his success in creating the Zionist Congress and for having sympathy for her charming but excitable husband. In any case, her daily gaze could not have been an activity designed to please her new spouse. The First Congress had convened from August 29 to 31, 1897, just weeks before the couple had met, and the Second Congress met just weeks after their marriage on June 20, 1898. Syrkin had been quietly present at the First Congress, but he was to play a contentious role at its second convocation. Nachman regarded Herzl and his cohort either as bourgeois or as clerical reactionaries; he himself represented the militant left — which consisted of a few socialist Zionists. At the First Congress, Syrkin sincerely believed it would be possible for the two factions to work together; but by the Second Congress, the differences had become too glaring to brush aside.

At the Second Congress an excitable and self-assured Syrkin burst onto the scene in explosive debate. This Congress began in anticipation of Herzl's upcoming meeting in Jerusalem with Kaiser Wilhelm II. One of the first orders of business was Herzl's proposal that the Congress send a telegram of appreciation to Czar Nicholas II for the international peace conference he had just called. Nachman Syrkin was enraged by what he thought was toadying to tyrants, and his boisterous protestations quickly created an unruly fracas among the delegates. A German delegate to the Congress, Ernst Calmus, has provided an eyewitness account of Syrkin's conduct and its brawling aftermath:

As is known Herzl suggested that the Congress send a letter of appreciation to the Czar. Syrkin, who sat in the first row on the left, acted as though a thunderbolt had struck him. He leapt up in violent excitement and protested against the proposal that the Jewish people should offer the honor to its oppressor. A disturbance arose. For a few minutes a storm broke loose. It seemed as though the Congress would break up. Herzl, the quiet, rational politician, had not expected such an occurrence. Quickly, he managed to stop the debate. . . . [Herzl] told me that he feared the incident might hurt all of Russian Jewry. Through his influence he managed to suppress publication of the incident. (*Memoir* 66)

And what was Syrkin's explanation for such shocking behavior? His own report commented sardonically that "Herzl glows like a heated stone and soon the suggestion is made that the Congress of that very oppressed nation which is seeking to throw off the Czar's yoke send a respectful, submissive telegram to Nicholas, naturally with the expectation of a donation. . . . As might have been expected this proposal precipitated a scandal among the few socialists" (*Memoir* 65).

The scandal was so fierce, escalating to actual fisticuffs, that Bassya herself approached Herzl's Hebrew secretary pleading, "Please, Mr. Secretary, save Syrkin; they want to kill him. Tell Herzl that Syrkin is in danger." Fortuitously, Herzl appeared on the scene and was able to calm the angry mob and rescue Syrkin; and when the delegates introduced a motion to expel all the socialists, Herzl refused to endorse it. Though he referred to Nachman Syrkin as "that *exaltado*" [hothead], (*Memoir* 69), he also seemed to like him. No wonder twenty-one-year-old Bassya gazed with admiration on the iconic Herzl's photograph.

Syrkin's disputatious behavior at the Second Congress, however provocative it may have been, was never a matter of personal pique. Yes, he was a man with a very short fuse; but his outrageous outbursts were the result of a sincere passionate belief in the cause of socialist Zionism. Undaunted by outright rejection and calls for his expulsion from the Congress, Nachman Syrkin continued to interrupt, to object, to oppose, to speak interminably, the better to spread his ideas and to persuade others to join his fledgling movement—which at this point had enlisted only a handful of members. But most of his remonstrances met with exasperation. With apologetic pride Marie Syrkin reports that the "number of *pfui*'s, hisses and *'grosser tummel'* (great uproar) which punctuate the minutes of the Zionist Congresses in connection with Syrkin's utterances is impressive. He had a genius for provocation, but in each instance it was because the cause was provocative—and indigestible at the time" (*Memoir* 69).

The second Zionist Congress of 1898 had been the venue for Syrkin's blistering words about sycophancy and for attacks on the preponderance of bourgeois and rabbinical elements in the Zionist organization, but all was not rancor; at this same Congress, he co-sponsored and submitted a successful resolution for a Jewish National Fund. Perhaps more to the point, 1898 was the year that Syrkin published his own seminal essay, "The Jewish Question and the Socialist Jewish State" (surely in response to Herzl's 1896 tract *The Jewish State*), which provided the theoretical basis for the synthesis of Zionism and socialism. Yet, despite the contention it caused at the Second Congress, by the time of the Third Congress in 1899, Syrkin's platform and lectures had begun to attract growing audiences.

Nachman Syrkin's public life had at last begun to bear fruit—and so had his private life. On March 22, 1899, in the city of Bern, Switzerland, Marie, the daughter of Nachman and Bassya Syrkin was born. Nachman was thirty-one and Bassya ten years younger. Their joy at parenthood undoubtedly was enhanced by the fact that the child was uncommonly beautiful—a full head of straight black hair, dark eyes, small nose—perfectly formed features. Despite Bassya's fixation, the baby did not resemble Herzl, though she did favor her father. What the Syrkins did not yet know was that Marie was extraordinarily gifted intellectually—and little Marie did not yet know that her parents' powerful influence would last a lifetime. Neither she nor they had any idea that she would be their only child, nor that her mother was destined to die at the age of thirty-six.

After Marie's birth, Bassya valiantly tried to continue her medical studies, but try as she did, her efforts were doomed to failure. First, there was the problem of her health. As a young girl, she had cared for a cousin who was dying of tuberculosis; inevitably Bassya contracted the disease herself. Though she recovered, and by the time she met

Nachman Syrkin she was convinced that she had fully recovered, the truth was that her physical condition was still fragile. Unfortunately for Bassya, her husband's burgeoning career called for frequent changes of location; thus, by the time Marie was a year old, the couple had moved to Charlottenburg, a culturally rich suburb of Berlin. Charlottenburg, probably named for Sophie-Charlotte, the wife of King Frederick I of Prussia, was the site of the Queen's palace, museums, art and music academies, and parks; but for the financially strapped Syrkins it meant living conditions that were cramped, damp, and lacking in the amenities needed to avoid a recurrence of Bassya's disease. Neither Nachman nor his wife seemed to understand this. It is hard to explain why two medical students failed to recognize the health hazards of their latest residential circumstances. Moreover, although Bassya Syrkin was granted permission to attend lectures at the University of Berlin, she could not take advantage of the permit because they hadn't the money to hire someone to care for Marie.

What was it that brought the Syrkins to Berlin? It could not have been simply Nachman's desire to abandon medical studies in order to complete his delayed doctoral dissertation in philosophy — though in fact he did manage to finish the dissertation in 1903. No, it appears that at this time, as he became more and more passionate about his political activities, the pursuit of medicine became not only impractical, but irrelevant. From this point on, he devoted his time and efforts to organizing Socialist-Zionist societies in Germany, Austria, and Switzerland. In this pursuit he had some small success.

In Berlin, Nachman Syrkin organized a group called *Hessiona* named after Moses Hess whose 1862 book, *Rome and Jerusalem,* is a founding text of modern Zionism. According to Marie Syrkin, *Hessiona* was a society that consisted of four members. "One of the original four was [Syrkin's] friend Mirkin. The combination of names proved irresistible to the local humorists who delighted in mocking the formation of a party which consisted of Syrkin, Mirkin and Manietchka (his two year old child)" (*Memoir* 71). Nonetheless, this tiny society publicized a lecture in Russian to be delivered by Nachman Syrkin, which was subsequently published as a pamphlet entitled "A Call to Jewish Youth." It turned out to be an extremely successful propaganda piece. Read and reread in Germany, Switzerland, England, France, and smuggled into Russia, it was copied by hand and circulated in student groups, where it was of such high voltage that it induced a cerebral jolt into action. Theory now became practice. Though the place of publication was listed as London, the pamphlet actually had been printed in Berlin. Marie Syrkin suspects that this "was to mystify the German police who might be ill disposed to revolutionary slogans" (*Memoir* 71). And thus the movement began to spread. Between 1901 and 1903, Syrkin organized a new group, *Heirut* (Freedom), published a journal *Der Hamoyn* (The Proletariat) in Yiddish, and another *Ha-Shachar* (The Dawn) in Hebrew—neither lasting beyond the first issue.

Amid the feverish political activity of the nascent Socialist-Zionist Movement, Nachman Syrkin tried to support his family through his writings while working on his doctoral dissertation, which he finally completed in 1903. Meanwhile, despite the increasing support for his ideas, he was also the object of a great deal of criticism from both the Jewish Socialist Bund and the Zionists. One journalist who signed his name "A. Coralnik" acidly observed in a 1903 review of *Ha-Shachar* in *Die Welt:* "Dr. Syrkin has one passion. Some people like to write books. He prefers to write magazines . . . composed exclusively of articles by Dr. Syrkin. He writes everything: philosophy, sociology, and even satire. And as he is the sole contributor of the journal, the issue will probably remain the only one, since he is its only reader" (*Memoir* 77).

From 1897 through 1901, the Zionist Congress met yearly, but the Fifth Congress passed a resolution to meet every other year. At the next meeting, however, in August 1903, a tragic pall hung heavily over the Congress. In April, the entire civilized world had been shocked by the horrifying brutality of the Kishinev pogrom. Over the two days following Easter Sunday, April 6, 1903 (which coincided with the last day of Pesach), rioters acted on a blood libel rumor as well as a rumor that the Czar had issued a secret edict as an Easter gift permitting the local population three days of brutalizing and plundering the Jews. Drunken villagers roamed the streets rioting—from pillage of property to desecration of Torah scrolls, from bodily attack to rape and murder. By Tuesday, April 8, 1903, when the army finally appeared on the scene to quell the violence, fifty Jews were dead and five hundred were clubbed with crowbars or otherwise severely wounded in this horrifying massacre to which the local police had turned a blind eye. The lament of the poet Hayim Nachman Bialik expressed the mood of the Jewish world:

> Arise and go to the city of
> slaughter;

Into its courtyard
and touch with your own hand
And see with the eyes of your own head
On trees, on stones, on fences, on walls,
The splattered blood and dried brains
of the dead Jews.
Walk into the ruins,
Pass by the shattered houses and broken walls,
Whose burned and barren brick, whose
charred stones reveal
the open mouths of such wounds that
No mending will ever mend,
Nor healing ever heal. There our feet will stumble
On wreckage doubly wrecked,
Torah scroll heaped on Talmudic manuscript,
Fragments again fragmented.[7]

To a post-Holocaust, twenty-first-century reader, the details of Bialik's poem are all too familiar, evoking the many eyewitness accounts and memoirs of atrocities that were doomed to follow. But in April 1903, the Kishinev Easter pogrom sent a seismic shock through the Jewish world. Four months later, when the Sixth Zionist Congress convened in August of 1903, the aftershock was still sending out tremors that blackened the mood of the delegates. In addition, the "charter" from the Sultan of Turkey that Herzl had sought for the establishment of a Jewish National Home in Palestine had failed to materialize. Added to this failure, the El Arish project — the British proposal for a territory in the Northern Sinai as a temporary settlement — had been rejected by Egypt on the grounds that it could not provide sufficient water for irrigation. Herzl did, however, have an offer from the British to apportion land in Uganda, East Africa, for autonomous settlement. The horror of Kishinev, as well as the failure of his efforts to secure a charter for land in the Middle East, led Herzl to take the Uganda proposal seriously enough to advance it for scrutiny at the Sixth Congress, though he never thought of it as anything more than a temporary solution. Uganda was not and never could be Zion. Consequently, Herzl did not put the proposal forward for an up-and-down vote, but offered it only as a vote to authorize a commission to examine the scheme and report the findings at the next Congress. Contemplated in the shadow of the horrendous situation in Russia, the seriousness of the issue was reflected in heated debate that caused those who opposed the idea to walk out of the hall, only to be brought back by Herzl himself, who pleaded with them not to destroy the Zionist Congress. The vote count further attested to the significance of the matter: 295 in favor, 178 against, 98 abstentions ("Zionist Congresses," *Judaica*).

The pro-Uganda contingent was led by the British writer Israel Zangwill, perhaps best known in America for coining the phrase "the melting pot" in his eponymous play. A pragmatic reformer of Jewish public and private life, Zangwill argued that "It is eighteen hundred and thirty-five years since we lost our fatherland, and the period of mourning should be about over. . . . Any territory which was Jewish, [and] under a Jewish flag . . . would save the Jew's body and the Jew's soul."[8] The opposing ideological camp was led by the moralist Ahad Ha'am and his *Hibbat Zion* (Love of Zion) followers, who argued that those in favor of the Uganda proposal (called "Territorialists"), had detached political Zionism from cultural values. One of Ahad Ha'am's followers, Yitzhak Gruenbaum (who was to become the first minister of the Interior of the State of Israel), argued that their goal was "to defend Zionism," which he defined as "not the Zionism of diplomacy and charity for the impoverished of the East, but the Zionism that is the full renaissance of the Jewish people in Erez Israel"(*Vital* 127). "What *united* the anti-Herzlians," David Vital maintains, "was that they all thought that continuity was crucial. The Jewish society at which they aimed, however vague and ill-focused their picture of it, had to contain within it the major elements of the Jewish heritage — [Hebrew] language, culture, history, and (with reservations) faith" (*Vital* 127). This of course meant that Eretz Israel was indispensable to their visionary idea of the rejuvenation of the Jewish civilization. Such a comprehensive program obviously could not be accomplished overnight, but the party of Ahad Ha'am was prepared to wait.

And where did Nachman Syrkin stand on this issue? Surprisingly, for someone who was regarded as a "romantic" and who had never seemed to have a practical turn of mind, he now argued in favor of "practical considerations." Syrkin came down on the side of those who favored the Uganda scheme, and he fulminated against those whom he claimed had "romantic attachments" (*Memoir* 87). In an address to the Congress (one of many that would follow), he said, "I greet with joy the idea of an autonomous Jewish settlement in East Africa. If you will grasp the scope of this idea, this Congress may become a turning point in Jewish history" (*Memoir* 87). In reporting her father's part in this debate, Marie Syrkin comments that the minutes of this meeting note that here Syrkin was greeted with applause. In words that betray her ambivalent pride and exasperation, she comments humorously, "For a change his appearances are being greeted with *lebhafter beifall* [lively applause] instead of the usual *grosser tummel* [much commotion]" (*Memoir* 87). Perhaps the explanation for Syrkin's surprising position is that for him the rescue of the suffering Jews was primary and the redemption of the Jews was secondary. One had to be accomplished immediately; the other could be a delayed dream.

Any action on the Uganda Scheme was put off until the Seventh Congress and the delegates were to go back to their home bases to campaign for their particular positions. Nachman Syrkin returned to Berlin to agitate for the East Africa scheme in fierce debate, in his letters, and in his publications. Regarding her father's activities at this moment, Marie comments, again with her customary blend of irritation and admiration, "A promising publicistic [*sic*] career was in the making, but most of his energy was as usual going into activities, written and oral, to which no taint of money could be attached. His family managed somehow" (*Memoir* 91).

The family may have had a roof over its head and enough calories to survive, but it was not enough to ward off a recurrence of Bassya's chronic illness. Her coughing had returned. Marie believes that her mother would have become mortally ill at this time had it not been for Nachman's mother, Zivia, who had arrived for a visit, surveyed the situation, and taken the required action. She knew just what the coughing meant and what could be the consequences, so she packed herself, Bassya, and four-year-old Marie off to the seaside resort of Nervi, Italy, for rest, rehabilitation, increased calories, and the healing powers of the sun and sea. The elder Syrkins obviously were in considerably better financial circumstances than their children. Bassya recovered, though Marie remarks with gentle sarcasm that this justified her father's "perpetual happy confidence that all would be well" (*Memoir* 91). Marie, incidentally, now had picked up a smattering of Italian.

The little group, however, did not to return to Berlin. While in Nervi, Bassya learned that her husband had been exiled from Germany for radical activities. He wrote to his wife that the Berlin police "'apparently thought more kindly of Zionism than of Socialist Zionism'"

(*Memoir* 91). In the spring of 1904, when Marie was five years old, mother and child joined Nachman in Paris, where they moved to a small apartment a few miles east of Paris, in Charenton. In his hasty departure from their Berlin domicile, Nachman had taken very little with him; thus, Bassya, who appeared to have recovered, set about creating at least a semblance of a home with the few items that remained from their prior residences. The small Paris apartment had the look of what today would be described as graduate student decor. Marie, now five, already had lived in four countries — Switzerland, Germany, Italy (albeit briefly), and now Paris. She asserts that for her, all these moves were not terribly disruptive. Life in each place was merely a continuation of what went before, except for the fact that in Berlin she was called Mariechen and in France she was Marie, though at home she most often was called by the Russian diminutive of Manya, "Manietchka." Russian was the language her parents spoke to one another, though Yiddish was sometimes spoken among friends.

Once established in their new apartment, Bassya embarked on her usual routine of taking her daughter to the nearest museum — in this case, the Louvre or the Luxembourg — and of buying opera tickets for herself and Nachman. The museum treks do not seem to have been a particularly pleasant childhood memory for Marie. "All this trudging in museums with my mother did not make me a true lover of the plastic arts," she later commented,

> but I knew that these were the things that were important. It was also important to try to get standing room for the Opera. I was too young to be taken, but the few discussions of finances that I recall did not revolve around such routine matters as unpaid bills for the day's necessities but the strategy for the Opera. The other important things were the "Revolution" and *Eivreistwo* [the Jewish people]; whoever came to tea and stayed for dinner, these were the themes loudly and excitedly discussed." (*Memoir* 94)

As it had been in Berlin, so it was in Paris — an apartment forever filled with argumentative "comrades" debating with Nachman in a variety of languages that Marie had been accustomed to hearing since infancy. All this was part of the unorthodox education of the bright young child of peripatetic, politically and ethically driven parents. It was her birthright.

Marie did, of course, attend school in Paris, though she claims to remember very little, except for the fact that the little girls wore "black aprons with ribbons of various colors to indicate their classes, and that one was given a piece of white bread and a piece of chocolate when one came home" (*Memoir* 92). It is not so surprising that the child deposited this into her memory bank to be withdrawn when she was a grown woman, for undoubtedly black bread was the more familiar staple of a Russian family; hence, sweets were forever to remain a craving. In addition to Marie's attendance at a French school, Nachman, who had taught his daughter to read and write German when they were in Berlin, now instructed her in those skills in French. It would be only a year or two later that he would begin her instruction in Russian. These languages were for practical considerations, of course—which begins to explain why Nachman did not try to teach her Hebrew at this time. Seventy-five years later, in a 1983 double interview in *Moment* magazine with Marie Syrkin and the journalist-scholar Trude Weiss-Rosmarin, Weiss-Rosmarin said to Marie: "You were fortunate in your upbringing. After all, to be the daughter of Nachman Syrkin. . . ." Marie sharply replied: "Yes, but one thing he failed to provide me. He did not teach me Hebrew at an age when I could have learned it. It's maddening. . . . So that's one thing I have against my father. . . . [T]hat he didn't teach me Hebrew was a serious loss" (*Moment* 9/83, 40). Nonetheless, Marie was an apt student, and by this time her parents regarded her as a prodigy, so they never thought twice about the psychological consequences for this tractable and certainly brilliant child, about the frequent moves from country to country with the requisite language changes. One useful result was that she became polylingual at a very early age.

Until the move to Paris, Marie's memories of family life are perforce sketchy, but by the time she was five her unusually active mind began to record events of daily life in considerable detail. Whereas it is true that what one remembers from childhood is often embellished by what one is told later, Marie's sharp recall of events does appear convincingly childlike, intensely personal, and probably accurate. In later years, however, as she recalled particular incidents of her childhood, she would include her interpretation of Nachman and Bassya's theory of parenting. Though her report of the event itself is undoubtedly factual, her language and style betray fond exasperation/admiration for her parents' commitment to deeply held values. Yet, whatever she may report in retrospect about her childhood docility, there lurks resentment at the cost to the three of them. Consider the following account:

My bringing up naturally reflected my parents' "advanced" views and was the kind of combination of the rationalist and romantic whose effects were not always happy. No base sop was ever thrown to the environment in which I might be thrust. Those ultra-romantics, my parents, sternly permitted me no infant illusions. I knew very early that fairies, gods, and angels were creations of ignorance and superstition and that there was no Santa Claus. In Berlin I was taken to see a Christmas tree — and to this day I feel the pang of delight at the shining globes and tinsel seen for the first time — but on *Weinachten* I knew that presents were not for me though other little girls on the street had new dolls; and there was no nonsense about Hanukah gifts as substitutes to soothe my spirit. The life of truth and reason had to be early embraced. The deprivation which modern parents fear for their children were offered to me as benefactions. Apparently I was tractable because I recall no four-year-old protests at pleasures denied. But the fact that I remember the holiday doll-less, not because I was Jewish and entitled to other festivals, but because there was no Santa Claus, indicates that the experience registered. (*Memoir* 93)

The years 1904 and 1905 provided Marie with never-to-be-forgotten memories. The first, and perhaps most intense, took place in July of 1904: as she describes it, Marie watches her mother arranging her hair in front of a mirror. Her father enters the room and says in Russian, "Herzl is dead." Marie, does not know who Herzl is or what his death means, but she feels the extreme tension in the room, and she knows that "something strange and terrible" has happened. The memory is so acute that some fifty years later she can describe the psychic experience of that moment: "My mother's illness, exile and whatever talk there must have been — in view of the family's unvarying indigence — of how to pay grocer or landlord — pale before that happening. This is the nature of the dreadful — Herzl is dead" (*Memoir* 93).

For Marie's father and mother, however, Herzl's death had both emotional and political meaning. This was not only the death of a great and revered iconic figure, but it heralded a battle royal between the two Zionist factions: those in favor of the Uganda scheme and those in favor of Palestine as the only geographic site for Zion. From the standpoint of Herzl and Zangwill — and Syrkin was with them — the issue was urgency. The masses had flocked to Herzl *because* he offered a solution to the increasingly desperate situation of the Jews in Eastern Europe. The 1903 Kishineff pogrom was proof-positive that the current situation was worsening. The leaders of the opposing contingent — Ahad Ha'am and

Menachem Mendel Ussishkin—were committed to the slower process of gradual settling of the land, and the renewal of Judaism's spiritual creativity through the cultural work of connection to their heritage. Ahad Ha'am had never held much faith in Herzl's political and diplomatic solutions, and he worried about the assimilated Viennese Herzl and his disciple Max Nordau's distance from traditional Jewish values and culture. Yet upon news of Herzl's death, the rank and file of Jews—intellectuals, religious leaders, creative artists, politicians, journalists, artisans, workers, peddlers—flocked to Vienna to publicly mourn the figure who had given them more hope than they had dared to hold for two thousand years. They massed in the street below the black-draped windows of Herzl's study where his coffin lay. Over six thousand mourners followed the bier to the cemetery, wailing and moaning, only to be jammed into a narrow space and to erupt into frenzied disorder. Uncountable messages of condolence were sent from Jews and non-Jews, from ordinary citizens as well as heads of State, expressing their shock and sorrow at the death of this larger-than-life leader. But Ahad Ha'am, recalling even at this time of grief, Herzl's Uganda proposal at the last Zionist Congress wrote, "His career and activities during the past seven years had the character of a romantic tale. If some great writer had written it, he too would have his hero die after the Sixth Congress."[9]

The two years between the Sixth Congress—Herzl's last, the one at which he had advanced the Uganda proposal as a temporary measure—and the Seventh Congress were marked by increasing conflict between the two factions. Before Herzl died, Nachman Syrkin had been spending his time in Paris passionately spreading the word, in print and in lectures, in favor of the "political Zionists" as opposed to the "Zion-Zionists." He was not always warmly welcomed and sometimes even enraged his audiences. His embrace of the British offer of Uganda even caused a split with his closest colleague, Mirkin. A few months after the Sixth Congress, Mirkin visited Palestine and wrote glowing letters to Syrkin about the land (including the difficulties):

The enchantment with Uganda will soon end; the notion of "general autonomie" will be bankrupt. A part of your party will go to the Bund; the others will return to Zionism. Remember my words. . . . Only in Palestine will the Jewish people be reborn! In that land where for the first time our great socialist-prophets proclaimed the ideals of social righteousness these ideals will be realized. This is my conviction. I believe it deeply. I cannot be in your *Heirut* because of Uganda." (*Memoir* 103–104)

Mirkin, it should be noted, now refers to *Heirut*, of which he was a charter member, as "your" *Heirut*.

Nachman Syrkin arrived at the first Congress after Herzl's death in July of 1905 prepared to continue the fight, but Mirkin's prophecy came to pass. Though the new leader, the philosopher-physician Max Nordau, called the session to order in solemn reverence with a eulogy for his beloved friend, Theodor Herzl, the opening stillness and silence in the room soon broke into angry debate over the still unresolved Uganda issue. Bitter and fierce emotions, restrained by the sheer strength of Herzl's charismatic power, now exploded with full force. In the two years that had passed since the last Congress, opposition to the Uganda proposal had been growing, especially since the return of the commission that had been studying the conditions of the East African territory and had pronounced it totally unacceptable for Jewish large-scale immigration and settlement. But Syrkin was undaunted and found himself in continual conflict with Nordau, causing disturbance and disruption, and calling down derision upon himself. In her account of the proceedings, Marie Syrkin once again displays her usual ambivalence regarding her father's "combination of naiveté, impertinence, and idealism." After reading the minutes of the meeting, she reports that the "outcries of '*pfui*,' '*hinaus*,' and 'down from the platform' addressed to Syrkin from the outraged delegates continue to multiply. . . ." provoking Nordau at one point to comment that "*pfui* is not a parliamentary expression" (*Memoir* 106).

When the vote was called, Uganda was soundly defeated. With this, Syrkin announced the withdrawal of his group of twenty-eight Socialist-Zionists from the Congress. His delegation of twenty-eight joined with the Territorialist group that called itself S.S. (Socialisti-Sionisti). A third faction, led by Israel Zangwill and comprised of members of the general Zionists, also walked out. Zangwill then organized this group into the ITO (Jewish Territorial Organization). After their departure, the Congress passed a resolution stating that practical work (political as well as philanthropic settlement) should not be delayed. Syrkin did not return to the General Zionist Organization for almost ten years; this partially explains his failure to emigrate to Palestine. Zangwill did not return until 1925, at which point he finally dissolved the ITO.

Meanwhile, revolutionary forces had been active in Russia, causing strikes and sabotage. Czar Nicholas II had ascended the throne in 1894 upon the death of his father, the deeply antisemitic Alexander III, under whom the brutal May Laws had come into being. Nicholas did not provide the improvement the Jews had hoped for. He had been tutored by one of his father's most rabid antisemitic advisors, Constantin Pobedonostev — a well-known jurist, legal expert, and Chief Procurator of the Holy Synod — who became the lay head of the Russian Orthodox Church. Nicholas, a weak and easily influenced personality, mastered his instruction in Jew hatred, with honors. Moreover, when he assumed the throne, the malevolent Pobedonostev was not his only tutor; there were two others skilled in evil counsel. First was "the notorious roué and blackmailer, Prince V. P. Mescherski, editor of the Slavophilist newspaper *Grazhdanin*. Above all, there was Nicholas' wife, the former Princess Alix of Hesse-Darmstadt, a woman ridden with fundamentalist superstitions and obsessions" (Sachar 246). In addition, both Czar and Czarina were much influenced by the mysterious holy mystic, Rasputin. So much, then, for the vaunted 1971 film romance of *Nicholas and Alexandra*. Moreover, under the power of these malevolent mentors, Czar Nicholas stated clearly that he would continue his father's autocratic rule in every respect.

The year before the Seventh Zionist Congress, in July of 1904, the Chief of the Secret Police, the notoriously antisemitic Wenzel von Plehve, had been assassinated. Nicholas, frightened by this event, had made a few gestures to the revolutionaries. But the strikes, sabotage, and assassinations still continued, as did the responses of the Czarist forces. On January 22, 1905, with the priest Georgy Gapon, the head of the Assembly of Russian Factory Workers, in the lead, the workers of St. Petersburg marched on the Winter Palace intending to present Nicholas with a petition of loyalty, but not without making some comprehensive demands. They were greeted, however, by Czarist police who fired on them. Approximately 130 men and women were killed and over a thousand wounded. Word of this massacre spread quickly and soon became known as "Bloody Sunday," inspiring other economic and ethnic groups to rise up in furor. The revolutionary movement caught fire, from pacific demonstrations to violent uprisings, from strikes to military mutiny, from political organization among the peasant population to the establishment of workers' *soviets* (assemblies of elected representative delegates). Furthermore, by 1905, Nicholas II had suffered a series of disastrous events: The Russo-Japanese War had gone very badly as the Russian fleet was virtually annihilated; strikes and terrorism were rampant; the interior minister and head of the secret police, Count Von Plehve, had been assassinated by a bomb thrown under his carriage; the massacre of Bloody Sunday had its retort from the Social Revolutionaries when Grand Duke Sergius was blown up in the Kremlin in Moscow. By October, the discontent had reached its peak and a monumental nationwide strike crippled the country. The thoroughly demoralized Nicholas (who had actually considered abdication) who was by now advised by the much more liberal Count Witte, issued his famous October manifesto. He promised the people of Russia a constitution, civil rights, and a parliament. The reaction was celebratory parades and joy and exultation in the streets and in homes everywhere. But it was not to last. In six months, the Czar issued a decree that restored almost all the power he had surrendered in the October Manifesto. For the Jews, this was devastating, for they knew that in the minds of the autocratic regime the words "revolutionary" and "Jew" were synonymous.

In October of 1905, however, the revolutionary events in Russia brought hope to Diaspora Jews that a solution to the Jewish Problem might yet be realized — perhaps now in the Diaspora, later in the homeland. For the moment, the task at hand for the socialist Syrkins, both Nachman and Bassya, was participation in the nascent revolution. Nachman's exit in a huff from the Zionist Congress did not mean that his work would cease.

Childhood in Four Languages

Not since the death of Czar Alexander I in 1855 (exactly fifty years earlier), had the Russian Jews entertained such great expectations. The Russian Revolution of 1905 brought hope and jubilation to a wide spectrum of Russian Jews. Both the autonomist *Sejmists* and the Marxist-Socialist Jewish Bundists dreamed optimistically about Jewish full and equal participation in Russian life; and both groups were opposed to the Zionists, who remained skeptical about life in *Galut*. Yet the Zionists themselves took heart at the events of 1905, because they believed it would now be easier to circulate their ideas about a Jewish national homeland without fear of government reprisal.

The Syrkin family, who had been in Paris for two years, shared the rising optimism of the moment. Nachman had not been back to Russia for eighteen years. Bassya, however, had returned in 1901, during their Berlin years. She had gone back with smuggled propaganda pamphlets that were intended to fertilize the seeds of the revolution as well as of Socialist Zionism. Bassya was then twenty-three, Marie not quite three. The task of baby-sitting at that time fell to Nachman, whose expertise in child care was just short of passable. Bassya was away for several months and as Marie later commented, Nachman "managed for several months in his devious way feeding us chiefly in the *Russische Kuche,* a restaurant for students. It was upon return from this venture that [Bassya] had fallen ill" (*Memoir* 95).

If Bassya was ready in 1901 to engage in dangerous revolutionary activity, by 1905, she certainly could not sit still. Nor could her husband. Conditions had become commanding. Bassya Syrkin fitted out a trunk with a false bottom containing political pamphlets and left for the land of her birth. Probably because Nachman expected to participate in the Seventh Zionist Congress in Basle in late July 1905, he and Marie remained behind with plans to meet up with Bassya later. This time, Marie's mother made sure that her daughter would not be restricted to student restaurants; Bassya's younger sister was drafted to share the domestic chores. "My mother's younger sister, Masha," Marie recalls, "a medical student at the University of Montpellier, came to look after me in the interim. Masha was still in her teens, but she valiantly took over her sister's menage in addition to her own studies. It all seemed eminently reasonable then. That was the way life should be lived" (*Memoir* 95–96).

The Seventh Zionist Congress convened on July 27, 1905. Before the end of the convocation, Syrkin had seceded from the Zionist Organization, a defection that left him free to become the leader of the Territorialist group *Sionisty-Sotsialisty* (Zionist-Socialists), and to return to Russia to participate in the Revolution. Syrkin regarded the emerging revolution as temporarily good for the Jews, but bad for Socialist Zionism. In an undated essay written in Yiddish, perhaps some time after he had allied himself with the American Poalei Zion Party, Syrkin wrote an analysis of the situation in 1905:

Before Socialist Zionism had a real opportunity to crystallize as an idea and a movement, a process of dissolution set in. The deepest crisis this fruitful idea was to encounter came in 1905, a year which was to have a decisive effect on the further development of Socialist Zionism. The Russian Revolution [1905] opened a free field of political activity for the Jewish working-class and aroused new hopes for the Jewish people in Russia. Theoretically at any rate, the *Galuth* had ceased to be the dark, hopeless vale of tears which the Zionist "deniers of Galuth" had painted. A dazzling prospect for Jewish economic and political independence unfolded. (*Memoir* 246)

In August of 1905, Marie and her father left Paris for Russia — leaving Masha to dispose of the "household effects, which she did by letting needy comrades help themselves to whatever they found useful" (*Memoir* 109). Masha, herself, then returned to the south of France to continue her studies in Montpellier, though she was destined to play a significant role in the Syrkins' lives many years in the future. The train ride from Paris to Vilna, where the Syrkins planned to settle, was long and frightening, particularly for six-year-old Marie. Even Nachman's usual optimistic disposition must have been disturbed by the perils ahead. Marie, however, had been prepared all along for the journey and relocation. Her mother, she was never to forget, had sung to her beautiful revolutionary lullabies with such "comforting" words as *"Na barricadi mi poedem ai mi rastroim csarky dom,"* which translates as "We will go to the barricades and we will destroy the house of the Czar." But on the long journey she was warned against humming it out loud; nor should she "chant the Marseillaise with its cry for 'liberte.'" She had been warned that "the dark land they were going to was ruled by a Czar, a tyrant whom one must destroy," and she had been thoroughly indoctrinated to worship young girls with names like "Sophie Provskaya and Vera Figner, revolutionary heroines, [who] had given their lives for 'freedom.'" Further, she was warned that in Russia one could not speak openly about one's opinion of the Czar because he "had a secret police which could hear even a discreet whisper. And then off one went to *katorga* (Siberian hard labor)" (*Memoir* 110). No wonder that in midlife, with innumerable frightening and dangerous experiences behind her, Marie could instantly summon the terror she felt as she and her father made the long journey to a place she had never seen:

Supposing one was indiscreet and said something out loud which should only be thought. This was something for a six-year-old child to worry about. And there were other worries. In the course of the long journey my father would get off at various stops to purchase food and papers at the station while I waited on the train. I would sit in agony afraid that the train might start off before he had returned and carry me off alone to the Czar's land. (*Memoir* 110)

Added to all these fears was the fact that Marie's mother did not accompany them on the first part of the train ride. She already was in Russia and was to meet them at the border. All that Marie Syrkin could recall about that meeting was that her mother seemed a little strange for a while. Whether this was due to fear or relief is not clear, but apparently "it soon passed" and they "were together again" — destination, Vilna (*Memoir* 110).

Why did the Syrkins choose to locate in Vilna? Given the fact that neither Nachman nor Bassya were born there or had family there, what was its lure? Undoubtedly the modernity, the vigor, excitement, and political centrality of this Lithuanian home to well over 65,000 Jews — almost 50 percent of the city's population — made it a powerful magnet. Vilna had been home to a Jewish community since 1633, when the Jews were granted a charter of privileges allowing them to engage in all manner of commerce and crafts that were not subject to guilds; but the charter also restricted them to specific areas of residence. When Napoleon passed through Vilna in November of 1812, he is reputed to have given the city the name "the Jerusalem of Lithuania." The epithet remained until the mid-twentieth century, when Hitler and the Soviets destroyed its people and erased its glorious past. Indeed, as the historian Lucy Dawidowicz laments in her memoir of her own experience in Vilna in 1938, "A visitor to today's Vilnius can no longer find a trace of what had once been the Jerusalem of Lithuania. . . . Vilna now exists only in memory and in history."[10]

Vilna Jewry, however, was not exempt from heated internecine conflict. In the eighteenth century, Vilna was the home of the great scholarly religious leader, Elijah b. Solomon Zalman, known as the "Vilna *Gaon*" (genius from Vilna) whose brilliant intellect was both profound and pragmatic. Until R. Elijah's appearance, in the latter part of the eighteenth century, Vilna had been primarily influenced in style, organizational methods, and systems of education by Polish Jewry. Interestingly, in the mid-seventeenth century, one of the first important rabbis called from the outside to officiate in Vilna was that famous forbear of Nachman Syrkin, the independent-thinking Rabbi Joel Sirkes of Cracow. But by the mid-eighteenth century, new ideas and religious philosophies began to penetrate the established ways of life and thought. *Hasidism* reached Vilna in the late eighteenth century and attracted a following. At the same time, a different breath of air blew in from Prussia in the West—*Haskalah*—bringing with it *maskilim,* who emphasized secular as well as Jewish skills—modernization without the loss of Jewish tradition.

By the seventeenth century, Vilna already had become known as an important center for rabbinical scholarship, but it was the Vilna *Gaon* more than anything or anyone else who gave the city its character and its fame as "the Jerusalem of Lithuania." A true phenomenon, R. Elijah's erudition encompassed the secular sciences, mathematics, geography, ten languages, Torah, Talmud, Midrash, Kabbalah, Zohar, Shulhan Arukh, Hebrew grammar, among other disciplines and subjects. Indeed, as one contemporary scholar has said in utter admiration, "there [was] no subject relevant to Judaism on which he did not write a book." (Elijah Ben Solomon Zalman, *Judaica*). Another historian called him "the most massive Jewish intellect since Baruch Spinoza" (Sachar 79). It was the Vilna *Gaon,* moreover, who led the ideological battle against the excesses of *Hasidism.* Under his powerful leadership, Vilna became the heart of opposition to the anti-intellectualism of the *Hasidim.* Elijah's followers, the *mitnaggedim* (opponents) continued the struggle against *Hasidism* until well after his death in 1797, developing the characteristic Lithuanian Jewish mind-set, notably skepticism and a harsh, critical attitude toward authoritarianism and disdain for ignorance— characteristics of the so-called *"Litvak."* The bitter feuding of the *mitnaggedim* and the *Hasidim* continued through the first half of the century until the two parties needed to compromise and present a united front against the inroads of an increasingly secularizing *Haskalah* and against the dangers of the antisemitism of the Russian government and church.

By the end of the nineteenth century, Vilna had developed into a bustling center for intellectual and political activity—despite the fact that in the face of government restrictions, pogroms, and high unemployment, large numbers of Jews in this congested city opted to emigrate either to America or Palestine. Vilna was the perfect venue for Nachman Syrkin and all that he hoped to accomplish. Syrkin may not have been a Vilna-ite by birth, but by temperament he was a *"Litvak" par excellence.* Moreover, his former roommate in his Berlin student days, Shmarya Levin, was one of the most prominent Jews in the city of Vilna. True, at the Sixth Zionist Congress in 1903, Levin had been one of the most outspoken leaders of the anti-Uganda opposition, but by 1905, Levin and Syrkin had apparently patched up their differences.

Shmarya Levin, of course, was not Nachman Syrkin's sole contact in Vilna. It appears that there was a woman Marie Syrkin remembered as a "bourgeois cousin." The freezing cold winter months in the city gave Marie little to remember or think upon fondly. There were horse-drawn sleigh rides, and she had been given a child's *shuba* (fur-lined coat) and a fur muff. "I still don't know how my parents managed to procure these delights," she comments. Most likely they were gifts of the bourgeois cousin. That same cousin, Marie recalls, had received a fresh pineapple from her son in St. Petersburg, which she kept on the mantelpiece "for the fragrance." Guests were invited to smell it. When it had ripened almost beyond eating, it was "transformed into preserves which would be prudently doled out. No one would dream of devouring the exotic fruit raw" (*Memoir* 110). Marie's gustatory memory was sharp — especially for sweets. Moreover, the pineapple episode stood in sharp sensory relief to the rest of the Syrkins' *basse-cuisine*. "The winter was bitterly cold," she recalls with no fondness. "We ate in the equivalent of one of those student kitchens which I had come to accept as the sum total of gastronomic delight. The room was frigid. The only bit of warmth radiated from the stove around which the lucky first comers would huddle" (*Memoir* 111).

If urban Vilna in winter held few pleasures to be tenderly remembered, summer in the suburbs outside Vilna was to be a wholly different experience. At the outset of an Arcadian retrospect, Marie states categorically, "The summer was different." Her recall of childhood life in the country is remarkably detailed:

We took a *dacha* (summer cottage) in the suburbs of Vilna together with Latski-Bertholdi, my father's friend and disciple, and his beautiful young wife, Bertha. The *dacha* was a plain pine-board bungalow with no amenities such as running water or inside plumbing. In these respects it was suitably proletarian, but we had a maid. It is difficult for me to understand now why the virtually penniless — or rather ruble-less — menage of four young adults and one child required a servant; at the time it seemed reasonable. It is only in retrospect that the economics of that summer appear puzzling.

So happy were these summer months that even the lack of food from time to time was regarded as a great adventure — not a grim hardship.

There were days when there literally was no food. But to the child, this was the occasion for going berry picking and mushroom hunting, and it often would result in "novel soups" made of freshly picked greens (*Memoir* 111–112).

Despite the fact that Marie has claimed that at the time the maid seemed a reasonable addition to the household, her account also suggests that this maid had perplexed her. This was not only because having a maid seemed inconsistent with the family socialist theory that she had begun to absorb, but also because she thought the maid was an unpleasant, faultfinding skeptic. The peckish woman rebelled against having to make meals for the ever-present fifteen or twenty comrades who continually arrived to debate the pros and cons of Territorialist theory and issues relating to the Jewish proletariat with their leaders, Nachman Syrkin and his protégé Jacob Ze'ev Wolf (Wilhelm) Latski-Bertholdi. It is hardly a wonder that a man with so long a name would be remembered by little Marie only as Latski-Bertholdi and later referred to only as Latski. A Jewish journalist and political activist, Latski, at the age of fifty-four, finally emigrated to *Eretz Israel*. But in 1905 he was holding court in a crude dacha on the outskirts of Vilna.

Among the fond remembrances of her summer idyll in the Vilna countryside, Marie intersperses a few less than pleasant moments. One involved a confrontation between the "captious" maid and Marie's weakness for delectable sweets. Reviving an old memory of this encounter, indignantly she recalled that

[W]hen I would describe the wonders of urban life to her she would sniff contemptuously and ask bitingly, "And what did you eat?" Then I would describe authentic splendid parties, particularly my last birthday party which had been celebrated in great style by the comrades. A cake, I said, and *tjaguchki,* a marvelous confection. Once she could contain herself no longer: "Who paid for it? Your father never has money." But I had a true and satisfactory answer: "Papa took his *shuba* [fur-lined coat] to the pawnshop." (*Memoir* 112)

There were three further episodes that were to remain in Marie's memory of that summer in the country. First, during a berry-picking outing with her mother and Bertha Latski, she overheard a conversation in which they discussed a rumor that "comrade P. had eaten a good dinner in a restaurant while on a trip to the editorial office in Vilna." To the child's mind, this was treachery. As she explains, "There was something undeniably base about eating in a restaurant while comrades at the dacha were munching wild strawberries." At the time that this recollection was written, the adult Marie Syrkin added, "The sinner, who was to rise to distinction, is long dead, and today I have a better perspective of his crime, but the childhood shock is so strong that I refrain from mentioning his name" (*Memoir* 112). There can be little doubt that this extremely intelligent six-year-old had been catechized well and could even interpret events accordingly.

The second vivid memory was of Latski and the local Jewish shop-keeper in vehement confrontation. The village storekeeper generously had been giving the Syrkin-Latski menage groceries on credit with extended latitude regarding payment. "After all," Marie explains, "we were no ordinary customers and a call for products would often result in a sociological discussion. As a typical representative of the non-laboring proletariat," the grocer was of particular interest to the theoreticians who were constantly demonstrating the need for his disappearance, "if the Jewish people was to be redeemed." But as the summer drew to a close, the shopkeeper began to worry about the "mounting unpaid bill due him from the 'intellectuals.' One night he came with his pregnant wife and grossly demanded his money. The outraged Latski threw him out bodily; the shopkeeper's wife had hysterics." Marie claims that she learned of this the next morning from "sotto voce discussions that went on." Both Bassya and Bertha decried Latski's terrible temper, especially because the shopkeeper's wife was pregnant. Yet, as Marie remembers it so many years later, "the villain of the piece appeared to be the miserable shopkeeper. He acted like a typical representative of his class — abject, grasping, unbelieving. But for socialists to have used violence was inexcusable. No doubt the bill was paid and the matter patched up, but somewhere theory had failed" (*Memoir* 113).

That pastoral summer of 1906 appears to have provided Marie Syrkin with two kinds of memories: the first, a short course in socialist theory with a heavy emphasis on the 1905 revolution and the fate of the Jews, a curriculum which, for a seven-year-old, Marie seems to have passed with astonishing success; the second, warm recollections about what she ate during that time. She recalls playing with a group of peasant children who lived in a nearby village. She showed her playmates three large green grapes that an uncle from Vilna had brought her, but she confesses that she did not share them. "Another time," she admits, "a tow-haired little girl told me that she ate only potatoes fried in lard, and that seemed a dull diet. If I was lucky I might get a kopek — sometimes to buy *sacharnaya morosheny* (ice cream) from an itinerant vendor. The peasant children never had a kopek; I ate while they watched. But we were friends" (*Memoir* 114).

In addition to Marie Syrkin's diet of theory and sweets, there was "something else" that the little girl ingested that summer — something that was not simply to be stored in her memory to be summoned from time to time, but an experience that was to reside permanently in active consciousness and that would give shape to her entire life and work. This was not a lesson that had been received secondhand from her father's instruction, nor had it been overheard in kitchen gossip; it had been one that she herself had learned firsthand. This was the lesson of antisemitism.

It is not that Marie had never before heard the words "pogrom" or "antisemitism." She knew that these terms suggested something base, "something fearful that happened in Czarist Russia." Calling up the emotions of her childhood self, she describes what she believes were her very thoughts at the time: "It had never happened in Paris where one went to museums and looked at the statue of Joan of Arc and sang the Marseillaise. Pogroms were not just base — to be ignored. If I let myself think of them, I was afraid, very afraid" (*Memoir* 114).

That same group of peasant children who watched while Marie ate, gave her some friendly advice:

There had been talk again of pogroms; there might be an outbreak even in these meadows. So one of the little girls who did not want me to be killed, said "It's easy. Just mark a cross on the door of your cottage. Then they won't hurt you." It did seem easy. Happy and relieved I ran to my mother and told her the good news. We did not have to be killed. We only had to paint a cross on the door. My mother smiled gently. I don't remember what she said but I understood, just as I had understood about Joan of Arc and the Marseillaise, that we would not paint a cross on the door" (*Memoir* 114–115).

Fifty-three years after the event, this story appears embedded within the chapter entitled "The Vilna Days" in Marie's biographical memoir of her father, *Nachman Syrkin: Socialist Zionist,* published in 1960. In 1980, seventy-three years after the event and twenty years after she first wrote of it in the memoir of her father, the little tale becomes the opening

salvo of Marie Syrkin's collected essays, *The State of the Jews.* Testifying
to the enduring power of that childhood experience, Marie Syrkin has
chosen to begin the introduction to this representative collection of her
life's writings as follows:

These essays and reports reflect a life-long concern with the riddle of Jewish experience in our times. I first encountered the riddle in its crudest form as a child
of six in Czarist Russia. There I learned the meaning of "pogrom" from friendly
village children who counseled me to paint a cross on our cottage should the
killing start. But when I brought these tidings of salvation to my father I discovered that this was not the right solution. The answer, I was taught and grew
up believing, lay in a Socialist society and a Socialist Jewish state.[11]

Despite the move from city to countryside, to yet another home, now
shared with others, the persistent lack of money, the fears of pogrom,
Marie remembers the summer of 1906 as a felicitous time in her life. Inevitably, it came to an end in the fall when the Syrkins moved back to
the city, for the time was right for Nachman Syrkin's activism to burst
forth. The October Revolution had dampened the appeal of Zionism
for the masses of Russian Jews who now hoped that socialism alone
would solve the problem at home, and so there would be no need for a
Jewish state. The Zionist movement itself was in disarray because of the
defection of the territorialists and the continued discord between the
"practical" Zionists who believed in immediate and continued practical
settlement in Palestine, as opposed to the "political Zionists," who still
hoped for a Herzlian diplomatic political success from Diaspora nations.
Herzl himself had believed that "any settlement activities in Palestine
before the grant of a 'Charter' by the Turks would be harmful and therefore should be discontinued" (*Essential Papers* 212). All this fed into
Nachman Syrkin's Territorialist program, and he furiously stepped up
his writing, lecturing, and agitating for the Zionist-Socialists (Sionisty-
Sotsialisty). Denouncing the weaknesses of the Russian liberals, the
Jewish bourgeoisie and the Zionist hypocrites in his customary acerbic
and now almost hysterical style, Syrkin, who held no illusions about the
future for Jews in the Diaspora, attacked the Zionist movement as "a
beaten bankrupt poverty-stricken band" (*Memoir* 120). In a scathing,
sardonic diatribe, Syrkin asks how "Zionist dreams can have any value
if they disappear once conditions in the Diaspora seem to improve?" Attacking even the dead Herzl, Syrkin lashed out:

The assimilator [Herzl] who knew not a word of Hebrew had been mistaken when he spoke of rescue from the Galuth. One must postpone Zionism for the future and the Messiah will come. True Zionism consists of dwelling in the Galuth, of making a snug living on the spot, of sending one's children to the *gymnasium,* of establishing Jewish kehillas [communities], of electing deputies to the Duma. The more firmly one sits on the spot, the more quickly one will get to *Eretz Israel.* This is called finding a bridge between today and tomorrow; this is called synthetic Zionism, evolutionary Zionism. (*Memoir* 121)

Years later, when Syrkin's daughter Marie wrote of these times, she called her father's tone "polemical ecstasy." She describes his attacks as vehement and intemperate, sounding merely frenzied — but she cautions her readers that the historic moment must be taken into account. Nachman Syrkin believed that in his insistence upon the Uganda project he was pragmatic; his daughter was convinced of his sincerity, despite his furious words. She admits that in "less than ten years Syrkin was to change his mind, if not rue his words, but in 1907 his bitterness at those who presumed to postpone the establishment of a Jewish state led him to accusations whose very recklessness makes one suspicious" (*Memoir* 121–122). Marie Syrkin asserts time and again that her father never lost his love for Palestine, that his frenzied behavior on behalf of a Jewish State outside of *Eretz Israel* was merely an act of realism. "Was he trying to outshout his own deep love for Palestine, never successfully stifled?" she asks. Or is Marie's psychologizing question merely an answer to help her come to terms with her father's outrageous behavior and apparent abandonment of *Eretz Israel?*

When the Syrkins returned to city life in the fall of 1907, the ephemeral hopes for Russian Jewry under the new dispensation were already in decline. The first Duma (Russian Parliament) that numbered twelve Jewish deputies (including five Zionists) had already been dissolved. Only four Jewish deputies were included in the Second Duma, which convened in February of 1907, and which was dissolved in June of that year. By this time, the brief sunlight of revolutionary promise had passed into shade. The Czar returned to his former reactionary ways and revoked what few liberal concessions he had granted — including shutting down the press. Not surprisingly, one of the casualties was Nachman Syrkin's journal *Das Wort.* In 1906, Count Peter Stolypin was named the new Minister of the Interior. He was, perhaps, the deadliest of those on the dishonor roll of Russian antisemites. A fierce warrior against the revolution, a zealous proponent of Russification, he organized a secret police force, encouraged terror groups, purged aliens from the civil service, sent out informers to hunt down all manner of revolutionaries, exploited Jew-hatred with extraordinary skill, and he was the architect of the infamous blood libel case against Mendel Beilis in 1911. This was a moment, to say the very least, not congenial for political activists. Indeed, to avoid arrest Nachman Syrkin found it prudent to leave Russia. And so it was that Nachman, Bassya, and Marie returned to Paris.

This, it would appear to us today, might have been the critical moment for Nachman Syrkin to emigrate to Palestine. Had he seized it, he would have been in the company of that great generation of pioneers, those of the Second Aliyah (1904–1914), who laid the foundation for the Labor Zionist movement in Palestine. He would have been among those whom he had inspired with his theory of socialist Zionism — the so-called founding fathers and mothers who came from all parts of Eastern Europe, such as Yitzhak Ben-Zvi of Poltava and his wife, Rahel Yanait, David Remez of Mogilev, Berl Katzenelson of Bobruisk, David Green (Ben-Gurion) of Plonsk, as well as A. D. Gordon, known as the "Tolstoi of Palestine," who had arrived in *Eretz Israel* in 1904 at the age of forty-eight to preach the philosophy of the return-to-soil movement and of human dignity through labor. But Syrkin did not choose to join his disciples. Instead, to escape the authorities, he fled Vilna for Paris to make preparations for departure for America. He had received an urgent plea from the American Socialist-Territorialist movement in the United States to come to New York to edit their journal, *Das Volk*. Nachman Syrkin accepted the offer, perhaps because New York would provide a freer atmosphere for the promulgation of his ideas, and would provide a new audience, and also would provide an income.

How does his daughter, who herself became a leader of American Labor Zionism, explain her father's peculiar choice? In a touching rumination on her father's decision and its many consequences, she hazards a guess. "Had my father not been possessed by the Territorialist illusion, which he then so stubbornly termed realism, I am certain that he would have left for Palestine instead of the United States, despite the fact that he was already thirty-nine years old. It is tempting" Marie muses, "and for me a poignant, speculation — to meditate on what life would have been like had my father returned to Zion sooner than he did" (*Memoir* 123).

Chapter 2

A Bronx Adolescence

❦

EXPLAINING HER FAMILY'S peripatetic life during her childhood, Marie Syrkin quipped, "Papa was always getting exiled, so we traveled a lot." For this reason in 1907, one step ahead of the Vilna authorities, the Syrkin family trio once more found itself on the move, and once more the family had to separate. By the fall of 1907, Nachman Syrkin set sail for America, leaving his twenty-nine-year-old wife, Bassya, and their eight-year-old daughter, Marie, to remain in Paris. There mother and daughter were to await Nachman's assessment of America as a promising venue for his Socialist-Territorialist work. It was a difficult time for Bassya — more difficult than during any other separation — because this time she was not occupied with her own revolutionary activity, and this time the distance between her husband and herself was not hundreds, but thousands of miles across the vast Atlantic, with no assurance of when or where they would reunite. The ever-optimistic Nachman Syrkin, however, took to America immediately, despite the fact that during his journey across the Atlantic, *Das Volk,* the weekly journal that he had been asked to edit had collapsed due to lack of funds. "Fortunately," as his daughter, Marie, later wryly commented, "another one, equally impecunious, was about to be started. There was to be no dearth of publications precariously teetering on the edge of bankruptcy at any stage in the Syrkin domestic economy" (*Memoir* 127). However sardonic her comment, she was correct. This was an era when every Jewish political, cultural, and labor group, even in the face of precarious finances, tried to promote its particular agenda in print; inevitably this resulted in a flood of short-lived publications.

It would be some weeks, however, before Nachman's enthusiastic letters written in Russian reached his wife. Postscripts to his eight-year-old

daughter were in French or German. This was one of his habitual pedagogic efforts; because Russian was spoken at home, he thought that his
French and German postscripts would help the child maintain fluency
in those languages. It did. Meanwhile, Bassya and Marie had settled in
at the Hotel Jeanne D'Arc located on the Rue de la Clef on the Left
Bank. This almost certainly was the area that the Syrkins had lived in before, for the Rue de la Clef, situated in the 5th Arrondissement of the
Latin Quarter, near the Sorbonne, the Jardin des Plantes, and the Natural History Museum, was a natural location for the under-financed but
intellectually voracious Syrkins. Not only were the prices cheaper, but
the Latin Quarter was also the haunt of bohemians and intellectuals,
and famous for its bookstores, cafes, and tree-lined streets. The apartment "was a modest place," Marie dryly recalls, "admirably suited to our
lack of means, and not too far from the museums which we were again
piously visiting. Comrades came frequently to cheer their leader's young
wife and small daughter, who while not exactly stranded were waiting
for a steamship ticket like many simpler immigrants" (*Memoir* 127).

Before long the tickets arrived. Yet, instead of bringing joy to Bassya,
it brought consternation. Her husband's voyage to America had been
paid for by the virtually resourceless Socialisti-Sionisti Party, which had
sent him on his own journey with a third-class ticket. It proved to be
a harsh crossing. In addition to his less than adequate quarters, the
weather was stormy, and inevitably, Nachman suffered acute seasick-
ness. Determined that his family should not have to endure these same
conditions, Syrkin purchased a first-class ticket for them, which he
bought on the installment plan. Never the practical one, he had not considered several facts that Bassya grasped immediately. First of all, she
had traveled in Europe enough to know that whatever were her husband's good intentions, this plan was bound to cause her distress. "Here
she was" Marie explains "with not a franc to spare and no clothes worth
mentioning, afflicted with this symbol of luxury!" Comrades from the
movement came to give advice. The first suggestion was that the tickets
be exchanged for second- or third-class ones, and then the difference
could be used for clothing and money for the trip; but, this solution was
soon seen to be out of the question because "nobody in Paris would accept tickets bought and not paid for in New York—the credit was too
remote" (*Memoir* 128).

With never-to-be-forgotten memories of this trip, Marie Syrkin later
would comment that "There are many immigrant tales of the pains of

steerage crossing to the Promised Land. Our saga of suffering in the first-class is funny only in retrospect." They were traveling on the *St. Paul* and everything, Marie remembers, turned out to be even worse than Bassya had anticipated. Through the rosy hue of hindsight, however, she recalls her own rather happy experience of the trip:

As far I was concerned, everything was delightful and I suffered only a reflected gloom. To have no money was a natural and not unhappy state of affairs, only distressing if it happened to you in the first class. Poverty had never been as oppressive as now. It seemed there was the matter of tips. One was surrounded by chamber maids, waiters, stewards, all of whom expected tips. And my mother had absolutely no francs for tips. Then, there was the matter of clothes. In the first class, my mother explained, the bourgeoisie indulged in ostentatious display. They dressed and undressed, and it seemed one could not go into the magnificent dining room unless one had suitable costumes. (*Memoir* 129)

Nine-year-old Marie, however, had glimpsed the beautiful table settings in the first-class dining room and so eager was she to "enjoy unknown pleasures" that she pleaded with her mother to go in her customary clothing. The child, thinking her mother looked fine, was baffled by Bassya's reluctance. Only later did Marie realize how shabby her mother's dress must have been if "despite her pride, she let herself be abashed by 'false forms.'" The upshot was that they took all their meals in their cabin. There were embarrassments aplenty on this voyage, from tips to rental of deck chairs — actually only one deck chair to be shared by Bassya and Marie. Through it all, like most children, Marie was able to disregard her mother's discomfort and search for her own pleasures, such as running around on the deck, or making friends with other passengers, who "though bourgeois, were very nice." Bassya, in the meantime, had warded off an offer of help from a charitable Jewish diamond merchant, though she welcomed the help of a third-class comrade who had heard of her peculiar situation. Finally, in March of 1908, Marie and Bassya Syrkin arrived in America just in time for Marie's ninth birthday, where they joined Nachman who awaited them and greeted them with joy and exuberance — though they "continued to pay for installments on that ticket for years after [their] arrival" (*Memoir* 131).

The failure of *Das Volk*, the journal Syrkin originally had come to the United States to edit, did not prove to be a great impediment to his new life in America, for it appears that almost immediately he received a new offer. This offer most probably came from Chaim Zhitlowsky, who had been a co-editor of *Das Volk*. After its demise, Zhitlowski became the editor of a new, highly intellectual journal, *Dos Naye Lebn* (*New Life*), a monthly periodical devoted to "science, literature, and socialism"[1] and that managed to remain in business for five years. Zhitlowsky, the chief theoretician of Yiddishism (the centrality of the Yiddish language and culture in modern Jewish life), was a proponent of Dubnow's autonomism[2] and national socialism, and since the Kishineff pogroms, sympathetic to Territorialism. Zhitlowsky must have recognized a kindred spirit in Nachman's politics as well as appreciated Syrkin's great intellect; consequently, he saw to it that the impractical Dr. Syrkin would not be without employment and finally would be paid a living wage.

This new position allowed Nachman to rent a four-room apartment on Charlotte Street, located between 172nd and 174th Street just southeast of Crotona Park, in the South Bronx. Though hardly luxurious, it was a decided improvement over past residences. The new apartment boasted gaslight in each room as well as central heating, and had been decorated with minimum furnishings bought on the installment plan. In 1908, Charlotte Street was a "pleasant block of small apartment houses, walkups, surrounded by unlittered lots bright with dandelions in the spring. Nearby Crotona Park was a safe, green playground and a place for picnics on summer days."[3] But in her 1983 essay about her years at Morris High School in the Bronx, Marie Syrkin could not avoid noting the fact that the fondly remembered Charlotte Street neighborhood of her youth now had become "a notorious symbol of urban decay" (Morris High 22).

As soon as the family was settled in their apartment, Marie, age nine, was sent off for formal education to P.S. 40, located only a few blocks from Charlotte Street. Among fellow students who were either recent immigrants or American-born children of recent immigrants, Marie Syrkin began her quick and easy process of Americanization. By all contemporary psychological measures the odds should be that Marie would have arrived in New York withdrawn and maladjusted. The Syrkins' peripatetic life before they came to America meant that by the time their daughter was nine she had already lived in four countries—Switzerland, Germany, France, and Russia—and could speak Russian, German, French, and Yiddish. For an ordinary child, such disruptions, accompanied by economic hardship, more than likely would have had serious emotional consequences; for Marie Syrkin, such was not the case. Some fifty years after her arrival in America, she herself examined and accounted for the equanimity of those early years spent in the face of the grim constants of poverty, danger, and exile. She confesses to having thought about it often in her maturity.

My parents violated all the rules of child psychology. My mother left me twice before I was six to transport contraband literature to Russia. My father never blasphemed Providence by trying to be provident when greater matters were at stake. The physical world as I knew it was mercurial, unsure — always slipping from one — countries, houses, possessions, even one's daily bread. And it was a threatened world — threatened because the Czar wanted to stifle the "revolution" and threatened because one was a Jew.

Any modern parent will tell you that grave personality problems from bedwetting to darker neuroses should have resulted and that a child who appeared cheerful under these circumstances was probably "repressing" with dire results for the future. Perhaps so, but on the conscious, surface level, at any rate, I accepted my world and was in that sense, "well adjusted." (*Memoir* 115–116)

The adult Marie asked herself several questions: How did her parents manage to develop such an accepting state of mind in their child? Why in her childhood did she often think how dull it would have been to be not Jewish; and why did the very thought of a non-Jewish life fill her "with a sense of emptiness and loss to which the knowledge that [she] was safe, that [she] was Jewish, would come with a rush of assurance"? It would have been explicable, Marie asserts, had she been brought up in a religious household — but there was "no trace of tradition" in her nurture. Nachman "felt too deeply about the Orthodox boyhood with which he had broken to permit any half-way pieties. A sentimental nostalgia was not permitted to replace a lost faith" (*Memoir* 116).

It is clear that Nachman Syrkin had broken with ritual pieties and superstition. However, his dedication to ethical principles, he freely admitted, were derived from prophetic Judaism. Moreover, Nachman's early, thorough Jewish education resulted in a deep knowledge of the tradition, which made the transmission of Jewish ethics — the part of Judaism that he never renounced — unselfconscious and natural. As a result, in Marie's attempt to explain the success of her father's educational methodology, she herself chooses a vocabulary central to the Jewish religion: election, "chosenness," and spiritual. She argues that her father imbued her with "a sense of election as surely as though he had been a medieval rabbi — only the basis for the 'chosenness' was different." The basis for election appeared to be twofold — at least to Marie as a child: suffering for an idea and poverty. With regard to her childhood understanding of the value of suffering, she explains, "Jews had such a special abundance of ideas for which they might suffer — the revolution, a land of their own, *samoborona* [self-defense during the pogroms] and other wonders." As for poverty, that too was a sign of election. "People who spent their time making money were bourgeois. Papa could make much money — of that I was certain — but the things he and his friends did were much more important." These were ideas that Marie did not question until much later, but that, she continued to maintain, was irrelevant. What was entirely relevant was that in order to understand her father

one must appreciate his genius for creating a spiritual atmosphere of a certain kind not only on the platform, but in the daily life of his home. . . . And there was nothing Bohemian about this life. Unpractical, improvident though it might have been, this existence had its discipline and its sanctities rigorously upheld. It had a code whose impress was so strong that its values were to remain substantially unaltered. In that sense the education was successful. . . . In my childhood there was never a sense of deprivation. That too, was a triumph of pedagogy." (*Memoir* 117)

Marie's talent for learning languages made her Americanization easier. Before long she could "chatter in English with the children on the block who seemed well disposed, though they would ask embarrassing questions. The chief of these was, 'What kind of a doctor is your father?'" Though she knew he was not a medical doctor, that he was a doctor of philosophy, she could not make clear "just what kind of a doctor that was" (*Memoir* 135). Enrolled at P.S. 40, Marie began her formal American education. In a description of how proficiency was achieved, she spells out the standard pedagogical techniques of elementary education in the first decades of the twentieth century:

Daily drills in spelling, recitals of multiplication tables, and practice in arithmetic occupied a sizable segment of the school day. The mystery of learning to read was addressed by straightforward phonetic exercises in the school primer. By third grade most pupils had grasped the relationship between letters and sounds. By sixth grade classroom blackboards were decorated with elaborate diagrams of sentences, subjunctive clauses, and adverbial phrases, studied in formal grammar lessons. By then we had also progressed to literature. This meant Longfellow's "Hiawatha" and such hortatory lyrics as "Excelsior" and "The Psalm of Life." We zestfully recited, "Life is real, life is earnest" before going on to more taxing passages from Shakespeare in the eighth grade. I recall no teacher who went beyond the prescribed subject matter, but the graduates, many of whom went straight to work, could manage the three R's; imbued with uncritical reverence for the Founding Fathers, they had learned a sanitized version of the history of their country; and they possessed as initial cultural baggage a number of famous poems all were expected to know. (Morris High 26)

Writing of this curriculum some seventy-five years after the fact, Marie poses the question, "Were the pupils stultified by these unimaginative techniques?" Her answer is to point out that the 1916 Morris High School graduation *Annual,* of which she was the literary editor, is filled with evidence of "accomplished teenagers . . . who had come from P.S. 40 or similar schools in the general area of Charlotte Street" (Morris High 26). Nor were the three Rs — reading, writing, and arithmetic — the sole focus of the pedagogy of the time. Marie's "moldering copy of *The Beacon,* March 1910, published by The Pupils of Public School No. 40, The Bronx, at five cents a copy, illustrates the relentless emphasis on the 'work ethic' to which the children were subjected." Lamenting the lack of self-expression and dullness in the student contributions "tolerable only to the parents of the authors," she remarks that what is startling these seventy years later is "the pupils uninhibited devotion to Effort, Proficiency, and Conduct, the three simple categories that used to appear on the monthly report card." In this remembrance of her early education, Syrkin insists that grade school and high school earnestness of those years regarding these three categories ought not be dismissed as "false 'middle class values,' alien to much of the present student body in urban centers. Few of my companions on Charlotte Street were middle class. I admit, however, that *values* — neither pretentiously absolute nor apologetically relative — existed. They served as checks on behavior and goads to aspiration. I suspect that they matter as much in the final result as the useful daily drills and foreign languages" (Morris High 27).

If Marie's Charlotte Street school life was considerably different from her European educational experience, her life at home with her parents had not appreciably changed. Her father continued to spend days at the New York Public Library and evenings at meetings. Friends from their Vilna or Berlin days who had come to America in these years of constant emigration continued their habit of congregating in Nachman Syrkin's apartment, some staying for the night, or even longer, until the guest had found some more permanent place to live. Marie always knew that when four chairs were arranged into an improvised bed, she would be the one to sleep on it. "Just as in other circles" she explains, where "it was taken for granted that relatives or 'landsmen' should be housed by those who had preceded them to America, in our midst the bond was ideology." She always knew that the telltale sign of a night of large quantities of tea, protracted talk, and "obscure excitement" was the arrangement of four chairs (*Memoir* 136).

The visitors to the Syrkin home would engage in a wide range of intellectual and political ideas of the day. Many of the frequent visitors to Nachman and Bassya's informal center for heated discourse were famous writers and important political leaders such as Baruch Zuckerman, one of the founders of the American Poalei Zion party who had joined the Territorialists in 1905, or Chaim Zhitlowsky, the brilliant and urbane theoretician of Yiddishism and Diaspora nationalism who often differed hotly with Syrkin over political opinions. Sholem Asch was yet another occasional visitor, characterized by Marie Syrkin as "moody and self-centered, already with an air of grandeur though not yet internationally famous." She also recalls a nearby neighbor, the Yiddish poet and editor Abraham Liessen, who participated in the founding of the Yiddish daily *Forward* and from 1913 until his death, was editor of the preeminent Jewish literary and cultural monthly in the U.S., *Zunkunft*. A number of attractive women from the Vilna days seemed to have made a deep impression, such as Zuckerman's beautiful wife Nina, a blonde beauty named Sonia Kamenetsky and "dark brooding Chaika Cohen" (*Memoir* 136–137). All these exciting people did not go unnoticed, for those friends who fussed over Nachman and Bassya Syrkin's beautiful and bright nine-year-old daughter with her large dark eyes and thick black hair were to remain vividly in Marie's mind until she re-met many of them professionally in her adult years.

Meantime her family's leisure activities also provided ideological nourishment. There were boat trips on the Hudson for *Po'ale Zion* members; there were meetings referred to as "balls," held for one cause or another, which fit the designation only insofar as after long speeches there would be dancing and refreshments; there were public lectures to which Marie would be subjected because her parents "felt that a bright ten-year-old should be able to appreciate political discourse at any hour." Moreover, at such locations one could meet celebrities such as Emma Goldman and Alexander Berkman who might turn up unaccountably "at a social-democratic ball despite their anarchism" (*Memoir* 137).

Though the Syrkins' social plate was full and satisfying, their financial cup was nearing empty. Paying the rent and grocery bills were becoming ever more problematic. Nachman Syrkin's approbation from his admirers in the local Jewish merchant community sometimes made payment dates flexible — but not always. Money issues were becoming so intrusive that even Marie became aware, if not worried, about them. Things came to a head when Bassya made a decision to take a job in a factory. This, of course, should not have caused any serious disturbance; after all, the Syrkins were socialist and egalitarian. But Marie argues that to understand Nachman's objection one must "reconstruct the state of mind of the European intellectuals of middle class origin to appreciate that for both [Nachman and Bassya] despite their socialism and 'proletarian' ideology, this represented social decline." Her ironic justification of her parents' attitudes argues:

To be a hungry student or a chronically indigent intellectual was proper and vaguely praiseworthy, but for my mother to seek work in a factory was as great a loss of caste as if my father had become a petty shopkeeper. To have become a peasant or farmer might have been in the *narodnik* or Tolstoyan tradition and tolerable as such. This was different. For the first time I was told to keep a secret. Our friends were not to know. (*Memoir* 138)

Bassya Syrkin, the former medical student, chose to apply for a job in a millinery factory because she was an excellent seamstress; even having made not-quite-stylish black alpaca suits for Nachman in Europe for appearances at Zionist Congresses and public events. (Herzl had set the standard for participants of the Zionist Congresses, requiring top hat and tails for the attendees). But she was instructed to make her work application under an alias, lest someone recognize her as the wife of the well-known Nachman Syrkin. Her tenure in the new position, however, was short-lived because, as Marie bitingly comments, "though the few dollars she earned were badly needed my father was so depressed by our solvency that the experiment was abandoned after a few weeks" (*Memoir* 139). Marie's mother left her job at her husband's insistence — though she would resume it again when the Socialist-Zionist party sent Nachman to Germany for the 1909 Zionist Congress.

Although Nachman Syrkin's political reputation was thriving, his finances were not improving. Fortuitously, however, a childhood friend of Nachman, Dr. I. Lourie, appeared on the scene. Nachman was delighted to renew his acquaintance with his childhood playmate from Mogilev. Dr. Lourie and his family were among the very few friends the Syrkins had who were not comrades "from the movement nor from the teacher-disciple relationship so common to [Syrkin's] circle" (*Memoir* 141). Lourie, moreover, offered certain benefits. Not only was he a medical doctor, but he owned real estate — apartment houses — in Brooklyn. And so it was that the year Marie entered sixth grade, the Syrkins moved to Gravesend Avenue in Flatbush. The new apartment was roomier than the Bronx apartment, but there were marked drawbacks. Though there were five rooms, rather than the four on Charlotte Street, there was no furniture for the extra room. More significantly, however, the new apartment did not have central heating. The only source of heat was a coal stove in the kitchen. Since this was a railroad flat, the rooms abutting the kitchen were the warmest. The room at the furthest end of the apartment, the living room, had only one piece of furniture — a piano, once again an installment-plan purchase, a plan that for the Syrkins seems to have been a version of the modern credit card which can be "maxed" out. As imprudent as that may seem in view of the family finances, its purpose was to see to it that Marie had music lessons. Marie's musical ability, however, was never to become one of her major attributes.

Perhaps more foolhardy than the purchase of the piano was assignment of the two bedrooms in the apartment. Only one had a window, and the Syrkins decided to give that one to their daughter. "The other" Marie clearly recalls, "was a windowless corridor between the dining room and the icy living room. Naturally," she reports with some puzzlement, "I was given the light room while my parents slept in the dark airless chamber. Both my parents had studied medicine; they were aware of my mother's tubercular history. Why were they so heedless?" (*Memoir* 142).

The family finances continued to have their ups and mostly downs, but Marie's experience of daily life was untroubled. She knew that her father spent each day in the Jewish Room at the Astor Library where he did his research and met with people eager to seek him out; she knew that her mother provided her husband with lunch sandwiches cut into bits so that he could eat them surreptitiously while doing his research; she knew that her mother would "dole out the exact change for carfare" because her father's prodigality needed to be restrained, lest he waste precious resources on some bauble for his daughter or "part with it to one of the hapless cranks who besieged him" (*Memoir* 142). At one point, Nachman became an enthusiast of the cooperative movement, lecturing and writing about its general merits as well as particular projects. For a brief period he actually held a job as a paid professional for a cooperative hat store. Earning fifteen dollars a week, Nachman suddenly felt like a millionaire, and unless Bassya kept her eye on him, he would arrive home with all sorts of luxuries for his wife and daughter. But after a few months, says Marie "the corruption of wealth" ended and "penury, less jolly as time went on . . . was restored" (*Memoir* 143). As for the effects on Marie herself, she readily accepted the fact that often she would walk for more than twenty minutes to Borough Park to buy four rolls for three cents because the same three cents would buy only three rolls just down the street on Gravesend Avenue. Looking back, Marie has insisted that she never experienced self-pity, nor did she ever think of her family as poor; yet she remembers and reports that her mother once gave her a bottle of homemade borscht and sent her to a friend's house with it. As Marie left, her mother added, "Perhaps they will invite you for supper." The words were not forgotten and in retrospect Marie comments that "I understood that there was nothing to eat in the house except that soup, but it did not occur to me then to wonder what she ate that evening because she had been careful to smile as she sent me off" (*Memoir* 144).

Although the tone of the Syrkin household was set by Nachman's "constant intellectual excitement" and "marvelous exuberance," it was Bassya who provided the practical ballast. The same Bassya who courageously left home to go to medical school in a foreign country, who left her husband and small child for weeks at a time to smuggle pamphlets hidden in the false bottom of her trunk in revolutionary Russia, who in America tried factory work to supplement her husband's meager income, now tried unsuccessfully to make women's hats to sell from her home. As strongly pragmatic as this physically compromised young mother became under the severe financial realities, she nonetheless remained a tender mother whose concern for her daughter showed itself in small episodes that Marie would long cherish. Writing of one moment that she would never forget, Marie recalls, "Once, when I was twelve, she bought me high-heeled shoes at a sale and I squealed with delight at the unaccustomed high heels. My mother's eyes filled with tears and she said gently, 'These are not the shoes I would buy you, if I had my choice'" (*Memoir* 143).

If, at this stage of her life, Marie loved her mother, she absolutely adored her father, accepting his outbursts and irascibility because she was never in doubt of his love for her. She consented to his severe tutelage in ethics with little argument because she never questioned his authoritative moral absolutism or his self-assurance. In later years, after attaining her own professional recognition, Marie asserted that one lesson that he taught her in childhood remained forever in her conscience and "proved costly." When her sixth grade class at P.S. 130 on Fort Hamilton Parkway decided to have a party, the class settled on a collection of ten cents each. A committee of three, including Marie, was chosen to buy the candy and favors. They set out one afternoon, and when their careful shopping was complete, the three shoppers discovered that they still had six cents. Tired from the experience, they talked about what to do with this leftover sum that was too small to divide with the rest of their classmates. Suddenly they had an inspiration. "It flashed on us that we had enough for a glass of cherry soda a piece. It seemed a reasonable reward for our efforts," Marie remembers as if it were yesterday. But clearly the reason for the clarity of recall was not just the soda, but her father's reaction when she gave her parents a full account of the day's events. Nachman fell into a fury—a condition she had witnessed many times before; and although she frequently did not know what "apparently innocent act might precipitate his indignation," it was never long until she found out her transgression.

This time it seemed I was an embezzler; my graceless committee and I had betrayed a sacred trust. We had used public money for private pleasure. This put a new light on the cherry soda. My father gave me six cents which, much abashed, I gave to the teacher the following morning with a complete confession. After restitution had been made I tried to collect four cents from the other members of the committee but they had no spare cash and had endured no equivalent moral qualms.

My father's anger was all the more impressive because, hot-tempered though he was, he was an adoring parent, more likely to embarrass me with extravagant praise than to reprove me. But in any question of principle he made no allowances for inexperience, age, or circumstances. Two cents misappropriated at the age of eleven from the public treasury was a breach of trust and had to be dealt with as such.

As Marie later maintains, this was a costly lesson, and not simply because of her father's rage over the lost pennies. The lesson had long range power. "It took me years," she would later lament, "before I learned to dine as well as a lecturer merited when an organization was paying, and I have never been able to pad an expense account intelligently" (*Memoir* 146).

If Nachman was the hard taskmaster in the matter of morals, he also assumed the role of home tutor. There were several subjects that he was certain his daughter would not be taught in an American elementary school, so he took up the job himself. But in this endeavor, he was not as thorough as he was in his ethics training. In Marie's exchange with the scholar-journalist Trude Weiss-Rosmarin many years later, when both women were retired and living in Santa Monica, Weiss-Rosmarin commented that Marie was very fortunate in her upbringing. "After all, to be the daughter of Nachman Syrkin." Marie quickly snapped back,

Yes, but one thing he failed to provide me. He did not teach me Hebrew at an age when I could have learned it. It's maddening. You know, when I was a child, a teenager, he would periodically get the feeling that he was neglecting me and he would take over my instruction. The books in question were *Das Kapital* in German, Spinoza's *Ethics* in Latin — I don't know why, except that I was precocious — and the Bible, where we never got beyond the first sentence. We'd get that far and Papa would suddenly be busy, and by the next time, I'd have forgotten what we'd done so we would start over. . . . So that's one thing I have against my father. . . . [T]hat he didn't teach me Hebrew was a serious loss. (*Moment* 8, 8)

Fortunately, Marie Syrkin was never tested in Marx, Spinoza, and Hebrew Bible at P.S. 130, for in 1912, at the age of twelve, four years after her emigration to America, she was scheduled to graduate from her elementary school. Despite the "embezzlement scandal" the year before, she had proven herself to be a very smart young girl, smart enough to have been chosen as valedictorian of her graduating class. The topic for the speech was selected by the teacher. Marie was to expatiate upon Julius Caesar's famous declaration, "*Veni, vidi, vici*," (I came, I saw, I conquered). Some seventy-five years later in one of her many self-deprecatory portraits, Marie described the process of writing her valedictory oration.

I began writing thunderingly some horrible stuff about "among the corridors of time the immortal words of Caesar ring out." This I remember. I remember that initial triumphant sentence which I thought was very brilliant. For some reason, when I was reaching my second paragraph, I remembered a passage from *Ivanhoe* in which Scott had phrased something admirably and it occurred to me that—should I use those words? Three or four sentences which said whatever it was that I wanted to say—which I really don't remember—I remember the fact that nowhere had I seen that particular thought better put. Or should I struggle to restate it? Something told me that I mustn't ask my father whether this is permissible. Some instinct warned me, so I decided to appease my conscience and ask my mother. When I put the case to her, she said she saw nothing wrong with this. Well, this oration, therefore, had a paragraph from Scott in it and then continued in my own sophomoric—not even sophomoric, but childish style.[4]

Many years later, Marie Syrkin, by this time well known for her superb prose style, reflected on this episode and bristled: "What amazes me now is the teachers who read it; the difference in style stuck out like a sore thumb." But her teacher, Marie recalled, was filled with admiration. "She probably admired my intellect more than the tight and elegant sentences of Scott. And I delivered the oration proudly—and that was my most triumphant moment for many years to come" (Personal interview).

The principal too was enamored. It offered him the opportunity to make a rousing speech about what America is capable of. He began with "Here is a little girl who came three years ago to this country and see what she has accomplished. She's gone to school and she's the valedictorian.'"

And what did Nachman Syrkin say when he heard his daughter's oration on graduation day with its plagiarized paragraph? His daughter reports that he said nothing. "He was too busy adoring his little daughter to take note of the text. Besides," she points out, "this was English, a language in which his sense of style was unsure" (*Memoir* 146–147).

This episode is contained in Marie Syrkin's biographical memoir of her father; but it also came up in a 1989 personal interview, sparking recall of another moment in her graduation year, one that does not appear in the memoir. At the end of the tale of the valedictory speech, Syrkin lost her train of thought. "I'm trying to remember the next point that I was going to make," she murmured, straining to recall; "yes-no." Suddenly with renewed assurance she says, "I still remember a teacher that I had there who thought I was wonderful. Miss Parsons." Syrkin named her in a soft reverential tone. "I thought her very old. I assume she must have been a woman of forty. I still remember what she wrote in my autograph book: Go where glory waits thee / and when fame elates thee / Oh, then remember me. / When the praise thou meetest / to thy ear is sweetest / Oh then remember me." Though Marie no longer had the book, she said that she clearly remembers the little poem. Again in an exercise of self-insight, Syrkin immediately interjects,

The interesting thing psychologically is that after that my life began to go downhill fast in many ways. In high school I was not working at all. . . . To return to my story, the notion of this brilliant beginning seemed to fade so utterly that I totally forgot what had been written to me at the age of twelve. But psychologically what is interesting—I have to jump many decades ahead. At the age of forty-two or forty-three, I wrote a very successful book on the public school system of New York. The book had rave reviews—front page stuff; there was an editorial about it in the *Herald Tribune,* and I had a sense at that moment—suddenly in that moment—that seemed to me victory, those words came back to me and I found myself reciting "Go where glory waits thee / and where fame elates thee / Oh then remember me." After a period of perhaps thirty years, I recalled Miss Parsons [again named reverentially] and those lines that had been written in the autograph book. (Personal interview)

Marie then proceeded to argue that "this justifies Freud" because she had completely suppressed the episode. When I asked her what the sudden recall meant to her, she snapped back that "it meant very clearly that Miss Parsons assumed that I would be famous. In the years to come I was anything but famous. I graduated from high school without any distinction."[5] With the passing years, until this book, Marie confessed, there was "nothing to warrant steadily the notion that I would ever accomplish anything except the most commonplace respectable things. And the dazzling promise whose peak appeared at age twelve was utterly gone—and my father of course was very much disappointed in me. I no longer had the autograph book, and Miss Parsons must have been long dead; she died certainly long before she ever saw my name in print, which she probably expected to see—and didn't"; but at that moment the words in the autograph album came back to Marie Syrkin completely. Whether or not this "justifies Freud," it is a revealing tale.

The last year before Marie's graduation from P.S. 130 was not a tranquil one. Though Nachman's capacity for wholehearted laughter and humor continued unabated, so did his capacity for intemperance and "furious impatience with every effort to pluck him momentarily from the cloud on which he dwelt" (*Memoir* 147). He would erupt unaccountably and out of proportion to the events which inspired them. Marie's relationship with her mother also had some peaks and valleys. In a story about the creation of her graduation dress, Marie says rather edgily that this will show the strict rearing her mother gave her. The girls in the graduating class were given the choice of either making their own dresses or having them made at home. Bassya, in the course of the family's financial misfortunes had developed a number of skills; she had become a superb seamstress, and quite naturally offered to make Marie's dress for her. In a sudden burst of independence, Marie refused the offer and said that she would rather spend the few dollars for the material and then make it herself. Bassya, however, had a great sense of discipline and told her daughter, "Remember, if you make it you'll have to wear it." As a result, Marie could never forget the consequence. Yes, she made the dress, but later lamented, "This little valedictorian had by far the worst dress of anyone in the class. And my mother stuck to her position. If we had invested three dollars and the dress was of my manufacture, that was that." It seemed to Marie that this was perfectly just. "I did not resent it and I had the dress which was not as nice as the other little girls. I was left with my choice and I did not cavil because it seemed to me fair. That was my mother; that was the kind of moral, ethical discipline you had to abide by" (Personal interview).

Bassya's Death

Whatever the pressures on Nachman Syrkin that caused his daughter to take note of his increasing mood swings, they came to a halt when Bassya developed a cough. Just a month before Marie's graduation in January, the attacks became severe enough to frighten Nachman into insisting that they move to a centrally heated apartment in the Bronx. Marie finished the term living in Brooklyn with Dr. Lourie's family.

Immediately upon graduation, Marie moved back with her parents who had taken an apartment on Charlotte Street, the same street they had come to upon their arrival in America. She was to begin her high school education in the February term at Morris High School. At first, her mother's health seemed to have improved, as did her father's state of mind. Nonetheless, Marie's view of her father began to grow increasingly judgmental. "The atmosphere of incense and gunpowder which always enveloped him — he was being either worshiped by his followers or attacked by his opponents — had stopped to impress me" Marie explains. Of course, this might be attributed to the typical attitudes of a thirteen-year-old girl to her parents — though Nachman Syrkin himself was far from typical. Her father embarrassed her. His public outrages humiliated her; his "weird pet names" for her, which he used when sticking his head out of the window to resoundingly call out "Pililee (or worse yet, Katiolochka), come home." He would also burst out into song in unlikely places such as a crowded subway train. Though he did not have a particularly good ear or a good voice, he would nonetheless sing out leitmotifs or bits of arias from operas — particularly Wagner. And if once she thought him lean and handsome, she now saw him as a short, stocky man wearing pince-nez and sporting a beard that took varying shapes, whose clothing looked rumpled and whose socks were sometimes unmatched. "He was irrepressible, full of exact, clear-cut plans for his abiding visions," contends Marie. Moreover, he seemed to his self-conscious teenage daughter, completely unaware that he often mortified her by his behavior (*Memoir* 148–149).

Nachman's irrepressible optimism prevailed even in the case of Bassya's health; his denial of his wife's true condition undoubtedly influenced his daughter's failure to see how sick her mother really was. Looking back Marie says, "Though I loved her very much. . . . I can't claim that I was as attached to her as my father. At the time that I was living with her, I was. But the psychology there is very curious. She really stopped being my mother when I was thirteen. . . . I was very devoted to my mother. I loved her — but she has not remained in my memory — I mean, I'm still obsessed with my father" (Personal interview).

The return to Charlotte Street turned out to be a brief one. One afternoon, before the end of the spring term at Morris High School, Marie came home from school to find both her parents seated in the kitchen awaiting her. She could tell that they had something to tell her. Bassya smiled and then gently told her daughter that her sickness had come back. She reassured Marie that it wasn't so bad, but the doctor had advised her to go to a better climate. "There was a hospital in Colorado called the Denver Hospital for Jewish Consumptives. Moreover, the doctor thought she should go there as soon as possible." Looking back, Marie claimed that this was a mistake; her mother should not have been "torn away from her family and sent to Colorado. But that seemed the wise course then." In addition to following the advice of the doctors, her parents thought that the move would protect Marie from infection, and the distance from New York was regarded as an advantage because "there would be less temptation to return before a total cure had been effected. Besides," Marie could not help but add to this exercise in hind-sight, "my father was assured that his wife would receive preferential treatment in any Jewish institution even though he had no money to pay" (*Memoir* 150–151).

The decision made, Bassya left for Denver and Marie remained to keep house for her father. From this point on Marie claims, Bassya stopped being her mother. She was only a source of worry and sickness and pain, and in an *ex post facto* analysis of her feelings at that time, Marie says, "I assume that I was selfish—self-centered enough to un-consciously resent it. Not consciously. I don't think I was a good daughter in any sense from the age of thirteen until her death" (Personal interview).

Still, with certain adjustments, life on Charlotte Street went on. Marie took over the housekeeping. Freely admitting that her domestic skills were "not of the most accomplished," she confessed that many girls of her age would have done better. Fortunately, it did not bother her father at all. Yet Marie pardons herself, arguing that "There had been little occasion in my wandering childhood to learn the domestic arts" (*Memoir* 151). These arts, in fact, were never to become a long suit.

During the period of her mother's stay in Denver, her father's de-spondency weighed on Marie more than did her mother's absence. Bassya wrote often—optimistically, and Marie simply assumed that her mother would return soon and all would be well. Nachman's suffering and sadness, however, was observable every day. It troubled Marie be-cause she knew that this was contrary to his naturally cheerful state of mind. Eventually, Syrkin had no choice but to break up the household. His own schedule included lecture tours, evening meetings, daytimes at work at the library; all these demands on his time made it impossible for him to attend to his daughter's comings and goings in her teenage years. There was nothing to be done but to dispose of the household furnish-ing and to find rooms with an appropriate family. Some of the house-hold items were parceled out to friends who told the sad little girl that they would give them back "when your mother gets better." The unpaid-for piano went back to the seller. The bedroom and dining room pieces were sold to a neighbor who heard that there was a second-hand sale. The woman took a quick look at the beds and the table and chairs and offered five dollars for the lot, perhaps expecting to get into a bargaining war with the owner. That moment was so excruciatingly painful that decades later, Marie could instantly summon up her father's despairing response. "I shall never forget the anguished bitterness with which he answered, 'All right. Take it away; take it away.'" "That," she comments, "was the end of my mother's American household. I sometimes wondered about the whereabouts of the Singer Sewing Machine, but no one remembered who had taken it" (*Memoir* 152).

The following two years were the blackest of Nachman Syrkin's life. Bassya did not improve. Even the Colorado treatment made no difference. As her health began its inevitable decline, the family clutched at any promise of palliation. Recalling that ten years before, Bassya had improved after her stay in Italy, Nachman decided to move her to a warm climate somewhere near New York. Bassya's brother, Minai Osnos, an extremely successful electrical engineer in Berlin, arranged to pay for a stay in a private sanitarium. Still, nothing seemed to help. Bassya was moved from place to place in quest of someplace "that would agree with her — Liberty, Lakewood, a town in the South — all were tried in a grim journeying to find health and quiet breathing" (*Memoir* 153). During the summer of 1915 Nachman at last brought Bassya home to New York. He finally acknowledged the dreaded prognosis. Though she could not be healed, at least she would not be alone.

If these were years of unrelieved pain and anxiety for Nachman Syrkin, the same was not entirely true for his daughter. Though she certainly felt her mother's absence deeply, she had no idea of the inevitable course it would take, and as she has put it, she sometimes resented the extra burden it placed on her — especially the responsibility for keeping up the apartment. But there were some moments of pleasure to provide respite from the bleak conditions. For one thing, the Syrkins had made some new friends — the family of David Ludins. Ludins was a Russian Jewish intellectual, and his wife Olga was a warm motherly figure who tried to mother Marie along with her own two daughters, Tima and Ryah, who became Marie's lifelong friends. "Though our apartment was in my charge," writes Marie, "and I tried to clean and cook, my father had the assurance that on many nights when he came home late from a meeting, I could wait for him at the warm Ludins home" (*Memoir* 151). Some seven decades later when Marie had retired to Santa Monica, she discovered that Tima Ludins, whose friendship she had retained on and off through the years, happened to be living in her neighborhood. "In our old age," she pointed out, "we are now living within several blocks of each other. She was my 'so-called' best friend. Unfortunately, politically we parted company in the thirties. I became a passionate Zionist, she a Communist, so we had endless difficulties. But the relationship of childhood and early youth remained. So we still see each other, but we invariably do battle" (Personal interview). Nonetheless, when Marie was fourteen, Tima was absolutely her best friend.

Once, when Marie's father was "feeling particularly rich," he gave her thirty cents. "That was a sum," she said, thinking back to those days, "whose dimensions I can't begin to describe. What did one do with thirty cents?" It did not take long before she settled on the best way to spend it. Marie's taste for sweets ruled the decision. She promptly invited Tima to join her for a heretofore unimagined delight — one that in their old age neither had ever forgotten.

Neither of us had ever eaten a Pineapple Temptation or a Banana Split which had come into being within that year. Well, they were impossible for us to purchase; they cost fifteen cents a piece. . . . This allowed for both a Pineapple Temptation *and* a Banana Split. And we went that day, the two of us fourteen-years-olds, on a real Saturnalia. One of us ordered the Banana Split, the other a Pineapple Temptation. We divided it, and we each, for the first time, tasted that extraordinary delight. Well there's never been anything quite like it — as you can imagine. A Banana Split and a Pineapple Temptation — all on the same day. (Personal interview)

The tale of two ice-cream sundaes told in her eighty-ninth year however, allowed Marie to take a jibe at contemporary affairs. Immediately upon exclaiming upon the joys of the two ice-cream dishes, Marie stressed the fact that "whereas children under similar circumstances today would view themselves as underprivileged . . . and that they are deprived, I had no sense of deprivation; this was an unheard of luxury, a beneficence which appeared, and if it wasn't there as a routine thing it was not particularly a deprivation" (Personal interview).

Marie's complete obliviousness to her lack of creature comforts, her ingenuous acceptance of near poverty, is affirmed in a story she tells about another unlikely childhood experience. In the early days of Marie's mother's absence, she had a glorious never-to-be-forgotten outing. It occurred in the summer, a few months after her graduation from P.S.

130 in Brooklyn. Somehow, Miss Parsons, the teacher who had written such praising lines in Marie's autograph album, must have gotten wind of the terrible news about Bassya Syrkin and the fact that her brilliant and lovely pupil Marie had now become a "latchkey" child. Marie Syrkin was still fresh in her memory, and though Miss Parsons was in Brooklyn and the Syrkins were now in the Bronx, she came to see Marie and told her that soon she would take her to "something fabulous." She said she was going to take her to Steeplechase in Coney Island. When the day came, Marie was wearing the dress that she had made for graduation. Miss Parsons arrived, took one look at the child and asked, "Why are you wearing that dress?" Marie explained that her mother was sick. "She looked at me with such compassion," Marie recalled,

and she said, "Well, you can't go with a dress that looks like this; we'll have to pin it up a little." Apparently, the dress was very long. I don't know how she managed to get the dress pinned up. . . . It seems to me we stopped somewhere and she explained, "this little girl's mother is sick and away." Suddenly I realized, I'm a little girl whose mother is sick and away. But I hadn't been thinking in those terms. And she took me to Steeplechase—I still recall that fabulous day with Miss Parsons. She got a fifty-cent ticket which enabled one to go on every ride. And she waited while I went on ride after ride. And I still remember, she took me to lunch to a place in Coney Island—I still recall that marvelous menu—steak and strawberry ice-cream. Fabulous! (Personal Interview)

Though Marie always insisted that as a child she had no sense of deprivation, the truth was that by the time she became a teenager, she began to understand "what a price [her] mother had paid for her life of dedicated hardship." Years later, reflecting on her mother's health and the hard life she had led, Marie mused poignantly: "She should have been given ease and comfort." Recalling again the episode of the borscht, Marie now stingingly accused herself of "unfeelingness" toward her mother: "I'm horrified at the insensibility of a twelve-year-old child, to whom it did not occur to say—I remember it now after all these decades—what a terrible thing it was that I didn't say 'No, Mama, I have to stay with you and we'll share the borscht.'" Marie maintained that she was not a particularly "vicious child," but she explained that whereas she herself had no sense of deprivation, "that obviously did not apply to her mother. She suffered a great deal." Yet, Marie marveled that even when her mother was already quite sick, and even with Bassya's recognition of Nachman's "deliberate poverty," of his insistence that he would not compromise with anything, that he would not undertake any type of work that "interfered with his cause," she proudly said to her daughter, "I would rather have lived one year with an eagle, than twenty years with a crow." Marie adds, "She had the temperament for it — this life. But she certainly suffered and I'm sure she fell victim to the terrible poverty which we endured and of which she was the victim, not I" (Personal interview).

Bassya's return to the Bronx, however, was not to the apartment, but to Montefiore Hospital. This was to be her last residence. The year was 1915; Nachman and Bassya had been married for seventeen years; Nachman was forty-seven, Bassya thirty-six. Marie, fifteen, would visit her mother several times a week after school. These were, of course, painful visits; yet one visit would never be forgotten. "One December afternoon," Marie achingly recalls, her mother

looked at her sixteen-year-old daughter in a transport of maternal love, and said "You are just the kind of daughter I dreamt of having." . . . That was the last time I saw her. Two days later she took an unexpected turn for the worse; pneumonia developed. All day the hospital authorities tried to reach my father who was somewhere at a meeting. By the time they located him, late in the afternoon, she was dead. She had died alone on December 19, 1915, at the age of thirty-six" (*Memoir* 153).

This recollection of the death of Bassya Syrkin captures the deep sorrow of a young girl separated from her sick mother for two years and now deprived of her altogether, as well as the enduring need of that child for her mother's approval and love. It also lays bare the blame she places on her father for not being present in her mother's final moments.

Chapter 3

That Fabulous Summer

Maurice

ON MARCH 28, 1915, a few days after her sixteenth birthday, Marie Syrkin began a diary that she kept for a little over two months. That, in any case, is all that she preserved. The last years of Bassya Syrkin's rapidly deteriorating health had been dark and depressing for Marie and her father. Psychologically, Bassya had stopped being Marie's mother when her daughter was thirteen, for precisely at that most vulnerable pubescent age, just as Marie entered Morris High School in the Bronx, Bassya Syrkin left home for the promised recuperative air of Denver, never to recuperate, and never again to be available to her daughter. She died just months before Marie's high school graduation. It is little wonder then, that the brilliant and beautiful child who been the valedictorian of her elementary school class, soon began to perform very much below capacity at Morris High School.

It does not require a license in psychology to diagnose the cause of Marie's academic decline. First, living conditions went from bad to worse. After dismantling their apartment, Nachman and his daughter became lodgers in other people's homes, with no expectation of establishing their own home ever again. They moved from place to place in the apartments of "kindly, impoverished ladies who offered room and board to paying guests" (*Memoir* 153). Typically there would be a small hall bedroom for Nachman and a slightly larger one for Marie. Marie particularly remembered one kind lady, a Mrs. Covan; but always Nachman made sure that there would be someone to cast an eye on the child. Furthermore, as painful a time as this was for Marie, it was utterly lonely and comfortless for her grieving father, "made endurable only by the unflagging intensity of his intellectual absorptions" (*Memoir* 154). The consequence of his despair and escape through "intellectual" painkillers, made Marie's anguish even more intense. Years later, in a tone not devoid of bitterness, Marie would describe how her father had seemed to her then: "Whatever his inner griefs, the pattern of his life remained unchanged. He would leave for the 42nd Street Library and come back in the evening, usually after a meeting. He had eaten alone in some cafeteria; if it were not too late he would come into my room for a report of the day's doings" (*Memoir* 154).

To say the least, the physical and emotional environment was not conducive to the intellectual progress of an adolescent girl. It was not that Nachman had lost interest in his daughter's academic development. He remained zealous about her education, and his expectations were high; but his methodology was highly irregular. "I had been a precocious child," Marie maintains,

and my father was not likely to be less enthusiastic about his daughter than about other matters which engaged his emotions. But I cannot say that his instruction was methodical.

Every once in a while, on a Saturday or Sunday when I was not in school and he was free, he would sit me down for an hour of learning; however, the interruptions were so many, the lapses between one lesson and the next so long, that I never seemed to get beyond the first chapter of these volumes. In addition, by the age of fifteen, I had developed a passion for the English romantic poets and my father was dismayed at my frivolity in preferring Shelley to Spinoza. (*Memoir* 154)

Nachman's failure to inspire Marie to academic heights, her worries about her poor grades, her addiction to romantic poetry, her attempts to write her own verse, her adolescent *weltschmerz* and romantic fantasizing, as well as her concerns about her awakening sexuality are all documented in detail in her two-month confessional journal.[1] There is little here to suggest either that she would develop a writing style that more often than not would be characterized as astringent and witty or that she would become a Zionist polemicist — though one can begin to detect her later fondness for irony. At the age of sixteen, she exhibits the usual teenage propensity for romantic sentimentality, albeit with an unusually lush and rich vocabulary. An adolescent *cri-de-coeur,* the diary begins with a topographical survey of her current emotional state: "Another year has begun replete with other woes. I see before me only dull, dull pain, with no relief. I am alone, all, all alone, alone in my grief and my joy. My mother is gone, I know not where, my father is away. The days pass by, a grey monotonous array, unproductive save of evil" (*Diary,* March 28).

But the source of this despair is not parental absence alone. It is accompanied by fear of ordinariness. "I am becoming common-place," she laments, "ordinary, the very thought of it maddens one." Perhaps the weight of Nachman and Bassya's treatment of Marie as a child prodigy, as well as Marie's grade school teacher Miss Parsons' support of their assessment, was too much baggage under the current circumstances. There are other issues too that show up throughout the entries. Marie is clearly not doing well in any subject but English. By April 6, her academic troubles become her main theme. "I shall commit suicide," she exclaims. "[T]here seems no other way of escaping my troubles, and I have not the slightest desire to bear them with heroic fortitude. My [worthy?] chemistry teacher publicly held me up as an example to the class of all that is obnoxious and despicable in a pupil. I cannot bear it." At this point, an early trace of what was later to become her rhetorical trademark pokes through—sardonic irony: "I have certainly realized my darling parents' hopes admirably. I shall most probably only fail in two subjects, so I decidedly have no cause to complain of my scholastic achievements" (*Diary,* April 6, 1915).

By April 7, however, Marie has a change of heart: "My life is a tragedy, ay a tragedy worthy of being enacted in the most exalted scenes. I have but one despairing thought haunting me now, that is my failure to make good in school. . . . I *shall* work, work so that all will perceive that I can yet become something."

Nachman and Bassya's expectations apparently have taken deep root. But the struggle between super-ego and libido has now begun. Though a wonder child, Marie was a very normal adolescent with growing sexual feelings, and as she matured into womanhood, sensuality would profoundly effect the events of her life. At this point, however, she expresses her newly discovered feelings in the overly sentimental language that she has read in novels but has not actually experienced herself. Now maternal loss and academic failure give way to a third and more prominent subject: awakened sexuality and its concomitant adolescent romantic fantasizing. Much has she "travell'd in the realms" of romance and poetry; in love with love, Marie's fancy falls on one after another object of desire. On March 28, she admits that she is "intensely interested in W." The rest of the name, "einstein" is crossed out. Though she says that she deliberately ignores him, she speculates about his feelings. In as purple a prose fantasy as she can produce, the barely sixteen-year-old Marie Syrkin pours out her real or imagined dream, "I dreamt of him tonight. The memories of that dream are vague, far off indistinct, but there is indelibly branded on my mind the certainty that in that dream I kissed him. I know that in that dream I kissed him. I know that our lips met in one long, torturous, passionate kiss, one mad embrace and all was over."

Two weeks later, Marie's passion for Weinstein has abated and now she confesses, "I am rather attracted towards B—." But the attraction, unbeknown to B(orodinsky), would not last long. Only six days later, on April 19, a new fancy overtakes this teenage ingenue. "I have at last met that ideal, of whom I dreamed. My fondest hopes were born. J. Kal. . . . Oh, I am so fickle, so incapable of any real [sincere?] feeling. . . . When I read the *Kreutzer Sonata,* I solemnly vowed to quench within myself all manifestations of the sex impulse, and yet how poorly I keep to my resolve."

Soon Weinstein reappears. Marie sees him in the library where he sits down at the neighboring table. "I did not raise my eyes," she admits,

though I felt a hot blush suffusing my cheeks. His presence inspired me to write several Byronian couplets, which was a most edifying occupation. Unfortunately, he almost destroyed the atmosphere — replete with desire (on my part at any rate) — by quite vulgarly blowing his nose in a decidedly unpoetic fashion, which caused me excruciating pain. He has a remarkable handkerchief ornamented profusely with an enormous and hideous brown border, which he took great pleasure in displaying in the French class last term. I wondered whether there [are] any tender associations connected with the execrable *mouchoir.*

Perhaps at this point Marie, after devouring the *Kreutzer Sonata,* has been reading *Othello.*

By April 23, Marie's mood becomes elevated when she discovers that she will not fail in the worrisome subjects. "Rejoice!" she writes. "The Gods are with me! Oh yes, indeed, I marvel at my miraculous good fortune! How my honorable pedagogues were deluded enough to give unto me the marks they did is a mystery to me! . . . Truly, such exultation is most inappropriate considering that the marks in question were anything but commendable. HA-HA-HA!" Marie may be unduly hard on herself regarding her academic performance; after all, she managed to become the literary editor of the Morris High School Annual. Moreover, if Marie had been unable to assess her own academic worth in 1916, she showed some signs of being on the road to emotional self knowledge. First of all, she was quite aware of her loneliness and the absence of any adult to guide her during these years of intense hormonal activity. "Oh mamma dear," is her poignant exclamation, "if I only had you now. I tremble when I think how horribly I acted towards you, my beloved. Again vain regrets! . . . I hear you calling me" (*Diary*, April 22).

Despite overblown expressions of adolescent emotional awakening, and effusively romantic poems, Marie is beginning to understand where the feelings come from. Uneasy about her own fickleness, about the worth of the objects of her affections, about the sincerity of her gushing poetic outpourings, she admits, "I am horrified at my sensuality. I, the purely intellectual, instead desire to experience the sweet sensation of a chaste embrace and soul felt kiss. How disgraceful! Ah, I have fallen indeed! There was a time when I would have hesitated to admit even to myself the faintest shadow of so gross a thought, and now I openly proclaim my shame in black and white." In a further sign of self insight and a soupçon of her later propensity for self-deprecation, on May 6, Marie berates herself: "Posh! I find my poetic imagination running away with me and ascribing sensations to myself which in reality I do not feel. I suppose all this nonsense is nothing more nor less than a particularly acute attack of spring fever. I would to heaven it were over as I stand excellent chances of flunking all my mids because of my er! temperamental nature." Adding a comment about her perception of the difference between the sexes, she claims, "It is maddening to realize that that which is for man but a passing by, is for woman all of life." Does Marie's private agon between "sense and sensibility" suggest that she has been reading Jane Austen?

How much did Nachman know about his daughter's daydreams? How aware was he of her emotional needs? How did his theory of egalitarianism extend to young women? There can be absolutely no doubt about his deep love for his daughter, but his parenting methods were decidedly Victorian. In his daughter's own understated comment, "he found the education of a young girl trying."

He had fed me the complete idealistic pablum of his generation: the freedom of women, the equality of the sexes, the absurdity of conventions, the innate goodness of man. To the pure all things are pure and the inner light is a maiden's best guide. Very fine, but by the time his daughter was fifteen he disclosed a troublesome inconsistency. A nice young man who invited me to a concert was informed that I might go provided a chaperone accompanied us to Carnegie Hall—to the discomfort of all three in the party. Another nice young man who wanted to call had to be informed by me that my father . . . considered me too young for callers; the young man could write letters. (*Memoir* 155)

The father-daughter conflict over proper behavior between male and female teenagers, fierce debates about "bourgeois deviation from principle," friendly advice from the reluctant Carnegie Hall chaperone, Mrs. Katz, and her admonition that Nachman was overly strict with his fifteen-year-old daughter, as well as Marie's own frequent reminders about Elizabeth Barrett and her father, continued throughout the year. Yet, by the approach of summer Nachman suddenly realized that school soon would be out for several months. Clearly, Syrkin had no intention of curtailing his own activities, so he had to come up with a plan that would keep Marie safely occupied and himself free to pursue his commitments. Contrary to his former mode of dealing with his daughter, Syrkin now decided that the best thing for her would be to spend the summer in Belmar, New Jersey, at the Atlantic Hotel—without him. This decision would be the beginning of Marie Syrkin's independent career as well as the cause of a crux in her personal life.

The Atlantic Hotel was a plain-looking Victorian three-story wood building. It had a large covered front porch where the summer guests could spend time outdoors protected from the sun, reading, or socializing. Its letterhead advertised that it was "On The Boardwalk," and it named Mrs. Mascha Strunsky as proprietress. Nachman Syrkin knew the owners of the Atlantic Hotel, the "fabled Strunskys" who were, as Marie later put it, "very liberal, very avant garde, and since they were friends of my father, he assumed that they would keep a paternal and maternal eye on my doings" (Personal interview). Moreover, the Strunskys knew Syrkin's circumstances and generously gave him reduced rates (*Memoir* 155). Mr. and Mrs. Strunsky also had several good-looking daughters who became Marie's friends that summer. Somewhat ungenerously, Marie recalled that the least attractive one, whose name she could not remember (it was Leonore), "at the time was very small," but was to marry Ira Gershwin. "The great beauty Emily, though pursued by every man who came around married less spectacularly" (Personal interview).

More importantly, the hotel was a well-known favorite resort for the Jewish intelligentsia. If the *hoy polloi,* fleeing the stifling summer heat and humidity of the Lower East Side, were attracted to the sweet air of the Catskill mountains of New York State, others, who perhaps thought of themselves as a little more refined and educated, chose to go south for the sun, sand, and salt air of the Jersey shore. Belmar, for example, was the summer retreat for the philosopher of Jewish Reconstructionism, Mordecai Kaplan and his four daughters. Although Kaplan was to have an intellectual encounter with Marie Syrkin some half century later, she did not recollect him from the Belmar years, but she clearly remembered seeing Sholem Aleichem at the Atlantic Hotel, "tiny and twinkling in a corner," and Sholem Asch "soulful and lumbering," as well as the famous Russian revolutionary and Zionist leader, Pinchas Rutenberg (*Memoir* 156). Nachman, too, came for a couple of weekends to observe his daughter's intellectual progress. On those occasions he would promptly sit her down with what she called "the *bêtes noirs* of her youth," perhaps Spinoza's *Ethics* in Latin, or, as she put it, to "start in on Marx in German—*Das Kapital,* or a bit of *Bereshit Bara* . . . ; we never got beyond those points." But there was one amusing encounter that the sixteen-year-old Marie would never forget: when Nachman Syrkin's friend Pinhas Rutenberg was visiting the Atlantic Hotel, he came upon father and daughter engaged in one of these lessons. Approaching them, he said, "Syrkin, what are you doing with her? Why don't you let her dance? Why are you keeping her at these things? Let her dance! Papa was very indignant," Marie recollected. "The notion that my intellectual capacity should be in any way minimized—and I was very troubled, and asked Rutenberg, 'Don't you think I dance well?' He smiled a little wryly and I got the feeling that he didn't think so well of my ability to do the fox trot or the fashionable dances of the time. I recall that as an implication which wounded me because I assumed I would be able to do it well" (Personal interview).

The month of July passed uneventfully and, as Marie Syrkin recollected it in later life, delightfully. She met all kinds of young men and women, and she was having a splendid social experience. But, over seven decades later, when recounting her sixteenth summer she was eager to explain in some detail, that none of the current mores were in practice then. The younger boys and girls managed to call each other by their first names, but otherwise one was on the Miss and Mr. basis. "Such a thing as 'necking' was utterly unknown—to me, at any rate,"

she insisted. "I don't know whether my contemporaries practiced it—
if they did it was certainly secret. There was on the one hand a certain
freedom, and on the other, a certain reticence in mores" (Personal
interview).

During the first weeks of her vacation, Marie poured out her heart to
her current high school best friend, Eugenia Shafran. Eugenia would remain one of her closest confidantes for some years and their correspondence, a good bit of which they both preserved, illuminates a number
of important moments in Marie's early life.[2] Eugenia appears to be the
first in a series of close friendships with women that Marie Syrkin
would make throughout her life. In a letter that appears to have been
written early in July 1915, Marie writes that she has been in "a state of
profound gloom . . . steeped in darkest dejection." The cause of her
melancholy, it appears is that old sense of "wounded vanity" caused by
lack of confidence in her intellectual ability. Going on at length about
her regret for not having worked hard in school and about her lost elementary school brilliance, her faded laurels in general, Marie reveals the
source of her now abandoned self-illusions.

Never till this summer did I so plainly perceive my absolute worthlessness and
mediocrity, never till this month was so clearly and convincingly demonstrated
to me the futility of my desires and expectations. . . . This summer I have met
great minds, great men. I am not alluding to the ancient celebrities that crowd
Belmar, Sholem Asch, Sholem Aleichem, Dr. Zhitlowsky etc. but to the young
geniuses who fill me with despair, and though I shudder to write it, with the
most demeaning jealousy.[3]

One young genius turns out to be a Dr. Levine. "I have once again seen
Dr. Levine who is simply marvellous, [*sic*] lectures in Columbia, writes
on Syndicalism Economics, . . . knows all the marvels extant and is
heartrenderingly paragonish. Have been introduced to a friend of his,
a quarter of a century old, horribly handsome, member of the *Fabians,*
lecturer, is attached to Columbia for whom he is writing some stupid
thing on economics—terribly learned and brilliant." But Marie's admiration for brains is not confined to young men. She now expatiates
upon the virtues of a Miss Hirschenson. "Then, the angelic one; I have
met Miss Hirs[c]hensohn. A graduate of Hunter in 1913. Winner of
the intercollegiate French Literature Prize, and at present teacher in
Hunter *College* at the tender age of about twenty-one. She looks

younger than I do, is pretty as a French doll, clever as the Gods, entrancing as a Lorelei." Though she is off by four years — Miss Hirschensohn was twenty-five at this time — Marie Syrkin recognized quality when she saw it; and she would continue to do so, attracting notable devotees, male and female, throughout her life. Tamar Hirschensohn later became the wife of Rabbi David De Sola Pool, the rabbi of Shearith Israel, the oldest Spanish and Portuguese Synagogue in New York City. After her marriage she gave up her position at Hunter College where she taught French, Latin, and Greek. She then went on to a glorious career as national President of Hadassah; she held leadership positions in many other facets of Jewish life and worked as a writer and lecturer in America and in Israel until her death at the age of eighty-nine. Tamar, it might be added, was the daughter of the respected Talmudic scholar Hayyim Hirschensohn who had two more daughters: Nina Adlerblum, the eldest, was a philosopher and scholar who worked closely with John Dewey; and Tehilla Lichtenstein, the middle daughter, was the first (non-ordained) woman rabbi in the United States. She took over her husband Rabbi Morris Lichtenstein's post as Rabbi of the Society for Jewish Science after his death, and she remained in that position for over thirty years. More than seven decades later, Marie Syrkin revisited her own awestruck impression of her first meeting with Tamar, whose acqaintance she would retain through the years, and who in 1942, would provide Marie with an extraordinary Passover experience. In 1915, however, Tamar, in Marie's eyes, was "an old lady" of twenty-four or -five.

But old lady though she was at twenty four, she was very, very pretty, very very cute, and very very clever. She was supposed to be "something" . . . between her looks and her attainments; she was quite wonderful — and I liked her very much. But she was already someone of the older generation, as far as I was concerned at sixteen. And that summer she showed no signs of the extreme orthodoxy that she would later assume. In fact her friend that summer was a very progressive, radical gentleman — but it was nothing serious, I gather, because the next I heard, she married Rabbi De Sola Pool. (Personal interview)

Belmar and the Atlantic Hotel had a heady clientele that from the standpoint of Dr. Nachman Syrkin had both positive and negative effects on his daughter. On the one hand, sixteen-year-old Marie became all too aware of her intellectual shortcomings, but she also became aware of women's accomplishments and independence. To Eugenia Marie confessed,

After this appalling list of intellectual giants you of course understand the extent of my misery, the depth of my conscious insignificance. When I was in the company of Dr. L. I felt so crushed and weighed down by my pitiful ignorance and stupidity that I could have almost howled. . . . Those four years of wasted High School life haunt me everywhere. My entire adolescence, marked only by the pettiest impulses and the profoundest lethargy maddens me. Whether I can ever atone for these precious years, whether I can by the dint of hard work compensate for that phenomenal brilliancy which is no longer mine, I don't know. I can hope to try. . . . (Shafran, Archives)

Despite her newfound freedom, July of 1915 appears to have been a month of self-doubt and self-criticism for sixteen-year-old Marie. But if it was July, could August be far behind? And without that August, the tale of Marie Syrkin's life would have had a quite different plot. She would not at the age of eighty-nine have evoked the summer of 1915 in heightened tones as "that fabulous summer." As she herself told it, "Sometime in August, there appeared on the scene a young man, Maurice, who by the accounts of my other friends was one of the old ones. He was twenty. He had just come recently from England, and he had come to visit the Atlantic Hotel with another friend of his who was in love with Emily [Strunsky], and she introduced me." Maurice, whom she always referred to as Morris, took Marie for a walk on the boardwalk. As she would tell of that time so many years later, "He was, of course Mr. and I was Miss — and . . . my great love at the time was poetry — contrary to my father's desires, who preferred more serious matters.

I discovered that every poem that I had ever loved he knew by heart. We walked that evening by the Atlantic Ocean and he recited from Poe, to Byron, to Shelley — one had only to mention a line; he knew the whole thing. He had a completely photographic memory — an extraordinary memory. In time he was to dazzle James Joyce by reciting pages of *Ulysses* to him. Joyce, on a visit to Paris, was startled to hear someone recite pages of that fairly difficult text. In any case, he also seemed extraordinarily handsome to me — he was very nice looking, though short; and in general, if one speaks of the *coup de foudre* "whoever loved, that loved not at first sight" — well, that was it. (Personal interview)

At this point in her narration, the telephone rang. Marie got up to answer it; and when she returned she asked, "Where were we?" I reminded her about that "fabulous summer" and asked if she wanted to finish the narrative about Maurice. Marie whispered her answer: "Yes — Maurice. . . . Well, yes, I'll finish that off — if I ever can." That interview was in 1989, and Marie was almost ninety.

Nonetheless, admitting that today no normal girl of sixteen would write as she did then, Marie repeated the words she wrote to her best friend Eugenia describing that sudden experience; "'I have just met someone who is as handsome as Apollo, as great a poet as Shelley, and as noble as Joan of Arc.' I offer no excuses for this — this is what I wrote," she snapped when confronted by my amused incredulity. "These were my standards of nobility, beauty, and poetry." Pouring out her heart to her best friend, she felt that Eugenia understood her perfectly, though in hindsight she admitted that to the present generation this is unbelievable. "I was on the one hand very precocious, and on the other very childish." Moreover, Marie further argues that "one has to bear in mind the mores of the time — which I took very seriously. Girls of that generation knew about sex, of course, but it troubled them — and there was also the dreadful possibility that one might get pregnant and what then? That would be a terrible calamity." She also pointed out that women were not respected if they allowed anyone liberties. "These were the mores of the time — except for a few bohemians." Marie allowed that she did not know whether the boys and girls that she knew indulged in greater liberties when they were alone, but she insisted that these were the mores that she held. "And this is what I must explain in regard to my own life." The change in sexual mores, she argued, did not really happen until 1920.

Eager to continue the narrative of her Belmar days, Marie's voice filled with emotion as she explained that this was an "enchanted summer." Maurice was not staying at Belmar, but in Averne, a little town nearby, giving English lessons. And he would "come every week and would walk on the boardwalk and he would recite poetry, and he called me Miss and I called him Mr. And we were both very much in love, but no word was said." It was a state of "rapture" for them. Marie, moreover, naturally assumed that Maurice was in the same sexual state as she, that is, that he had not had any sexual experience. Curiously, when retelling this part of the story of her first love, she stumbled over one word — "I was under the impression that he was a . . . a . . . Shall I use the word pure?" she stuttered. This hesitation is probably explained by an immediate *sotto voce* aside: "I was to learn otherwise later" (Personal interview).

When summer came to an end, Marie returned to life in New York. This meant going back to Morris High School in the Bronx for her last semester before graduation, despite the fact that she was now residing at 217 East 10th Street in Manhattan, in the apartment of a Mrs. Gischner. Though still on the Miss and Mr. basis, and despite the fact that Marie was a little troubled that she felt "unworthy" of Maurice, the two young lovers continued their chaste relationship. Apparently Nachman finally had given guarded consent for gentlemen callers, and Marie invited Maurice to visit her at home. In a charming note (though with a gentle jibe at Marie's tendency to use polysyllabic words), dated September 22, 1915, Maurice immediately sent his R.S.V.P.[4]

Dear Miss Syrkin:

Yours to hand. I shall be glad to come up on the eve of the day of rest. I shall call half an hour to eight. The day of rest here meant is not the day of rest of the Jews. I do not doubt but that you will feel quizzed at the strange tone of this note, but I wish to show you that length of words is not a need, and to this end I have used in this note — save where it could not be helped — no words of more than one part. I think — as you will find out when you try — that to write such a note is not a thing of ease, and in view of this fact, I am forced to cut it short. I hope, that you will take the hint to heart.

Yours unisyllabificatorilly
Maurice Samuel

Maurice Samuel who also had returned to New York after the summer found employment at a variety of odd jobs while trying to write. He introduced Marie to three of his friends: the two Ish-kishor sisters — Judith and Shulamith — and Samuel Roth. Judith Ish-kishor who later became a nurse, social worker, and writer of children's Jewish historical books, appeared to Marie as "an elderly character." When she revealed that she was twenty-four, it seemed inconceivable to Marie that anyone so "ancient would be tottering around" in their midst. Her sister, who would also become a children's book author, was eighteen, "so she was still under twenty and therefore tolerable" (Personal interview). It was a literary circle, and everyone in the group wrote poetry. Samuel Roth, however, would become notorious in subsequent years, but at the time he was, in Marie Syrkin's eyes, quite attractive — intellectually as well as physically, and he had won a scholarship to Columbia University on the basis of the quality of his poetry. But in her characterization seventy-three years later, she described him as "an ascetic looking young man, rather handsome, tall, thin, dark, always filled with prophetic fulminations. . . . I thought he was a very noble character — with my capacity to judge human nature," she was later to comment, with just a hint of a wink at her now-famous self-irony (Personal interview).

The five young aspiring intellectual poets formed a club. With laughter in her voice, Marie reported that the "brilliant name which Maurice thought up — of course it seems incredibly childish considering that these are people already past twenty— was Eigerkai." Eigerkai, it seems was their transformation of the Yiddish word *ugerkes,* that is, cucumbers. It sounded a little Greek, she explained, so they called themselves the Eigerkai Society. When recalling this youthful episode, Marie, in a tone of amusement, this time tinged with embarrassment, revealed that although it was called the Eigerkei Society "we knew it was *ugerkes* — and I can't explain the combination of childishness and sophistication."

The Eigerkeians met regularly to read their poems to one another. This practice was to give Marie Syrkin an essential lesson in the art of writing. As she explains it, she had taken very seriously the notion that one is inspired by the muses and from this inspiration, poetry flows. She felt that she would be cheating terribly if she really thought before she wrote a poem, and she admits, "I wrote the most dreadful drivel. However, when Marie realized that she would have to read her poetry aloud, she decided that she would "cheat the muses. I really began to think before I wrote, and the stuff was rather better," she explained. Marie already had experienced a disastrous episode a few years before as a consequence of taking too literally the notion that "the divine afflatus seizes you." She belonged to a debating club of "rather homely girls," giggling as she recalled this group who were called the "Aesthetes." Just before they were to engage in a debate on the topic of environment versus heredity, the faculty adviser asked Marie if she had prepared for it. Because she had read that Demosthenes opened his mouth and spoke, that Cicero opened his mouth and spoke, and thus they were inspired, thirteen-year-old Marie had answered immediately, "Oh no — you come in front of the audience and you are inspired." In this later recounting of her failed inspiration, she says incredulously, "Why the advisor didn't knock me over the head and say, 'you're an idiot my dear, and if you feel that way, for heavens sakes, don't undertake to represent this club.' Perhaps because I was considered so articulate and precocious, maybe he assumed that this girl knows what she's doing." What actually happened, however, was that although she had a general notion of her subject, when Marie was called on to present her case, the presence of the audience so terrified her that, absolutely tongue-tied, she could barely get out a few words. "I sat down in a state of utter shame and collapse," Marie shamefacedly recalled. But her colleague came to the rescue. Very properly prepared with notes and outlines, she took up the challenge, and though this girl had been considered "an also ran" she saved the day (Personal interview).

With her new understanding about the necessity for serious thinking about one's writing, Marie's poetry improved considerably. Presumably her deepening relationship with Maurice Samuel had not a little to do with that change for the better; and despite Maurice's epistolary corrective hint regarding Marie's multisyllabic writing style, she encouraged him to continue his visits. In the evenings, the two would go on long walks on the outskirts of the Bronx. Once when they were on one of those walks, they sat down on a bench, and some seven-plus decades later, recalling that auspicious moment, Marie's voice dropped and she whispered, "Of course, these are unforgettable words. He said to me, '*Je veut te dire je t'aime.*' I was so overwhelmed and so frightened, I said nothing. I looked at him, frightened to death — and awed; and we went back. He took me back to the house. I said nothing, and we parted at the house, and I never mentioned it and he never mentioned it. But the great thing had happened; he had said it to me." Suddenly, perhaps anticipating a surprised response from her interviewer, Marie's hushed tone rose in crescendo; in a harsh admonitory voice she burst out, "Now don't ask me why there were no . . . That's how — if you want to know how it was, that's how it was."

Returning to the events of the time as well as to a modulated voice, Marie Syrkin explained that not many months later, sometime in the spring of 1916, Maurice left for Ohio to look for a job doing some physical work so as to gather material for the naturalistic novel he was working on. Meantime, Samuel Roth, sardonically described by Marie as "that great poet and prophetic individual," decided to fill the space left by his friend. He would visit Marie and read poetry with her and write poems to her. "He seemed very nice and literary," she explained, so that when he suggested that they take the kind of walks that she had taken with Maurice, she readily agreed. They walked and after a while they sat down on a bench along the way. Suddenly, Marie said, he seized her in his arms and kissed her, offering suitable protestations, "I was so horrified; I felt absolutely violated—that was my first kiss in my life. I know," Marie added so many years later as she described this youthful episode, "that this is very hard to understand today about a girl who is practically seventeen. I was aghast; so I said, 'Well, we have to be engaged.' I didn't see how after such violence done to me—this man, his kisses, how I could just go on—So he said cheerfully, 'Wonderful, we're engaged.' He was all for it. But I didn't know what to do." Moreover, Marie didn't know that at that time Roth was engaged to someone else, to a woman named Pauline Alter.

In a self-amused description of her feelings at the time, Marie reports with amusement that she remembers rushing to tell her best friend Eugenia about her distress. "I don't know what to do. I'm engaged," Marie sobbed. They condoled with each other and were at a loss about what to do. Marie wrote promptly to Morris and said, "I must tell you that because of circumstances I'm now engaged to Sam." At this point in the narrative of her youthful romances, Marie Syrkin repressed a smile and looking directly at me said, "It's a crazy story—but it's the truth." When I asked how, given all her reading, she could have found herself in such a situation, she snapped back, "I can't help it. Do you want the story or do you want me to make it up?" Continuing this unusual saga, Marie declared that Eugenia completely understood the situation. Fortunately, however, the now seventeen-year-old Marie Syrkin would soon be saved from her secret engagement to Samuel Roth.

Since it was almost summer, once again Nachman Syrkin who did not yet know of Marie's predicament, sent his daughter off to the Jersey shore—this time in the care of a Mrs. Edlan, the wife of the editor of the newspaper Syrkin wrote for, *The Jewish Day*. Mrs. Edlan was, according to Marie, a very charming woman who told her some of the facts of life that she hadn't quite understood, at least "much more picturesquely" than she had known them. With the force of her father's feelings upon her, and with the security of some distance between New York and New Jersey, she would later gather courage to write to Roth, and inform him that they were "disengaged."

Within the year, Roth was married to Pauline Alter. But the details of Roth's future life go a long way to explain Marie's later repugnance at the very mention of his name. He went on to become an infamous figure in literature and law. Having pirated James Joyce's *Ulysses* in Paris and then publishing it in the United States, Samuel Roth was attacked in a public letter of outrage entitled "Stop Thief," (*Transition,* April, 1927) signed by scores of famous artists and writers from Sherwood Anderson and Albert Einstein to Thomas Mann and W. B. Yeats. He also went on to a career of jail sentences for violating obscenity statutes and has gone down in law literature as the "Roth" of the 1957 U.S. Supreme Court obscenity decision against his First Amendment argument.[5]

Of course, when Marie Syrkin found herself engaged to Samuel Roth in 1916, she could not see into his future. Repelled by his behavior at that time, she still was innocent enough to think that after his advances, she *had* to be engaged. It did not, however, take her long to realize that she absolutely *did not want* to marry him. Marie wrote to Maurice Samuel about her encounter with Roth and chastising herself for having planted a sisterly kiss on Roth's brow (a point she omitted when recollecting the episode), after which he seized her in his arms, kissed her and made his declaration of love. Marie received Maurice's response: from Akron, Ohio, Monday, July 10, 1916:

My dear Marie:

You can't imagine how gratified I am that you wrote me as you did, and how much more *grateful* I am than gratified: for even in the distress in which I read your letter, I saw things much more clearly than you can — for I know young men and I know Sammy.

Marie. You are little, or not at all, to blame in this. I unhesitatingly and vehemently lay the blame on Sammy. I say *blame* advisedly, for a foolish thing — if no worse, — has been committed.

To get things clear I will start way back.

I will not go into the subtleties of affections: I will not weigh up motives, results, impulses, etc. But *I will state one law which a man must keep.* The law is this: *that he shall not blurt out love to a girl or a woman merely because he feels it.* . . . To a man who is emotionally strong certain juxtapositions of circumstances are overwhelming. I will regret, so long as my memory will serve me, my own unmanly lapse, just as I will as long be grateful to you for that dignity and kindness which you gave me courage enough and strength enough to retrieve (as far as was possible) the foolish step [his earlier declaration of love]. The severity with which I censure myself I will not withhold from Sammy — rather will I increase it tenfold, for I hold that the position in which he is at present — affianced to Pauline, and still living in the latter twilights of a couple of his damned romances, — make his declaration intolerable to my sense of the noble.

Maurice ends his letter to Marie stating that in view of the current situation, he cannot continue to write to her (Samuel, Archives).

What Marie did not know was that after receiving her engagement announcement, Maurice immediately shot off a scathing letter to Samuel Roth in which he asked, "how can you, fresh from your whorehouses, venture to touch Marie?" Roth replied to Maurice, "And what about you and your whorehouses?" Not surprisingly, Roth wasted no time in informing Marie of the exchange. "He was very grieved" explained Marie, "because Maurice promptly broke with him." But this experience was a shocking lesson in sex education for seventeen-year-old Marie Syrkin. Decades later, in her explanation of the episode, the core of the drama and the trauma is patently exposed. Making a stammering shift from singular to plural, she explained, "Then I realized that . . . Maurice . . . that, that . . . that the lives of these young gentlemen were not exactly what I had assumed." Clearly, it was Maurice's "purity" that was the disappointment, then and forever.

Nonetheless, Marie wrote a second letter to Maurice later in July; and within three days Maurice responded, despite his earlier avowal that he could not continue the correspondence. Now he wrote that Marie's second letter

added a big burden of unhappiness to that which he first brought me: but that is as it should be, for I know that *you* must be very unhappy, too, over the whole affair.

You have come to a deadlock in the untangling of this business, and imagine you have Sam's word against mine. Were his so I should leave it as it stands. I would sooner forfeit your belief than purchase it by the humiliation of a recital of the circumstances in which Sam made a certain statement, in order that you might better confound him. I will have your implicit belief or none at all. However, (believe me, I burn with shame to parley in this way with my pride) it is no matter of Sam's word against mine. It is a matter of his memory against mine.

You say in your letter that you cannot as easily believe Sam to be a rascal: I will assert now what I had not dared say in my first letter. Sammy has behaved like a real scamp: not all this affection I have for him will alter this opinion, nor the consequences it must bring.

Let me rehearse some statements. Sammy is engaged to Pauline. He must give her one of two things: Love: Fidelity. Or else he should part with her. If he loves her how did he come to make any protestations to you? Or did he love her somewhat and you more? How could he protest to *you* before he had broken with her? Did he calculate out: "Well, if Marie doesn't love me I can always fall back on Pauline?" Had his love for you been accompanied by honor and strength (love without these is contemptible) he would have broken with Pauline before he ever spoke to you: and having received your negative, taken it like a man: without pursuing you and reiterating again and again that your love meant *so* much to him. Of course it did. That is what he meant when he said he loved you.

Therein I say Sam has acted like a cad. Do you think he will ever tell Pauline of this occurrence? That he will ever hint of it? (Samuel, Archives)

Samuel Roth did not bow out of his relationship with Marie Syrkin gracefully. Strange as it may seem, Roth had rented the room that Marie had vacated for the summer; when money is scarce, an unoccupied room is money lost. Thus, the young suitor found himself living under the same roof as his beloved's father. At this point, Nachman had absolutely no knowledge of Marie's predicament; sometime in August, however, he got wind of it, exploded, banished Roth from the premises, and forbade Marie ever to be in contact with the scurrilous wretch. Then, in a minutely cramped calligraphic missive (which Marie preserved), Sam spewed out a toxic and egoistic attack upon Nachman Syrkin's intellect, declared his undying love for Marie, and gave her some self-serving patronizing advice:

You must as a matter of fact choose between your father and me. I do not ask you to be unfaithful to your father but I ask you to have implicit faith in me, refuse to discuss me with him unless he is ready to do it in a spirit of fairness, and write to me and see me occasionally. Most of all get it out of your head that you are a child. Decidedly you are not. You are already a beautiful lithe woman, and you have a right to live as you dream living [big?] and noble. . . . You cannot be an obedient daughter and hope to be an individual of any meaning or power.[6]

It is hard to say how sincere Roth's letter is. Surely his manic protestations of love must have had some truth in them: "When you kissed my brow that day, I felt as though you crowned me. For the most beautiful thing in all my dreams, love, had become a reality. It was wonderful and I became a King throned in exalted consciousness of power" (Roth, Archives). And where is Pauline in all this time and tempest? One can, however, plausibly assume that when Marie received Roth's letter, she breathed a great sigh of relief. His accusation that Syrkin had resorted to a "mean lie" because Marie had "compromised" him in her discussions with her father, as she had "compromised" him with Maurice before, gave her the opening to extricate herself from the whole situation. In an attempt to get out gracefully, she sent him a ridiculously childish poem explaining her decision to become unengaged: "Because you are a flame and sear my ease, because you are too noble for me, I can't respond" (Personal interview). In 1989, however, when trying to recall the chronology of her unwanted engagement and the hiatus in her contact with Maurice Samuel, she never mentioned the August 23 letter from Sam Roth. She merely moved the whole episode back a month to July and claimed that after the mutual incriminations about "whorehouses," Maurice broke with her, and then she disengaged herself from Roth. At this, Marie bemoaned her plight: "So there I was minus this one, thank God, but I was also minus Maurice." Still, one has to wonder why she preserved Roth's letter for seventy three years. Vanity?

In essence, her account is correct. But she does not include Maurice's letter of July 21 in which he, from the wisdom of twenty-two years, proffers analysis and advice about the state of her affairs, along with a confession and apologia for his own sins. No doubt the confession is an attempt to rationalize Sam Roth's accusation regarding Maurice's sexual purity. Acknowledging his wrongdoings, he confesses, "I know of course that my own indiscretions have been infinitely greater than yours. I have done much which I would never venture to repeat to you: but I believe that my resilience, too, is greater than yours. I am unspeakably grateful for the ability which pulled me back, after many fruitless attempts into a life which cannot trouble me with after-disgusts, even though it is not, in the sense we have often mentioned, a solution to the unanswerable" (Samuel, Archives).

Maurice's confession has a tinge of Shakespere's sonnet "The expense of spirit in a waste of shame," but the fact remains that Maurice returned from Ohio and immediately resumed his relationship with Marie. She remembers with perfect clarity the second kiss of her life, but it was the first kiss from Maurice. "We were sitting together and [here, as she recalls it in 1989, her voice drops to double pianissimo], he suddenly took me in his arms and kissed me. [The tone of her voice now exudes pleasure mixed with regret]. I was seventeen, and it seemed very nice, and I kissed him back, and he said, 'You don't know quite how to kiss.' And he said, 'you have to purse your mouth' and I realized that I had to purse my mouth. And from then on it was love, love, love. But within the bounds of kissing" (Personal interview).

When challenged by the issue of what she had learned about Maurice's sexual experience and whether or not it tainted her feelings about him after the summer of 1916, first Marie confessed that she couldn't remember the exact sequence of events, and then she said quite matter of factly, "I accepted it, and realized that he had had mistresses, and that was rather shocking to me, but I said, 'Do you still have them?' and he said, 'Oh, no, no, no,' and years later he told me that of course, he kept right on, that during the years when he was wooing me, when he was supposedly only involved with me, he was not leading the life of Galahad, but that's what I assumed. My mistake. And so the romance went on until our elopement."

Chapter 4

Elopement and Annulment

DURING THE SUMMER of 1916 Marie Syrkin had learned some unpleasant facts about the lives of young men; yet, when she returned to
New York in the fall she decided not to break off her relationship with
one particular young man, Maurice Samuel — a decision that was to have
a profound effect on her life. For the time being, however, she simply
avoided thinking about his past and accepted his present proclamations
of fidelity along with his protestations of love. Simply put — she was
madly in love; and so, for that matter, was he.

In the fall Maurice returned from Akron, Ohio, where he had been
working in the Goodyear Rubber plant as part of his experiment in living an "authentic" American life while trying to write a naturalistic
novel. Once back in New York, he rented a room on West 126th Street,
sharing the quarters with his friends, Mick and Amy. These were the
years when many immigrants in need of housing, but without funds,
availed themselves of a current strategy; they would rent rooms in
someone else's apartment where, boardinghouse style, each would have
his or her own room, but they would share communal meals prepared
by the landlady. After the summer in Belmar, Marie returned to the
apartment on 124th Street where she and her father lived as boarders in
Mrs. Covan's rented rooms — one of which recently had been involun-
tarily vacated by the rejected lover Samuel Roth.

Maurice and Marie, who now lived only two blocks from one another, saw each other continually; and though the Eigerkai club no
longer met, they kept up with their old friends Eugenia Shafran, Judith
and Shulamith Ish-kishor, as well as Maurice's housemates, Mick and
Amy, among other acquaintances. Theirs was a busy and rich social life
made up of young intellectual compatibles, and with Sam Roth now oc-

cupied with his studies at Columbia and out of the picture, Maurice took center stage and assumed the role of sophisticated sage. Ever so serious about themselves, they were all certain that they would become writers — especially Maurice, Marie, and Eugenia Shafran. This little trio was a particularly tight group, vetting each other's writings, discussing the latest in literary currents, as well as pouring out their emotions and asking for advice — both literary and practical, not to mention personal.

It was the autumn of 1916, and the world was in turmoil. World War I had been raging for two years. The Russian Revolution was one year away, as was the British pronouncement of sympathy for the Zionist cause, the Balfour Declaration. America had not yet entered the war, and Woodrow Wilson was in his first term as president. The Jewish world also was also in a state of disarray. There was the continuing fractious debate about the national language of the Jews — should it be Hebrew or Yiddish? — and though the debate had already been won in Palestine in favor of Hebrew, in the United States Yiddish was the preferred tongue for the Jewish radicals who regarded the recently revived Hebrew as the defunct language of reactionary clerics. Nachman Syrkin, however, had absolute faith in the primacy of the Hebrew language — though he did acknowledge the need to use Yiddish as his chief propaganda medium because the vast majority of Jewish immigrants from Eastern Europe were Yiddish speakers and readers. Moreover, in this pre–World War I period in America there was the issue of where one stood on the opposing sides of the war — Germany, Austria-Hungary, and Turkey or France, Great Britain, and Russia. American Jews held strongly divided positions. The overriding sentiment of Syrkin's party, the Poalei Zion, as well as other socialists and pacifists, was against American entry into the war; it would be inconceivable even to consider taking part in the wars of the "munitions makers." Many American Jews, however, who would not and could not forget the land of pogroms under the bitterly despised Russian Czarist regime took a pro-German position. Furthermore, they would argue, from an intellectual and cultural perspective Jews had to admire the Germans for their *Aufklärung* (enlightenment) and *Kultur;* and the Emperor of the Austro-Hungarian Empire, Franz Joseph, familiarly referred to as Franz *Yussel* (Joseph), was sentimentally regarded as a beloved friend of the Jews. What is more, the Zionist headquarters were based in Germany; however, the Zionists themselves, to confound the matter further, were scattered in either neutral or Allied countries. And once again Nachman Syrkin found himself singing solo within his choir, the Poalei Zion. Arguing as early as 1915 against the pro-German position, and later for America's entry into the war on the side of the Allies, presciently Syrkin "fought against the delusion that emancipation would come from Germany. The contrary would be true. He warned that in the provinces it conquered, Germany was introducing 'draconic repressive measures' and a 'methodical system of persecution' and he drew attention to the anti-Semitic philosophy that was being formulated in the German Press" (*Memoir* 160).

The urgent contemporary events that so consumed the mind and passions of Marie Syrkin's father did not appear at this time to be making the same claims on the Samuel-Syrkin-and-friends clique; they seemed more occupied with the upheavals and revolutions in the world of arts and letters. Two movements had emerged during the late nineteenth and early twentieth century: naturalism and modernism. Naturalism assumed a scientific approach to the portrayal of human life, arguing against idealism and for disinterested objectivity, against free will and for the determinism of heredity and environment. Naturalism held that life ought to be depicted accurately, with frankness and with recognition of the Darwinian theories of evolution: the struggle for survival and the survival of the fittest. It was in this spirit that Maurice Samuels had spent the better part of the year working in a factory in the midwest. In France the great exponent of naturalism was Emile Zola, in America Frank Norris, Stephen Crane, and Theodore Dreiser. Maurice hoped to join that pantheon. Much later in life, looking back on his youthful principal compulsion to become a writer, he explained, "I used to think that the hunger for fame was the strongest element in [the compulsion]. . . . No, it is not the thing. The hunger for fame has died, with much else. To become famous in old age would be like getting cocktails after dinner."[1]

The second new movement was Modernism, a term attached to a set of dispositions in the arts that arose, like naturalism, in the late nineteenth century in reaction to the prevailing rules and values of romanticism. Modernism deliberately broke with the past to experiment with form, style, and content, to give shape and voice to the new focus on the consciousness of the individual. Among this explosion of new radical experimentalists who burst forth in every artistic form were Marcel Proust, Franz Kafka, James Joyce, Virginia Woolf, William Butler Yeats, Henry James, Ezra Pound, T. S. Eliot, William Faulkner, Paul Cezanne, Pablo Picasso, Henri Matisse, Igor Stravinsky, Arnold Schonberg, Erik Satie, Isadora Duncan, Michel Fokine, Sergei Diaghilev, and so on in literature, fine arts, music, and dance. Modernism would give rise to a dizzying list of subcategories that in a variety of radical movements — often in contradiction to one another — appeared one after the other throughout the twentieth century. A few example should make the point: symbolism, imagism, Dadaism, surrealism, free verse, Freudianism, Fauvism, Cubism, atonalism, serialism — all summed up in Ezra Pound's oft quoted manifesto: "Make it new!"

This was arguably the most exciting cultural moment in the twentieth century. Were the budding writers, Marie, Maurice, and Eugenia aware of these radical trends in literature? Did they try to write in the new style? It appears that at the very least Maurice, the self-styled mentor, and Eugenia, the gushing enthusiast, were acutely aware of some of the latest currents — Maurice was a naturalist, Eugenia, more theoretical, was drawn to the radical ideas of modernism. Marie, however, in a much later assessment of her own poetry, claimed that her early work was highly derivative, florid, and deeply indebted to nineteenth-century romanticism. Maurice's letter of September 22, 1915, which he had jestingly signed "unisyllabicificatorilly," makes the case in point. In this he gently pokes fun at Marie's nineteenth-century proclivity for polysyllablic words. Moreover, the evidence shows that she was still in thrall to nineteenth-century ideas about women as well as to ideas about poetic diction: that is, that a woman's identity is anchored through her relationship to the man she loves. As for Marie's best friend, the Francophile Eugenia, she percolates ideas through the filter of ingenuous earnestness and enthusiasm as she turns to Maurice for instruction, advice, and most especially as an outlet for her own literary speculations. A letter from Eugenia to Maurice at this time illustrates the deadly serious literary discussions among the Samuel-Syrkin-Shafran coterie.[2] But as sober as Shafran may have been about literature, she was, perhaps, less so about herself. As it was to turn out, Eugenia Shafran's life would be highly unconventional and plagued by poverty, bad relationships, and depression. Her friendship with Marie, which was very close, would end badly and sadly.[3]

And what of Marie's own obsession with literature? There seems to be no evidence that at this point in her young life she was at all concerned with theory. She simply loved poetry. She loved to read it, and she loved to write it. She especially loved to hear Maurice Samuel recite it. Marie had come to it quite early, reading the great writers in several languages. And though her father had plied her with the Bible, Spinoza, and Marx, a favorite uncle had given her a copy of Pushkin, which she read and re-read and which she kept throughout her life. Many years later, Marie Syrkin liked to tell a story that testified both to her devotion to books and to her father's disapproval of her passionate love affair with literature. It seems that in the early 1920s there was a particularly memorable moment when Nachman blazed out at his daughter because he thought she was frittering away her abilities. Marie, who had recently bobbed her black tresses in the current short style, was quietly stretched out on her bed, absorbed in a novel by H. G. Wells when her father came upon her. The newspapers at that time were full of the exploits of a young woman criminal who had been dubbed "the bobbed haired bandit."[4] When this female outlaw was not busy committing crimes, she was reputed to have spent her time reading novels. Syrkin, upon discovering his daughter leisurely reading her novel, exploded, "What difference is there between you and the bobbed haired bandit? She has short hair and you have short hair; she reads novels and you read novels!" It was just at this time, moreover, that Nachman Syrkin remarked somewhat sardonically, "There is a woman in our movement who is a remarkable speaker. I thought you'd be like her" (Personal interview). The unnamed woman was Golda Meir. Marie Syrkin was not destined to become a world-famous stateswoman, but eventually she would become Golda's close friend and biographer.

Nachman Syrkin's disapproval of almost everything related to his daughter's social and intellectual life notwithstanding, Marie and Maurice continued and deepened their *affaire de coeur* over the fall of 1916 and through the winter of 1917. It was not that Marie could completely overlook Maurice's unchaste past. The idea of it must have stuck to her sentimental and romantic skin like a nettle. Apparently, however, she was able to maintain her passion for Maurice while also delivering lectures to him about his morality; and Maurice had the emotional capacity to intensify his words of love to Marie when he apologized, expressed feelings of great guilt, and tried to explain his behavior: "So often," he pleaded, "I long to speak to you of simple things and am really ashamed. I am ashamed to tell you how much I long to be good, and how much so just because of you: not wholly and primarily so, but just because it is more fitting to associate it with the impulses you awake at moments in me than anything else I can think of. . . . I have mean desires sometimes, and sometimes they do go into action, but they only teach me how intense is my will for good. You do wrong, *always*, to chide the wrong I do, because I feel so keenly about it myself that your re-proaches are like sympathy offered to a friend at the very bedside of some-one just dead" (Archives, undated, ca. 1916). Nonetheless, in Marie's much later view of Maurice Samuel, he was either unable or unwilling to change his ways and always would be (Personal interview).

In the light of the moral standards of the first decades of the twenti-eth century, both positions are quite understandable. On the one hand, sexual morality had yet to undergo the radical changes that were to occur in the years after World War I; consequently, romantic Marie was under the sway of the still-prevailing Victorian mores that dictated sexual fidelity and abstention between lovers prior to marriage. At sev-enteen, this beautiful and super-intelligent young woman had no under-standing of the urgency of sexual expression for a young man of twenty-one — and she did have a tendency to be a scold. Maurice, on the other hand, had far more sophistication, having spent three years at Manchester University in England, followed by some months in Paris in 1914 where, determined to become a writer, he had settled himself. But on July 28, 1914, World War I broke out, and in the light of his current pacifist convictions, he emigrated to the United States, bringing with him sexual experience, as well socialist, atheist, and universalist convic-tions. Though he had been enrolled in Chaim Weizmann's chemistry course at Manchester University, he had not yet become a Zionist (*Little Did I Know* 181). Maurice Samuel was a young man of strong ego, great mood swings, and habitual womanizing. The combination of the two extraordinary personalities — Marie and Maurice — did not betoken a long life together in faithful domesticity.

Despite the volatility of their relationship, Marie and Maurice's ro-mance proceeded apace during the winter months as Maurice began to think seriously about the inescapable news of the war abroad. His pacificist views notwithstanding, in the late spring of 1917, just after the Selective Service Act was passed on May 18, 1917 authorizing President Wilson to temporarily increase the United States military through reg-istration and selection of men for military service, Samuel began to think about enlisting in the army. Before long he made the decision to register for the draft and then spent the next couple of months waiting for the results of the conscription.

Meantime, as summer approached Marie once again made ready to go to the seashore at Belmar. This, her eighteenth summer, was to be her third season at the Jersey shore, and she seems to have no activity in mind other than the social comings and goings of the young set of the Jewish intellectual elite. Although Nachman was sending her away to escape the New York heat as well as for what he believed would be intellectual stimulation, he preferred to ignore the fact that it also was the mating season. Today it is hard to imagine that there was not much else for most cultured young American women to do between the end of high school and marriage. And where better to go to meet eligible young men than the summer resort? There were, of course, those young women who had already enrolled in college — and Marie was one of them. Most of the women she knew who were at college were attending Hunter in New York, but, having met some young men in Belmar who were attending Cornell University, she hoped to transfer there. In the meantime Marie planned to spend the summer reading, writing, sunning herself, keeping up with the latest styles, meeting interesting young men, keeping up a correspondence with Maurice, and waiting for his visits.[5] His letters kept her apprised of affairs in the bustling Covan apartment where Nachman, as well as some of Marie's acquaintances, boarded. In an undated (but clearly written early in the summer of 1917) letter, Maurice, who it appears was taking meals at Mrs. Covan's, wrote to Marie, "I heard that you cut your hair short a la Russe. S'lam [Shulamith Ish-kishor] says it becomes you, but she reported that when your father saw you, he burst out, without preliminary greeting: 'Oy, Manitchka! [his nickname for Marie] How homely you look!' The information roused a storm of astonishment in the little Covan circle" (Archives, Summer 1917).

The summer correspondence seems to have begun with a letter from Marie inviting Maurice, despite their recent quarrels, to come to Belmar for a visit. He replies, "Dear, you have such a faculty for breaking into me with a written phrase. Most of the night I thought about you. Do you really want to see me as you say? Curiously I haven't that sharp, restless pain of separation now which I felt the first days of your absence. It is something much deeper and so much quieter. It is a soft, dear delight now to think of you — something like the glowing after-pain of a whiplash, or like a pleasant onset of the blues" (Archives, Summer 1917).

Whatever these rather curious images of longing suggest (perhaps the aftermath of stinging quarrels), Maurice continues his response with a reminder that soon they will have to part. Marie, presumably, will be going off to college, and he will be called up for army duty, and they will only have a "last two or three weeks together . . . it appears that I will be in the second or third section of the first quota. You know," he continues, "I asked my Exemption Board whether it would permit me to enlist in advance of my conscription, but the permission was refused. I am now going to ask that I be taken in the first section, first week of September. The delay and uncertainty are wearing on my nerves." The rest of the letter reveals the complexities of the attraction/repulsion character of their relationship. First, there was the tremendous physical attraction. Second, was a shared intellectuality. But this was complicated by gender inequality: Marie, though irritated by his arrogance, was awed and mostly submissive in the face of his apparent sophistication; Maurice asserted a superior and infantilizing attitude, displaying jealousy regarding her interest in other young men and Belmar social life and expressing impatience with her tendency to carelessness and lack of seriousness:

To me it's half amusing and half amazing that letters which you write in such obviously desperate carelessness should mean so much to me. You *must* surely write them all in frantic haste—words missing, sentences unended (don't be angry dear,) and phrases illegible. And yet your scribble (especially where you tell me that you love me,—even off hand, as you do) is deliciously pretty. I think that if you cared to sit down, and write carefully and with malice aforethought you would make me come dashing out there in my bathrobe. Please don't try.

It is unspeakably dull here in New York. Mrs. Covan has just gone away (today) for a week's vacation; and applicant after applicant comes up asking for your room. Such wretched human specimens, too. I don't know whether you'll find the room vacant for you when you do return.

I'm going to send this special delivery, because I should have sent it last night and didn't. I hate to ask you to write to me because I can see very easily that, as much as you want me to get letters from you, the actual writing of them is a burden. (Archives, Summer 1917)

Marie Syrkin seems to have swallowed this emotionally scrambled letter with a bit of honey, for she responded with yet another invitation to visit. In his turn, Maurice replied by adding sour lemon to the brew. Grateful for the invitation, he nevertheless sends his regrets: "Your papa is undoubtedly a dear, but he is going to Belmar this week-end." In addition to this, Maurice is broke. His employer has suspended payment until about August 10, and all he has at the moment is nine cents. "I have chronic blues all day and most of the night, and I'm just sick to have you here. I think I shall hate Belmar, because there'll be too many people watching. . . . [E]very day I'm more in love with you, and after having been near you so long this abrupt separation is cruel. . . . You know I'm really and truly afraid to come to Belmar to see you. If every fool on the boardwalk or in the hotel couldn't guess I'm madly in love with you when they see us together, or even see me watching you, human beings will have changed much in two years" (Archives, Summer 1917).

That Maurice Samuel loves Marie Syrkin there can be no doubt; but his kind of love is often prey to the green-eyed monster. In a series of paragraphs that veer between protestations of love and jealous sarcasms he declares, "All that I want to write about is how much I want to be near you again, and how I was tantalized reading 'Kiss I' [a poem by Marie]; but the very next sentence is a green-eyed accusation: "I know you are more interested in knowing what Myron what'shisname's address is. I have found it for you. It is 414 13th Ave., Belmar. Manitchka, don't let him fall in love with you." Next he romantically muses, "How glorious you must look in that white light dress of yours, on the sands"; nonetheless, the letter ends with a muted jibe: "Sweetheart, send me a letter for the weekend, and tell me something more than gossip. Devotedly, Maurice" (Archives, Summer 1917).

Another letter soon follows. In this one he complains about his impecunious lot. His finances are near rock-bottom, and so he will not be able to come out to see her. He has complained about this before, and on a couple of occasions Marie has sent him money. Maurice is longing just to look at her, but he can barely meet his daily expenses. In her absence, he will try to get over his blues by burying himself in work. "But," he calculates, "it is harder for me to forget you than it is for you, over there, to forget me: even if you care as much as I, which you don't. I'm just sick of not having you" (Archives, Summer 1917).

Marie's distance is not Maurice's only cause for anxiety. He is really worried about his conscription. "I will not, of course, lodge any appeal for exemption. That would be mean and stupid. Either I *go* or I *refuse* to go. I believe I shall go." He appears to have resolved the conflict between his pacifism and his belief that this is a just war. But it doesn't quiet the anxiety about his relationship with Marie. "Dear kiddy," he writes, "I miss even our squabbles, tho' I shall never, never, never squabble with you again. . . . How often I play that miserable waltz on the mandoline, and think that some dapper college boy is dancing with you to that melody. And then you go on the porch, and he's smart, or sentimental, or desperate — as I was, two years ago. Oh, Manitchka. . . . Dear, write me. A thousand kisses, Devotedly yours, Maurice" (Archives, Summer 1917).

Having received the report of Maurice's calamitous finances that prevented him from coming out to Belmar, Marie somehow seems to come up with some money, which she sent to him. He, it appears, accepted the money, but neglected to pay it back in a timely manner. Presumably Marie then sent a letter to remind him. "I am dreadfully sorry that this money should have slipped out of my mind," he apologizes, "but it did. I am sending it Special Delivery for despatch and safety." And once again, the table is turned — after a very brief letter explaining that he can't write at length because he is "wallowing in work and correspondence," Maurice manages to end the letter with "Dear, *do* send me a letter without any writing mistakes. I don't *care* about the mistakes. I only want evidence that you don't write to me standing on one leg at a counter" (Archives, Summer 1917).

Difficult as it is to imagine how this relationship could flourish with so many mutual recriminations, it clearly thrives. Soon after this letter, another typewritten one arrives for Marie. This time it contains the news that Maurice's number has been drawn for the first conscription draft — number 841. "I enclose the numbers with a mark opposite mean [a typo for "mine"]. Curious what that number means." What it *means* is clear. The reality had set in and Maurice complains of "feeling sick of things," not because of having been called with the first draft, because that is what he had applied for, "but just about now, when part of the suspense is ended, I have gotten sick of the business. I am feeling physically sick this evening" (Archives). For Maurice this appears to have been a "what have I done?" moment.

Shortly after, early in August, Maurice received a letter from the conscription board instructing him to report for his physical examination on the next Saturday. He calculated that if he passed the exam, which he believed he would, despite myopic eyes, he should be in camp by the first of September. One would think that such news would preclude all other concerns, but curiously, the letter begins with something quite different. The old issue of Samuel Roth has re-emerged. Apparently Maurice has never completely broken with Roth, and he knows that neither has Marie. Samuel seems to have written this to bring up the last year's unpleasant episode, and she, in turn, has responded to his present accusations. Oddly, Maurice begins this letter, containing the important news of his conscription, with the quarrel about Sam Roth: "The business which you think too old and too sickening to discuss I *had* to bring up, because I am dropping Sam—and Manitchka, I cannot tell you how happy I would be if *you* dropped him too. It isn't a question of your seeing him ever, or of your being away in Cornell.[6] It's the knowledge I want that you have nothing to do with him. I can't help asking you for this, because my feeling is so strong in the matter" (Archives, Summer 1917). Was the fact of their impending separation and his uncertain future causing such anxiety about Marie's constancy that he would attempt to control her social life in advance?

By the middle of August a new complication has arisen. "Dearest Manitchka," Maurice begins. His salutations, from "Dear" to "Dear Kiddy" to "Liebchen" and now "Dearest," chart the course of his escalating emotions, and in this letter there is news that drives him up one level in the language of love. . . . "I have very curious news for you—at least, I understand it's news," he begins.

This morning at table your father suddenly tells us that he has made his mind up definitely to return to Russia—permanently. Taking you with him. When I asked whether he didn't intend to let you finish your college course, he said "No, I can't leave her here alone." He said further that he was only waiting for certain arrangements—financial, I suppose—to be perfected, and he would go. He said that you knew nothing about it yet.

I simply cannot tell you of the effect this has produced on me. I never expected that our relationship would be put to this sudden and violent test. I cannot foresee the outcome and I can't venture to express any of my hopes, because now you will have to settle for good where it is you stand and what it is you expect to do. (Archives, Summer 1917)

The letter ends here; or, in any case, this is all that Marie Syrkin preserved. If it is the case that this page is all she held on to, that would suggest a self-conscious awareness that this was a crux in her life—as well it was. This is the take-off moment in the trajectory of Marie Syrkin's struggle to create her own life. In the face of her father's conventionality regarding his expectations and control over his daughter's social and intellectual life, despite the unconventionality of Nachman's own life, Marie was on the cusp of a decade of self assertions that will lead her to a life outside social norms that, willy-nilly, she will create for herself.

Why Nachman Syrkin should choose to go to Russia in July of 1917 is not a very hard puzzle to solve. After all, the United States was the fifth country that he had lived in since he left Russia twenty-nine years before. Now a lonely widower, his life had been one long peripatetic journey, and so why not return to Russia now that so much that he had worked for and dreamed of seemed to have become a reality? In February of 1917 there had been several days of protests and demonstrations in Petrograd (St. Petersburg) against the Czar's government; the government ordered its troops to fire on the crowds, but by the next day the troops themselves mutinied, and upon receiving the further bad news that the city of Moscow had joined the revolution, Czar Nicholas abdicated his throne. His abdication ushered in a nine-month season of fresh air for the Jews of Russia: the Provisional Government revoked all the restrictions on the Jews, and they were even given a chance to hold office, to practice law, and to become officers in the army. The old political weapon, antisemitism, now seen as incompatible with the revolution, was driven underground. Hence, Jews could be found in all the new democratic parties: the Constitutional Democratic Party, the Socialist Revolutionaries, the Mensheviks, and the Bolsheviks. The new participation and attitudes also made it possible for the general population from the religious to the secular nationalists to breathe freely; and the quickly growing Russian Zionist Movement, now numbering 140,000 members, boldly held its conference in Petrograd in May (*Judaica,* "Russia").

How gloriously full of hope and expectations were the Jews of Russia in the spring of 1917. Even more so was that great optimist, Nachman Syrkin, who had a good friend in Russia—Pinhas Rutenberg. Rutenberg was the kindly man at the Atlantic Hotel in Belmar who had advised Marie Syrkin's father to stop instructing his daughter in Marx and Spinoza and to "let her dance"; but Rutenberg also was the man who had marched with Father Gapon, the leader of the "Bloody Sunday" protest that inaugurated the 1905 Revolution; he was the man who then helped Gapon escape from Russia, but he was also the man appointed in 1906 by the Social Revolutionaries—who now believed that Gapon was a police agent—to organize his execution. Most importantly at present for Nachman Syrkin, Rutenberg had left the United States in 1917 to go to Petrograd where the head of the Provisional Government, Alexander Kerensky, had apponted him deputy governor of Petrograd in charge of civilian affairs.[7] Surely this seemed a propitious time for Syrkin to return to his homeland, Russia, to participate in the unfolding Revolution. And perhaps even more important, he also held the hope that he could offer a marriage proposal to Masha Osnos, the unmarried sister of his late wife Basha—the younger sister who years ago had filled in when Basha was away.

Maurice Samuel, however, was little interested in the explanation for Nachman Syrkin's sudden decision to leave America with his beautiful eighteen-year-old daughter. Samuel was determined to persuade Marie Syrkin to remain in America with him. "[N]ow you will have to settle for good where it is you stand and what you expect to do" (Archives, Summer 1917). Maurice, however, knew exactly where it is that he stood and quickly decided what he wished to do. He had been pondering the subject of love and the relations of the sexes for some time. In his notebook one finds an entry dated Monday, June 4, 1917 in which he says "There are certain conceptions of love, and of the relations between lovers, current amongst many cultured and intelligent persons, which are curious survivals of an age which has passed away almost completely."[8] He goes on to note that these conceptions are relics of the age of chivalry: "obsession with love, humility, lovesickness, rage, longing, dreaming, on the aggressive and never quiescent, full of quaint courtesies; the lovers do not premis [*sic*] mental equality in outlook." The conditions for such an expression of love have long passed away, he argues. "Modern thought and conditions call for free, equal, serene union. Neither has a part to play; 'he' and 'she' love each other: the rest is an adaptation to personal idiosyncracies and social conditions" (Samuel, *Diary*).

In Maurice's letters of the early weeks of the summer, it is obvious that there has been a small battle of the sexes—Marie insisting on conventional codes that she has found in literature and accepted, Maurice rejecting them in favor of the more radical mores he had experienced in France and had brought with him to America. But Marie was not yet ready for this. And so, undoubtedly doubly motivated by the twin future events—his entry into the American Army and her removal to Russia—all that he could do was to convince her to marry him.

On Friday, August 31, 1917 Marie Syrkin and Maurice Samuel eloped. They were married in the afternoon at the City Hall in the Borough of Manhattan. That night they consummated the marriage at the Theresa Hotel on 125th Street in Manhattan (Personal interview).

The next day when the newlyweds left the Theresa Hotel they were at once in a state of ecstasy and of fear. They knew that they would have to tell Nachman the news, and they also knew the fury that it would generate. Yet they agreed that it had to be done. Still, it did not have to be done on the spot. Nonetheless, they realized that in order to keep their elopement a secret, Marie would have to return to the Atlantic Hotel so that her absence would not be noticed. The only party to the secret was Mr. Strunsky, the owner of the hotel. Maurice would return to the apartment where he would proceed as if nothing at all had happened. But once he left Marie his mood plunged downward. Surely, everything from his trepidation regarding Nachman's reaction, to his gloom about having to leave for the army within weeks, his dread of being sent into combat, and his anxiety about his separation from Marie—all this sent him into a fit of depression that was summed up in the long letter that he sent that night to Marie, but that did not alleviate the despondency. The new bridgroom wrote to his bride: "There's a good deal to tell you apropos of everything. I'm not in the mood to write you a coherent account just now, because I have a very bad fit of the blues, and such an acute aching to see you that I can barely write of anything else. I'm unspeakably sorry I didn't go on with you to Belmar, instead of returning to this miserable place." When Maurice had returned to his apartment his two house-mates, Amy and Mick, pressed him to explain where he had been all night. Full of clues, they suspected the truth, but despite their clever detective work, Maurice did not divulge the details—though he reported all their deductions to Marie. His letter concludes with an ardent plea:

Marie: you must return to New York this [crossed out: evening] week-end. I shall simply go crazy otherwise. I don't think it at all manly to write to you in this way, and I know I am laying up a good deal of suffering for myself for the time when I shall be unable to see you for weeks or months at a stretch. But these last days I *must* see you often and be with you as long as I can. . . . Just at present my fierce headache of two days ago has returned, and I feel extraordinarily unhappy, though I do not know why, exactly. This new factor in my life is not self-contained: it overflows into the other hours and fills them with longings and jealousies and stinging recollections. I dare not stay alone. . . for I cannot read, or write (except to you, and that with difficulty) or do any work. I dare not come to you tonight, or I would, and you dare not return here before the week-end.

Marie, I feel deadly sick, I don't know what it is. The moment you went into the train this feeling seized on me, and it has not left me, a curious dizziness but—not in my head—in my body somewhere, below the heart. My dear

love, please think of me during these days. Be certain you will always, always be
with me.

Your unhappy lover.

(Archives, September [1?] 1917)

With great trepidation, on the following weekend, Maurice and Marie
confronted Nachman Syrkin with the news of their elopement. While
Marie remained outside the building, Maurice went up to the apartment to face his new father-in-law. The result was a furious explosion.
Nachman Syrkin did not take the news with equanimity. Marie was too
young, Maurice was not worthy; the bride was too beautiful and too intelligent to waste on a man with no means, no imaginable future, and
what's more with the immediate dangers of going off to war. No, Nachman erupted, as he detonated his final volley. He would have the marriage annulled. (Personal interview)

The End of a Brief Marriage

Nachman Syrkin's vow that he would have the marriage of his daughter Marie to his newly acquired son-in-law Maurice Samuel annulled
was not a mere threat. Yet, mindful that the bridegroom would be going
off to war almost immediately, Syrkin announced that although he certainly did not want them married, he would permit them to be engaged.
He also had not given up his own plans to go to Russia and take his
daughter with him. Knowing that this plan would put an ocean of space
between the two young lovers may be the reason that he agreed to their
engagement. Consequently, he immediately went ahead with his intentions. On September 17, Maurice Samuel was served with a court summons to answer the suit to annul the marriage filed by the plaintiff,
Nachman Syrkin, guardian *ad litem* of Marie Syrkin, against Maurice
Samuel. Samuel was given twenty days from September 17, 1917 (which
then would be October 7) to answer the complaint. Failure to appear or
to answer, would result in granting the annulment by default.[9] The
penalty nothwithstanding, less than a week later on September 23, Maurice Samuel acquired a new title and address: Private Maurice Samuel,
307th Infantry, Company F, Camp Upton, L.I. Here he would train in
the ways of war as he awaited notice of the trial to annul his marriage
to Marie Syrkin.

Camp Upton, located about sixty miles east of New York City in Yaphank, New York, on 10,000 acres of land in Suffolk County of Long Island, had been newly built in 1917 and opened, with the arrival of the first troops on September 10, as an induction and training center for new recruits. By November there would be a population of thirty-seven thousand men residing in the spare wooden barracks of this salt-marshy, rainy, mosquito-friendly, soggy terrain. Among the visiting personages to Camp Upton was the World Lightweight Champion Benny Leonard, who came to give the men boxing instruction. Maurice Samuel promptly enrolled in his course. Among the enlisted men was the not-yet-famous songwriter Irving Berlin whose negative attitude towards the bugler who blew Reveille every morning resulted in the hit tune "Oh, How I Hate to Get Up in the Morning."

Private Maurice Samuel received his first letter from Marie on September 28.[10] It was the first of a voluminous, almost daily correspondence of which only Maurice's letters are extant, though it is possible to surmise much of the substance of Marie's from Samuel's quotations from them and his references and responses to them. His response to her first letter suggests that Marie's letter had been capricious, whimsical, and full of sexual innuendo. "Dearest, dearest, liebchen," Private Samuel begins. "You're a wild crazy, sweet, *meshuggene* kid, and I got your first letter this morning. I reciprocate all your wicked thoughts, and hereby want to say that you're a teazing [*sic*], mocking imp, not fit for the society of the sane, the sober and the serious."

Sunday was the most popular visiting day at the camp, but Maurice did not choose to urge Marie to make the trip. Though the Long Island railroad ride to Camp Upton took only an hour and forty-five minutes, doubtless, one of his considerations in choosing not to press her was the number of hours the round trip would take. But when Sunday came and he stood by watching all the "kisses, handshakes and tears" he quickly bemoaned his own decision. As for Marie's explanation for her failure to visit, she informed Maurice that Nachman had forbidden it! Maurice shot back: "I think your papa is extraordinarily unreasonable. . . . [A]t a time like this, when to see you is an utter necessity to me, you surely ought to be permitted to come." In his next missive he pleads, "O child, if you don't come here next Sunday I shall go mad." Marie had now become the servant of two masters; it would take a while before she could become master of herself.

Marie did show up the following Sunday, and Maurice did not go mad, though he certainly continued to have serious mood swings. He would take his emotional temperature almost by the hour and report the ups and downs in detail in his letters to Marie. "Yesterday afternoon and part of the evening," he wrote to his love, "I suffered an extraordinary attack of the blues—not the softly melancholy kind, but that bitter, unrelentingly corrosive kind which drives one to the verge of tearless madness."

It is not difficult to explain the obvious emotional excesses of a young man who already had displayed unmistakable tendencies towards see-saw spirits: the normal stress of army life, with the further worry about being sent overseas to the war zone might be quite sufficient to stir up Maurice's emotional stew; but add to these anxieties the tense wait for the summons to a trial to annul his marriage to someone he truly loves, then add the bitter knowledge that his beloved's "papa" dislikes him intensely, and the sum of such ingredients adds up to a recipe for severe heartburn. Nevertheless, in the first few weeks Maurice Samuel impatiently awaited the summons. "I am awaiting instructions from you concerning the trial. As soon as the documents come, send them to me *special delivery and registered*." Only a day or two later, "I am worried because I have not heard from the lawyer yet," he writes to Marie, "and if the leave is to be granted me, I must have a day or two's notice. The summons to the trial should be here this afternoon or it will be too late." Too late, of course, to contest the suit.

The news finally arrives. In a postscript to yet another letter, again asking when the lawyer's letter would arrive, Maurice scribbles: *"Just received your S. D. [Special Delivery] letter. I laid my case before the captain. He gave me leave of absence at once. He's a brick. I'll be in N.Y. Wednesday afternoon or evening. Be at home."* This undoubtedly meant that the trial would occur on either Thursday or Friday, October 4 or 5, since the original summons had given him until Sunday, October 7, to appear. The summons had arrived just in the nick of time. Did Nachman hope that Maurice would be unable to arrange so hasty a leave?

Marie, of course, complied with Maurice's direction: she was at home. She was there, first and foremost, to greet Maurice—still her unanulled husband—and certainly, to stand as a buffer between the two men in her life—Maurice Samuel and Nachman Syrkin—thus to prevent a head on crash. But Marie herself was caught in the vise of two men vying to control her.

There was, however, a not-so-small matter of dates that would prove to have a profound long-term effect on the course of the lives of both Marie and Maurice. Nachman Syrkin had been named guardian *ad litem* for his daughter Marie, which meant that he was appointed her guardian for this particular action because she had not reached the age of twenty-one. The complaint was made on several grounds: first, that the plaintiff (Marie) was born on the twenty-second day of March, 1900 in Bern, Switzerland; second, that at "the time of the said marriage the plaintiff had not attained the age of eighteen years, and that the plaintiff now desires to annul her marriage with the defendant on the ground that at the time of such marriage she had not attained the age of legal consent;" third, that she "had not freely cohabited with the defendant since she had attained such age of legal consent." Obviously this last is a "boiler plate" contradiction, since it had already been stated that she had not yet attained the age of consent. There are at least three false statements in the above argument, leading to one inescapable speculation. First of all, the date of birth Nachman Syrkin supplied for his daughter is false. Marie Syrkin was born on March 22, 1899. Had she been born in 1900, it would have been in Charlottenberg, Germany, not (as Nachman Syrkin claimed) in Bern, Switzerland; Charlottenberg was where the Syrkin family was living in 1900. Second, the correct birth date would have made her eighteen; hence, she already *had* attained the age of legal consent. Third, since she already was at the age of legal consent, she *had* freely and legally cohabited with the defendant. These three points are indisputable. The document, however, closes with this sworn statement: "Marie Syrkin, being duly sworn, deposes and says that she is the plaintiff herein; that she has read the foregoing complaint and knows the contents thereof; that the same is true of her own knowledge, except as to the matters therein stated to be alleged upon information and belief, and as to those matters she believes it to be true." Could Marie really have believed that she had the wrong birth date or place of birth? Not likely. Did she already forget her wedding night at the Theresa Hotel on 125th Street? Again, no, since she spoke bittersweetly of it in an interview seventy years later. Yet she had sworn that she knew the contents of the complaint to be true, "except as to the matters therein stated to be alleged upon information and belief, and as to those matters she believes it to be true." Why would she so perjure herself? (Annulment documents). One can scarcely avoid speculating that Nachman Syrkin's power over her was too potent a force to resist. Such a conclusion, moreover, is strongly supported by words she wrote forty-three years later in her 1960 memoir of her father:

[A]s I grew into womanhood many personal conflicts were to arise between my father and me. In his relationship to his daughter he was as dramatic, self-willed and sure of his rightness as in all other aspects of his life. But the difficulty of that struggle is as much mine as his and its details, since they involve others still alive, must be omitted. (*Memoir* 156)

Adding weight to such a conclusion are Maurice Samuel's comments on this very paragraph; in a letter to Marie dated March 2, 1961, that is, forty-four years after the annulment, written after reading her newly published biographical memoir of Nachman Syrkin, Samuel writes:

It is a very beautiful book, Marie, because of its honesty, (am I misled by personal involvement?). . . . The central expression of your personal relationship to the subject is in the passage on page 156. . . . I remember vividly how great I knew your father to be, and how I hated his self-righteousness. I remember my *occasional* conviction that if he had been gentle, kind, 'understanding,' you and I would have remained together. (There's probably little foundation to the idea). But what strikes me now, strikes me down, in fact, as I read your account of him, is how much I must have made him suffer. I never really understood it. Perhaps you didn't at the time. What a terrible abyss of [?] there was between him and me [us?] because of that paragraph I quoted. (Archives)

There remains one further legality stated in the annulment document. Even if the annulment had been granted on the grounds that Marie had not attained the age of consent, it would have been possible for her, once she had attained such age—that is, some time in the future—to have the annulment reversed. But for many complicated reasons, this never happened. The trial was held and the marriage of Maurice Samuel and Marie Syrkin was thereby forever annulled. In her late years, when recounting this episode, Marie caustically commented, "And then, papa announced that we could be engaged!" (Personal interview).

Just before Maurice had to return to Camp Upton, he dashed off a note: "Dear Sweetheart: This letter I scribble immediately after leaving you. . . . My own, dear girl: we are passing thro' terrible days: they are the price of a clear conscience to me—the first big sacrifice I have made. We cannot help being unhappy, but let us both thank God that this unhappiness is not accidental misfortune, but a deliberate offering to the impulse of good." It was signed "Dead and living, Your lover, Maurice." Maurice Samuel had not contested the annulment. (Archives, October [5?] 1917)

When the returning soldier arrived at his camp, he had spent sufficient time on the train ride back to nurse his grievances. But the next day he wrote to Marie, "I sometimes think I am courting death by excess of love; is it possible to love many years as I love now? And if it is not, how will I find life tolerable?"

How Marie responded to Maurice's laments of love and life is not recorded, but it probably wouldn't be too far off the mark to guess that sympathy for his ups and downs and excesses eventually would begin to grow wearisome. After all, she was an optimistic eighteen-year-old, a bright college student yearning for freedom to discover herself. Held in check by tight reins gripped by her powerful father, wasn't she even more so trammeled by the demands of a lover who infantilized her with his barrage of reductive endearments?: darling child, childling, kiddy, little darling, baby, etc., to say nothing of burdening her with his unpredictable moods and demands? How to account for her attraction to him—one that would last a lifetime? Perhaps one must simply take her at her own words—her description of Maurice when she first met him— and immediately summoned up when she was eighty-nine years old: "He seemed extraordinarily handsome to me," she recalled nostalgically. "He was very nice looking, though short, and he had the most extraordinary, photographic memory. Every poem I loved, he knew by heart" (Personal interview). Then, in a mood of intense nostalgia, she repeated verbatim the very words she had written in 1915 to her best friend Eugenia about her "sudden experience": "I have just met someone who is as handsome as Apollo, as great a poet as Shelley, and as noble as Joan of Arc." Marie at eighty-nine allowed that no normal girl of sixteen "would write that way," and she could offer no explanation for the last attribute, but the whole suggests that the attraction was first and foremost, physical; second, it was his astounding command of the poetry that she so loved; and third, it is some attempt to find words for what she experienced as brilliance and an aristocratic bearing—perhaps suggested by his British accent. Ultimately, however, events were to diminish this *coup de foudre* into a distant persistent ostinato, but the force of that first thunderclap was never to die down.

For the next few months Maurice and Marie kept up their correspondence and continued to see each other on Sundays whenever Marie could visit Camp Upton or whenever Maurice could get a leave. The often contradictory letters to Marie carry on, singing the familiar personal refrains: he addresses her in infantilizing terms; waiting for her next visit is torture; he is deeply depressed; he worships her; she doesn't write often enough; his passion for her consumes him; he gives her instructions; he reproaches her; why does she reproach him?; why does she write such lecturing letters?; they really aren't compatible in terms of interests; he frets over her health; Papa is brilliant; Papa is a monster; she knows nothing of politics. This last accusation is curious because he takes the trouble to write detailed analyses of current events. These letters not only are evidence that his politics and Nachman Syrkin's politics are quite similar, but also, presumably—even if Marie's politics are deeply influenced by her father—she would know something about them, though she might not always agree with him. Moreover, it is more than likely that his detailed political observations are meant for Nachman's eyes as much as Marie's, the better to persuade Syrkin of his son-in-law-manqué's merit.

Yet Samuel's tiresome remonstrations to his beloved are not nearly as interesting as his epistolary comments on the events of the day. They reveal the mind of a thoughtful soldier in the midst of a fearful war who is struggling between the horror of killing and the impulse to goodness; they demonstrate the fright that accompanies bad news on the war front and great joy when the news is propitious. They also indicate the great significance of events in the war that appertain to Jews in particular. Yet, most importantly they express the conflicting feelings of a man who despises Germany but who supports the Bolshevik revolution in Russia. Under the Kerensky provisional government, Russia had continued to fight on the side of the Allies. But in October, after the Bolshevik coup, and now led by Lenin, the Russians were all too aware of their disastrous military losses and the exhaustion and hunger of their badly equipped and poorly led army; thus they entered negotiations to sign a separate peace treaty with Germany at Brest-Litovsk that would not only entail forfeiture of the territories of Ukraine, the Baltic lands, Finland, and Poland, but also would free up German troops to fight on the western front in their last effort to achieve the great victory that had thus far eluded them.

Private Maurice Samuel, the former pacifist, socialist, and universalist began to rethink his ideas; despite his past convictions, now he had

not a doubt about which side he was on. He writes to Marie about the
events in Russia and his feelings for the oppressed Russians, caught between the Provisional Government of the socialist Kerensky and the Bol-
sheviki led by Trotsky and Lenin: "Can any man look on unhappy Russia
and not desire either to lure the vile oppressors down to Cacus or die in
the attempt? . . . I have learned to love as teachers Trotzky and Lenin, and
learned to hate with insensate hatred . . . the German militarists. . . . I
feel unalterably happy that once more a Jew [Trotzky] should have proved
a teacher to the world. . . . I am more deeply depressed than I have ever
been before. I really begin to feel the menace of Germany." In a chill-
ingly prescient diatribe against pre-Holocaust Germany, he continues
his bitter critique: "There is something so terrible about the German
people, something so Godless and merciless, utterly devoid of human
softness and weakness, that when I allow my imagination to play on
the theme, these vast hordes seem not of this earth, but of some remote
planet. They do not care for human things, they look with indifference
or derision on our weaknesses; if they dislike us, they *exterminate* [ital-
ics mine] us, and all our efforts are childish and vain; we are a *flock of
sheep* [italics mine]. . . . I am beginning to grow intolerant of pacifists
and pro-Germans."

It is doubtful that at this moment Marie quite shared Samuel's intense hatred of Germany—that would come later; but almost surely she
shared his love of Jewish Jerusalem. On December 9, 1917 he writes in
exultation, "Nothing, since the beginning of the war, has so thrilled me
as the announcement of the capture of Jerusalem by the British, and the
subsequent pro-Jewish pronouncements of allied publicists. . . . Just
after the news of the fall of Jerusalem (God! 'The fall of Jerusalem!'
does that sound a possibility of today?) Think how the Jewish soldiers in
the English army must have felt when they stepped into the countr[y]?"
Moreover, he writes that this news came just as another piece of news
was announced—that the Germans were massing for a last tremendous
drive against the Allies, bringing to it troops from Russia, Rumania, and
from the Dutch border where they had been stationed for the last three
years. "Germany, the Efficient One is about to put all into the venture.
They mean to take Calais, perhaps even Paris, this winter, before American intervention becomes an important factor in the war. There will be
such a slaughter in this new drive as even this war-besotted generation
will stand aghast at. I would to God I could stand up against that German tide." He is so completely overcome with mixed emotions that he

declares to Marie, who could only fear for her fiancé's very life, "I cannot tell you how eager I am now to get to the fighting front. If I had a chance to get over in a month, to go on board this week-end, I would snatch at it with both hands." Then, turning again to his Zionist sentiments, "I feel that every Jewish soldier on the allied side adds something to the possibility of the realization of our dream." Maurice Samuel was a young man filled with an infinite variety of passionate emotions.

Maurice Samuel's letters to Marie constitute an extraordinary account of the tangle of ideas, sentiments, and interpretations of an acutely sensitive young intellectual caught up in the web of World War I. They surely deserve a volume of their own, but here Maurice Samuel's letters to his fiancée must serve mainly as background for Marie Syrkin's own struggle to achieve individuation. Paramount in her apparently unconscious effort to attain selfhood was the agon between her father and her lover. Nachman and Maurice might have been friends, had it not been for Marie. They agreed about Germany; they agreed about America's entry into the war on the side of the allies; they agreed about the importance of the Balfour Declaration; they agreed about the Zionist cause; they agreed about the Jewish Legion; but they did not agree about Marie! With respect to the Jewish Legion, however, Samuel, already in the American army, did not wish to transfer to the legion; but risibly, Nachman Syrkin immediately volunteered for it—at forty-nine years he was overage and overweight. He was, of course, rejected. But his daughter later made the claim that the offer was an honest one: "I cannot believe that he really expected to be taken in view of his age and physical condition, but the gesture was nonetheless honest. He would have gladly gone had they taken him. Always it was the idea that mattered; overweight and overage were unfortunate technicalities like so many other 'technicalities' which stood in the way of his visions" (*Memoir* 164).

The shared politics of the two men notwithstanding, Marie was caught between two opposing forces: Nachman Syrkin vacillated between being the adoring papa and behaving like a "Victorian ogre"; Maurice swung between besotted lover and modern libertine. Both father and fiancé recognized Marie's extraordinary combination of beauty and brains, yet they both treated her with reductive condescension; both were demanding; both exercised their masculine authority over her—moral, physical, and intellectual; and inevitably the controlling power of each of the men came into bitter conflict. Nothing could be clearer than the sentiments of a letter Maurice sent to Marie in early

December 1917. After a leave for the Hanukkah holiday that apparently included an acrimonious dispute with Nachman, Maurice shot off a brutal diatribe against Syrkin ending with this assessment: "I know for dead certain that papa has no sympathy for me. . . . What he says concerning his regard for my feeling—'since you are going to war, etc.' is pure self-deception. It is a manifestation of that faculty for self-convincing which, better applied, has helped him to do good work. Your papa has a vast and vague resentment of the intrusion of the world in general between him and you, and of my intrusion in particular." The letter ends with a final snipe at Marie who has "Altogether too much sympathy, too vaguely diffused and general. You emerge an impotent child from this all-around appreciation of other people's views." Samuel surely would not have believed that forty years later he would write to Marie: "But what strikes me now, strikes me down, in fact, as I read your account of [Nachman], is how much I must have made him suffer. I never understood it really" (Archives, March 2, 1961).

Maurice's solution to the problem is that he and Marie not see one another for the next few weeks and that they see each other only once before they part, when he will be transferred to a base in the south before being sent to France. The reason for this is that he is not prepared to give papa a "statement of our behavior during a tête-á-tête. . . . I will not see you on sufferance. . . . It is a question of dignity. . . . Your papa has succeeded in making our affection something ugly and clandestine. To prevent him from ruining it, we will circumvent him by not seeing each other." The last page of the letter is missing—but whatever the final words, these are the last extant sentences: ". . . your papa's anxiety to send you to Cornell has nothing to do with your health. I know, and I know from the bottom of my heart, that he is getting you away from me." These words are probably very close to the truth and will prove prophetic as well. Marie's matriculation at Cornell will not turn out to be felicitous for Maurice Samuel.

In January 1918, the eagerly anticipated move south from Camp Upton to Camp Greene, North Carolina, finally came to pass. It was to be the last stage before shipment to France—the move Maurice Samuel claimed he had been longing for since the day he had enlisted. The distance between the two lovers was now seven hundred literal miles and an equivalent number of emotional miles, growing more distant by the day. The dangers Maurice was soon to pass were becoming transparently clear, intensifying his every emotion, scaling every height and plunging to every depth. With little chance of meeting until after the war, Maurice's terrors became concentrated on Marie, and he knew it. "I am certain that this constant concentration of my attentions and thoughts on you is morbid and disastrous. . . . I have regular quarrels with you. . . . I carefully review all your faults and wonder what the deuce constitutes the unbreakable bond between us. . . . The thought of you quickens the beating of my heart, makes the rain sound deeper, casts me into deeper and deeper gloom and the stupidity of it angers me: because you are only a little girl, with a sentimental cast of mind, and a certain show of ability—and that's my honest opinion—coldly speaking."

But what could Marie herself be thinking as she read these words? Almost surely she asked herself the same question: What the deuce constituted her own commitment to the relationship? Why would she continue to feel such a powerful attraction to a man who constantly berated her for her childishness, her carelessness, for her failure to write as often as he wished, for her lack of political sophistication, for her sentimental Victorian sensibility, for her excessive loyalty to her father? Of course, she probably would have confessed to herself that, just possibly, she had overdone the continued reproaches for his past infidelities. Perhaps on the eve of his departure for the battlefield she should have held back, knowing that it could only anger him. And anger him it did: "Such a letter as the one I am returning makes me unspeakably angry," Maurice shot back after one of Marie's needling notes:

I am weary of hearing you repeat these things. It is mere impertinent priggishness. I suffer deeply enough for my shortcomings. Do you think by your constant allusions you add anything to my determination to put my life in order? I resent being told things by you. I have done bad things in my life such as you have never done. I have also done good things in my life the like of which you have never done. . . . If my love for you is such that it impels me to seek good, do not try to add to it by your baby-lectures and copy-book prattle.

And yet—how can a nineteen-year-old girl resist words like these: "Oh, Manitchka, Manitichka, everywhere you, you, you. Where are you now, brown-eyes? Laughing? Chattering? Reading? Or thinking of me, sentimentally, foolishly? When I will return from the war I shall not tell you of the exact day of my arrival, but I shall steal in on you, and surprise you. Are you longing for the day, dear?"

From February through April 1918, the letters from Camp Greene continue with regularity and with the same proportion of love and lambast—presumably on both sides of the correspondence. Admittedly, we have only Maurice's quotations from Marie's letters to go on, but the issues are clear enough. Many of the problems that had fed the flames of the conflict before the move to Camp Greene remain. Nachman's plans to go to Russia are still up in the air. Though Maurice's feelings are ambivalent—if Marie is at Cornell, she won't be in Russia, but if she is at Cornell, he will be envious of her education and fearful about her constancy: "How is it you are not at Cornell? The session opened a fortnight ago. Have you changed your mind or are you waiting for the settlement of the Russian business?" (Archives, Jan. 22, 1918). As it turned out, Marie would not begin her Cornell career until the summer session. But Marie's college studies make Maurice sharply conscious of his own educational deficiencies and time lost because of the war: "Let us not delude ourselves. This war will bring us nothing at all. I shall have lost (at best, darling) two years of my life, two years of you, two years of work, of study, of preparation, of making ready to go through life with you" (Archives, 1918). And the wounds from the marriage annulment have not healed. Responding to Marie statement "I wish you were back and we were married already. I find the excitement of courtship much too absorbing and enervating for a proper attention to my work," he mocks Marie's notion that their marriage was a way to avoid "the cheapening of the finest impulses" of which "we were rather proud," and launches into a frenzied tirade spitting out his own current reading of the event:

This is all balderash [*sic*], Manitchka. The marriage was a stupidity forced on us by our blindness to facts. It was stupid because we weren't prepared to back it up—or, rather, because it is a childish sop to certain vague (meaningless) morality views, which we didn't properly understand. It was stupid because you couldn't support yourself and I couldn't do it for you. It was stupid because it corresponded to *nothing* either of us really cared about. It was, in brief, a crazy act suddenly called for by events for which neither of us was wholly responsible but for which I must take the greater blame. . . . We cut a rather ridiculous figure, with the aid of your revered but excitable father. . . . I say again, the real stupidity (it was a laughable, a *stupid* stupidity) was in our flying to City Hall for to get the symbol of eternal and acknowledged love. Let's forget the ridiculous episode, and be more sensible in the future.

This is hardly a comforting good-bye from a battle-bound soldier to his erstwhile bride, now become bride-in-waiting. But he either realized that his words were too harsh or that he simply could not control his thoughts; thus, the letter continues with further analysis of the event of the past: "The root of much of the evils of the past," he now concludes, "was our youthfulness and dependence on others. I was rather afraid of your redoubtable father, and so were you. We didn't dare do things, and therefore shouldn't have done other things, which later we did. Also we lacked self control; I say advisedly, and blame myself more than you because I am older and should have been wiser. And I trust in time to shake of [*sic*] the fear of your father." Maurice is convinced that Nachman will martial all his energy to oppose their ultimate marriage. But the explanation for the fear of Nachman turns out to be fear of his own inadequacy: "I see no likelihood of my achieving great distinction or wealth on this side of middle age, and little likelihood of achieving more than a mediocre reputation (the thing beloved by you and positively insisted on by papa) . . . and he will strenuously deny that marrying an undistinguished, unpedigreed, unmoneyed, prospectless nobody like me will do you any good. So you see, Manitchka, we must grow up quickly and be ready to face his opposition with firmness, tolerance and dignity." This self analysis and pessimism comes from a man destined to become a prolific writer, admired lecturer and radio personality, and esteemed exponent for the Zionist cause.

Maurice Samuel sailed for France on March 30, 1918. His new address was Co. D., 1st Army Headquarters, Reg. American Expeditionary Forces. He would now spend one and a half years in the service of the U.S. Army in France—but not fighting at the front, as he had so ambivalently hoped. Instead, he was attached to the intelligence service and stationed in the town of Bordeaux. Here, the battle-ready Maurice Samuel was expected to do counterespionage work because he could speak French. Disappointed in being underused, he found the work dull and boring, and the people the same. Yet it gave him time to read, to study Hebrew with a Palestinian soldier, to write, to think—perhaps to think too much.

For the most part these letters across the ocean show the strain of this long-distance love affair. Marie and Maurice are a pair of Shakespearean style lovers—somewhere between Beatrice and Benedict and Petruchio and Katherina; their verbal battles are furious; they are magnets that both repel and attract—but, the Bard's comic spirit is in short supply. By

September 1918, despite his utter contempt for his work and surround-
ings, he has been promoted to the rank of sergeant, but it is not clear
that this new status has provided him any more onerous tasks. It certainly hasn't stopped him from his opinionated correspondence. He is
an out-and-out worshiper at the feet of Woodrow Wilson's "lofty idealism," which he compares to the " barbarian interpretation of Zionism
which most of us have held until now . . . a thing of the dark ages—a
thing almost of the slime—a querulous, strutting, spear-shaking thing."
He asserts that "Zionism as represented by its leaders in America is
simply godless." This is not the Zionism he wants Zionism to be. The
former secular, pacifist universalist has turned spiritual. Zionism, he
declares,

"means nothing to my views on art, on social reform, on love and friendship.
Judaism means everything to me in its relation to those things: Judaism means
to me the immanence of God, continuous ecstasy, life ever active, ever true,
ever magnificent. My Judaism—my inherited capacity for communing with
God—drives me in all my thoughts, makes me hate the present social system,
makes me love Shelley, makes me loathe the ugliness of our marriage system, makes me pray for the disappearance of stupidity and meanness. But
did Zionism ever have any such relation to my spiritual totality? To yours? . . .
Yes, there is need of inspiring Zionism so that it shall be Jewish, so that it shall
be "peculiar." If our national existence is to be different from the national existence of the Goyim (and otherwise we *are* Goyim) Zionism must be holy and
spiritual, must be a cult, not merely an organisation, must be a faith, a mighty
inward impulse, must be identified with the Bible. At present it is an imitation
(and result) of the wave of nationalism which came in Europe in the 19th century."

It is hard to argue against such a visionary conception of Zionism, a
conception that seems presciently in advance of the late-twentieth-
century resurgence of religious spirituality.

But of course, this dream of Zionism was dreamed before the Holocaust and before the State of Israel, when Zionism's mission would have
to attend to other demands—more in tune with Nachman Syrkin's
ideas. It is apparent, however, that much of what Samuel rejects is
Syrkin's "rescue" Zionism. Wasn't Syrkin's primary concern the *physical*
safety of the Jewish people, so much so that he could endorse the
Uganda movement when Palestine seemed an ever-elusive goal? And as

for Jewish spirituality, Marie's father had grown up within Eastern European orthodoxy and that sent him headlong into secularism, socialism, and political Zionism. But Samuel, it seems clear, had been reading Ahad Ha'am and had been thrilled by the idea of "cultural Zionism"—the argument that Zionism's mission was certainly to protect the physical safety of the Jews, but even more so to reinvigorate the spirit of Judaism as well.

There is no need to speculate what this letter inspired in its recipient. The writer himself tells us directly: "Yours of October 24 received today." With apparent sweetness and light Samuel begins, "It is altogether a fine letter," but the sentence immediately shifts tone, "despite (or perhaps because of) the violence of your repudiations and your counter attacks. I have already remarked, and the observation will bear repetition, that the only way to rouse you to real, valuable thinking pitch is to be brutal about the ineffable nonsense which you allow yourself. As a rule, when you write on wars, ethics, Zionism, poetry, etc. you have the most exasperating habit of allowing a keen, clear and powerful mentality to debauch itself with sobs and enthusiasms." As the letter continues, Maurice responds to Marie's accusations. She has at various times, Samuel reports, accused him of brutality, reproached him for cynicism, rebuked him for sanctimoniousness, admonished him for egotism, reproved him for pedantry. To some of the denunciations he admits, but some he not only indignantly rejects, but also accuses Marie of those very shortcomings.

With such a barrage of charges and countercharges, one can but wonder how Marie could even consider continuing the relationship—particularly when her fiancé ends his letter with the fact that he is still not sure about his future, that he doesn't know when he will be able to return to America because America is going to have a large army of occupation in Germany "stationed there for God knows how long," and he thinks he will be part of that army because of his "knowledge of German(!)." The parentheses is meant to indicate that the German he knows is not really German, but Yiddish. Finally, he would be "very much astonished if the last troops should have left France nine months after the order for demobilization—not the suspension of hostilities, mind you."

Perhaps at this point, Marie's heart was, if not hardening, at the very least, congealing. She may very well have been thinking that the annulment was a blessing, and that in the contest for control between her father and her fiancé, at this moment her father had the advantage. Given the mutual emotional bruising that had been increasing since Maurice's time at Camp Greene and was subsequently stepped-up in France, the news that he might have to remain in Europe for some time was not an effective balm.

Chapter Five

Marriage, Motherhood, and Tragedy

Broken Engagement and Life at Cornell

MARIE SYRKIN WENT to Cornell for orientation in the first week of July 1918, and had a taste of what glorious times might be in the offing. She was nineteen, very intelligent, and extraordinarily beautiful: a finely shaped face, framed with thick, dark hair, large, deep-brown eyes punctuated by black eyebrows, a perfectly formed small, straight nose, and gently curved lips that could bend upwards into a beguiling smile or just as easily turn down in seriousness or irritation. A photograph taken at the time shows her with an enigmatic Mona Lisa look — is she smiling or not? Her huge dark eyes look away somewhere in the distance. And the beauty of her face is crowned by a large broadbrimmed straw hat with a wide band of flowers around the crown. She knew she was beautiful and she knew she was smart. She also knew that she had been hemmed in by two powerful men — and now she was free.

Never having been farther from the New York Jewish world than the New Jersey Jewish world, she was now free to flirt, to be silly, to breathe the air of a different America, an America of towns, not cities; homes, not apartments; green trees and gardens, not pavements and subways; native Americans, not immigrant Jews.[1] True, Marie was aware of the unfamiliar demography of Cornell and Ithaca before she chose to go there. She had met a number of bright young men in Belmar who were students at Cornell, and although she did not know any women there, Cornell was far from a casual choice. After a mediocre high school experience, Marie now was dead serious about her studies. She longed to get a Ph.D. in English Literature and she aspired to write fine poetry. She wanted the prestigious Ph.D. in order to be self-supporting; but most importantly, she yearned to be part of an intellectually exciting academic community. Cornell was regarded as the only institution in New York that could rival the Ivy League Columbia University; but Columbia was not coeducational and Cornell had been so since 1872. Marie was not interested in the prestigious northeastern women's colleges, such as Vassar, Mount Holyoke, Wellesley, or Smith; and since she expected to do graduate work, she carefully chose a University. Finances also may have had something to do with it because, as a land grant college, Cornell's tuition was a rather manageable $200 a year. More importantly, perhaps, the choice may have arisen out of the liberal reputation Cornell held — particularly among Jews. The proposed charter of 1865 had stated that the University was to be nonsectarian and that a majority of the board of trustees was never to be of one particular religious sect or of no religious sect and that persons of every religious denomination or of no religious affiliation should be equally eligible for all offices and appointments. The proposal was bitterly opposed by the press and the denominational colleges, but they were overruled and Cornell was granted its charter.[2]

Just a little less than a year after her elopement, on July 6, 1918, after a ten-hour ride to upstate New York, Marie Syrkin, accompanied by her father Nachman, stepped off the train at Ithaca. "I left my angel of a father looking so mournful and adorable that I felt like a heartless brute for three minutes," she quipped the following day in a full report to Eugenia Shafran from her new residence at 120 Oak Avenue, Ithaca. Because Eugenia had been in correspondence with Maurice over the last year and had remained Marie's closest confidante, she undoubtedly was aware of the problems in her friends' relationship. But Marie's letter mentions nothing about the state of that affair. Explaining that she spent the first day at Cornell "reconnoitering," Marie's letter is a hymn to her new found liberty. "Ithaca is heaven, if heaven is anything like what I want it to be — a real, green, quiet dreamy place with unexpected rivers and crazy bridges and two funny streetcars. . . . I know little of the university yet, save that it consists of magnificent buildings spread over a tremendous campus on which soldiers squat picturesquely, though alas unapproachably." Her own particular soldier in France to whom she was still engaged, and who at least figuratively was approachable, is not even mentioned in this report to Eugenia. Moreover, Marie already had some male acquaintances at Cornell who had been there for a couple of years. Apparently a quite "jovial" fellow, one Mr. Goldberg, immediately offered his services as an escort around the campus. First, because dormitories for women would not be built until 1927, Marie had to look for authorized off-campus housing. She secured a large windowed, furnished room for three dollars a week in a cottage near the campus. "My room is on the ground floor so that I am surrounded by the arms of trees stretching into my window." she ecstatically reports to Eugenia. "My landlady is a fat, efficient, genteel American who has been brought up on college girls and has the lingo and their needs *par coeur*. . . . I also have a chaperone—that is the cottage has, who glowers white-hairedly from her room which faces mine and is right by the entrance to the house—an excellent observation point—she keeps her door open. The other girls gave me a cabbagy impression, rather rustic and thin and stupid. I don't know any yet. I should love to know them well." After securing her room, Goldberg took her to a country vaudeville show, which Marie mocked and reported to Eugenia that it was risibly crude. But she was having fun (Shafran, Archives f. 6).

At the end of the orientation session at Cornell, Marie returned to Belmar where she would spend the remainder of the summer and then would return to New York to wait for the fall semester to begin sometime in early October of 1918. For several months, Marie had been struggling with guilty feelings over her failure to participate in the war in some active way. She had written to Maurice about several different courses of action she might take. Private Samuel had been shipped to France in early April, and by August had been promoted to sergeant. In September, Marie wrote to Sgt. Maurice Samuel in France that she planned to work in a munitions factory. Maurice's response to that was a decidedly negative and vicious attack on her plan: "You ask me with pathetic fear, not to make fun in advance of your intention to go and work ten hours a day in a munitions factory. I insist on making fun of it. Without having heard the results, I assert that, if you got as far as the factory, you didn't work there three consecutive days: to that I'll swear." He was not quite correct; Marie did not last the day. Marie's letter, however, also contained the fact that at Cornell, Goldberg had assumed a "proprietorial attitude" toward her. Maurice nastily responded that he was "not astonished, and I only wonder," he adds, "that it did not manifest itself before. He is, of course, an excellent fellow, as far as I can make out, but a bourgeois," and warns her against trusting men like Goldberg (Archives, September, f. 12).

Though Marie gave up the munitions plant attempt, her impulse to do good did not dissipate entirely. Next, she thought of nursing the wounded. This too did not survive the month. October came quickly— and Marie returned to Cornell to complete her studies in English Literature for her B.A. degree. The letters between Marie and Maurice began to slow down. The mail appears to have been sporadically delivered to Maurice, for in a letter dated November 2, he writes to Marie that he has just received two letters from her from early October at Cornell. The November letter is full of recriminations on Maurice's side and excuses on Marie's side. In December, he admits having received "a whole bundle of letters from you which explains your recent seeming silence. These letters were dated 8–11 and 16 November, the most exciting of recent days" (Archives f. 12). Exciting they certainly were, for on Monday, November 11, 1918, The *New York Times* headline, in bold black letters, announced: "Armistice Signed, End of the War! Berlin Seized by Revolutionists; Chancellor Begs for Order; Ousted Kaiser Flees to Holland."

One might imagine, that with this great news Maurice would fill his next letter with grand hopes for their future, but such was not the case. Instead, he ripped off a seven-page missive, the first pages of which vilify Theodore Roosevelt and the Republican Party for their campaign against the League of Nations, and then at great length, glorify Wilson's idealism, which he believes is in "holy earnest." Finally, after his hymn of "glory to Wilson in the highest" (he would have been shocked to learn from later twentieth-century scholarship that Wilson was also a racist and antisemite), Samuel turns to matters personal. Marie has inquired, now that the war is over, what does her intended husband intend regarding his return to America? Certainly she has been thinking about this. He informs her that not only will it not be soon—"probably not before June." As for what he intends to do in America when he returns, "God alone knows," he writes (Archives f. 12).

If all of this uncertainty did not hearten Marie to wait eagerly for the return of her fiancé, his next certainty, was most dissuading: "I am not as confident of the future as you. Sudden heavy responsibilities have fallen on me; could I be relieved of them (which I cannot) I would face the future with utter, careless confidence." His next letter, dated December 7, tells Marie exactly what those responsibilities would be. "It is highly probable that when the war is over my mother, younger brother and younger sister will want to join me in America—and for various reasons I am anxious that they should do so. I would be their one mainstay in those circumstances—and even if they remain in England—which is unlikely—and I in America, my obligations, if somewhat lighter, will be none the less real." All that being said, the true *coup de grace* was probably Maurice's statement about the future for the two of them: "To live away from you is impossible: to live near you and not with you seems equally impossible. But all events now insist at least on the second impossibility and in the face of them I am acutely unhappy." And when will all of this come to pass? "I think" he speculates, "I shall be back in the States before you finish Cornell. But this only serves to accentuate impossibility number two. What have you to say?"[3]

What Marie had to say is clear. The substance is contained in Maurice Samuel's last letter to Marie—last, that is, until years later. On February 4, 1919, a cold winter's day in upstate New York, Marie Syrkin wrote a heated letter to her fiancé calling a halt to their engagement. Maurice received it on February 25 and replied that he spent the night almost entirely with the question of whether her letter left room for a reply. "Its tone is final," he concludes. "I inspire you with violent dislike. You have no faith either in my kindness or my decency. I have been disloyal and cruel, and life with me would be one long torture for you." His refutation of himself, among a number defenses, is that he has had crises in his life that have long since passed, that she has been completely unsympathetic and there have been some misunderstandings. The letter ends with a mild hope for change: "I shall be waiting for a considerable time, probably three or four years, let us say, to hear from you again. I accept your letter unconditionally without complaint. I have not the remotest intention of urging anything on you. But if you decide that certain obstacles can be overcome, and are worth overcoming (at present a questionable assumption) I could not want to think that this letter of yours prevents you from writing to me. . . . I will not write to you again." Maurice adds that his movements after demobilization in Europe or in America are uncertain, so if she wants to write to him he leaves his mother's address in Manchester. "If I do not answer, you will know that it is for one reason only; that the letter didn't reach me."[4] Marie did not respond.

And thus, the correspondence that had obsessively occupied Marie and Maurice for the past two years came to an end. But as the letters from Maurice ceased, in their place came the frequent letters of Nachman Syrkin to his daughter. On December 31, 1918, Syrkin sent a New Year's letter to his daughter at Cornell. "Darling Maryetchka!" he begins. "Happy New Year! I hope to see you around me with a good and strong will for everything that is just, beautiful and true in life." He tells her that he expects to leave for Europe in about ten days and anticipates that "the trip is considered meanwhile on the basis of 2–3 months, but I think I will have to go somewhere else after those 2–3 months. . . . I wish you moral strength and poetical inspiration for the coming year. Papa" (Archives f. 1). Two weeks later, on January 15, just before he is to sail for Europe to attend the Versailles Peace Conference and a Zionist Conference in London, Nachman Syrkin again wrote to his daughter; this time to clear up details, particularly regarding the money to pay a Cornell bill that was immediately due: "why did you not write a few days before that the last day is approaching?" Nachman asked reprovingly. Then, in questions that echo and simply replace the ones that Maurice habitually had asked, Marie's father bombards her with worried-parent inquiries. "How is your health? How is the ear? Write me please the whole truth. Your condition does not stop to worry me day and night. If you will not write me a few times a week, while I will be in Europe, I am afraid my depression will check all my energy and work" (Archives f. 1). Health and epistolary negligence had been two irritating questions that appeared with regularity in Maurice's letters. Now Nachman will add questions about finances to the list. Marie, of course, has no income of her own, yet she does not appear to be especially cautious about financial matters, nor does she seem to understand that her father does not have readily available funds.

Surely, during the weeks before and after Marie's letter of February 4 to Maurice Samuel terminating their engagement, she must have sent her father a response to his letters of December and January, and one would suppose that she had written to him at least sometime in February, but Marie appears to have deliberately withheld the disengagement information from him. Papa Syrkin would not be the first to find out about his daughter's change of heart, though the news certainly would have cheered him up. Marie did not write to her father about the breakup until the very end of February. Instead, she chose her friend, Eugenia, as the immediate recipient of the tidings. Marie wrote to her on February 10, 1919, only four days after writing to Maurice. "I have written Maurice and told him I no longer loved him. I sometimes wonder now if it is true," she confesses to her closest confidante. She also admits it to herself and would ask herself the same question many times over the years. But, she had done it and was really none the worse for the *angst,* for she blithely goes on to a name a new man in her life. Reporting on the overnight train trip, apparently from New York to Cornell after the Christmas vacation, Marie is in high comic form as she describes her sleeping arrangements in the upper berth on the train. A fellow she knew named "Schmidt" had been given the lower berth. Embarrassed by this, he sat in another car and Marie "retired with unbecoming speed."

My new dress, was something of a hindrance. I had to partially remove it and expose two legs to the knee before the porter could shove me into my berth. As the train was filled chiefly with young masculine Cornellians, I felt that I was undressing *en famille*. I am certain that they too were struck by the propriety of the incident. Several other professorial eyes loaned further dignity and respectability.

In the morning, the admirable Bodansky came to meet me, per order. He went thru [*sic*] the Pullman to discover where I was, and whispered sweet nothings indiscriminately at all the berths in order to extract the proper answer. I had no means of warning him that Schmidt was reposing curiously and delightedly underneath. Bodansky afterwards assured me that he had called me by my first name in public in order not to announce my presence to everyone in the car which the shouting of my second name would have done (Shafran, Archives f. 6).

Marie could not have been exceedingly discomposed by the breakup of her love affair, marriage, and engagement (in that order), though she had admitted to some uncertainty. The letter to Eugenia suggests that Marie had been having a high time in the seven months at Cornell; and her epithet "the admirable Bodansky" implies that Eugenia was not unfamiliar with the name. What and whenever she had been writing to Maurice—and he did complain of its sporadic nature—it is clear that she had also been on the replacement lookout. Mr. Aaron Bodansky, a thirty-year-old lecturer in biochemistry was about to assume a front-and-center place in Marie's life.

Meanwhile, Marie was enjoying herself, becoming at ease in the Cornell community, making all sorts of friends male and female; her closest woman friend was Laura Reichenthal, who would later be known as Laura Riding, the renowned poet and muse of Robert Graves. Nevertheless, despite all her socializing, Marie certainly was not neglecting her studies. Unusual as her ambition to become a Ph.D. in literature was for a young Jewish woman, she saw it as the major station on her route to intellectual autonomy. Her correspondence with Eugenia (quite a bit of which is extant) reveals the fact that, despite her flair for fun, a flair that was so often ironic and sometimes self-deprecatory, she also possessed a dead-earnest, serious, literary, critical faculty — quite impressive for one so young. Eugenia had been trying off and on to write a novel, and she sent the manuscript to her friend for an evaluation before she left for Cornell. On December 7, Marie responded with a detailed critique that was honest, but kind. Beginning with the accent on the positive, she tells Eugenia, "I read the manuscript several times, and I shall give you my impressions as carefully as possible. Most important of all, I think, is the fact that I was interested thruout [*sic*]. Whether this interest may have been aroused because you were the writer, I do not know. I don't believe this was the case, though it may have been a contributing factor. The writing has one excellent quality — passion and strength." Marie believes it shows the possibilities for "significant work." And then — the real criticism begins: "*However,* it is formless. I do not mean by formless merely a carelessness of thought and expression. I use the word form in the sense of an architectural idea, a creative idea which determines the shape of your thought. A work of art must strain to one end." Marie suggests that the manuscript be boiled down by about half, and that she has found a tendency in several cases, "to cheapness of expression. For instance, No more would I 'yearningly scrutinize infinity' or 'silver stars that sing' or 'make music, etc. . . . [B]y now, infinity has been scrutinized yearningly so often, that if you want to convey any idea to your reader, you will have to [find other words]" (Shafran, Archives f. 5). This critique is one of the earliest examples of what will become Marie's strongest suit — critical analysis, whether literary or political.

The letter to her friend, moreover, illustrates some of Marie Syrkin's best personal characteristics. She has remained loyal to Eugenia through some terribly difficult times. Eugenia is undoubtedly an emotionally unstable young woman; she suffers periods of deep, sometimes suicidal depression in which she is brought low by physical symptoms; she always finds herself in severe financial straits; she cannot seem to hold on to a job; from time to time, she cuts off communication with friends. Nonetheless, Marie has remained loyal to her. Her serious attention to her friend's needs and the gentleness with which she begins what will be an honest, objective, and not entirely positive critique, is a hallmark of her capacity for empathy, kindness, and honesty.

Eugenia, it appears, accepted the criticism good naturedly, for a month later she received a facetious account of a basketball game Marie had attended between Cornell and Buffalo. "It was a delightful spring day despite the calendar. I had been reading Heine all day and felt properly mournful. Hence I went to the game *ganz allein*. It is an interesting experience. The teams wear dirty trunks and were hideous — without exception. A member of the Cornell team seemed to be an idiot — he dashed up and down in a manner which no athletic exigencies would explain. The shining flower of the Buffalo team was a very Jewish little Jew. A sort of plump and juvenile Abe Kabibble." Though Marie had been convinced to join the athletic association so that she could attend events, neither participatory nor spectator sports ever became a favorite pastime (Shafran, Archives f. 6).

Aaron

By the end of February, Marie's relationship with Aaron Bodansky was proceeding apace, and that is when Marie finally decided to let her traveling father know that she had broken her engagement to Maurice Samuel. Nachman Syrkin at this moment was thousands of miles away, fully occupied with his official duties. He had been elected by the recently formed American Jewish Congress to be a delegate to the Versailles Peace Conference. Until 1918, the American Jewish Committee, an elite and anti-Zionist organization established in 1906, functioned as a Jewish defense organization "to prevent the infraction of the civil and religious rights of Jews in any part of the world." Founded by a small group of prominent German Jews, including such notables as Jacob Schiff, Cyrus Adler, Mayer Sulzberger, Oscar Straus, and Louis Marshall, and acting out of a sense of *noblesse oblige,* they exercised their enormous wealth and diplomatic skills to gain access to high places. They were an American-style group of self appointed "court Jews" who intended to solve the crises of pogroms and the terrible conditions of the Jewish communities in Eastern Europe in the early years of the twentieth century. They were the very "establishment" against which Maurice Samuel and Nachman Syrkin had vented their spleen.

The American Jewish Congress, however, was formed in 1918 to provide a voice at the Versailles Conference for the postwar Jews of Europe. World War I had exacerbated the suffering of Eastern European Jews beyond the capacities of the American Jewish Committee, and though relief work had been expanded through feverish philanthropic activism and applied to a wider geographic area, it was not enough.

Since 1914, Chaim Weizmann had been pressing British political leaders for a public endorsement of the Zionist intentions in Palestine, and finally, in November of 1917, the British issued the Balfour Declaration, supporting the establishment of a national home for the Jews in Palestine. In the United States, Supreme Court Justice Louis Brandeis, the leader of the American Zionist movement, Rabbi Stephen Wise, and Supreme Court Justice Felix Frankfurter pressed Wilson for similar endorsement, which he promised to give. Moreover, given the weakened postwar condition of the Jewish communities of Europe, these communities would have to be defended at the Paris Peace Conference — but not by the hegemonic American Jewish Committee that most Jews in America felt was too elitist and openly anti-Zionist to adequately represent them. The active American Jewish community now pressed for a democratically elected Jewish "parliament" to argue for the rights of Jews during the peace deliberations. Though Nachman Syrkin had written about such an idea in the Zionist journal *Yiddishes Folk* as early as 1909, it wasn't until 1915 that the powerful lawyer Louis Brandeis (appointed Supreme Court Justice in 1916) came forward to head a committee to create a democratically elected body to represent the entire American Jewish community (*Memoir* 168–169). "The new organization would be designed to deal with matters affecting the welfare of Jews everywhere. But the highest priority was given to securing civil and political rights for Jewish communities in reconstructed postwar Europe." Brandeis was not universally applauded for his efforts. Many members of the American Jewish Committee accused him of splintering the Jewish community in America. Brandeis' response was "that only an American Jewry united in a body organized on the principle of Jewish peoplehood and dedicated to mass democratic participation would have the power to obtain equal rights for their brethren in Europe."[5]

Scarcely one month before the European nations were scheduled to meet in Versailles, the first democratically elected American Jewish Congress, representing the variety of Jewish groups in America — from the Yiddishists to the Zionists, from the religious to the secular, from the fraternal organizations even to the American Jewish Committee — convened in Philadelphia in December 1918, to elect a delegation to speak for American Jewry at the Peace Conference in Paris. The nearly four hundred votes cast by "over thirty Jewish organizations and more than eighty cities" elected nine men to be their representatives: Chairman Judge Julian Mack for the Zionists, Nachman Syrkin and Professor Hayim Fineman for the Labor Zionists, the labor leader Joseph Barondess, attorney Louis Marshall and Colonel Harry Cutler for the AJC, Reform Rabbi Stephen Wise, and B. L. Levinthal for the religious Zionists, and the poet Morris Vinchevsky (*Memoir* 168).

Marie Syrkin reports in her biography of her father that she herself had not attended the Philadelphia Convention where her father was chosen to represent the Socialist Zionists at Versailles. Though it was a foregone conclusion that he would be chosen, she explains that she was "busy at Cornell University where [she] was an undergraduate immersed in English Romantic poets. But," she adds, "a remarkably able and politically alert young girl among the Poalei Zion delegates, Golda Mabovitch (later Meir), years later told me of a circumstance in the election that then impressed her. When nominations were made at the party caucus, Syrkin did something unprecedented. He spoke for himself, pointing out all the reasons why he was the most suitable candidate. And instead of shocking the sensibilities of his comrades, his simplicity and earnestness moved them deeply," Golda reported. What would have been an intolerable display of bad taste in most men appeared in Syrkin, by virtue of his absolute childlike honesty, completely fitting and "natural" (*Memoir* 169).

Upon receiving Marie's letter sometime in early March, Nachman wrote to his daughter from London where he was participating in a Zionist Conference, which had sorely disappointed him. "Zionism has suffered in this conference a great moral defeat as so many rich Jews are displaying now their appetites to get the control over the country and to bury all the great hopes and promises of Zionism. I have, therefore, a bad time on this conference" (Archives f. 1). It is not surprising that Syrkin had a "bad time." The split between the Weizmann and Brandeis factions of the Zionist movement already had emerged. Louis D. Brandeis, the leader of American Zionism, had challenged Weizmann's leadership and his European Zionist view that antisemitism was inevitable and that unless the Jews had their own state they could never live normal lives. It was Weizmann's tireless diplomatic efforts that had brought about the Balfour Declaration, but he was also an adherent to Ahad Ha'am's Zionist philosophy of spiritual as well as political renewal. Brandeis, however, argued that this ignored the "exceptional" position of the American Jewish community; American antisemitism was not as strong in America as it was in Europe and it did not stand in the way of the Jews' remarkable social and economic mobility; therefore he did not feel the need of mass migration to Palestine. A "practical" Zionist, Brandeis' conception of Zionism was largely philanthropic, and he felt no need for spiritual renewal, though he did believe that there should be a national home for Jews who needed to be rescued. In hindsight, perhaps both were right: on the one hand, the Holocaust only two decades later proved the urgency for emigration from Europe; on the other hand, American Jewish life kept a steady pace of improvement and provided good reason for the existence of a strong diaspora—though the rate of assimilation and loss of cultural traditions kept an equally steady pace.[6]

Nachman Syrkin, representing the socialist Zionists, of course had no sympathy for the "rich Jews," and thus, his "bad time." Nevertheless, with respect to his daughter, he begins his letter in a euphoric mood because Marie had written him the one thing that he had so longed to hear her say—that she had broken with Maurice. "My darling Maryetchka!" he exclaims, "I received your both letters at once and was really happy. The same day I sent you per cable 100 dollars, so that you are not more broken. . . . I think you acted in full accordance with your inward moral sense, if you have broken with M," was the careful reaction. But Papa Syrkin could not let it rest there, for his next sentence is a paternal caveat: "But, darling Maryietchka, please do not pledge yourself and do not give your word to anybody, before I will return." The admonition continues, "You realize sufficiently how serious and at the same time how labile all these love affairs are, and not every affection must necessarily wind up immediately into life companionship and marriage. If you would not be only so exceedingly enthusiastic" (Archives f. 1).

It was only much later in life that Marie would be able to admit that although her father was "dramatic, self-willed and sure of his rightness" in his relationship to her, the conflict between them owed as much to herself as to him (*Memoir* 156). Marie was, just as he had described her, "exceedingly enthusiastic"; she was also, at this time in her life, easily distracted from work, very social, somewhat careless about details and money, and not an especially keen judge of character. Though she loved her father, she also struggled against him, and she knew just what sweet-talk would persuade him. By the end of March, Marie had received her father's letter of caution, a letter that also noted the fact that her birthday was only a few days hence, and that he regretted so much that he was far from her. "Accept my greetings and congratulations," he wrote. "The day and moment you were born is so much in my imagination!

Which tremendous way, filled with misery and hope, humanity went through during that time, and how tragical formed itself my own personal life. You, Maryetchka, are my only happiness and consolation, my anchor of salvation in life" (Archives f. 1). On March 26, four days after her birthday, Marie seized the opening his congratulations had given her; his birthday greeting would serve her purpose. "Dearest Papa," she began: "I am twenty years old already. Isn't that aged? Did you send me anything for my birthday? How are you feeling dearest? I am so worried about you because of the influenza which is raging in Europe. How is the good cause? Write me about the activities which you are undertaking." A good opening paragraph to woo a father whom she knew would not like the rest of her letter. The letter plainly displays Marie's mix of childish protestation and explanation, fear of her father's reaction and his power over her, as well as a clear awareness of her own strong intellectual capabilities and ambition — but thus far only an *unconscious* desire to break through her willing acceptance of the conventional marriage myth in which domination by her father would be transferred to a husband. Thus, Marie's transparent letter, here quoted in full, continues:

I wish to speak to you about a serious matter. I shall write to you as frankly as if you were a friend of mine, instead of my father. You know that I broke with Maurice, because I felt I could not be happy with him. I have now decided to marry Bodansky as soon as possible. I am no longer a child. I am a grown-up girl of twenty (the age mamma was when she married you) and practically out of college. My marriage will in no way interfere with my career, as I propose to get my M.A. in Cornell next year, and then to go to New York so that you can live with me and I will get my Ph.D. in Columbia. My dearest Papa, I don't want you to feel that I will be in any way less yours, if I marry. But after all, you married and Momma married and all children marry. After I get my Ph.D. we will all three go to Palestine, if you want to go. If you would like to stay in Ithaca, you could live with me already next year, instead of waiting a year till I come to New York.

However there is this difficulty. You do not know when you will return. It may be in June or in September or later. I will find it exceedingly hard to wait until you return. Dear papa, be reasonable. Don't think of human situations as if they were mathematical equations to which you can apply a rule and judge by that rule. You did not wait to marry Momma. You married her before she was thru [*sic*] with college (I am graduating) and before you had met her parents and she had met your parents. Try to remember that I am a grown-up person with desires of my own and with a sense of what is best for me. You, like some parents, are inclined to a tyranny of love. It is this attitude on the part of parents which has caused the breaking up of families — why Sophy and Helen left home — why Judith and Sulamith left home, why Amy left home, etc.

I love *no one* better than *you*, so I will do nothing that will hurt you, but I beg you to be considerate and accept my judgement on affairs which concern me so vitally. When Helen, at the age of eighteen decided to marry a little boy of eighteen, her mother said to me "her life is hers. If she wants to marry, she can." Most of the girls I know deliberately deceive their parents, because of the ridiculous attitude of proprietorship which most parents assume, or else they simply openly disobey. *All of my friends,* except Eugenia, are either married or *living secretly* with some man. Eugenia, who is not, is a nervous wreck in a really tragic state of mind. This year, she almost entered *a convent to become a nun.* With the greatest difficulty she was persuaded not to do so by her friends. I am telling you all these things, so that you should realize that instead of being unusual I am rather milder than most of the girls you and I know — the girls who are my friends.

I don't want to waste my time and energy the way they do. I am exceedingly anxious to work and study, because I know I have excellent abilities which I intend to put to good use. I am tired of fritting away my time in emotional messes like Amy or Judith or any of them. I intend to amount to something, and I will, if you won't force me to shape my life as you want it. If I am mistaken, I'll abide by the consequences — but it is immoral to force my choice.

Dearest papa, if we wait till you return, you will not know Aaron better than you do now. You will simply create a *great deal of unhappiness,* if you insist that I wait till your indefinite return. And so, dear papa, I beg you let me marry Aaron now. Remember I am grown-up — twenty years old and a college graduate!!! If you agree, *wire* your blessing.

My darling, it is only because I love you so much that I defer to your wishes. I beg you don't use my love for you to unfair advantage. *I will always live with you* [triple underscore] and instead of losing me, you will gain me better and wiser. (Archives f. 4)

This long letter marks a crux in Marie's struggle to distance herself from her father without losing him. The fact that he is so far away no doubt emboldens her to speak her mind. True, she no longer needs her father's legal consent as she supposedly did eighteen months earlier in her marriage to Maurice Samuel, but she still needs Nachman's emotional assent, despite her insistence on the fact that now at the age of twenty she is "no longer a child" but "a grown-up girl of twenty." The ambivalence is clear in the plea "I beg you, *let me* marry Aaron now" [italics mine] followed soon after by the last sentence of the letter "My dearest, if this makes you unhappy, I won't do it."

Is there something else of interest that one can infer from this emotional plea? At the least, it challenges ideas about the lives of intelligent young women in the post-Victorian first decades of the twentieth century. Apparently, all were not living chaste lives in protected homes, postponing sex until the man of their parents' choice showed up to set them free. We learn even more about what women of this era knew and discussed from a letter Marie appears to have dashed off to Eugenia and from Eugenia's reply to it. Marie's letter is undated and is missing a salutation. "I have just been told something tragic," she scrawls.

Gracie [Grombecher?] (whom you probably remember) is some place in Germany, pregnant and penniless. She claims that the husband left in America is the father. If that is true, he will probably not believe her because she did not tell him of her pregnancy when she left. Now she claims that she kept her condition secret because she feared he would urge her to have an abortion (she has already had two). She has written to her mother for money to return. The whole story is pitiful beyond words. A woman has to be cold and clever to get away with the slightest irregularity — at which point imagine as eloquent a descant as you can manufacture in the injustice of the double standard. Women are so soft and vulnerable and they become strong only at the expense of their womanhood. What a hell! (Archives f. 6)

Marie's letter reveals a strong proto-feminist attitude, but Eugenia's high-minded reply argues a very different, though also feminist, position: "As to Gracie, it is no 'slight irregularity' that is involved, I think. And if Gracie has lived with others since leaving U.S.A. it doesn't really matter who the father is. A man cannot be responsible for a woman's passionate moments."[7] The exchange between these two young women, even more than among Marie's list of friends who had left home, attests to the shift in sexual mores that had begun (at least among educated women) just after World War I on the threshold of the famously freewheeling Jazz Age.

Nonetheless, discovery of women's sexual desire but fear of pregnancy and abortion undoubtedly was a compelling reason for women's early marriage. In Marie's case, one can only surmise that it is the hidden agenda in her letter to her father, dated April 7, regarding her marriage plans: "Dearest Papa: I suppose by this time you have received my *passionate* [italics mine] plea for a swift consent and I suppose you have sent the right answer. Really, darling, I shall be so happy if you agree — and I shall study so hard because I will have *nothing to distract me*" [italics mine]. Marie's periphrasis and choice of words reveal not a little about her emotional condition. The letter quickly moves on to a subject Marie knew would be certain to claim her father's sympathetic attention — her academic curriculum. "This term I am continuing Hebrew, Italian, Greek, English and I am beginning physiology and philosophy." From the perspective of twenty-first century undergraduate curricula, her program is indeed impressive and leaves one in near wonderment that there is room for a social life at all. Nonetheless, having outlined her current syllabus, she then informs her father of her future academic plans.

I'll take some more science during the summer. I have been thinking about my work for the M.A. thesis and it seems to me that *Yiddish Poetry* would be an excellent subject. I could take Heb [word crossed out] Yiddish Literature as a whole, for my Ph.D. thesis. However I am afraid I will not have enough books and instruction for such a subject and anyhow I wish to continue my Greek and Italian. Next year I'll take Dante. What do you think about those subjects. As I have to plan my work soon, I wish you would write me about it. Aaron [Bodansky] thinks they are excellent topics. (Archives f. 4)

It is difficult to assess the sincerity of this quasi–love letter to her father. Is Marie really as devoted to her college work as she insists? Her choice of Yiddish literature for her graduate work might have been merely a strategem to please her father. There is the crossed out "Heb" before the word "Yiddish;" had she changed the word because she knew her father would know that she did not have enough Hebrew to write such a dissertation? Still, Marie very soon did begin to publish English translations of Yiddish poetry; indeed, she was among the very first to do so, and it would be quite some time before anyone would write a Ph.D. dissertation on Yiddish literature. Ultimately, however, she would write her Master's thesis on the English poems of Francis Thompson, — whose poetry she first heard when Maurice Samuel recited "The Hound of Heaven" to her when she was sixteen. At the age of eighty-nine, she could still quote long sections of "The Hound of Heaven" from memory.

The last few lines of this letter take a sharp turn toward the amusingly pragmatic: "I received your $100. I told you I needed $200. You left me with so many debts, that I have not paid them yet. Besides I have a dentist bill which I have to pay." Nachman's daughter immediately softens her request for money with information no doubt designed to butter up her father: "I entered the poetry competition but I am afraid I won't get it. As soon as I hear the results, I'll begin sending my poems to magazines. Wish me luck!" (Archives f. 4). Marie Syrkin's struggle for self-realization has begun in earnest. Whatever her motivation for the description of her studies, an intuited sense of vocation provided the fuel for her drive to pursue a career. But the necessary analysis of her relationship to men has not yet taken place. She has made a lover of her father and a father of her lovers, mixing the categories such that dependency was inevitable and personal freedom near to impossible.

Two Marriages: Father and Daughter

Marie had not yet received Nachman's letters of March 26 and 31 when she wrote her letter of April 7. Both of her father's letters had complained that Marie had not written; and after the obligatory questions about health and finances, Nachman inquired on March 26, "Why do you not write me anything about your *affaires du coeur,* if you will excuse me that step forwards into the realm of your intimacy. Any way I repeat you again and again, Keep your promise to me and do not decide anything even morally for yourself, till I will come back, so you will have then the possibility to tell or ask me something. I hope you will take into consideration my words." The March 31 letter is more of the same, but Nachman begins to tighten the screws:

If you are healthy and do not write, you do me the greatest injustice, not to speak about the fact that you suppress by this way and attitude all your feelings of love and duty to your father who is crazy over you. If you love me still to some degree, write immediately a good letter. Your health, work, self consciousness, *les affaires du coeur?* Be prudent my child, take life just as life imposes itself on the men of spirit: cheerful, serious and tragical. Our responsibilities are so endless and so deep, but to realize our responsibilities is also some moral gain. But, *helas,* it is so easy to *lecture* to other people. . . . Remember the pledge you gave me concerning your affairs of heart. Wait till I will come and be prudent, reserved and my child. (Archives 1)

Syrkin ends this letter stating that he will probably go to Palestine from Paris and will return to New York in September. He will, however, continue to send her money as well as a birthday present.

It is true that Marie had withheld her *"affaires du coeur"* from her father, but he in turn did not disclose his own *"affaires du coeur."* Before Marie's father had left for Paris, he had written to her that "the trip is considered meanwhile on the basis of 2–3 months." The two or three months would turn out to be more than a year—for not only will the Conference last much longer than he expected, and not only will Nachman Syrkin make his first trip to Palestine, but as he shyly hinted to his daughter, "I think I will have to go somewhere else after those 2–3 months." The "somewhere else," Marie later will learn, is to persuade Masha Osnos—the younger sister of his late wife Basha, the sister who had helped the family when Basha was away, and whom Nachman had not seen since he had left for America in 1907—to marry him. Though Nachman had lost touch with her after Basha's death, he knew that if she had survived the war she would be in Russia, Poland, or France. When Nachman left for the Versailles Conference in 1919, he had decided to find her, and if she were not married, to ask her to be his wife. At the conclusion of the Paris Peace Conference, Syrkin went on to the first World Conference of the Poale Zion to be held after the war in Stockholm, in August of 1919. There it was decided to send an international Poale Zion Commission to Palestine to analyze the conditions there and to plan for mass immigration. Syrkin was chosen to represent the United States. This was followed by travels in Europe, then on to Palestine where, on April 4, 1920, he witnessed pogrom-like Arab attacks on Jews in the Old City, and then to Alexandria. But while in Europe, Nachman had learned that Masha Osnos was single and that she had left Russia after the revolution and was living in Poland with her brother. He began writing to her at once, and his letters continued from each new place he would visit, from Rome to Palestine. Though Masha was eighteen years his junior, he had fixated on her as the object of his capacity for love and as a solution to his bleak and lonely life. Later, Marie would explain this May-December romance:

His imagination fixed itself increasingly on the sister of the lost wife of his youth. He remembered Masha as a gentle, reticent girl, intelligent, disciplined. True she was nearly eighteen years his junior, a woman in her early thirties, but that, from a man's point of view, was hardly an objection. He assured me sub-

sequently that he would have married my mother's sister whatever her age —
even if she had been the older sister. Whether or not this was true, age was irrelevant to this particular choice. There were plenty of young and youngish
women in the United States who would have been pleased to accept his name.
But as he told me naively on his return, he could not let himself marry 'a strange
woman.' Masha was a projection and renewal of the old love, a continuation
and development of his whole life. He could love her passionately in her own
right with no sense of break or loss. (*Memoir* 195–196)

When Nachman Syrkin arrived in Warsaw to claim his bride, he was
in no way disappointed. After thirteen years she was just as he remembered her and "all that he had dreamed — sweet, modest, good. . . .
Faced by her ardent wooer she made a few mild demurrers, but all suggestions of delay or deliberation shriveled in the blaze of Syrkin's
courtship" (*Memoir* 195). The two would marry within the year, on May
25, 1920, whereupon they would leave for the United States.

Marie had written to her father that when he returned she, he, and
Aaron will live happily ever after, either in Ithaca or Palestine. But at
that time she was unaware that her father had tracked down her
mother's sister Masha and had found her living with her brother in
Poland, having left Russia after the Revolution; nor did Marie know
that Nachman had been writing to and courting Masha from all over
Europe and the Middle East with the *idée fixe* of marrying her.

Many years later, when writing about her father's pursuit of Masha
Osnos, Marie tenderly interpreted what she found in the letters that
Nachman had written in Russian to Bassya's sister:

They are what I suppose every woman dreams of and rarely gets when she
thinks of a love letter — ardent, tender, devout. All the poetry and phantasy of
his nature, fresh and uncorrupted, are concentrated in his desire and he pleads
his case vehemently, without cautious probings. Missing are the polite preliminaries suitable to the occasion. Nor is he suggesting a reasonable arrangement
such as a man past his youth might discreetly offer to a woman he has not seen
for thirteen years and with whom he has had no previous emotional relationship. Though he voices the fear that she may find his suit precipitate or unwel-
come, that does not hold him back. As in his entire intellectual and spiritual life,
he has fallen in love with an idea and found its form." (*Memoir* 192–193)

In retrospect, Marie finds her father's epistolary emotions and his
actions poignant and praiseworthy. Could she have been comparing

them to the mercurial love letters she had received from Maurice
Samuel?

Nonetheless, just as Nachman was ardently pleading his case to
Masha Osnos, his daughter was fervidly pleading her own case to her father. Either Nachman Syrkin had not yet received Marie's letter of intention or he was deliberately ignoring it. In either case, his letters were
certain to cause resistance and his daughter's "passionate plea" of April
7, was the result. She would not wait until her father's September return,
and it is not likely that she ever made a serious "pledge" to that effect, or
if she did, she was not going to honor it. On April 25, 1919, Marie
Syrkin, just twenty years of age, married Aaron Bodansky, age thirty.
She did not wait for her father's blessing.

Marie married Aaron less than three months after she had broken
with Maurice Samuel. On the surface, her action seems capricious, almost frivolous. Yet it was not a simple case of on-the-rebound. Aaron
seems to have been in the picture even before the break with Maurice.
What was it about Aaron that attracted Marie? A circa 1920 photograph
presents a youngish man of about thirty, nice looking, but not handsome; a long angular face topped by full, black wavy hair, two arcs of
thick black eyebrows perch just above steel-rimmed bespectacled dark
eyes, a thin aquiline nose flares slightly at the nostrils above gently smiling lips, but contradicted by a prominent jutting chin. He is dressed in
a three-piece wool suit, striped tie, and white shirt with an unstarched
collar. Very professorial. Marie's new love was ten years older than she.
Was this a case of "father substitute," or did she think that because Bodansky was an instructor at Cornell, he would please her father more than
her first choice had? Though he was pursuing an academic career in biochemistry, Aaron's credentials, at this point, however, were hardly likely
to impress Papa. Bodansky had immigrated to America from Elizabeth-
grad in the Ukraine when he was seventeen; and in the years between
1904 and 1911, while going to school, he had worked part-time as a printer
for the Yiddish and the English press to support his family. At the end of
1918, at the age of twenty-nine, he served a brief stint in the Chemical
Corps of the American Army; after this, he went on to pursue graduate
work at Cornell where, as a poorly paid instructor, he taught. Bodansky
did not receive his Ph.D. until after he and Marie had married.

Perhaps Marie's attraction to Aaron Bodansky was cerebral. Besides,
what undergraduate is not flattered by the attentions of a "professor"?
Though not at all religious, Aaron had Zionist interests, leftist politics,

and wide-ranging readings in history and literature. Some eighty-five years in the future, Aaron's son, David Bodansky, would comment that he had not known how extraordinarily comprehensive was his father's library until he began to dispose of it, one that included a collection of small and miniature Bibles in many languages and an impressive collection of books on literature and history—though he always knew that his father had a wide interest in politics. And although Aaron never completely rid himself of a trace of an accent in English, he was a bit pedantic about his knowledge of and insistence on correct grammar, not only in English but in German, French, Yiddish, and a few other languages as well. Perhaps the force of Marie's attraction to Aaron Bodansky was intellectual—his unusual polymathic intelligence. As for Aaron—whatever Marie's intellectual talents, her physical beauty was not a small thing. Indeed, in answer to the question of why Marie entered so precipitately into her marriage to Aaron Bodansky, their son David remarked softly, "He was persistent" (Personal interview, August 2007).

Nor did Marie give her father advance notice; and when she finally did write to him about the event, it was two weeks *ex post facto,* for on May 24, Nachman was still completely in the dark. After complaining that all his letters and cables had gone unanswered, he asks "What is now your intention to be? Did you marry, as you insisted on it. Did you decide to wait until I return? You have my blessing to your marriage, although I would like that you should wait until my return. . . . I think that I did wrong leaving you alone without any help and advice, as I should not take serious your oral promise. But I hope you made a good choice, as everybody can only himself forge the fate of his life." But Nachman cannot let it go; after launching into a disquisition on the state of her teeth, the need for a root canal, the importance of a New York City specialist, and the relationship of these items to his sleepless nights, Nachman tells her that he will cover the costs. Then, "I ask Aaron, that he shall take good care of that matter and shall go himself to a doctor with you. Write me all the details" (Archives f. 1).

Aaron himself, however, already had written to Nachman Syrkin to ask for his approval of the marriage. And on May 26, Nachman sent a brutal reply: "I read your letter with deep emotions and disinquietude [*sic*], as you can imagine. Maryetchka is young, she is almost a baby, especially in experience and practical things of life. On the other hand she is exceptionally gifted and could make an unusual career, if the external circumstances will be favorable. I hope her choice was good and I give my consent and paternal blessing." Syrkin goes on to state that he concludes that Aaron has "abilities, energy, and the sense of duty." But he hopes that Aaron realizes "the tremendous responsibility before Manya, before her beauty and her talents." Without hesitation, Nachman expresses his major worry: "It is the rather poor status of your finances. Even if you will get an increase of your salary, I do not see how you will be able to support Manya even modestly. If Manya will start to wash and scrub in poverty, it will be terrible for all of us" (Archives f. 1). Nachman Syrkin seems to have forgotten that when he married Bassya Osnos, the facts were comparable. Nachman was ten years Bassya's senior. He had not completed either his medical studies or his Ph.D. in philosophy. He was deeply engaged with a precarious political movement that had a tiny constituency — and he certainly didn't have very much money. Yet Syrkin did not hesitate to marry a woman he had met only months before. If the father was given to precipitous enthusiastic action, the daughter appeared to have inherited the tendency.

When Nachman received Marie's letter informing him that her marriage to Aaron was a *fait accompli,* he responded with a mixture of happiness for her new status, notice of a great change that has come over her, concern for her welfare, belief in her talents, advice about reading, and questions about Aaron's ability to support her. "I am so proud of the nobel [*sic*] desires, which are filling your exceptional soul. Maryetchka, if nobody believes in you, I believe in your talents and your future. Some deep feeling, an intuition, prophesies me that you will develop great abilities of writing and thinking and you will display a nobel and sublime attitude of life." These are loving and proud words coming from father to daughter. How could she fail to be buoyed up by such faith in her abilities? But Nachman can never resist pedagogic instruction. "Read only good inspiring books," he advises, "every book in its original text, read and reread every book and try to conceive not only what the great writer has outspoken, but what he has concealed, what filled his heart, what was even stronger and deeper than his style and gift of expression. We shall not only read the great books, but we shall assimilate ourselves with the great creators of truth and beauty, and therefore we must reread their books as many times as possible." Wise words indeed; but surely not the words a twenty-year-old bride wants to read in a letter of congratulations from her father. He does go on to praise her for writing her own poetry and asks her to send him some of her "new things." But again, he cannot leave well enough alone. On the subject of his daughter's new husband, Nachman asks that Aaron write him a few lines in every letter that Marie writes — adding, "Of course, I must confess that I did not do it in respect to my father in law." Then, Papa Syrkin ends his letter with some questions that were sure to alienate his new son-in-law. "How do you make meet the both ends? I like to be enlightened about it in detail. If Aaron has only 20 dollars a week and you need at least 50 a week, how are your finances 'all right'? That worries me to the highest extent." The letter ends with an infuriating undermining of Aaron's ability to provide for his wife and a suggestion that their meager means would deprive his beloved daughter of her basic needs. Though he is in Europe and will be traveling for some time, he will see to her needs and has sent her an extra 100 dollars. "You shall not deprive yourself of anything, especially you shall have enough milk, eggs butter, vegetables, fruit. Have you enough dresses and hats for the summer? If you did not require them, buy them now. I will pay the bill. How is now with your teeth? Do you have still pains? How is your health in general? . . . I kiss you and send my paternal greetings to Aaron. Papa" (Archives f. 1). Paternal indeed!

One month later, on July 11, Marie wrote a letter to her father excusing herself for not writing to him for some time. "I had read that you left for Palestine, for which reason I did not write." She tells him that she and Aaron had gone to New York and placed flowers on her mother's grave. Is this simply an act of ritual reverence, or does it also mark a first and unconscious step toward distancing a controlling father and seeking a female model for Act Two of her life? By the end of her letter, Marie tells her father that she is very happy, that she is working hard, and that at the end of the summer semester she will get her degree. Her grades have been excellent, she "stands well" with the English department in which she will do her graduate work. Her plans are to get her Ph.D. in three years. "I can apply for university teaching, so that I may become a professor yet — the only disadvantage is my sex. Women cannot get positions in any except women's colleges — for the most part." These words were sure to please Nachman, the better to request of him $200 for tuition and another hundred for books and clothes "and we will get along quite comfortably." Assuring him that if it is a hardship she would not accept it, she does hope that he can at least pay tuition which, she notes, "as you see is quite an expense." Sending her father her tenderest love, she gives the letter to Aaron to read and mail. Having read it, Aaron is moved to add a postscript.

As if in response to Nachman's letters to him and to Marie, as well as to Marie's current reply, Aaron appends the letter with these controlled remarks: "I hesitate to intrude, but I must assure you that Manya's education, comfort and happiness will not be sacrificed, if you are unable to extend to her any aid. And may I add that I should feel happier if I were allowed to provide for our needs through my own efforts? Please do not accept this as an attempt at interference. I shall make all necessary sacrifices for Manya's happiness, but I hesitate to agree to further sacrifices on your part without making my attitude understood" (Archives f. 1). Aaron's polite postscript is a double invitation to his father-in-law: first, to accept Marie's transfer from father to husband; and second, for Nachman not to interfere in their lives. The conflict between Nachman and the man who loves his daughter is about to repeat an earlier version. Could any man have had Nachman's approval? Or did he understand his daughter better than she thought he did? The conflict between father and son-in-law has begun, but the actual combat will have to wait until they are *vis-a-vis.*

Beginning of the End

Marie had expressed the joys of married life to her father who was far away, but her words to her friend Eugenia on June 17, two months after her marriage, were a bit more honest. After listing her current course work, Anglo-Saxon, Greek philosophy, and geology, as well as satirically describing the professors of these studies, Marie turns serious. "At the present moment I am rather wretched," she confesses. "Marriage has this in common with most situations, that is, not a bed of roses. Marriage entails all the petty annoyances that any close association of two persons brings with it, and in addition demands the adjustment of an individual, in all his serious and intimate phases, to another individual. Marriage as a partnership of convenience is ugly. As a protracted love affair, it is nerve-wracking and stifling. The plane of adjustment of all these forces, small and great, is a damned elusive business. I question seriously whether marriage is feasible for the woman who does not wish to make home and children the basis of her life" (Shafran, Archives f. 6).

So harsh an assessment after only two months of marriage did not promise a long life of wedded bliss. What could have caused such an evaluation? It could not have been Nachman's assessment of Aaron's character because he had not yet met him. It also was not likely to have been disagreement about Marie's growing commitment to Jewish life and Zionism. In a letter to her father just a few months earlier, Marie had referred to her father's dedication to Zionism rather flippantly as "the good cause," but by this time she was beginning to write her own articles about that cause, and both Marie and Aaron had agreed to make *aliyah* to Palestine in the near future. Many decades later, speaking of her own early Zionist attitudes, she reported that she and Aaron had bought collapsible wooden folding chairs for their first home so that they could easily ship them to Palestine when they emigrated (Personal interview). Moreover, in a letter written from Alexandria on April 28, Syrkin wrote that he had gotten word from a friend that Marie had delivered a lecture on Zionism at Cornell, "at which," he was proud to write, "you, Maryetchka, presided and Aaron participated on the discussion."[8] Further, it was not likely that Marie's marital disappointments were because Aaron objected to her desire to write and publish her own poetry and translations, for he openly supported her in those efforts. The question remains, then, what was really going wrong with this marriage? The answer would clearly be given in a letter to the one person Marie knew who would totally understand and would be sympathetic — Eugenia. It is an undated letter, but it is probably sometime in July of 1920, soon after Marie's father, with his new bride, returned to the United States.

Nachman and Masha had been married on May 25, 1920, in Warsaw, surprisingly in an Orthodox Jewish wedding, and as his daughter drily commented later, "quite unlike the simple student ceremony in Switzerland two decades earlier"(*Memoir* 195). Marie and Aaron met them in New York where they arrived. In the biographical memoir of her father written forty years later, Marie insists absolutely that "[m]y delight at seeing my father and the young aunt whom I remembered with the utmost affection from my childhood was genuine and complete. For me as for my father there was no strangeness, rather a sense of something once more given. . . . My father's friends, too, were glad that his solitary life was at an end, though a few ladies of mature years made some tart comments to me about my father's belated fancy for youth. I felt a bit sorry for my aunt: papa was fifty-two, an advanced age, hardly suitable for romance." The bridegroom was, of course, not unaware of the eighteen-year difference, and in his accommodation to this fact, he returned to America *sans* beard — a feature his daughter had never seen him without. And of course, when Nachman first saw Marie upon his return, there *was* some strangeness, for by this time Marie had been married for more than a year.

Marie's recollections of this period have been tempered by time. Some of what she wrote in her 1960 memoir of her father is less harsh than letters she wrote contemporaneously with the events. Her attitude toward her father and her aunt soon after they had arrived in America, for example, has a sharper tone when she describes it to her friend Eugenia: "I was in N.Y. to help my father and aunt get settled," she told her. "Papa is the typical elderly doting husband with young wife, and is letting himself into expenditures which terrify me" (Shafran, Archives f. 6, July 1920). Marie's revision in the memoir of an explosion she had with her father immediately after his return from Europe is also challenged by contemporaneous epistolary accounts. When Nachman left for Paris, he had stored his library and possessions in the basement of the apartment house in which he had roomed. While he was in Europe, the woman in charge of the flat decided to move and asked Marie to remove the trunk stored in the basement. Marie later claimed that it contained his library, which was too large to store in its entirety. In an attempt to be "practical," she decided to sell many of his books to a secondhand dealer — but she admitted that because she based her choice on her own taste for "belles lettres" and her father's library was topheavy with works on philosophy, history and economics in German, Russian, and Hebrew, she made some bad choices (*Memoir* 196). But on July 21, just after he had returned, Syrkin wrote a scathing sardonic letter to his daughter in Ithaca:

Many thanks, my little practical girl, for your various advices, but I want to let you know that the trunk cannot be found in Cowan's cellar. It is a great calamity for me, as all my life work is lost. You never underwent the painful work to investigate about the trunk and to write me about it, although I asked you for it many and many times. How I was mad at you, you will find out from the letter which I wrote you from the house of Cowan's in New York. I did not send you that letter but I want that you shall read it, and you find it thereby enclosed. Do not consider that letter as sent to you, it was written in a moment of great pain and sorrow. At present I love you just as the trunk would be found and nothing would happen. Why should I trust you such matters and it is only my own fault. How is your work, my darling? How is Aaron? (Archives f. 1)

That Marie did not save the enclosed letter is hardly surprising. What is surprising is that she did save the letter in which it was enclosed. Marie's

negligence in the whole matter is beyond explanation, and it is not difficult to empathize with her frantic father in this situation. In fact, that he
did not send the letter immediately, and that he forgave her so quickly,
is testimony to his overwhelming love for his daughter, as well as to his
capacity for emotional acrobatics.

In this same letter Nachman wrote to Marie and Aaron that "we hope
to see you in your little home in Ithaca" within a week. Marie's father
and his new bride did, in fact, make the visit, but it was a most unpleasant experience. Once again, the details of the event and the tremblings
of Marie's heart were poured out to Eugenia. It is in this letter that the
fundamental reason for Marie's marital distress is made clear. She explains that she has not written lately because of "the amount of real
trouble which [she has] suffered recently.

As you know, my folks visited me for several weeks. As you do not know, that
visit was complicated by very unpleasant developments. Papa disapproves completely of Aaron. Papa's intense and desperate imagination has made Aaron's 32
yrs., lack of beauty, and quiet behavior, a monster of age, ugliness, and stupidity. That Aaron is far from dazzling, I appreciate perfectly, but of course papa's
characterization is absurd, particularly on the score of brains. In short papa is
urging me to leave Aaron. As stated, the solution seems to be an indignant reply
to my father and continued dove-cote happiness with Aaron. Unfortunately the
situation is complicated by the following factors:

1. Foremost, my lack of passionate love for Aaron — a very serious consideration in marriage, though generally discounted as romantic nonsense by the in-
experienced or the insensitive.

2. Aaron's difficult and exacting temperament.

3. My desire for greater personal freedom which I believe essential for development.

My father's arguments have had a twofold effect upon me. On the one hand,
the actual reasons that he advances, which amount simply to saying that Aaron
is not a good match for me, his "bright & beautiful daughter," seem to me to be
infinitely mean considerations and arouse all my loyalty to Aaron. On the other
hand, papa's apparent acceptance of the possibility of a rupture (something from
which my after-all conventional soul recoiled per se) has given me the moral
courage to weigh the factors that I enumerated.

Then there are ethical implications which confuse me. I do not know which
is the greater moral loss — sexual life with a man for whom one feels no sexual
attraction, or the cheapening of faithfulness and intimacy in which a break with

Aaron would result. I mean whether such an act would not indicate a complete lack of spiritual earnestness in me; whether the modern woman's sensitiveness as to the priority and ardour of her sexual experiences and concern for the dignity of her individuality compensate for the perhaps higher virtue of constancy and simple affection. . . . As I review my entire blundering (and to many, shocking) past, I wonder seriously whether my actions and perhaps even more important, my doubts and almost actions, were due to a particularly impulsive, intrepid soul, or a tendency to trifle with holy things. What do you think of it all?" (Shafran, Archives f. 6)

Undoubtedly Eugenia was sympathetic, having written her own evaluation of the relationship between personal ambition and marriage. Years before, she had told Marie that she did not think she was cut out for family life. Eugenia's own situation was still very unsettled: she had moved out of the home she been living in with the man who had taken her in when she thought she was pregnant, but whom she did not love; she was unhappy in her work, she had severe bouts of depression, and she often felt that she needed to go away somewhere. Marie knew all of this about Eugenia's emotional and financial problems, but continued to care about her well-being. Despite her own marital issues, or perhaps, because of them, Marie invited her friend to come to Ithaca for the summer and to stay in the spare room in her house. She thought that this might encourage Eugenia to study at Cornell and work toward something practical.

Eugenia did come, but apparently it did not work out very well. She returned to New York, but her health declined considerably and once again, Marie invited her to return to Ithaca to recuperate; this time, however, to find lodging in a boarding house. Once again, the two friends quarreled very badly. Eugenia, it appears, wrote a long letter immediately after the event — though she probably never sent it. Nonetheless, it provides a picture window onto the early deterioration of the Syrkin-Bodansky marriage.

My position at your house last year was so unbearable, I do not know how I ever stood it. And Aaron's general attitude toward you and toward me makes friendliness, and pleasurable relations impossible. Constant complication, constant complication. There is the memory of so many discourtesies, so much that really should not be pardoned, in my mind, and then you and Aaron tell me that I am touchy. The most primitive courtesies have been denied me, and yet I am repeatedly invited to your house. I am invited at times when I am not needed, when I should not be there at all. . . . I eat with you and hear the matter of who is to wash my plate discussed. . . and every move I make is the subject of mean and harrowing discussion. I take a drink and somehow mysteriously all that has been going on between you and Aaron. Or else Aaron offers me something not because he wants me to have it, but so as to tease you.

The letter continues on in this vein for two more pages as Eugenia complains of their mutual failure to tolerate intimacies, misunderstandings, her own touchiness, and the unnamed cause for which she has given Marie displeasure and which caused Marie's bitter and cruel words. What indeed could have been the unnamed cause that so displeased Marie? One can only speculate, but it is very tempting to conclude that the subject was Maurice Samuel. Eugenia had been in friendly correspondence with Maurice while he was in the army and had visited him at Camp Upton. She had last heard from him in late 1918 — just before the break with Marie. But three years later, on October 18, 1921, back in the United States after several years in Europe, and after marriage and fatherhood, Samuel got back in touch with Eugenia. It seems altogether possible that Eugenia had told Marie that she was presently in contact with Maurice, that Marie thought this inappropriate, to say the least, and perhaps even a betrayal because Marie only too well knew the sexual proclivities of her annulled husband and those of her friend — or it might even have been jealousy and regret.[9]

During these years, Marie continued to study, to translate, and to write her own poetry. More than fifty years later, she published a volume of poetry, *Gleanings: A Diary in Verse,* poems written during a period of over fifty years, from the age of eighteen to the 1970s. The subtitle, she explains in the foreword, "indicates that the poems were written at various periods in response to a personal crisis and put aside."[10] She selected them from a very large body of works and grouped them into categories beginning with the latest poems and ending with "Written in Youth." Placed in the middle of the last category is a poem, "Old Letters," that appears to have been written precisely at the time of her quarrel with Eugenia:

> All ignorant your letters lie
> In my attic near the birds.
> Bold and sure, unknowingly
> They warble their wild lovely words.

O it's not easy to forget
That always, out of sight, above,
Your breathless letters babble yet
The blind and dreadful speech of love.
(*Gleanings* 103)

Could these letters be anything other than the voluminous collection of
letters that Maurice Samuel had written to Marie over the years 1915 to
1919, which she kept until her death in 1989? The poem must have been
written during the stormy episode with Eugenia and Aaron (unless the
"attic" is purely metaphoric), because this was the only time that Marie
actually had an attic. It also follows a poem called "Maternity." In that
year, 1921, Marie Syrkin became pregnant with her first child.

Zivia

In the year since Nachman had returned to America with his wife,
Machette, he continued to write to Marie at Cornell with the same infantilizing badgering admonitions about her failure to write, her health,
money, and work. Syrkin remained unhappy about her marriage, and
what he regarded as a frittering away of her talents. He and Machette
(she is now called "Machette" instead of "Masha"), he writes, miss her,
"but it makes in us a special pleasure to talk about you, to admire your
extraordinary abilities and talents, your modesty. Only when it comes to
your craziness I feel myself beaten. . . . I plan many many great things
for you, and the first is a travel to Europe to study there. Of course, you
will do better if you will make previously your Ph.D. in America. How
is it with your M.A.?" (Archives f. 1). Meantime, Nachman's own wife
has become pregnant and Syrkin, worried that Marie will feel supplanted,
writes to reassure her of his everlasting love for his "first daughter" and
praises Machette for the very things he warns Marie against — that is, his
pleasure when his wife "became active and busy in her feminine and maternal duties so that it is just as amusing as rejoicing to observe her sweet
good mastership in the house" (Archives f. 1). He seems to have forgotten that she has given up her career as a medical doctor. When Nachman's second child was born, Marie sent flowers and her father responded, "Do not worry, my first one! Everything is fine, Machette feels
splendid." The child

will be called Zivia in memory of my mother. Who was, as you know, a very re-marcable [*sic*] intellect and character. You read once the testament she left to her children before she died, it is a very fine literary letter, where mother tried to be above all the pettiness of life and grasp the eternal immortal idea. Zivia is Bib-lical and in English it will be pronounced rather exotic. Anyway she, it means, Zivia, is now an exemplary child, she is an individual by herself and she has in her appearance, in crying, in the voice and in all her attitude quite different char-acter from you at her age. I am looking at her and drawing parallels between Malala [his pet name for Marie] and Zivia. (Archives f. 1)

Nachman, the worrier, may have been apprehensive about Marie's re-sponse to the birth of her sister, but he need not have been. The child turned out to be a gift to Marie. Zivia and Marie developed an intense lifelong relationship that partook of the triple bond of sister, mother-daughter, and friend. In later years, Marie wrote of the birth of Zivia:

Within a few months Masha was pregnant. She had expressed some natural misgivings in regard to maternity. The difference in age, my father's uncertain financial status of which she now had a more realistic understanding than in Warsaw, the interruption of her medical career for an indefinite period — all these seemed weighty objections. To have a child under these circumstances seemed a piece of juvenile recklessness but Syrkin as usual declined to consider practical consideration. These he dismissed as irrelevant. What mattered were essentials, and what was more essential than a woman's deep longing for a child? "You will want a child" he told his wife, and, Zivia, his second daughter was born in April 1921. Of course this time he wanted a son; a girl, as he knew, might not fulfill her promise or his hopes. But the wonderfully pretty, bright baby soon stilled that pang. (*Memoir* 203–204)

There is nothing in this paragraph to contradict the depth of feeling for Zivia and her family that Marie would possess and unabashedly display all her life. Furthermore, Zivia would not have disappointed her father with regard to "her promise or his hopes;" she followed in her mother's scientific footsteps and chose the path of mathematics to lead her to a long successful career. Her father had named her for his mother who had written "a very fine and literary letter," but that would be the path for his first daughter, Marie. And this Nachman understood; not only did he encourage, but he badgered his daughter to venture forth on this road not yet taken.

Meanwhile, Marie herself was pregnant and unhappy. Her father perceived this only too well, and in July he wrote from Belmar, New Jersey, where his family was spending the summer, "Darling, how is your situation? How is your health? . . . Do not worry, my Maryetchka, you will soon overcome with God's help your troubles. . . ." But Nachman, being Nachman, could not resist his importuning and pedagogical instruction. "Darling," he implores her, "abstain a little bit from eating. That will do you good. How is it with your Greek? Your Greek studying would give some Aristotelian structure to the breeding of your infant who is already very dear to me" (Archives f. 1). Is he jesting, or is he serious — or perhaps a little bit of both.

As Marie's domestic life continued to deteriorate, her father's life flourished (though not financially, for he had made a few bad business and employment decisions). Years later, Marie remarked that the family used to say, "Papa doesn't understand real life." This meant that he could be cheated mercilessly by any petty tradesman, but hand-in-hand with the trivial absurdities went a profound wisdom. "However, no matter how absurd he could be in trivia, he was often sublimely right in essentials. He was wonderfully happy in his marriage, and the silver candlesticks that Masha blessed each Sabbath in answer to his wish, were an expression of a long thwarted need for the sanctities of home and tradition" (*Memoir* 203).

Describing a home and life that she herself would never really quite achieve, Marie recalls that her "father's modest apartment in the Bronx — not too far from the original American domicile on Charlotte Street — now had the order and graciousness so long absent from his life." Is there some tone of regret in this statement (made in 1960,) that despite her personal struggle to free herself from the men who held control of her earlier years, she too might have yearned for an ordered family life? "There was nothing Bohemian about Masha despite student days in Paris," Marie explained. "Her household was kept as meticulously as her lecture notes. My father marveled at the display of unfamiliar domestic arts — my mother's housekeeping had been inventive rather than punctilious — and noted the unsuspected capacity of pots to shine and glass to gleam with the enthusiasm he always accorded fresh revelations in any sphere of human experience. 'You see,' he would say with the air of a Galileo, 'they shine'" (*Memoir* 203).

During the nine months of her pregnancy, from January through September 1921, Marie continued to pursue her studies and to write her poetry. Her father wrote to her regularly urging her to continue to work toward one aim, "to make good use of your talents which nature gave you. All other things must be subordinated to that worthy aim." Nachman, moreover, is acutely aware of the discord in Marie's marriage, and he cannot resist cryptic comments about her current situation and future possibilities. In May, he tells her that he and Machette speak so often about her, "always admiring your abilities, your talents, your power of concentration, your generosity. Even," he continues with some biting sarcasm, "the unpardonable stupidities which you committed against yourself and your future seem to us now as temporary mistakes which you will have courage and will to make good. I am sure you will regain your self and arise to real height. What is about your M.A. If it is hard to write the thesis at present, you will, of course, better postpone it." Worrying about what she plans to do for the summer while Aaron, it appears, will have to be away, Nachman suggests that, given her present condition and the fact that she will be in her third trimester by the summer, she should come back to New York. "I am so worried about it," he lets her know, "Anyway, write about your plans for the summer and we will still see what is to be done" (Archives f. 1).

Benya

On September 6, 1921, Marie and Aaron's son was born. They named him Benya. Once again, the truth of Marie's marital, maternal, and intellectual life is exposed in a letter to her erratic but constant friend, Eugenia. In this sardonic report, one can hear her despair and irritation born of her helpless incapacity for the requirements of traditional maternal and wifely activities and emotions. If Eugenia had previously admitted that she had no desire for motherhood, this letter, written when Benya was six months old, would do nothing to encourage her to change her mind.

Everything here is *comme toujours,* only more so. I embroider little rompers and devote myself to household duties with zest, particularly the rompers. They are very cunning and decorated with ingenious designs. If you should wish to wear rompers I shall embroider a pair for you in all approved colours.

Benya is an amiable child with a love for theory divorced from practice which distresses me. I refer in particular to his academic announcement of certain interesting functions post facto, and no amount of reproachful exhortation can induce him to put his knowledge to practical use. When he perceives the receptacle devoted to exclusive uses, he charmingly makes euphonious sounds indicative of the purpose for which said receptacle (in vulgar parlance — potty) was designed, but he will not approach it for any save contemplative motives. So you see, I am busy with this and that. My misery flourishes as lively as ever and shows no signs of needing cod liver oil." (Shafran, Archives f. 6)

Marie turns to questions about Eugenia's life and exhorts her to "write me a decent letter." She gives her friend a rundown of her recent reading, including a very dull play by Bjornson. "I was forced to read it," Marie explains, "because there was no *Saturday Evening Post* around. As a matter of fact, I much prefer the *Ladies Home Journal* which contains much exciting information on rompers and can therefore be incorporated into the days work, but that journal is not around." The letter ends with the bald statement, "On the morrow I am 24" (Shafron, Archives f. 6).

To Marie at this moment, it must have felt as if the life of her mind had come to a dead stop. But that wasn't quite the case, for she had already inaugurated her journalistic and poetic career, and her public commitment to Jewish life and Zionism were beginning to emerge. While at Cornell, she had been a member (though not an active one) of the pan-collegiate International Zionist Association. Her merely tangential association with the I.Z.A. is explained in an article she was to publish in the *New Palestine,* in which she praises the new Jewish student movement *Avuka.* In a prose style that both improves on the clever sardonicism of her letter to Eugenia and foreshadows the sharp ironic wit alongside a roseate idealism that would later characterize her writing, she describes the I.Z.A. as

a kind of painless dentistry which temporarily filled spiritual cavities of a special nature. . . . A Jewish student of a certain type went to the I.Z.A. meeting to sing the *Hatikvah* when he remembered Zion. To remember Zion in a vague ineffable way, was the chief function of the Zionist student groups. . . . A too platonic love for Zion, rather than a sense of living alliance with a concrete Palestine was the unsubstantial basis on which the I.Z.A. failed to flourish.[11]

In praise of *Avuka,* the new Jewish student movement, Marie points out that the prewar student movement was animated by the desire for conformity and full Americanization; but the new movement arose out of postmandate conditions and was quickened by the "beat of the *Cha-lutzim* [pioneer] pickaxes in Palestine." *Avuka* arose when "Zion emerged from the hazy distance of a Utopia to the disconcerting clarity of a reality. To declare oneself a Zionist meant more than merely to sing the *Hatikvah* or bethink oneself of Israel. It was the definite statement of national allegiance. It was also the affirmation of national individuality" (Avuka 140).

Although the grim letter to Eugenia bears the seeds of the witty sardonic style of the *New Palestine* article, it lacks its opposite mode: exuberant idealism. The article, moreover, appears to be the earliest example of Marie Syrkin's Zionist writing. Stylistically, it is embryonic Syrkin; that is, a mode that seesaws between extravagant idealism and sharp riposte. In recent years, Syrkin has been criticized for having spoken in the language of naive and sentimental ideological early Zionism, but this overlooks the point that such a double-sided rhetorical style is characteristic of the zealous writer from the prophets through John Milton and the polemicists of the 1960s. Only the idealist with a sense of high moral purpose can turn the smooth carpet over to expose a rough side of moral indignation. The cynic—which Marie Syrkin was not—has only one texture.

It was during these early years of the twenties—both of the century and Marie—that Marie began to publish her translations of poetry from the Yiddish into English. Among the very first to do so, she was very much in the vanguard. For her, it was one way of reconciling her love of poetry and her emerging sense of Jewish purpose. By the time she had written to Eugenia, "on the morrow I am 24," she had already published translations of the poetry of the important Yiddish poet Yehoash in *Menorah Journal*. Henry Hurwitz, the editor, had sent her a note asking for biographical data. Syrkin wrote back, and perhaps recalling her father's request upon news of her marriage that she should "wear the name Bodansky-Syrkin and write under that name," she submitted the following revealing self-description: "As to myself, I am the daughter of Dr. Syrkin and the wife of A. Bodansky who teaches here. I have my B.A. and M.A. from Cornell and, God willing, I may some day get a Ph.D." (Shafran, Archives f. 14).

God, it seems, was not willing, for Marie Syrkin never did get a Ph.D. Too many other things intervened. Here one might speculate about what was keeping Marie's marriage to Aaron alive, though certainly not thriving. Once again, in a letter just upon her twenty-fourth birthday, she confesses to Eugenia, "As to myself, sorrow and wretchedness. Flunked Practical in English but am receiving requests for credentials from B.of E. So don't know what's up. . . . I'm so appalled at the notion of a divorce—the fact that it's the second practically in my young life throws me into such fits that I am determined to do my utmost in the way of housekeeping efficiency, gentle femininity—good wifeness— etc. If then my consort does not improve I shall consider myself among the world's unfortunate but blameless" (Archives f. 6). The Ph.D. will have to be shelved, it seems, and a teaching license will have to do. Is this a practicality in the face of Aaron's small salary, or is it some unconscious preparation for a divorce that at this moment "appalls" her? Nonetheless, Marie's conscious life is telling her not to disrupt her present situation. So much does she want to avoid a rupture that by June of 1923 she is pregnant again. The ties of connection are beginning to bind beyond escape.

In December, Benya, then two years and three months old, developed a terrible cough and fever. Nachman wrote to his daughter on December 20, "We received your last letter and you can imagine how worried we are, I and Machette. Darling, wooping [*sic*] cough is not at all dangerous, but you in your present condition must take the greatest care, in order that you shall not be infected" (Archives f. 1). Nachman's encouraging assessment, no doubt the product of his wife's medical knowledge and his own natural optimism, was to prove wrong. Benya died three days later.

There is no personal tragedy greater than the death of one's child, no grief more inconsolable. No matter the age of the child, the experience and maturity of the parent, such a loss is too horrendous, so inconceivable that even nightmares must be repressed. Marie was a young woman of twenty-four, herself barely emerging from childish irresponsibilties, dependencies, and self-absorption, and despite an enormous intellectual capacity, she seemed unable to make appropriate and sustaining relationships. Her maternal instinct seemed blunted as she described with flippant sardonicism her motherly chores. She could not even acknowledge Aaron's fatherly concerns. "Baby is a cutavitch!" Marie had quipped to Eugenia. "But wilful and opposed to spinach & eggs & fond of strawberries. To a monstrous extent and generally mixed up about this universe so that I have my hands full and so far he seems to emerge victorious from all our combats. Aaron hovers over him like a bird of ill omen dolefully prophesying all sorts of things unless I stuff spinach into

the kid and has weird ideas about putting spinach into strawberries —
but the kid hates wisdom & will not of the corrupt strawberry." How
clever and cold this is. How intensely Marie works at covering unhappiness with arch style.

Years later, Marie Syrkin would say that she was to blame for the
death of her child. Saying no more than that she was too absorbed in
her own work to be a careful mother, she took the calamity upon herself. Marie's immediate state of mind is available for all to see in a final
extant letter to her friend and confidante. It is impossible to condense
this grief-stricken, unmediated outpouring of her stricken heart. The
letter, dated December 29, 1923, appears here in full:

Dear Eugenia

Your postal card came on the day my little boy died. He had gotten whoop-
ing cough — there was an epidemic of it in Ithaca — and on Monday he was taken
ill with pneumonia — a common complication and on Thursday at 4:32 in the
afternoon he died. He was buried on Friday — yesterday.

It is strange that I got the postal just as I came home from the hospital after
his death. I had not expected to hear from you or to write from [*sic*] you but
now all the things and the evil which came between us seems infinitely trivial
and far away. The only thing I remember is that we were friends when we were
both young with life before us and that every step of my life seems to have
tended to this and that you knew him when he was a little baby. You did not
know him afterwards when he was beginning to be a little human being and
walking and thinking and making every trivial object and act infinitely dear.
That is where the memories are terrible. One cannot touch a piece of bread or
an orange or look out of the window or take a bath without remembering some
darling baby way in which he asked for it or said something about it. The couple
of weeks before he died he had learned a lot of rhymes — Jack & Jill — Tom
Tucker — Georgie Porgie and when he was very ill I soothed him and made him
take medicine by reciting about Georgie Porgie and Tom Tucker. The whoop-
ing cough choked him. He was too weak to cough because of the pneumonia
and he had to cough or choke. I saw him die. Aaron and I sat beside his bed all
day and watched him die. We could not do anything. His fever went up to 107
2/5 the last time it was taken. It was probably more by the time he died. I took
him in my arms when he was dead and although he was dead he was hot as fire.
When he was dying he was in a slight convulsion all the time and his little hot
hand in mine felt just as the beating of him felt in my body before he was born.
The last real thing I remember his saying was looking out of the window on

Tuesday morning and saying with joy "white snow." When he was born papa brought white roses. We put white roses on his grave. The Jews of the town were very good. As a mitzvah they gave him a Jewish burial and the shop keepers left their stores to form a minion for the services. There is no regular synagogue here and Aaron said Kaddish over him who should have said Kaddish over Aaron and me in the years to come.

My only hope now is that the child I will bear — if he lives — will be a little boy like Benya. I remember when Benya was only about two months old going to a play with you — I think it was Romeo and Juliet and seeing a little boy of 10 or 12 and saying to you how sweet and strange it was to think that the years would pass and I would have a big little boy, and then we left because I had to get back to nurse him. And now all is over and gone and the only thing left are memories in every trivial object and act and a few toys and a few old dresses. The rest we are giving to charity. I wanted to snatch at things and it seemed so economical and quick to have two babies and I was so proud when I thought that by the time I was twenty-five I would have a little boy and another baby — but there is no use snatching at things or taking things unless you deserve them and are ready for them — for now all these years are gone and I have no little boy and the desolation is greater than anything I would have imagined. I thought I knew suffering but all the things that grieved me in the past and the things I thought I wanted from life have in two days turned meaningless as smoke. The only real thing that mattered is gone.

If I have a live baby I shall be happy to wash diapers for it and every little service at which I rebelled would seem very sweet now. It seems strange that he should have died just as the hard part of raising him was over. He was a happy fat little fellow and the things he said and did were very sweet. I would keep on writing like this all day but there is no use and it would not mean much to you.

You write that you can not get your license and want to go into the wilds and write. Don't Eugenia. If teaching H.S. is the best way for you to make a living, don't shirk it, don't run away. Evil will overtake you. Fight it out like others who try for licenses till they get it. That's the only way to live.

I got my license — I don't know why — but I don't think it will be of any use to me. Good luck, Marie (Shafran, Archives f. 6)

Gone is the flippant quip, gone the self-conscious style, gone the put-upon complaint, and in their place is utter sincerity, truth of feeling, sad realization that plans are only plans, and a sudden awareness of life's darkest side. The death of Benya was the moment that transformed Marie Syrkin's life.

Chapter 6

David, Divorce, and the Death of Nachman

EVEN FREUD MIGHT have agreed that the "family romance" of the Syrkins, circa 1921 to 1923, was quite out of the ordinary. Nachman Syrkin had married the sister of his late wife, Masha, who was eighteen years his junior — young enough to be his daughter; she not only was Marie's aunt, but now had become her stepmother as well. Nachman and Masha had recently become parents of a healthy baby girl named Zivia; Zivia became at once Marie's half-sister and also her half-cousin; Marie, herself, had thus become an elder daughter; she had married Aaron Bodansky and they had a son, Benya, who was Nachman's first grandchild, and was but a few months younger than his grandfather's daughter Zivia. All this would be an amusing "I-am-my-own-grandpa" account but for the tragic event that occurred in the sixth month of Marie's pregnancy with her second child: the death of her first child, Benya.

"My Maryetchka! You were never so near and dear to me as now in your despair," wrote Nachman Syrkin to his daughter after receiving the news of the death of Benya. His letter is short, for he knows that there are no words in English or in any other language to express such personal grief and such utter anguish in the face of his daughter's despair, for her despair is his first concern. "I implore you, be brave," he writes. "Do it for yourself, the newcomer, for all of us. We are all in God's hands. Let us all start a new life, full of love, duty, responsibility and truth. Benya is remaining in my memory as long as I will live. Write immediately about your health. Did you fumigate everything? Be brave, my darling, my child! Papa. P.S. Machette loves you more than we all think, she will write tomorrow" (Archives f. 1). Nachman's instruction to fumigate everything seems a rude intrusion, but he was probably acting on his wife Masha's cautionary professional medical advice. More telling is the absence of any mention of, or sympathy for his daughter's husband, Aaron. Most probably one can account for this lapse of civility as his undisguised desire for Marie to leave Aaron and return to New York City.

Marie did return to New York early in 1924 to await the birth of her child, staying with her father and his family until her son David was born on March 10, 1924. According to her son, David Bodansky, upon leaving the hospital his mother returned to her father's home. He further speculates, "I think she may have gone back to Ithaca occasionally after this, but I am not sure."[1] In her memoir of her father, however, Marie says that she was summoned to New York from Ithaca on September 3 when her father had been taken to Mount Sinai hospital after suffering a heart attack. In any case, it appears that by this time the break between Marie and Aaron Bodansky had effectively been made. David's impression is that his mother's "departure from Ithaca was not a single well-defined time. Rather," he thinks, "it was intermittent before becoming final" (E-mail, May 17, 2005). It did not become legal until 1930.

When Marie arrived at Mount Sinai hospital, her father was already on his deathbed. She found him weak, barely able to speak above a whisper, in constant pain, but in total command of his mental faculties (*Memoir* 222). His death, Marie later recalled,

had a kind of story-book character. . . . He knew that he was dying; he brushed aside all attempts at deception and few were so insensitive as to offend him with cheap and futile assurances; only the nurses and medical staff exuded their synthetic sick-bed comfort. His family and friends accepted the terms he set; his high awareness of the drama in which he was the actor. He would not let us dim the solemnity of a man's passing by trivial pretenses or a jab of the doctor's needle. Death was the final experience before him and we had to live it with him as intensely and greatly as he desired. And when I write "we" I mean not only his wife and daughter but all those with whom he had shared the mystery of being alive in common thought and action. (*Memoir* 223)

Syrkin's grave illness had been reported on the front pages of the Yiddish press, causing a steady flow of visitors to the hospital who had come to say a final farewell. Remaining conscious throughout, but weak of body and voice, Syrkin said goodbye to his comrades one by one, and each in the language in which he customarily addressed them. To Masha he spoke Russian, to Marie he spoke English, and "when a doctor came in he whispered in Latin, '*Pontifex, pontificorum,*'" but his daughter drily adds, "the doctor did not understand, and he was too weak to repeat that last joke." Nachman Syrkin, in his faint last hours, sent messages to his life's compatriots in the cause of Jewish nationalism who were unable to attend his death, friends and foes as well, to Pinhas Rutenberg, to Chaim Weizmann, and even to his great but respected opponent, Vladimir Jabotinsky. And to his beloved and devoted disciple, Baruch Zuckerman, Marie later would recall, "he dictated a letter to Leon Trotsky urging him to fight for socialism as a son of his people. He was beyond being troubled by Trotsky's probable and possibly contemptuous indifference; it was his last plea to the Jewish anti-Zionist 'internationalists.'" Affixing a typically "Syrkinistic" comment, Marie adds, "His comrades honoring the memory of their leader sought, perhaps mistakenly, to spare him a posthumous slight" (*Memoir* 224).

That Nachman Syrkin knew his time of death had come is evidenced by his composition of a Hebrew prayer, *Birkat ha-Mavet* (Blessing of Death). Syrkin was a secularist, that is true; but he also was a profoundly spiritual man. That might lead one to argue that a spiritual secularist is an oxymoron, but in the words of his daughter, Marie, "His battle with orthodoxy had long been won; a rigid clericalism no longer petrified Jewish life. As he grew older the rebel could allow his deep religious sense to assume traditional forms." He had confessed to his daughter on many occasions that he was tempted to go to a synagogue on holy days as he did in his boyhood and that privately he would listen to recordings of cantorial music. His was not mere nostalgia, for "the strong mystical strain which had enabled him to write reverently of 'God' in the period of his fiercest anti-clericalism together with his sense of Jewish tradition grew stronger from year to year. It did not surprise me," wrote his daughter so many years later, "that he chose to die observing Jewish ritual, so proclaiming his identity with the generations before him." Asserting this absolute identity with his heritage, Syrkin composed his *Birkat ha-Mavet* in Hebrew; the English translation follows:

> Praised be Thou, O Lord,
> Spirit [*ruach*] of the universe,
> Who brought me across the Yabok bridge of life.

When the dim light of my own self
Will sink and merge
Within the light which illumines
The world and eternity,
I shall conclude the order of my days,
In this twilight glow of my life,
I stand before the dawn of my new sun
With tense consciousness,
A man about to die and to live,
Who feels at one with the universe and eternity,
As in the ancient words:
"Hear O Israel, the Lord our God
The Lord is One,"
Praised be the God of Life and Death
Of light and love.

As Marie Syrkin later pointed out, "The prayer though beginning with the traditional 'Praised be Thou [*Baruch Atah Adonoi, Eloheynu . . .*]' has his stamp. For the second line should have been *Melech ha Olam* (King of the Universe). But the dying man changed King to Spirit. He would pray his own way to the end."

The following night, the night before his death, Nachman Syrkin summoned Dr. Chaim Tchernowitz, the renowned scholar and professor of Talmud at the Jewish Institute for Religion in New York. Syrkin wished to say the traditional orthodox prayer before death, the *Viddui*, the communal confession of sins said on Yom Kippur, but in the face of death, he transposed it from the plural to the singular. When knowledge of Syrkin's dying act of prayer was reported to the orthodox, they contended that it was an act of "deathbed conversion on the part of an atheist radical." Horrified by the orthodox claim, the secularists countered that Syrkin certainly had not renounced his belief in nonbelief, but it was simply a case of failure of nerve in the throes of death agony. Later, Marie, who was present at the occasion, insisted that neither camp was correct. "There was no sudden illumination—or darkening—at the end." The struggle with rigid orthodoxy had been won, and Jewish religious life had evolved far enough for him to "allow his deep religious sense to assume traditional forms" (*Memoir* 224–228).

It was 1924, and American Judaism, in an effort to reconcile itself with modernity, had already created new forms of worship: The Reform movement's Hebrew Union College had been established by Rabbi Isaac Mayer Wise fifty years before; Solomon Schechter, the great scholar, Zionist, and architect of Conservative Judaism became President of the Jewish Theological Seminary in 1902; in 1909 he had hired Mordecai Kaplan who had already begun to articulate ideas that later would inform nonsupernatural and egalitarian Reconstructionist Judaism; in 1922, Kaplan's daughter, Judith, had become the first Bat Mitzvah in America; and in 1922, Rabbi Stephen Wise had established the Jewish Institute of Religion for the training of rabbis for education, research, and community work. Wise, a pluralist, encouraged Jews of all theological persuasions to participate in the work of the J.I.R. Not surprisingly, when Syrkin in his last hours wished to express his religiosity, it was to Chaim Tchernowitz that he turned. Tchernowitz had been a renowned European traditional scholar who had come to the J.I.R. as Professor of Talmud in the hope of transforming Jewish studies by combining traditional study with modern research techniques. No doubt Nachman Syrkin's desire to say the *Viddui* prayer as he lay dying in the hospital was a deliberate moral act as well as his imprimatur for the new forms that traditional Judaism was creating in liberal America. Though Marie Syrkin plainly understood the meaning of her father's deathbed act, it was not something that she herself would ever be able to repeat; with all the pedagogic effort that her father had spent on his daughter's education, he had not given her any useful knowledge of Hebrew or of traditional Judaism. So many years later, in a poem written in the 1970s entitled "Quotations," she acknowledges this insufficiency:

> We'll to the woods no more,
> We'll go no more a-walking,
> True, they were dark and lovely
> But there three beasts were stalking.
> How they clawed at my heart,
> The lion, wolf, and leopard.
> Green pastures, quiet waters?
> I never found the shepherd.
> (*Gleanings* 14)

September 6 was Syrkin's last day of life. He grew increasingly weak, so weak that he could not complete the sentences that he began. Yet his mind, Marie would recall, remained "preternaturally keen." He was sufficiently lucid to whisper to his daughter, "You will always remember the day of my death [September 6] because it is Benyah's birthday." Years later, recalling these very words, Marie wrote, "And so it was. Always through the years birth and death have been one for me on this day" (*Memoir* 227).

But even these were not Syrkin's last thoughts. He went on to dictate to his wife in Russian. He dictated a one-sentence definition of socialism and he took his leave of his "mortal experience" proclaiming, "one last word—I embrace my wife and kiss her; this is the end."

"But," his daughter Marie demurs,

it was not the end; he could still gasp single words. And again imperiously he motioned that we write down ideas for his family, three-year-old Zivia and his infant grandson David, to cherish—the patrimony that he left. And there went on that literally breathless catalogue of thinkers to be studied, ideals to be honored. I kept jotting down the names and phrases, disconnected, no longer explained: Tutankhamen, Moses, Jewish prophets (all named), Plato, Aristotle, Phidias, Venus of Milo, Arab philosophers, Maimonides, Goethe, Marx. . . . So the long list went, as though with each name he sought to create a last contact with what he had loved best. He dictated the inscription for his tombstone: "Each man dies with his work unfinished." (*Memoir* 227)

Nachman Syrkin's huge funeral inspired a public outpouring of mourners, speeches, articles in the press, memorial meetings in the Diaspora and in Palestine, and tributes from friends and opponents everywhere. Yet for Nachman Syrkin's daughter, Marie, the "true moment" of memorial came twenty-seven years later in 1951, when Syrkin was reinterred in Israel. As the "brief and austere" service came to a close, the Prime Minister of the new State, David Ben-Gurion, unexpectedly stepped out of the shadows on the shore of Kinnereth "to the edge of the open grave and said in Hebrew, Syrkin, *hazonikha yitkayem,* 'your vision will be fulfilled'; then he drew back into the shadows just as swiftly as he had emerged" (*Memoir* 9).

The death of Nachman Syrkin was the third in a series of grievous traumas that Marie suffered within a few years (excluding the annulment of her elopement). The first blow was her almost immediate realization of the failure of her marriage in 1919 to Aaron Bodansky. The second and undoubtedly the most heartbreaking shock was the death of her first child in 1923. The *coup de grace* was the death of her father less than one year later in 1924. Marie herself had confessed to Eugenia that she had imagined that by the time she was twenty-five she would have "a little boy and another baby." But as life and death would have it, at twenty-five, she would have no marriage, no parents, no Benyah. After the baby's death, in her letter to Eugenia, she mourned her profound loss: "the desolation is greater than anything I could have imagined. I thought I knew suffering but all the things that grieved me in the past and all the things I thought I wanted from life have in two days turned meaningless as smoke. The only real thing that mattered is gone" (Shafran, Archives f. 6). By September of 1924, at the tender age of twenty five, Marie Syrkin was virtually alone with a new baby. Her imagined paradise had been lost; and in the words of the poet John Milton, "the world was all before [her], where to choose."

Alone in New York

By 1925, Marie and her infant son, David, had left the not-so-Edenic Ithaca and had moved permanently to New York City, moving in at first with Masha and Zivia. "At some point," David Bodansky speculates, "she moved out and lived with an older woman who served as baby-sitter. Eventually (roughly 1927, I would guess) she joined Masha at the home of Mrs. Epstein, who was the widow of a family friend and a godsend to all of us — as homemaker and child caretaker" (E-mail, May 17, 2005). This was an absolutely necessary move, for Masha had returned to her work as a doctor, and by 1925 Marie had taken a position as an English teacher at Textile High School on 18th Street in Manhattan. The letter that Marie had written to Eugenia immediately after the death of Benyah ended with these words: "I got my license — I don't know why — but I don't think it will be of any use to me." Now she knew why. Moreover, the other passing remark to Eugenia that Marie had made, that she had "flunked" the Practical in English but that she was receiving requests for credentials from the Board of Education, meant that evidently and fortunately the Board had decided in her favor. Fortunately, because she needed to support herself; but unfortunately, because for the twenty-five years that she would remain in it, she detested this work. She did not get her Ph.D., this was not the glorious academic career she had dreamed of, nor were her colleagues the poets and scholars she had imagined they would be. Her students were not the brilliant, eager to learn, knowledge-hungry youths she had wanted to teach. Instead she had to face the daily grind of classes filled with adolescents of a variety of ethnic and social backgrounds who were not always prepared or terribly interested in what she had to tell them, for whom she did not always have great patience or sympathy. Perhaps that is why she had "flunked" the Practical. Her general posture regarding her experience as a high school teacher in a basically commercial high school environment was one of toleration and is evinced in a poem about the classroom written during that period, titled "Shirley":

> Her name is Shirley and not Deborah.
> There's one in every class, I know the look.
> She'll never read what's called a worthwhile book.
> She'll stay at home on Yom Kippur but not fast.
> She tinkles when she walks — bells, bracelets, charms but with the rest
> Of late, a Shield of David on her breast.
> I ask her why; she knows no word sublime;
> She hesitates, "I guess it is the time.
> Besides, the other girls wear crosses now."
> I bow.
> What makes these little girls
> With heavy lipstick and with silly curls,
> With voice too loud,
> So proud?
> (*Gleanings* 47)

By the beginning of 1925, Marie began her teaching career at Textile High School, commuting daily between the Bronx and 18th Street in Manhattan. Her son, David, was nine months old. The break between Marie and Aaron was now permanent, but not yet legal. Aaron remained in Ithaca as an instructor in chemistry for the year, but, because of his Jewishness, could not find a permanent academic position. He then moved to Kalamazoo, Michigan, where he worked for the Upjohn Company for two years. But separation from his son David, to whom he was extremely devoted, was too painful, and he returned to New York City and took a position at the Hospital for Joint Diseases as a supervisor of a diagnostic laboratory and as a research chemist. He remained there until his retirement in 1954. Aaron Bodansky became a very productive chemist, and among his numerous research findings one can find a listing in the *Dorlands Medical Dictionary* under the entry "Bodansky unit." As his son, David, was later to characterize his parents, his father "was an exceptionally well-read person with wide intellectual and political interests — a good match to my mother in intelligence and (perhaps not for the best) in strength of mind" (Personal conversation). Ironically, however, the "chemistry" was wrong.

When Marie took up permanent residence in New York to begin her teaching duties, her life became extremely constrained. That beautiful and brilliant young woman who, only a few years before at Cornell, had found personal freedom, had made such interesting friends as the poet Laura Reichenthal (later, Riding), had intellectual stimulation, literary encouragement, and academic success, now perforce kept a rigid domestic and work schedule with little time left for socializing. She did, however, keep up with a few old friends — Tima Ludins, who would remain her friend for life, and Eugenia Shafran, with whom she continued a stormy but intimate and important relationship, but who ultimately would disappear from her life, leaving behind only a box full of letters.[2] Marie continued to write her poetry, translate, maintain contact with the Zionist Movement, write for publications such as *The New Palestine* and *Menorah Journal.* Having learned early on from her father about the pleasures of the serene facilities at the New York Public Library (which had afforded him many quiet hours of reading and writing), Marie began to spend time at the library as well. Here, she could insulate herself from the demands of her daily chores and concentrate on her continuing commitment to literature. It was during one of these library visits that she was spotted by another reader — one who had not seen her for the past six years. That person was Maurice Samuel.

Samuel had been demobilized from the U.S. Army on September 22, 1919, nine months after Marie had broken with him. He had remained in Europe, living in Paris for a year and working with the Reparations Commissions in Berlin and Vienna. While in Berlin in 1920, a year after he had learned the news of Marie's marriage to Aaron Bodansky, Samuel married a cousin, Gertrude Kahn, whom he had met in Frankfurt. His daughter, Eva, was born in September of 1921, but his wife suffered from emotional instability and had been in a sanitarium.[3] Now living in New York, he worked for the Jewish newspaper *The Day* and published his first novel, *The Outsider,* about the demobilized servicemen in postwar Paris. Contrary to Nachman Syrkin's expectancy, Samuel's professional stars seemed to be in the ascendency.

Maurice Redux

One of the first things Maurice Samuel did when he set up his new life in New York was to get in touch with some old friends. On October 18, 1921, he wrote a note to Eugenia informing her of his return and his wish to renew their friendship. By the end of October, he received her reply, and on November 2, he wrote in return, telling Eugenia that "Of all the old friends, [he] really values her friendship," thus beginning a renewed correspondence that continued for some years.[4] Sometime late in 1924, Eugenia wrote a letter to Maurice that, it appears, suggested that either they intensify their relationship or break it off. It provoked an astounding reaction. Maurice's response is a long and bitter misogynist fulmination that must have appalled its recipient, and undoubtedly will unnerve the many latter-day admirers of Maurice Samuel who read his words:

Dear Eugenia:
[I]t may surprise you to know that your short note has hit me so hard that I have responded with a kind of recklessness. There is something vicious in my attitude toward women. I will not admit that they mean anything to me except body. I cannot admit that they have a hold on me such as they once had. It is brutal to think so; it is perhaps the exclusion of a great deal of good. But I cannot help myself. I desire women, and dislike them. Unless a woman means to me physical enjoyment I seem to feel a kind of fierce, submerged principle bidding me keep away from her. You do not know, I have never admitted, (I have perhaps said the very contrary) with what pain I remember my faculty for true loving: not perhaps that I was ever good, but that I could be utterly mastered by beauty. But I cannot conceive a return of this faculty in me; it is completely atrophied. . . . I do not know what part Marie played and plays in this condition of mine; I am utterly incapable of disentangling the threads of various developments that have gone on simultaneously in me. I cannot bear anything but the simplest, most brutal relationship, soon begun and soon ended. And yet . . . I am [not] content. I am as hungry for something which I despise and deride as I was when I was eighteen or nineteen. At that, if a mere touch of it were to return, I should bungle it, I do not doubt, as I bungled it years ago.

I couldn't have conceived myself saying to you what I am about to say, but I do it under the very curious influence of your letter, and because I do not want ever to see you again. I saw Marie in the library a few weeks ago, and I tell you simply that if I had not been sitting when she passed I should have fainted. Yet I do not want to meet her again, would not want to meet her even if both of us were free. I cannot manage my life properly in these matters. All that I have ever spoken to you in regard to Marie wipe out of your memory. It was talk, and meant nothing. She has not been out of my mind one day since at least I returned to this country, and yet I cannot say what I think. I say I do not know what part she plays in my condition, but she plays a dominant part. I do not understand myself. I sometimes think I hate women as I do (it is a very real hatred) in spite, out of a hunger for revenge, a very stupid, stupid hunger. I am brutally self satisfied and superior in my attitude from a similar feeling. At bottom I am horribly insecure and I have the feeling that I have spoiled my life utterly, utterly, utterly, so that it is loathsome, and there is no way of going back. I have never wanted to talk to you like this, and have never talked to anyone so since — six years ago or so. Because of all this sickening misery I don't want to have a woman friend, with all its implications, and recollections, and the rest of it. Please do not suggest to me that we should meet again. If you reply to this perhaps I shall answer you, perhaps I shall not. It does not matter any more.

Yours, Maurice (Samuel, Box)

This brutally candid letter almost certainly was written in 1924. Samuel had seen Marie in the library, which means she had to have been in New York — as well she was during and after the death of her father on September 6, 1924. Whatever the case, it is clear from his letter that Maurice is still profoundly bound up with Marie. It is also true that both parties, Marie and Maurice, are deeply unhappy at this moment in their personal lives. One absolute fact, in the light of all these speculations, is that by late April 1925, Maurice Samuel and Marie Syrkin had, in Marie's own words, "resumed their relationship" (Personal interview).

Many years later, Marie spoke briefly of the renewed affair, but she did not wish to speak at length about it. She did, however, reveal that there were letters testifying to this, and she disclosed their whereabouts. She had given them to Brandeis University, not to be opened until after her death or by authorization. Among those letters is a fragment that points to Maurice as the initiator of the "resumed relationship." Marie had saved only the last paragraph: "longevity. But whenever it ends I want, if you will let me, to resume our friendship. It may be, of course, that by that time you will have grown utterly indifferent to me: if that should not be so I want you [word missing] let me know. If I am not yet in New York I will receive and reply to your letter in all happiness; if I have returned I will come and see you. Affectionately yours, Maurice" (Brandeis, Letters).

Whether this letter was written just before the resumed relationship or some years later is not absolutely verifiable. What cannot be controverted, however, is that sometime in late 1924 or early 1925 the two renewed their relationship. When Maurice had returned to the United States in 1921, he not only took up work for the newspaper *The Day,* but he also worked for the Zionist Organization of America, then under the leadership of Meyer Weisgal. Weisgal was the first friend Maurice had made when he came to the United States. From 1918 to 1921, Weisgal had been the editor of *The Maccabean* and from 1921 to 1930 of *The New Palestine;* both Marie and Maurice were contributors to these publications. Moreover, Weisgal served from 1921 to 1938 as national secretary of the Zionist Organization of America and became Chaim Weizmann's personal representative in the United States. Maurice, it might be noted, in as much as he would later collaborate with Weizmann on his autobiography *Trial and Error,* had been a student in Weizmann's class in chemistry at Manchester University in England—though Samuel did not stay in the course for more than a few classes "because he could not understand Weizmann's Yiddish-accented lectures."[5] Maurice Samuel's third book, *I the Jew* (1927) was dedicated to Weizmann.

With such connections, as well as the fact that Samuel was a gifted speaker, Weisgal sent Maurice to the Midwest and the West on a lecture-fund-raising tour for the Zionist Organization of America. Maurice's first stop and first letter to Marie is in late April of 1925. Marie was now twenty-six and Maurice, thirty. Much had happened to both to change them since their last contact in 1919, yet the "chemistry" had not weakened the force of the combustion produced by their combination. Maurice writes from his hotel room in Leamington, Minneapolis:

Marie, my lost one and found one. . . . I try to think, of course, of clandestine loves that have been long and happy. I try to see ourselves from the outside. But nothing succeeds in removing the misery from my heart. There is no way of getting around it, no way of fooling ourselves, of making a sort of setting to our love which will give it comfort. . . . For years I sneered at [our love] and deliberately outraged it, and now find it stronger than I believed any emotion could be. . . . I am waiting in a kind of agony for your first letter.

Your lover, always, Maurice (Brandeis, Letters)

After receiving news of the birth of his brother Joe's baby boy (Joe's first child had died), and after receiving further news of it from Marie, who surely empathized deeply, Maurice writes:

I think as you do, of the future, and the much that we ought to be building now. . . . You have, of course, materialised it at once, as women do — a child! A boy of ours! Do you think it means nothing to me that Marie should bear me a child? Yet I stave off the fear of the future, and I say, if it were otherwise, even if we were free to have a child — we would wait a year or two, surely. And I try to create the illusion of something nearer to perfection. . . . But of one thing I am sure, Marie and try to believe me despite a woman's distrust of a man: I know that it is too late for me ever to disentangle you from my heart. Whatever you should do, some day love someone else perhaps, marry perhaps, I shall feel that my best is yours. Well — let that go. (Brandeis, Letters)

Whatever else this letter may contain, it is written in the language of the conditional, of uncertainty — In this case that; if that, then this. How could Marie have read his letter and not have been thrown even deeper into the abyss? She had made her own decision about marriage; she would seek a divorce. But Maurice's letters — despite his protestations of love (which doubtless were sincere) — do not go beyond the "*if* we were married" condition. On the other hand, however, he can write from a different perspective — her pain and his inability to make any commitment to her: "Dearest, kindest of all, you have left a bruise in me, that heroic restraint of yours. After all, things do even up. I think I suffer more, because of your strength, than if you were weak. When that flush passes over your face, and I know tears are coming and you hold them back, then I grow cold with a kind of self contempt. It is very wrong of me to write even this" (Brandeis, Letters).

Maurice's circuit of Jewish communities across the country lasted several months, ending in Norfolk, Virginia, where he wrote: "I can't go to sleep without a word to you." Time and distance had not diminished Maurice's ardor, and he ends this note with "I don't know what I'm writing to you, and don't care so long as it's to you and tells you direct or otherwise, that I am wildly and outrageously in love with you, out of all proportion to my merits — but not to your dear loveliness. Yours, as never before, Maurice" (Brandeis, Letters).

One might imagine from the passionate avowals of these letters that Maurice would soon begin to consider leaving his wife — but such was not the case. Despite his apparent colossal mood shifts, and his affirmation of liberated sexual mores, he appears to be unable to sever his unhappy spousal relationship. Perhaps he cannot bear to separate himself from his children; perhaps he feels obligated — though trapped — by his wife's illness; but whatever the cause, by December of 1925, it appears that Marie could no longer continue in the uncertainties of the present.

Between 1920 and 1925, Marie Syrkin had suffered a series of seismic existential shocks. Two failed marriages, two births, two deaths inside of five years. These might have crushed a weaker soul, but in Marie's case, they transformed her. She had been a young woman bound by the dream of a conventional Victorian rite of passage — the safe transfer from loving father to loving husband. Marie, however, had begun to challenge that loving but overbearing father's domination: first, by unconventional behavior leading to an unconventional elopement, though followed by acquiescence to a forced annulment; next, by a hasty second marriage in her father's absence to a father substitute. But her struggle faltered; for although she realized early that the second marriage lacked the "chemistry" of the first, she nonetheless found it difficult to part with that old romantic fantasy of hearth and home, of *mater familias*. But the veneer of her conventional marriage was mostly decorative, overlaying a strong-minded intellect and will that was beginning to express itself in personal poetry and public Zionist journalism. The death of her first child, however, had dealt the mortal blow to her dreams of happiness ever after; the death of her father left her free to choose her own ever-after.

There was one more mopping-up measure that Marie Syrkin took to, clear the stage for the next act. Though there is no parting letter from Marie to Maurice extant, she preserved a letter from him that, in effect, reveals just what Marie had written:

I read your letter and I tried several times to reply to it — repeating the effort until I became altogether confused and hardly knew what I was writing. Perhaps I ought not to try and write anything for the thing you make of me in the letter is so unclean and imbecilic that it is impossible to say anything at all, though the best that I have to say does not clear me of guilt, just as I cannot find a way of making reparation. Of course you need fear nothing in regard to your position in the office. If what you say of me is true (could any person believe it of himself and live?) you must be perverse and corrupt to nourish any affection for me. If it is untrue, you are the most venomous person I have ever known. I am not a good person. I have wronged you deeply. I do not know what to do in this ghastly complex of my life. But to twit me with henpecking, with "great man" complexes — naive or otherwise — and to link up this debacle with all that, is — I can't find a word for it. It doesn't matter. I wish I could help you some way. In the essential I cannot, as I cannot help myself. I can only offer that brute assistance which you despise. I wish you would not, even if you feel it would give me a feeling of relief. (Brandeis, Letters)

Finally, it appears that Maurice was no George Henry Lewes; because Lewes could not divorce his legal wife, he chose to live unconventionally, as if married, to the woman he loved, George Eliot. And so the Marie-Maurice affair ended in much the same way as it had seven years before, with a kiss-off letter.

Marie Syrkin now found herself to be totally on her own — no husband, no father, no lover, and no resources save her own intellectual and emotional assets. In the next few years, she would teach high school English, write and translate, and begin to involve herself in Zionist concerns. Many decades later, when Marie had been dubbed "the doyenne of labor Zionism," she was asked to explain the development of her ideology. Questioned about the beginnings of her lifelong role in the history of Zionism, she replied that she was "brought up with a sense of Jewishness and belonging to a certain type of family with certain convictions." And though, she explained, her inclination in her earlier years tended more toward the literary, she always was interested in the socialist Zionism she grew up with. But, she continued, " a recrudescence of a sense of direct involvement again, comes with my first visit to Palestine in 1933." Cutting off her interviewer, she self-interrogated — "but why did it take me so long to get to Palestine?" Answering her own question, she tossed off all the pain and sorrows and difficulties that she had suffered into one brief phrase, "because of personal complications." Proof of an early impulse to Zionism — although admitting that in her twenties it was not "all-consuming" — she insisted, can be traced by a series of facts. First of all, she pointed out that in 1917 she was present at the ceremony when the 39th battalion of the American Jewish Legion was sent off. Then she pointed to the fact that, when she married Aaron Bodansky, they bought collapsible furniture that could be shipped to Palestine when they emigrated. Then she added that while at Cornell, she joined the student leftist Zionist group *Avuka* and began writing for *The Maccabean*. The interviewer posed two more personal questions that were met with sharp denials: how much influence did her correspondence with Maurice Samuel (who was very much a Zionist) have, and how much did distance from her father have on her increasing political awareness? Marie's answer to the former was "Yes, Maurice was Zionist—he wrote poems about Palestine and things about Zion and so on—pretty rotten ones, I must say." As to the latter question, her riposte was a sharp "No. I don't think it required distancing—that's too biopsychology, you know." Indeed, it may have been, for Marie's ability to avoid rigid ideology and to entertain shifts of position argues against a mere "anxiety of influence" (Personal interview).

Career Beginnings

As advertised, there is ample evidence that Marie's Jewish self-awareness was growing stronger—though at this point it was still mainly literary. Her long association with *Menorah Journal* began with a letter she wrote to the editor, Henry Hurwitz, in April of 1923, in which Marie offered him her translations of Yehoash, followed by a May letter asking whether or not Hurwitz would be interested in translations of Yiddish poets other than Yehoash and a blank verse translation of Beer-Hoffman's "magnificent poetic drama (German) 'Jacob's Traum.'" Apparently, Hurwitz was interested. Only then did Marie identify herself: "As to myself, I am the daughter of Dr. Syrkin and the wife of A. Bodansky who teaches here [Cornell]." The correspondence grew, over the years, as the salutation, "Dear Mr. Hurwitz" became, by the end of the thirties, "Dear Henry"; and by June of 1942, Hurwitz would write thanking Marie for "a beautiful review of a beautiful subject. I expected no less of you," he continues, "In fact, you never disappoint me! Which I must take care to note in my 'ethical will,' for thus only can I repay you. Even so, that'll be more selfish on my part than anything else; I might hope to survive a little if in after years it will be noted, in the *Life and Letters of Marie Syrkin*, that she was spoken of also by the fellow who was for some years editor of an obscure and precarious candelabrum periodical" (Archives f. 14).

A graph of Marie's sense of herself, both as a woman and as an intellectual, would depict inclines as well as some slumps; her maturation was neither in a straight line nor did it occur overnight. True, the disastrous years between 1920 and 1924 had left her in a weakened emotional condition, but not so weak that she could not take the first steps to recovery—and as the proverbial caution says, the first step is the hardest. Her first step was her move to New York and separation from Aaron Bodansky. Fortunately, shoring up her shaky self-image at this critical time were several invitations to join new publications, as well as bids to participate in public Jewish events. Later, in the 1980s when I asked about the development of her growing reputation in the mid to late 1920s, she summoned up a number of events that, she said, testified to her growing reputation. Quite proudly, she mentioned that the first of these was in connection with the opening of the Hebrew University in Jerusalem. Although twelve foundation stones for the University had been set on Mount Scopus on July 24, 1918, and the first faculty did not begin teaching until seven years later, when Albert Einstein provided the very first lecture in 1923, the ceremonial opening of the institution had to wait until April 1, 1925. Arthur Balfour had opened that dramatic and moving convocation, attended by such dignitaries as the High Commissioner Sir Herbert Samuel, General Allenby, Chaim Weizmann, Hayim Bialik, Ahad Ha'am, Chief Rabbi Kook, and the Chancellor, Rabbi Judah Magnes. Marie did not attend the actual ceremonies in Palestine, but she was invited by Meyer Weisgal to participate in the creation of a special commemorative issue of the *New Palestine* that was devoted entirely to the opening of the Hebrew University. This, she insisted, showed that by the mid 1920s she had already established herself as a committed Zionist.

True, by the time Marie had broken with Maurice Samuel, her reputation in the Zionist world was beginning to grow, but in the world of Yiddish literature her translations of articles and poetry from the Yiddish and Russian had already made her name quite prominent. As proof-tale of her growing literary reputation at the time, she offered a self-ironic anecdote that she regarded as an "hilarious story." The famous Soviet poet of the early years of the Russian Revolution, Vladimir Mayakovsky, arrived in New York in 1926 and was met by a group of Yiddish poets. No one else, Marie claimed, was interested in attending. But to the Yiddish poets, she explains, "he is their *tovarisch;* they are his *tovarishki.*" Marie has been invited on the strength of her burgeoning reputation as a translator. The group immediately went to a café on the Lower East Side—a favorite haunt of the immigrant literati, where they sat around a table drinking tea in glasses with lemon and cubes of sugar. Mayakovsky, however, was disgruntled because this was not what he came to America for; he felt slighted by the Americans. These were only Yiddish poets. In his irritation, he turned to Marie and said something sexually provocative — to which she responded in Russian, "Go to hell!" But that response seemed to please him and he became apologetic. Knowing that she was considered to be a fine translator, he baited her to come to his hotel so he could discuss her translations. "He is an absolutely stunning guy," she explained, "tall, magnificent." Now, admitting that she was tremendously flattered and thrilled to be doing something so scandalous, she confessed that she naively agreed. But as soon as she entered the room, he tried to embrace her. Horrified, she resisted, and tried to say something in Russian, "but," she reported regretfully, "I didn't know how to express myself very well so it came out as 'it's not serious,' and Mayakovsky replied 'Oh God! Nothing serious.'" Laughing at herself, Marie concludes her tale as Mayakovsky backed off and "using the *carpe diem* method" said in Russian, "You're pretty, but your teeth are a little black." Moreover, she claimed that she had convinced him completely that she had no intentions of accepting his philanderings, but she still wished to do the translations. They made an appointment for that, but she never showed up (Personal interview).

In 1989, when Marie recounted this episode, she used it to illustrate her growing reputation. But in her self-deprecatory mode of telling, it revealed something more about her history and personality: At the age of almost ninety, she continued to think of herself in sexual terms and to enjoy spinning yarns of her youthful romantic adventures, though they often ended in self-deprecation. It is perhaps for these reasons that Marie added a totally private recollection to the tale of Marie versus Mayakovsky. The event had taken place a month or two before the termination of her resumed affair with Maurice. She immediately reported the Mayakovsky story to her lover, who, she said, "behaved as if his heart were broken." So, she asked him what *he* would do if a great poet with a great reputation who was very beautiful had made a pass at him. His instant reply was, "You couldn't hold me down." But he added, "Nevertheless, it hurts me." "So I didn't keep the appointment," Marie admitted. "Well, this was my true love — was I going to be false to my true love? If it hurts him? And, I think, two months later [Maurice] was giving me the . . . he was through — or something like that" (Personal interview).

Adding to her contention that the breakthrough in her journalistic career had already occurred by the late 1920s, Marie embarked on another signature self-ironic yarn. This one concerned her invitation to join the editorial staff of *Reflex,* a new monthly Jewish magazine with cultural interests. Begun in 1927 by S. M. Melamed, its mission as stated in its editorial was "to report and interpret the realities of modern American Jewish life. . . . It sponsors no creed or doctrine. It pretends no mission. . . . Every phenomenon of importance, every creative figure will be viewed." At the outset, the articles were timely in subject, and had been written by well-known figures in the Jewish world, both European and American, including Alexander Goldenweiser, Moses Gaster, S. A. Dubnow, Isaac Goldberg, Franz Oppenheimer, Maximilian Harder, Maurice Samuel, and Marie Syrkin.[6] It is interesting to note that by 1927, Maurice Samuel already had distinguished himself as a writer and speaker; and although Marie was beginning to be known, she did not yet have the prominence of the other figures. "My name was on it as an assistant editor," Syrkin stated, "and I was very proud of myself—it seemed so wonderful to me, to be named as an editor—a big shot" (Personal interview). Yet, the only things that she could remember—or that she cared to speak of—regarding her brief employment at *Reflex* was that the editor was a scoundrel and the theater critic took advantage of her by promising her theater tickets if she would write the reviews. He never gave her the tickets, he signed the reviews she wrote, and she was never reimbursed. But when asked if she might have been invited to join the staff because of her father's notability she strongly demurred.

Marie Syrkin's third proof-tale in her case that she had begun to make a name for herself by the late 1920s was an improbable but true account of her "encounter with Jabotinsky." Marie had no trouble recalling this episode and launched into it without hesitation and with anticipatory amusement—though it was not a very good piece of evidence. Vladimir Jabotinsky was a commanding figure in the history of Zionist activism. A quintessential Renaissance Jew, polylingual and charismatic, he was the architect and leader of the Revisionist movement; he also was a scholar of the Hebrew language, a poet, a dramatist, a compelling orator, a polemical journalist, the founder of the Jewish legion in World War I, the mentor of the Zionist youth movement *Betar,* the organizer of the underground Jewish self-defense organization in mandatory Palestine known as the *Haganah,* a disciple of Herzl's vision of Zionism—hence, a proponent of a Jewish State (not a national homeland), and one that would be established on "both banks of the Jordan." Moreover, Jabotinsky was an opponent of socialist-Zionism, and an antagonist of

David Ben-Gurion. In 1935, he took the Revisionist movement out of the World Zionist Organization and formed the New Zionist Organization, which was dedicated to the evacuation of 1.5 million East European Jews to Palestine, to opposition to the partition plan of the British Peel Comission in favor of militant self-defense and anti-Arab terrorist tactics, as well as to opposition to the Zionist policy of *Havlaga* (self-restraint). Jabotinsky often has been credited as the ideological ancestor of the Israeli political right.[7]

With regard to the adventures of Marie Syrkin in 1927, why did this enemy of Ben-Gurion and socialist Zionism come calling on a fledgling American woman poet *cum* journalist? Jabotinsky had come to America on one of his many fund-raising lecture tours, perhaps as well as to activate Jewish American youth for *Betar*, the militaristic Revisionist youth movement. A man of many ideas, he also thought that there ought to be an English language journal devoted to his recently formed Revisionist movement. He contacted Marie Syrkin and her friend Joseph Brainin, the son of the well-known Hebrew language journalist and literary critic, Reuven Brainin, and invited them to be on the editorial board of the new publication he had envisioned. The two were more than pleased to be asked; indeed, they were flattered that such a celebrity had contacted them. Of course, they knew his politics and were opposed to it, but Jabotinsky's fame and glamour were too much to withstand. "He was irresistible," Marie confessed. She was starstruck enough to agree to meet this highly sophisticated, urbane man of the world, for dinner. But little could she imagine that he would take her to the Cotton Club in Harlem.

It was the 1920s Jazz Age and the height of the Harlem Renaissance when, as the poet Langston Hughes put it, "the Negro was in vogue." Harlem became a major attraction for New Yorkers and tourists as black American artists, such as Countee Cullen, James Weldon Johnson, Langston Hughes, Zora Neale Hurston, Duke Ellington, Ethel Waters, among a catalogue of now celebrated African-American names, began to express their unique culture in music, painting, literature, and all varieties of art and entertainment. It was also a time when white American artists such as as George Gershwin, Jerome Kern, and Marc Connelly began to tap the African-American culture for new forms and idioms. And it was prohibition as well, and speakeasies were blossoming throughout the Harlem streets, sprouting exotic nightflowers known as clubs, such as the celebrated Cotton Club on Lenox Avenue, clubs that made Harlem a mecca not only for blacks, but for whites too, who were drawn to this indigenous culture of nightlife, jazz, blues, erotic dancing, and open rebellion against the regnant sexual mores.

As improbable as it seems, Vladimir Jabotinsky escorted Marie Syrkin to one of these clubs on the evening that she agreed to meet with him. It is not very hard to understand why the urbane Jabotinsky wanted to patronize so trendy an establishment, but why he thought it would be appropriate for Marie is open to conjecture.

When the Jabotinsky party arrived at the club, Marie recalled, she was ushered into a dimly lit smoke-filled room. "There were only black people in the place," she recalled. People were sitting at tables and drinking; men and women were on the dance floor, engaging in what Marie thought was outrageously erotic. Although by this time, Marie had been married twice and had had a return engagement with her first love, she appears to have been surprisingly prudish. In fact, her report of this event some six decades later continued to express discomfort. In addition to Marie's shock at the Harlem club's licentious ambience, she also overheard someone in the party whisper to Jabotinsky, "Why are you bothering with this girl?" To which Jabotinsky answered, *sotto voce,* "her name is important." Marie was horrified and the next day she told Joe Brainin what had happened; the two now acknowledged the truth—it was "Brainin" and "Syrkin" that Jabotinsky was after. Not Marie and Joe. They were ashamed of their acquiescence, appalled at their own naiveté, and quickly agreed not to be seduced by fame. Then they had to decide who would break the news to the great man, as Marie put it, "Naturally, it fell to me." She made an appointment to meet Jabotinsky the next day. This time he suggested an ice cream parlor. When they met, she quickly broke the news of their defection. Jabotinsky's response was avuncularly patronizing. He patted her on the head and said, "That's all right little girl—would you like an ice cream?" It was a put-down Marie never forgot; she consigned it to her inventory of self-deprecating tales of woe, and she enjoyed the telling of it (Personal interview).

Although Marie Syrkin chose to use this episode to demonstrate her growing reputation in the world of journalism, she knew that it wasn't a very good piece of evidence. But it was a very good story; and as a good journalist, she knew it.

Despite the humiliation of the Jabotinsky episode, it *was* true that by 1927 Marie Syrkin had begun to make a name for herself. In addition to her high school teaching, she had been writing and editing for *The New*

Palestine since she had returned to New York after the death of her father. Moreover, her living situation had become easier. As her son, David Bodansky, remembers, in 1927, "she joined Masha at the home of Mrs. Epstein, who was the widow of a family friend, and a godsend to all of us—as home maker and child caretaker" (E-mail, June 11, 2005).

But what about Marie's social life now that Maurice Samuel once again was out of the picture, as was Eugenia Shafran who had met and soon married a painter named Marc Peter Ganbarg, a devout socialist (probably communist) who had absolutely no sympathy for Zionism. Marc insisted that Eugenia completely break her ties to her current friends. She did; but not before she entrusted Marie with a box of letters from her friends and family, asking her to keep them for her. This Marie did, not knowing that the trove included some significant letters to and from herself, as well as from Maurice Samuel. Marie kept the box throughout her life, though Eugenia had all but disappeared from Marie's world by the late 1920s.

Enter, Charles

Marie Syrkin now was free to move on, to make new friends and remake her life. Sometime in 1927, she received a phone call from a gentleman named Charles Reznikoff. His was not a completely unfamiliar name; while doing graduate work at Cornell, she had come across a slim volume of poetry, privately printed, written by one Charles Reznikoff. Marie was not terribly impressed because, at the time, she had been working on the poetry of Francis Thompson, whose romantic verse seemed to her the epitome of poetic accomplishment. "I remember thinking patronizingly of the vanity of private publication," Marie was later to write in her personal memoir for a volume of essays devoted to Charles Reznikoff (Hindus). "My particular friend at Cornell was Laura Reichenthal, later Laura Riding, and I had already been exposed to strains of modernist verse. But the culture had not taken. My first reaction to Charles' free verse was negative. Today more than sixty years later," she confessed, "I like to think that anyone with the prescience to hang on to one of the little books I dismissed would have had a valuable collector's item."[8]

Back in 1920, with a flick of her hand, the book of verse by Reznikoff was closed. And it remained closed for seven years. Then, in 1927, Marie

Syrkin came across another poem by Charles Reznikoff. This time his poem entitled "Rashi" had been published in a special edition of *The New Palestine*. Inevitably, she saw it. "A friend who knew the poet told me that he was a curious chap with a sense of his poetic vocation, and a lawyer admitted to the bar who declined to practice.[9] We agreed that, whatever the idiosyncrasies of the author, 'Rashi' had some splendid, quotable lines" (*Man and Poet* 37). A few months later, Charles Reznikoff called Marie regarding a literary project that later she could not recall. She invited him to come see her. "First impression?" Marie asks herself in her memoir of Charles. She immediately answers:

A neatly dressed moderately nice-looking young man, average in height, dark hair, soft nearsighted brown eyes, with no striking features and nothing in his appearance to suggest bohemian non-conformity. In fact he was quite unlike my vision of a literary man; a vision formed by having met a number of unruly specimens. But I was promptly re-assured. Whatever the original purpose of his visit, this got lost in a conversation during which, with few preliminaries, I was given an outline of his life. (*Man and Poet* 38)

Charles told her that he was thirty-three years old—she was twenty eight. He also told her that he had become a lawyer—but did not wish to practice. A cousin insisted on procuring his services, but Charles lost the case. Regarding this event, Marie comments, "a happy development that freed him from further family solicitations." At sixteen, he had enrolled in the school of journalism at the University of Missouri "under the impression that journalism was the road to a writer's career. Realizing his error after his freshman year, he had returned home to Brooklyn to explain to his bewildered parents, hard-working Russian Jewish immigrants, that writing and journalism were antithetical crafts." Marie's account next points out that, after much parental insistence, he began to study law at night while working in the family millinery business by day. In 1927, however, he no longer sold hats, but he did receive an allowance of twenty-five dollars a week from the family business, as Marie put it, "for labors past." Now, she added, "he could devote himself wholly to his poetry. And the heartaches of not being published no longer troubled him. No more rejection slips. He was his own printer and publisher. To a drudge like myself," Marie confessed, "this was the liberated life. I was charmed by his simplicity and impressed by his assurance" (*Man and Poet* 37–38). And so began the love of Charles and Marie. It would last, on and off, for more than forty-five years. Nonetheless, the semi-amused, semi-ironic tone of Marie's description of their first meeting, written after his death in 1975, reveals the strains of marriage to a man she loved, but whose utter impracticality could try her patience and send her packing.

Chapter 7

A New Life

Charles

WITHIN A YEAR of their first meeting, Marie Syrkin and Charles Reznikoff decided to marry. But that did not—could not—happen for two more years. In 1928, divorce law required consent of both parties, and even this long after their separation Aaron Bodansky withheld his consent. During the first two years of their relationship, Marie and Charles wrote to each other a couple of times: once after her birthday; again when he was sick; and then during the summer of 1929, when Marie and her son David had gone to spend the school vacation at the beach in Averne, near the Rockaways on the south shore of Long Island. The Rockaway peninsula during the 1920s and 1930s was a beach town with hotels, bungalows, and rooming houses that catered to New Yorkers looking for an escape from the heat and humidity of airless New York City apartments. It was closer to the city than Belmar, New Jersey, which might have had unpleasant associations for Marie, and no doubt Averne was cheaper. Marie's first letters to Charles betray a certain restraint, some lack of emotional color. The first extant letter from Marie to Charles is dated March 22, 1928. It was her twenty-ninth birthday and the two had been seeing each other for about a year. Here is Marie's thank-you letter to a man who obviously cares for her: "As you did not come up to-night I wanted to thank you for the collection of charming things you left with me yesterday when I was too excited to do them justice. The roses are beautiful; the scarf, a woolen gossamer, and the honey from Hymettus, bland to the palate and lovely to look at. I suppose I will see you just a little after you get this note, but I felt the con-

trast between my last night's abruptness and your graciousness so dis-
agreeably that I wanted to make some amends."

This cool apology is immediately followed by a self-question begging
for an answer:

Why the devil do I sound so formal? . . . I feel that I ought to continue an
epistolary tradition started by you — so if you'll wait a second, I'll think of
something.

> Intermission (3 minutes)
> Chorus to be chanted by love-lorn ladies clad in Greek robes:
> "The sweetest thing that a guy
>> can get us
> Is surely honey from Mt. Hymettus!!"

I hope you don't crack a knuckle from laughing at the neat wit of this couplet.

Having concluded in a blaze of informality, I consider the situation saved on
all fronts and remain,
> Lovingly yours,

Marie
XXXXX (Archives f. 15)

This is a cute letter, but not one that promises high passion. Indeed,
the "lovingly" of the sign-off is formulaic — it is the very phrase that
Marie will use throughout her life to close her letters to many friends —
male and female — whom she favors. And the five *X*s placed in the lower
left-hand corner have the feeling of afterthought. As for the verse itself,
Marie would be addicted to this mode of witty ditty all her life — even
under extremely serious circumstances.

It is true that Marie Syrkin has stated that within a year of their meeting in 1927, she and Charles Reznikoff made the decision to marry; and,
as Marie herself many years later pointed out, it is also true that "initial
formalities took a bit longer than is now the fashion" (*Man and Poet*,
38). Nevertheless, her self-consciously facetious letter of January 7, 1929,
written about two years after they had met, still retains those early initial formalities. Marie writes to Charles that his brother had called her
to tell her that Charles would be confined to bed for a number of days.
"It was a most inauspicious conversation," she reports: "He said, 'He is
in bed,' and I, alarmed at your failure to speak in person, misunderstood

him (think of the most disagreeable rhyme for 'bed'). However he proceeded to reassure me, but I was left sorely shaken" (Archives f. 15).

In the year between their meeting in 1927, the time between the birthday letter of March 22, 1928, and the letter of January 1929, the emotional level of Marie's involvement with Charles seems to have remained static. Her light-hearted letter is self-consciously chipper, dryly
witty, and a bit precious; her premarital ardor appears surprisingly tame.
Of course, one can understand that Marie might not want to jeopard-
ize her divorce situation, for in 1929 adultery was a major issue; moreover, there is a suggestion of secrecy regarding Charles's open receipt of
mail from Marie. Charles was living at home with his parents and his
brother and sister. Perhaps he was reluctant to tell them about his plans.
Would they leak the secret to someone who might know Aaron? Not
likely. Whatever the explanation, nothing in Marie's next letter to Charles
from Averne calls to mind ardent love, except for a few suggestions for
a way that he might visit her while Aaron would be away at a scientific
conference and not likely to show up to see his son. (Is this a forbidden
interlude?) After a long account of her conflict with her landlady, she
adds "And how are you, my friend? I have thought much and kindly
about you these days" (Archives f. 15). Even in this late summer note,
Marie's style remains seasonably dry.

In any case, despite several obstacles that stood in the way, Charles
and Marie remained committed to their marital plans. First was the
issue of Aaron's refusal to give consent. Second, the two of them realized that they had a problematic financial situation. Charles had the
twenty-five dollars a week that he received from the family business;
Marie had her teaching salary, sixty dollars a week that barely covered
living expenses, as she set aside half for her son. Marie has explained her
acceptance of their fiscal complications as follows:

One role that Charles was never prepared to assume was the bourgeois one of
a good provider. Superficially there was nothing bohemian in his behavior: he
did not womanize, drink or even smoke; he was often prissily prudish. All in all
quite the reverse of the stereotype of the manic poet. But on a more fundamental level he rejected the basic conventions as to how life should be led. He would
assume no obligations, such as support of a family, that might hamper his true
vocation. I respected his poetry enough to sympathize wholly with his view,
particularly as I found myself in economic bondage because of my responsibilities. So we agreed lightheartedly that since he had enough income to meet his

share — the $25 a week — we would set up housekeeping as soon as I could get a divorce. (*Man and Poet* 40)

Reno

Getting the divorce, however, was not so simple. In order to accomplish this as quickly as possible, Marie had to establish residence in Reno, Nevada, by living there for three months. Reno law was notorious for its "quickie divorce" conditions. During the early nineteenth century, Nevada and other frontier territories had very loose residency requirements for divorce, but by the later decades of the century, perhaps due to progressively stringent Victorian moral attitudes, divorce law in the United States began to grow increasingly rigid. Nevada, which became a state in 1864, had a six-months residency law until 1913. By the end of the nineteenth century, however, clever Eastern divorce attorneys were taking great advantage of the "quickie divorce" laws available in Nevada. In 1913 reformers convinced the legislature to change the requirement of six-months residency to a one-year requirement; this, however, made Nevada no easier than most of the other states, hence, it resulted in big financial losses to local businesses. Two years later, in 1915, successful business lobbies forced residency back to six months, and by 1927, the tremendous increase in income from the divorce enterprise drove the requirement back even further to three months. Marie Syrkin's divorce came three years later, in 1930, but had she waited one more year, in 1931 the residency requirement was further reduced to only six weeks![1]

Legendary Reno, the so-called "Divorce Capital of the World," became the infamous oasis for the unhappy marriages of the rich and famous, such as "America's Sweetheart," Mary Pickford, or the millionaire Cornelius Vanderbilt, bringing millions of dollars to the State of Nevada as well as to attorneys throughout the United States. In the mid-twentieth century, such contemporary ideas as equitable distribution, no-fault divorce, and pre-nuptial agreements were nowhere to be seen on the radar screen of spousal strife.

Marie Syrkin Bodansky arrived in Reno on February 6, 1930. She began a three-month correspondence with Charles Reznikoff during her train ride to Nevada on the San Francisco Limited. After her arrival in "divorce city," she wrote to Charles that she had gone immediately to see her Reno lawyer, whom she described as a "big, florid fellow who, I trust, knows his business. He made no attempt to raise the fees specified but indicated that I was getting rates so low-cut, that I began to feel like a charity patient. I was on the verge of giving him an additional $50, but restrained that impulse." Following the encounter with the lawyer, she set about to find a place to stay and settled on a rooming house at 132 Island Avenue, Reno. This first letter, dated February 6, 1930, written to Charles from Reno, ends with the fact that she is too weary and too lonely to write any more. "I wish you were here." Marie laments, "We could have a lovely time. There are mountains and snow. It would be nice. I venture to enclose my love" (Archives f. 16).

Marie's temporary quarters did very little to cheer her up. She rented "a large dingy room with 3 windows" for which she paid thirty dollars a month. "This sum," she informs Charles in her letter of February 8, "includes housekeeping privileges. The room is furnished with derelict remnants of all eras — mostly early American patched up with later American. There is a plenitude of doilies, cushions, bureaus, rocking chairs, decorative lamps in pink and blue gauze, floral wall-paper, etc." The house was owned by a Swedish woman and, despite Marie's "pathetic efforts to become acquainted with [her] fellow room-mates," she does not yet "know a soul in the house. . . . The strange, painted ancient female across the way makes no effort to meet me half-way," she complains, and "neither do the equally bepainted younger females whom I glimpse hopefully *en route* to the bathroom. If the lawyer had not assured me that this was a respectable house I would be very skeptical of my milieu. As far as I can tell, these seem to be native low-class 'goyim.' My sense of direction being what it is, I suppose I shall discover on the eve of my departure that I have been living with the grandmother of Woodrow Wilson who married a Viking. The landlady's name is Jensen" (Archives f. 16).

The subsequent correspondence between Marie Syrkin and Charles Reznikoff provides a much clearer picture of their relationship than does the extant one-sided correspondence between Maurice Samuel and Marie. This time, since both sides of the exchange of letters have been preserved, there is an unobstructed window on the nature of their romantic involvement as well as their individual personalities. That they love each other is apparent; but it is a form of love quite different from Marie's ardent passion for Maurice Samuel or her cooler marriage to Aaron Bodansky. It is quieter, more restrained, more aware of very clear differences. On the whole, Charles was gentler and almost ingenuous, less demanding, not so volatile, but then, perhaps, less exciting than Maurice; he also was much more aware of and accepting of Marie's needs than Aaron — unless provoked. He was in no way a father figure, as Aaron Bodansky may have been. Milton Hindus, the Reznikoff scholar and close friend of Marie and Charles, has observed, "it is amply evident that the marriage was far from being purely romantic and uncalculated (at least on her part)."[2] There is another difference that bears noting: At thirty-one, this was Marie's third marriage; at thirty-six it was Charles' first. As Hindus has commented, "it was an unequal match" (*Letters* 11).

Charles Reznikoff presented a stark contrast to the other men who had figured in Marie's life up until this point, including her father. An intensely private man, Charles Reznikoff was a poet of the simple life, of ordinary things. His work was a fanfare for the common man played on an oboe. But he could be provoked, and then his dry humor would slyly slip into sarcasm; and he could be provoked most of all by jealousy. Of course, he was quite aware of Marie's prior marriages; nonetheless, in a letter written to her just after she had arrived in Reno, his jealousy fairly springs off the page. Charles had been invited to dinner at the home of Elliot Cohen, the managing editor of *Menorah Journal,* an important publication that had begun in association with the Jewish college student organization, the Harvard Menorah Society. Organized by Henry Hurwitz in 1906, it later grew into an American, campus-wide Menorah Association. Hurwitz, the founder and editor of *Menorah Journal,* had come to America from Lithuania at the age of six, and later was greatly influenced at Harvard by the humanist philosophy of George Santayana and William James. Deeply conscious of the values of his own heritage and sensitive to the antisemitism around him, Hurwitz hoped to promote the study of humanistic values in Judaism in the Association and to dedicate the *Journal* to these values as well. Among *Menorah*'s early contributors were people of great distinction, such as Louis Brandeis, Mordecai Kaplan, Harry Wolfson, Charles W. Eliot, Solomon Schechter, and Israel Zangwill. From the very outset, under the direction of Henry Hurwitz, a man of creative intellect and taste, the publication was devoted to *belles lettres,* fine arts, music, and philosophy. The roster of those published in the pages of *Menorah Journal* was an encyclopedic list of great names in Jewish as well as non-Jewish art and thought in America. It was certainly not accidental that Marie Syrkin published her earliest work (translations of Yiddish poetry into

English) and Charles Reznikoff published some of his early poems in this wide-ranging cultural record of contemporary Jewish creativity. The peak of *Menorah's* influence came in 1929, at a dinner given by wealthy contributors—such as New York Congressman Lucius N. Littauer and Chicago investment banker S. W. Straus—when the establishment of a Menorah Foundation was announced. Sadly, seven months later, the Crash of 1929 would be a major cause of the gradual decline of *Menorah's* strength. It ceased publication in 1962.[3]

It was Reznikoff's long association with *Menorah Journal* that prompted Elliot Cohen's dinner invitation to Charles, though the details of the letter make one wonder whether Cohen had some kind of a mischievous motive in his choice of guests. Two days after Marie had arrived in Reno, on February 9, Charles reported to her:

At Elliot's I found he had another guest for dinner—Maurice Samuel. During the dinner Samuel was telling us about a book he was writing on culture: the theme, I understood him to say, was that culture must be divorced from government and a general condemnation of the mob. He used big words and important names—Spinoza and the modern philosophers. He was very glib. Elliot and I picked his arguments to pieces: they were very feeble stuff. We were all very good-natured about it; and he ended up by saying, that if he were not so sure of himself, we two might disturb him. He is furious at what he calls the mob and their idols—such as [Rabbi Stephen] Wise and [Rabbi] Hillel Silver. "Oh no," I said, "these are very small idols, local gods: Herzl was a fraud." The man is an out-and-out charlatan, Marie, I mean Samuel.

Charles' jealousy is barefaced, and he did not hide it from Marie. The entire exchange between Maurice Samuel and Charles Reznikoff is electric with male posturing—two rival male peacocks strutting for first place with the female. The face-off began as the ardent Zionist, Maurice Samuel, lashed out at two enormously popular American Zionist leaders, Rabbis Wise and Silver. Charles' report of his rejoinder to Maurice that the two rabbis are merely local gods, followed by his barb that Herzl was a fraud, is as much about Reznikoff's dispassionate Zionism as it is about his green-eyed view of Samuel. Marie's name is never mentioned in the entire exchange (though Charles reports that Samuel told a "beautiful story" about Nachman Syrkin). Charles was all too aware of the part Maurice Samuel had played in Marie's life, and Samuel knew that presently Charles was much involved with Marie.

Extremely unsettled by the episode, Reznikoff's letter continues:

I won't go into Samuel's ideas: they are shallow and false as ideas and as history—
well, I won't go into them. After Samuel was gone, Elliot said to me, "Do you
still see Marie Syrkin?" I suppose we have been seen together, "Yes," I said.
"Where is she now?" "In Reno" I said. Then he talked about you for some time.
I was uncertain whether to tell him that we were going to be married, but I decided not to, since that might make trouble now if it got about. . . . But on the
way home, I was very sorry I told him that you were in Reno. When I thought
that Samuel might come out to see you, by the anguish I felt and still feel, I
know how I feel about you. I am not jealous of him; but I am afraid that taking you by surprise in your loneliness—I think of it as of a snake creeping on
its belly toward a dove. O, I know Samuel isn't a snake, but, sometimes, in your
generosity, in your simplicity, you are such a dove.

Despite his disclaimer, Reznikoff's jealousy knew little restraint. This,
in the face of the fact that in the early 1920s Samuel had written a very
positive review in *Jewish Tradition* of Reznikoff's *Three Plays*. Charles'
emotional imagination see-saws down and up, alternately from invec-
tive directed at Maurice Samuel to sentiments of adoration for Marie.
"I cannot begin to tell you how I feel about you," he maintains. But he
does tell her:

Perhaps it will take me the rest of my life. To begin with, I feel towards you like
a father. I want desperately to shield you, to feed you, to clothe you, to take care
of you—and yours; and then I feel toward you like a son, I want to tell you all
my petty victories and my defeats, to have you reproach me and give me your
advice; and then, of course, always, I think of you as companion and wife.
(When we are married, we must be married by a rabbi; it would be intolerable
to be married by a clerk.) You are all woman in one to me—all women I ever
saw, that ever passed me in the street, that I ever wanted to meet. I have only
one wish: to be wise, do the best for yourself. Now that you are away, I see
clearly how much you mean, I see all your beauty, nobility, and innocence.
When I think how often I used to say that my work meant more to me than
anybody, I see how childish that was: I kiss your hand, the hem of your dress,
the ground before your feet.

Still, the smarting Charles can't let it go. Straightaway, he launches a
new attack on his rival as he reports further inquiries from Elliot Cohen:

Elliot said, "What a fool that supposedly great and wise man Dr. Syrkin was to
break up the marriage of his daughter and Samuel." I wonder what he would say
now if he saw what Samuel is now? "What would he say," I answered, "what
would a man trained in philosophy as Dr. Syrkin was say if he heard the twaddle
Samuel was talking so pompously tonight? . . . However, I am sure Dr. Syrkin
would not have thought much of me either as a son-in-law—and he may be right.

That assessment is no doubt correct. Charles' barely visible reputation
in 1930 was certainly not anything to write home about, nor was his
pedigree: his immigrant parents had a millinery business in Brooklyn;
his maternal grandfather, according to family tradition, "had also been
a poet, but his verses in Hebrew had been lost, for he had made his living as a peddler and had died on one of his trips" (*Man and Poet* 16). But
as Reznikoff's chief advocate, Milton Hindus had to admit when refer-
ring to Nachman Syrkin's interference and annulment of Marie's marriage to Maurice Samuel, "It was a decision, however justified at the time,
that would haunt his daughter for the rest of her life, despite the almost
worshipful attitude she had towards her great father. . . . Her resentment
was no doubt exacerbated by the fact that her young lover [Samuel] soon
attained celebrity as a writer not only in the Jewish circles frequented by
her father and his comrades but in the larger arena of American literature"
(*Letters* 19). Ironically, by the beginning of the twenty-first century, with
all parties long dead, it is Reznikoff who has the more lasting reputation—a name that rests mainly on the kind of poetry that he had included in this letter of February 1930, a verse that seeks to express his
longings for Marie through image, brevity, irony, and point:

> It is stupid to be thinking about you
> As much as I do; for such thoughts
> Do nobody good: it is not even wool-gathering.
> I sat in the reading room as I used to,
> But instead of reading, thought of you:
> I thought if I should wait for you
> As in other days, I'd have to wait a long time.

He adds:

> I meant to send you something cheerful; forgive me—
> But laughter is gone in a second, tears last a minute or two
> (*Letters* 75–78).

What woman could resist the soft-spoken seduction of such tender thoughts? Certainly not Marie, whose love for Charles had so much to do with her love for his poetry.

Charles' needs appeared to be rather simple to Marie. First and foremost, he wanted the freedom to write; he wanted no responsibilities that would prevent this, including the responsibilities of finances and family. But this did not mean that he loved Marie any less. She thought that these were conditions that would not stand in the way of the development of her own autonomy. Milton Hindus, friend to both parties, has suggested that although on Marie's part the marriage was deliberately thought-out, "it was also far from being the tragic mismatch depicted in the posthumously published [Reznikoff novel] *The Manner Music*. What bound them together most was the love they shared for literature" (*Letters* 11). Charles loved Marie deeply and fully, that she knew; but neither one knew then, that years later he would be hurt deeply, fully, by her.

From the outset, Marie's side of the Reno correspondence shows emotional restraint. Of course she still had real fears that if Aaron knew of their intention to marry he might revoke his needed consent. Indeed, so careful was she to maintain secrecy that at this late date, Charles had not yet met Marie's son David for fear he might expose their plans. Apparently, he had not accepted Marie's summer invitation to Averne for he describes his first meeting with David in his letter of March 2, 1930. Charles had arrived at Marie's Bronx apartment and rang the bell, unaware that Aaron, who had taken David and Zivia for the day, had not yet left.

It seems that my coming was something of a mistake; your aunt intended that I should call *up* at that hour, not call. However, it was a happy mistake. Your aunt and Mrs. Epstein were at the head of the stairs, and I walked into the front room. In bounced your little sister, tricked out with red cloth, a piece wound about her waist and another about her head, full of laughter. She stopped and looked at me with a slightly amused glance. Following her was a boy, almost as tall as she, and I knew, of course that it was David. . . . (I had expected a tiny "puny" child, to use your expression). He wore a dark blue sweater with a thin red stripe in it (it seems he had just come back with Aaron), and yellow battered shoes. . . . He had just had a haircut and his black hair, so much like yours, was neatly combed. His dark eyes — just like yours, too — were full of fun." (*Letters*)

On March 5 Marie responded:

You are an angel. There is no doubt about it. Your account of the visit to my
home, and the evening with my aunt entitles you to heavenly honors — may
they long be kept waiting. I am glad that you had a pleasant evening and I am
glad that you saw David, but I think you had better not appear at the house. I
don't want Aaron to suspect anything until after May. (Archives f. 16)

Reno was a very dull place. It offered almost no pleasures to Marie,
who was trapped in this desert town for three months. There was little
to do and no place to go except the library, which she visited almost
daily. Deciding to make the most of her leisure, Marie set herself a plan:
she would read through all of Shakespeare — many of the plays she had
never before read — in search of a dissertation topic. Apparently, her
dreams of a Ph.D. in literature were still alive and she regularly reported
to Charles her findings regarding the plays. Marie's voracious reading
during her three months in Reno was extremely ecumenical. In addition
to Shakespeare, the list includes the contemporary imagist poet and
friend of Ezra Pound, Richard Aldington, the play *The Old Wives Tale*
by the Renaissance dramatist George Peele, the modern poet Edna St.
Vincent Millay (whom Marie admired and Charles disliked), *Farewell to
Arms* by Ernest Hemingway, a best-seller novel, *Ex-Wife,* by Ursula
Parrott — at first published anonymously in 1929 because of its seami-
ness. It was so popular that in 1930 pre-Code Hollywood, it was made
into a film for which Norma Shearer won an Oscar. In turn, Charles sent
her a report of his own writings — poems, prose, plays — all manner of
composition, and he urged her to continue her own poetry; Marie,
however, never refers to her own creative writing, although after her
death the creative work she had been doing on the quiet in Reno would
be discovered. They discuss Charles' financial situation. He now had
taken a job with the American Law Book Company, publishers of *Corpus Juris,* an encyclopedia of legal terms. His job was to compose
definitions and he says he is bedeviled by "proximate cause" among
other technical terms and would like to reduce his employment to half-
time so as to leave adequate time for what he considered his real
work — his writing. His employer, however, is reluctant to make such
an arrangement. It is 1930, after all, and the stock market crash of 1929
has made it very easy for employers to find replacements everywhere
(*Letters* 123–124).

Social Life in Reno

Marie's stint in Reno may not have afforded her much intellectual companionship, but it did provide her with the opportunity to meet the
kinds of people she otherwise never would have had the inclination to
befriend. One such woman was an oversized Jewish saleslady named
Jeanette. Marie writes that she keeps meeting this lady, and "she is incredibly funny." Jeanette is in Reno to get a divorce from Bertram because she fell in love with Max; but while in Reno she met a cantor who
was there to get a divorce and who began to woo her and make many
promises. Jeanette has told Marie that the cantor eats steak, and in so
doing does not observe the rules of kashrut (Archives f. 16).

Reno, in addition to being the divorce capitol of the country, was
also a hunting ground for the soon-to-be single man or woman. Marie
herself had been approached by a Jewish tailor whom she politely had
refused and about whom she had written to Charles. In the letter about
the lovelorn Jeanette, Marie adds, "It transpires that by refusing the attentions of the tailor . . . I refused the attention of the Sheik of the Jewish population. My sales-lady was aghast. I should have felt honored.
'He doesn't ask every Tom, Dick and Harry to go out; where do you see
a well dressed man?'" (Archives f. 16).

Marie Syrkin had a true gift for the comic. She had sharp eyes and
ears, and a satiric wit, but much of the time her routines would be at
her own expense. Charles wrote sketches too, but his, less comic, were
powerfully effective. One tremendously moving narrative sketch appears
in his letter of March 8, 1930. The time is four months post–October 29,
1929 — known as Black Tuesday — the worst day in U.S. Stock Market
history, the onset of the Great Depression. Although most of the letters
between the two do not reflect the rampant pathos and misery of the
time, and are primarily concerned with personal considerations and daily
routine, this vignette is a valuable social document and at the same time
attests to Charles' capacity for empathy and compassion; as such, it de-
serves full quotation. "Marie darling," he begins:

It is a habit of writers, I suppose to forget their own troubles by watching those
of others, and so I want to tell you — I suppose you have seen in the papers that
there is a lot of suffering in New York, many homeless men, many out of work.
They are not like the professional beggars — they don't come up to you and beg,

but pass you for the most part looking straight ahead. Last Sunday my cousin took us—father, sister, and myself—to the Bronx, in his automobile and he went through the Bowery. It was about 5 in the afternoon and there were many breadlines: the first I saw—the men were standing in squads of four or six close together and the line was all of a block long and turned around the corner. They were lined up next to the curb, and as we went swiftly past, I saw that one man was dead or had fainted. He was propped stiffly against a stoop—an old man, his hat off, and I could see his white hair and face white as limestone. No one was near him, he was all alone on the stoop, and the army of men in the bread-line stood in their places alongside the curb.

Charles continues his meditation on the suffering of destitute men in New York with an account of a more personal experience that he had with an impoverished gentleman. A few days later, he was about to enter Bickford's cafeteria for a cup of coffee, when

a man at the door murmured something about coffee. I put my hand in my pocket to give him a dime. "May I go in with you?" he said. "Certainly," I answered, and we went in together. He was a man of about fifty, his hair all grey, for he took his cap off as we went in, wearing rough clean clothes, his face extremely thin. We walked up to the counter, and I said to him, "What will you have?" He pointed to a cruller and said—timidly, the way a child might ask his father, "May I have one of these, sir, with my coffee?" "Don't you want something else first" I said. "How about some soup" "That would be fine sir." Bickford's serve[s] rolls instead of crackers with their soup. Now their soup is taste-less, I think, but their rolls are fine. I was thinking that heavier food might be bad for a hungry man, and, besides, I felt he ought to eat a little at a time. "Suppose you eat the soup now," I said, "and later we'll have something else." I ordered a cup of coffee and a slice of pineapple (thinking, here I am buying lux-uries) and followed him to his table. "I'll be sitting over there," he said as he left me with the soup. He was waiting for me, and began eating in the greatest hurry, "Take your time," I said, "I can't sir, I'm nervous" he answered. Then as he ate he said to me, "I was at the waterfront all day trying to get on a boat to work my way home to Maine. I come from Portland. I never thought I'd come to this." "One can never tell" I said just to show that I was interested.

After exchanging a few more sentences with the man, Charles thought he would go on to an art exhibit at the Modern Gallery on 57th Street and so excused himself saying that, although he had to go, the man

could remain in Bickford's as long as he wished. The little narrative continues as Charles apologetically tells Marie what he next said to the impoverished man:

"Now your check is 15c, here is 50c and get a cup of coffee and whatever else
you want," and . . . I wished him luck. He looked up at me and his face lit up
and his dull blue Yankee eyes glowed. I felt a little ashamed of myself because I
could have given him more than 50c (you would have); I felt cheap for having
bought so much thankfulness for so little—and went on to the pictures. . . . I
knew this man was genuinely in need; still, I could not at the moment think of
how to give him a little more help gracefully; because I was anxious to make
him feel that I was just a friend, that it was only an accident that I was not in his
place and he in mine and so I did nothing. (*Letters* 104–106)

Marie's response to this poignant and compassionate rendering of an
all-too-common depression story, as well as to Charles' own self scrutiny,
reveals her own capacity for empathetic kindness, as it establishes their
shared sensibility to human suffering. "Your letter," Marie responds,

describing your encounter with a starving man made me feel, as I often feel, the
indecent futility of publishing words and phrases when there is such a world
of misery at one's door. Yes, you should have given him more than fifty cents.
If it ever happens again please, honey, add an equal sum from me to what you
would normally give. I promise to refund faithfully. Though of course a few
cents are no solution. I suppose the valiant enter the struggle—as my father did
and so many of his friends. We are a craven breed unworthy of our ancestors.
(Archives f. 16)

This response underscores their common compassionate dispositions as well as their different temperaments. They are both deeply
moved by pity, that is true—but that pity urges Marie toward an as-yet-
untapped resource: her growing need to "enter the struggle" in an active manner. For Charles, there is no such need; they also serve who only
sit and write.

Marie's remark about the valiant who enter the struggle, however,
suggests a bit of guilty conscience as well as it provides a clue to her instinctive calling. "We are a craven breed unworthy of our ancestors," she
had concluded. Was Marie unconsciously preparing for a life that would

reflect her father's activism, but one that would be played out on her own terms; one that would acknowledge Charles' tendency to quiescence, but that would accommodate her activism to his essentially solitary nature?

Events in the World

Despite the fact that Marie Syrkin had been writing about Zionism in *New Palestine* for some time, her correspondence with Charles Reznikoff is astonishingly devoid of references to current events in the outside world. In the year just passed, 1929 to 1930, events in Palestine, in America, and in Europe, had been ominous. There had been a wave of violent Arab riots in Palestine in 1929, known as the disturbances, that had been incited by the Supreme Moslem Council. On August 23, more than a thousand Arabs fanned out from the Arab section of Jerusalem and attacked all the Jews they encountered in the Jewish sections of the city, ultimately killing 133 Jews and wounding 339. The British response to this was to refuse permission for the Jews to set up self-defense groups to protect their settlements. It was a pivotal moment in Palestinian Jewish/Arab problems. Because the Arab and Moslem countries gave financial and moral support to the Arab Palestinians, the conflict turned from a local problem into a pan-Arab, pan-Moslem issue. On the other side of the globe, on what has notoriously become known as Black Tuesday, October 29, 1929, the American stock market experienced the worst day in its history. By December 1, investors had lost $100 billion in assets, almost 50 percent of their value, bringing to an end the famous Roaring Twenties and signaling the beginning of the Great Depression. The market would continue its precipitous decline until it bottomed out in July of 1932, and it would take years for it to recover. Across the Atlantic, in Germany, there had been menacing signs. Hitler had been released in 1924 from Landsberg Prison, where he had written his infamous autobiography *Mein Kampf*. The volume expressed his repudiation of the humiliation of the World War I Versailles *Diktat* in a formulation of a political philosophy that called for the need for expansion of German land, the necessity of Aryanization, the vilification of the Jews as the source of corruption (hence the need to get rid of them), all to be accomplished through the medium of the Nazi Party. The ten years following Hitler's release were, in the words of Howard Sachar, a nightmare of inflation, then of depression, and always of corrosive, embittered nationalism. It was during this period that Hitler's hysterical and hypnotic oratory convinced hundreds of thousands of distraught German lower *Mittelstand* white-collar workers, the class which was the principal victim of the economic crisis of the 1920's, that the Nazi party was the one dependable instrument of Germany's salvation. . . . In 1930, when the world Depression forced hundreds of German banks and factories to close their doors, the Nazi's won 107 seats in the Reichstag and became Germany's second largest political power. (Sachar 509)

These were ominous times in 1930, and almost none of this is mentioned in the three months of letters between Marie and Charles. Instead, as the weeks of waiting crawl by, sentimental and generous Charles tried to bolster Marie's flagging spirits by sending her little gifts. He would like to buy her a watch, but she demurs and suggests a modest ring instead. To indicate the size, she measures her finger with a piece of string and sends it on to him with a further request: candy. Marie's birthday, March 22, approaches. Although Charles has mistaken the date of her birthday as March 25th, on the twentieth of the month, one part of his gift — perhaps the part she relishes most — arrives. "The candy arrived and is delicious," she exclaims. "At first I valiantly strove not to open it till the appointed day, but decided that the vexation of struggling with temptation would nullify the pleasure of the candy. On which philosophic note, I opened the box" (Archives f. 16). The old childhood craving for sweets has not abated; it has simply become the mature craving for sweets. Marie, however, is not in this alone; Charles apparently likes good food and tempting desserts as well, leading to a tendency to gain weight. Wishing to be attractive to Marie, on March 16, he confesses all: "I hope I can lose about ten pounds, for I am getting too fat." To this confession, the confessor replies on March 19, "So the capital is waning and the flesh is gaining!" (Archives f. 16).

The letters continue their back-and-forth banter: Charles tells her about his work, his friends, his critics, his continuing love for her. He tells her that Sam Roth, the villain of Marie's teenage love life, who also had published Reznikoff's *Poems* in 1920, has been sent to prison for pirating and publishing James Joyce's *Ulysses*. Charles writes further that he would like to come out to Nevada to meet Marie, but he doesn't say when; that his closest friend, the poet Louis Zukofsky, has applied for a job at Textile High School and doesn't get it; that Zukofsky also has applied for a Guggenheim fellowship, but doesn't get that either; that upon Zukofsky's suggestion, Charles has sent two of his stories to Ezra Pound who has been asked by a French magazine to translate them; and Zukofsky has told him that Clifton Fadiman "has informed [Lionel] Trilling and [Elliot] Cohen that he has no use for any of [Charles'] writing including the prose" (*Letters*, March 18).

In 1930, Clifton Fadiman and Lionel Trilling, both in their mid-twenties, were part of the group of writers who cohered around the *Menorah Journal*. They would soon move on to highly successful careers: Trilling will be the first Jew to hold the position of Professor of English Literature at Columbia University and will become the celebrated literary critic; Fadiman will assume the position of book editor of *The New Yorker* and will achieve wide, popular fame as an intellectual on the well-known radio program of the 1940s, *Information Please*. In October of 1930, however, Trilling published "Genuine Writing," a review in *Menorah Journal* in which he praises Reznikoff's short novel *By the Waters of Manhattan* for being "remarkable and original in American literature" (*Letters* 79). As their careers burgeoned and flourished, Trilling and Fadiman would distance themselves from *Menorah Journal*, Jewish interests, and Jewish subjects. But Trilling's early appreciation of Charles Reznikoff indicated his great gift of literary insight.

The month of March passed slowly. The library was seeing much of Marie. "I am reading 'War and Peace,'" she tells Charles. "It is a great book. The opening chapters are magnificent even though the translation is inept. The flavour of the style is missed entirely. . . . I took out a volume of *Twentieth Century Poetry* compiled by Drinkwater and Benet. Laura Riding is included. I didn't understand a word of either of her poems — literally not a word. Do you wonder that I blush at my weak-minded affection for the conventional giants. Well, it can't be helped."

Marie's assessment of Riding (nee Reichenthal) may not be altogether objective; perhaps there is an ounce or two of envy. Throughout the years after they left Cornell, the two women kept up a sporadic correspondence. Marie knew that Laura Riding, had gone off to Egypt with Robert Graves and his wife in 1926 (and later, would famously become Graves' "muse" for his celebrated book, *The White Goddess: A historical Grammar of Poetic Myth*). But by 1930, her poems had been appearing in Robert Penn Warren and Allen Tate's publication *The Fugitive* and Harriet Monroe's *Poetry*. Her own volumes, *The Close Chaplet* (1926) and *Voltaire: A Biographical Fantasy* (1927) were both published

by Virginia and Leonard Woolf. In 1926, Laura had written to Marie
that she had seen an old copy of the *New Palestine* and had learned of
the death of Nachman Syrkin. "Had I known of this sooner you should
certainly have heard from me sooner were it only the tiniest note," Riding apologizes. "I am deeply sorry, distressed for you." Laura Riding's
next words indicate that the two had certainly been in touch and that
Laura knew and cared about other troubles in her friend's life. "Life
hasn't been very good to you and death hasn't done much better by you,
has it? There is always the third of the trinity, but you are a quaint para-
dox who will, I'm afraid, always love Love better than loving." Discern-
ing words indeed. They must have been quite close in those Cornell
years, because so well did Laura Riding understand her college friend
that in 1926, she guessed at Marie's present living situation and gave her
some perceptive advice that may have lingered in the crannies of Marie's
mind for years, perhaps helping her to make certain decisions leading at
last to a self-directed life.

I am guessing that you have gone to New York and are living with your Aunt.
What is she doing, and have the two of you, I wonder, made some sort of
womanish household together. If only you can pull out. Marie, it doesn't matter
how, what the handle is you hang to. All the dignity goes out of life in a situation in which you can't even fool yourself. If you were temperamentally a cynic,
you would be safe, because in his own way the pessimist is a sort of romanticist
and has his refuges. But you do ask for every-day bread and not dreams, and the
sooner you make up your mind at least to try for it, the happier you'll be on the
whole. I've seen enough of it to feel this desperately for you. For the sake of
self-love or whatever else will move you, perhaps principally for David's sake,
stir out of it, no matter how. (Archives f. 13)

Marie may not have been able to "understand a word" of Laura Riding's poetry, but she understood all too well her friend's epistolary
words; and perhaps, they came back to her when she found Laura Riding's poems anthologized in the volume of *Twentieth Century Poetry*.
Perhaps, by contrast, Laura's career reminded Marie of her own desire
to do creative work and suggested that there could be an alternative to
the pursuit of academia for her too, for the very next paragraph in her
letter to Charles is a rejection of her academic plans: "My work in
Shakespeare is very enjoyable but frankly I don't see how I shall contrive

a PhD out of it. My most ingenuous observations have all been observed before. A PhD requires *terra nova*."

Marie's language betrays her failing self-confidence in her ability to say something original about Shakespeare. Why does she choose the word "contrive?" Doesn't that suggest some insincerity or artifice? And why "ingenuous" (i.e., sincere) observations? In other words, a contrived Ph.D. topic on Shakespeare would be disingenuous; a sincere one would not be original. Ergo — drop the project.

The very next day, Marie reported to Charles that she was getting increasingly restless, with her mind "fixed on the day of deliverance," which will be May 12. She sits around with the other women at the post office that has become the "center of existence." There "the ladies congregate and read their love letters to each other — they are curiously alike — and contrive appropriately impassioned answers. At the same time there are local intrigues despite the perfervid correspondence. Will the cantor marry me or must I go back to Max? Shall I marry Nate or return to the rich manufacturer who sent me here? My role is that of the mentor. I am assumed to be fancy free and a credit to the female sex. . . . Tomorrow my salesladies get their divorces and depart. The occasion is to be celebrated with a party" (Archives f. 17).

The comic mode is Marie's escape, but it is not a long-lasting palliative. She wishes Charles could meet her in Reno on May 12 and go to the coast with her, but she admits that it would be deliriously expensive. "I have asked you a number of times as to your plans. You keep writing as though you proposed to come here in May. Please write me about this. . . . If you do not come here, I will go to Los Angeles between May 5–12. There is no reason why I should hang around here and have more time and expense later." Marie has yet to learn that Charles is not inclined to travel unless it is in the pursuit of livelihood (Archives f. 17).

Charles' response to Marie's self-doubt is a bit tepid. "As for your PhD in Shakespeare," he replies, "I suppose if you work steadily at it something will occur to you — besides you do enjoy the work." This follows a request regarding the kind of home they will establish: "Darling, won't you like to keep an orthodox Jewish home? Bless candles on Friday, keep all the holidays? I like to think of you blessing the candles in our home. I kiss you a hundred times. Good night until tomorrow" (*Letters*, March 24, 25). There is no response to this in Marie's letters. The best she can do is to report that she went to the local synagogue for Purim and but for the communal shouts at Haman's name, she found the whole experience wanting. Undoubtedly, she went out of loneliness and boredom, certainly not for any emerging religiosity. Her satiric account of a timid rabbi imported from Palestine, a community of hapless shopkeepers and divorcees, with the rich element absent, a dance following the reading of the *Megillah* that offended an influential family in mourning, is followed by her flat statement, "There was no Hamentaschen" (Archives f. 17).

A Long-Distance Spat

Meantime, Marie has been spending time with Jeanette, the saleslady. Apparently, Charles disapproves and believes Marie is wasting her time. His own worries about getting permission to work half-time, writing exact definitions of legal terms, getting his work published, translating his father's memoirs, feeling loneliness and yearning for Marie, begin to manifest themselves in worries about Marie and her peculiar environment. On March 27, Marie's response to a recent letter exposes a new frayed edge in their separation:

I received a woeful letter from you this morning in which you indicate gently that I am wallowing in filth, drinking polluted water and bathing in pits of darkness. Fortunately, you suggest that perhaps you exaggerate — All this precipitated by my acquaintance with an estimable saleslady with the proverbial heart of gold. If you are afraid that my saleslady friendship may lead to plumbers and firemen, I forgive you because jealousy is a curiously illogical emotion; though I confess that even such an interpretation is hardly flattering to me. However, if your objections are to the saleslady herself — her vulgarity, her loud shouting voice, her atrocious table manners, her lack of self-control, her perpetual hysteria, I consider such objections invalid. . . . I am afraid I have little sympathy with your point of view. I assure you that her vulgarity was at least as disagreeable to me as it is to you, but she was a human soul in pain, and though I probably would not have been equal to much more of her unfailing society, I was perfectly willing to spend 2 or 3 days with her.

Darling, I beg you to remember as you have often informed me in regard to yourself — that I am as I am. The older I grow the more I discover how trivial the differences between human beings are. In their fundamental reactions they are alike psychologically. It's only in the frills that they differ — but it is the frills that matter. (Archives f. 17)

An irritated tension in Marie's tone shows in her obvious exaggeration of his criticism. Is this the result of boredom, or is there something as yet unnamed working on her state of mind?

After the new divorcees leave, Marie still is unable to marshall any scholarly impetus: "I shipped off my salesladies yesterday, and shall now return to quiet meditation. I was glad of the interlude because the printed page was beginning to pall fearfully. Today I shall visit the library and take out the second volume of 'War and Peace.' Not Shakespeare for scholarly investigation, but Tolstoy for sheer pleasure of reading."

The almost daily letters carry on—some less serious than others. Some with ardent professions of love from Charles: "My darling girl, beloved, I hold you and kiss you a thousand times!" and "Loveliest, dearest, darlingest—forgive me, I am lovesick." Perhaps in an effort to encourage Marie's Shakespeare studies, he sends her a sonnet; but she does not respond. "By the way," Charles complains on March 26, "I do not know why I assume so 'blithely' as you say, that you are going to marry me. I notice that you said nothing of the Marie Reznikoff sonnet—even the fact that it had 14 lines did not seem to please you overmuch. Honey, darling will you marry me?" (Letters). He had written her a somewhat mixed Petrarchan/Shakespearean sonnet, with a decided echo of Shakespeare's carpe diem Sonnet #73 ("That time of year") in the phrase "few, or none." The final lines were:

> Kisses are best, but if they must be few,
> Or none—well, then I'll scribble rhyming stuff—
> Forgive it if it is rough but it is true—
> For you a new Marie—soon Reznikoff.
> (*Letters* 85–86)

It may be that Marie did not like the sonnet in general, despite her love of Shakespeare and romantic poetry. That is not what she loved about Charles' poetry which shunned rhyme, romantic excess, and obscure symbols in favor of simplicity and verbal craftsmanship. More than likely, she did not mention the sonnet because she did not like its last line. She had no plans to change her name—she intended to remain Marie Syrkin.

Nonetheless, Marie did respond to Charles' words of proposal. "Will I marry you?" she writes in return. "Having at last extracted a formal offer of marriage, let me tell you, honey, that I consider myself married

already. You mean—will I take out a marriage license? I confess that
Reno has not increased my affection for that document, but if you insist, of course your honor will be safeguarded by all the ramparts of the
law." Then, all unselfconsciously, on March 30 Marie describes her
evening activity of the night before. Had she known the consequences
of sending Charles her vignettes about her efforts to break the boredom of her Reno incarceration, she might have withheld her report.
Had she forgotten his earlier condemnation of the low company she
was keeping?

Last night I went to Tony's Dance Hall. Couples are $1.10 and extra ladies are 10c.
I was the extra lady. The floor was enchanting, the music first-rate and the local
Adonises all they are cracked up to be. How they dance. Why do ignorant numb-
skulls dance like angels? I told a number of gentlemen coyly in answer to simple,
straightforward questioning, that I had a "sweetie back East and hence could not
accept their kindly proffered attentions and a good time was had by all.

No—she had not forgotten Charles' earlier admonition, for her description of the dance is followed immediately by her recall of those words:
"Now, my angel, walk around the room thrice, count till a hundred, and
don't send me a letter about iniquity, cesspools, degradation, predatory
wolves and guileless lambs. My behavior would have been approved by
the sternest canons of decorum" (Archives f. 16). Thinking that this will
take care of Charles' peculiar anxieties and flights of jealous imagination, the next letter tells him that the day before, her landlady took
her for a drive through the mountains.

Talk about the trail of the lonesome pine, canyons, sun, hail, clouds, vistas,
color!—Lord, what beauty. How I wish you were here. What a glorious time
we could have—you know me, the intrepid hiker. We'll thrust the rattlesnakes
out of our path and laugh scornfully at the coyotes.
    Oh, boy! . . . I am enclosing violets plucked in the mountains yesterday. I sup-
pose they will be dry, yellow stalks by the time they arrive, but as I enclose them
now they are purple and lavender, fresh and dewy and delicately scented. . . .
Maybe you think sending violets is unduly sentimental, but then again, maybe
you don't. I kiss you, my precious. You are an excellent person, if a little *meshuge*.
Pardon this last. I kiss you again to atone. (Archives f. 16, March 31)

    Upon receipt of Marie's letters regarding Tony's Dance Hall and her
drive through the Nevada mountains, Charles fell into a fit of paranoid

anxiety. Not surprisingly, his first instinct was to write a poem, "To Marie," which he then sent on to her:

1

If you are my wife you are cruel to me, if you are my friend you are kind;
If you are my friend be cruel for all I care, but if you are my wife be kind.

2

I wrote you that I loved you, that when I thought of you I sighed;
Perhaps it merely pleased your vanity and putting the letter down
You went up to the mirror and smiled at your pretty face.

3

I can think of names that would cause your heart to leap;
But at mine you would merely turn your head and smile a welcome —
You try to be kind to me and in your kindness call your kindness love.
(*Letters* April 2)

In his next communication, Charles explains his bitter poem:

"Your letter informing me that you go to Tony's dance-hall where you coyly repulse the advances of the men there was received this morning. It has made me furious and miserable all day. Do not regret that you have written this because I deserve at least the truth at your hands. (Your letter informing me that your landlady has begun to take you out on motor trips was received this evening!) I cannot write any more tonight; I feel sick at heart and I have a rotten taste in my mouth, [handwritten] a very rotten taste.

Charles Reznikoff
[handwritten] Marie!

And so began a silly but serious quarrel (and one in which the United States mail is complicit due to several letters that criss-cross each other). Marie, of course, wrote impassioned defenses of her perfectly proper conduct at Tony's Dance Hall and on the mountain drive with her landlady; but before Charles received her explanation, she received the following astonishing note from him finally disclosing the source of his anxiety: "I lay awake most of last night thinking of you at Tony's dance hall, of you on the automobile trip Monday with your landlady picking violets. If you love me somewhat as you loved Maurice a good deal, my unhappiness will not displease you; if you do not care about Aaron, it will merely annoy you. If you love me you would not do what would hurt me if I knew about it, even though I may never know about it. I used to love your frankness and always forgave you; please do not learn all from the salesladies, be frank now" (*Letters,* April 3). There is no salutation and no closing signature.

Had Marie received this sooner, she doubtless would have understood that Charles had been suffering from a raging case of delusional jealousy worthy of Othello. In the next week the two exchanged letters of accusation and anger, bitter words zooming past each other on east and west railroad tracks. The mail service was playing havoc with Charles Reznikoff and Marie Syrkin's relationship. The evening of the day that Marie wrote a letter of termination, she had to sign and acknowledge receipt of Charles' special delivery letter. Meantime, Charles had sent two letters of apology, a telegram, and a third letter of apology. In the last of the apologies, he pleads: "Darling, even in my angriest letters you must have seen how I love you. Very soon now I hope we will be husband and wife, and if any differences should arise, God forbid! We will be able to settle them at once, and not through the medium of letters and intolerable delays and what 'a sick fancy' may feed on. Dear wife, I kiss you good-night—if you will let me" (*Letters,* April 10).

The kiss of course is immaterial, but Charles knows a more substantial route to pardon. In a final expression of his pleading regrets, Charles promises to send a package including a pound box of candy for Marie's landlady." Then a further enticement: "I hope to send you a parcel. I hoped I could include some Passover dainties, but I suppose the stores where I buy these things do not carry them. I am really including a box of candy which I want you to give to the landlady for taking you on rides." And two days later, "I have just had sent you from 'Glass' some Droste's *creme de caraque,* some French nougat (ready cut), and some candied grapefruit peel . . . . I have also included a box of French chocolate intended for your landlady. However, if you wish to give her the nougat instead, do as you like" (*Letters,* April 12). How could Marie resist this sweet-giver and his gift of sweets?

In the afternoon mail, Marie received Charles' irresistible peace offering and she instantly returned bona fide words of acceptance. Her side of the accord began: "This morning I wrote a sad imploring letter—which you will probably receive with this one. Darling, I just received your Special Delivery. You haven't insulted me, and it sounds as though

you still love me. I have been so infinitely wretched these days. I hope
that all my answers haven't precipitated a new series. If they have I shall
go to a hospital or a mad-house. I don't feel so well and have done nothing but weep in public places (park, restaurant) since yesterday — not so
nice! . . . I kiss you — and don't do it again" (Archives f. 17).

Indeed, Marie had not been feeling well. Now that her tiff with
Charles was resolved, she felt able to send him a letter about her worries
about their financial future. Charles had been working tirelessly at his
Corpus Juris definitions and could not see how it would be possible for
him to be finished before the end of May — which, of course, made it
impossible for him to come out west in time for the final divorce. Moreover, he was still considering asking for half-time work so that he would
be able to spend more time on his writing. His mother thought he
ought to give up the law definitions entirely. Marie, however, had her
own opinion about the situation, which would prove to be an issue
throughout their marriage. She thought that if the firm offered him
half-time at the end of the few months left on the current project, he
should "stick it out." She argues that "married or not married I feel more
strongly than ever that a man of your age should be self-supporting on
no matter how modest a scale. I *hate* the thought of you returning to
the status of a little boy asking papa for pocket-money. For this reason,
if half-time is promised you at the close of a comparatively brief period,
I think you should stay. I make about $60 a week. Of these $60, I must
set $30 aside for David. Your thirty and my thirty=$60 — on which we
can manage modestly. Such are my eminently practical views" (Archives
f. 17). This is strong language, but it reveals how far she has come towards the pragmatic management of her own life and future.

The argument with Charles and the financial worries were com-
pounded by a health scare. For several days, Marie was experiencing a
severe pain in her right breast and right arm down to her fingertips, but,
she writes to Charles on April 7, that because she had been so "mentally
distraught" she put off going to a doctor. When she finally went, he told
her that it was a "kind of nerve strain that would take several days to improve." On April 10, panic stricken, she wrote to Charles again and di-
vulged that she has bad news for him. She went to another doctor who
said she had mastitis, which is "frequently the precursor of cancer, and
if the mastitis does not improve within a few weeks, he advises the removal of the breast because mastitis surgery is simpler than a cancer
mastectomy." Marie assures Charles that the reason she writes him of

this is to let him know that she will not marry him with such a possibility "hanging over" them. "I might as well get the divorce" she adds, "since I am so near it." The next day, she dashed off another bulletin in which she reported that "people here assure me that the doctor in question is an alarmist, that to speak of removing a breast years before cancer will develop is crazy — etc." On April 12, however, Marie telegraphed Charles with a message that could only have left him totally baffled. "Disregard letters April Tenth Eleventh Explanatory Letter Follows Happy Passover. Marie." Whatever his immediate reaction to this — which could only have been great alarm and mystification — he immediately replied that he just returned from the post office where he had posted his letter only to receive her letter of April 10 and her telegram. He had not yet received her explanatory letter, but

whatever that letter contains, good news or bad news, *you are my wife,* your troubles are mine, and what you say about not considering marriage, because of this, whatever it is, is nonsense: you are married. If you are running no risk by staying until you get a divorce, stay on *by all means,* but if you do, come back at once. Certainly, you do not intend to have anything surgical in any event done to you in Reno, do you? . . . I want you to understand this, Marie, that I am your husband now — and only one thing can divorce us, your real wish, but nothing that happens to you can: you are my wife, my money is your money, your sickness is mine. It is agony to be away from you now. (*Letters,* April 12)

The United States Postal Service was tormenting the two because of the unavoidable gap between getting and sending. No sooner would one of them dispatch a heavy-hearted message, than the other would simultaneously respond to the prior letter. It was hard to resolve problems and emotions in this way. But Marie did send an explanation on April 12: After being told that cancer was in her future and that she might as well have her breast removed now, she admits to Charles, "I naturally almost went crazy." But after this, three other doctors examined her and all three agreed that "there was not the slightest evidence of anything being the matter with me except severe nervous strain and that the pain is a nerve pain aggravated by anxiety." Although the three medical doctors agreed that the cause of the pain was nerve strain due to anxiety, they ventured no further. What, then, could have been the cause of such anxiety? Furthermore, Marie adds that "They also agreed that the first doctor 'is an alarmist,' a 'quack,' an 's. o. b.' — that he's 'crazy' and that he 'ought to be shot.'" Finally, she tells Charles, they all thought "his theory was to run up a nice bill." It was an undoubted relief, of course; nonetheless, she planned that when she got back to New York City she would go to a "first-rate physician and be thumped and bumped some more." Marie apologizes to Charles for the anxiety she has caused him and assures him that if she is okay "we shall marry and, God willing, live happily ever after. If not——" (Archives f. 17).

Charles Reznikoff's intense feelings for Marie radiate from so many of his letters. In them, he confesses that he has two loves in his life: his writing and his love for Marie. At this moment, however, as he sits down to write a letter of support and encouragement to her, love for Marie trumps the writing: she is far away, she is in pain, the cause of the pain is not yet clear, and he has not yet received the promised explanatory telegram. If there was ever any doubt about Charles' love for Marie, this letter bears witness to it. He begins "Dear Wife:"

I came home expecting to find the explanatory letter of your telegram, but it has not come as yet. Perhaps tomorrow. . . . Dearest, I have a great faith in the power of emotions: at one time hate enabled me to do what I would otherwise have found impossible. Likewise, love for you has grown so great that I feel strong enough to climb — and carry you — anywhere. Darling our love should make us unafraid and joyful in the face of anything. Darling, how I wish that I were in pain instead of you — at least I am home among friends. Dearest when you come home and we marry, we shall never be parted again! I kiss you, and writing this my heart beats faster. Hand in hand through everything! (*Letters*, April 14)

After this, Marie's mood changed and expressions of her own love became more open. Having received the above letter, the greeting on her reply is "Dearest Charles!" She has never used that term of endearment before and the exclamation point sets it in relief. Though her physical condition has improved, her mental state is "numb." Moreover, her more cheerful tone may have been influenced by the receipt of Charles' package: "The candy arrived and is of overwhelming elegance & deliciousness. I gave the Creme de Caraque to the landlady as I could bear to part neither with the nougat nor the chocolates. She thanks you accordingly."

Included in this installment of her daily report to Charles is a subject that has not appeared in their correspondence before. "I asked the doctor if he thought I could marry, have children, etc. He assured me vigorously in the affirmative, though I carefully explained that the guy in question couldn't afford an invalid wife." So—Marie has been thinking of having another child. But this does not seem to be in Charles' plans. He makes no mention of it in his letters, and years and years later Marie would say, speaking of Charles' attitude about their married life, "he rejected the basic convention as to how life should be led. He would assume no obligations, such as support of a family, that might hamper his true vocation" (*Man and Poet* 40). There would, then, be no children other than David, who would always be her responsibility shared with Aaron; the divorce would prescribe joint custody. Yet, Marie always insisted that she respected Charles' poetry enough to "sympathize wholly with his view, particularly," she added, "as I found myself in economic bondage because of my responsibilities" (*Man and Poet* 40).

As the days dragged on, Marie waited for the news that her trial would take place on May 6 rather than May 12. "It is funny," she comments to Charles, "that 6 days should matter so much, but you cannot begin to understand how intolerable the days have been, especially since I have devoted myself to idleness. I have no desire, at present to take up my Shakespearean labors and I shall not force myself to do so" (Archives f. 17). In order to pass the time, Marie joined a group of people on a visit to an Indian School on a nearby reservation. It is the first time that she has gone anywhere since her illness and she tells Charles that "it was delightful to be out again and alive to impressions. The school—I saw the primary grades—seems about as advanced as the similar grade of a N.Y. school—though there was a touch of pathos in hearing the little Indian kids sing stolidly 'The Pilgrims came to Plymouth Rock in 1620.' As a finishing touch of unconscious irony, the drawing project for that class was the landing of the white man in America. The purpose I suppose, was to instill patriotic responses" (Archives f. 17). This small paragraph was a harbinger of works to come. In her prescient sensitivity to the feelings of the Indian students, in anticipation of what would later become the banner of multiculturalism, Marie Syrkin was unconsciously gathering material for the celebrated book about the American public school system that she would write fifteen years later.

As the time drew nearer for the divorce trial, which Marie had learned would almost certainly take place on May 6, she began to make plans for a visit to the West Coast—one that she had hoped to share with Charles, but now knows that she will have to take on her own. Charles has declined the invitation on the grounds that work and finances will not permit him to accompany her. Though he did not accompany Marie to San Francisco and Los Angeles, Charles did suggest that she contact his friends who lived there. The most important contact was Albert Lewin in Los Angeles. Lewin was Charles' childhood friend who had gone to Harvard and there was encouraged by Professor George Kittredge to become an academic, but who chose instead to go to Hollywood. There he became a screenwriter, director, and producer and served as an assistant to the great film director, Irving Thalberg. Lewin later achieved great success with such films as *Mutiny on the Bounty, The Good Earth, The Portrait of Dorian Gray,* and *The Moon and Sixpence.* In 1930 he had not been in contact with Charles for a few years and though Charles thought Marie should get in touch with him, he was not altogether confident that Lewin would have the time or inclination to see her—especially since Charles had not been in contact with him for some time. As it would turn out, the reconnection made at this time would result in a much needed opportunity for Charles a few years later.

On May 3, Marie sent a telegram to Charles to inform him that her case was set for May 6. Three days later she wrote, "My dear, the divorce was granted this morning. It was a solemn and mournful affair and I wept. I hope, as one prays, that I shall be able to do well by David, and by you, and by myself—and that I shall have the health for my responsibilities. I am leaving tonight for San Francisco." She had planned a sightseeing tour during which she would visit San Francisco for a day, Los Angeles for a few days, San Diego, Tia Juana and the Grand Canyon. "These things," she asserts, "must be seen apparently." Marie tells Charles that he must inform her family of her imminent return, and he must ask her aunt to "keep it quiet" because she wants to be sure that Charles will be at the train and no one else—not even David. "I want to meet you," she says, "alone, and then go home." Marie returned to Reno on May 15th for a final visit to her doctor, who told her nothing was wrong and promptly discharged her. "As to the future, they can offer no guarantees" she adds, "I being of mortal flesh" (Archives f. 17).

Reno had been a border crossing in Marie Syrkin's quest for selfhood. Her friend, Laura Riding, had put it well when she wrote that Marie was not "temperamentally a cynic" and that she does "ask for every-day bread and not dreams." Riding had advised her friend that "the sooner you make up your mind at least to try for it, the happier you'll be on the whole. . . . [S]tir out of it now."

Those are tough words that surely came back to Marie during the
Reno months. Until now, her haphazard life had brought her too much
sorrow, too many failed relationships, too many losses, and not enough
satisfaction, let alone happiness. Willy-nilly she had been sinking deeper
and deeper into a sea of troubles. But the seemingly interminable three
months in Reno unexpectedly turned out to be a rehabilitation facility,
a decompression chamber that gradually reduced the emotional pressure that had been building for fifteen years since the death of Marie's
mother. Reno provided the perfect atmosphere for her to "make up her
mind to try for it . . . to stir out of it."

What, however, is the "it?" For Marie, Laura Riding's "*it*" is a Janus
pronoun: "it" refers to both "every-day bread," and "dreams," too—
paradoxical as that may seem. Marie had been scrambling towards a practical idealism; that is, turning dreams into a reality, rather than the other
way round. During the months of February, March, and April, Marie
Syrkin came to certain critical conclusions: she would give up her plans
to pursue a Ph.D. with a dissertation on Shakespeare; she would continue in her job as a high school teacher (a job she never really liked);
she would continue to write her own poetry; and she would continue to
write for Zionist publications. Despite some obvious problems, she
would marry Charles Reznikoff as soon as she returned to New York;
but she would delay her return to New York so that she would not miss
out on the opportunity to travel in the West. She would, at last, manage
her own life.

Was it merely the distance from New York that freed Marie to make
these changes? Or was it the lack of responsibilities, or, possibly, the absence of male authorities that led her to reject a conventional plot for
her own life story? Perhaps at thirty years of age, it was simply the end
of her developmental period. Or was there a major event, a specific activity that begged Marie Syrkin to rewrite the script?

There is unexpected evidence that during her enforced residence in
Nevada, Marie had been engaged in a private activity—one that she did
not speak of in her letters to Charles and had not revealed during her
lifetime. After Marie's death in 1989, an unfinished and undated handwritten manuscript of an autobiographical novel was discovered among
her papers. David Bodansky, Marie Syrkin's son, believes from internal
evidence that this was composed during those months (Personal conversation). The over five hundred pages end with a scribbled account of
the illness, death and funeral of two-year-old Jackie, the protagonist's

child. Marie's clipped, chilling account is as cold as the December earth that she describes.

They sealed the coffin. It was time to get in the car. Judith and Jim got in. At their feet an attendant placed a wooden box. It was not larger than the crate for a kiddy-car. In this box was Jackie. If she moved her foot, it touched the wood. They had put her child in a box. And now she had to go and watch them put the box into cold December earth, under cold, December snow. There was no escape.

Marie wrote no more; for the author, that moment was a dead end, and she was in search of a new beginning. Perhaps at this moment she recalled her father's consolatory words: "Let us all start a new life, full of love, duty, responsibility and truth." Perhaps the writing of the novel was a purgation, a classical catharsis, an unburying of psychic forces that finally liberated Marie (Samuel–Bodansky–soon to be Reznikoff) to make her considerable way in the world as Marie Syrkin—a self-directed woman who would be able to choose life.

PART II

Chapter 8

An Unorthodox Marriage

Palestine and Hollywood

IN MID-MAY OF 1930, after her divorce became final and after her sightseeing trip to the West Coast had been completed, Marie Syrkin returned to New York to begin a new—perhaps the most important chapter—in her life. On May 27, 1930 Charles Reznikoff and Marie Syrkin were married in an Orthodox Jewish ceremony. It was already apparent, however, that this would be a most *un*orthodox marriage. Nonetheless, Charles and Marie were completely confident that the unique aspects of their life together would not cause discord in their marital harmony. Marie understood that her husband would not take on responsibilities that might interfere with his "creative freedom," and although Marie never said explicitly (in print) that this included fatherhood, it was a condition that she could not have found easy to accept. Charles, in turn, had to accept certain disagreeable consequences of his wife's divorce agreement. As she herself has explained:

He . . . was a partner willing to accept the peculiarites of our domestic arrangements. As part of the divorce agreement my former husband and I had full shared custody. One year my son was with me; the next with his father. Each of us had unlimited daily visiting privileges. In practice this meant that in the alternate year either parent could visit at any time. Whatever the difficulties of this enforced intimacy Charles agreed that a child was entitled to both his parents. In retrospect the pitfalls in such an agreement are obvious but I was not going to deprive my son of his father through legalistic circumscription of the time to be spent together. And vice-versa. Few husbands would be so understanding. That Charles agreed throws light on his character. (*Man and Poet* 41)

Accommodating as Charles may have been, the arrangements inevitably created some uncomfortable moments for the three adults involved. Marie was teaching at Textile High School, which was on 18th
Street in Manhattan; Charles continued his work at *Corpus Juris,* which
was in Brooklyn; Aaron was living in Riverdale, where David's school
was located. To make things easier for Marie, Charles agreed to live in
Riverdale, a decision that made Marie's subway ride long but spared
seven-year-old David the problem of changing schools and making new
friends. Decades later, David cited his mother's decision to live so far
from her work and Charles' work as proof of his mother's loving devotion to her son (Personal conversation). Marie and Charles rented a
two-room-with-kitchenette apartment at 225 McClellan Street in the
Riverdale section of the Bronx and began their daily routine. Leaving
home at 7:00 A.M., together they would board the subway; Marie
would get off at 14th Street and Charles would continue on to Brooklyn. There was, however, one hitch in the routine. As per this most unusual divorce agreement, each parent had unlimited daily visiting rights,
and most times when Charles would arrive home, Aaron was in the
apartment visiting his son. "This," Marie has explained,

proved more embarrassing to Charles than he had expected, but his solution
was simple and to him agreeable. Instead of coming home for dinner like a
proper husband, he would walk across the Brooklyn Bridge in the twilight and
continue along Riverside Drive as far as he could manage. He would reinforce
himself *en route* at some automat and appear when the danger of uncomfortable encounters was past. I could not protest with any grace. Charles had found
an incontrovertible excuse for swerving from the usual domestic pattern. (*Man
and Poet* 41–42)

In reality, this was more blessing than curse for Charles. If his wife and
his poetry were his first two passions in life, walking was absolutely his
third. Walking was Charles' religion, his renewal of spirit, the source of
his creative life. His wife has declared that unless he walked a number of
miles a day "dwindling through the years from twenty to six daily, he
suffered psychic deprivation. 'I did not walk today,' he would announce
with an air of tragic loss that the simple fact did not seem to justify."
Walking was an obsession that had begun in childhood and now became
the fount of his poetic experience. "[H]e saw, he felt, he wrote" com-
prises Marie's commentary on her husband's creative process. Hence,

his walking from Brooklyn to Riverdale were miles of spiritual intoxication rather than forced march; the stops and sights along Reznikoff's
route were realized into masterful word images, "Feast, you who cross
the bridge / this cold twilight / on these honeycombs of light, the buildings of Manhattan"[1] (*Poems* I, 118). "The whole poem," in the keen words
of the poet Michael Heller, "attains to the condition of the photograph
rather than the lyric—the photograph, in the words of Walter Ben-
jamin, as 'the posthumous moment,' the moment rescued from time"
(*Man and Poet* 165).

From the start, Marie Syrkin had recognized the poetic originality and
the moral vision of Charles Reznikoff's art; thus, at this slightly later stage
of her life she was learning to live with her husband's eccentricities—as
long as these did not hinder her freedom to pursue her own interests.
Essentially, Charles was a solitary man, but together the couple did have
a small circle of friends whom they saw socially from time to time. The
closest were two poets often grouped together with Charles under
the umbrella of Objectivism: George Oppen, and Louis Zukofsky. "Mary
and George Oppen," Marie has recalled, "appeared on the scene some
time in 1930—Mary in the golden beauty of her youth, and George,
dark, handsome, and reverential to Charles as the older poet. Louis
Zukofsky, elongated like an El Greco painting, the quintessential poet
in appearance and manner, was also one of the group." However, as
Marie was quick to point out, "The Objectivists are often described as a
school. Though they all shared the same literary values, scrupulous fidelity
to the subject or idea, in practice each interpreted these values in his individual fashion, as a comparison of Zukofsky and Reznikoff would
indicate" (*Man and Poet* 43). The group also published books under
the Objectivist Press imprint; their principal poet was William Carlos
Williams. In fact, Marie Syrkin's own poetry which began under the
influence of nineteenth-century romanticism, would, over the decades,
owe a decided debt to the influence of Charles Reznikoff.

Although Charles was very nearly a loner—occupied with his daily
work, his long walks, and his writing—Marie's nature was more social.
She made friends easily and had been accustomed to a wide circle of
friends and confidants, although at this time she was limited by her daily
teaching obligations, and she was becoming increasingly involved in
Zionist activities and writing. On weekends, however, she and Charles
liked to take a ride down 5th Avenue on an open-top double-decker bus,
or they enjoyed roaming the streets of bustling, bohemian Greenwich

Village, where they could observe an aggregation of beautiful, or not-so-beautiful people, and they might treat themselves to a delicious fish lunch or an Italian dinner for less than a dollar. But their best form of entertainment and relaxation was reading poetry aloud to one another. Marie has recalled that on several New Year's Eves they got together with the Oppens and would read "old favorites loved in adolescence and revisited as a special dispensation" (*Man and Poet* 43), and sometimes would read aloud a new discovery, such as Rilke.

Although it was 1930 and money worries were inescapable, the first months of Charles and Marie's marriage passed relatively uneventfully; but only a few months after their marriage their income became significantly reduced. Charles' father lost some of his business property, and with it went the twenty-five dollars a week that had been part of Charles' contribution to their shared income. Moreover, the loss left the elder Reznikoffs with debts that had to be paid off. Fortunately, two of the three Reznikoff children were fairly comfortable, but that did not let Charles off the hook — nor, as Marie adamantly insisted, did he expect to "request exemption on the grounds that he was an impecunious artist." Furthermore, unable to secure a half-time position, his full-time work at *Corpus Juris* left him very little time or energy at day's end to add to their income from some other source, for he was a scrupulous worker who exercised exacting and painstaking analysis in his search for precise definitions of legal terminology. Marie puts it this way: "With no gift for easy generalizations, he would ponder fine points slowly and cautiously. Trying to aid him in his laborious perplexities, a well-disposed head at *Corpus Juris* once admonished him kindly: 'When I hire a carpenter, I don't want a cabinet maker.'" But Charles was incapable of carpentry, and before long a new superior decided that Reznikoff would never be able to nail definitions on the head at a greater speed. "I remember his shock," Marie recalls, "when he came home to tell me that he had been 'fired' with two weeks notice. Though he detested the drudgery, he had tried faithfully" (*Man and Poet* 45). The failure, however, was a persistent irritation.

On May 6, 1930, Charles Reznikoff had written to Marie as she prepared to leave Reno, "This, Marie darling, is the last letter I expect to write to you for a long time, I hope" (*Letters*). He assured her that it would be a very long time until they would again be apart. But hopes too often are crushed by hard realities. Although the elder Reznikoff's debts had been settled, by 1931 — just one year after their marriage — the younger Reznikoffs were facing their appreciable financial problems. Boni publishers had paid Charles one thousand dollars for the novel, *By the Waters of Manhattan,* but they nearly lost the money "because," as Marie tells it, "Charles, though openly doubtful of the stability of a new bank in the neighborhood, chose to deposit the whole in that questionable institution — he had known a member of the firm in Brooklyn so loyalty overcame prudence." Breathing an almost audible *ex post facto* sigh of relief, Marie later wrote, "By a lucky stroke we rescued our fortune just hours before a bank run closed the place" (*Man and Poet* 41).

The money worries were not new, although Charles all along had been trying his hand at low-paying odd jobs, such as translations or occasional articles. In fact, in the penultimate letter that he had written to Marie in Reno on May 6, 1930, he acknowledged that he ought to find a job that would provide a regular source of income: "I have just finished the first 15 pages of the Boni book and at this rate I should be finished in about a month. In about four hours a day I can do all the writing I want to do, in two hours all the reading. I know that I can do some kind of work — such as selling — that will give me a steady income and not interfere with my work" (*Letters*). Then, after a gestation period of almost a year, Charles produced his highly improbable solution to their financial problems. He would go on the road. He decided to try his hand as a traveling salesman for his parents' millinery business. Thus, as out of character it may seem, hat in hand, in early April he set out, by bus, across the country to sell the latest fashions in headwear. Somewhat naively, Charles began his cross-country itinerary with cheerful optimism. On April 16, he wrote, "Bus riding is fine — but there's a little too much of it. And, of course, there will be much more — I hope. . . . When I see something beautiful — and I have seen so much — I think of you and reach for your hand, dearest. I am tired tonight and must be up very early. I kiss you a thousand times, dear wife, and hope that our separation will not be useless" (*Letters*).

Charles' hopes, however, did not bring useful results, though he tried to make the best of bad business by soaking in the sights as he proceeded on through Harrisburg, Pittsburgh, Columbus, Indianapolis, St. Louis, and then on to Oklahoma, New Mexico, Texas, and finally Los Angeles; but he failed to make many sales. Charles Reznikoff, the would-be hat salesman was faring much worse than Charles Reznikoff the poet who reported on April 24, from his stay in St. Louis: "I have seen much, expect to see more and feel richly repaid by the bus mode of travel. . . . The jubilation about the millinery business has been quite premature, as you no doubt realize" (*Letters*).

Charles in Hollywood

In a move that would turn out to bear fruit a few years later, the day after his arrival in Los Angeles, Charles telephoned his boyhood friend, Al Lewin. Lewin, who had become a highly successful screen writer, director, and producer asked Reznikoff to come right over to his Hollywood studio. Although Al and his wife Milly were leaving that night for a ten-day trip to the East Coast, they invited Charles to stay at their home. "They both were so friendly," Charles reports the next day, on May 3, from the Lewins' home in Beverly Hills, "and urged me to stay here at their home at least until they return. There is a maid. A cook, a chauffeur. I am in a sort of wing, all to myself and have a private bath — a kind of Hollywood bath." The rich quarters at 714 North Roxbury Drive, Beverly Hills, were impressive, but they had nothing to do with the main purpose of Charles' trip — the pursuit of business success. Two days later, Charles informed Marie, "I went to Los Angeles today and tried to sell hats — but did nothing. Until the return of the home-owners, there is nothing for Charles to do but see a couple of Hollywood acquaintances, look at the ocean, and write. The absurdity of Charles Reznikoff's situation evokes visions of another Charles, and the comparison is evident to Reznikoff himself: "I am leading a fantastic life," he reports to Marie, "and since you saw Charlie Chaplin in *City Lights* — the beggar in the automobile, you'll understand. I am served dinner — alone — every evening in style by a butler in a white coat. I have a large touring car to ride wherever I please. The whole thing is Arabian nightish, but I really don't care much because I prefer the bus — the top out in the open air — to the closed limousine. Anyway, I feel silly. When Al comes back, I'll find a cheap room and a good cafeteria" (*Letters*, May 5).

On May 17, Al Lewin returned home; Charles did not move out. Instead, he spent his time chatting with Al, continuing to write, and living the social high life at night. He had been unable to make any hat sales for a variety of reasons: one hat is too heavy for the climate; another has been copied from an original by many other hat manufacturers; a third is too expensive for the general Los Angeles population. No doubt, one more reason was Charles' dislike for the work and his utter lack of selling talent. But the failure to sell hats did not interfere with the enjoyment of his visit. He writes to Marie that he finds Al Lewin "clever as ever" and one of the most intelligent men he has ever met, "but he and I feel he is wasted in the work he does" (*Letters,* May 18). This assessment—for the man who will go on to write, direct, or produce over fifty films including *Mutiny on the Bounty, The Picture of Dorian Gray,* and *The Moon and Sixpence,* and whose career is charted on ten pages of Google websites!

Back in New York, Marie Syrkin surely had to think that Charles was wasting his time. She was working hard and complaining that her Textile High boredom was leading to exhaustion. What could have been going through her mind as she rose early each morning to catch the subway downtown to teach at least five classes a day of mostly unwilling students, only to return at day's end to tend to her son, do domestic chores, grade a stack of student exams, write articles for Zionist publications, and read Charles' latest report from the western front? Writing almost every day of how he misses her, he shows no sign of leaving, but complains that it is hard for him to work in California:

I have not gone to bed before 2 o'clock for a week. Whether friendly or not, and when they get drunk some . . . become unfriendly (though none to me because I am still a guest), everybody is extremely sociable: there are always the people of your circle—which is usually a small one—dropping in or inviting you out. Now, last night we went to a Chinese restaurant where the food was most disgusting and then we picked up a gang of strangers—negroes—male and female—and went to their house. I, as you imagine, was not the life of the party—and I don't give a damn. During the day, I sit on the patio: here it is pleasant, though no pleasanter than many other places. It is very hot until evening, there is a palm tree, flowers etc. enclosed by a high whitewashed wall, it belongs to the house and no one enters it all day but I—green turf, easy chairs—however there are also flies: some bite, others just crawl on your hands and neck and face. However, I prefer it to the house, which is cool and screened. Well then, if I cannot stay on and on decently, I should get a room. But every place is so far from every other place in this city—Beverly Hills is 6 miles from Santa Monica, 4 from Culver City, 10 from Los Angeles, 4 from Hollywood. I thought of stopping at one of the beaches, bathing is best during the middle of the day, but I am not so keen about it. In other words, in another week I should have had enough of Los Angeles, and I would leave today were it not for my friendship for Al Lewin and the feeling that to leave almost as soon as he returns would be unfriendly. (*Letters,* May 18)

It would have been superhuman for Charles' wife of one year not to have bridled at her husband's reports of passing his time apart from her by going to previews and dinner parties, socializing with Hollywood characters, sitting on a Beverly Hills patio in the afternoon, and not selling any hats. But by the end of May, even patient Charles had had enough. Despite Al Lewin's invitation that Charles stay all summer in his house, he feels that he should leave. "We have now resumed our ancient harmony of mind, but it is not easy for me to work here — during the day it is hot and at night, there is almost a constant round of entertainment — and the only way I'll ever make any money is through the sale of my books — if and when." Moreover, he misses her intensely, writing "Marie, if others have gone west to be divorced, I have gone west to feel myself completely married, now and forever. I kiss your hand and your mouth (I have no cold)" (*Letters,* May 23).

It was time to leave; by May 27, he was on his way. After a short trip to see an old friend in San Francisco, Charles began his cross-country meander by bus, with about fifteen stops along the way, taking a little over two weeks. From Boise, Idaho, he writes, "Dearest, morning star in the east, towards which the buses I ride in travel, I suppose my schedules are as uncertain as my mother's recipes." If one listens hard, it is not difficult to hear Marie's deeply ambivalent sigh as she read these words. Charles reached New York about June 10.

By the end of the month, Charles Reznikoff and Marie Syrkin moved some five miles north of McClellan Street, to a larger apartment at 3615 Greystone Avenue, in order to provide better accommodations for David and to be only a mile away from his school, the Ethical Culture private school, Fieldston. The next two years, as Marie herself has insisted, were the happiest years of their married life. Charles continued his writing, he returned to his job at *Corpus Juris,* and to his walking; Marie continued teaching and began to develop a significant reputation as a journalist and activist for the Labor Zionist Movement in America, and though she continued to try to write poetry, the past dreams of a literary career were pushed to the back of the desk in the face of the urgencies of the present situations in Palestine and Europe. It was not without some regret, however, that during an interview in 1989, in the middle of a discussion of her participation in Zionist activities in the thirties, Marie remembered that one of the great moments of her life was at Cornell, when she was taking a graduate course in English, in which she was the only student, and her English professor told her to "just write poetry. He saw some of my poems which I showed him," she recalled with pride and pleasure in that memory. "He said 'you're a real poet.' . . . That was one of the most delirious moments of my life. I remember that very well." Then she whispered, "I was a great disappointment to him. And when he heard that I was teaching school he said to Aaron, 'what a great pity.'" When I asked Marie if her move into the world of polemical journalism was compensation for not doing more creative writing, her answer was both immediate and sharp: "No. I don't think so. I had this compulsion, this feeling, as today, that something has to be done; and I know how to do it" (Personal interview). Marie's phrase is repeated by Irving Howe, who years later wrote in a tribute to Marie, "I value the occasional troubled, eager phone call: *something must be done!* And she usually was right: something must be done. Whether I can help do it, or know what to do, is another matter; but she is right: it must be done."[2] As for her poetry, she later called it a self-indulgence: "There was a period in my life," she explained, "when I felt that to be sitting writing poetry was a self indulgence. You know, I used to write [it] only under tremendous emotional impulse, and as an indulgence" (Personal interview).

Despite these demurrals, Marie Syrkin did publish poetry throughout her life, in the *Menorah Journal,* the *Palestine Post,* the *Jewish Frontier,* the *Jerusalem Post,* and the *New York Times,* which included several of her poems in the *Anthology of the New York Times Best Poems.* But in the first years of the 1930s other compulsions were more pressing. Dire reports from Germany had begun to trickle in; the increasingly ominous National Socialist (Nazi Party) election figures pointed to the end of the post–World War I Weimar Republic. The party had garnered 800,000 votes in the 1923 election; in 1930, the number rose to 6.5 million; and in 1932, the figure spiked to 14 million out of a total 45 million. On January 31, 1933, President Paul von Hindenburg named Adolf Hitler as Chancellor of the German Republic. This was reported on page three of the *New York Times* on January 31, with the headline "Hitler Puts Aside Aim To Be Dictator." But in the words of the eminent historian of the Holocaust, Lucy Dawidowicz, "National Socialism was the consummation toward which the omnifarious anti-Semitic movements had striven for 150 years."[3]

The *New York Times* may have buried the appalling event on page three, but in Marie Syrkin's understanding, this foreboding news had front-page significance — though she later confessed that in 1933 she could not yet perceive the unimaginable atrocities that were about to unfold. Still, it was obvious to her that there was an ineluctable link between the events in Europe and the events in Palestine, where the Jews were creating a country in a land controlled by the British Mandate and shared with the Arabs. There had been increasing Jewish immigration to Palestine in the years between 1922 and 1929. The 1922 census calculated that the Jewish population of Palestine was 83,780 and the Moslem Arab population was 589,177. By the 1931 census, the Jewish population had more than doubled to 174,606 — 100 percent plus — and the Moslem Arab population increased only about 35 percent to 759,700.[4] These figures (which over the years have been challenged by both sides) partly explain the series of massacres that occurred in 1929. The disproportional increase in the Jewish numbers caused Arab fears that such growth, along with Jewish economic, political, and technological resources, ultimately would swallow them. The majority of the Arabs were concentrated mainly in the hill areas of the northern and central parts of the land and were tenant farmers for the small clans of elite Arab families who owned almost all the land and controlled the economic and political life of the community. In sharp contrast to this semi-feudal state of affairs, Article 4 of the Palestine Mandate as approved by the League of Nations in 1922 had authorized the establishment of "an appropriate Jewish Agency" to be recognized as a

public body for the purpose of advising and cooperating with the Administration of Palestine in such economic, social and other matters as may affect the establishment of the Jewish national home and the interests of the Jewish population in Palestine, and subject always to the control of the Administration, to assist and take part in the development of the country. The Zionist Organization, so long as its organization and constitution are in the opinion of the mandatory appropriate, shall be recognized as such agency.[5]

The Arabs of Palestine were ruled by a few powerful families or clans — most especially, the Husseini clan; the *fellahin* (peasants), who were virtual serfs to the clans, reaped none of the economic benefits of the sizable financial activity of the Jews of Palestine and remained poor and ignorant; and the Arab professional and mercantile class worried about competition from the Jews. As one historian has put it, they "viewed the Zionist experiment with growing concern. They frankly feared that these European Jews, with apparently limitless and technological resources, would someday engulf all of Palestine, and transform the country into a Jewish state, a dagger poised at the Arab heart" (Sachar 385).

Between 1922, the date of the Mandate, and 1929, the Jews of Palestine had developed a quasi-self-government through the Jewish Agency. They were experimenting with new social forms such as the kibbutzim (collectives); they had produced agricultural innovation as well as industrial organizations; they had created a national culture, including the revival of the Hebrew language, as well as an indigenous literature and other art forms. All of these Jewish achievements gave small comfort to the Arab oligarchy and middle class, who were quite content with the status quo. As for the illiterate, superstitious, and unsophisticated *fellahin,* they regarded the Zionists as followers of an infidel religion. Their impassioned feelings were ignited by the Grand Mufti of Jerusalem, Amin al-Husseini, the Islamic legal scholar, and religious and political leader who was appointed to his political position by the British in 1921. For all these reasons and more, bitter anti-Zionist feelings and rhetoric flourished and was disseminated through the Arab communities, whipping up hot hostility until it resulted in the bloody riots of 1929, known euphemistically as the Arab disturbances (Sachar 461–462).

The response of the British Colonial Secretary, Sidney Webb (later Lord Passfield), to these riots was to send two commissions to investigate the situation. The first commission cleared the Mufti and the Arab Executive of any wrongdoing, and suggested that there was no further room in the territory for Jewish immigration and that the rights of the non-Jewish communities were being threatened. The second commission was even more draconian in its recommendation: that Jewish immigration and land acquisition be severely restricted. The sudden shock stunned the Zionist community. But more was to come. Lord Passfield himself issued a White Paper in which the underlying premise was that both the Balfour Declaration and the Mandate held that the whole enterprise had a double purpose, to the Jewish people and to the non-Jewish population, and it rejected any idea that the passages about the Jewish National Home were the essential aspects of the Mandate. Hence, the Passfield White Paper declared that arable land was too scarce to support new immigrants, and any further purchase of agricultural land in Palestine would need the approval of the British authorities who would make their determination on the basis of the unemployment level of the Jews and the Arabs. Since the Jews were ideologically committed to employing only Jewish labor, the effect on the employment figures is obvious. And the effect on further immigration is equally obvious. It is surprising, on the surface, that Sidney Webb/Lord Passfield, who himself was a Fabian socialist, was not the least swayed by the fact that the Jewish community of Palestine was building a Socialist political economy that should have been the envy of British Labor. Instead, he chose to favor the Arabs' feudal oligarchy. The only explanation could be inherent antisemitism of the kind that led Webb's wife and collaborator, Beatrice Potter Webb, to remark to Chaim Weizmann, "I can't understand why the Jews make such a fuss over a few dozen of their people killed in Palestine. As many are killed every week in London in traffic accidents, and no one pays any attention" (Sachar 462–463).

Chaim Weizmann, however, was so incensed by the Passfield Paper that he resigned from the presidency of the Jewish Agency, protesting that the White Paper not only was a divergence from the obligations of the British Mandate, but that it was inching close to "denying the rights and sterilizing the hopes of the Jewish people in regard to the National Home" and that the development of that home would be frozen at the present stage of development (*Judaica* "Passfield White Paper"). Fortunately, in the face of overwhelming protests from Jews and others throughout the British Empire, Ramsey MacDonald, the Labor Party Prime Minister, interceded. He sent a letter to Chaim Weizmann assuring him that there would be no change in the British Government's interpretation of the Balfour Declaration or the dictates of the Mandate, and that there would be no prohibitions on the normal growth of the Jewish National Homeland.

The Seventeenth Zionist Congress met in June of 1931 under the shadow of the Passfield White Paper, and despite Macdonald's intervention, the Zionist leaders were all too aware of the continuing Arab opposition. The Revisionists among other delegates strongly protested Weizmann's policy, which called for maximum cooperation with the British government. Vladimir Jabotinsky, the powerful and unchallenged leader of the Revisionists, demanded and put forward a resolution stating that the main goal of Zionism was the creation of a Jewish majority within a Jewish State in Palestine on both sides of the Jordan River. When his proposal was rejected by the majority, Jabotinsky tore up his delegate card and shouted that "This is not a Zionist Congress." The Seventeenth Zionist Congress elected Nahum Sokolow the new President, and it adopted a resolution that called for action to re-establish good relations and peace with the Arabs of Palestine, a resolution that had little chance of success because of the Arabs' unalterable objection to the Jews being granted any political rights at all in Palestine (*Judaica* "Zionist Congresses").

More and more the maelstrom of ominous world events in the early 1930s occupied the central place in Marie Syrkin's intellectual and political thought, no less in her emotional life. She was still teaching at Textile High, but her extracurricular work was increasingly absorbed in Zionist activities and the writing that those issues inspired. One can almost hear the agitated voice that so many years later Irving Howe would report: "Something must be done!" In fact, in speaking some thirty-five years later about her early journalistic work, Marie Syrkin invoked these precise words, and then added: "And I knew how to do it!"

Marie Syrkin Meets Goldie Meyerson

Marie's determination to do what she knew she could do may have been strengthened by another event that happened much closer to home. It was at this very time, 1932, that she met Goldie Meyerson, who would later take the Hebrew name Golda Meir. This meeting was the beginning of a profound, deep, and most important friendship. The relationship of the two women was natural and complementary, for as much as Syrkin admired Golda Meir for her rare effective combination of activism and idealism, Meir, in turn, admired Marie for her combination of intellect and idealism. They were, furthermore, both unselfconscious feminists of the same stripe. It would be a very long, lifetime relationship; a personal, intellectual, political, mutually admiring, and loving friendship, though with one or two late disappointments for Marie Syrkin.

In 1989, Marie said that Goldie Mabowitch Meyerson had, at the age of seventeen, already become a propagandist for the movement. The thought of the young Golda (who was only one year older than Marie) triggered the memory of her father Nachman Syrkin's admiration for the young woman from Milwaukee: "Some time around 1919," Marie mused, "my father said to me, 'There's a young woman in our movement (and it could only be she) who is a remarkable speaker.' He then said, 'I thought you would be like that'" (Personal interview). Though Marie did not learn the young woman's name at that time, the episode remained fixed in her memory, and seventy years later she was forced to confess that it had made her feel a little guilty. Moreover, if Nachman Syrkin was highly impressed by the ardent young Zionist woman, Golda had been deeply influenced by him. In her 1975 autobiography, Golda Meir speaks of those men who made the strongest impression on her:

I think first of all of such Jews as Nachman Syrkin who was one of the most fiery ideologists of Labor Zionism. A Russian Jew who had studied philosophy and psychology in Berlin, Syrkin returned to Russia after the 1905 Revolution and then emigrated to the United States, where he became the leader of the American *Poalei Zion* (Labor Zionists). Syrkin believed that the sole hope of the Jewish proletariat (which he labeled the "slave of slaves" or the "proletariat of the proletariats") lay in mass immigration to Palestine, and he wrote and spoke brilliantly on this subject throughout Europe and the States.[6]

Meir notes here that his "daughter Marie became my close friend and later my biographer" (Meir 56).

Marie Syrkin and Golda Meir first met in New York, circa 1932. Golda's daughter had been very ill with what had been diagnosed in Palestine as a kidney problem, and Golda decided to bring her to the United States for medical treatment. She approached the Women's Labor Council and asked if she could be sent as a *shlichah,* an emissary, to the Pioneer Women's Organization in America. This group founded by Rachel Yanait Ben-Zvi (wife of Yitzhak Ben-Zvi, the future President of the State of Israel) was a worldwide labor Zionist organization with a decidedly socialist-feminist ideology that had begun in New York in 1925. Its goal was to provide social services to women and children in Palestine, to help absorb immigrants, and to encourage Jewish women in America to become active in Jewish and American affairs. When the movement first began, its affairs mainly were carried out in Yiddish, but as the immigrant population became more acculturated, the organization switched to English. Goldie Meyerson was fluent in both, as was another regular contributor to the *Pioneer Women's Journal* — Marie Syrkin.

It was inevitable that the two women should meet. Golda's main mission was to go on tour and address groups of women in Yiddish or in English — and both groups listened intently to her, for she was a mesmerizing speaker. But she was also an editor of the *Pioneer Women's Journal,* and in this capacity she also had to write. The art of writing, however, was not Golda's forte. As Marie has put it: "Her directness and simplicity — her outstanding oratorical virtues enriched by her voice and the force of her personality — became matter of fact and undistinguished when she had to write rather than speak. But if her exposition was tame, her oral eloquence was unforgettable."[7] In a remembrance of Golda written just after former Prime Minister Meir's death, her longtime friend and champion, Marie Syrkin, wrote these words:

I first met Golda in the thirties when she returned from Palestine to serve as an emissary to the Pioneer Women. Her audience in those days was limited to the small circle of the faithful — Labor Zionists like herself whom she addressed in Yiddish and English. American Jewry as a whole was as yet largely untouched by the Zionist idea and amazingly ignorant of the small pioneer settlement of the *Yishuv*. The kibbutz was a barely known, exotic concept. But if she had no multitudes to captivate, Golda's effect on the members of her movement was immediate. Labor Palestine could have had no more impassioned and persuasive exponent than Golda. All that subsequently became the trite rhetoric of Zionist oratory — making the desert bloom, renewing an oppressed people in a just, cooperative society — was both challenge and revelation when she spoke. Though an unknown young woman, she required no panoply of office to reveal her unique force, and I like others, came under her spell.[8]

The magic spell of Golda's oratory no doubt impelled Marie Syrkin to intensify her determination to use her own verbal skills in the service of the Jewish people; but it was her prose, not her poetry, that was called for at this moment in history. And a fortunate decision it was: if Golda's written skills were not her strength, Marie's powerful way with the written word could be used to broadcast their mutual cause. What is more, as it would turn out not far in the future, the text that Marie crafted would become the written word that Golda spoke.

Having been inspired by Golda and having made the decision to use her own skills in the service of Zionism and the Jewish people, Marie began seriously to consider her school sabbatical plans for the next year, 1933. She would go to Palestine. She felt she did not want to report on events in the Middle East in the abstract, from thousands of miles away from the action. She wanted to do eyewitness reporting from the Palestinian zone of creativity as well as conflict. Personal considerations did not seem insurmountable. The very unusual custody arrangement that Marie and Aaron had devised was both equitable and practical: both parents had intense careers, both were completely devoted to their child, and neither wished to sacrifice one for the other. It was David's year to be with his father, and Charles, who had done his own cross-country traveling for several months the year after they were married, could hardly object to Marie's plans; and if he so wished, he could accompany her to Palestine. His deep Jewish interests had been expressed very clearly in his poetry. Indeed, the very first of his poems that Marie had ever encountered was the intensely Jewish poem, "Rashi." Yet when she asked him to join her on her trip he assured her "in all gravity that he was too busy; he had not yet explored Central Park to the full." He promised her that they would "set out on a walking tour of England, Wales, and Ireland; and then [they] would go to Paris, Rome, Jerusalem — all in some indefinite future." It never happened; and Marie later would report that her response to his long-term plans was, "I did not wait and he did not object" (*Man and Poet* 44). Nor was she stricken, she would claim, by his ready acquiescence in her departures.

Years later, Marie was called upon to write a memoir of her life with Charles Reznikoff. Recognizing that their separations were not usual for the newly married and might be misunderstood, and wishing to make the picture of their relationship "whole" she wrote, "I shall allow myself to quote from a letter that serves as a corrective to what otherwise would be a misleading account of a complex relationship." The quotation is from a letter Charles had written to her in Palestine in 1933:

I feel a compulsion, which I shall not resist, to write my lament for Israel. I am thinking of nothing else in my spare time, and though nothing may come of it, I must do what I can. . . . I wish you to see everything and enjoy everything slowly, unhurriedly to soak in as much as possible. Somehow I feel as if I as well as you am in Palestine, that is that you are my alter ego, and so I know that we really have become one flesh. As I sit here thinking of you and looking at times at your picture on the desk, I am very thankful that after so many delays, so many twists and turns, we have found each other, at least that I have found you, and curiously enough, alone in our house I do not feel lonely. . . . I have come to think that of all states of human happiness that of being happily married is not to be despised, as I once despised it — before I knew you, there is quiet glow in me whenever I think of you; I feel its warmth to my fingertips, to the roots of my thoughts. (*Man and Poet* 44)

Marie in Palestine

At the end of March — just days after her thirty-fourth birthday — Marie Syrkin set off on her trans-Atlantic voyage on board the S.S. *Manhattan*. After a brief stop in Paris, she then set sail on April 2, aboard the French ship *Marietta Pacha,* for Palestine. Exclaiming enthusiastically to Charles about the blandishments of the Mediterranean Sea from which venue she writes, she is in no way seduced by the means of travel. "The French boat, on which I am, is supposed to be one of the finest of the Mediterranean craft — deluxe in fact. But French de luxe is very low American. I cannot eat the food at all. I am probably the fussiest person in the party declining all the French viands, all of them elaborate and horrible, resolutely."

This banter about the weather and the cuisine, however, shifts abruptly to the very serious. If Marie had planned this trip so that she could be eyewitness to the events of the times, the plan went into action almost immediately. "We had a great deal of excitement on board because of the German Jews," she tells Charles.

We have a number who have just escaped from Germany. They tell the most dreadful stories. A protest meeting was held at which I spoke among others. To put it modestly my remarks were well-received. At the meeting it was decided to give the stories we had heard some publicity by writing to various publications. I had written a letter planning to mail it to *The Nation* from Alexandria, where we have a one day stop. However last night a bulletin was received to the effect that the boycott had been lifted. In view of this, I am mailing the letter to you. If the situation does not improve, please mail it to *The Nation* yourself. (Archives 1 f. 18)

The letter to *The Nation* may be one of the earliest examples of Marie's instinctive journalistic responses to the looming Nazi perils and the subsequent fate of the European Jews. The triad of intertwined locales, Germany, Palestine, and America, would absorb her polemical powers for the rest of her life, but were especially dominant in the years between 1933 and 1950.

Marie Syrkin arrived in Palestine on April 6, 1933. She disembarked at the port of Haifa, though she had been booked for Tel Aviv. There the ship could not go directly to Jaffa because there was no harbor and, as she described it in a letter to Charles, "little boats come up with Arabs, who [put] in the passengers with no regard for life, limb or baggage. When the sea is at all rough it is impossible to disembark. The ship goes on cheerily to Haifa — four hours further on." Once in Haifa, after much hubbub and confusion on the ship and while going ashore, Marie was met at the port by her uncle — Nachman's brother, Isaac, who had emigrated to Palestine. She would be staying with him and his wife for several days. Despite the great confusion, babble of languages, ship captain's commands, crew's orders, indignant passengers, Marie reacted at once to the fact of finally touching ground on the soil she had known in her heart and mind since infancy. Sitting on the little front porch of her uncle's "primitive" house on top of Mount Carmel, surrounded by a profusion of red poppies, with the Mediterranean spread out below, she is moved to write, "The great thrill comes when I walk a step toward the back and see the blue harbor below. It's terribly beautiful. I wonder if the Jews wrote great poetry in Biblical times because they were situated in such an extraordinary setting of mountain and sea." The letter is, of course, to Charles; hence, in a comic but edgy *caveat* as much to herself as to him, she adds, "I know you think I am gushy and your puritanical nature revolts" (Archives 1 f. 18).

Passover occurred in early April that year, which gave Marie her first opportunity to experience Jewish life on a secular Palestinian *kibbutz* — though she referred to it then as a *kvuzah*. The *kvuzah* was the earliest form of small, voluntary, agricultural, collective community, its small size arising from the principle that the community should function as an extended family. The first *kvuzah* was founded in 1909, at Deganyah, by a small group of *chalutzim* (pioneers). Five years later, there were eleven *kevutzot* (plural), and by 1918, there were twenty-nine. But after World War I, as a new and larger number of settlers (known as the Third *Aliyah*) began to arrive, the idea of a larger form of collective, the *kibbutz,* was proposed. The *kibbutz* would be a bigger and a more self-sufficient collective village that could combine agriculture with industry. Ein Harod, founded in 1921, was the first of the *kibbutzim*.

It was to Ein Harod that Marie accompanied her old friend Sonia Kamenetsky, a feminist Labor Zionist who had emigrated to Palestine in 1931. Marie explained to Charles, "I spent the Seder not at Tel Aviv as I had originally planned but in Ein Harod, one of the oldest *kvutzahs* [*sic*], communes. My friend Sonia Kamenetsky was going there so I decided to accompany her as Ein Harod is very near Haifa." The overnight visit absolutely enthralled Marie. If she thought the prose of her prior letter to Charles might have been a bit too purple, this one is glossy aubergine. Enraptured by her first eyewitness experience of secular socialist Zionism in action, rather than in the abstract, she instructs Charles: "It was an extraordinary experience. I suppose you know that the kvutzahs [*sic*] are workers colonies which have been built up on the purest [communist is crossed out] socialist ideal of a cooperative communal life" (Archives 1 f. 18).

Marie's letter is a prefiguration of what will become signature Marie Syrkin; that is, a rhetorical mode that see-saws between extravagant idealism and stinging attack. Syrkin has sometimes been criticized for having spoken in the language of naive and sentimental early Zionists, but this misses the point that her double-sided rhetorical style is characteristic of the zealous writer from the prophets onward through the centuries. Only the idealist with a sense of high moral purpose can turn the polemical carpet over to expose a rough underside of moral indignation. The cynic, however, has only one texture. Stylistically, Marie Syrkin was a pragmatic idealist, capable of soaring flights of enthusiasm as well as hard-nosed judgment.

After a lengthy description of the hardships and the spare living conditions of the adults on the *kibbutz*, then the children's "ideal existence," their playrooms "as charming as those of any American kindergarten in a progressive school . . . decorated with flowers, pictures, brightly painted walls, etc." Marie further points out that if Charles had seen the central dining room of the parents "with its long bare tables, tin spoons, enamel plates thrown in piles and then saw the charmingly set tables of the children [he] would realize what that meant. The children have a carefully worked out diet—an egg daily and milk—vegetables—etc. The adults hardly ever see an egg despite the fact that they are an agricultural commune. Whatever excess there is must be sold for the improvement of the *meshekh* [kibbutz economy]" (Archives 1 f. 18).

Not surprisingly, Marie was bowled over, despite the hardships, by the apparent zealous commitment of the *kibbutzniks* of Ein Harod to the ideals of socialist Zionism. This was her first look at the fruits of communal life. Many years later, in response to the growing criticism of weaknesses, mistakes, and failures of the *kibbutz* system, and in the light of her own recognition of many of these developments, she would continue to argue for the lasting value of the *kibbutz*'s original intent and experience in the history of the Jews and the State of Israel.

But in 1933, it was a revelation, a wonderment. Having come primarily to participate in the Passover ritual of secular Jews (paradoxical as that might seem), Marie describes the event to Charles in detail:

The seder was extraordinary. There was nothing of the traditional orthodox celebration. The long tables of the mess had table-cloths of a yellowish whiteness. The enamel plates were placed neatly with an occasional tin spoon and fork (there is a scarcity of knives). A festive touch was given by sprays of green leaves. In the center of the hall were small tables for the children. Passover is the one night of the year when the children eat together with the adults in the common mess. We came in and sat down. After the adults were seated, the children came in two processions carrying sheaves of grain and singing in Hebrew. The text was explained to me as follows. "We bring the first [offering, crossed out] grains [ear?] of the fields. It is not full because of the drought. . . . May next year be better." They circled around repeating this prayer and then sat down. To the workers of the commune, it must have been very affecting because they have suffered terribly for the past two years on account of the drought. The song "a better harvest for next year" has replaced the ancient "next year in Jerusalem." Afterwards a small child asked "kashas" [questions]. The following were asked:

1. Why are some people poor and some rich?
2. Why do great winds and small winds blow?
3. Why do the Arabs always live on a hill?
4. Why are there wars?

The answers were naturally of a socialist, ethical character. In addition, some children read about Moses from the Bible, and two others recited poems of Bialik (of course everything was in Hebrew, one hears nothing else unless one is an unfortunate tourist who compels people to speak Yiddish, Russian) the food served was supposed to be unusually fine — meat, soup, kugel, and compote — I found it far from good though infinitely better than the really ghastly lunch and breakfast at which even the weak tea has a vile and peculiar taste.

After the meal, they danced the Hora. The Hora is a typical peasant dance which calls for as much endurance as enthusiasm. Hour after hour the circle goes around singing and stepping to the self-same rhythm. I tried it and fell out in two minutes half-dead. My companions and I retired to real beds, donated by the workers, very early. But the young folks danced the hora and sang till dawn. I probably disgraced myself as a weakling but one day there exhausted me. Today I am at my uncle's. Tomorrow I expect to go to Tel Aviv.

I don't know whether you are interested in all this, but I cannot tell you how exciting I find it. It is a real Jewish land. We need never again say that we

have no land. One feels that instantly. As far as the Arabs are concerned the sentiment of all those to whom I have spoken is one of quiet fortitude. "If they
attack, we will fight." It is not like being slaughtered in Germany, aliens in an
alien country. The feeling is "We are at home, we will fight for our home." I
have never seen such Jews before. The features are those with which we are familiar, but the bearing, the color, the spirit — that is something we have not
known. (Archives 1 f. 18)

Marie Syrkin's report to her husband ends with a question. Would he
like to live in Palestine? She is thinking of using the $500 she has saved
up to build a house in the Yishuv. She triple-underlines the sentence "We
must learn Hebrew." None of this will happen. Finally, Marie adds a
postscript: "Are these letters awful? You know my epistolary weakness —
tell me and I will try to improve" (Archives 1 f. 18).

Marie's next stop was Tel Aviv, from where she reported on life in this
exciting city. "It's a completely modern city with American bustle. Of
course it's new and white and glistening, directly on the beach. . . .
People sit about on beach chairs and bathe, but just as the illusion of
perfect Westernization is complete, you see a slow string of camels
driven by an Arab walking at the edge of the sea." Yet, for Marie the attractive contemporaneity ornamented with Middle Eastern local color
is not its true allure.

"I was shown about very graciously," she explains to Charles, "by the
local Poale Zion. One is impressed by the strength of the labor movement in the country, and the character of the workers. They are as
impressive in the city as they are in the *kvutzah* — a really chosen group."
Syrkin also reported on a "superb" production of Stefan Zweig's *Jere-
miah* given by the worker's theatre *Ohel* in an open air stadium, "as opposed to *Habimah* which is professional."

Does Marie believe at this point that active dedication to the ideals of
socialism and Zionism are the only attitudes to be found among the
Jews of Palestine? Though she certainly waxes rhapsodic over "authentic native art" and boldly asserts that "whatever one sees, no matter what
one's ideology, is Jewish, and that to me is terribly exciting," it quickly
becomes clear that she is not so easily beguiled:

Of course one is conscious of other elements also. I visited a wealthy Tel Aviv
family — very "*balabotish*" [respectable, goodstanding], where the talk was of
sales of "*pardessim*" (orange groves) and real estate instead of a socialist Pales-

tine. One is also conscious of the Revisionists and their antics. There happened to be a Revisionist convention in Tel Aviv while I was there so the streets were full of brown shirted youths. When I first saw the brown shirts I was aghast. I wondered what Nazis had the temerity to enter Tel-Aviv—the 100% Jewish City. I was told that the brown shirts are the regalia of Jabotinsky's darlings—an additional evidence of their wisdom and tact. I was pleased to observe that the only puny, undersized youths that I have seen in Palestine are the Revisionists. It's funny to think that the fire-eating Revisionists are physically far below the standard of the chalutzim,—who are magnificent—an inferiority-complex I suppose. And these damned brats act as strike breakers when the workers maintain their struggle for a higher standard of living despite the recent capitalist immigration from Germany and other countries. The place is seething with Germans, who are seeking refuge.

Undoubtedly, at this moment, Marie would have recalled her own personal experience with Vladimir Jabotinsky some seven years earlier. Although at that time she was not so utterly hostile to him, not so many years later, by 1940, Marie Syrkin would write a trenchant analysis of the history of the Revisionist organization and its activities. Published as a pamphlet by the Emergency Committee for Zionist Affairs in which were represented all the Zionist organizations in the United States, its purpose was "to inform the public of the true nature of this organization and to refute the misleading propaganda being circulated by the Revisionists and their "front" organization, the "American Friends of a Jewish Palestine" and the "Tel Hai Fund." But in 1933, what Marie probably had witnessed was a Betar (a self-defense-Revisionist-Zionist *youth* movement) demonstration—which might account for their "puny" physical appearance. Moreover, Marie's hostility to the brown shirts was shared by most socialist Zionists who said that the brown shirts expressed its fascist elements, although the costume had been in use since the early 1920s (Archives 1 f. 18, April 17 1933).

After a bucolic day in the country, visiting an old friend of her father in Rehovot, Marie went on to Jerusalem. If Tel Aviv had inspired a Syrkinesque hymn to the worker's paradise, the Holy City left her decidedly underwhelmed. "Curiously enough" she confesses to Charles, "Jerusalem made a slighter impression on me than any of the other places that I have visited. That's sheer cussedness on my part, because Jerusalem is supposed to be the pièce de resistance of Palestine." There are too many tourists like herself; the modern residential section outside the gates is only about eighty years old. The University, however, dazzles her senses. Marie's words of awe express feelings that generations of visitors to the site continue to affirm: "When I sat in the white amphitheater on Mt. Scopus on a sunny morning," she exclaims, "and looked out over the Judean desert and the Judean 'hills' to the Dead Sea, I felt an uplift of the spirit and such as nothing that I have seen has given me. . . . There could be no better place for a University" (Archives 1 f. 18).

Marie's next stop is the ancient city, which she finds extraordinary; it is "hard to believe that one is in the presence of reality and not a museum piece." Charles is then treated to a well-written travelogue of the ugly and the colorful sights, smells, and sounds of the old city: "The incredibly steep, narrow streets winding in dark alleys downhill and uphill—the bazaars . . . where the shops are black holes full of flies, filth and oriental wares, the little blond boys with 'zizis' and 'payes'—everything out of the sun—one can't quite assimilate it. It's what is known as 'picturesque' with a vengeance—a fearful mixture of live babies crawling in the dung, blind Arabs, vendors squatting in their dark doorways" (Archives 1 f. 18).

The travelogue continues with a roll call of the famous historical and religious landmarks that Marie had visited, from the Mount of Olives and the graves of Absalom and the prophets, to the Mosque of Omar, the Church of the Holy Sepulcher, and the stations of the cross. Marie found all this impressive but she was not terribly moved; however, she had yet to visit the wailing wall, which she had reserved as the climax of the visit. She finally went on a Friday afternoon, as she described it, "breaking my neck along the crooked, crazy streets unevenly paved, cobble stones worn slippery by the pedestrians. It's just an old gray wall,—a small one at that. Some Jews were praying and wailing. I felt nothing to my great disgust." The following day Marie decided to make one last visit to the old city, and despite yesterday's repulsion she would revisit the wall. Astonished at her own revised reaction, she admits to Charles, "I stood there listening to Jewish laments till tears trickled out of my eyes. Before I knew it I was getting more emotion than I had bargained for. I felt like sobbing out loud. My guide, with whom I had maintained a professional distance throughout our meanderings, was so affected by my tears that he invited me to the movies—an invitation which I declined without difficulty." She continues,

The Jews are an extraordinary people. I can not help marveling at a people so pure and strong that it can make the center of its longing for centuries a hideous, bare wall, whereas every other people requires the stimulus of every art for the places of its remembrance. You have no idea how beautiful the Mosque is, how seductively glorious the Catholic, Armenian, and even Protestant churches are, with their Madonnas, candles, incense, paintings, draperies. But the Jews have only an ugly narrow little street, with a corner of a broken wall, and to that they cling. I take my hat off to them. Anybody would pray in the Mosque of Omar or the Church of the nativity. Only an exceptionally fanciful and tenacious spirit could find its emotional moment at the wall. (Archives 1 f. 18)

Marie Syrkin's first of many, many visits to the Middle East concluded on May 3. Her last week took her through the Galilee, to Tiberias, the Kinneret, Mt. Hermon, Mt. Tabor, Degania, Tel Hai, among other places of natural, historic, and social interest. In the letter she wrote to Charles aboard the S.S. *Martha Washington,* bound for Italy, Switzerland, and France, Marie sounds a couple of characteristic notes: first, "Despite my unfortunate past experiences [the violets sent from Reno] I cannot resist sending you some poppies plucked from my uncle's garden on Mt. Carmel. I picked them just before I stepped into the automobile, taking me to the harbor. . . . But all jokes and provocative remarks aside, these are red poppies — very scarlet when picked — from me and Palestine;" and second, "I congratulate you your third wedding anniversary, which transpires, as you don't know, on May 27." The letter ends with a little local linguistic joke: "*L'hitraot* — (Hebrew for '*auf wiedersehn*' — the German Jews say L'hitleraus" (Archives 1 f. 18).

Chapter 9

At the Nexus of
the "Jewish Problem"

❧

MARIE SYRKIN LEFT Palestine on May 5 bound for Brindisi, then Naples, Rome, Florence, and Venice; from there she traveled on to Bern, Switzerland — her birthplace — and finally to Paris, where she would stay with her frail, elderly aunt and uncle. Marie was sorry to leave Palestine, but not because she wished to do more sightseeing. Rather, she explained in a letter to her husband, "Palestine draws every Jew with a particular tenderness," and her curious reaction to the beauty of the Italian landscape was surely a consequence of her overpowering sojourn in Palestine. Perhaps recalling the oft-quoted Yiddish proverb, *A khasuren die kalleh is tsu sheyn* (a fault that the bride is too beautiful), she protests that "In fact, Italy is too beautiful." In Palestine, Marie had savored the hard-won fruits of a different, a more unforgiving terrain, and later found it emotionally difficult to digest the richness of Italy's natural *abbondanza*. On May 15, she wrote to Charles:

The extraordinary luxuriance of its vegetation, the abundance of mountains (real ones) flowers, sea, panorama, gives me a slightly vertiginous feeling. Naples, Capri, Fiesole, are simply too much. Especially after Palestine, where every tree is a human triumph, every hill a holy mountain, I had a sense of surfeit. Maybe it's jealousy, but nature has been very spendthrift of her loveliness in Italy. Perhaps that's why the Italians are emotionally superficial. There is too much to love anything deeply. How could they approximate the rapture with which one *chalutzah* in a measly little colony showed me a radish — a red radish grown on the barren soil of Palestine? There are many earthly paradises in Italy — Capri or the Poslippi [*sic*] in Naples — there is no heaven left to long for." (Archives 1 f. 18)

Despite her emotional indigestion, however, Marie does manage to make the most of her quite extensive and mostly appreciative sightseeing in the great cities of Italy.

Traveling from Italy to Switzerland, Marie reports to Charles, "the little I saw of Switzerland" was like a breath of cool air after Italy. It is beautiful—but nobly beautiful—high mountains, pure blue lakes. The people are quiet and not over-courteous. These are villainous generalizations, and no doubt quite untrue. I think I shall stop." From Switzerland, on to Paris. Here, staying at the apartment of her very frail and sick elderly aunt and uncle, she hears quite a few not-so-charming tales about her father's childhood. Unlike the reception she had in Palestine, when at every mention of Nachman Syrkin's name, people fell into reverential raptures—"the 'prophet,' the 'great idealist' among other pet appellations for papa," this time, she writes to Charles, her Aunt Vera was "full of his villainous exploits as a boy." Marie seems particularly charmed by a story she had never before heard and which she recounts in her letter: "[A]t the age of 13 he managed to get himself expelled from gymnasium for no nobler reason than that he said 'Kiss my _____.' To his teacher. [the letter A is crossed out in favor of the _____.] He was expelled thoroughly—despite his excellent scholastic record—and could go to no gymnasium in Russia—hence Germany later, from which in due time he also got himself expelled, though for worthier causes. You might show this to Machette. It will encourage her about Sylvia [her sister Zivia's American name]. She is following in a good tradition" (Archives 1 f. 18, May 22, 1933).

Marie sailed from Le Havre on June 8 on the *Manhattan*, the same ship that had carried her to Europe. In her last letter to Charles from Europe, she writes, "By now, I am terribly impatient to be home. I should be delighted to take an earlier boat if there were one, so with the grace of God, I will be back in your arms in two weeks" (Archives 1 f. 18, May 29, 1933). She arrived in New York on June 15, eager to write about what she had learned in her peregrinations abroad: whenever she knew that "something must be done," she would do what she could do. Almost immediately, something had to be done. On June 16, the day after her return to New York, the newspapers reported the shocking assassination of the influential and popular Labor Zionist leader Chaim Arlosoroff, a leading figure within the Mapai Party which had been founded in 1930 and which by 1931, had become the dominant party. In 1931, the quiet academic-like Arlosoroff was elected to be a member of

The Syrkin family in 1907, before they came to America: Nachman, Bassya, Marie (age 9).

Maurice Samuel (ca. 1917, age 22).
Approximately at the time of his
elopement with Marie.

Strunsky's Hotel, Belmar, New Jersey, (ca. 1915). Where Marie Syrkin spent her
fabulous sixteenth summer.

Aaron Bodansky (ca. 1920s, age 32) when he and Marie Syrkin married.

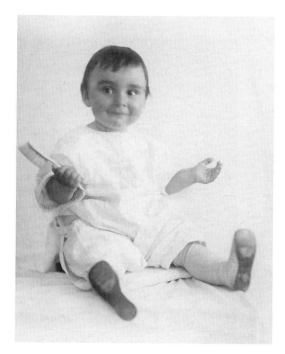

Benya, age one year. Marie Syrkin and Aaron Bodansky's first child who died at the age of two.

Charles Reznikoff (ca. 1935).
Marie Syrkin and Charles
Reznikoff were married in
1930.

David Bodansky (age 19, 1943).
Marie Syrkin and Aaron
Bodansky's son.

Marie Syrkin in a DP camp in the American Zone in Germany, 1947.

Zivia Syrkin Wurtele (ca. 1950). Marie's sister.

Marie Syrkin during her first years at Brandeis (ca. 1950).

Charrles Reznikoff in the 1960s after Marie Syrkin retired to New York.

Marie Syrkin and Golda Meir holding a copy of Syrkin's biography Golda Meir Israel's Leader.

Marie Syrkin receiving honorary degree at Brandeis in 1979. (Pictured with Carole Kessner and Professor Milton Hindus.)

Marie Syrkin (ca. late 1980s) in retirement in Santa Monica.

Marie Syrkin's descendants (ca. 2002). Her son and his wife; her two grandsons and their wives; her five great-grandchildren.

the Jewish Agency Executive and to head its Political Department. On June 16, 1933, while taking an evening stroll with his wife on the beach in Tel Aviv, he was murdered by two unknown assassins in Arab garb. Though two rank-and-file Revisionists were accused of the crime, the murder was never solved. The British tried the two men and acquitted them for lack of evidence, but the Labor Party continued to believe they were guilty. The case, however, greatly stepped up the political tensions in Palestine and within the Zionist movement in general. There already had been angry clashes to settle other scores — economic, political, and moral between the Labor Party and the Revisionists. As Walter Laqueur has described the situation:

hardly anyone on the Left doubted for a moment that Revisionists were behind the crime, even though the Revisionists themselves emphatically denied responsibility. The murder had been preceded by a hate campaign against Labour in the Revisionist press. "Traitors," and "despicable lackeys of the British," were among the epithets hurled at Weizmann, Arlosoroff, and the other leaders of the Zionist movement. For a while it seemed as if Jewish Palestine was on the eve of civil war.[1]

To make matters between the Labor Zionists and the Revisionists even more explosive, Chaim Arlosoroff had devised a strategy known as the "Transfer Plan," a scheme to get the endangered German Jews out of Nazi Germany as well as to promote emigration to Palestine. As head of the political department of the Jewish Agency Executive, he spent the last few months of his life implementing this plan that called for negotiating with the Nazis and establishing a public company named *Transfer*,

whose sole business was to transfer the property of German Jews from Germany to Palestine, with the hope that the owners would be able to follow it. This arrangement lasted from 1934 to 1938. The company, a non-Jewish firm directed and managed by two respected English businessmen, would buy Jewish property, which the Jews themselves could sell only at a fraction of its worth, and barter it for German goods exported to Palestine, where the proceeds of their sale were reimbursed to the German Jews who had immigrated there. This was the only way German Jews could save part of their possessions. The interim financing was handled by a special Jewish Agency Executive budget.[2]

While it is quite true that negotiations with the Nazis, which had begun in secret in April of 1933, were necessary to accomplish the goal of getting Jews out of Germany, into Palestine, and providing them with some means of existence once in Palestine, it was a plan that caused enormous controversy. When the news became known, the Zionists split in two, with Mapai on the left and their adversaries, the Revisionists on the right, causing riots, antiphonal screaming, protest marches, rancor, and threats. On June 16, 1933, the Revisionist newspaper *Hazit Ha-am* printed the following: "There will be no forgiveness for those who for greed have sold out the honor of their people to madmen and anti-Semites. . . . The Jewish people have always known how to size up betrayers, . . . and it will know how to react to this crime"("Chaim Arlosoroff," *Judaica*). To some in the Labor Party, this statement certainly sounded like a death threat.

News of the murder reached Marie immediately. She knew that without question this would be a major issue at the forthcoming Eighteenth Zionist Congress. Not only was the Congress meeting under the ominous shadow of the Nazis' rising power in Germany, with its concomitant dire consequences for German Jewry, but the Congress would also have to deal with galloping inflation in the *Yishuv,* and now, certainly, the assassination of Arlosoroff, which brought the conflict between Labor and the Revisionists to Fahrenheit 212. In preparation for the Congress, which was to meet in Prague on August 21, Mapai was scheduled to hold its convention a few weeks in advance when it would elect members to the Eighteenth Zionist Congress. Moreover, someone would have to be elected to fill Arlosoroff's position. That someone was to be the secretary general of the *Histadrut,* David Ben-Gurion — the man who would later become, effectively, the Prime Minister of the *Yishuv,* then the Prime Minister of the State of Israel; he was also the man who, two years later, would take Marie Syrkin to dinner and the movies.

A Triad of Topics

Surely these events were important enough for Marie to consider returning at once to Palestine and Europe. This was where the action was, and would be; as a serious journalist covering the current events of the Jewish people, it was without doubt where she *should* be. Her teaching obligations would not begin until after Labor Day; her son was with his father; her husband had said he would not stand in her way. Since the

1920s, Marie had been contributing poetry, translations, drama criticism, and articles for Jewish and Zionist publications, but this, she felt,
would be the beginning of something quite new: eye-witness reports
and commentary on critical events in the history of the Jewish people.
During the 1920s her personal life had been so fragmented, disturbed,
and tragic that she could not devote herself wholeheartedly to events in
the world outside. In August of 1933, however, Marie Syrkin was confident enough to assume that whatever she covered in the Congress, and
whatever new information she gleaned, would find its way into print, in
one place or another.

When Marie returned to America from the Eighteenth Zionist Congress, she had a triad of topics begging for journalistic reportage: Palestine, America, Nazi Germany. To begin with, this had been the first
Congress in which her own party, the Labor Party, outnumbered the
General Zionists; second, there was galloping inflation in the *Yishuv;*
third, there was the murder of Arlosoroff; fourth, there was the conflict
between those who supported the American Jewish Congress' endorsement of an anti-Nazi boycott and those who were in favor of Arlosoroff's Transfer scheme, which would undercut the boycott. In addition to all this, there was Hitler's increasingly restrictive anti-Jewish
laws, which in two years' time would be further escalated and forever
known as the draconic Nuremberg Laws. Marie Syrkin had enough material for a lifetime. And as it was to be, the Middle East, America, and
Europe would be her lifetime interest.

In the year that Marie returned to America from Europe and Palestine,
however, Zionism was not front and center in the ordinary American
Jew's consciousness. Second-generation Jews in America were distancing
themselves from the world of their parents; they were responding to the
immigrant "cult of gratitude" or in Max Lerner's phrase, "the slaying of
the European father," by assimilating and striving to be upwardly mobile and socially acceptable.[3] Moreover, American Jews in the 1930s
were in the midst of the Great Depression and facing new versions of
antisemitism. Despite the economic conditions, they had moved on
from blue-collar to white-collar work, advanced in the fields of profes-
sionalism, and were trying to penetrate the corporate world. Women
also had entered the white-collar and professional worlds, no longer
seamstresses and domestics, but now as secretaries, teachers, and small-
business owners. Yet, in all these fields, Jews faced discrimination and
sometimes quotas, especially in higher education. It was true that Roo-

sevelt had brought Jews such as Henry Morgenthau, Judge Samuel
Rosenman, and David K. Niles into his inner circle of trusted friends,
with many others brought into lower levels of public service; and it was
true that his liberal policies of social reform, the New Deal, were reflec-
tive of his Jewish advisors' liberal thought; but it was also a fact that the
enemies of the New Deal began to mockingly call it the "Jew Deal." The
Roosevelt bashers spoke of Franklin "Rosenfeld," and well-known
figures, such as H. L. Mencken, Theodore Dreiser, Charles Lindbergh,
and Father Coughlin spoke out against the foreigner Jews who were
labeled at one and the same time communists, capitalists, war mongers,
social climbers, anti-Christian Bolsheviks, cosmopolitans, and international financiers. Sporting its menacing, white-hooded costume, the Ku
Klux Klan geared up for action as numerous other organizations spouted
vile slogans of hatred—many of them financed and supported by cor-
porations that also funneled money to congressional demagogues. To
make matters even worse, antisemitism in the United States was given
financial support by Nazi Germany. "Hitler's most dependable agents
in this campaign," Howard Sachar explains, "were German-Americans,
many of them recent immigrants to the United States, veterans of the
Kaiser's army and now ardent partisans of the Third Reich. The Nazi
propaganda bureau supplied them with organizational leadership,
funds, and endless quantities of uniforms, insignia, and propaganda literature. In 1934, many of America's culture *vereinen* were reorganized
and centralized in the German-American Bund" (Sachar 405–406). The
effort to evangelize Hitler's gospel of hate continued through the 1930s,
ultimately counterbalanced by journalists' reports of Nazi brutality and
America's entry into the war against Hitler and his obscene ideology.

Against this background, Marie Syrkin returned to America in September of 1933—just in time for the opening of the school year. She was
armed with information gathered from her visits to Palestine and the
Zionist Convention in Prague, inspired with enthusiasm, hot with per-
turbation, and with a burning desire to do something. The specific
"something" was the spread of the word about the developments and
achievements of the Palestinian *chalutzim* (pioneers) and the recent success of Mapai—the Labor Zionists having become the largest voting
bloc in the World Zionist Organization. Despite her growing concerns
about the situation in Germany, Marie seemed to privilege what she *saw*
in Palestine over what she *heard* about the Nazis. Years later, she would
admit this: "In . . . 1933 I took my first trip to Palestine" she wrote in

1980. "The ship's radio carried the news of fresh measures enacted by Hitler, newly come to power. Yet the Nazi menace in its initial unfolding seemed somehow unreal. It was too preposterous; it would blow over" (*State* 2). In fact, in the early 1930s Marie composed a humorous satiric verse about the state of affairs in Germany after the first six months of Hitler's appointment as Chancellor; it was also after the burning of the Reichstag and its aftermath, after the suspension of individual rights and civil liberties, after the passage of the Enabling Act that gave dictatorial power to Adolf Hitler, after the enactment of the boycott of Jewish businesses, after the burning of books, after the spread of hate propaganda against Jews, after the formation of secret courts of no appeal, after the establishment of concentration camps, the dissolution of opposition political parties, and the Law for the Prevention of Hereditary and Defective Offspring — among othe draconian measures — Marie Syrkin in all her naiveté still thought she could respond with mockery and wit. In a parody of Christopher Marlowe's "Come Live With Me and Be My Love," she wrote her "Aryan Love Song":

> Come live with me and be my mate,
> But bring your birth certificate,
> And prove by Grandma's wedding papers
> She cut no oriental capers.

> When in my arms you'll softly nestle,
> I'll sing you lyrics of Horst Wessel,
> As we will sit beside the falls
> Of Marxists, Jews, and liberals.

> And I will make you beds of bear skins
> Like the ancient forest fairskins;
> A little club, a cap of brown
> And swastikas for every gown.

> Love, should you ever lack for fuel
> For Siegfried or Brunhilde's gruel,
> I know that every "echt" librarian
> Will furnish kindling for an Aryan.

While I protect with ax and sabre
The revelation, "Hate your neighbor!"
Come live with me and be my mate
But bring your birth certificate.[4]

Read today, Marie's clever sardonic verses appear far too facile in the face of such impending doom. As early as 1933, after Hitler had come to power, the great liberal rabbi of Germany, Leo Baeck, had prophesied the future: "The thousand-year history of the German Jews has come to an end" (Dawidowicz 169). But like almost everyone else in the world, Marie was unable to grasp the nightmare of annihilation ahead. Out of an understandable failure of imagination, in 1933, she did not foresee the monstrous future.

Instead, Marie Syrkin focused her work on trying to inform the mostly disinterested American Jewish population about the actual marvels of the Palestinian pioneers. In 1980, Marie confessed that in 1933, more real to her than the reports from Germany "were the kibbutzim that I saw in the Valley of the Jordan and Galilee, the rapture of a young woman who ran up to me with the first radish grown in her settlement, the *hora* danced on the Sabbath on the streets of still uncrowded Tel Aviv along whose shore camels slowly made their way. Each accomplishment was still a victory to be celebrated in the popular pioneer songs of the time (*State* 2). In later years, the Yiddish ironic adage "*Die kalleh is tsu shayn*" (the bride is too beautiful), the one that she had seemed to paraphrase regarding Italy would be turned on her: Marie Syrkin would be criticized by the American and Israeli left for the "too beautiful," naive, sentimental, rhetorical style of her early writings about Palestine. She was taken to task, perhaps unfairly, for having omitted the warts.

On the Frontier

By the fall of 1934, the League for Labor Palestine decided to discontinue its publication *Labor Palestine,* but something would have to take its place. A committee was formed with Marie Syrkin and Hayim Fineman as co-chairpersons to work out the details for the new journal. The Yiddish language organ of the American Poale Zion Party, the distinguished Labor Zionist journal, *Der Yiddisher Kemfer,* had a loyal, but not very sizable, following of Yiddish speakers and readers. It had been in existence since 1906, under the editorship of very eminent figures, including the much-admired disciple of Nachman Syrkin, the Marxist Zionist theoretician Ber Borochov. It appeared irregularly as a weekly until 1923, and then as a bi-weekly under the name *Yidisher Arbeter* until 1931, when it resumed as a weekly under the brilliant editorship of Hayim Greenberg. The journal had long been an internationally important political and social think tank for Labor Zionism, but its readership was aging, the world's Jewish population was quickly moving westward to America, and the next generation was replacing Yiddish with English. And while it is true that under the extraordinary leadership of Greenberg, the readership began to extend beyond movement devotees, it was also true that the movement itself was not growing particularly fast.[5] Non-Labor Zionists read the journal because of its unusually high quality — not for its ideology. Statistics show that in the mid-1930s the Jewish population in the United States stood at 4.28 million. The American Zionist movement numbered only 63,850 — barely 1.5 percent of the total Jewish population (Raider 58). One reason for the low membership numbers was obvious: it was the Depression and money to pay for membership was too hard to come by. But it also was the result of the march of assimilation. Second-generation Jews did not read the Yiddish Press; they spoke English, read American newspapers, and took a keen interest in American politics. Yet the leaders of the Labor Zionist Party were convinced that a high-quality, English-language publication could engage the younger generation.

The committee to discuss plans for the new journal met in October of 1934, and first on the agenda was the choice of an editor-in-chief. Though he was already the editor of the *Kemfer,* when Hayim Greenberg was asked to add the new publication to his work schedule, he readily agreed. Greenberg was at the height of his career. Far more than an editor, he was a brilliant essayist who wrote in four languages: Hebrew, Yiddish, Russian, and English. A *wunderkind,* by the age of fifteen, he had already made a reputation as a superb speaker for Zionism; by the time he was thirty, having displayed an acute philosophical and political mind as a journalist, essayist, and lecturer, he had become one of the most influential figures among the cultured intelligentsia of Russian Jewry. Perhaps most of all, this slightly built, ascetic-appearing, meditative intellectual with an ever-present cigarette held between two fingers as he spoke, this cosmopolitan, deeply Jewish, nonreligious, anti-Marxist socialist Zionist, pacifist (at the moment), idealist, was, as Greenberg's contemporary, Maurice Samuel, put it, "a sage. . . . [H]e had a grave and affectionate understanding of man's needs. His *sagesse* did not derive from his learning: on the contrary, he had accumulated his vast learning in the practice of his *sagesse*" (qtd. in *Other* 46). Two generations later, Robert Seltzer described Hayim Greenberg as a "classical Jewish moralist who called for a restoration of ethical values in light of a realistic perception of the sins of the age: indifference to the suffering of concrete human beings" (*Other* 47). Finally, it can be said that the new editor of the *Jewish Frontier* was a spiritual and moral leader for his generation. He was revered by those who knew or knew about him, and not the least by his new associate, Marie Syrkin. In the introduction to her edited anthology of the writings of Hayim Greenberg, Syrkin writes, "no matter how surprisingly effective this delicate and reticent thinker proved to be as a political thinker, his abiding influence lay in his dual role of writer and spiritual spokesman of the Socialist-Zionist movement in the United States. His essays, of which three volumes have appeared in Yiddish and two in English, reveal, if only partially the richness of a mind too often deflected from its natural course by the responsibilities of political leadership in a tragic and heroic time."[6] Marie was smitten at once and for all time.

All this having been said in praise of Hayim Greenberg, it does seem surprising that he would accept such a risky position. In Marie Syrkin's own words, "That a writer and theoretician of Greenberg's brilliance and reputation should have undertaken to head the mostly volunteer staff of an ill-financed journal that would speak for an obscure movement was a stroke of rare luck." The mostly volunteer staff included Marie and her committee co-chair, Hayim Fineman, a longtime Labor Zionist and Professor of English at the University of Pennsylvania. Dedication was their motivation. "The only professional," Syrkin recalls, "was a managing editor who received only a pittance. (In this respect the *Jewish Frontier* was not to change.) Greenberg . . . began at some point to receive $75 a month."[7] Marie, however, never did take a salary, even after she herself became the editor-in-chief.

Doubtless, readers accustomed to the miasma of twenty-first century journalistic cynicism and Orwellian obscurantism will be unaccustomed to the declarations of purpose of the first editorial in the *Jewish Frontier*. This unabashedly idealistic agenda probably was written by Hayim Greenberg, and almost certainly translated by Marie Syrkin, as she would do for many of his future writings. The telltale clue is the choice of the word "rapture," a Syrkin signature word that first appeared in her 1933 letter to Charles from Palestine, and appears in a similar context in the editorial:

We believe that the new values created in Palestine — the rapture of pioneering, the ennobling of human labor, the heroic attempt to elevate social relationships — are beginning to stimulate Jewish life everywhere. We seek to strengthen the dynamic influence of Palestine Labor on Jewish life in America by means of an informed, alert, public opinion. Particularly today, when reaction and suicidal cupidity threaten to invalidate all that has been achieved in Palestine, we feel that there must be a publication which will interpret contemporary events in Palestine and take its stand on the frontiers of Jewish life throughout the world. We represent that synthesis in Jewish thought that is nationalist without being chauvinist, and which stands for fundamental economic reconstruction without being communist. Only such a synthesis can answer the need of the disorientated modern Jew. (*Frontier*, "Our Stand," December 1934)

These were heady days, indeed. Marie was standing firmly on her own frontier; having left ideas of conventional marriage and family behind, she now embraced an exciting life in the service of a vocation powerfully felt. Electricity was in the air when the small battery of editorial assistants was charged by the intellectual power of their editor-in-chief. Writing in 1979 of those first days in 1934, Marie Syrkin clearly recalled that "[t]he excitement of our editorial meetings in the early years was generated by our assurance that we had something urgent and important to say for which we were the only available voice. Greenberg was not so much a task-master as a moral force. We may have had no money and a small readership, but he never let his assistants forget that we had the magnitude of our purpose" (*Frontier*, January/February 1983, 41).

The *Frontier*, however, was not the only serious Jewish publication on the market. It is curious that in these very economically constrained times, within a few years, several new English language Jewish publications appeared on the scene. There was, of course, the much older *Menorah Journal*, but in 1935, Mordecai Kaplan launched *Reconstructionist*; in 1936, Trude Weiss-Rosmarin began her publication, the *Jewish Spectator*; and in 1938, the American Jewish Committee began its bimonthly *Contemporary Jewish Record* that in 1945 would become *Commentary*. Moreover, in 1936, under the founding editorship of Philip

Rahv, William Phillips, and Sidney Hook, the non-Communist Marxist, avant-garde literary magazine, *Partisan Review*, began publication. Though this publication was not associated with any Jewish denomination or cause, and included such non-Jews as Mary McCarthy, Dwight MacDonald, and Edmund Wilson, one of its founding contributors, Irving Howe, said (somewhat self-servingly) of the group that cohered around *Partisan Review*, "They are, or until recently have been, anti-Communist; they are, or until some time ago were, radicals; they have a fondness for ideological speculation; they write literary criticism with a strong social emphasis; they revel in polemic; they strive self-consciously to be 'brilliant'; and by birth or osmosis, they are Jews."[8] All of the new publications were of high intellectual caliber, but there was one further distinction to be made between *Partisan Review* and all the others. Howe further argued that this was "the first group of Jewish writers to come out of the immigrant milieu who did not define themselves through a relationship nostalgic or hostile to memories of Jewishness" ("Intellectuals" 29). If they did not define themselves in terms of nostalgia or hostility, how then *did* they define themselves Jewishly? Was it simply through the accident of birth? More probably it was through their alienation from their Jewishness, for these were Jews who were taking the high intellectual road to conquer America. America was their subject; whether like Delmore Schwartz or Bernard Malamud, they wrote about Jews, or whether like Rhilip Rahv or Irving Howe, they wrote about American literature, their true interest was America. Moreover, influenced by Thorstein Veblen's emphasis on the benefits of Jewish marginality in his 1919 essay, "The Intellectual Pre-Eminence of Jews in Modern Europe," and by the philosophy of existentialism, alienation became the intellectual coin of the *Partisan Review* cohort. Who better to speak of this condition than the doubly alienated, the doubly marginal Jew? This stance obviously put them at odds with those writers associated with the overtly Jewish journals. One might sum up the difference between them as "nominal" rather than "nominative" Jews. Moreover, some of the *Partisan Review* group, such as Lionel Trilling and Hannah Arendt, did publish early in their careers in *Jewish Frontier* and *Menorah Journal*, but writers associated with these journals were not invited to write for *Partisan Review*. Yet, the twain finally would meet about twenty years hence, in the 1950s, when representatives of both groups found themselves employed at Brandeis University.

In 1934, however, Marie was at the ready, poised to publish what she had learned in her Palestinian sojourns and to bring the agenda of the Labor Zionist program to English-speaking readers. One of her first assignments was to seek out the well-known liberal social commentator and scholar Max Lerner, then the editor of *The Nation,* to suggest an article about the social experiment in Palestine. "When I approached Lerner," she later recalled, "he informed me with utmost kindness that he had never heard of a kibbutz. I still remember the pall that fell on our editorial collective. If Lerner was uninformed, what liberal American intellectual might be expected to be interested in the cooperatives of Palestine?" (*State* 3).

The tale of Max Lerner's total ignorance of the *kibbutzim* in Palestine today may appear implausible, but the fact is that in 1934, and up until the State of Israel was established in 1948, American Jewish interest in Zionism was negligible and even less than neglible among non-Jews. That said, in 1950, when Max Lerner and Marie Syrkin found themselves as colleagues at Brandeis University, Marie no longer had to instruct him on the subject of *kibbutzim* in Israel.

The fact that Lerner declined Marie Syrkin's offer did nothing to dampen her enthusiasm and commitment to the program of the *Jewish Frontier.* She was in total accord with Greenberg's words in the first editorial "What We Stand For."

In the midst of a growing social and economic awareness among the Jewish masses it aims to present a magazine of character and courage. The pages of the *Jewish Frontier* will attempt to analyze and solve Jewish problems by correlating them to the cultural, political and economic renaissance in Jewish life and to the efforts for creating in Palestine a free society rooted in agriculture and industry. . . . We hope to build up a clearing house for writers who, whether in polemics, poetry, fiction or criticism, are aware of responsibilities.

In the December 1978 issue of the *Frontier,* an issue in tribute to Marie Syrkin, in her own article entitled "That First Decade," Marie was to comment that from the perspective of hindsight, Greenberg's words "hardly seem earthshaking today." Four decades later, she wrote:

However, its propositions were far from hackneyed in 1934. What could sound more tired today than the first sentence? "The thoughtful Jew can no longer escape the conviction that he must take a definite stand in regard to the pressing Jewish problems of our time." No self-respecting scribe would today permit himself such a banality. But in 1934 the stirring of Jewish awareness in reaction to what was happening in Germany had barely begun. "Thoughtful Jews" were not taking a stand. (*Frontier,* January/February 1983, 42)

Marie, of course, was taking a stand, but even more so on the significance of the ascetic life in the remote *kibbutz* collectives halfway round the world. Whereas it is true that her stand on the German situation was not quite as firm as it was on Palestine, she certainly kept up with the increasingly dismaying news as it was reported in the newspapers. On August 20, 1934, the *New York Times* reported that Germany had held a plebiscite to further expand Hitler's powers and that 90 percent of the German voters voted to endorse Hitler's assumption of greater powers. Marie chose to respond to this dreadful turn of events with a poem (published in the *Jewish Frontier*) titled "On the Record," which is quoted here for historical reasons, not for its very weak poetic value. It begins with an epigraphic quotation from the *New York Times* article: "In all Bavaria Chancellor Hitler received the largest vote in his favor in the concentration camp at Dachau."

> Let congressmen and president
>   Abandon tactics truculent
> And emulate the brotherly
>   When hit, I'll turn the otherly
> Cheek — of across the sea.
>
> Because so loud the country calls,
>   Secure the loudest behind walls;
> Take office ere encountering the glad electorate
>   Then each Republican in haste
> Acquires a Democratic taste.
>   For getting out a record vote, there's nothing like a camp!
>   Because you'll be the singular and only candidate.
>
> And should there be a backward mite
>   Who hasn't learned to plebiscite,
> In Sing Sing's bracing woodland air, he'll his approval stamp
>   He'll ja with all the camp-fire boys
> When concentration he enjoys.
> (*Frontier,* n.d.)

Of course, Marie knew that the reason for the heavily favorable vote from Dachau was that it would have been dangerous for the prisoners to vote "no." Presumably, when she wrote her poem in 1934, she also knew that Dachau had been established on March 10, 1933, as the first concentration camp — a forced labor camp of over 5,000 people imprisoned for a variety of political offenses; but what she did not know was that by 1937, Dachau would hold over 13,000 prisoners, that political prisoners were no longer mainly Social Democrats and German Communists, but then would include Jews, Jehovah's Witnesses, gypsies, and homosexuals. She did not know that the number of Jewish inmates would increase to over 10,000 in the wake of Kristallnacht in 1938, and that the number of prisoners incarcerated in the camp between 1933 and 1945 would be in excess of 188,000. Nor in 1934 did Marie Syrkin know that Dachau would become a training center for S.S. concentration camp guards, that gruesome and fatal medical experiments would be performed on the prisoners, that the camp was surrounded by an electrified barbed-wire fence, with a wall with seven guard towers strategically placed, and that its iron gates would be emblazoned with the bitter message, "*Arbeit Macht Frei.*" But perhaps most tragically of all that she did not yet know, was that Dachau would become a death camp. Though it had gas chambers, most of those who were killed at Dachau would be shot or hung; those selected to die would be shipped off on death transports to satellite camps, as Dachau would continue as a major center for German armaments production produced by its overwhelmingly Jewish population and it would serve as a model for the administration of all Nazi concentration camps. Marie did not know that in the end, on April 26, 1945, as American forces of liberation approached Dachau, the Nazis would force more than 7,000 prisoners on a death march south, killing anyone who was too weak to continue and allowing an untold number to die along the way of hunger, frailty, cold, and utter exhaustion. Marie Syrkin did not know yet that when the Americans would arrive, they would liberate those still alive, but they would find over thirty railroad cars piled high with decomposing dead bodies, like stacks of wood for burning. She did not know that Dachau would become shorthand for Holocaust — a word yet to be coined.

Marie Syrkin's response was to publish a less-than-mediocre poem in a light, sardonic mode. Like most Americans who deplored what they heard of Nazi Germany, she thought it wouldn't last. In the introduction to her collected essays, *The State of the Jews* (1980), Syrkin openly admitted that she came late to full comprehension: "the ship's radio carried news of fresh measures enacted by Hitler, newly come to power. Yet the Nazi menace in its initial unfolding seemed somehow unreal. It was too preposterous; it would blow over. More real were the kibbutzim" (*State* 2).

Marital Happiness

The first years of the 1930s were precipitous years in world history, but they were also the first years of Marie's marriage to Charles Reznikoff — years that she later insisted were the happiest of their marriage — with the exception of their last years together, after her retirement. During this time period, however, the newlyweds spent an unusual amount of time separated from one another. After Marie's 1933 trip to Palestine and Europe, and after she assumed her editorial position on the *Jewish Frontier,* she became increasingly caught up in the current events in Palestine and in Europe, all the while continuing her daily teaching job. Charles remained at his dull *Corpus Juris* job, which he seemed to regard as an insult to his dignity as well as an imposition on his real work: poetry. He continued his long walks from Brooklyn to Riverdale, gathering the objective details for his subjective experience: "This smoky winter morning / do not despise the green jewel / shining among the twigs / because it is a traffic light" (*Poems* 116).

At first glance, it might seem that Marie's sense of a Jewish urgency, the call for political activism in the form of on-the-spot reporting and public activity, would be utterly incompatible with Charles' quiet, unassuming, stay-at-home manner, his passive rootedness in the New York City landscape, and despite his own deeply felt Jewishness and avid study of Jewish history, his refusal to become engaged in any mode or manner other than poetry. In the very years when his wife was busy sailing back and forth to the Middle East and to Europe, producing polemical arguments, Charles Reznikoff sat in his study and wrote:

> I will write songs against you,
> enemies of my people; I will pelt you
> with the winged seeds of the dandelion;

> I will marshal against you
> the fireflies of the dusk.
> (*Poems* 168)

The poem was published in 1936. Yet, the two so-different personalities seemed to thrive under conditions that would have severed most marriages. There were several reasons for its stability in these years: first, Charles and Marie truly respected and admired one another; second, they loved one another; third, they allowed each other the freedom to pursue their own vocations; fourth, despite Charles' rocky road to recognition, his wife always recognized his poetic gift. She knew then what the poet-critic Adam Kirsch wrote seventy-five years later: "what makes Reznikoff a significant Jewish poet is the same thing that makes him a significant poet: his successful representation in verse of a sensibility shaped by a particular "Jewish, American, urban" milieu. For Reznikoff, as for all true poets, the route to the universal begins in the local, and the best symbol is the most concrete."[9]

As for Charles' deep love for Marie, in addition to his admiration for her intellect and his love of her appealing personality, he was powerfully attracted to her physical beauty. In 1935, Marie was thirty-six years old — no longer a young girl, but hardly in the autumn of her life. Still Charles, taking note of the passing years, wrote this poem:

> Malicious women greet you saying, So this is Marie!
> She was such a beautiful girl, my dears.
> And afterwards you study your glass for wrinkles and hair graying.
> As if the face of a Greek goddess were less beautiful
> because its paint has been washed away a thousand years;
> your beauty is like that of a tree whose beauty outlasts the flowers,
> like that of a light constantly
> losing its rays through the hours
> and seasons, and still aglow
> through twilight and darkness, through moths and snow.
> (*Poems* 168)

At thirty-six, Marie was still an extremely beautiful woman — still lovely enough to attract powerful men whom she would meet in her professional activities. By 1935, she had been successfully displaying her considerable polemical and linguistic talents for over a year at *Jewish Frontier* and was admired and trusted by her colleagues enough to be sent on

an important new assignment. David Ben-Gurion had come to the
United States and was in New York. He had contacted the *Jewish Frontier* and invited Marie Syrkin to come to see him. He wanted her to
write an article about current issues facing the *Yishuv* at this time.

As leader of the largest political party in the *Yishuv,* Mapai, as secretary general of Histadrut, and as chairman of the Jewish Agency Executive, he was the *de facto* Prime Minister of the *de facto* government of
the Jewish community in Mandatory Palestine. Despite all the positive
events in his rise to prominence since the formation of the Mapai party
in 1930, by 1935 Ben-Gurion now found himself facing crisis upon crisis: Within the Zionist movement, he continued his fight to prevent
the Revisionists from gaining power; in Nazi Germany, stringent anti-
Jewish laws accompanied by policies of terror tactics and brutality had
resulted in peak immigration to Palestine; in Palestine itself, this statis-
tic had not been missed by the hostile, often-violent, emerging Arab
nationalism that held total objection to any political rights at all for
Jews, including an objection to a British proposal for a measure of
home rule. The British had proposed a Palestinian legislative council
with proportional representation that could further restrict immigration and land purchase, but even this the Arabs rejected. In response,
Ben-Gurion was prepared to battle Britain's policy of mollification of
the Palestinian Arabs, while he remained committed to an effort to engage in dialogue with the Arabs themselves.

Early in his career, David Ben-Gurion had held a curious romantic
though Marxist view of his Arab neighbors. As Amnon Rubinstein has
explained:

Ben-Gurion believed that the local Arab fellahin were descended from the ancient Jews who in time of trouble and strife "preferred to deny their religion
rather than leave their homeland." When these allegedly "Jewish" Arabs refused
to make any compromises with the new Jews, Ben-Gurion and his colleagues
saw in this a typical "class struggle" in which the landed effendi class exploits the
friction with the Jews in order to divert the attention of the masses from their
real class interests. . . . On the other hand, a common interest—and a future
common front—would unite Jewish and Arab workers. Eventually class consciousness would prevail and only then would Arabs and Jews co-exist in their
common land.[10]

It took the bloody riots of 1929 for Ben-Gurion to give up his Marxist interpretation. Yet, he was not alone in the belief in the long-lost

brotherhood of the two Semitic peoples, that the Arab was "a freshly re-discovered brother who has kept the family tradition and, in many re-spects, was regarded as a model for the new Jew." Such a romanticized view can be found in much of the *Yishuv*'s early literature. Rubinstein suggests that "if the Jews sought a release from *galut* images and searched for their new, authentic identity, the distant relative rediscovered, the uninhibited Arab, was a figure worthy of emulation." This peculiar brand of Jewish "Orientalism" is undoubtedly part of the explanation for Ben-Gurion's effort to engage in Arab-Jewish dialogue, even as he fought British policy and witnessed fresh skirmishes with Arab farmers and workers who remained immune to Jewish overtures (*Zionist Dream* 56).

As if all these political problems were not enough, Ben-Gurion also had to deal with the *Yishuv*'s considerable financial problems due to re-duced contributions from America, which was in the midst of the Great Depression. It was a tough agenda for Ben-Gurion, now the leader of a small settlement of about 350,000 Jews in an unforgiving region of the Middle East.

There was no denying it — David Ben-Gurion did not cut a very pre-possessing figure. Very short, stocky, balding (later with a halo of un-kempt white hair), he was not very physically attractive; but a more im-portant descriptive fact is that he was magnificent in self assurance, magnetically charismatic, and possessed of great vision. It was surely a leap of resourcefulness if not imagination for a man who so plainly had rejected the Diaspora and had mocked American Jews, to come to these United States in 1935 to ask for financial assistance and political aid. But he really saw no alternative. As early as 1930, Rabbi Steven Wise "had spoken of England's 'great betrayal' of Zionism; by the mid-1930s Ben Gurion had also become convinced that the first country to champion the Jewish national movement [in the Balfour Declaration] was turning into its adversary, although many in the Zionist camp refused to ac-knowledge the change."[11] Ben-Gurion understood that if he could no longer count on London, the only logical place to turn to for help was the large Jewish population in America, with its money, its unique ac-cess to political power, and its investments in Palestine. Furthermore, the fact that America had supported both the Balfour Declaration and the award to Britain of the Palestine Mandate made America the obvi-ous and necessary partner of the *Yishuv*. What is more, Ben-Gurion al-ready knew Supreme Court Justice Louis Brandeis and held in him in high esteem; Brandeis returned the admiration.

Justice Brandeis had been appointed to the Court by Woodrow Wilson in 1916. He had become committed to the Zionist cause early in his career and had served as chairman of the Provisional Committee for General Zionist Affairs. He also had been a strong supporter of an American Jewish Congress. Though Brandeis had resigned his Zionist leadership role in 1920 in his conflict with Chaim Weizmann essentially over Zionist philosophy, by 1935, he and his American followers, Felix Frankfurter, Judge Julian Mack, Robert Szold, and Rabbi Stephen S. Wise, had returned to active participation in the Zionist Movement. Now, David Ben-Gurion had come to the United States intending to get its government to put pressure on England. Presuming on his friendships with Brandeis, Frankfurter, Wise, and others in political high places, Ben-Gurion wanted them to urge President Roosevelt to press the British to live up to their Balfour Declaration and Mandatory obligations and not to restrict Jewish immigration. Ben-Gurion's activities in the United States on this 1935 visit were the beginning of a strong American-Jewish political relationship with the *Yishuv* and later with the State of Israel. David Ben-Gurion would become an enormously popular figure for American Jews, a heroic exemplar of the new Jew — tough, aggressive, and smart. For all these reasons, Ben-Gurion was in New York; and in order to disseminate his ideas (with which she thoroughly agreed) in the *Jewish Frontier,* Marie Syrkin went to see him.

In a late 1980s interview, expecting Marie to speak about the reasons for Ben-Gurion's important visit to the United States, I asked her how well she knew Ben-Gurion at this time and what were the subjects they discussed. But her answer immediately took a personal tack: fifty years after the event, in a narration that bore the signature marks of the many self-deprecating anecdotes she was fond of telling, Marie Syrkin recounted an amusing story of an "aborted affair with the great Ben-Gurion."

"He seemed very much interested in me" she began, "and I was not interested in him." Surprised, I asked if she meant "personally interested?" She replied flatly, "I had the feeling that he was. He was apparently a susceptible man — he had said he would like to meet me and talk to me." Flattered, but in all innocence, Marie claimed, when she went to his hotel, he immediately asked her if she would like to go to dinner and the movies. At dinner, she was unnerved by his table manners. In the movies, he tried three times to hold her hand, but she kept taking it away. "I was so shocked. The great Ben-Gurion wants to hold hands," she recalled. Finally, Marie told him that she was married, and after that, she confessed, Ben-Gurion lost interest in her. "When I next came to Israel," she recalled, "presuming on our old friendship, thinking he must remember those moments, he was completely indifferent. But I saw him occasionally." And although in 1935, Marie Syrkin's dinner companion was not to her taste, as a political personality he almost always would be—except some years later, when the Prime Minister and the American journalist would have a public disagreement on an important political issue, the Lavon affair, which would be played out in the press.[12]

Chapter 10

On the *Jewish Frontier*

The Twenty-First Zionist Congress

WHEN MARIE SYRKIN began her long association with the *Jewish Frontier,* she was poised at the nexus of the age-old "Jewish Problem" and the much more recent "Arab-Jewish conflict." Her father, Nachman Syrkin, had understood the Jewish "problem" to be the oppression of the Jewish people who had been exiled and homeless, whose insistence upon retaining their Jewish uniqueness and whose refusal to conform to the demands of their host nations resulted in their persecution. Nachman Syrkin noted in his 1901 "Call to Jewish Youth" that "[p]ogroms and mass discrimination have become commonplace, and everywhere the human dignity of the Jew is trodden underfoot. The fundamental cause of Jewish oppression is that of all human oppression: the unequal alignment of economic and political forces: the class character of modern society. But the specific, immediate cause is to be found in the social and political impotence of the Jews as a people" (*Memoir* 294–305). Syrkin's solution to the socio-economic-political Jewish problem was Zionism in general, socialist Zionism in particular.

Nachman Syrkin's daughter had learned this lesson at her father's knee. In the opening paragraph of the "Introduction" to her collected essays, *The State of the Jews,* she writes that she has had a "lifelong concern with the riddle of Jewish experience in our times."

I first encountered the riddle in its crudest form as a child of six in Czarist Russia. There I learned the meaning of "pogrom" from friendly village children who counseled me to paint a cross on our cottage should the killing start. But when I brought these tidings of salvation to my father I discovered that this was not the right solution. The answer, I was taught and grew up believing, lay in a Socialist society and a Socialist Jewish state. (*State* 1)

By the time Marie herself became professionally and personally active in the struggle for an answer to the riddle, some progress had been made: there had been the Balfour Declaration, then the Palestine Mandate, which (despite some late revocations) was obliged to observe the principles of the Balfour document; the Jewish population of the *Yishuv* had grown from 85,000 in 1914 to 400,000 in 1936; and in 1933, the socialist Zionist Party, Mapai, had emerged as the dominant party in the *Yishuv*. An optimist might even have believed that socialist Zionism *would* solve the Jewish problem.

There had been a variety of solutions to the "problem" over the centuries of diaspora and persecution, but there was to be another, just on this cusp of history, that would indeed go far to solve it: the "Final Solution" as conceived by Adolf Hitler and his Nazi Party. This euphemism—Hitler's answer to the older euphemism "Jewish problem"—called for nothing short of the total annihilation of the Jewish "race." Hitler, fortunately, did not accomplish his demonic worldwide vision; but he did manage to make European Jewry smaller by six million deaths, and he devastated Zionism by murdering the most likely immigrants to Palestine/Israel.

The "Jewish problem," which began in ancient history and had found "solutions" in Europe through the Crusades, the Inquisition, and even emancipation, now seemed to some in the early 1930s on the brink of a resolution. Between 1931 and 1939, despite all sorts of immigration restrictions, 276,000 Jews managed to emigrate to Mandatory Palestine. Just on the eve of Kristallnacht, November 9, 1938, the total population of Jews in Palestine stood at 450,000 — approximately the same number of Jews who resided in prewar Germany. The consequence of this steady increase of Jews into the Palestinian neighborhood, however, turned out to inspire a chain of hostilities and violence that began with the dawn of the twentieth century and has persisted into the new dawn of the twenty-first century. The bitter irony was that as the "Final Solution" of Europe's "Jewish problem" violently exploded, and ultimately imploded in bloody defeat, a new hostile environment for the Jews had already cast its shadow in the shape of the Arab-Israeli conflict.

Another Summer in Palestine

In 1936, Marie Syrkin chose to put herself in the midst of these dangers. She decided to spend her summer vacation in Palestine and then go on to Geneva, Switzerland, for the World Congress of Jewish Organizations. Sailing aboard the Cunard ship *Aquitania,* she landed in Cherbourg on July 3. On July 2, aboard ship, she wrote to Charles that the crossing was smooth and that she had a good rest. In an undoubtedly ironic barb she explained, "You know, or perhaps you don't, the complete illusion of unreality that one displays aboard ship. Everything behind one and before one seems remote." Charles, once again, had declined her invitation to join her on this trip. The letter also suggests that Charles had been out of sorts in recent days. "I hope you have gotten to work and that you are in good spirits. I was very happy to see the good mood you were in when I left. I hope it stays. I think you are quite right in feeling that what has happened will probably be for the best — not in the sour grapes sense either" (Archives 1 f. 19).

What has happened is that Charles has lost his job. He explains to his old friend, Al Lewin, with whom he had been corresponding since his 1931 visit to Hollywood, "I have been, believe it, on excellent terms with both my immediate superiors. However that may be, in this week's clash of executive wills, I am out — 'at liberty' if that is the phrase for it. Of course they would let me stay a while until I make some other 'connection,' but I have no stomach nor urgent need for a couple of weeks salary on such terms. Luckily, despite my ill-timed printing, I have some money saved and, of course Marie has a job with 'tenure of office.' (She is leaving this Saturday for a trip abroad from which she is not due to return until September)" (*Letters,* June 24, 1936).

Marie had not returned to Palestine or Europe since her first visits abroad in 1933. She had taken that trip with the conviction that if she was going to report on events, she had to be a shoe-leather reporter, not an armchair analyst. Yet the next two years proved to be relatively uneventful years spent at home. Marie did not go away for any length of time, nor did Charles. In 1934, she had been appointed an associate editor for the *Jewish Frontier* and was steadily making her name known as an important journalist for the *Frontier* as well as for other publications. Marie Syrkin soon became familiar to Jewish audiences as a lecturer on events in Palestine and as a spokesman for the Labor Zionists, all the while keeping up her teaching at Textile High, filling in the small gaps with some translations, and with her own poetry and keeping up her domestic duties and care for her son. While it was true that Marie Syrkin and Aaron Bodansky kept up their mutual unique arrangement of alternate-year living arrangements for their son, David, there was never an alternate year decrease in caring about his welfare. In a late retrospective analysis of his childhood and adolescent years, David Bodansky easily recalled that he always believed that both his parents were completely devoted to him, that he was made to feel that he was an absolute priority. There was, however, a clear division of labor: his mother was in charge of his physical well-being; his father was in charge of his mental development. As a result, David thought of his father as much the domineering and dominant figure, and his mother seemed not as intellectual. If in his youth he were asked to describe what his mother and father did, he would have said that she was a high school teacher and he was a scientist. Both, he added, were equally strong-minded. As to his parents' relationship in his teenage years, David admitted that there was the stock friction of such circumstances, but it abated in later years, and he believed that his mother actually felt affection for his father. When asked the blunt question about what may have been the cause of the divorce, David added that, in addition to both parties being strong minded, there also had been the intensity of the Maurice Samuel experience (Telephone interview, 2007).

In the winter of 1935, Marie had published an article in *Menorah Journal* about the Arab outbreaks and the Revisionists. In a letter to Henry Hurwitz, the editor of *Menorah Journal,* she explains, "As to the Arab outbreaks — my charge is one of the stock charges against the Revisionists. General opinion seems to agree that their march 'precipitated' the riots. Of course they deny it as insistently as we claim it. The charge has been made so often that it will be no news to the British press (which you mention)." For this article, Marie filled out a form dated 2-28-35 with her credentials, and she signed it Marie Reznikoff, but the Reznikoff is crossed out and replaced with Syrkin. In her next communication to Hurwitz on March 10, she wrote, "From a purely journalistic view point, I think it might be interesting to add in connection with this article that the writer is the daughter of Dr. Nachman Syrkin, founder of the Socialist-Zionist movement (in the biographical note.) Please use your judgement in this matter" (Archives, Hurwitz Coll.). But was it purely journalistic or an act of self-assertion? Or perhaps a pragmatic decision to accept whatever cachet her father's name afforded?

Charles, meanwhile, had kept up his work at *Corpus Juris* while working hard at his own writing. From 1933 to 1934, *Objectivist Press* had published two volumes of his poetry, *Jerusalem the Golden,* and *In Memoriam,* and a prose work, *Testimony.* He had hoped that *In Memoriam 1933* would be accepted by Harriet Monroe for her magazine *Poetry,* but when he did not hear from her, he wrote, "About two months ago I sent you a bulky manuscript 'If I forget you, Jerusalem: In Memoriam 1933.' I am in no hurry about a reply, but knowing your promptness, I cannot help wondering if the manuscript ever reached you" (*Letters,* July 7, 1934). Presumably it did, but she didn't accept it— Henry Hurwitz of *Menorah Journal,* however, did. On November 9, 1934, Charles had written to his friend and Hollywood connection, Al Lewin, "I have asked that a copy of the *Menorah Journal* with 'In Memoriam: 1933' be sent to you, and no doubt you will receive it soon. I am having it reprinted in book form and will send you a copy and as many more as you like." More importantly, Charles' letter speaks of a script that Lewin had asked him to write about the eleventh- and twelfth-century philosopher-theologian Pierre Abelard and his tragic love for Heloise. Charles has had trouble focusing on it and apologizes, "though I have no trouble throwing off verse now and then, I find it hard to do any 'muscle' work, as I must with Abelard or any prose" (*Letters* 206).

Since his stint in Hollywood in 1931, Reznikoff had kept in touch with the Lewins, exchanging letters, receiving Christmas gifts from them—though Al was Jewish. This is perhaps explained by the fact that in the 1930s and 1940s rampant assimilation attracted many Jews to the blandishments of and at least minimal participation in the American holiday, Christmas, which they rationalized as merely an enchanting secular celebration. Charles and Marie's letter of December 29, 1935, to the Lewins punningly begins: "Dear Milly and Al, We feel quite showered and dowered. You have us Jews completely benighted—Arabian. We wish you a very happy new year. Charles" Marie adds to this note:

You have this Jew completely overwhelmed. What a swanky bag! And what pajamas! Charles was all dressed, ready for one of his gruesome hikes, when they arrived on Xmas morning, and—this is the gospel truth—he promptly undressed, took a bath (to be worthy of Jean Harlow) and spent the day at home in the pajamas. This being the first thing I have ever encountered powerful enough to deflect Charles from a projected hike, you can judge how generally overcome the Reznikoff household is. . . . Greetings of the season, including Chanukah!

Marie (*Letters* 212)

But more and more Charles had been falling into low spirits. He really detested his work on *Corpus Juris,* he wished to be free to write his verse, and he didn't seem highly motivated to work on Abelard. Yet, he did not want to rebuff Lewin—probably for more than reasons of personal obligation; times were economically tough and physically grueling. In a letter worth quoting at length, Charles described his daily routine—a *modus operandi* that was certainly no way to promote marital togetherness:

My own way of living (week-days) is now something like this: I must leave the house at seven to get to my job in Brooklyn at eight forty-five. We work under constant supervision, which is kept for the most part in velvet gloves, until five thirty, reading and writing steadily, with an interval for lunch, of course. Every once in a while—every other week or so—if our pace seems to slacken, pressure is put upon us to raise our blood pressure, and we have to step lively or find our heels stepped on; but since the NRA and for the time being we have our Saturdays free. Our place of work was originally in a fairly quiet neighborhood which has since become the busiest and noisiest in Brooklyn, since it is on the best way from Manhattan. The steady analysis of cases and careful writing beside the traffic is—if you can remember your days on Fifth Avenue—pretty tiring; it takes me an hour or so in the evening to rest up. This I do while eating, reading the newspaper, and riding part of the way home. I usually get off at 72nd Street at about seven o'clock and walk along Riverside Drive as far as I can go—usually all the way. This is the time I do my own work, and when I reach home after ten, I am usually too tired to do more than glance at some Hebrew, if I do that. On this walk I find it easiest to do verse. Which more or less writes itself or not at all, and does not bulk; for even a thousand lines, enough to make a small volume, will have no more than about five thousand words. Perhaps, this will partly explain why I have been so dilatory with Abelard. . . . (Our organization has become so strict and jobs so desirable that to ask for a leave of absence is to quit.) (*Letters,* August 17, 1935)

To Hollywood Again

Al Lewin no doubt was appalled by this depressing account of his gifted friend's daily routine and he responded almost immediately, urging Charles to move out to Hollywood and take a job with the studio. It was an offer that Charles did not refuse out of hand, for he wrote to Lewin, "When I told Marie that she might have to live in Los Angeles, she said that she could not give up her job, particularly because she has her boy to think of. But, in any event, there is no need for her to give up her job in New York. I can come out to Los Angeles in the spring, if you wish it, and she can get a leave of absence for the next year, and have it renewed, if necessary. I think this should amplify my answer with respect to Marie's teaching in California. I realize, of course, that our talk was merely exploratory and need go no further" (*Letters*, October 19, 1935).

Certainly the thought of leaving New York would have been inconceivable for Marie. Yes, she had security in her teaching job, and no, she would not disrupt her son's life, nor would she leave him; but an equally persuasive reason for staying put was that New York was where the action was; New York was where the *Frontier* was located, New York was where Hayim Greenberg, a man she revered and worked with, was situated; New York was essential to her journalistic career, which perhaps was even more important to her than her paid job.

Marie stayed on in New York until the end of June 1936, embarking on July 3, 1936, for her summer trip abroad. She landed in Cherbourg, France, and from there would go on to Palestine. On July 28th Marie wrote to her husband from Palestine describing conditions there due to the ongoing Arab revolt that had begun in April. Her words could scarcely have been balm for Charles' multiple woes:

I suppose you have wondered why I have written so little from Palestine. I expect to leave the day after tomorrow — by the time you get this letter, I will have already left Palestine. I did not write to tell you now in detail because conditions in the country are dangerous, and as I traveled from point to point I did not want to worry you with detailed accounts. When I say dangerous, I mean that no day passes without shooting and bombings at various points. Nevertheless, the population is remarkably calm. The Jews refuse to be terrorized. They travel with or without military convoys — according to the taste of the individual. The workers in the *kvutzahs* work all day in the fields and watch all night — frequently they have to fight off the attacks of Arab bands. Even Tel-Aviv — the supposed completely safe spot — has had bombs thrown in school-yards. Of course, a kind of miracle has so far protected the Jewish population. A very small percentage of the bombs explode — very few of the bullets hit their target. Were the marksmanship or the craftsmanship of the Arabs better, the number of calamities would have been a thousand fold. Sometimes chance intervenes. A huge and for a change, not defective bomb was discovered accidently [*sic*] on the Tel-Aviv beach by a girl who tripped over the wires which went through the sand till Jaffa. The Jews go about their business with a mingled fatalism and courage. The courage — as all good qualities — is mostly evident in the youth and the *krutzah* settlers who as usual bear the brunt of the situation. If heroism and patience are political assets, then the Zionist future is assured — unfortunately, the higher-ups seem to consider the political "conjunktur" as unpromising.

I went to Jerusalem from Tel Aviv and back with the David Pinskis. These two old people insisted on going in a small private auto — they belong to the school that scorns convoys — I was amazed at these convoys. We went through the winding mountains toward Jerusalem, through Arab villages noted for their kindliness, passing Arab brigands who scowled affectionately at us, and I shook like a leaf (a large one) but the Pinskis sang Hebrew songs cheerfully — *Emek, Emek, avodah Emek, Emek, hora*. (Archives 1 f. 19)

"I am very glad I came at this time," Marie concludes. "One cannot understand Zionism unless one sees the people at this moment. I don't think I am being unduly sentimental." The last sentence is an acknowledgment of Charles' scorn for the sentimental; it is also a rebuttal *ex ante facto* to latecomers in the twenty-first century who would be critical of such emotional rhetoric. Years later, Marie would answer the charge that she was among the "myth-makers" of the founders of the State with the rebarbative refutation: "Those who now proclaim that the 'myth' of Israel is dead are mistaken. Israel is an exemplar of what *can* be done. Even if it lasts only forty, fifty, years, what that State achieved can never be erased because it shows the potential of idealism. . . . The adaptation of the dream to realities is merely the price of survival" (Personal interview). She might have added that the adaptation of realities to myth is also a contribution to survival. What might she have said in response to Zeev Sternhell, whose 1998 book, *The Founding Myths of Israel*, argues that it was the Labor Zionist Founding Fathers' espousal of nationalism more than socialism that created many of the problems that now face the State and that prevent it from being a truly liberal democracy? In his preface, Sternhell writes, "To analyze social and political realities one has to give priority to the raw material of the period and not to the eye-witnesses' memories of it. Those who take part in unfolding events have an unfortunate tendency to wax sentimental about their far-off youth and to embellish the realities of those years. Memory is not only a filter; it also has a regrettable way of reflecting the needs of the present."[1] Marie Syrkin might have responded to this, had she lived a bit longer, with the words she said a few weeks before her death: "The term 'myth of Israel' was created by those who never participated." She might well have added, "Historiography too has a regrettable way of reflecting the needs of the present. Read what I wrote at the very time that it happened." She could have suggested the above letter as a case in point.

With her Palestine adventures now behind her, Marie Syrkin left Haifa on the S.S. *Esperia* on July 30, 1936. She would land in Naples on August 4, and then go on to Geneva. On August 3, the day before she was to disembark, she wrote to her husband, "My dear, Tomorrow I land at Naples. Palestine is behind me and the European installment begins. Till now each moment has been so crowded with impressions that I find it difficult to write." Arguing that she has already told him about "the extraordinary heroism and discipline of the Jewish population [of Palestine] under constant provocation," Marie now promises to tell him everything in detail when she sees him. The letter continues with a long description of a side trip she took when her ship stopped at Alexandria. A group of Americans Jews, herself, and a honeymooning rabbi and his bride, motored from Alexandria to Cairo and back within twenty-four hours. They traveled for six hours each way,

leaped on a camel — took snap shots beside the Sphinx, and motored back to catch the boat, having had 2 hrs. sleep in Cairo and hardly so much as a glance at the pyramids, the 15 minutes we spent there having been devoted to snapshots and arguing with the guide about "baksheesh." This, of course, sounds crazy and you're shaking your head about my folly. But be still. I am willing to give you the Sphinx and the camel and the pyramids as a bit of tourist madness, but that ride along the Nile at twilight, then in the bright sun the following day! It was glorious — though at the time, occasionally terrifying (riding through Egypt along the river bank at night, passing only occasional cities here and there, clay huts, seeing strange groups of dim human beings, having stones thrown at one by playful little Egyptian boys — a rabbi who had passed through

Palestine unscathed had his glasses broken — everything moonlit and marvelous. Well — you get the idea).

You must forgive me for my manner of writing. It's in my worst and most characteristic style, but at the present, I haven't the patience to formulate my impression with any exactness. I can only gasp. Perhaps we can go together soon again.

Once more, Marie has critiqued her own writing. But it is probably only a very conscious act of ironic self-deprecation, another aspect of her "characteristic style" (Archives 1 f. 19).

A Brief Resumption of an Old Affair

The previous letter is dated August 3, 1936. It shows no sign at all that aboard ship she had just received a letter from Tel Aviv, dated Monday, July 27 with the salutation, "Dearest Marie" and signed, "Ever your Maurice." But the accompanying cover page reads "Mrs. Marie Reznikoff, S.S. *Esperia,* 2nd class. Sailing from Haifa Thursday, July 30, 1936." Its very existence attests to the fact that it had been delivered, received, and preserved. There is nothing in the extant letters of Marie to Charles or to anyone else indicating that she and Samuel had met in Palestine, nor was there an intimation in any of the interviews I had with her about an earlier 1933 meeting with Maurice. There was, however, her hint to me that I would find some interesting information in the group of letters that she already had given to Brandeis University. At the time of our last interview in 1989, the bulk of her papers were as yet unassigned. Indeed, she asked me then where I thought she should donate them.

The first sentence of the letter is quite astounding and immediately prompts a question: "I won't repeat the mistake of two years ago," Maurice asserts. What mistake was made during the earlier meeting? And was that meeting in Palestine? Perhaps it was in America — though not likely, for during the ten years from 1929 to 1939, Maurice Samuel resided in Tel Aviv. His letter continues:

My heart is still full, and I know that one of the best things in my life has happened to me with the resumption of our friendship. Perhaps if I had had the courage two years ago, we would by now have found out exactly how it can all be made to fit into our lives. But I lacked the courage because I had been so guilty. I am still aware of this guilt, but you've helped me over its bad effects. Of course I don't see yet what we shall do in America. You can't just say that if Charles isn't perturbed by our friendship then nothing matters: because there is the world that talks, and there are Charles's parents, and all the rest of it.

When we first spoke about Charles, here in these last few days, I forced my friendly feelings for him a little. Only later, when you told me how you'd lived with him, did I have a free flow of feeling toward him. And this came about most in the last conversation, which was trifling on the surface, but which brought up many echoes from far below.

I hope that these books which I'm sending you will mean as much to you as they have to me. Write me when you get to Europe. I'm very unclear as to how we shall meet in America, (and in fact whether it will not seem best to us that we should not meet except on rare half-accidental occasions) but out of my love for you I long to add whatever I can to your life.[2]

As in the earlier correspondence between Maurice and Marie, there exists only Maurice's side of the exchange; consequently, Marie's responses only can be inferred. There are many more questions than answers, and the only real certainty is that they met and they still had strong feelings for one another. Yet now, Maurice refers to their relationship as a "friendship." Does this mean that they have agreed that the sexual aspect of it is over? And what does his guilt refer to? His refusal in 1926 to leave his wife so that he and Marie could marry? Has Marie suggested that when he returns to America they can just go on being friends, and that would be acceptable to Charles? And if that is true, what does it say about Charles, or about Marie's attitude toward him? And what does Samuel's remark about Marie's life with Charles mean? Is the hardship because of Charles inability to make a living, or is it their mutual absences, or his long walks that brought him home each night late and tired? Or something else? And what were those "echoes from far below?" Finally, what were the books he sent? Were they the three books he had published since they had broken with each other, the last a novel entitled *Beyond Women*?

Marie's ship anchored at Naples; from there she went on to Geneva, Switzerland, for the first convention of the World Jewish Congress where 280 delegates representing the Jewish communities of thirty-two countries were in attendance, led by Rabbi Stephen Wise and Nahum Goldmann. The concept of a World Jewish Congress originated much earlier in the century, when Jewish communities around the world sought to cooperate when confronted with political, legal, and religious matters as well as in relief work for refugees and victims of pogroms. The events of the past few years — Nazism and the Arab disturbances — made the need for cooperative political activity urgent. "Jewish organizations in the West initiated a widespread boycott of German goods. In order to co-ordinate defense and aid activity [the] World Jewish Congress . . . passed resolutions regarding propaganda, boycott activities, the struggle against discrimination, constructive activity for rehabilitation of Jewish refugees and the changing of Jewish occupations, particularly among the younger generation."[3]

Sadly, two Jewish communities were not present at the convention: German Jewry and Soviet Jewry, both of whose governments did not permit them to leave their countries. The American Zionist leader, Rabbi Stephen Wise, fired up the members of the convention with passionate words of urgency and resolve:

Such national bodies as there are among Jews — B'nai B'rith, the *Hilfsverein,* the Board of Deputies, the American Jewish Committee — each works separately and alone in the land of which it is a part and amid the citizenship in which its members are included. But it is not the Englishmen who are attacked, nor Frenchmen, nor Americans, nor Belgians, nor Dutch, but Jews, Jews, Jews. Not French Jews, nor British Jews, nor American Jews, not even German Jews, but Jews as Jews. Even the war of Hitlerism is not directed against German Jews. That phase of the struggle was little more than an election expedient to bring the Nazis to power. Hitlerism's real war is against World Jewry. Hitler said, *"Wir werden die Juden ausrotten"* ("we will root out the Jews"). Through the voice of the World Jewish Congress we answer: "You shall not destroy Jews, though you may uproot them from your own land." For the Jew has within him the very essence of imperishableness. What Haman and Titus and Pobiedonosteff failed to achieve Hitler will not do. (Ben-Sasson 986)

On August 4, Marie Syrkin sent a letter to Charles telling him that she was waiting for the opening of the World Jewish Congress; she cautions him to address his letters to the World Congress of "Jewish Organizations" because "our fraction [*sic*] is going to wage a desperate struggle to have that the official name because the Congress was not elected through democratic elections." It is a brief letter and ends with her travel plans. She is tired of traveling and longs "desperately for the boat back home." One month of "concentrated travel and new impressions" is her maximum. The Congress will be over in the middle of August and if she can change her booking for an earlier one she is again thinking of skipping England. "Next time I'll take England first. However, I shall see" (Archives 1 f. 19). Of course, no word about Maurice Samuel.

Unable to change her booking, Marie has until September 2 to sail on the *Queen Mary* from South Hampton, England. Meantime, she informs Charles that she will remain in Geneva until August 20 and will attend a world conference of the *Poale Zion* that has just begun. The Congress of World Jewish Organizations is over, she reports, and she found it horribly dull, but probably useful. "I comforted myself" Marie adds, "with much excellent Swiss cooking, the result being disastrous to my shape. The pounds I have put on are the best indication of the placidity of the Congress and my existence." After August 20, Marie plans to go to Paris, where she certainly will not find the food less seductive. From thence she will go on to England; there the cuisine doubtless will tempt her less (Archives 1 f. 19).

Once aboard the S.S. *Queen Mary*, Marie Syrkin received a second letter from Tel Aviv dated August 27, addressed to Mrs. Marie Reznikoff and signed "yours, Maurice." The letter is both personal and political. Samuel's description of the events in Palestine in late August of 1936 elaborates on the conditions Marie had described in her letter to Charles. In it, he gives his own eye-witness details of the continuing Arab uprising against the Jews and the British, which began in April of that year with a general strike of Arab workers and continued with increasing intensity through the next six months. It would not let up until October 3, 1936.

During this period of revolt and riots, the Arab High Command — a loosely connected coalition of Arab political parties — had been formed, led by the Mufti Haj Amin al-Husseini, and it continued to represent the Palestinian Arabs until 1948. The campaign against the Jews began with the workers strike and a boycott of Jewish goods, and it soon intensified into terrorist attacks on the Jews and their property. During the month of June, 75,000 Jewish trees in citrus groves and orchards were destroyed, as well as 3,500 grapevines; buses were ambushed and bombed, unarmed Jews were shot as they were driving along the main roads. Bands of marauding Arabs roamed the countryside, killing the British as well as Jews. In early June, the Arab Supreme Council de-

manded a total halt to Jewish immigration and engaged in guerilla warfare against the British in order to end what they regarded as the Zionist
influence in London. Faced with deteriorating conditions, the British
took stronger and stronger measures, fast becoming engaged in uninter-
rupted battle with the Arabs, killing them in their efforts to stanch the
violence.[4] Meanwhile, the Jewish self-defense forces began to mature
into a full-fledged military force—the *Haganah*. At the beginning of
the riots, the *Haganah* under the directive of the Jewish Agency took
the position that the *Yishuv*'s response to the terrorism should be one
of *Havlagah* (restraint)—not a position supported by Jabotinsky's
Revisionist militia. It was both a moral and a practical policy against re-
taliatory terrorism as well as in the hope that it would influence the
British to support the underarmed Jews not only with words, but with
weapons. At the outset, the British did cooperate and even helped them
with uniforms and arms to form an auxiliary police. It was in the heat of
these frightening summer days, that Maurice Samuel wrote to Marie.
"Dear Marie," he began:

I received your letter from Geneva two days ago, after what seemed to be a long,
long wait. I thought that perhaps (whether or not you'd received my wire and
the books) you'd thought it best not to write to me. God knows it's a muddled
situation. And I suppose it ought to be—I mishandled it consistently for more
than twenty years, so what can I expect? But there's some sort of grace in the
world if I can still have your friendship. That matters most, and details can wait.

You can't have had much joy of that Congress. It seems, in fact, to have been
worse than I expected, and I expected pretty nearly the worst. But I'd rather
have been there than here. If you've been getting reports (though I don't see
how you can: we're small fry, and the world's newspapers don't pay much attention to us) you'll know what I mean. The last ten days have been hideous: the
killing of two nurses, a girl in one of the colonies, sundry workers—and
the spread becomes so wide that it touches the circles of friendship or acquaintance of many thousands. On top of it, a feeling of utter helplessness and bewilderment. Yesterday 25 of the Arab leaders were released from Sarafend. The
killings go on. The split among the British administrators becomes more and
more obvious. No one knows what anyone is driving at: is it really just a double
crossing game, or is it the same kind of driveling indecision as resulted in the
retreat before Italy? I felt better in 1929—I could join the Haganah. Now I'm
too old. And it makes one feel sick to tell others to go ahead and be courageous
and fight back. On top of it all, as a reaction from self-disgust, there comes

callousness. To hell with it all. There are more important events on the *Tagesor-dnung*. It matters infinitely more to the future of the world whether the Government or the rebels win out in Spain than whether we have a Jewish Homeland or not.

Gertrude and I are leaving here September 4, as I think I told you. She is staying in Italy for a month, I'm going on via England (I shall arrive in Manchester September 17, and stay for three weeks) to America. Will you send me a letter there — even the shortest, — telling me of your journey and arrival home? It would make me very happy.

I'm wondering when I shall see you, and my heart is full of good wishes for you. (Brandeis Library)

The events Maurice Samuel describes were not unknown to Marie; she had described them in her letter of July 28 to Charles, and though she knew he would be frightened and appalled by the details, she also was certain that he was unacquainted with the situation on the ground. She shared a love for the Jewish people with Charles, but not the experience and the politics of life in the *Yishuv*. That she shared with Maurice Samuel.

Marie Syrkin Reznikoff arrived home on Labor Day, Monday, September 7, 1936, just in time to return to her school responsibilities. On September 10, Charles informed his friend Al that Marie had arrived on September 7 and duly came down with a cold. "I expect to leave Friday and should be in Beverly Hills by the first of next week. On September 27, only three weeks after she had arrived home, having been away for two months, she wrote to him in Hollywood, chiding him for insisting that he would write only once a week. "How much longer are you staying in Hollywood?" she asks. "It's pretty lonely here, and I wish you were back. I have gotten used to sleeping alone, but I don't like being alone, even though David tries to be the 'man of the house.' He watches my expenditures with an eagle eye." David, at this moment, was twelve years old. Al Lewin must have encouraged Charles to come out to the West Coast to work on the Abelard play, though Al himself had just resigned from the studio. By October 3, Marie has begun to lose patience and she urges him to come home. "I think if it's a question of sitting around and waiting for off moments with Al, you should come home and work here till his arrival [in New York]. Furthermore, it occurs to me that I may be of some assistance. I make this suggestion quite seriously at the risk of seeming presumptuous. Perhaps together we could do something which would please Al. . . . I think that I have in generous measure that degree of interest in emotional situations which you lack and cannot simulate. I urge you to come home at once and work with me till Al's arrival" (Archives 1 f. 19). Though Marie herself had just returned from a two-month stay away from New York, she is palpably exasperated by Charles' indecisiveness and impracticality. Theirs was the very model of a modern matrimonial, multicoastal arrangement.

Back at the Frontier

Marie may have been peeved, but she did not brood over it. Her own work eclipsed the annoyance. The world was too much with her, and she felt a compulsion to spread the bad word. Immediately upon her return from Europe, Marie Syrkin faced an overflowing agenda. Perhaps daunted, she nonetheless knew that something had to be done and that she knew how to do it; she would marshal the facts, analyze, and disseminate her findings to the American Jewish public in writing and in speeches. There were two deeply interconnected major events that demanded world Jewry's attention — one in the Middle East and one in Europe. First, the Arab riots, followed by the British government's appointment of a Royal Commission headed by Lord Robert Peel to investigate the causes of the so-called Palestinian "disturbances." The second was the Nazi enactment of the Nuremberg Laws and their inevitable ghastly consequences. There would soon be a third event, in the Soviet Union; Marie Syrkin would be the first to translate and analyze the transcript of the Moscow purge trials of January 1937.

In Palestine, after a year of investigation, in July of 1937, the Peel Commission finally issued its report. It recommended the partition of Palestine into two separate states, one Jewish and one Arab, with a corridor from Jaffa to Jerusalem that would remain under British control. Although the territory assigned to the Jews would be quite small — approximately one-fifth of the size of that mapped out for the Arabs, the Palestinian Jews reluctantly accepted the proposal, and the 1937 Zionist Congress accepted it for further discussion; but the Palestinian Arabs flatly turned it down. There were, however, some Palestinian Jews who opposed the idea. Not surprisingly, one of these groups was the Revisionists; a second was *Brit Shalom*, a group that had been formed in the mid-1920s in answer to increasing Arab hostilities to the growing Jewish immigration. *Brit Shalom*'s solution to the Arab-Jewish conflict was the utopian dream of a bi-national State. By 1936, Judah Magnes, the President of Hebrew University, led a group of intellectuals who supported *Brit Shalom,* to oppose the Peel Commission's call for Partition. In later years, Marie Syrkin would contribute to a volume dedicated to the life of Magnes in which she remarked that "Like Magnes [Golda Meir] opposed partition when it was first proposed by the British Royal Commission in 1937, but she changed in response to the catastrophe of the Holocaust when partition became the official policy of the Jewish Agency."[5] Syrkin always supported partition and wrote about it from the very start, as did David Ben-Gurion who, responding positively to the Peel Commission on January 7, said "It is our belief that a great Jewish community, a free Jewish nation, in Palestine with a large scope for its activities, will be of great benefit to our Arab neighbors. . . . We need each other. We can benefit each other." Six days later on January 13, the Arab leader, Awni Bey Aboulhadi, also replied to the Peel Commission, "Every Arab in Palestine will do everything in his power to crush down Zionism, because Zionism and Arabism can never be united together" (Gilbert 25). Sadly, this was a prognostication worthy of that truth teller, Cassandra.

Many years later, when I visited Marie Syrkin, then living in Santa Monica, I brought a house gift with me: *The Birth of the Palestinian Refugee Problem,* by Benny Morris, then the "dean" of the new revisionist historians. After reading the book, Marie commented that she certainly admired Morris' great ability as a journalist-historian, but "his father [a founding father of the Labor Zionists] must be turning in his grave." By this she meant that Morris, a pioneer of the "new historians," had set out to "demythologize" the regnant Zionist narrative. By taking a fresh critical look at history, he would provide a counternarrative that exposed what he regarded as the fatal flaws of the founding myths. But Syrkin argued that there really was not much new in his exposé. There always had been dissenters. Ten years later, in his new book, *The Birth of the Palestinian Refugee Problem Revisited,* to the astonishment of his admirers and his detractors, Morris took a new view of his old view and made a critical about-face. In a review of Morris' counter-counternarrative, Anita Shapira, the eminent scholar of Zionism, cleverly reworded the gist of Syrkin's 1989 words: "one can say that what is bad is not new and what is new is not bad." What is more, it would not be long before Morris would write words that would no longer cause Marie Syrkin to worry about his father's eternal peace. His words would contradict the implication of some of the new historiographers of Israel and Zionism that the Zionist movement never wanted or accepted the idea of partition. Morris writes:

Until 1936–1937, certainly the Zionist mainstream sought to establish a Jewish state over all Palestine. But something began to change fundamentally during the Arab revolt of 1936–1939, which was conducted against the background of resurgent anti-Semitism in Europe and the threat of genocide. In July 1937, the British royal commission headed by Lord Peel recommended the partition of Palestine with the Jews to establish their own state on some 20 percent of the land and the bulk of the remainder to fall under Arab sovereignty (Ultimately to be conjoined to the Emirate of Transjordan, ruled by the Emir Abdullah). The commission also recommended the transfer — by agreement or "voluntarily" and if necessary by force — of all or most of the Arabs from the area destined for Jewish statehood. The Zionist right, the Revisionist movement, rejected the proposal. But mainstream Zionism, representing 80 to 90 percent of the movement, was thrown into ferocious debate; and shepherded by David Ben-Gurion and Chaim Weizmann, the Zionist leadership ended up formally accepting the principle of partition, if not the actual award of 20 percent of the land. The movement resolved that the Peel proposals were a basis for further negotiation. (*New Republic,* May 8, 2006, 26)

The British government's response to the Peel Commission reflected its own precarious position. Whereas the government did not overtly repudiate the Balfour Declaration or the intentions of the Mandate, in the face of conditions on the European ground, the ferocity of the Arab revolt prompted a change of direction toward the Arabs. Britain, by 1937, was aware of the "gathering storm" and began making preparations for the probability of World War II. Recent events in Italy and in Germany were dire indicators of events to come. In 1935, Italy, under Mussolini, ignoring the terms of the Versailles Treaty and against wide international protest, attacked Ethiopia; with this aggression Italy lost the support of the democracies, only to enter into rapprochement with Nazi Germany. On March 7, 1936, also in blatant disregard for the terms of the Versailles Treaty, Hitler, with the support of Italy and betting on the weakness of England and France, took the great gamble of occupying and remilitarizing the Rhineland. Then, in June of 1936, the Span-

ish Civil war erupted. The two dictators, Hitler and Mussolini, sent aid
to the leader of the Fascist faction, General Franco, who was fighting
against the legitimately elected government of Spain; within a few
months, on October 25, 1936, Germany and Italy signed the Rome-
Berlin Axis Agreement. By the fall of 1936, Britain could not deny the
forbidding signs, and as the threat of war intensified, Britain's war strate-
gists became ever more conscious of the nation's dependence on Middle
Eastern oil. *Plus ça change, plus c'est la même chose.* Given these threatening conditions, the British chose to ignore these words of the July 1937,
Palestine Royal Commission Report: "It is true of course that in times
of disturbance the Jews, as compared with the Arabs, are the law-abiding
section of the population, and indeed, throughout the whole series of
outbreaks, and under very great provocation, they have shown a notable
capacity for discipline and self restraint" (Gilbert 22). The long and detailed report stated that it had not found any basis for the Arab claim of
exploitation by the Jews, and moreover, that the Arab population had
considerably benefitted from the growth of the Jewish settlement
(Sachar 468). London undoubtedly felt certain that given the tragic current events in Germany, it would automatically receive the cooperation
of the Jews, but they also knew that they would need to accede to Arab
demands. Thus, along with the report of the Peel Commission, the government issued its own policy statement declaring that, in principle, it
accepted the Peel Commission's partition plan and would do what was
needed to implement it. However, until the two states were established,
the British government would continue in its Mandatory responsibilities of maintaining order and keeping the peace between Arabs and
Jews. During this time, it would prohibit any land transactions that
might prejudice the partition plan, and it would limit immigration between August of 1937 to March of 1938 to 8,000. Whatever positive
statements Lord Peel's Commission had made, and whatever good news
the partition plan may have been for the Jews, the last two conditions
were met with utter dismay and despair. At the very moment that Jewish emigration and land on which to settle the immigrants was of critical importance, the means to help the threatened Jews of Germany and
to build the State that the partition plan envisioned, were now severely
diminished.

   This situation was at the head of Marie's list of things to think
about, write about, and speak about. It is not hard to imagine that in
these months she would frequently buttonhole friends and colleagues

exclaiming, "Something has to be done!" Yet the Arab-Jewish conflict was matched in intensity and crisis by the worsening situation of the Jewish population in Germany. The Nuremberg Laws of 1935 were proliferating—spawning new rules and regulations, bearing undeniable witness to Rabbi Leo Baeck's 1933 prophetic utterance that "The end of German Jewry has arrived." As the historian Michael Berenbaum has pointed out, there would be "four hundred separate pieces of legislation enacted between 1933 and 1939 that defined, isolated, excluded, segregated, and impoverished German Jews."[6] Within these six black years, Hitler's will to power, his seizure and exercise of power, and his uncontrolled abuse of power, helped him to execute his mad dream of a *Judenrein*, one-party Aryan Police State—all at the tragic expense of its suffering Jewish population. These facts Marie Syrkin now understood. By 1937, she could no longer write witty little ditties about the surreal events in Germany, and any complacency or expectation that things would blow over had evaporated. So, the Arabs who would soon make league with the Nazis, and the British, who were traveling the road of self-interest in their mollification of the Palestinian Arabs, became the trio of Marie's polemics. The continuo was the Jews. She had plenty to write about.

Suddenly, however, the trio became four-part discord. At the offices of the *Jewish Frontier,* Hayim Greenberg had received the 600-page Russian-language stenographic transcript of Stalin's January Moscow trial, which he handed over to Marie Syrkin to translate and write about. Her analysis may have been the first to call a purge a purge. By May 1937, there had been two open trials and in March 1938, there would be one more, plus a secret trial before a military tribunal in June 1937. Quite a few Western journalists observed the trials and concluded that they had been fair, that they had proven the guilt of the accused, and that there had been no evidence of coercion. Marie Syrkin's closely argued analysis, based on the written text, appeared in the May 1937 issue of the *Frontier.*

After reading the nearly 600 pages of stenographic report of the January Moscow trial, one begins to understand why so many correspondents, like Walter Duranty, wrote home that the testimony rang true. The grotesque accusations, the incredible self-flagellation of the defendants, which stood out in such naked relief in the brief news dispatches, are submerged by the flow of detail. Dates, meetings, descriptions of specific localities, reports of conversations—the sheer volume of trivial and significant incidents — have an inherent persuasiveness, irrespective of accuracy. The most fabulous plot seems a little far-fetched if we announce that it was hatched at Childs' on Broadway, and if we describe the buckwheat cakes the plotters ate. Some of the reality of the maple syrup clings to the story.

By now everyone is familiar with the setup. The chief figures of the Bolshevik revolution admit to a collection of crimes among which murder is the most attractive. This wholesale confession of crimes is indulged in by all of Lenin's closest associates and collaborators with two exceptions — Stalin and Trotsky. Stalin is in the Kremlin, Trotsky in Mexico, the rest are in their graves or about to repose in them. Just how complete the liquidation of the Old Bolsheviks has been, may be judged from glancing at the memberhsip of the Central Committee of the Communist party during the crucial years' of 1917 to 1920. With the exception of a few who retired from politicial life, all the surviving members have been shot as counter-revolutionaries — again barring Trotsky and Stalin. Immediately after the death of Lenin, in 1924, the Political Bureau of the Communist Party consisted of seven members — Stalin, and his six counter-revolutionaries; Bukharin, Zinoviev, Kamenek, Rykov, Tomsky, and Trotsky. At the time they were shot, most of the defendants occupied positions of great importance in the country. Obviously, we have here not only treason on a colossal scale, but a riddle of human behavior, towards whose solution one scans the long records of the trials eagerly. What have they to tell?

Syrkin argues that "it is impossible to disassociate the Radek-Pyatakov trial from the August trial of Kamenev-Zinoviev. The second proceeds from the first, just as a third trial involving Bukharin and Rykov is now unfolding." She goes on to point out the similarities as well as the differences, but contends that the confessions sound "phony" and further concludes that the "record of the January trials would seem to indicate that there is a much greater amount of dissaffection in Soviet Russia than one had suspected. The fanatical insistence throughout the trial on the dangers of intellectual opposition or deviation from the party line forces one to the conclusion. It also forces one to the conclusion that the regime will not be squeamish about 'liquidating' any opposition." Arguing that her conclusions, though unpleasant, are inescapable, she finally asserts that

no service is done to socialism or to Soviet Russia by refusing to face what one conceives to be the truth. Both Socialism and Soviet Russia are greater than the actions of any given group of men or regime. They are best served by an honest attempt to understand what is happening in the first country that is "building socialism." Certainly the lesson would seem to be that dictatorship and political repression are fatal means, no matter how noble the end. (*Frontier,* May 1937)

Marie Syrkin did not live to see her lesson fully played out; however, she did see the beginning of *perestroika,* Gorbachev's program of economic, political, and social reform introduced at the Twenty-Seventh Party Congress in 1986; but Syrkin died in 1989, before the dismantling of the totalitarian Marxist-Leninist-Stalinist Soviet Union, before the fall of the Communist Party and the rise of independent republics. Socialist that she remained to the end of her life, she would not have mourned the death of Communism. Probably her analysis of the transcript had been influenced by her mentor Hayim Greenberg's thinking, but the words Marie chose to describe Greenberg's attitude toward Marxism in the introduction to her 1968 anthology of his writings were her opinions as well: "[Greenberg] was a socialist and always called himself one, but he rejected the dogmatism of the Marxist. The notion that man was solely a social or economic animal whose needs could be met purely in economic or social terms seemed to him the ultimate blasphemy" (Greenberg 11). Her own statement that "no service is done to socialism or to Soviet Russia by refusing to face what one conceives to be the truth" was not so easily faced by the Left. And when some early believers in the Revolution finally did, it required a complete repudiation not only of Stalinism but of socialism, and then of liberalism as well.

With the year 1937 only one-fourth over and her journalist docket crammed with critical world events, Marie made the rather surprising decision not to attend the forthcoming meeting of the Twentieth Zionist Congress that would be held in Zurich from August 3 to August 16. Instead, she would spend the summer months with Charles in Santa Monica. It undoubtedly was going to be a contentious and crucial Congress because the main issue on the agenda was a discussion of the Peel Commission report. Mindful of the fact that the Balfour Declaration had stated that the Jewish National Home should comprise the "field of the whole of Palestine including Transjordan," most of the Congress delegates understood that this "field" was no longer in play. Ben-Gurion was scheduled to speak in favor of the current partition proposal, and Berl Katznelson had said he would oppose it. Ultimately, the Congress would vote to empower the Executive to negotiate with the British government, hoping that it could extract a more favorable division of land than the Peel Commission had proposed. Despite the urgency of this topic, and despite Marie Syrkin's total commitment to partition (she would write persuasively about the subject several times), this time, personal issues argued against another trip abroad.

Charles had received an invitation from Al Lewin to return to Los Angeles to do some work for him. On March 13, 1937, Charles had written to him "Your letter came yesterday. I expect to be in Los Angeles Saturday. It was kind of you to offer to advance the fare, but I still can manage" (*Letters* 215). Marie and her husband Charles had been together without separation for the past five months. Now he found it necessary to part again, but they planned to get together for the summer either in Los Angeles or New York.

By Saturday, March 20, Charles had settled in at the Hotel Carmel in Santa Monica. A few weeks later he wrote to Henry Hurwitz at the *Menorah Journal*, "The job came through after all. Will send you some verse, or what I have, when I come to. In the meantime, hard at work but finding it exciting—and very pleasant" (*Letters* 215). Charles, it appears, has found a patron. Lewin had remained amply enamored of Charles' poetics and sufficiently devoted to their long friendship to offer him employment as a script writer for the Abelard project, with time available to work on his own poetry. As much as the scenario, "Reznikoff in Hollywood," appears to be the tale of a man completely out of his milieu, he did compose some of his best work while there, including the now famous "Kaddish." Marie and Charles' relationship in these late years of the decade are, at best, irregular: the contemplative and the active trying to make a life together, but mostly living apart. Charles loved Marie deeply—but he may have loved his poetic work just about as much, enough to spend long periods of time thousands of miles away, with jet airplanes and e-mail years in the future. Marie loved Charles too (yet she was willing to travel for long periods of time for her own work), but she also felt some disdain for his impracticality and inability (perhaps, unwillingness) to make a living. The disdain however, was softened by her conviction that his poetry was wonderfully original and important. It was her total support of his literary gifts that prevented her complete contempt, in the knowledge that while she traveled far and wide to be an active, on-the-spot reporter of some of the worst events of the decade—especially for Jews—he had been sitting under the palms and fig trees of sunny California writing about the bitter-sweet love of the twelfth century's Heloise and Abelard. Yet, while he toiled at the script that never was to be finished, he too spoke to the tragic events of his own time in superb and moving verse. The poem, "Kaddish," an expansion and interpretation of the traditional "*Kaddish de Rabbanan*" as translated by R. Travers Herford, is worth full quotation as testimonial evidence in the clear case of Marie Syrkin's total devotion to the power of Charles Reznikoff's poetry despite other things being unequal.

Upon Israel and upon the rabbis
and upon the disciples and upon all the disciples of their disciples
and upon all who study the Torah in this place and in every place,
to them and to you
peace;

upon Israel and upon all who meet with unfriendly glances,
    sticks and stones and names —
on posters, in newspapers, or in books to last,
chalked on asphalt or in acid on glass,
shouted from a thousand thousand windows by radio;
who are pushed out of classrooms and rushing trains,
whom the hundred hands of a mob strike,
and whom jailers strike with bunches of keys, with revolver butts;
to them and to you
in this place and in every place
safety;

upon Israel and upon all who live
as the sparrows of the streets
under the cornices of the houses of others,
and as rabbits
in the fields of strangers
on the grace of the seasons
and what the gleaners leave in the corners;
you children of the wind —
birds
that feed on the tree of knowledge
in this place and in every place

to them and to you
a living;

upon Israel
and upon their children and upon all the children
in this place and in every place
to them and to you
life.
(*Poems* I 185)

It cannot be denied that both Marie Syrkin and Charles Reznikoff
were lovers of Zion, but they expressed it in different forms. Charles
was a lover of Jewish history, which permeated his contemporary poetry
and sometimes his prose. Marie had experienced more recent Jewish
history, which made her acutely sensitive to barometric changes in the
current Jewish atmosphere. That informed her prose and sometimes her
poetry. For all their differences, they professed love for each other and
they both loved their Jewishness.

The routine of parting and returning continued through the next
two years. In 1937, Albert Lewin assumed a new position. He had been
the famed producer Irving Thalberg's personal assistant, but after Thalberg's death in September 1936 Lewin joined Paramount Pictures as a
producer, where he would produce some of Paramount's biggest films
of the 1930s. He had not forgotten his friend; he still believed in his poetic ability, and wishing to extend a helping hand, he offered him a job
for which he undoubtedly knew Reznikoff was not especially suited.
Charles left for Hollywood, checked into the Hotel Carmel, Santa Monica, but soon moved to an apartment at 1147 Sixth Street. He seems to
have returned to the Bronx by the fall, but not for very long. By the
spring, he was back in Santa Monica and Marie joined him at the end of
the school year. "During the two summers that Charles was in Hollywood [1937, 1938] I spent my vacations there," Marie has written. "We
had a one-room efficiency facing the ocean above what is now Bellevue
restaurant in Santa Monica. The bed came out of the wall. Charles introduced me to the delights of a long street car ride to Boo's cafeteria,
his favorite, in the heart of Los Angeles. In the thirties the Los Angeles
sky was brilliantly blue and the air smog-free. Santa Monica seemed a bit
of paradise after a winter in New York" (*Man and Poet* 50). This recollection appears in the 1984 memoir of her husband that she wrote from

her spacious two-bedroom apartment with balcony on Fifth Street. Syrkin retired to Santa Monica shortly after Charles' death. In the same memoir, she recalls Charles' Hollywood experience:

In [1937], when he was a producer with Paramount, Al, aware of Charles' difficulties invited him to Hollywood. Charles' assignment was to be determined by whatever talents he might display as a reader, re-write man, or scenario writer. In an exuberant moment Charles saw himself alternately as a fledgling director or writer of Hollywood hits. Anyhow, with the offer of $75 a week for unspecified services as Al's assistant, he set out by train for California. With Al's concurrence we agreed that until Charles' capacity was tested I had better keep my teaching job in New York. His salary [75 dollars a week] — non-existent by Hollywood standards — was a clue to his realistic prospects. . . . At first, the studio hierarchy, unsure of his exact standing, gave Charles the deference due a friend and assistant of Al. That stage, as Charles wryly indicated in his letters, soon passed. (*Man and Poet* 46)

At work, Charles had been given a sizable office and secretarial help. He hobnobbed with celebrities when he lunched with Al, which he did frequently. He had plenty of time to work on his own poetry and his historical novel in progress, *The Lionhearted,* about the massacre of the Jews of York, England. At night, he attended parties where there was much drinking and witty repartee — neither with which he felt comfortable. But there was a certain kind of fascination and perhaps some headiness at being included in so celebrified an atmosphere. In the 1984 memoir, Marie notes, the parties were "social distractions that he probably enjoyed more than he admitted — he always noted the occasions when he was not invited." But to make the point, she chose one particular selection from a letter to include. It describes Charles' reaction to a party at the home of the Hollywood composer Herbert Stothard:

Here we found Rosa Ponselle, the opera singer, and an assortment of followers: a fat Italian who was her accompanyist, utterly bored; a middle aged and short Russian Jew who was her secretary or agent, utterly bored; and her husband, an American polo-player, tall and a rich man's son, who was already pretty well in liquor and, his feet resting on a commode, sprawled in the middle of the sitting room, dozing off with a large cognac glass, which he had just replenished, in his hand. After a while, she began to sing as if to sing the walls down — a powerful beautiful voice; dressed in a flame colored gown, very tall, slender, moving her beautiful body about as she sang, sang phony Neopolitan songs ("like paper carnations" Angna Enters said), sang arty French songs, sang German; she was very attractive, despite the peasant's face. (*Man and Poet* 49)

From April 1937 through June 1939, Charles Reznikoff lived in Santa Monica with intermittent trips to New York, and with Marie spending the two summers in California. Surely those two summers were Marie's accommodations to the facts on the home ground. Those two years from 1937 to 1939, however, were the years of the inexorable march of dire events in Europe without knowledge that the "final solution" lay ahead. War had not yet erupted, but Hitler's plans for *lebensraum* (expansion) were unfolding apace. Three major events in 1937 to 1938 set the German machine into full acceleration: The *Anschluss,* the annexation of the Sudetenland, and the Munich Conference. Shifting into first gear on March 12, 1938, Hitler marched his German troops into Austria to the accompaniment of a rousing welcome from the native population that had its own long history of antisemitism. Hitler, himself a native of Austria knew that his homecoming would be greeted with flowers and cheers upon arrival and that the Nuremberg laws would be imposed with little difficulty. At the time of the *Anschluss* (the German takeover of Austria), there were approximately 180,000 Austrian Jews — 170,000 in Vienna. By the time war broke out in September of 1939, 120,000 had already left and by the end of the year another 6,000 had fled. "The terror that now followed," explains Howard Sachar, "surpassed the brutality of the purge of German Jewry; for the Nazis were now quite certain of the impotence of world opinion" (Sachar 525). Those with foresight made every effort to leave.

After his easy victory in Austria, Hitler shifted his war machine into second gear and veered north toward Czechoslovakia's Sudetenland, home to three million German-speaking Czechs. Czechoslovakia, which had been created by the Versailles Peace Conference following Germany's defeat in World War I, quickly became one of the most successful creations of the Conference. "Its base was the Czech people, steady, industrious, intelligent," Sachar writes. "Czechoslovakia's government under the direction of the astute statesmen Tomáš Masaryk and Eduard Běnes [*sic*] was democratic; its army was well-disciplined and efficient. Within this thriving oasis of equality and opportunity lived 350,000 Jews. . . . All the Czechoslovakian Jews, whatever their economic status, enjoyed complete political and economic freedom. . . . Any basic threat to security seemed quite remote" (Sachar 526). But Adolf Hitler claimed provocation, at least as far as the Sudetenland and its 3 million ethnic Germans were concerned. Emboldened by his conquest of Austria, Hitler called on the Czechoslovak government to grant autonomy to the Sudetenland. With the help of the Sudeten Nazi party leader, Konrad Henlein, Hitler instigated a barrage of antisemitic propaganda, and boycotts of Jewish businesses; and exploited those with German loyalties and encouraged them to protest against Czechoslovakian rule. With the German armies marching up and down the borders, Hitler threatened President Beneš with invasion if he did not turn over the Sudetenland to Germany. Beneš declined, but could not keep control of the chaos. Throughout the summer of 1938, the crisis worsened as the Germans of the Sudetenland responded to Nazi propaganda and brought the territory to the cusp of civil war. In response, the British Prime Minister, Neville Chamberlain, continued the policy of appeasement that he had followed in the face of the *Anschluss.*

As the summer of 1938 drew to a close Marie Syrkin knew that she had to leave Hollywood. Certainly she felt conflicting emotions: her love for Charles, his needs, her irritations, her desire to make their marriage work, her responsibilities to her son, David, to her teaching job, to her work at the *Frontier;* and at this moment especially, her uncompromising commitment to the plight of the Jewish people. The scales weighed heavily on the side of what could be best accomplished from New York. So at summer's end, Marie Syrkin bought a ticket for a train traveling east.

Chapter 11

The War, the White Paper, and the Rescue of Jews

❦

IT WAS AUGUST 1938; Marie Syrkin and her husband Charles Reznik-off had been enjoying the balmy Los Angeles weather: lows in the six-ties, highs in the eighties, clear skies, low humidity, a view of the Pacific and lush, tropical vegetation — a virtual paradise compared to the choking heat, humidity, and blistering concrete sidewalks of New York that Marie was preparing to return to at the end of the month. There — as Saul Bellow so vividly described the neighborhood of those years: "the sunshine of upper Broadway, not clear but throbbing through the dust and fumes, a false air of gas visible at eye level as it spurted from bursting buses" and "the carnival of the street — push-carts, accordion and fiddle, shoeshine, begging, the dust going round like a woman on stilts" — there on the Upper West Side of Manhattan, summer sizzled.[1] Yet, regardless of the seductions of Hollywood, whatever the satisfactions of spousal companionship, it was to the hot Upper West Side of Manhattan that Marie returned in time for the 1938 to 1939 school year.

This was to be David's last year at home before he would leave for col-lege at Harvard University. In September, just after Marie left for New York, Charles, still in Hollywood, still working at Paramount for his friend and patron, Al Lewin, still working on his novels and his poetry, wrote to Marie, "I am very sorry that you have to be going back to teach and I hope with David in college you will feel able to take the plunge of giving up work and salary" (*Letters* 220). Did Charles really expect to work for the movie industry indefinitely, to live in Hollywood perma-nently, to be a successful screenwriter immediately, and so to ask Marie

to join him there? Though none of these aspirations seem in the least realistic, Charles appears to have caught the tinseltown virus — and he
knows it. The September letter begins with a taste of the many letters
that he filled with tales of Hollywood *machers* (big shots) and hangers-
on whom he grudgingly held in some awe:

> To begin with trifles, the grand party on Sunday was all right. Cukor and Helen
> Westley and even Nazimova were amusing. Milly served champagne to begin
> with. I had none because I had had some sherry and was a little afraid of get-
> ting sick inopportunely. They told some funny stories: of Tallulah Bankhead
> who insisted that cocaine was not habit forming and who said she knew because
> she had been taking it for seventeen years; there were several others but I have
> forgotten them.

Charles admits that although late September has been very hot for
Hollywood, "it is nevertheless livable and, I suppose, even pleasant. I
write you this little detail to let you know how easy it is to soften
and, after a while, how hard to leave the rouge-pots of Hollywood"
(*Letters* 218). Thus, Charles Reznikoff became one more on the list of esteemed East Coast literati to answer the call of California-the-Golden:
F. Scott Fitzgerald, William Faulkner, Tennessee Williams, Nathaniel
West, Clifford Odets, Daniel Fuchs, George and Ira Gershwin, among
many, many others — not to mention the roster of displaced European
artists who succumbed to the irresistible lure of celebrity and sunshine.
Marie's husband would remain in Hollywood until December, only to
return the following April. Marie went home to New York, not to return to live in California for many years.

    Despite the social trivialities recorded in Charles Reznikoff's letters,
he did keep up with the increasingly frightening events in the world that
thoroughly absorbed his wife, and he would sometimes comment on
them in his letters. Marie, of course, remained immersed in the crises of
the time and certainly was not about to "take the plunge and give up her
salary." She held tight to her paying job — which she freely admitted she
detested but needed — all the while traveling to make speeches and to
write about the terrible triangle: Zionism, Hitler, and the Jews. Marie
Syrkin's alertness to the deep connection of events in Palestine and
events in Europe is evinced by an article in *The Nation*, dated February
11, 1939; she had kept a copy of it for fifty years and gave it to me in 1989,
noting that she had made check marks in the margin calling attention to

two paragraphs in particular. The article is headed by a parenthetical explanation:

[News reports of the National Socialist Party Congress at Nurnberg last September made brief mention of the presence of a sizable group of Arab sheiks. The following letter, written by the nephew of one of those sheiks to Al-ford ibn Roos, who translated and passed it along to us, sheds light on their mission to Germany and on the activities of the Nazis in the Near East. We have had the original document, written in Arabic, carefully examined by a competent scholar and feel assured of its authenticity. While we cannot vouch for the information it presents, the letter seems important if only for what it reveals of the attitude and expectations of the Arabs themselves. . . . Editors of *The Nation*]

The first checked paragraph is as follows:

My uncle, the Sheik . . . who was honored together with more than a hundred other of all the *dar al Islam,* hath returned from a visit to the ruler of the Germans. And they did sit in council with the viziers of the ruler, and when my uncle related the great things that were arranged there I was permitted to sit in the ring of the elders of Bir el Melosah. And we all rejoice to know that the High Vizier of the Germans, one Yussuf Goebbels, gave assurance that the ruler Hitler and all the viziers and the *sipah-silar* [army commanders] have accepted the tenets of the Prophet, upon whom be blessings, and are actually true believers, though for purposes of state and temporarily this has not been promulgated in their countries and must be disseminated throughout Islam. All Islam rejoices to know that Allah hath inclined the hearts of the Germans to accept Allah's Prophet and become believers, just as he inclined the heart of the Wolf in the land of the Italians; so we have two former infidel rulers who are vowed and committed to champion our cause of justice. (*The Nation,* Feb. 11, 1939)

The second highlighted paragraph points out that the young Arab men of

Jebel ed Druse can scarcely be restrained against the French, for they remember well the French massacre of not many years ago, and all our own young men are avid for war against the infidel English, who would give El Kuds, the Holy, to the Jews and let the Dome of the Rock be desecrated by unbelievers.

My uncle was told that all the world would be at war soon." (*The Nation,* Feb. 11, 1939)

The writer's uncle hit the bull's eye.

The Sudetentland: Hitler, and Chamberlain in Munich

Almost immediately after Marie returned in September of 1938 from her Hollywood sojourn, events in Europe began to heat up to Celsius 100. Hitler had been screaming his venomous, bellicose orations to rallies of fanatical Nazis, attacking the Czechs and demanding that "the Czech government give 'justice' to the Sudeten Germans. If it didn't, Germany would have to see to it that it did."[2] Fearing the dire consequences of Hitler's plainly announced plans to annex the Czech territory, Prime Minister Chamberlain sent a pressing communiqué to Hitler requesting a meeting. "In view of the increasingly critical situation I propose to come over at once to see you with a view to trying to find a peaceful solution. I propose to come by air and am ready to start tomorrow. Please indicate the earliest time at which you can see me and suggest place of meeting. I should be grateful for a very early reply" (Shirer 384). William Shirer has reported that when Hitler received this message, he exclaimed "Ich bin vom Himmel gefallen!"; Hitler was astounded by Chamberlain's pleading tone and the fact that this important British statesman who was "sixty-nine years old and had never traveled in an airplane before should make the long seven hours' flight to Berchtesgaden at the farthest extremity of Germany" (Shirer 384). Further exhilarated by his recent successes and encouraged by the obvious weakness of the European democracies, Hitler up-geared once again.

On September 28, 1938, Mussolini, not quite ready for war, called for a conference including Britain, France, Germany, and Italy to be held in Munich. The subject was the resolution of the political status of the Sudeten Germans in Czechoslovakia, but the Czech government was not included. The British and French, believing that they were preventing all-out European war, acceded to Hitler's demands (though they both had treaty agreements with Czechoslovakia in the event of attack) and agreed to the German annexation of the Sudetenland. Neville Chamberlain and his French yes-man Daladier naively believed that this would satisfy Hitler's hunger for *lebensraum.* Chamberlain returned home to proudly proclaim that his appeasement of Germany was for the sake of "peace in our time." It was, it can, and has been argued, the most pusillanimous act of political diplomacy, the worst betrayal of moral statecraft in modernity. With this deluge of dire events crowding out all other thoughts in Marie Syrkin's mind, she received another letter from Charles with his own comments on world events. Though most of his letters had been reports about what was news on the Rialto, he was not so removed from the outside world as to be unaffected by it. In mid-September, he wrote:

I am here, as you are, of course, greatly excited by the news from abroad. I feel that England is right in trying to postpone war in every possible way and, providing it piles up its strength in the meantime so that there can be no question about the outcome and so ultimately no issue by force, England can afford to give ground little by little only to regain it all and much more at once. They will probably give the Sudeten to Germany after they have stripped the territory of all that can be beneficial immediately to Germany, but though this is a setback it is not a defeat. A war is as destructive to the winner as to the loser unless it is brief and the conquest of Germany will not be brief so that even if, as I think, Germany will lose in a long war, England and France will probably win only a victory that will not last in the face of an inevitable third war waged by an angrier and greater Germany with a population then greater than both England and France put together. As for me, I am for England and for France and am very skeptical of the future of humanity generally or of the Jews in particular in Russia; whatever victories for humanity have been won there are fine, but the future under the present leadership is uncertain. (*Letters* 219)

Not surprisingly, Marie's husband also was quick to admit his lack of political expertise, "Of course, I stick my neck out when I discuss foreign affairs in these letters," he confessed in a letter dated September 24, 1938, four days before the Munich Conference. "By the time you get them, you have read the morning papers and are much smarter than I. However, the events going on now are so astonishing that it is hard to keep still. I wonder why Hitler is taking the attitude that he does since everything will be in his hands in a few weeks or months" (*Letters*). Four days later, the Sudetenland was in the hands of the Germans, and however bitter the Czechs may have been at the loss of their territory and border fortifications, they were powerless to withstand the Nazi assault that was proceeding month by month.

Charles Reznikoff was a very fine poet indeed, but not very good at prophecy. Within days, the German troops occupied the Sudetenland. Marie, however, held a view different from her husband. Not too long after she received his letter she wrote an analysis of *Mein Kampf* for the *Jewish Frontier* entitled "Spreading the Nazi Gospel." The opening paragraph reads:

Whether Mr. Chamberlain was an ingenuous blunderer who really believed that he was securing "peace in our time" by the Munich sell-out, or whether he was a cynical trickster consciously surrendering the world to fascism to protect the interests of the Cliveden set, only Mr. Chamberlain is in a position to reveal. The rest of us can only surmise. However, though the impulses at work in the British mind may be debatable, in one field at least all is clear. We need have no doubts whatever as to what is going on in the Nazi mind. Those curious to know just how much "appeasement" will appease or how bright the prospects for peace actually are, need only consult the frankly avowed and endlessly repeated Nazi Program.

. . . The immediate results of the Munich peace are obvious enough. Germany bestrides Central and Eastern Europe, and those states which have not yet been gobbled up, are rushing to come to terms—to enter the German orbit rather than jaw. The Road to Bagdad lies wide open and the signposts, lettered in gothic say, "Verboten." It looks like a good day's work, and perhaps Chamberlain really believes that Hitler will require "peace in our time" to digest his gains. But that is a forlorn hope. The three fundamental Nazi tenets, the belief in a master race, the belief in a master state, and the glorification of war, allow of no respite. They form an exacting Trinity whose devotees are in perpetual service.

No longer was Marie Syrkin writing amusing little verses about the soon-to-blow-over lunatic antics of the overblown hysteric of Western Europe; now she read the fateful signs with Tiresian truth. "On the basis of their own statements," Syrkin warns, "Hitler and his cohorts will not be satisfied with South-Eastern Europe and the Danube region already within their grasp. They will not be satisfied with the wheat-fields of the Ukraine for which they hanker so openly. They will reach the happy condition of 'appeasement' only when they have attained world-dominion. They have a world mission, and Nazidom has embarked on a crusade to fulfill its mission" (*Frontier*, December 1938, 12–15).

Only Winston Churchill seemed to understand the meaning of the

Chamberlain cave-in; five days after the Munich debacle, Churchill — out of power — addressed the House of Commons:

We have sustained a total and unmitigated defeat. . . . We are in the midst of a disaster of the first magnitude. The road down the Danube . . . the road to the Black Sea has been opened. . . . All the countries of Mittel Europa and the Danube valley, one after another will be drawn in the vast system of Nazi politics . . . radiating from Berlin. . . . And do not suppose that this is the end. It is only the beginning. (Shirer 423)

Churchill, almost alone, had the foresight to see what, in hindsight, history has proven to be tragically too true; it *was* only the beginning. By October 21, Hitler conveyed his "Top Secret" program to his military commanders announcing his plan for "the liquidation of the remainder of Czechoslovakia" (Shirer 428).

Evian and Its Consequences

In July of 1938, only two months prior to the annexation of the Sudetenland (and with the Kristallnacht pogrom yet to come), President Franklin Roosevelt had convened a conference to deal with an already increasing refugee problem. Held at Evian on Lake Geneva, delegates from thirty-two countries were in attendance. Despite the fact that the Governor of New York, Herbert Lehman, himself a Jew, sent Roosevelt a note with a single word, "Splendid," Roosevelt wanted to restrict immigration — particularly during these Depression years and with rising antisemitism in America. Henry Feingold has pointed out that "Jewish leaders were so overjoyed at this development [the Evian Conference] that few noted that the invitation to thirty two nations was circumscribed so as not to conflict with the immigration laws of the participating nations. Moreover, the British would not permit Palestine, the obvious place for Jewish immigration, to be discussed and the American presiding over the conference denied Chaim Weizmann permission to speak to the convened group. This preordained the conference to failure, since a hoped-for initiative from the Latin-American republics, which the administration counted on, would not materialize."[3] Only the dictator, Generalissimo Trujillo, of the Dominican Republic made the great-hearted offer of asylum for one hundred thousand "political refugees" of all religions—an obvious euphemism for Jews.

Tragically, in the end the conference accomplished nothing. Roosevelt had sent a minor diplomat to represent the United States, which the others took as a signal that he simply had been playing to public opinion. It was a photo-op event that need not cause any fears for the delegates; hence, there would be no humanitarian rescue. No one was willing to make more than a token adjustment. Canada said it would accept farmers, but there were few farmers among the mostly urban Jews fleeing Hitler. The long and bitter lead editorial in the August 1938 issue of the *Jewish Frontier*, most probably written by Marie Syrkin (but at the very least her translation from Hayim Greenberg's Yiddish), called the atmosphere and results of the conference political cowardice, but on the opposite page there was a small poem entitled "Refugee Conference" (from *Canadian Forum*), by one John Smalacomee:

> Nephews and cousins of Our Lord,
> Taught by the cudgel and the cord
> To dread and shun their Aryan kin
> Turn with fresh hope to newer skies;
> And promptly Canada replies,
> "Too bad. There's no room at the inn."
> (*Frontier* 2–5)

Apparently someone across the border got the message. But across the ocean there was another message: this one the official response to the conference from the German Foreign Office; "Since in many countries it was recently regarded as wholly incomprehensible why Germany did not wish to preserve in its population an element like the Jews . . . it appears astounding that countries seem in no way anxious to make use of these elements themselves now that the opportunity offers" (Berenbaum 50). There would be no reverse, no neutral, but only a matter of months before the Fuehrer's war machine would shift into an even higher gear.

Now, month by month, Hitler's hidden agenda—*lebensraum* and the war against the alien Jews—began to emerge from the shadows into full view. Living space for the Aryan nation would be accomplished by conquering territory and evacuating Jews in conquered lands and inside the *heimland* itself. Wherever and whatever lands the Nazis occupied, the

Nuremberg Laws would root out the bad blood. In a brilliantly acerbic article in the July 1938 issue of *Jewish Frontier,* Marie Syrkin took a creative approach by which to expose the Nazi racial laws and to warn the American Jews of what was yet to come. In the March 1938 issue of the popular *Woman's Home Companion,* the mother of the famous Jewish violinist Yehudi Menuhin had confessed that contrary to received information, *she* was not Jewish. Her father, she claimed, was a Tartar and her mother was Italian, but her husband happened to be a Jew. This made her son only a half-Jew. Marie Syrkin writes in her article, "Grandpa Was a Tartar," that Mrs. Menuhin explained this odd mixture "to ladies eager to produce genius," because that "accounts for the musical talents of her children. . . . Naturally we feel let down," laments Syrkin, "because . . . so much had been made of the Jewishness of Menuhin." It was widely known that Yehudi's grandfather was a Hebrew teacher, born in the Crimea, but with a Palestinian background; that he and his wife had made sure "the son of a genius must wear a sign — *Yehudi,* 'the Jew'; the daughter of a genius will bear a strange Biblical name — Hepzibah — not Shirley or Myrtle. And their speech will be Hebrew." But, Marie continues, "Of course there are sceptics. There are people with unkind memories who knew the Menuhins in their early days when they were struggling with their gifted children — the days when Jewish emphasis was broad and brave." These people, Marie points out, remember the [maternal] grandfather as a member of a synagogue in Chicago who collected for a Jewish charity in Palestine. He was an Orthodox Jew "and gave no evidence of hiding an Italian wife behind his beard. Friends recall his joy at his daughter's marriage to the worthy Hebrew scholar, Moshe Menuhin — a curious predilection for a descendant of Genghis Kahn." Syrkin then ironically points out that if Yehudi's father, Moshe, would discover that his mother was really an Arab from stock "lightened by some Teutonic Crusader . . . a further reduction in the Jewish blood-count would be achieved." Marie was not being cute. Her satire was prickling with urgency: Directed to uninformed or complacent Americans, Syrkin was using Mrs. Menuhin's genealogy in the service of an exposé of the Nuremberg racial laws as well as a goad for those who in these terrifying times would deny their Jewish origins. The central point of the satire explains:

In general, since Hitler's advent there has been much curious scanning of the family tree. The Nazis, of course, are trying to detect any Semite hidden in the eaves, but many a half Jew in Germany shakes the branches eagerly, peering for an Aryan interloper. According to Nazi law, a Jewish father or grandfather, means classification as a Jew, even if your Aryan mother brought you up as a devout Lutheran. But there is a loop-hole. If you can prove that your grandfather was not Siegfried Cohen, the lawful spouse of your Aryan grandmother, but really Fritz, the traveling salesman, then you have redeemed the honor of your name, and may be certified as an Aryan. It is reported that German officials are beset by petitions seeking to establish the adulterous connections of the petitioner's female relatives. A well-authenticated lapse from virtue on the part of an Aryan granny is worth a lot to her descendant, who can thus be cleansed from the taint of Jewish blood. Prove that the fleet was in town, and you may yet be saved the degradation of belonging to the Jewish people.

Marie, however, does not fail to call attention to the "other side of the picture" — the brave Christians and Jews who had been brought up as Christians and who identified themselves with or as Jews. And, she reports, "there was the Aryan German Professor who accepted Judaism with his whole family as a protest against Hitler." (Marie did *not* mean the philosopher Professor Martin Heidegger, who famously joined the Nazi Party and did their bidding). As to the Menuhins,

we hate to believe that their early insistence on courage, on dignity, on one's own identity, was only a hoax; a clever publicity scheme calculated to rally the enthusiasm and support of the sentimental Jewish public behind the young Jewish genius. Once perhaps, the idealism was real. But the destruction of the last five years has been pervasive and incalculable. Much has been lost that is not in the books. Besides the lost lives, lost jobs, the lost possessions, who can chalk up the loss of assurance of mental balance, which is part of the havoc? The tide rises and threatens to engulf. So one clutches at straws, even so frail and pathetic a straw as Tartar masquerade. Yet surely the old "*Shamas*" must have told his daughter that the only salvation in the deluge is to be found in the strictly Hebraic vessel built by Jewish hands — the ark. (*Frontier* 24)

Despite her signature witty, sardonic tone, Marie Syrkin's trumpet call alerting American Jews to the present dangers in Nazi Germany was deadly serious — and it was without full knowledge of the grave tragedy yet to come. What is more, Marie had written her alarum several months before that November 9 catastrophe infamously known as *Kristallnacht*.

Between September and March, Hitler moved ahead with the plans that long before he had clearly stated in *Mein Kampf:* expansion of Germany and the war against the Jews. Each month brought further preparations for his target date for war with Poland (known as Case White); the chosen date to be no later than October 1, 1939. The war against the Jews, however, took on stunning immediacy and clarity in the month of November 1938.

During September and October, Marie had kept up her dizzying schedule of home work, school work, and *Frontier* work, while Charles remained in Hollywood and wrote his wife letters about the lives of the rich and famous, about the progress of his creative writing, and about how eager he was to get back to New York to spend the holidays with her — at first Thanksgiving, and when that proved unmanageable, Christmas. But during those weeks, the *coup de grace* for the Jews was struck. On November 9, 1938, the Jews of the German Reich — Germany, Austria, and the Sudetenland — became the victims of the merciless violence of the notorious *Kristallnacht* — the night of the broken glass.

From this moment on, Marie Syrkin's life was welded to the events of the time. Jewish survival in Europe and in the Middle East now shaped the essential text of her life story. To understand Marie, one must understand the historical circumstances that occupied her body, mind, and soul. Irving Howe, once her detractor, by 1983, came to say in tribute to her, "I believe in Marie Syrkin. I believe in the kind of life she has led, a life of commitment to values beyond the self."[4] The world events of 1939 are her biography; and to narrate her history, is to narrate the history of her world.

Kristallnacht

Hitler claimed provocation for the *Kristallnacht* pogrom, blaming it on the murder of a minor German official in Paris by the seventeen-year-old Herschel Grynszpan; the boy's Polish born parents had been stranded on the border between the Germany that deported them and the Poland that would not take back its Jewish citizens. Mr. and Mrs. Grynszpan wrote of their plight to their son, who blind with rage, sought revenge in the murder of the German diplomat. Exploiting this unfortunate event as a fortunate excuse, the *Fuehrer*'s Gestapo carried out its 3D pogrom of destruction, desecration, and death. For the repair of the "broken glass" and its corollary damages, a fine of one billion *Reichmarks* was imposed upon the victimized Jewish communities of Germany, Austria, and the Sudetenland. All but the politically naive, morally blind, or self-delusional knew that it was one minute till midnight — time to leave. And there would be no glass slipper.

But where to go? The Evian debacle had been followed by German expulsions of Polish Jews and Slovakian expulsions of Hungarian Jews into no-man's lands; ill-fated ships carrying fleeing Jews, ships like the S.S. *Königstein,* or the *Caribia,* or the *St. Louis,* became "floating communities . . . that had left Hamburg in 1938 for Latin America with many hundreds of passengers on board, but were not permitted to land in their countries of destination," though the Nazis were willing to take the voyagers back — into concentration camps. "And so these ghost ships continued their macabre voyage between Europe and Latin America, between the Balkans and Palestine, treated as if they were the carriers of the plague" (Sachar 507).

The options were virtually nil.

January 1939 — the first month of the new year that ushered in the last year of the whole appalling decade — did not augur well for the months ahead. On January 24, Hermann Goering, the head of the Gestapo, ordered Reinhard Heydrich, the leader of the S.S. to accelerate forced emigration of Jews from German-occupied territories. After the Vienna *Anschluss,* Adolf Eichmann, the Nazi expert on Zionism, had initiated the program of forcible departure as an alternative to terror tactics. Three days after this, Neville Chamberlain announced his recognition of the fascist Franco government in Spain and was harshly criticized by many in Parliament. On January 30, on the sixth anniversary of his accession to power, Hitler prophesied, in a speech to the Reichstag, "[I]f the international Jewish financiers in and outside Europe should succeed in plunging the nations once more into a world war, then the result will not be the Bolshevising of the earth and thus the victory of Jewry, but the annihilation of the Jewish race in Europe!" (Berenbaum 61). The next month proved no better; in the war for expansion, on February 14, the German battleship Bismarck was launched; a week later, in the war against the Jews, the Nazis compelled the Jews to hand over all their gold and silver. On February 27, Neville Chamberlain announced the official recognition of Franco's government. In early March, Stalin began to make noises about the natural relationship between Nazism and Communism. Political events in Europe clearly were not pointing toward peace and resolution. Nor were they much better in the Middle East, which had seen the publication in November of 1938 of the Woodhead Commission's findings, effectively nullifying the partition recommendations of the Peel Commission.

Then, in March of 1939, only six months after the Sudetenland takeover, and four months after Kristallnacht, the Nazi machine ratcheted up yet another notch and drove its forces of occupation into the rest of Czechoslovakia. Under Hitler and Goering's threat of bombardment of Prague, the Czech President Hácha declared the provinces of Bohemia and Moravia a German Protectorate, as Slovakia seceded and became a separate state. It has since been widely noted that Czechoslovakia was the first non-German territory that Hitler seized.

The consequence of Hitler's occupation for the Czech Jews was no different from that of Germany or Austria. Of course, the 118,000 Jews of Bohemia and Moravia knew they now faced mortal danger; between the March 15 takeover and September 1 the outbreak of war, about 26,000 Jews emigrated. That left 90,000 in the Protectorate — the home of the infamous Theresienstadt "ghetto" or "model camp," where most of them would be sent. "It was a Potemkin village," explains Lucy Dawidowicz, "purporting to be an autonomous Jewish community. Among its inmates were many prominent German Jews whose disappearance would prove embarrassing to the Germans in case of international inquiries about their welfare. In reality Theresienstadt was, for most of its inmates, just a stopping place before their final destination at Auschwitz" (Dawidowicz 137). At the end of the war, only 10,000 Czechoslovakian Jews — almost a tenth of those who had remained in the Protectorate, had survived (Dawidowicz 377). By 1939, Jews from Germany, Austria, and Czechoslovakia were taking flight and going to whatever country would take them in; though most would not. After the *Anschluss*, there were too many Jews seeking a haven in the Western democracies to consider admitting them.

Adolf Hitler's brazen landgrabs, however, had at least one positive effect; it incensed the British public who now saw clearly the wages of Neville Chamberlain's appeasement. By March 31, the British Prime Minister, in a reversal of his prior policies, "made his historic declaration in the House of Commons that Britain and France 'would lend the Polish Government all support in their power' if Poland were attacked and resisted" (Shirer 465). They signed an agreement on April 6. The British-French position, however, did not change Hitler's plans to destroy Poland; so infuriated was he by their action that his response was to demand that Poland turn over the town of Danzig and the Polish Corridor to Germany. Poland, quite naturally, rejected Hitler's arrogant demand. And, finally, Neville Chamberlain conceded to his cabinet that any further negotiations with Adolf Hitler would be impossible. Hitler's response to Poland however, was to seize some more land, occupying the once-Prussian port city of Memel, which Germany had lost to Lithuania in the Versailles Treaty. On March 23, Memel fell to the German Navy at 1:30 in the afternoon. The scrupulous historian of the German Third Reich, William Shirer, reports that "at 2:30 a seasick Hitler, debarked from the battleship *Deutschland* and made another of his triumphant entries into a newly occupied city and at the Stadttheater in Memel again addressed a delirious 'liberated' German throng. Another provision of the Versailles Treaty had been torn up. Another bloodless conquest had been made. Although the Fuehrer could not know it, it was to be the last" (Shirer 462).

Within the next few weeks, Europe's threatening and threatened countries began furious preparations for impending war: Britain signed a mutual assistance pact with Poland; in response, Hitler denounced the Anglo-Polish pact as having been aimed exclusively against Germany and he nullified the 1934 ten-year non-aggression pact with Poland as well as the Anglo-German Naval Agreement of June 1935; both Britain and France promised support for Greece and Rumania in case they were attacked. Meanwhile, Madrid had fallen to Franco's fascist forces, thus ending the Civil War in Spain; Mussolini, both envious and emboldened by Hitler's landgrabs, sent troops into Albania and added it to his prior conquest of Ethiopia; in Germany, Hitler sent a communique to his Army chiefs to prepare Case White — the attack on Poland — for implementation by September 1. And across the Atlantic, in the United States, President Roosevelt, under the constraints of the 1935 to 1937 Neutrality Acts made vain attempts to wangle guarantees from Hitler and Mussolini that they would make no further attacks on European countries.[5]

Most of these dizzyingly menacing events happened between the end of 1938 and mid-April 1939 — the months that Charles Reznikoff had spent in New York with his wife Marie Syrkin until his return to Hollywood in mid-April. Obviously, there is no correspondence between the two during the three months they were together to tell us how Charles was reacting to the mounting world perils, though we do know that around this time, he was in the process of writing a sequence of poems titled "Autobiography: Hollywood." If Charles leaves no record of his thoughts about events in the world at this time, Marie's responses are clear and can be found in her frequent and furious writings appearing in the pages of the *Frontier* and other publications.

On March 25, Marie Syrkin turned forty. She was thirty when the decade began, newly married and working to establish her credentials as a journalist, convinced that she knew what to do in these serious and critical times: she would react, research, and respond in print and in speech. Her words, however, were never like Charles' homely "dandelions," but were roses, blood-red and pungent with very prickly thorns. By her fortieth birthday, Marie was now a mature woman, but still beautiful, with finely chiseled features, flashing dark eyes, perhaps a bit fuller of figure, and with one or two grey strands in her thick black hair—though now more fashionably coiffed with a few curls; her reputation as a sharp polemicist had become substantial, and she was known in the Jewish world as an opinion-maker whose articles were a "must read." Here, for example, are some of those pungent thoughts written just after *Kristallnacht* in December 1938, entitled: "Spreading the Nazi Gospel":

Since the belated discovery of *Mein Kampf* by American journalists, the air is heavy with quotations from that opus as though *Mein Kampf* were an isolated phenomenon and the sole source of light on Nazi intentions. "What will Hitler do next?" And the answer is produced pat and formidable, from what is beginning to seem the most unassuming autobiography of the century. By now these citations smell of the grave. We stand around the corpse and caw: "So he did exactly what he said he would do on page 143, or page 247." And yet, despite the elegiac mood which colors our reading, Nazi literature is still of more than posthumous interest, particularly if we realize that Hitler is merely the exceedingly shrewd and able popularizer of an elaborate body of dogma. It is a mistake to assume that the vision which animates *Mein Kampf* is original with its author or necessarily dependent on him. He is the supreme exponent in speech and action of a philosophy whose implications the civilized cannot evade, if it proposes to survive. . . . The time has passed when we can afford to be amused at, or scornful of, Nazi pronouncements. . . . It is too late to shed tears for Austria or Czechoslovakia, but it is not too late to try to understand what the future holds in store. (*Frontier,* Dec. 1938, 12–15)

In mid-April, Charles was back in Hollywood, though he was wise enough to do as the Psalmist recommended, to "number his days." Al

Lewin's hearing was worsening, and so was his relationship with Paramount. He told Charles that he believed that the studio was trying to get him to resign and added "I am surprised that they don't fire you. If I have nothing to do, obviously I don't need an assistant." On May 2, 1939, Charles wrote to Marie that "There has been a change in my relationship with A—very slight but perceptible. Now that the position of master and man is about to be terminated, if not this week this year, but most likely in a week or two, we have become equals again; in fact, I act the superior when it comes to writing—give suggestions as to practical methods, 'daily dozen,' etc." (*Letters* 249).

For the next few weeks, the uncertainty persisted, and Charles' letters remained mostly shop talk and social talk, with little to say about the outside world—except for one or two items: "I am keeping the information with respect to your uncle and aunt but am afraid to broach the subject of an affidavit just now.[6] As soon as I can I'll do so but, as you can gather from the attached sheets and those I sent you, I am completely up in the air. However, this weekend ought to clear matters up— and probably terminate my job. I shall let you know as soon as anything is definite" (*Letters,* May 4). A week later, he wrote to Marie about her summer plans: "It looks, although tomorrow may change all this and I may be on my way to New York, that I will be here for the summer if things work out as they seem to be tending. In that event you should come here, of course. Going to Europe or Palestine now is taking quite a chance of being marooned there for four years although, if there is no war this year, I think the chances for peace are good as England and France grow in strength and allies" (*Letters,* May 12).

By May 18, things are still in flux: "Dearest," Charles greets her, "There is really nothing definite yet—as you can see from the enclosed. I am glad you liked the nougat and will send a larger box when I am near the place again. The newspapers, even in California, are almost as exciting as in New York: the good news about England and Russia's approchement (if that is correct) is balanced by the news from Palestine. However, it is clear that the Moslems are more important for England than the Jews and will win out every time in Palestine. I hope the Jews will be able to wangle a better territory than British Guiana out of England for settling besides Palestine" (*Letters*). Surely at this late date, Charles could not have thought that Marie would turn territorialist! He may not have understood precisely his wife's brand of Zionism, but it is clear that he continued to share her taste in sweets.

Marie's attitude toward the British offer of Guiana for Jewish colonization, which excluded the coastal belt, was limited to the jungle areas of the inferior interior territory, and had no access to the sea, was not hard to deduce: first, there was the Palestinian Jews' difficulties with Arab demands and the continuing riots; second, there was Malcolm MacDonald's White Paper of May 1939, which had renounced the earlier partition proposal as impractical and offered an alternate policy which stated that "His Majesty's Government now declares that it is not part of their policy that Palestine should become a Jewish State" and that such a policy would be "contrary to their obligations to the Arabs under the Mandate" (worldwar-2). And finally, there was the failure of the Evian Conference, which left thousands upon thousands of displaced Jewish refugees looking for a safe haven. Marie saw the new policy as a blatant British betrayal of the spirit of the Balfour Declaration and the intent of the Mandate, and as such, an obvious pro-Arab political ploy. The June issue of *Jewish Frontier* contained an editorial most likely written by Marie (the style is hers), with the heading "The 'Promised Land' in Guiana." The opening paragraph leaves nothing in doubt regarding the position of the writer and the publication:

It cannot be said that the experiment in Jewish colonization in British Guiana which may commence this fall will begin under auspicious circumstances. The justifiable suspicion concerning the legitimacy of its paternity will continue to haunt this project, particularly if the White Paper policy concerning Palestine will be enforced to any degree. The feeling that this stretch of jungle is intended as a sop for the betrayal of Jewish hopes and efforts in Palestine cannot be so easily eradicated from the minds of Jews everywhere. Yet no responsible person will say in view of the present needs that this Greek offer should be rejected because of the arrogance and brutality of the appeasers in England. There are by far graver reasons for doubting the success of this new plan or the extent to which it can serve as a solution for the refugee problem. (*Frontier* 7–8)

Neither Marie, nor any other Zionist was unaware of the cause of this situation. With war already showing its halberd and helmet above the horizon line, Britain would take no chances. Arab oil was the requisite then, as it would be in the future.

On June 12, Charles finally lost his Hollywood job. "This means I am out of the studio by June 24th at the latest," he wrote to Marie. "As I thought, they called Al down this morning and incidentally asked him to let me go. He asked for leave to give me two weeks notice and they consented. On the whole, the return trip, carfare and all, was not so bad" (*Letters* 275). By mid-June, Charles had returned to New York to resume his life with Marie at 410 West 24th Street. By the end of the month, June 28, Charles wrote to his sometime patron Al Lewin that "Marie has changed her mind about going to Palestine—or even Switzerland. I'll go with her (and my typewriter) to the Adirondacks after school closes. However I think the dryad will have enough of trees in a week or two" (*Letters* 276). It is hard to say whether or not both Reznikoffs had a pleasant vacation in the Northeast, but Charles seems to have had quite an enjoyable trip. Six weeks after he had written to Al that Marie had decided not to go abroad, he wrote again on August 12 with the news that "Marie left for Switzerland on Wednesday. She should be back September 4th. We went up to the Adirondacks, through the Green Mountains, and another week in Maine (Ogunquit), and came back about the middle of July. The trip did Marie a lot of good and now, rested and brave, she has gone (the darling!), a delegate to the Zionist Convention, to rescue captive Israel" (*Letters* 276). It is not clear whether Charles' comments are patronizing, or sarcastic, or simply oblivious—or all of the above. One thing, however, does seem clear: there is tension between the two that has much to do with conflicting work ethics. Much light is shed on the subject from Marie's later account of that period in their lives—though admittedly, it is seen through the bifocal lenses of hindsight:

On Charles' return from Hollywood we had a small apartment on 18th Street [her memory failed slightly—its was on 24th Street] in Manhattan near my high school on the corner of Ninth Avenue—not a choice neighborhood in those days [a year later they moved to 18th Street]. As my son was getting ready for college the need for the remote Riverdale residence was over. This made life easier. This was also a time when Charles decided unilaterally that he would make no further effort to find a regular job but would devote himself wholly to writing lucrative fiction, "a best seller." He took it for granted that I would agree in this course as policy, rather than in the past as temporary necessity. My scepticism as to the commercial viability of Charles' writing and my resentment at what I viewed as my own bondage, made me what Charles termed "uncooperative"—a charge not likely to soothe under the circumstances. Perhaps I should have been more generous in spirit because the objective reality was not appreciably altered by my lack of enthusiasm for his program. I was being cast in the role of Xantippe. I thought unfairly. (*Man and Poet* 51)

Marie adds that "Though not precisely Xantippe I always felt that the lady had gotten a bad press." She found the image of the Proverbial Jewish "woman of valor" equally irritating — "surely one of the earliest though most revered exemplars of male chauvinism!" (One questions, then, why Marie originally titled her biography of Golda Meir, *Way of Valor* only to change it to *Israel's Leader* in a later edition; perhaps she realized that her title evoked images of the Proverbial praise of women that she so disliked.) Marie next points to the long Jewish tradition of the true Talmudic scholar spending his days in pious study "while his barely literate wife uncomplainingly ran the family store." Charles, she explains, "viewed his vocation as a sacred study" (*Man and Poet* 51).

Despite Charles' barely disguised patronizing comments in his letter to Lewin ("the darling") and the slightly sardonic "rescue of captive Israel," his displeasure with and distance from the concerns that impelled his wife's decision are all too obvious. Marie, however, had no choice — not that she wanted one. Marie Syrkin had been elected as a delegate to the Twenty-First Zionist Congress, as part of a small group of Americans representing the Labor Party, and given the grave political crises of 1939, she was not about to turn it down. Moreover, in 1989 when she spoke of this Congress, she seemed to remember (at first she wondered if she was confusing it with a later Congress) that both Golda Meir and Ben-Gurion had sent a letter insisting that she be sent by the Party as a delegate. When asked about the number of women delegates to the Congress, Marie could not give the exact figure, but she did recall that there were many women delegates from Israel, a few from other European countries, and the largest group of women from America were representatives of Hadassah. Women, however, had not always been part of the official delegation. Indeed, a photograph of the delegates to the First Zionist Congress shows only one woman, Rosa Sonneschein, the founder of the magazine *The American Jewess,* standing behind Herzl. Sonneschein, it should be noted, was not a voting delegate, but had been given observer status. Rosa Sonneschein, a friend of Theodor Herzl, was there to observe and afterwards to report in her publication, and thus she may be thought of as the herald of Marie Syrkin, who also came to observe and to report — and who had never forgotten that her parents had met at that First Zionist Congress.

The Twenty-First Congress was to meet in Geneva from August 16 to 26. It was the very eve of World War II, and Marie as well as all the other delegates and attendees knew it. The present moment was terrifying, for the Jewish world was teetering on the edge of a deep chasm in the earth's surface that gaped from Europe to the Middle East. The delegates were all aware that something had to be done. But what? The central issue of the Congress was the White Paper of May 17, 1939, which in effect nullified the Balfour Declaration and the obligations of the British Mandate. Though the delegates unanimously expressed their intense opposition to the document and vowed to fight it, they were far from unanimous in their ideas about *how* to fight it, and the various factions spoke up with conflicting opinions. Later, in her capacity as journalist, Marie Syrkin reported in the pages of the September 1939, issue of the *Frontier* about the events she had observed in Geneva. She began the account with a personal statement about the context in which the Congress was held:

In the light of the present, much of what happened at the Zionist Congress seems remote. The squabbles about the shekel, the clamour for additional mandates, the paradoxical attack on Labor by American General Zionists and Hadassah, the party maneuvers which loomed so large, occasionally, at Geneva become ludicrous and pathetic in retrospect. Neither the victories nor defeats of one fraction [*sic*] or another matter now, when many of the decisions, so bitterly arrived at, must wait for some indefinite future.

I do not wish to say that the Congress itself is unreal in retrospect. Only the noisy trivialities assume their true proportion. The core of the Congress — that in it which was heroic and tragic — is unforgettable. And even though much of the discussion, as well as the fundamental theme, is no longer immediately relevant, the 21st Zionist Congress, convening as it did in modern Jewry's blackest hour, and concluding in the flame of a World War, has significance which must not be obscured by the barrenness and futility of some of the proceedings. How did Zionism act in a crucial hour? What were its resources of mind and spirit? . . . The Congress was faced by two terrible challenges — the crisis in Zionism [the White Paper] and the crisis in European Civilization [Adolf Hitler]. I think it is not too much to say that on the whole, the Congress met both challenges with courage and with a high sense of responsibility. It is this moral temper which it is essential for us to retrace because by its quality we must live as Zionists and as individuals in the coming time. (*Frontier* 10–13)

Syrkin's report contained a précis of the numerous speeches, the most important presented by Chaim Weizmann, Solomon Goldman, Abba Hillel Silver, Meir Grossman, Ben-Gurion, and Berl Katznelson. "Since these speeches represented divergent intellectual attitudes," she explained, "not only in the Congress but in Jewish life as a whole, it seems worthwhile to consider them." Weizmann, who presided over the meeting, Marie reports, "gave an impression of great weariness and passivity" and restated his familiar position: "We have been betrayed but we must continue our constructive work." After stating his opposition to the use of arms except in self-defense, he called for the systematic education of public opinion for "economic development within the framework of the White Paper which should be exploited to the full."

Marie characterized Ben-Gurion's rebuttal, given at the meeting of the closed session of the labor fraction, as a "great speech" and "one of the two most moving at the Congress — the other being that of Berel Katznelson." After acknowledging Ben-Gurion's detractors' accusations of his rigidity and obstinacy, Marie went on to describe the man and his words as "the speech of a small white-haired man with an *idée fixe,* the speech of a fanatic, and in the last analysis, the speech of a great man, with vision, with tenacity, and above all with a course of action." Syrkin then summed up his position : "A bold assertion by Jewry of its right to Palestine will have a positive political effect. Economic progress is important, but at this moment, a change in the political picture is of paramount importance. This change will best be brought about by a daring patriotism expressing itself in an insistence on continued immigration under all circumstances, whether it leads to clashes with the authorities or not and colonization in remote outposts, with or without government sanction. The heroic mood which dares to perish in order to live!" These words, in contradistinction to Weizmann's, referred to the central issue of the day, *Aliyah Bet,* the unauthorized immigration "whose existence is an open secret."

There were other reported speeches as well: Meir Grossman of the Jewish State Party called for an end to *Havlaga* and an implicit condonation of terrorism; Solomon Goldman, a Conservative rabbi and President of the American Zionist Organization was against the use of force in any form, reminding the Congress that in Jewish history, "Johanan ben Zakkai, the apostle of peace, has been viewed as a greater hero than the military leader Bar-Kochbah." Goldman was in favor of constructive (economic) work. Rabbi Abba Hillel Silver's speech provoked a great

deal of resentment; he opposed all extremist measures and openly attacked unauthorized immigration (later he would change his position).
And in answer to Ben-Gurion who had said in regard to *Aliyah Bet* that
"Jews should act as though we were the State in Palestine, and should
act so until there will be a Jewish State there," Silver "warned emphatically against acting 'as if you are the State,' when you are actually powerless, when you are not the State." Marie Syrkin also commented that
during the policy sessions, "timidity increased in direct proportion to
the distance from Palestine. The Americans were the most wary, the
most cautious, and the most hesitant" and the Palestinians, she said,
were "psychologically the most prepared for an active fight against
the White Paper no matter what forms such a struggle might assume"
(*Frontier* 10–13).

Ben-Gurion's central attitude can be summed up in the epigram he
famously issued a few days after the Congress when Hitler attacked
Poland, and the war broke out: "We will fight with the British against
Hitler as if there were no White Paper; we will fight the White Paper as
if there were no war" (Teveth 54).

The answer to Grossman, Goldman, Silver, and others who con-
curred with them was provided by Berl Katznelson. There can be no
mistake about Marie Syrkin's approbatory response to Katznelson; she
revered this beloved Palestinian leader and intellectual. She put it this
way: "Without oratory, without any of the stock in trade of the supposed 'eloquent' speaker he stirred the Congress as no one else had
done. He stood on the platform, a short stocky man, speaking rapidly
between gulps of water, pausing to look at his notes and he held his audience tense." Katznelson attacked those who advocated violence, as he
reminded Grossman's party of *Havlaga;* he responded to Silver by in-
voking "the higher law which must violate temporary law restrictions, if
Zionism is to survive," and to Goldman, "he retorted that it was the mission of Zionism to restore that of which the Diaspora had deprived us,"
and he rejected the proposal for economic work alone. The heart of his
argument, however, was *Aliyah Bet.* He declared that the "center of our
struggle was not in London but on the sea, that sea which was more
merciful to the refugees than those who spoke of stopping the ships
which bore them, that sea which incredibly let so many cargoes of the
wretched land in safety." Marie wrote that the "Congress was stirred as
at no moment in the sessions" (*Frontier* 10–13).

Fifty years later, recalling Katznelson's presence at the Congress,

Marie spoke in hushed and almost reverential tones and in the present tense: "In thirty-nine Berel [*sic*] is a great figure; he stands there sipping water or occasionally tea—not an orator in the sense that others are great orators, and he is explaining why it is necessary to have illegal—any immigration to get in" (Personal interview).

Marie Syrkin's long report on the proceedings of the Twenty-First Zionist Congress was a clear presentation and analysis of the various policy differences among the parties. Her own position—that of Labor—was also patent and passionate. It had to be, for this profoundly dark hour in the history of the Jews was the here and now of life or death. Surprisingly, however, there is no mention in her report of an astonishing event that occurred three days before the close of the conference: In Moscow on August 23, Germany and the USSR signed a non-aggression pact. It included a death-blow to Poland, for the two signatories agreed to split Poland between them "in the event of a territorial and political transformation of the territories belonging to the Polish State." Hitler no doubt had in mind his target date, September 1, for an attack on Poland. The pact further suggests that it would not be in the interest of the two parties to maintain an independent Poland. William Shirer comments that "Once again Germany and Russia, as in the days of the German Kings and Russian emperors, had agreed to partition Poland. And Hitler had given Stalin a free hand in the eastern Baltic" (Shirer 541). None of this could be construed as "good for the Jews." It was, moreover, an electric shock for those radical American Jews who, despite the 1938 Moscow trials that Marie had exposed, still held sympathies for the Soviet Union.

Despite all the intra-faction controversies of the meetings, Chaim Weizmann closed the Twenty-First Zionist Congress with the emotionally heavy words "I have no prayer but this; that we will all meet again alive" ("Twenty First Congress," *Judaica*). Later, Marie would add that "this was really his farewell to us." The Congress did not meet again until 1946. Marie Syrkin knew that her own task in 1939 was to use her considerable verbal skills to inform American Jews of the impending dire fate of the Jews of Poland and elsewhere in Europe, and of the grave difficulties in finding a *modus operandi* in a hostile or unconcerned world.

Syrkin's experience as a delegate to the Twenty-First Zionist Congress was unforgettable, though when she described it fifty years later, she could not remember whether it was held in Geneva or in Zurich. She was certain that it was Zurich because she remembered the train station from which she left. She was wrong. It was Geneva. But the important details were still as clear as if they had been recorded on a modern video camera. Furthermore, in 1989, the then almost-ninety-year-old Marie insisted upon telling a post-Congress story she recalled in deadly serious, but sometimes hilarious detail. She also wanted to add this story to her written account, not only because there were personal details that would not be appropriate for a strictly journalistic report, but also because that instant in history was of such tremendous consequence as to be worthy of lengthy inclusion. Her narrative began with Chaim Weizmann telling the delegates that the Congress would have to be closed because it was possible that they would be stranded — war will break out. "I was very alarmed," Marie confessed to me, "and they called me Nervous Nellie. They also said Cassandra; they forgot that Cassandra foretold the truth — that little element." Nonetheless, when the decision was made to continue the Congress, Marie was determined to remain until its end. "There were contrary currents among the delegates; — those who till the last minute would say nothing will happen, and the few who said it would. But, the irony of it was that the Zionists — nobody wanted to give up their place in the *General Debate*. They had to say their bit," she explained with an amused chuckle in her voice. "The notion of giving up your right to join in the *General Debate* of the Congress — this endless debate — no one would forego it for the sake of curtailing the Congress. Weizmann didn't win on that. So at the last possible minute we parted."

Marie, at this point, interrupted her tale to mention *sotto voce* that she and Maurice Samuel also parted at that moment, for he had been in attendance at the conference (not as a delegate but as an observer) and as she put it, "we met again." Perhaps that is the reason that she confessed that she had skipped a few meetings at the Congress; and it was those missed meetings that triggered her recall of a fondly treasured encounter with Berl Katzenelson whom she so greatly admired.

It was on the day after Weizmann's announcement, Marie recalled, that she had been absent from some of the meetings. Then on the last day of the Congress, she ran into Berl Katznelson who had been a champion of her ideas and of her contributions as a delegate of the Labor Party. He said at once, "Oh — you're here," and when she replied in surprise, "Of course," Katznelson said with relief, "Marie, I'm so glad. It was a big disappointment to me when I thought you had departed." Her immediate response was that she would not dream of leaving before the close of the Congress. But it appears that Marie's tale of this encounter was not simply to show Berl Katznelson's esteem for her (which, incidentally, she cherished) or to showcase her own courage, but to make a current political point regarding the role of the Palestinians in the Holocaust. Around the time of my interview with Marie, she had been challenged in the pages of *Tikkun* and elsewhere for whitewashing the role of the *Yishuv* during the Holocaust. Again, Marie reminded me that this was the last Congress before the war, and it was the Palestinians — particularly now, in the glaring light of the German-USSR non-agression pact — who stayed on longer than anyone else to meet with the delegates from Poland:

the young people, very young people — people like Zivia Lubetkin [a heroine of the Warsaw ghetto] — a separate group of young people who were determined to remain — the Americans did not tell them to try to leave with us because they already had said no, they were going back to be with their people; and Golda and the Labor people stayed on later too, because they were making plans to maintain contact with each other. They all know that once war breaks out communications are closed. So the Palestinians are the ones who get back last. The Americans manage to get out either before or on time. That's the crucial difference between what the Palestinians and the Diaspora Jews did. The Americans were eager to get home, and either they left early or they were honorable and stayed until the end. The Palestinians' lives were a calculated risk all the time. But the most important thing was to work out systems by which they could maintain contact — whatever the situation. In every crisis it was the Palestinians who had a sense of identity.

Syrkin would use this story again as evidence in her rebuttals to the contemporary new historians' accusations regarding the Palestinians failure to act during the Holocaust.

Returning to the post-Congress narrative, Marie recalled that the American delegates went to the consulate and were given the official advice that the consul was told to say: all Americans are to go to their port of embarkation. The delegates all had questions, such as "should one go up to Mount Blanc for which one had a ticket, or should one forgo it? Or things of that nature." But the repeated advice was to "go to your port of embarkation."

It was August 27. The delegates began to go to their ports of embarkation. Now summoning up the never-forgotten high emotions of fifty years prior, Marie burst out with a volley of details: "It is complete bewilderment! You get out of your train in Paris, and Paris is already black; they expect either a gas attack or a bomb attack at the outbreak. I find a taxi driver, and I say to him go to some hotel. It's pitch dark and he says in French—nothing will happen—it is a false alarm. At the same time he also says 'there is nothing to worry about; we have the best army.'" In a tone of amazement, Marie comments: "these contrary emotions of human beings in moments of stress!"

"Paris is a black hell-hole," she continues, "so I decide there is nothing to be gained by hanging around Paris and I go to the consul in Paris and I ask, 'what shall I do?' He says 'nothing will happen.' . . . I decide that there is nothing to be done, despite the fact that the consul says nothing will happen, and you can stay where you like." Marie decided that she would go to her port of embarkation, which was Cherbourg, where she was to take the last trip of the *Queen Mary*. When I asked her why she would even have considered staying in Paris (wasn't she eager to go home immediately?) she answered dismissively that things were not so simple; it was already very hard to get out, hard to get a train, hard to get anything, and there were other personal considerations" about which she clearly did not want to say more. "There I was," she went on,

I had two suitcases and there was no such thing as getting a porter or anything. Things are so bad—I get on the train and I think I see the soldiers—nothing will happen, because there are the soldiers. The French soldiers—they look like such a disheveled worthless group and I say to myself, brilliantly, it is amazing, they certainly have no spit and polish, look how weak they look. I was told they were the best army in Europe. I get off in Cherbourg—absolutely dark—a woman alone in the dark and I can't see anything. I have two heavy suitcases. Not a soul to ask and it is pitch dark. So what should I do now? You ask a Frenchman—he says 'je ne sais pas, madame.' They are busy saving their own skin; they give not the slightest attempt to assist you. They're glad that *they* have a place to go to—*they* know where to go.

Just then, Marie spotted a young French boy of about thirteen or fourteen and asked him to help her carry her suitcases and accompany her from hotel to hotel until she found a place to stay so that she wouldn't have to sleep on a bench in the port. At every hotel the answer

is *"pas de place, pas de place."* Marie explained that "everyone, all the dele-
gates have been coming to the port of embarkation; everything is taken.
I go to one, and I am absolutely desperate, and I'm there with my two
suitcases and the boy, and I'm told there is no way to sleep in this hotel.
I'll have to spend it on the dock, and just as I'm told *'pas de place'* Shlomo
Grodzensky [the Palestinian literary critic, journalist, and editor] appears." Grodzensky told Marie that a very prominent and foresighted
American General Zionist delegate whose name she could no longer remember, but to whom she would be eternally grateful, had gotten there
early and said to himself that a lot of delegates to the Congress will be
stranded, and immediately he reserved a number of rooms. Shlomo
Grodzensky had one and as soon as he saw Marie, he told her that there
would be a room for her too. Marie now sighed as if it were happening
just at this moment and not fifty years ago, and she said: "My sense of
relief and marvel at that; I would have a place to rest my head." With
parenthetic irony, she added a characteristic comment: "The man who
had reserved the rooms was not a Labor Zionist—he was a very practical man." Continuing her tale of fright and frustration, she explained
that "in the morning, since a gas attack was expected, it was thought
that one should go and get gas masks from the French government.
They said that they had gas masks only for French citizens. So we had
no gas masks. What will be, will be." In the meantime, Marie discovered
that Tamar de Sola Pool, her old friend from Atlantic Hotel days, (now
the wife of Rabbi David de Sola Pool of the Spanish and Portuguese
Congregation in New York) had "brought a whole delegation of Hadassah ladies to a place not precisely in Cherbourg, but to a charming pensione right on the outskirts." So, Marie happily continued, "one could
go there and have meals there, and the Hadassah delegates would be
perfectly delighted." When I asked how Tamar De Sola Pool had made
such a wise decision, Marie answered, "She was a very, very practical
woman; she engaged the whole place—not in Cherbourg proper, but a
delightful pensione in the environs. There was no war there. You didn't
feel the tension of Cherbourg. And the funny part there was that all
Zionist delegates, regardless of their Party would go there during the
day because it was a pleasant place to be, but [Tamar] had managed to
go off for some reason and, I remember that they were offering the most
delicious things to eat from their French menu—fresh lobsters. I saw
them on the menu and I said I would like some. But I was told, Oh no—
Madame de Sola Pool said that no Zionist delegate was to be given lob-

ster. When Marie said, "I don't care," the waiter immediately replied, 'No. No—Madame de Sola Pool said you can't have them.' So one sees these delicious dishes going around, and we couldn't have them. [Tamar] in the meanwhile had departed for I don't know what reason. It was hilarious."

The *Queen Mary*, in the meanwhile, had gone to England for some reason unknown to the delegates, but would come back to pick up the passengers in Cherbourg. "Now," Marie continued, "comes the terrible moment where you don't know whether the *Queen Mary* will come to pick you up or not. It might already have been requisitioned as a troopship—as it was immediately after. When we saw that the *Queen Mary was* coming in, the joy of the Americans was what is known as unbounded. Instantly the need to leave the doomed continent—and we didn't know how doomed—was so strong." And then, with laughter in her voice, Marie asked, "on that last day, do you know what all the Americans did?" The group was told that one could still get "liquor unlimited, and the most delicious things, and one was allowed to take in five bottles. And one had to get perfume, and chocolates, and all such things. So everyone went shopping. So there I was," Marie lamented, "with five bottles of liqueurs, perfume, and whatnot that were really a curse to handle. They were things that I later gave away, of course, because I didn't use them myself. But when the *Queen Mary* came in, there was the sense on the one hand that salvation had come and we really are leaving, yet there was also a feeling of uncomfortableness—not guilt,—but discomfort. Still Marie admitted that she was very glad to depart. "And how" she exclaimed. After three days at sea, the declaration of war was announced. It was the last trip of the *Queen Mary* and Marie said she "marveled at the behavior of the British, their courage at once—I can imagine that on a French ship the yelling that would go on—the silence, the stoicism—all right, that's it, we'll show them. Marvelous, I mean. You felt that the essence of a people comes out in a moment of crisis magnificently, just as the French were completely discombobulated, or whatever the word is. The control of the British, the proverbial stoicism, this was all there." Even fifty years after the event, Marie Syrkin's prejudices were in plain view. The wonder, however, is that the White Paper—the central subject of the Twenty-First Zionist Congress—did not appear to influence her admiration for the British or her disdain for the French (Personal interview).

By the time Marie arrived home, the war that had begun on September 1 was underway. Despite her amusing and sometimes self-deprecatory anecdotes, Marie's experiences between mid-August and the first days of September had been a mixture of fear and courage, dread and determination, anguish and strength. On September 5, Charles sent a note to Al and Milly Lewin: "Marie came back on the Queen Mary after a lot of excitement in Switzerland and France, suspense and all that, but none the worse. We send our love. Charles." That was all. Perhaps she hadn't gotten around to the details and their inevitable consequences.

For the next few months, Marie's life was occupied with writing important informative articles, such as "Aliyah Beth," that appeared in the autumn issue of *Menorah Journal* (336–342), lecturing, and teaching. In late December, her son David had a minor operation for a cyst but by the next day was running a fever of 104 degrees. Though the fever slowly abated, Marie spent most of her time during the school holiday hovering over her sick son. She did not take his condition easily, for the loss of her first child had been too deep a wound ever to heal without a permanent scar.

Charles, in the meanwhile, kept in touch with Al, hoping that he, who had just entered into a partnership with David Loew, the founder of the Loew's theater chain, would find some work for him. "If you think I could be of any use, I should like to work for you again. Really work. I don't suppose it is possible to work for you two years without becoming a partisan of yours, if one is not a partisan to begin with, as I was. As for salary, that never bothers me," he wrote on October 18. The suggestion did not bear fruit, and on November 29, he sent Al his writing schedule for his novel, his verse, and his prose. "As for what I am to do for a living, if anything at present, I am quite uncertain. I have not really tried to find anything and am divided between planning to live very carefully on very little, using up the money I have saved and doing nothing but writing or — and this I have always thought sensible and no hindrance to doing much real writing as I have it in me to do — working at a job. Unfortunately, all the publishers of law books (except for the one I worked for) are out-of-town" (*Letters* 279). From his wife's point of view, he was looking for a job by knocking on doors with a sponge. Charles' point of view with respect to his wife's work can be found in the roman-a-clef that was discovered among his papers after his death.[7] Though written in the 1950s, it takes place in the late 1930s. In it, a major theme is Hollywood; the protagonist, Jude Dalsimer, is an unsuccessful composer, and the composer's wife is a very unsympathetic Zionist high school teacher who constantly complains about being tired and does not appreciate her husband's talents. The intensity of Charles' pain and bitterness is inescapable. Eight years after Charles Reznikoff's death Marie wrote,

I read Charles' novel in 1976 in sorrow at the intensity of the suffering revealed. I had not suspected his anguished sense of abandonment because while the fundamental problem depicted in the book was searingly real, the actual facts were far less dramatic than the fiction. I could well understand why, though the novel was the most powerful and accomplished prose work he ever wrote, he never breathed a word of its existence to me even in the years after my return from Brandeis. (*Man and Poet* 52)

Chapter 12

Wartime Horrors

Personal Unhappiness

"THE FORTIES WERE an unhappy time for us personally," Marie wrote in 1984. "My absorption in the unfolding Jewish catastrophe — Charles' own deep involvement expressed itself in verse not public activities — and our basic discontents led to a growing estrangement. Yet neither of us wanted a divorce" (*Man and Poet* 51). The 1940s were, indeed, the ten years when Marie Syrkin's work hit its stride and held its pace for the entire decade; if the 1940s was, as she said, the nadir of the couple's personal life, those same years were the zenith of Marie's professional life. For Charles, the decade undoubtedly was as personally unhappy as it was for his wife. His writing was his outlet, traversing an internal route. He was preoccupied with four projects during these catastrophic years — three of them were prose. He finished his long autobiographical novel, *Family Chronicle*,[1] he was working on an historical novel, and researching a history of the Jewish community of Charleston, South Carolina (the only project for which he was paid a modest sum), and each day he worked on his verse. *Family Chronicle* ran more than one hundred thousand words, but by the end of 1939, he had completed it. Writing to his friend Al Lewin at the end of December, he reported: "I turned my book over to an agent and hoped to forget about it for a while, but he returned it in a week, refusing to show it to any publisher" (*Letters* 281). Two months later, he wrote again: "I am still at the new book. The other one is resting quietly in a drawer except when Marie lets fly at it one of her bolts from the blue. But the dead shall arise; verily I believe in the resurrection and the life" (*Letters,* February 24, 1940).

What had caused this "bolt from the blue"? One can but speculate that Charles' faith in his work and his passivity—his manuscript "resting quietly in a drawer"—provoked it. Passive he may have been in his deeds, but he knew quite well how to express aggression in his words. Anger crackles the paper of this poem written during those years:

> I remember very well when I asked you—
> as if you were a friend—whether or not
> I should go somewhere or other.
> you answered: "It does not matter
> you are not at all important."
> That was true. But I wonder
> whom you thought important.
> He who has been in his grave
> these ten years or more?
> He is not important now.
> Or he who is wearing out a path
> in the carpet of his room
> as he paces it
> like a shabby coyote in a cage
> an old man hopelessly mad?
> Yourself no doubt;
> looking like one
> who has been a great beauty.[2]

The two men mentioned in the poem doubtlessly are first, Marie's father, and second, Charles himself. Milton Hindus has said of this verse, "Sometimes the poet is bitterly ironical and pins his victims wriggling against the wall" (*Other* 259). Nonetheless, the poet dedicated the whole volume to his wife.

Charles and Marie had been living together in the small apartment on 24th Street since her return from Europe in September. A year later, they moved to 18th Street to a better neighborhood, on the same street as her school, and with slightly larger quarters. Perhaps the cramped space on 24th Street also cramped their relationship—though the new space did nothing of note to improve their discordant companionship. They were the *L'Allegro* and *Il Pensero* of Jewish life and letters.

Although war had not yet been declared in America, there were plenty of serious issues for Marie to write about. By the 1940s it was obvious to all who read the newspapers or saw the newsreels that the Nazi

virulence had become pandemic and that the failure of the 1938 Evian
Conference had made voluntary emigration the next thing to impossible. In May of 1939, the German ship *St. Louis* had left with 930 Jewish refugees on board. Sailing to Cuba and having been denied shelter
by the Cuban government, then denied refuge from Chile, Paraguay,
Argentina, and Colombia, it went on to Florida, sailing along the East
Coast of the United States, waiting in vain for President Roosevelt to
respond to a plea for help. With no reply, it sailed back to Europe where
Britain, Holland, France, and Belgium finally agreed to take the desperate group; 819 dispirited passengers disembarked in Antwerp, where
after Germany occupied Belgium, they undoubtedly ended up in concentration camps; 287 refugees were deposited on the Isle of Man,
where a year later they would be interned as enemy aliens. But these 287
at least would survive the war. The *St. Louis*' search for a haven ended on
June 17, 1939. But there would be more ships that would make the same
fearful search.

From Marie Syrkin's perspective, the only real escape for fleeing Jews
was, now more than ever, Palestine. But even here the plot was complicated by leaky ships, British quotas and blockades, and Arab hostility.
Americans Jews would have to learn the meaning of the two Hebrew
words, "*Aliyah Bet*"—illegal immigration. Immediately after her return
from the Twenty-First Zionist Congress, on September 25, 1939, Marie
sent an article describing the program of illegal emigration to Henry
Hurwitz of *Menorah Journal.* Two days later, he wrote back: "Just the
thing! Clearly and beautifully done. I cannot tell you how grateful I am
for your cooperating with *Menorah* in this way. . . . With all good
wishes to you and Charles for the best possible New Year in a brutal and
insensate world (Archives, Hurwitz, Box 57 f. 25).

During the next few months, events in Europe continued to worsen:
France, Britain, Australia, New Zealand, and Canada had declared war
on Germany; the United States remained neutral; the Soviets invaded
Poland; Poland surrendered; and Germany and Russia divided up Poland
according to the terms of the Nazi-Soviet non-Aggression Treaty of August 1939. In addition to the agreement that Russia would not interfere
with Hitler's war in the West, there was a secret protocol in which the
two signatories divided up Europe into spheres of influence. In a
fiendish game of World Monopoly, Stalin traded two Polish provinces
for four Baltic States. "Hitler," William Shirer explains, "fought and
won the war in Poland, but the greater winner was Stalin, whose troops

scarcely fired a shot. The Soviet Union got nearly half of Poland and a stranglehold on the Baltic States" (Shirer 632). The independent countries of Finland, Estonia, Latvia, Lithuania, Romania, and part of Poland thus became Soviet property. On November 30, 1939, the Soviets attacked Finland and on December 14, the Soviet Union was expelled from the League of Nations. These were the events that ushered in the new decade.

The first six months of 1940 brought a rush of Nazi invasions and quick conquests: April 9, Denmark and Norway; May 10, France, Belgium, Luxembourg, the Netherlands. By June, Holland, Belgium, and Norway had surrendered. On June 14, Hitler's troops entered Paris and by June 22, France had signed an armistice with Germany. The Soviets, in the meanwhile, began their takeover of the Baltic States. Hitler and Mussolini were solidly in charge of the Axis powers, with Stalin newly signed-on, but elsewhere, there were some changes: In May, Winston Churchill became the Prime Minister of England; in June, a weak eighty-four-year-old Marshal Petain, once the hero of Verdun, now became Prime Minister of the collaborationist French State at Vichy in the unoccupied southern zone that Hitler had left to the French to self-govern; but it was General Charles De Gaulle whom Britain recognized as the leader of the Free French. By July 10 the Battle of Britain had begun and would last until September. During those months after France fell, the British, especially in London, were subjected to intense air raids intended to destroy the RAF, followed by the German bombing of other cities, with London suffering fifty-seven consecutive attacks in September and October, which continued sporadically until April. These months became famously known as the time of the "Blitz."

Back in August, when Marie Syrkin left the Zionist Congress just before the outbreak of war, she closely observed the French as she traveled from Paris to Cherbourg. After boarding the British liner, *Queen Mary,* to return home, she took note of the ship's stiff-upper-lip English seamen and officers. Her immediate reaction to the two nations was quite clear: feckless French and intrepid English. Later, when she compared Britain's aerial success through its superior technology, better defenses, cracking of the German code, and the sheer will of the outnumbered RAF forces against the vaunted German air force, the ignominy of France's quick capitulation and its Vichy government's collaboration further diminished the defeatist French in her eyes. Marie may have been fluent in the French language, but in these days she found it difficult to speak to or for them.

The American Scene

Much had happened since the 1939 Zionist Congress in Geneva; the catastrophic events that followed made it impossible for Marie to return to
Palestine for another half-dozen years. Though she had plenty to write
about concerning the Nazis, the Arabs, and the Jews, now, forced to
stay put in America, Marie Syrkin turned to an issue in her own back
yard: antisemitism in America. Here, she had a ready-made laboratory:
the very school she taught in where on-the-spot reporting needed no
binoculars. As Marie would write many years later,

The forties were to introduce old terrors into the consciousness of American
Jewry. For the first time native-born American Jews were nervous. Home-grown
rabble rousers, emboldened by Nazi victories, had come out of the closet. Pro-
Nazi Father Coughlin rallied his disciples in popular radio broadcasts that
influenced a periphery extending far beyond the circles of such rabidly anti-
Semitic groups as the Christian Front or the Silver Shirts. The German American Bund strutted openly in full storm trooper regalia in Madison Square Garden at huge meetings called to demonstrate against American involvement in
World War II, and just as openly against American Jews scheming to inveigle
the United States into the conflict." (*State* 4)

Until the United States entered the war after the Japanese attack on
Pearl Harbor on December 7, 1941, the First Amendment had protected
open pro-Nazi speech and antisemitic propaganda and agitation with
no regard for its opprobrious content. Even the students in Marie's high
school current events classes defended the right of their pro-Nazi
schoolmates to express themselves, justifying it by declaring that "It's
their opinion." Appalled by the timidity of her fellow teachers to rise to
the challenge (though she hinted that it might have been less timidity
and more knee-jerk American toleration of "tolerance"), Marie began to
write about the subject in a variety of publications, including *Common
Ground* and *Look* magazine, and of course, in the *Jewish Frontier. Common Ground* was the perfect venue for her reports. Published by the
Common Council for American Unity, with a pluralist advisory editorial board that included Van Wyck Brooks, Pearl Buck, Mary Ellen
Chase, Langston Hughes, Alvin Johnson, Thomas Mann, and Lin Yu-
tang, its primary purpose was "to help create among the American

people the unity and mutual understanding resulting from a common citizenship, a common belief in democracy and the ideals of liberty, the placing of the common good before the interests of any group, and the acceptance, in fact as well as in law, of all citizens, whatever their national or racial origins, as equal partners in American life."[3] It was particularly interested in helping the foreign-born adjust to American life while knowing and valuing their particular cultural heritage. *Common Ground* was a truly multicultural publication forty years before the explosion of late-twentieth-century multiculturalism. And it was tailor-made for Marie Syrkin. Those who in recent times have sought to portray Marie Syrkin as a hide-bound Zionist ideologue and alienated American, have not recognized her deep love of America. She was a charter member of the immigrant culture that Max Lerner once dubbed as "the cult of gratitude." *Common Ground* spoke to her as much as she spoke for it. A late piece she wrote for them identifies her at the end of the article with these words: "Marie Syrkin is an old friend of *Common Ground* readers." Ultimately the article Syrkin wrote for *Common Ground* and some other periodicals of the time would become the heart of her important book, *Your Schools, Your Children*.[4]

Marie's first article for *Common Ground* appeared in 1940 and reported on the difficulties she faced as the faculty advisor of the Jewish club at Textile High. "The club is not a success" she lamented, "possibly due to a lack of organizational talent on my part, and also due to a lack of Jewish zeal on the part of the members" (Autumn 1940, 86). The students, who were not intellectual, and few of whom would go on to college, really wanted to socialize, not to listen to lectures or engage with interesting speakers. Another article, "How Not To Solve 'The Jewish Problem'" attacked the *Atlantic Monthly* for printing two articles by Albert Jay Nock, identified as a "conscientious Gentile" (*Common*, Autumn 1941, 73). In the Spring of 1942, Marie placed an article entitled "Morale Begins at School" in *Common Ground*. This one opens, "When I entered my classroom the morning after Pearl Harbor, I was worried. I teach in a large New York high school where isolationist sentiment has been strong. My students are of predominantly Italian and Irish backgrounds, with a good sprinkling of Slav, Greek, German and whatever else goes to make up America. I know the inevitable tensions and conflicts at work in this conglomerate, and I also know how shrewdly these have been exploited by pro-Axis elements." The point of the essay, however, is to show that however successful the subversive organizations had been prior to December 7, the morning after Pearl Harbor "in their whole-hearted simple patriotism my youngsters sounded like the theme song of 'Americans All'" (*Common*, Spring 1942, 98–102).

Propaganda and subversive activity was a major subject for Marie Syrkin during the war years. In a later essay in *Common Ground* titled "Goebbels' Favorite Weapon," she explains the technique and purpose of antisemitic parodies of "well-loved, patriotic songs whose melody is familiar and whose sentiments are part of every American child's heritage" that have been slipped into the public schools by subversive groups. "No aspect of Nazi psychological warfare is more diabolically clever than the practical use to which Goebbels and his associates have put the findings of modern psychology in their exploitation of anti-Semitism." She offers a few illustrations of these jingles that invariably suggest that "Jews are staying home, waxing rich, while Gentiles are fighting the Jews' war." A few verses that had appeared on the schoolroom blackboards illustrate the point:

> Oh say can you see, by the dawn's early light,
> To save the Jew's skins, all we Gentiles must fight.

Or to the tune of the "Marine's Hymn":

> From the shores of Coney Island
> Looking out into the sea,
> Stands a kosher air-raid warden,
> Wearing V for victory
> who chants:
> Let those Christian saps go fight the Japs
> In the uniforms we've made.

Or "Praise the Lord and draft another Christian."
In a shrewd analysis of this technique, Syrkin explains that

In each case a framework hallowed by previous associations has been filled with a new vicious context. Every young American is conditioned to an automatic favorable response when he hears the "Star Spangled Banner." The natural revulsion from the ugly and false is stilled by the familiar melody and rhythm. Some of the agreeable associations of the original are carried over instinctively and help give a spurious validity to the parody. The process is an unconscious one, but it is precisely in the exploitation of the recesses of the unconscious that the Goebbels' technique is most effective. Furthermore, since the parody follows a familiar word pattern, the words are more easily retained and have a greater opportunity to leave a dent in the mind. (*Common*, Summer 1943, 17, 18)

In yet another chilling piece, which she later chose to include in *The State of the Jews* under the title "Nazi Kultur in Yorkville," Marie describes a visit to a German movie theater in the Yorkville section of Manhattan, where on a Friday afternoon at 3 P.M. she went to see *Sieg im Westen,* the "Nazi film record of the conquest of western Europe." Instead of the usual afternoon audience of children and retirees, the audience was comprised of "husky, close-cropped, well dressed Germans of all ages" there to thoroughly enjoy the triumphs of the German military. When she left the theater, a long line stretched outside the movie house. Her final point was "when avowed Nazi groups are allowed to flourish unrestrained and to propagandize the population not subtly but with a sledge hammer, then it is time to suggest that government agencies investigating subversive activities stop picking at herring, red, black or any other shade, and take a poke at the whales spouting under their noses" (*State* 221–225).

In 1940, Marie Syrkin's son David left New York for Harvard; three years later, at the age of nineteen, he would graduate with a B.S., magna cum laude, in electronic physics and enter the signal corps of the United States Army, where he would serve until 1946. The variety of Marie's concerns ranged from the domestic to the global—from her son at Harvard to the fate of the Jews in the world, which seems to have left small space for her husband on 18th Street. In his own space, Charles kept up with his writing, kept up with the news, and kept up with his epistolary relationship with Al Lewin: "I thought of writing you time and again," Charles wrote to his friend in Hollywood, "but the news has been so bad—and daily worse—that everything else seemed too trivial. . . . Marie will probably go to Bermuda for three weeks in July. She has a sabbatical leave until February. When she returns from Bermuda, she will go away again. I have been suggesting Alaska" (*Letters,* June 25, 1940). Despite Charles' sardonicism, this trip to Bermuda does appear to be a real vacation trip; there will be another trip to Bermuda in 1943 for a Refugee Conference.

In 1941, however, Marie Syrkin chose not take her husband's advice. Instead of Alaska, she went to the Dominican Republic. President

Trujillo's offer at the Evian Conference to accept 100,000 refugees had not been acted upon until 1940, when he generously deeded 26,000 acres of land in the area known as Sosua to the Dominican Republic Settlement Association Inc. (DORSA), sponsored by the American Jewish Joint Distribution Committee. Located on the northern coast of the country, it was fertile and richly wooded land, and was to be a rent-free and tax-free agricultural settlement. Settlers would be chosen from those countries of Europe from which emigration was still possible. Marie went there in January 1941, and in February, she wrote an article describing in careful detail what she saw. She concludes, "Any plan which proposes to save refugees from the hell of Hitler's Europe merits support. No reasonable prospect of rescue can be dismissed." But her final words are: "Assuming that it will be possible to increase the tempo of immigration, Sosua can in no sense be viewed as a rival of Palestine. It does not pretend to solve the Jewish problem or to build a Jewish future. If it is successful it will give some refugees a chance to re-establish their broken lives and to become good Dominicans, far from the current of European and American civilization. Such a prospect fails to fill me with enthusiasm, but then I live in the United States, not Germany (*State* 62).

Though Charles' sympathy for Marie's travels was fast eroding, his sympathy for the world's troubles and the Jewish catastrophe in Europe and Palestine was increasing. Charles was not then, and never would be, a public personality; every idea, every emotion, all his intellect and feeling were poured into his writings. His profound love of the Jewish people with its glorious but tragic history was marrow-deep, and his empathy for all the world's working poor, disenfranchised, disabled, unemployed, marginal was fathoms-deep, but he insisted that he was a writer, and as a writer he was under no obligation to try to *solve* the problems. His wife knew that when she declared, "Something must be done," her husband was not likely to do it. Even his attempt to participate in the prewar preparation was unsuccessful. He had tried to enlist in an army training camp for civilians, he wrote to Al Lewin on June 25, 1940, "for truly I want to learn how to shoot and kill, but unfortunately, my eyes have gotten worse — although almost perfect with glasses — and are below the army's present minimum (20/100 without glasses). Should this minimum requirement be lowered, I will enlist in anything" (*Letters* 286). At the time, he was forty-six years old. Four months later, in another letter to Al, after reporting that he and Marie have moved to "a rather nice flat, a little nicer than where we lived and a little cheaper," he added that "Marie has been to Mexico and come back, and written an article for her paper which *World Digest* wants to reprint on Jewish Indians in Mexico," (*Letters,* October 27, 1940). Marie, it appears, did not feel obliged to stay put for very long. Charles' little epistolary comments give a small indication of his state of mind, but it is in his poems that the anguish is unmistakable.

> Though our thoughts often, we ourselves
> are seldom together.
> We have told each other
> All that has happened; it seems to me —
> for want of a better word —
> that we are both unlucky.
> Even our meetings have been brief
> we should call them partings, and of our words
> I remember most "good-by."
> (*Poems* 119)

Charles' aim was sure; he hit the mark with a wounding accuracy that might have been fatal, had the poems themselves not been an anodyne. She knew that he had also written:

> It was in my heart to give her wine and dainties,
> silken gowns, furs against the wind;
> a woolen scarf,
> coffee and bread was all that I could buy:
> It is enough, she said.
>
> It was in my heart to show her foreign lands,
> at least the fields beyond the city:
> I could not pay our way:
> when she would see a row of street-lamps shining,
> How beautiful, she would say.
> (*Poems* 118)

Wartime and Passover

Despite the frequent partings, the temperamental divide, Marie and Charles did manage some shared time and experiences, particularly at holiday time. Neither one was religiously observant, but both have written poetry about the Jewish holidays. Charles' poems are philosophical meditations on the meaning of the holy days; Marie wrote satirical verse about the loss of that meaning in contemporary worship. Obviously, the Jewish holidays in the abstract meant something to them. In a conversation I had with Marie Syrkin in the last weeks of her life, we talked about the role of religion in her own experience. She repeated the fact that in her childhood there were no religious observances at all; in fact, she was obliged to go to school on Yom Kippur. Asked whether, at the least, she went to Passover Seders, she said "in New York, no one that we knew was making seders. Seders entered my life when I was in my twenties and was living with Mrs. Epstein. She made a Seder every year — not that she was a great believer in the tradition; it was a miserable Seder — it was the kind of thing where the emphasis was on the food, and we tried to rush through the *Haggadah* that was an awful bore, because nobody could understand it."

Suddenly, Marie took a breath, her eyes brightened, her voice modulated; "the first Seder in my life that I appreciated, when I understood for the first time what it *could* be, was in [1941] during the Holocaust, and Charles and I were invited to the Seder of Rabbi de Sola Pool. I was very friendly with Tamar de Sola Pool," Marie reminded me. She had known Tamar since her sixteenth summer in Belmar, New Jersey, when she had looked up to the twenty-five-year-old Tamar (Hirschensohn) — a very pretty, very intelligent, sophisticated "older woman" who taught Latin and Greek," and she had kept up with her through the years. "Their Seder was something that I had never seen before in my life. It was held in the banquet hall of the synagogue — at long tables. The food was de-emphasized" (unlike the Seders Marie had attended in the past), and "where you ate those delicious *knaidlach* and just wanted to get through the *Haggadah* as quickly as possible." With this, Marie lowered her voice to barely more than a whisper as she described the chanting of the *Haggadah* in the Sephardic tradition by Rabbi De Sola Pool and the assistant rabbis. Marie grew wide-eyed: "It was so beautiful and so impressive. For the first time I realized that this was a great ceremony — that the *knaidlach* was only a minimal part. It was pretty late to realize this," she admitted. (She was forty-two years old.) "Then another thing happened at that Seder that was immensely impressive." By this point in her narrative, Marie became overwhelmed with emotion, "The French Rothschilds had just gotten to the United States, and they were invited to this Seder; and one thinks of the situation of that historical moment; the situation of the Jews was at its nadir. The Rothchilds had escaped with their lives." [In 1940, the Nazis tried to capture members of the family, but they all escaped and spent the war years either in England or in the United States.] "It was the moment of absolute hopelessness," Marie went on,

and just before the beginning of the chanting of the Haggadah, three or four Rothschilds appeared. I'd never seen anything like it; they appeared not as hangdog, unhappy people who had been deprived of their fortune; they apparently had saved their jewels [This is said in a surprised voice] — because the women came in *blazing* with diamonds, and when one saw that resplendent assertion of power and beauty and the refusal to be cowed — and they sat at the head table beside De Sola Pool, literally *shining — blazing*. . . . It seemed an affirmation of the Jewish will. That Seder was an incredible Seder. It meant to me a new dimension by which I was ever after to regard a Seder. Of course I have never been to a Seder quite like it, before or after, because there was never a Seder when the fortunes of the Jews was so low. Or a Seder at which the Rothschilds blazing with diamonds came in, in a kind of gesture of defiance at the whole world. It was a tremendous experience for me. (Personal interview)

These days some might be tempted to say that Marie's narrative was naive or melodramatic, but this was her style; though its tone might be extravagantly idealistic, it was never a put-on. Her instinctive analytic and poetic powers connected the Rothschilds, the grandeur of the Sephardic synagogue, and the beauty of the Passover service as all together the embodiment of the inner meaning of the Passover ritual: oppression; liberation; responsibility. Perhaps she thought of Charles' verse, "Passover."

> "Begin with the disgrace and end with the glory," the rabbis say.
> The disgrace was not in being a slave —
> that may happen to any one —
> but to remain such.
> What was the glory?
> To choose the Lord:
> that is, the bread of affliction and freedom.[5]

In later years, Marie and Charles, when not invited to someone else's Seder, would observe it just for the two of them. They "would have

Matzos and would read through the *Haggadah* and consider that a Seder." But they would celebrate it (Personal interview).

During the weeks of our interviews and private conversations, Marie would often dig out of her files some off-print that she thought I ought to read. One that took me by surprise was titled "The Gentling of the *Haggadah*," which appeared in the April 25, 1941, issue of *Congress Weekly*. What surprised me was the subject; the one area of Jewish life that had never interested Marie Syrkin was religion — and it was one area that she knew very little about. So why this review? The first edition of *The New Haggadah* (Behrman House, Inc.), Mordecai Kaplan's innovative Reconstructionist revision of the traditional Passover text, had sold out almost immediately. The forward explains that the editors have "prepared a text which enunciates the essential message of *Pesah* clearly and unmistakably, [they] have steadily kept in mind the needs of the young American Jew, and have striven to offer him such gems of Rabbinic fancy, such readings and responses, poems, and songs, as would stir in him that devotion to freedom which our forefathers gained from the *Pesach Haggadah* of tradition." Oddly, Marie was very critical of this new *Haggadah* that wished to engage the attention of the young, but that in the face of the ongoing Nazi atrocities, omitted traditional texts that expressed cruelty and vengeance. This included omitting the ten plagues and the verse "Pour out your wrath upon the nations which know you not." It also eliminated any references to "the chosen people." Kaplan argued that during these years of the Nazi inhumanity, "all references to events, real or imagined, in the Exodus story which might conflict with our own highest ethical standards have been omitted." Given Marie Syrkin's earlier caustic comments about waiting for the *knaidlach,* it was no surprise to read in her review

Give the Jewish boy or girl modern thought or idiom and he will be able to keep his mind on the significance of the festival rather than on delayed *knaidlach.* No one will deny that the Seder, as frequently celebrated, is a shocking travesty of a great religious and historic holiday. . . . Even under the impact of our present agony, the average Jew is powerless to express his dread and hope through the eternal symbolism of the Passover narrative. He retreats hastily to the fish and matzo-balls because he does not understand the language, he does not know the chants, and the undignified hocus-pocus of an uncomprehended text is something from which he instinctively shrinks.

So far, nothing surprising. Marie has indeed described her own situation.

But then she launches into her real critique: "*The New Haggadah* omits the description and enumeration of the plagues that struck the Egyptians; it omits the denunciatory 'Pour out thy wrath upon the heathen'; it omits all references to the special 'chosen' character of the Jewish people. In short anything that might be construed as vindictive or boastful is carefully strained out, leaving only the pure milk of human kindness to flow gently for friend and foe alike." There are further textual and stylistic criticisms, but Syrkin's main point is that

The New Haggadah is a polite and pretty piece of work but it is not the food we need today. Anyone who has seen an orthodox Seder conducted with dignity and reverence knows how much more the traditional *Hagaddah* has to offer in an evil hour. The whole spirit of *The New Haggadah* may be summed up by its translation of *L'shana haba b'Yerushalayim*. What could be simpler or stronger than the few plain words, "Next year in Jerusalem"? This appears as "May the coming year witness the rebuilding of Zion and the redemption of Israel." Instead of the direct, passionate statement of the individual's desire to be "next year in Jerusalem," we get a testimonial of approbation which calls for no commitments and will antagonize no one. Our time needs sterner stuff.

This last sentiment is not at all surprising — it is the obvious critique of a committed Labor Zionist. But what about the strong reaction to the omissions? Why, indeed, was Marie Syrkin so intensely upset by Kaplan's reconstruction of the traditional *Haggadah,* one she had never before taken the trouble to examine? (One remembers, however, that she had written ecstatically about the secular kibbutz Haggadah she encountered on her first visit to Palestine.) The answer, however, is not far to seek. The Passover Seder that Marie had attended at Rabbi De Sola Pool's synagogue was held on April 10, 1941; the review appeared two weeks later. Doubtless, Marie's reaction to the *Haggadah* was inspired by her experience at the Seder where the Rothschilds appeared in a "gesture of defiance at the world." Interestingly, she took an "I told you so" attitude when I informed her that in later years the plagues had been restored to the Reconstructionist *Haggadah.*

This leaves one further question. How did Marie suddenly become so informed about the traditional Haggadah? And why did she choose to review Kaplan's revision? These were not her areas of expertise — and as she had always freely admitted, she knew little Hebrew and less

ritual. The answer is more than suggested in a paragraph in the autobiography of Mordecai Kaplan's son-in-law and intellectual disciple,
Ira Eisenstein, who was one of the three editors of *The New Haggadah*. Eisenstein describes the variety of attacks that Kaplan received
from the Jewish Theological Seminary. "A letter signed by every member of the faculty was sent to Kaplan protesting the publication of a
liturgical text which violated *halakhic* regulations." Eisenstein says that
he always knew that Kaplan's views were unpopular with the JTS faculty, but he was "truly amazed by the content and tone of this round-
robin letter." Rabbi Eisenstein then speaks of a criticism from another
source.

I believe the man whose objections to portions of the text disturbed me most
was Maurice Samuel, and perhaps that is why I took his criticisms seriously. He
felt that we had knuckled under to the adherents of the good will movement by
deleting from the text the verse "*Shefokh hamatekha al ha goyim*," "Pour out Thy
wrath upon the nations which know Thee not." He insisted that at that moment
when the world was called upon to resist and destroy Nazism, the quotation
from the Psalms was all the more needed. He made no apologies for calling
upon God to pour out His wrath upon Hitler and his murderers. . . . Our
omission of the Ten Plagues annoyed Samuel almost as much. What was wrong
with perpetuating the folk custom of pouring out a drop of wine with the mention of each plague? In fact, there was much to be said in favor of it because
in the Midrash the Sages had specifically ordained that the cup of joy must be
less than full since the Israelites' emancipation had been accomplished at the expense of God's (Egyptian) creatures.[6]

All of Samuel's criticisms appeared in Marie's review.

A postscript to this subject: When Mordecai Kaplan read Marie
Syrkin's review, he invited her to come to his office to discuss it. She
confessed to me that she was terrified. Kaplan's reputation as a stern
taskmaster whose teaching techniques frightened generations of future
rabbis was not unknown to her. Perhaps he would think it *chutzpah*
for her to have written as she did. But, to her surprise, Dr. Kaplan was
warm, friendly, and eager to quietly counter her arguments with his own.
In fact, he invited her to teach a course in homiletics at the Seminary —
which she declined. And just possibly, he was not altogether immune to
her obvious combination of beauty and brains.

The World at War

The *Haggadah* episode, however, should not be taken as merely an amusing diversion from the story of the main events in Marie Syrkin's life in the 1940s. To the contrary, it emphasizes the fact that for her, all roads led to Jerusalem. The fate of the Jews was her primary concern in these bitter years as the world was increasingly swept up in a vortex of deterioration, destruction, and death. Hitler had been scoring victory after victory in the West: Hungary and Romania joined the Axis in November of 1940; the German "Afrika Korps" under General Rommel arrived in North Africa in February 1941; an Axis government was set up in Iraq in April 1941; Greece and Yugoslavia surrendered in April 1941; and the blitzkrieg of London and other British cities continued unabated. Hitler was, so to speak, on a roll. Meanwhile, the Fuehrer's ally, wily Josef Stalin, believing that Hitler was too busy in the West to interfere, began to gobble up territories in the East, moving into the Baltic and Balkan States. One year after the Nazi-Soviet pact, Stalin, having studied the Hitler model, incorporated Lithuania, Latvia, and Estonia into the Soviet Union. Stalin was certain that Hitler, having drawn the blueprint, would have no objection to further Soviet aggression; in June, Soviet troops invaded and took the Rumanian territories of Bessarabia and northern Bucovina.

"Relations between Berlin and Moscow," writes William Shirer, "had for some months been souring. It was one thing for Stalin and Hitler to double-cross third parties, but quite another when they began to double-cross each other. Hitler had been helpless to prevent the Russians from grabbing the Baltic States and two Rumanian provinces, and his frustration only added to his growing resentment. The Russian drive westward would have to be stopped" (Shirer 800). Shirer also asserts that although Stalin was determined to get all he could in Eastern Europe while Hitler was tied up in the West, he "did not wish or contemplate a break with Hitler"(Shirer 795). What the cunning, crafty, crude, but unwary Russian dictator did not know was that for some time Hitler had been planning to break with *him*. Stalin should have known from Hitler's past words and actions that he was not to be trusted. But then, neither was Stalin. They were a matched pair of potentates. What Stalin did not know was that as early as December of 1940, Hitler had issued his *"Top Secret, Directive No. 21"* (Operation Barbarossa): "The German

Armed Forces must be prepared to *crush Soviet Russia in a quick campaign* [Hitler's italics] before the end of the war against England" (Shirer 810). Operation Barbarossa was nothing less than the willful shredding of the 1939 Molotov-Ribbentrop Non-Aggression Pact by a surprise brutal invasion and blitzkrieg of Russia. Almost with perfect fidelity to the plans outlined in *"Secret Directive 21,"* the Germany Army drove its way through Soviet Russia, capturing major cities in Latvia, Lithuania, Estonia, the Ukraine, and the Crimea. By September, there were only thirty-seven miles between the Germans and Moscow. The cities of Leningrad, Moscow, and Stalingrad were the treasures Hitler wished to capture at the end of the brutal hunt.

The Soviets, however, were tough and fought with an unexpected ferocity in the defense of their country. Then winter came, and like Napoleon's army before them, the Germans were unprepared for such bitterly freezing cold conditions. Poorly equipped, with supplies slow in coming, they also were not prepared for their tremendous casualties; nor had they anticipated the fierce resistance of the Soviets who, accustomed to the Russian winters, were able to hold out. Hitler's expectations for a "shock and awe" victory as he unleashed the combined forces of the *Wehrmacht* did not happen, and he had to wait for the spring of 1942 to begin another offensive. On December 5, the Nazis abandoned their attack on Moscow; on December 6, the Soviets mounted a strong counter-offensive around the Soviet capital.

Meantime, in the United States, Franklin Roosevelt, who had been re-elected for a third term in 1940, disclosed his plan to give financial aid to the Allies in their fight against the Axis powers. On March 11, 1941, Congress passed the Lend-Lease Act, which gave the President the power to sell, lend, exchange, and transfer equipment to help countries defend themselves against the Nazi powers. Nonetheless, in America, isolationism and antisemitism continued as swastika-uniformed German-American Bund members, funded and supplied by the Third Reich, continued to spew out their poison bill of fare: the New Aryan Order. The nativist "America Firsters" wolfed it down. But American isolationism, neutrality, and a sense of distance from the actual fight underwent a radical change on December 7, 1941, when the Japanese attacked Pearl Harbor. The next day, the United States and Britain declared war on Japan. Three days later on December 11, Germany declared war on the United States. On January 1, twenty-six allied nations signed a Joint Declaration of United Nations. The signatories declared that they subscribed to the purpose and principles of the Atlantic Charter of August 1941, as propounded by Roosevelt and Churchill: "Being convinced that complete victory over their enemies is essential to defend life, liberty, independence and religious freedom, and to preserve human rights and justice in their own lands as well as in other lands, and that they are now engaged in a common struggle against savage and brutal forces seeking to subjugate the world," the twenty-six nations declared that it would "employ its full resources, military, or economic, against those members of the Tripartite Pact, now Germany, Italy and Japan and its adherents with which such government is at war and that they would not make a separate peace or armistice with the enemies."[7] It was now truly a World War.

By December of 1941, the German frontier and areas of control and occupation had expanded beyond its 1933 borders to include Austria, Czechoslovakia, Poland, Ukraine, France, Belgium, Holland, the Baltic States, and parts of Russia. It included a litany of great cities with large Jewish populations: Vienna, Prague, Paris, Amsterdam, Antwerp, Riga, Kovno, Vilna, Minsk, Lodz, Cracow, Warsaw, Lvov, Kiev, Kharkov, and too many others to name here, though not to disregard. The Jews had become an endangered species. The conquering Nazi military forces were known as the *Wehrmacht,* but it also included the Nazi Party's internal private army, the S.A. (storm troops), and the S.S. (the elite corps of the S.A. under the command of Himmler). There was also the military body known as the *Einsatzgruppen* (special action squads), who were small units recruited from the S.S., S.D., Gestapo (the police), among other groups. Ultimately, it hired Ukrainians, White Russians, Latvians, and Lithuanians. The *Einsatzgruppen* training included intensive indoctrination in Nazi ideology: "Their special task, transmitted orally, was to kill the Jews, to perform the mission entrusted to Himmler by the Fuhrer" (Dawidowicz 125). And kill the Jews they did; and they did it well.

There were, then, two wars; the war for *lebensraum* (living space) and the war against the Jews (and other inferior groups). The forces of depravity accomplished their goal, the destruction of the Jews, through a variety of old and new techniques: Jews were herded into ghettos, where starvation, the chief means of destruction, was exacerbated by epidemic disease, lack of clothing, hot weather, frigid weather, little employment, slave labor, overcrowded living quarters, poor sanitation, humiliating punishments and arbitrary shootings by the S.S. All these unbearable conditions resulted in daily deaths, with dead bodies left lying on the streets, waiting for the Jewish burial societies to pick them up. The first of these ghettos was the Polish city of Lodz, which was enclosed on May 1, 1940; the Warsaw ghetto came next in November 1940; by April 1941, the job had been completed and almost every Jew in Poland had been ghettoized. And so it was in the rest of the Eastern European countries that were invaded and conquered by the German forces. Ghettos were an old institution, but ghettos like these were of a new demonic design. Another new method of killing Jews and other subhumans and inferiors were mobile killing squads that rounded up Jews, herded them into vans, took them to the woods, there to murder thousands upon thousands by shooting them *en masse* and throwing them into execution pits. Those still alive in the ghettos who had not succumbed to despair would try to survive by their wits, but it would not be long before they too would be on their way to the very newest form of mass killing—the concentration camps that soon would become death factories. There, Hitler would implement his mad fantasy of a Jewless world.

Wannsee and the Final Solution

Mass killing had been in process since the German invasion of the Soviets, but the technique to kill vast numbers quickly had not yet been perfected. "On December 8, the day after Pearl Harbor, the gassing of Jews began in mobile gas vans at Chelmno, a Polish town forty miles west of Lodz. Gas chambers were already under construction at Auschwitz and Belzec. Although the policy of mass extermination was not yet articulated, it was in fact being carried out" (Berenbaum 104).

The formal articulation of the policy of mass annihilation, otherwise known as the "Final Solution," occurred on January 20, 1942, at a conference held in a villa located in Wannsee, a wealthy suburb of Berlin, in the atmosphere of an executive corporate meeting at a private club where drinks, lunch, and after-dinner brandy and cigars were on the menu. In attendance were fifteen men holding the highest positions in the Nazi government, including the presiding officer, Reinhard Heydrich, the head of the Security Office, and the head of his Jewish Office, Adolf Eichmann. It was here that the euphemism "Final Solution" was first spoken in Heydrich's ignominious understatement that already "practical experience is being collected which is of greatest importance in view of the coming Final Solution of the Jewish Question." Heydrich had called the conference in order to coordinate the various offices and to discuss Goering's order that went out with the letters of invitation (Dawidowicz 136). That directive read as follows:

I hereby commission you to carry out all necessary preparations with regard to organizational, substantive, and financial viewpoints for a total solution of the Jewish question in the German sphere of influence in Europe. . . . I further commission you to submit to me promptly an overall plan showing the preliminary organizational, substantive and financial measures for the execution of the intended final solution of the Jewish question.[8]

"Here," Yehuda Bauer emphasizes, "'final solution' is used for the first time to describe mass murder" (Bauer 201).

Reinhard Heydrich was put in charge of the coordination of the Final Solution and it was quartered in the Office of Jewish Affairs and Evacuation, overseen by Adolf Eichmann. And thus a watershed had been reached: slave labor in concentration camps as the norm gave way to murder en masse in gas chambers as the policy of the State. In addition to the six million Jews, an equal number of non-Jews were killed for reasons of racial prejudice — particularly Slavs and gypsies, mental and physical defectives, homosexuals, political activists (communists), criminals, and so on. Concentration camps had been established in Germany, East Prussia, Czechoslovakia, Holland, Austria, and Poland. There was now an added station to the Holocaust itinerary: first, into the ghetto; second, deportation from the ghetto (called "resettlement") to the slave labor camps; third, regular selection of those unfit to work to the Zyklon B gas chambers. It was a long and ghastly one way journey. Within months of the Wannsee Conference, six camps — all in Poland — Auschwitz/Birkenau, Belzec, Chelmno, Majdanek, Sobibor, and Treblinka became active killing centers for the gassing of concentration camp victims.

What did the neighbors in the nearby towns know of the activity in the camps next door? They knew, but did not admit it. The smell of the chimneys, the odor of sickness and rotting flesh by and large were ignored as they went about their daily lives. And what did the outside world know about the Nazi extermination program? What did American Jews know about the extent of the tragedy? And when did informed and activist Jews — such as Marie Syrkin — learn the incredible appalling truth? But perhaps first one should ask the question, when did the American government begin its rescue of the Jews? Perhaps the even more interesting question is, when did the American government first *hear* of it?

On August 8, 1942, Gerhart Riegner, a Berlin-born Jew who now was a representative of the World Jewish Congress in Bern, Switzerland, sent a secret cable to the State Department and to the British Foreign Office to be transmitted to the influential Zionist leader and President of the American Jewish Congress, Rabbi Stephen Wise. The cable informed the American officials that the Nazis planned to exterminate all Jews from Germany and German-controlled areas in Europe, numbering about three and half to four million, after deportation and concentration in the East. It specified the use of prussic acid (Zyklon B) to exterminate the Jews "at one blow" and to "resolve once and for all the Jewish question in Europe" (Teveth 15). This was, of course, the plan adopted at the secret Wannsee Conference in January of that year. By the time Riegner sent his cable, deportations from Warsaw to the death camp at Treblinka had been underway for almost a month.

The U.S. State Department withheld the cable from Stephen Wise, but Wise had already received the information from Samuel Silverman (a member of the British Parliament and British section chief of the World Jewish Congress) who had learned of it from the British Consulate. On August 28, Wise inquired about it of the American State Department, and only then was he shown the cable, but asked not to publicize the information until it could be confirmed. The State department ultimately determined that because Riegner's cable was based on a report from a German industrialist named Edward Schulte, a high executive of a mining company that employed 30,000 workers, and because this very specific report came from such a highly placed German who had access to the top Nazi officials (rather than testimony from Jewish victims) it had to be taken seriously. Thus, the incredible official German policy of the annihilation of the Jews was made credible (Berenbaum 161).

In an article written forty years later, entitled "What American Jews Did During the Holocaust,"[9] Marie Syrkin addresses a "new area of research: the behavior of American Jews during the Holocaust." In response to a whole host of questions about the apparent docility of the Jewish organizations and leaders, she writes, "The failure appears base and inexplicable to a generation conditioned to direct action. Diligent researchers have come up with dates and quotations that prove incontrovertibly how early American Jews must have known what was happening—from the beginning of 1942 according to Yehuda Bauer, Walter Laqueur, and other historians." But, Syrkin asserts, all agree that the turning point came with the cable that Riegner sent to the State Department on August 8, 1942. "Did Jewish leaders docilely remain quiet for three to six months, depending on which dates are accepted?" She answers by arguing that "only those who were involved in the misery of those years can attempt an answer. A catalogue of dates is no guide to comprehension." Thus she proposes to begin her refutation with a personal experience:

Towards the end of August 1942 Hayim Greenberg and I, as editors of the Labor Zionist monthly *Jewish Frontier* were invited by Leon Kubowitzsky, a member of the staff of the World Jewish Congress, to a small, private meeting of Jewish writers and journalists. He told us of a bewildering report received from the Geneva office: Hitler intended to exterminate all the Jews of Europe; the plan was already being implemented.

We listened in numb disbelief. The individuals who heard these tidings had since 1933 been deeply involved in the struggle against Nazi persecution through articles, meetings, political pressure. That was why we were invited. But we could not take in what we heard. It should be noted that Hayim Greenberg, the foremost Zionist writer in the United States at the time, has been repeatedly singled out by students of the period . . . as an exception to the supposed apathy of American Jewry. Yet he, too, left the meeting stunned and dubious. All the words we had written about the Nazi atrocities had not prepared us for this horrifying revelation.

During the previous week a document from the Jewish Socialist Bund purporting to be a circumstantial account of the mass gassing of Jews in the Polish town of Chelmno had reached the office of the *Frontier.* Now I come to an incredible disclosure. We were as unable to assimilate the written words as the spoken ones of Kubowitsky. We hit on what in retrospect appears a disgraceful compromise: we buried the fearful report in the back page of the September issue in small type, thus indicating that we could not vouch for its accuracy.

Throughout September information multiplied. Some Polish women, exchanged for German war-prisoners, had reached Palestine in mid-August. They were the bearers of first-hand accounts. There was no further evading the truth. It had to be faced. We skipped the October issue. Throughout that month our small staff gathered whatever material could be found at that time. Our special issue appeared in black borders. The editorial minced no words:

In the occupied countries of Europe a policy is now being put into effect whose avowed object is the extermination of a whole people. It is a policy of systematic murder of innocent civilians which in its ferocity, its dimensions and its organization is unique in the history of mankind. . . . We print this somber record to acquaint the free world with these facts and to call on the governments of the Allied Nations to do whatever may be done to prevent the fulfillment of the horror that broods over the blood-engulfed continent of Europe.

The document from the Bund which a month earlier had been relegated to the back page appeared in its proper place.

The following paragraph, however, is the heart of her attempt to describe the psychology of committed American Jews of the early 1940s to the questioning young Jewish scholars of the more sophisticated 1980s:

The September and November issues of *Jewish Frontier* only a month apart, indicate dramatically the emotional space that had to be traversed before even those who, whatever their failings, could not be accused of indifference to the Jewish tragedy, were able to assimilate the idea of total extermination as a considered program. Even in retrospect I think that this inability reflects more on our intelligence than on our moral obtuseness. Today when genocide, gas chamber, and mass extermination are the small coin of language, it is hard to reconstruct the more innocent state of mind when American Jews, like the Jews in Europe's ghettos, could not immediately grasp that the ascending series of Nazi persecutions had reached this apex.

It is hard to read these last words from the vantage point of this, our twenty-first century, when words such as "mass extermination" and "genocide" have become ubiquitous currency expended throughout world geography, marked out in dark colors on television newscast maps, debated in the United States Congress. Genocide — first coined by Dr. Raphael Lumkin in 1944 — was first described to an unbelieving world in an editorial written by Marie Syrkin in the *Jewish Frontier* in November of 1942. Stephen Wise had written to President Roosevelt "about the most overwhelming disaster in Jewish history," asking him to meet with a delegation of Jewish leaders. On December 8, a group of representatives of Jewish organizations presented Roosevelt with a twenty-page document, "Blue Print for Extermination." A memorandum cried out to Roosevelt to "save those who may yet be saved." It begged him to "Speak the word! Institute the action!" (Feingold 233). Roosevelt appeared to be sympathetic and "assured the delegation that the Nazis would be held to 'strict accountability,' [but] there was no change in rescue policy. Nine days after the meeting, the Allies issued their first warning on war crimes. It contained no clue that they were aware of the 'final solution' or that there would be accountability for crimes against Jews." (Feingold 233)

The shameful role of the United States in the rescue of the Jews was further debased when, on February of 1943, Undersecretary of State Sumner Welles sent a telegram to American consulates in neutral countries in which he shut down the secret channel of communications that passed on information about the situation of the Jews and "signaled to American embassies abroad that the State Department was uninterested in information concerning the Jews" (Berenbaum 162). In the face of the newly confirmed information, Marie Syrkin reported that the American rabbinate "proclaimed a day of mourning and fasting. The protests and demonstrations Jews had been organizing for the past eight years assumed a new urgency. At a huge 'Stop Hitler Now' rally at Madison Square Garden on March 1, 1943, Chaim Weizmann, president of the Jewish Agency for Palestine, called on the democracies to negotiate with Germany through neutral countries for the release of Jews: 'Let havens be assigned in the vast territories of the United Nations. . . . Let the gates of Palestine be opened'" (*Midstream,* October 1982, 7).

The information about the ongoing genocide could no longer be kept secret, nor could the outrage of the American Jews and empathic non-Jews continue to be suppressed. Thus, the Anglo-American Conference on Refugees was convened in Bermuda on April 19, 1943. And as Marie Syrkin correctly points out, it was held "during the very days when the Warsaw Ghetto was in its death throes." In a devastating passage from the diary of Breckenridge Long, whom she identifies as "the steadfast opponent of any liberalization of the immigrant quota and strategically in charge of the Visa Department division of the State Department," Marie quotes:

The Bermuda Conference on Refugees has been born. . . . One Jewish faction under the leadership of Rabbi Stephen Wise has been so assiduous in pushing their particular cause — in letters and telegrams to the President, the Secretary and

Welles—in public meetings to arouse emotions—in full page advertisements—in resolutions to be presented at the Conference—that they are apt to produce a reaction against their interest. . . one danger in it all is that their activities may lend color to the charges of Hitler that we are fighting this war on account of and at the instigation and direction of our Jewish citizens.

Marie Syrkin's comment on this diary entry is "Obviously Long found Jews uncomfortably active—in fact, pushy—rather than the reverse." This is obviously a strong point in her rebuttal to those who accused the American Jews of abject passivity, and that their leaders "timidly abetted the American government's conspiracy of silence" (*Midstream*, October 1982, 6).

Pressure on the governments of America and Britain rapidly intensified; open indignation, expressed not only by Jews, but also in church sermons, and in newspaper and magazine articles, began to inform the public and exposed the failure of the governments to do anything about the rescue and refugee problems. But the response was shockingly belated. Finally, on January 22, 1944, at the urging of the Jewish secretary of the treasury, Henry Morgenthau, Jr., President Roosevelt established the War Refugee Board. Henry Feingold has written that "Financed primarily with JDC [Joint Distribution Committee] funds, the WRB embarked on an effort to rescue the Jews of Hungary, the last sizable Jewish community surviving in Europe. On 12 June 1944 the immigration laws, thought by rescue advocates to be immutable, were also circumvented. The admission of over nine hundred primarily Jewish refugees, temporarily housed in an Army Relocation Authority camp in Oswego, New York [Fort Ontario], until they could be returned to Europe after the war, was supposed to serve as an example for other receiving countries to follow suit. Few did" (Feingold 233). Marie Syrkin's comment on the Fort Ontario project appeared in two articles, one in June and one in July, in the *Frontier*. In July, after bitter words about the meaning of "visa" and "quotas" and statistical arguments rationalizing the world's failure to save millions of Jews, and the fact that since 1933 the United States had actually admitted a million *fewer* immigrants than would have been permitted by the quotas if they had been filled, she argues that "if the United States can permit itself to declare to the world that its maximum contribution to the refugee problem is the admission of 1,000 people, what answer can be expected from smaller and poorer nations who have coped with sporadic streams of refugees for years? If the

United States really accepts the moral responsibility of offering sanctuary to Hitler's victims, then only one principle can be viewed as valid. We will provide free ports, or temporary havens to whomever can escape, and we will do all in our power to assist in this escape. Everything else is a mockery" (*State* 245). It should be recalled that only two years before this, Marie had personally witnessed in the tiny country of the Dominican Republic, the generosity of President Trujillo who had agreed to accept one hundred times Roosevelt's offer of one thousand.

During these war years, it became increasingly difficult for Marie to travel abroad, but she was totally immersed in the turbulence of the events in Europe. In July of 1941, as Charles put it in his July 27 letter to Al Lewin, "Marie went to England for a brief vacation" (*Letters* 302). England seems an odd choice for rest and recuperation from the work she had been doing. Though the United States was not yet at war, London had just been through the famous blitzkrieg; and other cities, especially Coventry, had suffered appalling damage throughout the fall and winter months. Moreover, she had to know that the transatlantic crossing was dangerous. But Marie had always been a great admirer of the stiff-upper-lip British and undoubtedly was eager to visit England in the moment of its mixed emotions; the bombings had been horrific, but the British RAF had been spectacularly successful. William Shirer comments that despite the terrible damage, "British morale did not collapse nor armament production fall off, as Hitler had so confidently expected. Just the opposite. . . . Hitler's bomber losses over England had been so severe that they could never be made up, and in fact the Luftwaffe . . . never fully recovered from the blow it received in the skies over Britain that late summer and fall" of 1940. Churchill, speaking of the spectacular achievement of the RAF to the House of Commons in August of 1940, proclaimed famously that "never in the field of human conflict was so much owed by so many to so few" (Shirer 782).

But, as Marie Syrkin has pointed out, at this moment her threefold interests — Europe, Palestine, and America — were of equal importance, and she was given to quoting the words of her friend Golda Meir who, after watching (as an observer) the disgraceful proceedings of the Evian Conference, had defined the charge of Zionism: "There is no Zionism except the rescue of Jews." Again, in response to those who years later accused the Zionism of the war years of being more interested in the idea of statehood than in rescue operations, Marie's vehement rebuttal was that the "slogan of the Jewish struggle against the Mandatory

Power was not 'A Jewish State' but 'Open the Gates'" (*Midstream,* October 1982, 7). Here, Marie alludes to the resolution adopted by the extraordinary Zionist Conference held at the Biltmore Hotel from May 6 to 11, 1942. Because of the war, there could be no regular meeting of the Zionist Congress; hence, this convention called for by the American Emergency Committee for Zionist Affairs assumed the authority of an official meeting. By now, the truth about the Holocaust had been made clear, as had the conclusion that Zionism could not achieve its needs and aims under the British Mandate. Consequently, the announced policy of the Biltmore Program was the resolution "that Palestine be established as a Jewish Commonwealth integrated into the structure of the new democratic world [after World War II]" (*P.D.* 61). This was first time that the Zionist Organization officially had called for a Jewish State. Six hundred delegates attended from the Zionist organizations in America and Canada, as well as available leaders from Europe and Palestine, including Chaim Weizmann and David Ben-Gurion, the main speaker. Marie Syrkin, of course, was in attendance.

Shortly thereafter, Syrkin wrote an essay entitled "Why A Jewish Commonwealth," published and widely distributed by the Political and Education Committees of *Hadassah,* the Women's Zionist Organization of America, Inc. In this thirty-one-page polemic, Syrkin argued that "It is because the various bi-national schemes fail to meet the major issue of immigration that they have been rejected by the official Zionist bodies which have endorsed the program for a Jewish Commonwealth embodied in the Biltmore Manifesto." Next, Marie itemizes the main points of the platform. The first item on the list became her strong eyewitness evidence against the accusatory words of later historians who questioned the priorities of the Zionists during the war.

The most significant provisions of this platform are:

1. That the gates of Palestine be opened.

2. That the Jewish Agency be vested with control of immigration into Palestine and with the necessary authority for upbuilding the country, including the development of its un-occupied and uncultivated lands.

3. That Palestine be established as a Jewish Commonwealth integrated in the structure of the democratic world.

The Biltmore Manifesto is based on the experience of the past decades under the Mandate, and on a realistic appraisal of present Jewish needs. It recognizes that there now exist in Palestine the manpower, the training and the skills which, if controlled by the Jews themselves, can be exploited for rehabilitating Palestine as the Jewish National Home. It is based on the belief that only the Jews themselves, driven by the desperate need of establishing a land where Jews may enter as of right and not on sufferance, can bring forward the ingenuity, the intensive effort and the inspired planning necessary to transform a backward land of the Near East into a country that is part of the modern world, geared to the needs of an industrialized twentieth century civilization.

The resolution was opposed by several Zionist and non-Zionist groups, such as the bi-nationalists, those who thought it was premature, those who wanted to work toward the repeal of the White Paper, and those who pointed out that no boundaries were mentioned, and in Walter Laqueur's words, "Weizmann is said to have thought that nothing should be done to antagonise the Arabs and thus to damage the British War effort." Laqueur, however, also argues that "both adherents and opponents of the Biltmore programme were mistaken in believing that it was a decisive turning point in the history of Zionism. It failed to materialise because it was based on premises that were not realistic. Nor did it do much harm, as critics at the time believed" (Laqueur 548).

Churchill regarded the White Paper as "a gross breach of faith," and the Arabs always "believed the worst as far as Zionist intentions were concerned, and did not need the Biltmore programme to confirm their suspicions. In the last resort Biltmore was not a policy but a symbol, a slogan, reflecting the radicalization of the Zionist movement as a result of the war and of the losses suffered by the Jewish people. It foreshadowed the bitter postwar conflict with the British government" (Laqueur 548). But for Marie Syrkin, the program was incontrovertible evidence in her own case against her detractors. In her 1982 article, "What American Jews Did During the Holocaust," she wasted no niceties:

[I]n view of the obdurate rejection of any rescue measure by the international community, there was no gainsaying the argument of Zionist Rabbi Abba Hillel Silver: "We cannot truly rescue the Jews of Europe unless we have free immigration into Palestine." The conference established three commissions: one for rescue wherever possible; one for Palestine; and one for post-war problems. Nevertheless, despite this clear record, the current dossier against American Zionists includes the canard that the commission on rescue was slipped in as a casual afterthought. Such distortions savor more of belated psychoanalysis than objective history. (*Midstream,* October 1982, 10)

Your School: Your Children

Clearly, Marie's energies in this period were directed mainly to the issues of the rescue of European Jews and the "opening of the gates" — the interdependency of Europe and Palestine. But as it would turn out, despite her intense focus abroad, she did not neglect mainstream American issues. Indeed it was at this very moment — in the midst of the war, in 1944 — that Marie published the book that would bring her to the attention of the wider American public. The purpose of the book was to disclose the problems of instilling the democratic idea given the present conditions in the world. The book was titled, *Your School, Your Children,* a rather tepid title for an explosive book. So explosive that the reviewer in the *Chicago Sun Times* wrote, "This book is dynamite. It's the sort of dynamite which could be set with profit under the greater part of our school system and the fuse lighted." But the benign title has an accusatory subtitle: *A Teacher Looks at What's Wrong with Our Schools.* Hence, it is immediately apparent that this will be a critique of the American public school system, gleaned from material collected and experienced over eighteen years of teaching in that system. Yet, the fact that it was written during the midst of World War II has much to do with the content of that critique. Even in this book about the school system, Marie's eye remained trained on the fallout of wartime horrors.

Divided into three main sections: "The School: Its Social Function," "The School: Its Intellectual Function," and "Synthesis," Syrkin's book searches for the way schools can translate the abstractions of democratic principles into their day-to-day routine. Her quest is to find a *modus operandi* for teaching democracy in the schools so as to turn ordinary students into useful citizens. And she is not afraid to use the word "indoctrination."

Buttressed by all the current intellectual and philosophical thought of her era — from John Dewey's progressive education to the liberal group "Education for Freedom, Inc." that included Robert Hutchins, Mortimer Adler, and Mark Van Doren, who advocated a return to the classical curriculum, which effectively meant the "Great Books" list — Syrkin's laboratory was Textile High School, where she taught classrooms filled with mostly average students, 90 percent of whom would not go to college, but most of the male students would upon graduation enter the armed forces. Setting the argument in the context of the history and the hopes of the Founding Fathers' dream of a public liberal system of education in America, the author asks the question, how well has the present system fulfilled those hopes? Quite courageously, Syrkin outspokenly describes the Fascist influences in the schools, Jim Crow, anti-black and antisemitic hatreds that have spread to the classrooms, and the skeptical attitudes of ordinary teenagers who regard all stories of devotion to a cause as "bunk" or "propaganda." The second part of the book attempts to diagnose these appalling symptoms; the major virus being the massive size of the expanding public school system. "We have learned," Syrkin asserts, "that mass education is not synonymous with education of the masses." Questioning the methods of both the Progressive Movement and the "Great Books" movement, her "hands-on" analysis concludes that neither one alone can help to improve public education; then she presents one successful program, known as the "Springfield Plan."

All this is written without restraint and with Syrkin's customary wit and common sense. And once again, she is one step ahead of the group — in the course of her analysis, she has presented an early argument for the revision of the literary canon. She suggests that particularly in non-academic curricula, the dusty, traditional Goldsmith poem *The Deserted Village* might well be replaced by a narrative by the war reporter, Ernie Pyle. The book was an enormous critical success. It was reviewed in glowing terms by large and small newspapers and magazines, including the *New York Herald Tribune, PM,* the *New York Post,* the *Chicago Tribune, Saturday Review,* and dozens of publications around the country, including the Yiddish and Anglo-Jewish Press. Marie received letters of admiration from ordinary readers as well as famous writers and artists such as John Dewey, who wrote a book blurb for it, the composer John Alden Carpenter, Dorothy Canfield Fisher, Horace Kallen, Max Lerner, George Shuster, the President of Hunter College, and so on. *Book of the Month Club News* singled it out for high praise; Dorothy Canfield wrote the review, in which she said "We have had other books on this piercingly vital matter. But never such a one as this, which is simply not to be missed. The author is a frontline fighter in active service in the never-ending battle to civilize by education each oncoming generation, a teacher in one of the New York City public high schools." Max Lerner claimed in *PM,* "It is a more important book on urban American education than all the solemn treatises and the pretentious educational manifestoes to which we have been recently exposed" (October 18, 1944, 2).

In the first five years of the 1940s, Marie's life was anything but dull. Absorbed by the events of World War II, haunted by the unfolding of the Holocaust atrocities, terrified by the terrorists in Palestine, fearful for her son in the army, intent on doing her job at school and in print, only her home life was unfulfilling. Charles had been working steadily at his poetry, privately publishing a volume entitled *Going To and Fro and Walking Up and Down* (1941) that included some poems originally published in *Menorah Journal*. He did not publish another collection of his poetry until 1959, when he collected poems that had appeared in such journals as *Commentary, Menorah Journal,* and *Jewish Frontier* under the title, *Inscriptions: 1944–1956*. He was also working in collaboration with Uriah Z. Engleman on a history of the Jews of Charleston, as well as a short story about the Jews of Georgia in the colonial period. During these years, however, while Reznikoff worked continuously at his writing (both poetry and prose), he also held down a variety of jobs in research, translation, and editing for such organizations and publications as the American Jewish Committee, *The Jewish Publication Society,* and *Jewish Frontier.* He had even gone back to work in 1943, at *Corpus Juris* for the American Law Book Company. This last was not something that he wished to do. In a letter of February 26, 1943, to Al Lewin, Reznikoff unpacks his feelings, both financial and marital:

I went [to Corpus Juris] most unwillingly. . . . I remember telling you that I had been asked to resign and that this had been unfair, for I never did a better piece of work at the law than my last. Of course nobody believed this — except my immediate chief. Well. He's the head of the department now. And he asked me to come back. I remember telling you that if I were not married I would not work at all but just do my writing. I could carry myself for another year at my present scale of living but then I'd be flat broke. This is generally supposed to be uncomfortable. If I were not married, I think I could make my money last two, three, or even four years, and that would give me more chance to get a book over. But I am married and of the two books I have finished since I came back from the Coast, the Jewish Publication Society's editor says that they will probably publish one next year but won't promise anything and the other book can't be read by the rockets' red glare. (*Letters* 310)

In 1944, Charles Reznikoff published the novel he had been working on for some years, *The Lionhearted*. The work dealt with the massacre and expulsion of the Jews of York in the the twelfth century. Reznikoff's chief champion in later years, Milton Hindus, reviewed the book for *Contemporary Jewish Record* negatively when it came out. Later he would explain: "The irony of the title appealed to me, but little else did. The title had been expropriated from the famous Crusader King Richard and bestowed upon the fugitive small people of strangers in his realm, who were hunted down and killed by an inflamed, envious population, welcoming the opportunity of improving their own lot by taking the lead against the helpless from the hands of the lords of church and state" (*Other* 253). Hindus thought that, though he "sympathized heartily with the subject of the book and what the writer was attempting to do with it," Reznikoff did not succeed in his aim. One might be tempted to smile patronizingly at Charles' immersion in a tale of medieval England while millions were burning in contemporary Europe; but Charles' method had antecedents. Weren't Shakespeare's history plays intended to allude to analogous contemporary English concerns? Reznikoff meant the reader to understand the twelfth-century massacre as a parallel to the twentieth-century slaughter of the Jews. Curiously, in the *Book of the Month Club News* that features Marie Syrkin's *Your School, Your Children* on page 11, Charles Reznikoff's novel, *The Lionhearted,* is reviewed on page 12. The reviewer writes, "Despite its time and place, this is no tale of faraway and long ago; one need turn only to yesterday's newspaper for fresh news of this old evil."

As Marie traveled "to and fro," Charles continued "walking up and down." They were the yin and yang, the micro and the macro, the interior and the exterior—two contraries making a life apart, together. Charles' gift was for meticulous detail that causes the concentration in his verse and prose. "He looked upon no job which he was called upon to do as beneath him, and he never performed it shoddily," says Milton Hindus. "Perhaps it is this humility which is the secret spring of the sympathetic identification with which he always portrays the humblest members of the social order; the scrubwoman, the elevator operator, the poor shoemaker, the overworked servant-girl, the millhand hurt in an industrial accident, helpless children, immigrants, members of vulnerable minorities (Jews, Blacks, Orientals), people in the grip of overwhelming passion as well as the victims hurt or destroyed by them. He always refuses the inherent invitation of his material to sentimentality. If Reznikoff errs at all, it is on the side of understatement and restraint, never melodramatic exaggeration" (*Man and Poet* 29).

Marie's gift was for larger gestures, expansive ideas, piercing insights,

but no less compassion than that of her husband. One of Charles'
now perhaps most famous poems is called "Te Deum." Hindus comments that "The refusal to be competitive explains much . . . about
Reznikoff's life and work. It certainly explains why his most oft-quoted
reticent utterances in verse were recommendations of the joys of a
simple, uncompetitive life in which one was content to do one's work
and to enjoy to the full nature and everyday life as it presents itself to
every one of us." Hindus offers "Te Deum" as an example of Reznikoff's
prayer of triumph.

> Not because of victories
> I sing,
> having none
> but for the common sunshine,
> the breeze,
> the largess of the spring.
>
> Not for victory
> but for the day's work done
> as well as I was able;
> not for a seat upon the dais
> but at the common table.
> (*Other* 255)

Though she agreed wholeheartedly with Milton Hindus' reading of the
poem, Marie felt the need to add a personal note. "Because of my official position, I generally sat at the dais. While Charles would be seated
elsewhere. I never thought that mattered to him. When I read his lovely
'Te Deum,' I wondered: the distinction in the seating had not gone unnoticed. Whether or not this rankled, the poem illustrates his ability to
turn every experience, no matter how trivial, to his purpose. . . . In 'Te
Deum,' obscurity, the minor role appears to be philosophically, even joy-
ously, accepted." But Marie immediately adds "In another mood he
writes more bitterly":

> Scrap of paper
> blown across the street,
> you would like to be cherished, I suppose,
> like a banknote.
> (*Man and Poet* 60–61)

Chapter 13

Postwar Projects

DP Camps, Blessed Is the Match, *Israel*

LIKE THE PIANIST who keeps his fingers nimble by practicing every day, Charles Reznikoff kept his poetic skills sharp by writing some verse every day. His wife, Marie, however, always insisted that she wrote her verse only when she felt compelled to do it — that is, when her emotion was so great that she had to bring it to birth in poetry. She asserted that much as she wanted to go on writing poetry, she considered it an indulgence — especially during the dreadful years of the 1940s. Nonetheless, her increasing awareness of the ghettos, the camps, the gas chambers, the refugees, and the silence of the world, turned into poems she could not and would not suppress. Along with all her polemical essays and articles in journals and newspapers, she gave voice to her personal griefs and bitterness in a group of poems collected in her 1978 volume, *Gleanings: A Diary in Verse* under the heading "In a Time of Massacre." A threnody entitled "To a Christian Friend" calls to account the Christian West's betrayal of the true meaning of Jesus. The opening lines suggest that once there was a respectful understanding between the Jew and the Christian, but now it has been severed by silence.

> There is something between us now,
> The cry you did not raise,
>
> You have washed your hands again.
> Put down the pitcher.
> The water will flow between us.

Give me back Jesus;
He is my brother.
He will walk with me
Behind the gray ghetto-wall
Into the slaughter house.
I will lead him into the lethal chamber;
He will lie down upon the poisoned stone.
The little children pricked with the death-bubble
Will come unto him.

Return to him the yellow badge.
Give me back Jesus;
He is not yours.
(*Gleanings* 53)

Syrkin's ironic use of Christian imagery and New Testament references later would become ubiquitous in post-Holocaust Jewish literature and art, most famously in Elie Wiesel's *Night* or Marc Chagall's paintings. It is also worth noting that, whereas in these years Marie's marital relationship with Charles Reznikoff was in serious decline, her poem, "To a Christian Friend," shows the strong influence of his verse on her politically engaged poetry. No matter what the condition of their personal affairs, she would always believe in his considerable poetic gift.

Marie's poem probably was inspired by the knowledge that finally had been made public in the November 1942 issue of *Frontier;* any lingering doubt about the gravity of the situation was impossible following the unending reports of the Nazi atrocities. In July, deportations from the Warsaw ghetto began and the Treblinka death camp was opened. Mass killings in gas chambers were added to mass graves at shooting pits in places like Ponary and Babi Yar. "Before the mobile killing units of various types finished their work, approximately 1.2 million Jews were killed, one by one by one. Their bodies were piled high in mass graves throughout the occupied Soviet territories from the Baltic to the Ukraine" (Berenbaum 98). The Nazi *Einsatzgruppen,* aided by complicit officials and ordinary folk in France, Belgium, Poland, Russia, Lithuania, Latvia, Ukraine, Romania, Hungary — everywhere in German-occupied Europe — rounded up starving, terrified Jews wherever they came upon them.

By the autumn of 1942 the rising tide in the affairs of the Axis suddenly ebbed. The Nazis' early emboldening military feats turned into a series of devastating defeats: British General Bernard Montgomery, in command of the Eighth Army in North Africa, drove back the much-vaunted German General Rommel in November of 1942, and utterly defeated him in the desert of North Africa at El Alamein. On November 8, the American forces began its successful invasion of North Africa. Meanwhile, in Europe, the Soviets defeated the Italian troops on the River Don in December, and by February 2, the German army met its greatest defeat when it surrendered to the Russians at Stalingrad, though only after there had been an enormous human toll on that bloody, corpse-laden, frozen wasteland of a battleground; but indeed, the war's tide had turned. The consensus among reputable historians' accounts after the war is that the victorious Allied battles of El Alamein and Stalingrad, followed by the surrender of the German and Italian troops in North Africa in May of 1943 and the Allied landings in Sicily in July 1943, mark the reversal of the fortunes of World War II in favor of the Allies. From this point on, the Germans were at best only holding onto a piece of rotting flotsam. After the massive Allied D-Day invasion of the European mainland, the German military leaders knew that they had lost the war. After the devastating February 13 and 14 Allied bombing raid on Dresden, and after the successive Allied victories of major German cities and strongholds, on April 28, 1945, Mussolini and his mistress were captured and hanged by Italian partisans. A day later, on April 29 and 30, in the secret underground *Fuerhrerbunker* fifty feet below the Berlin Chancellery "whose great marble halls were now in ruins from Allied bombing" (Shirer 1108), in a grotesque reprise of Wagner's *Liebestod,* the Love-Death music of *Tristan and Isolde,* Hitler married Eva Braun, his mistress of twelve years; the two then committed suicide and were reduced to ashes on a funeral pyre. Not long after, on May 23, Himmler committed suicide followed by Goebbels' and Goering's suicides. The end of the catastrophic European War was proclaimed on V-E Day, May 8, 1945. Three months later, on August 6, the United States dropped the first atomic bomb on Hiroshima; Japan surrendered on August 14, 1945, after the second atomic bomb fell on Nagasaki.

There had been two summit conferences of "the Big Three"—Churchill, Stalin, and Roosevelt—during the war. The first post-V-E Day conference of the Allied leaders was convened at Potsdam on July 16, 1945, just after the United States, British, and French troops moved into Berlin; this time the participants were Truman, Stalin, Churchill, plus Clement Atlee, who had just been elected to replace Churchill as Prime Minister. The main subject was the administration of postwar Nazi Germany. Many historians regard this conference primarily as the origin of the Cold War; others remember it because the new British Prime Minister, Clement Atlee, had resisted all pleas to open the gates of Palestine to the now-displaced Holocaust survivors. In early June, the Allies had begun implementing their postwar plans by dividing Germany among the victors. As a consequence of the German Reich's unconditional surrender, it was truncated and divided into four zones of occupation. The Soviets took Eastern Germany and established it as a Stalinist socialist state; the United States, Britain, and France divided the West. Berlin was also divided into East and West. The war was over and the fallout had begun.

The Soviets had been the first of the allies to enter the concentration camps: in July 1944, they had liberated Majdanek, a death camp on the outskirts of Lublin, Poland; on January 26, 1945, they liberated Auschwitz; on April 12, 1945, the day of Roosevelt's death, the Allies, led by General Eisenhower, liberated Buchenwald and Bergen-Belsen concentration camps. Indeed, the European war was over and the maniacal Axis protagonists were gone, but the residuum was too ghastly to face all at once. The unimagined extent of the Holocaust had been revealed to the world when the first concentration camps were liberated in 1944. The many attempts of various Jewish individuals and groups in America, Europe, and Palestine who had pressed the free world for help during the catastrophe and the failure of the democratic governments to make a serious effort to save the Jews during the years of slaughter made Zionists of Jews who had never before been drawn to the cause. It is true that at the moment of victory in Europe, Americans — Marie Syrkin certainly among them — celebrated the triumph with exuberant joy, relief, and pride. Yet, at this great long-awaited moment, Jews — again, Marie Syrkin among them — felt emotions different from their non-Jewish fellow citizens. Facing the graveyard of Europe, the Zionist hope for a mass postwar emigration to Palestine literally lay in ashes. Six million were dead. Yet, there were those who had survived and had been liberated; the operative epithet for them was "the walking dead," and they desperately needed immediate asylum. After their liberation, the displaced began to search for their families and relatives who had survived the Holocaust. The Allied governments were ready to repatriate them to their prewar homes, but most of the Displaced Persons (or DPs, as they were called) refused to return to the Germany that had caused their agonies or to the Poland that after the war, in July of 1946, vented their ingrained antisemitism in a blood-libel pogrom by the secret police and villagers of the town of Kielce. The pogrom left forty-two Jews dead and eighty-two wounded out of the two hundred Holocaust survivors who had returned to their town. It was not the largest pogrom ever to have befallen the Jews of Poland, but for the Polish Jews of the DP camps it was an event that put to rest any ideas of going home to Poland (Bauer 341). The obvious answer to the survivors' desperation lay in the power of the British to rescind the White Paper and to permit emigration to Palestine for all who wished to do so. This, however, was never to happen.

The British refused, despite the fact that by the end of the war, 32,000 Palestinian Jewish men and women had been in active service with the British armed forces, many in the Jewish British Brigade, which had been permitted to fly its own Zionist flag, "a standard which bore as its emblem the yellow Star of David, the ghetto badge of the medieval and Nazi eras" (Sachar 558). Curiously, despite the fact that the Arab states had thrown in their lot with the Axis forces, the British still refused to revoke the White Paper. Thus, immediately after the war, when a quarter of a million Jews were facing the bald fact that they were once again trapped in squalid prison-like conditions in the European DP camps, when the countries to which they might be repatriated were the charnel houses of their recent miseries, when other more hospitable places had strict quotas, and worst of all, when the one place in the world that truly wanted them was unavailable due to the British ban on open immigration, illegal immigration to Palestine became the only possible avenue of escape.

Blessed Is the Match

Marie Syrkin's repeated refrain in time of crisis surely was on her tongue now: "Something must be done!" But *what* was to be done about the survivors, the barely survived, and the nearly dead displaced? She did not know what others would do, but she did know what she could and certainly would do. She would write a book, and it would be a book not about death and destruction, but about survival and heroic resistance.

The poetry would wait. These broken, yet still human, lives became the focus of Marie's passionate effort to find out how, indeed, they were still human. Who were the living souls behind the cold numbers? Indeed, how *did* they survive? How did they resist; who were their leaders; what was the role of the *Haganah* of Palestine? Marie was determined to see them, to speak with them face to face, to hear their sometimes ghastly, sometimes proudly heroic stories of how they remained alive and how they resisted the Nazis. To do this, she determined to go to Palestine, to gather material for her book about the Palestinian parachutists who "leapt down into the Nazi-held Balkans in order to bring help to the surviving Jews of Europe,"[1] and then about the underground network, the ghetto fighters, the partisans in Eastern and in Western Europe, and the resistance in Palestine. Marie also planned to make her way to Europe to see the ruins—both architectural and human—for herself.

In the introduction to *Blessed Is the Match,* Syrkin explains her original intent: "In the Fall of 1945, immediately upon the conclusion of World War II, I left for Palestine on the M.S. *Gripsholm,* the first ship from New York to sail for the Middle East with civilians since the outbreak of hostilities in 1939. My purpose was to interview survivors of the death camps and participants in Jewish resistance, who at that time were to be found primarily in Palestine. *Blessed Is the Match* was the result of that voyage" (*Blessed* vii). In the 1974 reissue of the book, Marie freely admits that since the first publication of the book in 1947, "a huge literature on all aspects of the Holocaust" had arisen. "Indeed, what followed were major volumes of historical research, memoirs, diaries, archival material provided by the Nuremberg Trials, poems, fiction. But in 1946, none of this material was yet available, and the only resource at hand for Marie was "the immediate memories, not recollected in tranquillity, of the sufferers" (*Blessed* vii–viii). The truths inherent in the immediacy of her encounters with survivors for *Blessed Is the Match* later would become important evidential material for her critique of Hannah Arendt's *Eichmann in Jerusalem.* In 1945, however, Marie's main purpose was to document the story of Jewish resistance in order to understand the hearts of those who had resisted the darkness.

Syrkin's motivation was to find the life behind the abstractions, so to penetrate the psychological wall of those who protected themselves from the meaning of the stupefying quantitative data; so also to reach those whose excess of sorrow had numbed their nerves and turned them away from facing the truth and its consequences. She did not wish to

focus on the mortifications, the details of the crematoria; no—Marie
Syrkin's focal point was resistance, the incredible stories of how these
women and men tried not to die, but to live, and to help others to live.
Marie wanted her book to give her readers a new roster of Jewish heroes
and heroines—ordinary people whose feats of nobility, courage, and
selflessness deserved a place of honor in the world's *Zikhronot* (remembrance). Those names include the Palestinian parachutists, Enzo Sereni
and Hanna Senesz; the women ghetto fighters, Renya of Bendin and
Ruzhka of Vilna; the three leaders of the Warsaw ghetto uprising, Mordecai Anilewitz, Yitzhak Zuckerman, and Zivia Lubetkin; Hayka Grossman, a leader of the Bialystok revolt; Anatol Belsky, the partisan from
the White Russian woods; the Warsaw historian, Emanuel Ringelblum;
the diarist, Chaim Kaplan; and also Joel Brand, whose failed negotiation
with Eichmann for the ransom of Jews in Hungary in a "goods for blood"
(Eichmann's phrase) exchange is controversial even at this writing.

Blessed Is the Match begins in Palestine with a story of a baby named
Ud (the last brand) born in *Eretz Israel* to survivors of the Warsaw
ghetto uprising. This introduction is neither surprising nor overly sentimental, for it is written both in the dark memory of the loss of her
own child and in the light of mature hope. Years later, in the early years
of the State of Israel, Marie would compose a memorial poem for the
dead son of her own youth in which she writes:

> I have never gone back to Ithaca
> Afraid of the small headstone, the weed choked plot.
> Now there is a plaque with your name
> In a kindergarten in Jerusalem.
> In Jerusalem
> In a house for children
> With eyes dark as yours,
> Prattling in Hebrew
> and laughing
> I took heart to face your name:
> Benyah.
> (*Gleanings* 94)

Syrkin's account moves on to the Palestinian parachutists (all members of *kibbutzim*) who leapt from the skies behind the lines in Yugoslavia to work with the partisans. It continues with the stories of the

underground networks and the details of negotiations with Adolf Eichmann, moves on to the ghetto battles, and the Eastern European Partisans in Vilna, in the forests of Poland, Galicia, and White Russsia, then
to Western Europe, in Holland, and France, with the Jewish Maquis,
and finally back to Palestine to hear the narratives of *Haganah* resistance
and *Ha'apalah* (illegal immigration). Finally it ends with a short account
of a meeting with a young man with a heavy German accent who, like
all the others on the yet-unfinished settlement, came to Israel from Youth
Aliyah and settled on the new *kibbutz* Geser. The boy told her that here,
Joshua "had blown his trumpet. From beneath this soil," he noted, "ar-
chaeologists had excavated the remains of six ancient cities. . . . He
looked at the dry, scorched soil and the few scattered tents and barracks
and said proudly: 'And this is the seventh city, and the last'" (*Blessed* 361).

Marie Syrkin explains her deliberate decision to end with this story:
"the spirit of Jewish resistance is not truly portrayed if one ends on a
note of death, even heroic death. For it is not the mood of Masada that
animates those who dash themselves against the apparently impossible.
The fury of despair may be a factor, but it is not the decisive one. The
banner under which Palestine fights is not Masada. When I seek a fitting
symbol, I do not think of the suicidal stand at the ancient citadel, but of
a new, unknown settlement — Geser" (*Blessed* 360). Her choice of first
and last chapters — the promise of rebirth — should not be brushed aside
as mere sentimentality, but rather as an expression of her natural optimism, a tendency to dwell on hope rather than to fall into despair. In his
review of the book, Ben Halpern, Marie's colleague at the *Frontier,* asserted that "*Blessed Is the Match* is American in its fundamental approach.
It begins with, and maintains throughout, the stunned incredulity of the
American in the face of the monstrousness and the perversity of the suffering, and the inner tension of the book lies in the continuous effort of
the author to understand what happened to these people, how they survived or how they died, how they fought or how they passively succumbed, in circumstances which would be normally unintelligible to her."

A word about the title. "Blessed is the match" is the first line of a
poem by Hanna Senesz, the young Hungarian from Palestine who para-
chuted into Hungary to bring comfort to the trapped Jewish communities, to let them know that someone cared. Ultimately, Hanna Senesz
was executed by a Nazi firing squad, but she left behind a collection of
her poems. Her mother survived her, and in a hotel room in Tel Aviv,
Mrs. Senesz told Marie Syrkin of her daughter's last days in prison;

how, from a prison waiting room, Mrs. Senesz had heard the shot in the courtyard below that killed her daughter at the age of twenty-three. Syrkin translated Senesz's Hebrew poem (*Ashrei Ha Gafrur*) into English and pointed out that "every Jew in Palestine can recite the four simple lines of the poem Hanna wrote shortly before she was executed" (*Blessed* 23).

> Blessed is the match that is consumed in kindling flame.
> Blessed is the flame that burns in the secret fastness of the heart.
> Blessed is the heart with the strength to stop its beating for honor's sake.
> Blessed is the match that is consumed in kindling flame.
> (*Blessed* 24)

The original Hebrew of the repeated first word "*ashrei*" (happy) of Senesz's quatrain evokes the first word of Psalm One, imparting a liturgical spirit. "The poem celebrates the self-immolation of the hero," Marie wrote. "There is no assurance that the ultimate issue will be life. There is only insistence on the sacrifice. That such a sentiment can be described as the national slogan of Palestine Jewry indicates the bitter lesson learned from the Nazi decade" (*Blessed* 24).

The chapter entitled "Blessed Is the Match" begins with Marie Syrkin's statement that when she arrived in Palestine she kept hearing people say of Hanna Senesz, "At last Jews have their Joan of Arc." But Syrkin, a rational romantic, quickly admits that Hanna was no Joan of Arc. "She did not conquer the enemy," Marie points out,

> nor did she save the Jews of Europe. I stress the obvious not because I believe that the legend of the young and charming Hungarian girl, who valiantly sacrificed her life, should be kept within rational limits. The romantic enthusiasm aroused by the girl's history is natural enough. I mention what Hanna did not do and could not do, to underscore the point that even if Hanna had been the equal of Joan in vision and power, she would have been essentially helpless, for she was the heroine of a people without armies to be led and without a land on which to lead them. (*Blessed* 22, 23)

Despite Marie's demurrer, she, herself, seems to have had a curious lifelong attraction to Joan of Arc. During a 1989 interview with Marie, she had confessed to me that when she was sixteen she had written to her best friend: "I have just met someone [Maurice Samuel] who is as handsome as Apollo, as great a poet as Shelley, and as noble as Joan of Arc." In another curious instance, the earliest poem in Syrkin's *Gleanings: A Diary in Verse* (which begins with the latest poems and ends with the earliest) is titled "Saint Joan," but it is a rejection of heavenly reward for martyrdom and an affirmation of the earthly blessings of peace, beauty, and love. Nonetheless, the noble image of Joan of Arc seems to have had a peculiar hold on the very rational pysche of Marie Syrkin.

Ben Halpern's 1947 review of *Blessed Is the Match* ends with words of praise for Marie's optimism but he speaks words of despair because the painful work of illegal immigration carried out by the *Haganah* had not yet been relieved: "It is perhaps, too much to hope that our State Department officials will read Miss Syrkin's book and then note how similar the characters in it are to the 4,400 now sweating it out on the *Exodus 1947* and other British prison ships. But one may hope that the general public will read it. Then Americans may understand why Yitzhak Zukerman, a hero of the Warsaw ghetto uprising, wrote in the year *after* his liberation, 'Were a dog to lick my heart, he would be poisoned.'"[2]

Blessed Is the Match was reissued in 1974. Syrkin offers several reasons for the reissue; one being the heretofore unavailablity of archival material and the many major historical studies since its first publication. But she asserts that even with the full advantage of all the new knowledge, there is little that she would omit in her narrative as she gathered it in firsthand encounters, but much that she would add. That said, there also was a not-very-hidden agenda. The reissue is in the face of the growing politicized debate over who and what was done or not done by the *Yishuv* and American Jews to rescue the Jews of Europe. Marie had actively participated in one of the earliest revisions of the role of the Jewish leadership during the Holocaust, when verbally and in print she attacked Hannah Arendt's 1961 account of the Eichmann trial in *The New Yorker*. By 1974, the debate had grown into what Ben-Gurion's biographer, Shabtai Teveth, has called a Rashomon-like drama (Teveth 23). But back in 1974, Marie Syrkin took the opportunity in the introduction to the reissue of *Blessed Is the Match* to state unequivocally that those who had recounted their experiences, and she herself who wrote their stories, did so in innocence. She explains,

By this I mean that our emotions were pure; we could still feel horror, and we judged with absolute clarity as to who were the guilty and who the sufferers. The murky metaphysics of later decades, in which the "guilt" or complicity of the victim became a kind of extenuation of the criminal, had not as yet evolved. The systematic denigration of the tormented with a consequent implicit rehabilitation of the tormentor was not underway. The symbiosis of the sufferer with the perpetrator of the suffering was a refinement of perception to be evolved by future analysts, and the confusion of roles fashionable in some contemporary writing about the Holocaust was wholly absent.

Having said this, Syrkin added that, of course "All the dark notes were sounded." She was told about ambiguous *Judenrate,* brutal ghetto police, Jewish collaborators, and savage behavior for survival in the camps. "But the overriding theme was Nazi bestiality not Jewish degradation. . . . So, at any rate, did those whose wounds were still raw speak to me in 1945 and 1946. The simple woman who said, 'Understand it humanly,' was wiser as well as more compassionate than many a more sophisticated future student of the Nazi era" (*Blessed* viii). No doubt Marie has in mind Hannah Arendt, whom she had accused in 1963 of "failing so signally in sympathy and imagination."

The Secret Radio of the Underground

While in Palestine in 1945, Marie had the opportunity to closely observe the resistance work of the *Haganah* and to get to know some of the young men and women who filled its ranks. She has written that she "often wondered whether the British had any inkling as to how young, how ill prepared and ill armed were their antagonists." Her personal connection came during an unexpected brief stint with the underground. One evening, Golda Meir mentioned to Marie that a secret radio station was in the works that was to be called *Kol Israel* (the Voice of Israel). "Its purpose," Marie later explained "would be to keep the Yishuv informed despite British censorship and to present the Jewish side of the struggle to the British soldiers and Arabs. For this reason the broadcast would be given in Hebrew, English, and Arabic. The number of English speaking people in Tel Aviv who could be entrusted with such a broadcast was limited at that time, so [she] offered to do the English broadcast." The set-up for this mission was conspiratorial and secretive.

The broadcasts would be made from various apartments in the heart of the city. The place would be shifted from day to day so as to confuse the British. The broadcast had to be completed, the set dismantled and the participants out of the house within a given number of minutes. A longer period would give the British a chance to pinpoint the place of origin and surround the house. If our precautions should fail and the British police arrive, I need not worry. The entire block of the apartment house would be patrolled by Haganah boys who would sound a warning whistle in good time. The boys would at once hide the set and run to the roof. "Don't worry about them," said my adviser, "they are limber." So I ventured to ask: "What about me?" My friend assured me that this too, had been arranged. It was taken for granted that a middle-aged, American lady [she was forty-six] would not be able to scamper along the rooftops. Should we be caught, I was to go into the living room. . . . The family would be sitting, drinking a cup of tea, and I would explain to the British that I was a visitor — an aunt or a cousin. . . . The text had to be composed on the morning of the broadcast so that fresh news could receive immediate comment and evaluation. . . . The day of the first broadcast was — I can think of no brighter word — memorable. This was my first, belated taste of conspiracy, and the preliminary precautions were surrounded by a suitable aura of mystery. (*Woman* 137–141)

The strategy called for all sorts of precautions: goings and comings from one apartment building to another, people arriving and departing, plans made and changed, cover-ups prepared. Marie confessed that she brought a cake of American soap and a "wad" of toilet paper with her to the broadcasts in case she was caught and had to go to prison; fortunately, the British never arrived. Marie Syrkin's contact with the *Kol Israel* did not last very long because a number of people recognized her voice, but the clandestine radio station continued on "till the establishment of a powerful station." The broadcasters were never caught, and she continued assisting in the preparation of the texts for the broadcasts. More than forty years later, as Marie told me this story, her voice took on the hushed whisper of conspiracy and dangerous undertakings as she remembered those exciting, but also frightening, times. Suddenly, her voice modulated to the crisper tone of proof as well as pride, as she showed me two books of Holocaust drawings and woodcuts. "These books," she very proudly said, "were given to me in 1946 in Israel by comrades of the *Haganah* because of my English broadcasts on the secret radio of the Voice of Israel — my only venture into underground activity. The dedication to the book says: "Receive the blessings of the sons of the homeland for your voice that added color to the announcement of the redemption. When the day comes when the wall of evil crumbles in the storm your reward will be the opening of the gates" (Personal interview).

Marie Syrkin left Palestine to return to the United States in the winter of 1946, making a stopover in Europe before sailing home from Marseilles. This indirect route would give her a chance to witness the ruins of postwar Europe, but there was a more important personal reason why she wished to stop in Europe at this time. Her son, Second Lieutenant David Bodansky, had not yet been demobilized from the U.S. Army and had been sent to Europe in early 1946. He spent a few weeks in Naples before being shipped to Rome. While there, he learned that his mother was coming on a ship from Palestine. Bodansky concedes that after so many years, he is not sure how he first learned about her visit, but he does remember that it was the Red Cross that facilitated the meeting while his mother's ship was briefly docked in Naples. With Red Cross help, David got leave and transportation to the port where he was on hand to meet the ship. Sixty years later, remembering that meeting, David writes,

Of course it was dramatic to see my mother under these special, fortuitous, circumstances. However, what I remember most vividly was meeting some young [Jewish] Palestinians with whom my mother was very friendly and who she explained were going to France to do something to help refugees. That was all vague and innocuous, but in retrospect it seems obvious that they were Haganah organizers of "illegal" immigration. They were all about my age (21) and my present image of them is of vigorous congenial contemporaries. (Email, 9/23/06)

Marie's meeting with her son was surely emotional. For all the world's troubles that had occupied her in the prior decade, the fact that her young son was in the Army during the war years added personal anxiety to her list of "things to worry about." She mentioned to me that Golda Meir (at that time, Goldie Meyerson), who was then head of the political department of the Histadrut, had helped to arrange the Naples meeting. David Bodansky says that although he never heard anything about it, it was certainly possible that Mrs. Meir was the intermediary between his mother and the Red Cross. "I would guess," he concurs, "that at the time the Red Cross was geared up to unite people, and what could be better than uniting a U.S. Soldier with his mother?"

The Plea to "Open the Gates": Bevin and Truman

David's guess about the young people who arrived on the ship with his mother was undoubtedly correct. The most pressing issue of the day was illegal immigration. Three years before in November of 1943, at a meeting of the Executive of *Mapai* (the dominant Zionist Labor Party), Golda Meir declared that "There is no Zionism save the rescue of Jews." As Marie would later write, "This dynamic conception, by which Zionism became not only the means of securing a shelter for the rescued but the major instrument of rescue, became a popular slogan, repeated in the Diaspora, acted upon by the *Yishuv*."[3] In 1946, the war in Europe was over, but in Palestine the fight for the rescue of Jews was still raging. Marie had seen for herself the *Haganah*'s heroic postwar work of illegal immigration as it increased its activities and as ships bearing refugees began to be seen regularly along the coastline. But not very many of these ships were able to break the British blockade; instead, the authorities apprehended them and either detained them or sent them back to Europe. Marie Syrkin's traveling companions had come to help displaced persons in Europe get to Palestine to start new lives.

Marie had arrived in the Middle East in the fall of 1945, but as early as May—just after the European war was over—the executive of the Jewish Agency had sent a petition to the British government asking it outright to declare Palestine a Jewish state—a request first made in 1942 as part of the Biltmore Program. In addition, the Agency sent a proposal to the conference of the United Nations in San Francisco outlining a plan for a free and democratic Jewish commonwealth. "The appeal to Britain was no doubt made for the record; there was not the slightest chance of a favorable response," writes Walter Laqueur. "Anglo-Zionist relations had reached their nadir" (Laqueur 564). Across the ocean in Washington, however, through the efforts of Secretary of the Treasury Henry Morgenthau, Truman signed on to a State Department proposal to send Earl Harrison to Europe to investigate the situation of the DPs, "particularly the Jews."[4]

Harrison reported that the situation was deplorable and referred back "to the proposal made by the Jewish agency to the British government that 100,000 additional immigration certificates [to Palestine] be made available. . . . Truman forwarded Harrison's report to Clement Atlee in London on August 21, 1945, together with his own conclusion that 'the main solution' to the problem of the DPs was 'the quick evacuation of as many as possible of the non-repatriable Jews who wished it, to Palestine'" (*Truman* 112). With the new Labor government now in power, one might have expected some sympathy for the socialist government-manque in Jewish Palestine, and that at least was the hope of an editorial in the August issue of the *Jewish Frontier.* To the contrary, however, the Labor government—especially the newly appointed foreign secretary, Ernest Bevin—remained hostile. Walter Laqueur describes the scene as follows: "Bevin, like his chief Attlee, was neither pro- nor anti-Jewish. He simply believed that the Jews, unlike the Arabs, were not a nation and did not need a state of their own. The Jews, as he and Atlee saw it—and as the Foreign Office had told him—were ungrateful, devious, and cantankerous. The Arabs, on the other hand, were a straightforward people with a deep liking for Britain" (Laqueur 565). The rationale during the war was the need for Arab oil; postwar it appears to have became an argument about character. It is hardly a wonder that when Bevin visited the United States, he was booed at Yankee Stadium, picketed at his disembarkation at the Cunard Line, the target of vegetable throwers, and the object of terrorist threats. New York, the home of the organized labor of the ILGWU (International Ladies Garment Workers Union) and other labor unions was no place for what was perceived as blatant antisemitism. Bevin's refusal to negotiate, his dismissal of Truman's request as simply an electoral ploy to woo the New York Jewish vote, resulted in his declaration that the White Paper was still in force. The absolute need for Jewish sovereignty could not have been clearer.

Though Truman continued to press London for the 100,000 certificates, the only response of the British government was to propose an investigative committee, the Anglo-American Committee of Inquiry. Bevin's rationale was obvious, as exhibited in such antisemitic remarks as, "If the Jews, with all their sufferings want to get too much ahead of the queue, you have the danger of another anti-Semitic reaction through it all" (Sachar 562). Or his snide remark that the Americans supported the admission of 100,000 Jews into Palestine because they didn't want too many of them in New York (Sachar 562). Some historians, however, suggest that this actually might have been to the good, because it gave the Zionists continued ammunition. If Bevin *had* acceded to Truman's request, some of the urgency would have been lost and the push for a Jewish State would have lost its punch. The historian, Joseph Heller, has argued, "the very failure to implement [the Anglo-American Committee's] recommendations, specifically the British refusal to permit the entry of 100,000 refugees, according to [Abba] Eban, enabled the Zionists to keep their strongest and vital card, and Bevin became Israel's George III" (*Essential Papers*, 690).

British actions energized resistance. In Palestine, the reaction to Bevin's postwar policies was an increase in anti-British activities. Not only did illegal immigration continue apace, but so did terrorist attacks by the *IZL* (*Irgun Zva'i Le'umi*), the underground military defense and resistance organization founded in 1931 because of a dispute with the *Haganah* over tactics and policies. By 1937, the *IZL* was almost exclusively comprised of militant Revisionists under the command of Ze'ev Jabotinsky. Menahem Begin, later to become the Likud Party Prime Minister of Israel, was appointed in 1943 as the new *IZL* commander; but, after the war in 1945, out of complete frustration with British policy, the *Irgun* joined with the *Haganah* and the even more extreme terrorist group *Lehi* (a.k.a. Stern Gang) to form the Hebrew Resistance Movement. However, the *Haganah,* which historically had espoused the principle of self-restraint, withdrew from the group in July 1946, immediately after the infamous attack on the King David Hotel in Jerusalem in which ninety-one people — British, Jewish, and Arab — were killed. The *Haganah* had cancelled the whole operation just before it was to be implemented, but the *Irgun* and *Lehi* went ahead with the plans anyway. With a reward of 10,000 pounds for his capture on his head, Begin evaded arrest, and while on the run, continued to direct *IZL* operations until 1948 and the establishment of the state. The terrorist groups were repudiated by the majority of the Palestinian Jews, but there was also a certain amount of sympathy for them; Jews in Palestine and in the rest of the world had been provoked into a state of outrage and rancor against Britain's callous intransigence in the face of the obvious suffering of the survivors of the Holocaust. In the United States, during the early 1940s, the well-known playwright, Ben Hecht, and many other celebrities (but not the mainline Zionists) had supported the Revisionist, *IZL* member, Peter Bergson's (a.k.a. Hillel Kook) Emergency Committee to Save the Jewish People of Europe and his sometimes-underhanded techniques. In Palestine, even though Ben-Gurion fiercely opposed their actions, he too, well understood the frustrated anger that motivated the *IZL* to terrorist activity.[5]

Such were the conditions in Palestine when Marie Syrkin arrived there in 1945 and when she left for Europe in early 1946 to meet up with her son. Marie's own description of the immediately postwar scene in Palestine appears in the introduction to *The State of the Jews* (1980):

While [in Palestine] I saw the beginnings of the armed struggle against the British. The scruples that had inhibited reprisals against Arab terrorism in the thirties were again in evidence. Determined to "open the gates" of the Jewish homeland to survivors in defiance of British restrictions, the Haganah nevertheless adopted a strict code: military action to bring in refugees reaching the shores of Palestine and to aid in their settlement should be taken whenever necessary; however, indiscriminate violence such as characterized the dissident Irgun and Stern was opposed. Those who witnessed the heart-searchings and qualms of visionary Socialists whose pacifist dreams had to make way for the realities of armed battle know how profound was the spiritual crisis undergone by young kibbutzniks who made up the bulk of the Haganah. The tough years ahead were to bring pride in military prowess, but Golda Meir and others of her generation never stopped mourning the original vision: "We wanted to be good farmers, not good soldiers." (*State* 6, 7)

It would turn out to be a little of both, for even the controversial military leader, Prime Minister Ariel Sharon, was also a farmer of sorts. And conversely, the farmers of the *kibbutz* had turned out to be extremely good soldiers. Moreover, at this writing, Moshe Halbertal, Hebrew University Professor of Philosophy and consultant to the Israeli Defense Forces (IDF), has asserted that today the IDF has adopted the same official code of combat that was held by the *Haganah* in the 1930s, as well as at the time that Marie Syrkin wrote the above description. The main point remains *havlaga:* proportionality of response; who may be deemed a legitimate target; the exclusion of civilians as targets; and the avoidance of murder or massacre. Strategy and morality must operate together.[6]

Marie and Golda: Friendship Deepens

The months in Palestine had a further personal dimension for Marie. It was during this period that she grew closer to Goldie Meyerson — later known worldwide as Golda Meir. True, Marie had known and admired Golda since the 1930s when Golda had spent two years in America as an emissary to the Pioneer Women's Organization, but Marie's 1945 to

1946 visit to Palestine brought the two women into deeper understanding. In the first edition of her book *Way of Valor: A Biography of Golda Meyerson,* published in 1955, Marie recalls her experience of Golda at that time. That time is, of course, before the rise of the women's movement (Betty Friedan's pioneering work, *The Feminine Mystique* was ten years in the future), but Marie's assessment was, in fact, somewhat in advance of the times. Marie had a room in the same worker's cooperative as Golda and had frequent opportunities to see her friend in the intimacy of daily life. Though the building faced the beauty of the Mediterranean, the apartment itself was three flights up. The three rooms and kitchen were occupied by Golda, her children, and a friend, Leah Biskin, yet the place looked uncluttered. (In the later edition of the book, Marie points out that "by now Golda and her husband Morris were separated with no further attempts at reconciliation.") Genuinely struck by her friend's multiple roles on an ordinary Sabbath evening, Marie recalls the active scene:

On Friday, when the *Vaad-Hapoel* (Workers' Council) would close early in preparation for the Sabbath, one could see Golda baking and cooking like any good Tel Aviv housewife. At first I used to be indignant at the sight of Golda, exhausted by a harrowing week of crucial decisions, conferences and public meetings, stirring a batter, seasoning a carp, or carefully ironing the white blouse which she had washed the night before. The egalitarian concepts of the *Histadrut* allowed for no such luxuries as adequate domestic help for its chief executives. Golda knew that when her masculine colleagues came home after a strenuous day and evening they were not expected to shop, cook, and clean the house. Nor did they mend and iron for a family. A wife, sister, or mother presided over these activities. And to that extent feminine equality was proving a one-sided affair with double the responsibility and half the perquisites. One may safely assume that none of her distinguished male comrades were tempted to bake a cake or stuff a carp. Golda, on the other hand, enjoyed domesticity. . . . On Friday night and all day Saturday unannounced guests would keep dropping in. Golda would be busy most of the Sabbath clearing away dishes and serving more tea and cake, as new guests would arrive. (*Valor* 127–129)

If Marie's admiration for Golda is obvious, it is not exactly the hagiography that Sarah Schmidt and others would have it.[7] Schmidt argues in her critique of Marie Syrkin's biographical writings about Meir that, although Syrkin "played a major role in publicizing the facts of Meir's life and in helping to keep her memory alive," it is "not clear . . . to what extent Marie Syrkin understood that she was writing from an especially hagiographic perspective, intent on creating and perpetuating a myth that to an extensive degree she helped invent" (Schmidt 159).

It is clear as day that Marie Syrkin admired Golda enormously, but she certainly was not "intent upon creating and perpetuating a myth." She was intent on telling the story of a unique woman whom she had closely observed over a long period of time. Marie's many writings about Golda are evolutionary. They begin in awe, that is true; but as the years pass and the relationship develops, Marie's assessment of her friend, written and verbal, reflects her own personal experience, maturity, and rationality. When the two women first met, they were both in their early thirties. In 1932, Golda had come to the United States primarily because her daughter Sarah had been extremely ill and she felt she could get better medical treatment in America; for this reason she asked of the Women's Labor Council that she be sent to the United States as a *shlichah* (emissary) to the Pioneer Women. Once there, she arranged for Sarah, who was at this point wasting away from a kidney ailment, to be admitted to Beth Israel Hospital on the Lower East Side of Manhattan. Golda Meir has written, "No one who has ever hospitalized a child needs to be told what it is like to leave a small son or daughter in a hospital ward." These are words that did not have to be spoken to Marie Syrkin, whose own young son had died in a hospital. In 1946, the relationship that had begun in 1932 between two women who had experienced similar personal disappointments as well as professional satisfactions, grew stronger as they found in each other complementary strengths. As Marie would put it later, "Golda was stronger, but I was more intellectual" (Personal interview). Or, as Syrkin wrote in the foreword to the first edition of the biography, Meir was a rare type — an effective idealist. "Among the remarkable personalities who created the state of Israel I met a number of such men and women — individuals who responded to a world in chaos neither passively as "alienated" intellectuals, nor actively as energetic cynics. For me, this translation of belief into life became one of the few sources of moral affirmation in our time" (*Valor* 7).

After Marie's longed-for reunion with her son, David, in Naples in 1946, she went on to Marseilles to embark on her journey back to America, to her life at the *Jewish Frontier,* to public activism, to resume her iffy life with Charles Reznikoff, and to go back to her high school teaching — probably in order of personal satisfaction. As she has openly said, it was a period of many discontents for herself and her husband, yet they did not wish to divorce. Marie sublimated this unhappiness in, among other things, furious activity related to the horrendous postwar condition of the Jews in Europe and in Palestine. "Charles' own deep involvement," Marie has written, "expressed itself in verse not public activities" (*Man and Poet* 51), and these differences led to growing estrangement. Moreover, perhaps because of his domestic unhappiness, or perhaps as Milton Hindus argues, "Reznikoff was too self-critical to be very productive as a poet and what he did produce too often succumbed to his passion for revision" (*Man and Poet* 29). The fact is that between 1941 and 1959, Charles Reznikoff did not publish any collection of his verse, though he did publish individual poems in magazines, as well as a history of the Jews of Charleston, and some miscellaneous translations and editorial work.

In the DP Camps

Marie, on the other hand, continued her daunting agenda. Even her poetry, which she said she wrote only under compulsion, flourished in this period. In 1945, surely after her postwar trip to Palestine and Europe, she felt compelled to express her personal connection to the death camp at Treblinka:

My Uncle in Treblinka

My uncle, man of science in Berlin,
Grew old in Honor,
Having prospered.

In the evil days,
With neither work nor visa —
No land wanting him —
He wrote:
I spend my time
Solving problems and reading Scripture;
I seek truth.

The Germans led my uncle to Treblinka.
He went with his prayers and equations,
His psalms and logarithms

At the door of the slaughter-house
Both were with him —
The angels at his side.

God of Israel
Light of reason,
In the chamber of gas, in the pit of lime,
Did my uncle, gentle and hard of hearing,
Feel their pinions
Over his head?

To the seat of justice,
Where prayers are heard
And problems solved,
I, ignorant alike
Of Hebrew and mathematics,
Send these words for my uncle,
Murdered at Treblinka.
(*Gleanings* 61)

This poem is an open window to Marie Syrkin's state of mind in 1945. Cold numbers turn achingly individual in these tender words of grief; and so, in those days of communal and personal mourning, Marie made the decision to apply for permission to visit the DP camps in the American zone of Germany. Describing the refugee situation in 1946, Marie explains:

Jewish survivors began flocking to these camps in 1945. The British had closed their camps to survivors in June 1946; consequently most of the Jewish DPs found their way to camps in the American Zone of Germany. The refugees elected a "Central Committee of Liberated Jews in the United States Zone of Germany" with headquarters in Munich. The American authorities gave this body official recognition as the representative of Jewish DPs.

The camps became a center of Zionist sentiment and a source of Aliyah Bet, the "illegal" immigration to Palestine. The Central Committee issued a proclamation demanding the abrogation of the 1939 British White Paper. . . . The proclamation also called for the establishment of a Jewish State. (*State* 10)

Syrkin's application to visit the DP camps was accepted, and she was authorized to go in January of 1947. But investigative journalism was not her sole purpose. Marie had been asked by Dr. Abram L. Sachar, then the Director of the National B'Nai Brith Hillel Foundations, to visit the DP camps to find suitable applicants for available scholarships that would be above and beyond the immigration quota. The successful candidates "would have their transportation paid to the United States and would be maintained at an American university. When their studies were completed, they would be obliged to return to Germany or leave for some country for which they obtained a visa. But in the meantime," Syrkin writes in a 1965 account, "a respite from D.P. existence would be granted and opportunities for a college education given" (*State* 28).

Coincidentally, a few weeks before the time Marie would be leaving for the camps, the first full-scale Zionist Congress since 1939 was to be held in Basle, December 9 to 24, 1946. Surprisingly, however, she had not been planning to attend the Twenty-Second Zionist Congress, though it was to be the first post–World War II, post-Holocaust Congress. Years later, Marie informed me that she had readily accepted Abram Sachar's invitation to go to the DP camps, and she quickly added, "but that doesn't necessarily mean also going to the Congress. And I wasn't sure as to whether I should go to the Zionist Congress." Naturally assuming that she would have been chafing at the bit to get to this momentous meeting, I immediately asked her to explain. Very quietly Marie answered, "I had personal reasons against it." Though I attempted to learn what those personal reasons were, she hesitated, cleared her throat and finally told me to turn off my tape machine. Which I did. When I turned it back on, Marie resumed her narrative,

I was not sure I would be able to go to the Congress, but I was determined to go to the DP camps. However, in Israel, when they heard that I was not going as a delegate, I received a telegram signed by Ben-Gurion and Golda urging me to go at their expense — they would refund my expenses — they wanted me to go as a delegate. And their request was *force majeure*. Forty-six, of course, is the trauma of meeting the people one had said goodbye to in '39 — and they're not there. The comrades to whom we had said goodbye are missing. They are gone. The Jews of the DP camps are there, but Polish Jewry is not there — except for those few who have survived. The survivors have made their way from the various DP camps as a special group — and *they* were at this Congress. You had *them*. Not the people to whom we had said farewell. The young people had perished. (Personal interview)

Marie paused. She told me that she had been informed when she arrived in Basle that Zivia Lubetkin, the heroine of the Warsaw ghetto had died, only to discover later that she had made her way to Palestine at the end of 1946; consequently Marie did not include Lubetkin's story in *Blessed Is the Match*. But in the epilogue to the 1976 edition, Syrkin remedied the error. "Crawling through the sewers under the flaming ruins of the Warsaw ghetto," she now wrote, "Zivia led the exhausted survivors of the uprising to the dubious safety of a fighting unit in the forest. Even after the German defeat, Zivia had remained for a year in Poland in order to gather whatever members of the youth groups had remained alive. . . . In Israel with her husband, Yitzhak Zukerman, a commander of the ghetto uprising, Zivia became one of the founders of *Kibbutz Lohame Hageta'ot* (Ghetto Fighters) in Upper Galilee" (*Blessed* 360). Marie Syrkin grew to know Zivia Lubetkin quite well, particularly after Lubetkin attained prominence as a member of the World Zionist Executive. In passing, Marie said to me, "I wrote about her somewhere — *Ms.* magazine — as a great feminist." Lubetkin had been accorded a seat in Marie's pantheon of great heroines.

Whatever the reasons for Marie Syrkin's earlier inclination to skip the Twenty-Second Congress, once she arrived in Basle, she had to have been energized by the moment, dismayed by the dissension, but certainly not sorry that she had changed her mind. The issues were too important and the conflicts too glaring for an ambitious and responsible journalist to have missed it all. The first major issue on the agenda was the call for a Jewish Commonwealth as it was outlined in the 1942 Biltmore program and approved in 1945 at the international Zionist conference in London as the official program of the Zionist movement. But an even more crucial issue was partition.

Why Partition?

After the London conference, but a month before the Twenty-Second Congress, in an article in the *Jewish Frontier* titled "Why Partition?" Marie Syrkin published a powerful argument in favor of partition. "There is a strong likelihood" she wrote, "that the coming twenty-second Zionist Congress . . . will be another 'Partition Congress.' That is to say, the question of a Jewish state in a part of Palestine will probably be among the acute issues before the delegates. This has resulted in a re-alignment of forces; parties are going on record in their official plat-forms as to whether they oppose or accept partition; Zionist leaders are committing themselves *pro* and *con,* and Zionist meetings are being prodded to make their sentiments known so that the 'entrenched bu-reaucracy' will not be able to betray the will of the Jewish masses." Pointing out that the atmosphere surrounding the partition debate is highly charged, and with a swipe at the Revisionist position, Marie Syrkin adds that "every member of the Jewish Agency Executive in Paris who voted for the partition formula did so with a full sense of the im-mense and bitter sacrifice of Jewish rights implicit in the proposal. . . . The situation both of the *Yishuv* and of the Jews of Europe is too grave to admit of a rhetorical maximalism which has no prospect of realiza-tion within the predictable future" (*State* 74–75).

Marie's essay reviews the original territorial intent envisioned by the Balfour Declaration, its gradual boundary diminution, and the subse-quent development of the partition debate that had begun nine years before. The British plans for partition drawn up by the Peel Commis-sion in 1937 had been provisionally accepted by the Jews and rejected by the Arabs; in 1938, the Woodhead Commission presented three alterna-tive plans, each of which would have awarded the Arabs a far greater ter-ritory than the Jews, though both territories would have been further diminished to the advantage of the British area. The British ultimately scrapped the three plans because they were unworkable. In 1939, Cham-berlain issued his White Paper before the next Congress of 1939 could convene, and when it met, "it had to content itself with denouncing the annihilation of Zionism begun by the British in the panic engendered by Hitler's designs in Europe and the Middle East." For the time being, the talk of a Jewish State had to be abandoned, though the Zionist Executive adopted the Biltmore program of 1942 calling for a Jewish commonwealth. After the war, from December 1945 to April 1946, the Anglo-American Inquiry Committee looked into the matter once again in the light of the Jewish need for immigration for those who had sur-vived the Holocaust; its proposal was for a binational single mandatory territory under the control of Great Britain and with the immediate grant of 100,000 immigration certificates and the revocation of restric-tions on land purchase. The Bevin government rejected this plan, and then put forward yet another one: the Morrison-Grady scheme for cantonization, which would even further reduce the territory. Of this plan, Marie was compelled to point out that "according to its provisions the Zionist district would include 1500 square miles instead of the 2600 recommended in the partition proposal of a decade earlier, and that this so-called 'province' would be deprived of virtually all political auton-omy. Compare this travesty," she argued, "with the 45,000 square miles of Palestine when it was originally promised as a Jewish 'national home' and you get the measure of the deterioration of the Zionist and Jewish position, through a variety of international factors which it would be beside the point to review now" (*State* 76–77).

The Jewish Agency, not surprisingly, met this last proposal with con-demnation, and in August 1946, put forward a new plan for partition. This new plan envisioned a two-state solution with the Jewish territory including Nahariya, Haifa, Tiberias, and Safed in the north; a coastal territory including Tel Aviv and Gaza; in the south, the Negev, Ein Gedi, and the western shore of the Dead Sea; in the east, Jaffa as an Arab enclave, and Jerusalem under international control. This was the map that was in play just before the Twenty-Second Zionist Congress that met in Basle in December of 1946. This was the plan that Marie Syrkin endorsed in her polemical argument "Why Partition?" which concludes with these words:

Partition must not become a stick with which to attack the Zionist Executive or the Jewish Agency. Personal antagonisms and party rivalries can no more be avoided in the Zionist movement than in other movements. But there are mo-ments in history which impose their responsibilities and restraints. This is one of them. Every Zionist aware of the desperate plight of the Jews of Europe and of Palestine must bear in mind that partition may represent the only immedi-ate, realistic means of preventing the British from carrying out their uncon-cealed effort to liquidate Zionism. In 1937 partition was called a Solomon's judgement. Today we must perhaps consider that the child is a Siamese twin whose life can only be saved by a drastic operation. (*State* 80)

The issue of partition was then, as it would be for the very long future, the critical issue. In November 2006 — sixty years to the very month after Syrkin's plea in the November 1946 issue of the *Jewish Frontier* — at the memorial gathering in Tel Aviv marking the eleventh anniversary of the assassination of Prime Minister Yitzhak Rabin, the Israeli writer David Grossman, whose son had been killed in Lebanon in August, spoke these words: "The vast majority of Israel's citizens . . . know what the outline for the resolution of the conflict would look like. Most of us understand, therefore, that the land would be divided, that a Palestinian state would be established. . . . I call on those who listen, the young who came back from the war, on citizens, Jew and Arab, people on the right and the left, the secular, the religious, stop for a moment, take a look into the abyss. Think of how close we are to losing all that we have created here."[8] Sixty years after the Jewish Agency put forward its new partition plan that envisioned an Arab State as well as a Jewish State, the conflict was still raging and the dangers greater than at any other time. Partition had not yet been achieved. There was no Palestinian State and the Arabs still refused to recognize the nearly sixty-year-old Jewish State and the "maximalists" persisted.

The great urgency of the call for partition at the 1946 Congress was the intolerable situation of the DPs in Europe; thus, an equally important item on the agenda was the continuation of *Aliyah Bet* (illegal immigration) until Britain abolished the restrictions of the White Paper. Another item was the increase in armed resistance and violence in the *Yishuv* and the call for the release of the leaders of the *Yishuv* and the Jewish Agency who had been caught in acts of resistance and whom the British had arrested. Also on the agenda was the rejection of the Morrison-Grady (Anglo-American) plan that proposed the cantonization of Palestine into four areas (Arab and Jewish provinces, a Jerusalem district, and a Negev district with the British as the central government, with a high commissioner as highest authority). Such a plan obviously ruled out a Jewish State. Confrontation flared between the moderates and the activists, between those who supported Weizmann's conciliatory attitude toward London, and those who thought his too pro-British policies had failed and now were turning to Truman and America for signs of encouragement. On the evening of Yom Kippur 1946, just prior to the New York elections, President Truman issued a public statement in which he once again called for the British to issue 100,000 certificates for entry into Palestine; he called for liberalization of U.S. immigration quotas; and "for the first time, mentioned the idea of a "viable Jewish state in an adequate area of Palestine" (Laqueur 573). The statement had heartened the Zionists—and angered Bevin. Of course, the Arabs were furious, and the anti-Zionists in Truman's administration were incensed.

After bitter criticism of his policies of constraint and conciliation, Chaim Weizmann, in furious anger, resigned his presidency of the Congress, and for the first time in the Zionist Congress' history, no new president was elected. With that, on December 24, 1946, the Twenty-

Second Zionist Congress closed. Marie Syrkin immediately left for the
American Zone in Germany, where she was scheduled to travel through
the DP camps in Stuttgart, Munich, and Frankfurt, and to survey the
conditions, talk to the survivors, and fulfill her commitment to find students for the Hillel scholarships "who could prove themselves qualified
to enter an American university and to adjust to American college life."
The task was excruciatingly difficult. These were students who recently
had barely escaped selection for death, and now Marie was to submit
them to selection for a new life! In 1965, recalling the responsibility,
hence the agony, of being cast in the role of such a selector, she described her situation: "As the maximum program for all of Europe called
for only several hundred scholarships, and a number of these had already been filled, I could recommend no more than approximately fifty
students to be chosen from the entire American zone in Germany. It was
a heartbreaking as well as responsible assignment in the course of which
I became intimately acquainted with another sector of DP life — that of
the young students and the problems peculiar to them." Marie's first
challenge was to devise some method of measuring the qualifications of
the innumerable applicants. "It stood to reason," she wrote, "that many
boys and girls confined in a D.P. Camp would welcome the chance to
study at an American university. Each would adduce need; each had a
past so tragic that it became impossible as well as presumptuous to seek
to measure the extent of suffering or to use that as a criterion. The de-
termining consideration had to be the individual's ability to meet the
academic standards of an American university. It would have been mis-
guided kindness to award a scholarship to someone who would fail in
the first semester. 'You must not be emotional,' I had been warned"
(*State* 28–29). Certainly, she had to use all the restraint in her emotional
arsenal, and some of her anguished accounts later would appear in
print. But despite her personal torment, Marie Syrkin did an admirable
job; in 1982 she received a packet of documents relating to the work she
had done in 1947 from Rabbi Oscar Groner, then the current Director
of the Hillel International Program with the following note: "Dear Dr.
Syrkin: Your influence is pervasive in the Hillel Foreign Student Program. Even after 40 years your memoranda read as if they were written
today. I thought you might want to refresh your memory, which is why
I am sending you a copy of the documents we prepared." Among the
documents were letters from Albert Einstein recommending several
young men for scholarships, a description of a typical case written by

Marie Syrkin, a postwar list of students brought to America, a list of the schools that had accepted them, available information on what had happened to the students and where they presently resided, and a letter from one of the recipients just after he arrived in the United States. The letter is as follows:

I am so happy and glad that it is impossible to find the proper words to thank you for everything. Since I am in this country everybody is so good and kind to me that I simply don't want to believe it. In New York Mr. and Mrs. Freyberg treated me as their child. Marilyn is a real angel and at Rabbi Horowitz's home I feel as well as at home.

I have passed my English examination successfully and learn very hard. Rabbi Horowitz will find some job for me so I'll be able to help my aunt and uncle. I am perfectly satisfied for having the opportunity of learning, working and for having a warm home. Now I can fully realize what is the meaning of this word: Hillel. Goodness, warmth and love, those feelings what we so desperately miss in the morally destroyed Europe.

I'll write you soon and thank you very much for having given me a warm home and aims for the future.

With every good wish,

Gratefully yours
Tommy Lantos[9]

Tom Lantos (who announced his retirement in 2008) served for thirteen terms as a Congressman from California. First elected in 1980, Lantos was the Chairman and senior Democratic member of the House Committee on Foreign Affairs. He died on February 11, 2008. He was the only Holocaust survivor in the Congress.

At the end of December 1946, Marie had sent off a letter apparently describing the Congress as well as her own reasons for remaining in Europe; "*apparently*," because the contents of her letter can only be deduced from the contents of the reply. The recipient of this letter was not her husband, Charles Reznikoff, but rather Maurice Samuel. Though Samuel's response is mistakenly dated January 17, 1946, the details indicate that it is 1947. Moreover, his subsequent letter has the correct date, February 28, 1947 (Archives 1 f. 12). Both letters are on the letterhead stationery of the Hotel Berkley on 74th Street in New York City. "Dearest Marie:" Samuel begins:

Your letter of January 1st has just reached me, and has left me feeling queer and depressed. Apart from other matters, this enterprise of yours simply floors me. I don't know where you get the strength and persistence to carry on like that. I personally face the prospect of a long journey to (and through) Europe and Palestine in the spring with a sinking at the stomach. And you are condemned to Europe in the winter, and to those sights and memories which under the most favorable physical circumstances would be an unbearable strain. I think a lot about you, and wish to God you'd cut the ordeal as short as possible, so that you may come out of it without harm.

I read the reports of the Congress, and I've had personal reports too, of course. We foresaw it would be a miserable business; but worse than the Congress is the moral and spiritual condition of the movement as a whole. Zionism is becoming unrecognizable; and those of us who have cared about it as an expression of social-ethical-national as well as sociological impulses have to make some sort of stand against its frightful deterioration. You know that Wise has resigned all his offices in the American Organization, in protest. It was the wrong thing to do. All of us are responsible for the movement, whatever happens to it; and if it threatens to become, or has almost become, a mob manifestation, we can't step aside and say, "we wash our hands of it."

After remarking on the appalling destruction of cities like his own home city—Manchester, England—and even more so, Frankfurt, as well as the people in them, he laments, "I often decide that since there has been no great mass revulsion and *t'shuvah* [repentance] everything is hopeless. Only we have to carry on as if it weren't; because if it is, what's the difference?"

Marie's letter seems to have mentioned her plans to go to Frankfurt, for it reminds Maurice that he had met his wife, Gertrude, in Frankfurt in 1913. That, of course, would have been two years before he had met Marie in 1915, when she was sixteen and he, twenty. Now, thirty years after their elopement and annulment, Marie has had two more marriages and is two months shy of forty-eight; Maurice is still married to his emotionally disturbed wife, and he is fifty-two years of age. What is it that has kept this intermittent relationship going all these years?

Perhaps the fourth paragraph in his letter of January 17 offers a key to their long-lasting mutual attraction. Maurice continues:

I believe that the worst conclusion people like you and I could reach is—that our efforts are not worth-while because they can't make a head against mass corruption: the worst conclusion, because the next step is to seek mass counter-measures, and these are always corrupting. We do what we can, with books and speeches (God help us) and we are not responsible for more than we can do; for when we try to assume world responsibility, we become megalomaniacs. Well, we've got a few years before us yet, and we'll keep on honestly to the end. . . .

On February 28, Maurice writes again:

Dearest Marie: I was immensely relieved to get your letter of the 3rd. This whole matter of your European trip at a time like this depresses me continuously; and it's no good my reminding myself that others are hungrier, or perhaps colder. I can't take a philosophic attitude about it; and I wish I knew when you were coming back. There is no mention of that in your letter. . . . I leave for Europe (England first) and Palestine on the Queen Elizabeth April 24. Will you be back by then? If not, shall we meet in Europe? I am much concerned for you and fear terribly that this experience will undermine your health. Do let me know what your approximate schedule is.

The bulk of Samuel's letter is about Jewish problems and the politics of rescue and immigration, and the reception of his 1947 novel, *The Web of Lucifer,* a novel of the Renaissance Borgias, but its sub-text is an analysis of more contemporary dictators: Hitler, Mussolini, Stalin, and so on.

Perhaps the glue that still held Maurice and Marie together was their brilliance as polemicists. "Polemics is the chief instrument, the illustrious and ancient mode, of the explainer," explains Cynthia Ozick. "Maurice Samuel is above all a polemicist, assuredly the best of our time. . . . Samuel is a polemicist from beginning to end: which is to say an unrelenting critic of thought — and always from the Jewish standpoint. For Samuel the Jewish view is almost never yielded up through simple declaration or exposition; it is wrested out of engagement with, and finally a disengagement from, an alternative world view."[10] Or, perhaps, as Irving Howe has put it, "Samuel wrote 25 books: historical works, novels, tracts, literary criticism, almost all on Jewish themes but few, if any, narrowly parochial. He regarded himself as an unofficial, sometimes dissident spokesman for the values of Yiddish and the moral universe it recorded; but he was usually free of ethnic defensiveness and irritability."[11] Both Ozick and Howe point to Samuel's polemic against Arnold Toynbee, *The Professor and the Fossil* (1956), as his masterpiece.

Coincidentally — or perhaps not — Marie herself had published a celebrated sharp rejoinder to Toynbee in 1955. Was it the shared aesthetic of the art of polemics that attracted them to one another at this moment of their lives, not to mention the insight of Proverbs 5:17: "rejoice with the wife of your youth"?

During the winter months of 1947, Marie had worked hard to fulfill her onerous task of screening young applicants in the DP Camps for Hillel scholarships. She faced a population of survivors that had sunk into despair. "Not only because physical conditions were bad — and they were wretched," she wrote some years later.

The Jewish DPs were no longer gaunt figures with tragic hollow eyes we had seen in newsreels immediately after liberation; the graveyard look was gone. They could walk freely in and out of the former SS barracks that housed them. Yet the men and women I met were more bitter than in May 1945. They talked constantly about the days when Eisenhower's troops had liberated them and the GIs had showered the starvelings of Buchenwald and Dachau with sympathy, chocolate and cigarettes. *Then* the American soldiers were friendly and the Germans afraid if not ashamed; and *then* the survivors of the Nazi holocaust were sure that the world would be eager to make good the wrongs they had suffered. "We thought all doors would be opened to us," person after person said to me. Now they knew better. Their early naive hopefulness had given way to a mixture of despair, cynicism and resolution. Sick of visitors, skeptical of Committees of Inquiry, abandoned and betrayed, they were somehow determined to get out. (*State* 11, 12)

And now a selected few would have the Hillel scholarships as a ticket to liberation.

When her work in Germany was complete, Marie returned home in 1947 to continue her regular routine of teaching, writing, and lecturing. Though she remained in New York, her mind concentrated on the events in Palestine. The Zionist Congress had passed its resolution stating, "Only the establishment of a Jewish State will fulfill the original aim of the mandate. The Congress opposes any form of trusteeship to replace the mandate. It calls on the United Nations Organization and all its member states to support the demand of the Jewish people for the establishment of their own State in the Land of Israel, and their acceptance into the family of nations" (Teveth 57). There had been a conference in London at which Bevin tried to find some compromise for the

Arab-Jewish conflict, but he was unsuccessful, realizing at last that "the Arab delegation was not only opposed to the idea of a Jewish State in principle, but rejected Jewish immigration and land sales under any circumstances." Bevin and his counselors, perhaps tired of the burden of the mandate, finally threw up their hands in surrender, and in February announced in the House of Commons that the only solution for the British was to submit the problem to the United Nations, arguing that Britain "had no power under the terms of the mandate to award the country either to Jews or Arabs or to partition it between them" (Laqueur 577).

The End of the British Mandate: The UN Votes for Partition

Back in New York, the domestic home front had not changed for Marie. As she concentrated on the present world crises, her husband Charles seems to have been much absorbed in the history of the Jews of Charleston, a detailed work of nonfiction, which he published in 1950 and for which he was paid. Nothing had happened to improve their estrangement. Marie, however, was glad to be where the action was; the United Nations in 1947 was located at Lake Success on Long Island, where she could keep watch on the political jockeying. For the Zionists, the work at hand was to drum up support for the Jewish position. In April, Trygvie Lie, the Secretary General of the United Nations, summoned the first special session of the General Assembly at Flushing Meadow, New York, to address an agenda of one item: "Constituting and instructing a special committee to prepare for the consideration of the question of Palestine at the second regular session" (Official Records of the second session of the General Assembly, Supplement no. 11 United Nations Special Committee On Palestine, UNISPAL Home). The General Assembly created an eleven-member committee, the United Nations Special Committee on Palestine (UNSCOP) to investigate the Palestinian stalemate. The committee comprised delegates from Australia, Canada, Czechoslovakia, Guatemala, India, Iran, the Netherlands, Uruguay, and Yugoslavia. Over the emphatic objections of the Arabs, the UNSCOP put together an agenda of study that included a close investigation of the DP camps; the members would also visit Palestine and they would look into the current situation of the broken-down American river boat SS *Exodus 1947*, (previously, the *President Garfield*) carrying 4,500 refugees from German DP camps. On July 18, the *Exodus* was attacked and boarded by the British and instead of sending the passengers to the nearby detention camp in Cyprus, they routed them back to the French port of Sete, from which they had embarked. And when the French refused to force them to leave, the British sent them on to Hamburg where they arrived on September 8. The UNSCOP group also heard or read Golda Meir's statement of August, 26, 1947 to the National Council of Jewish Palestine, before the final destination of the *Exodus* was known. Meir pleaded,

There is almost nothing left to say about this ship which dramatically symbolizes the state not only of the Jewish people, but of the entire world as well. What has been happening these past weeks, ever since *Exodus 1947* reached the shores of Palestine and earlier, when the boat still stood outside Palestine's territorial waters, could not have taken place had not the world, after its victory over Hitler, continued to live in the moral climate created by Hitler. Most shocking, perhaps, is not what happened to the thousands in the boats, the infants, the pregnant women, the young and old. Even more shocking is the fact that not a single country, no statesman cried out in bitter protest against a world in which such events can take place.[12]

Perhaps because of ships like the *Exodus,* perhaps because of the growing information about the extent of the Holocaust, perhaps because Britain wished to extricate itself from the problems of the Mandate, perhaps because the Soviet Union desired a foothold in the Middle East, perhaps this, perhaps that, but whatever the explanation, on Saturday, November 29, 1947, the General Assembly of the United Nations voted by a majority of thirty-three to thirteen, with ten abstentions, for UNSCOP's recommendations to partition Palestine into a Jewish and Arab state, and to internationalize Jerusalem. With the Cold War at zero degrees Celsius in Moscow and thirty-two degrees Fahrenheit in Washington, with the balance of power at stake in the UN, the world was astonished to learn of the two superpowers' joint support for partition. With this, the British, hated by both sides in Palestine, prepared to depart the territory.

In Palestine, in New York, in London, in the DP camps of Europe, wherever there were Jews, there euphoria reigned. There in the streets of Jerusalem, all the alliterative synonyms together could be heard: elation, exaltation, exhilaration, and more. In his memoir, *A Tale of Love and Darkness,* Amoz Oz powerfully describes in brilliant detail that stunning Jewish moment:

There was dancing and weeping in Amos Street, in the whole of Kerem Avraham, and in all the Jewish neighborhoods, flags appeared, and slogans written on strips of cloth, car horns blared, and "Raise the banner high to Zion" and "Here in the Land our Fathers Loved," shofar blasts sounded from all the synagogues, and Torah scrolls were taken out of holy arks and were caught up in the dancing, and "God will rebuild Galilee" and "Come and behold / how great is this day." . . . the bars opened up all over the city and handed out soft drinks and snacks and even alcoholic drinks until the first light of dawn, bottles of fruit drink, beer and wine passed from hand to hand and from mouth to mouth, strangers hugged each other in the streets and kissed each other with tears, and startled English policemen were also dragged into the circles of dancers and softened up with cans of beer and sweet liqueurs, and frenzied revelers climbed on British armoured cars and waved the flag of the state that had not been established yet, but tonight, over there in Lake Success, it had been decided that it had a right to be established.[13]

This scene is a glorious description of the psychic electricity charging the neighborhood streets after the UN vote had been announced; but perhaps the most intense memory for Oz, who was a small child at the time, is his vivid recall of his father's primeval wordless outcry: "My father and mother were standing there hugging one another like two children lost in the wood, as I had never seen them before or since, and for a moment I was between them inside their hug and a moment later I was back on Father's shoulders and my very cultured, polite father was standing there shouting at the top of his voice, not words or word play or Zionist slogans, not even cries of joy, but one long naked shout like before words were invented" (*Tale* 343).

The instant response of the Arabs was rejection of the partition plan, with immediate attacks on Jewish settlements from Beirut in Lebanon to Beersheva in the south. The day following the UN's announcement, the Syrian delegate to the UN said "Arabs and Moslems throughout the world will obstruct it, and all Asia with its thousand million people will oppose it" (Gilbert 39).

The British also were opposed to partition, but they were still responsible for keeping law and order while preparing for their inevitable evacuation. They had about 100,000 troops remaining in the area, yet they did not quell the uprising, intervening only sporadically "primarily to safeguard the security of British forces and installations" (*P.D.* 313). Buses were fired upon, the Arab Higher Committee called a general strike that provoked the burning and looting of the Jewish business area near the Jaffa Gate (*P.D.* 313). There were Arab attacks, Jewish terrorist counterattacks; Arabs, Jews, and British soldiers killed and were killed in increasingly high numbers as the chaos in Palestine raged and grew increasingly savage as the months went on.

At the outset, the Arabs seized the initiative and maneuvered to cut off the roads and isolate the cities from the outlying settlements. By February, the Arabs were on the rampage throughout the country, and on March 11, 1948 they set off a bomb at the Jewish Agency in the Jerusalem city center, killing and wounding many more. The Jews tried to defend themselves, but, in Walter Laqueur's assessment of the conditions, the

Hagana was by no means as well equipped and trained a fighting detachment, as was commonly believed. Its forces and equipment were sufficient to cope with civil war, but they seemed inadequate to defend the Yishuv against regular armies. [Many of the Arabs were soldiers in the Syrian and Iraqi armies.] While Britain continued to supply arms to the neighboring Arab countries, and America had declared a general arms embargo, the Jewish forces had great difficulty in obtaining supplies. . . . Jerusalem was about to become a besieged city. The Jewish relief force sent to help the Ezion settlements had been wiped out to the last man, a terrible loss by the standards of those days. (Laqueur 583)

Yet, during the following months, even as the British moved toward relinquishing the mandate, and even after the U.S. Ambassador to the UN suggested that partition might be suspended in favor of a UN trusteeship of Palestine, and as American support (Truman included) for partition began to waiver, military conditions for the Zionists began to improve. By April, the *Haganah* assumed the offensive. There was escalating violence on both sides: the Stern Gang massacred 254 inhabitants of the Arab village of Deir Yassin; three days later the Arabs ambushed a convoy of Jewish doctors, nurses, and students on the way to Hadassah Hospital on Mount Scopus. In the fierce battle for the Jerusalem–Tel Aviv road, as the Arabs attempted to cut the city of Jerusalem off from all supplies, weapons, water, food, there was no slack in determination, no equivocation of purpose for the Jews of Palestine. They appeared to have an inspired rush of combat adrenalin.

Ben-Gurion and the Declaration of Independence

An unlikely appearing hero emerged on the international scene at this moment: the short, stocky, wild-, white-, halo-haired, tough-looking, blunt speaking, farm worker, trade unionist, autodidact inspired by the Yishuv's beloved cultural/educator Berl Katzenelson, alumnus of the British Army's 38th Battalion Jewish Legion, chairman of the Zionist Executive — David Ben-Gurion, was introduced to the outside world as the personification of the unbending will of the Jews of Palestine. First, at the end of March, Ben-Gurion formally notified the United Nations Palestine Commission that the Jews were going ahead with the organization of a provisional government. Then, at the beginning of April, the *Haganah* seized the offensive with Operation Nachshon (named after the legendary first Hebrew to set foot in the Red Sea), which was designed to open the road to Jerusalem, and for the next six weeks the *Haganah* captured Arab sections of Tiberias, Haifa, and Safed. With the battle still raging throughout April and into May, with Arabs forces from Syria, Iraq, and Egypt mounting attacks to push the Jews out of the Negev and the Galilee, the battle for the Jerusalem roads making them impassable again, and Egyptian warplanes overhead, with the British troops gradually departing, on May 14, Ben-Gurion gathered his council together in the Tel Aviv Art Museum. In his diary entry of that day, in short declarative sentences, Ben-Gurion flatly recorded the counterbalancing facts that at 11:00 A.M. he had learned of the fall of the embattled Etzion Bloc (four *kibbutzim* high on the hills between Hebron and Bethlehem), and at 4:00 P.M. the State was proclaimed:

At 11 A.M. Katriel Katz announced that the Etzion Bloc had fallen. The women were taken to Jerusalem and the men taken prisoner. At 1 P.M. the National Council met. The text of the Declaration of Independence was approved. At 4 o'clock independence was declared. The country went wild with joy. But, as on November 29, I refrained from rejoicing. The state was established. Our fate now rests in the hands of the defense forces.[14]

Because the Declaration was proclaimed late on Friday, just before the Sabbath, the *Palestine Post* had to wait until Sunday, May 16, to announce in the bold letters of its headline: "State of Israel Is Born," followed by the statement "The first independent Jewish State in 19 centuries was born in Tel Aviv as the British Mandate over Palestine came to an end at midnight on Friday, and it was immediately subjected to the test of fire. As '*Medinat Yisrael*' [State of Israel] was proclaimed, the battle for Jerusalem raged, with most of the city falling to the Jews."

Upon the termination of the British Mandate at midnight of May 14, the sovereign Jewish State of Israel came into being in Palestine on the stroke of twelve. Although Ben-Gurion had reacted with great restraint, and although the ceremony ended with Rabbi Fishman pronouncing the traditional "*Shehekheyanu*" benediction (we have lived to see this day), with everyone silently standing at attention as the Palestine Philharmonic played the national anthem *Hatikvah*, the throngs in the streets reacted with exuberance. "Outside, the fever of nationalism was spreading with fond embraces, warm handshakes and kisses. Street vendors were selling flags, crowds gathered to read posted bulletins, and newspapers were being sold everywhere. As the Sabbath had started there was not the degree of public rejoicing that there would have been any other day," the *New York Times* correspondent reported. But when word was received that President Truman of the United States had changed course and *de facto* recognized the new government, "there was great cheering and drinking of toasts in this blackened city. . . . The effect on the people, especially those drinking late in Tel Aviv's coffee houses, was electric. They even ran into the blackness of the streets shouting, cheering and toasting the United States" (*New York Times*, May 15, p. 2).

President Truman's recognition came at 6:00 P.M. Washington, D.C., time — eleven minutes after the Declaration had been read. Two days later, Dr. Chaim Weizmann, who had sent a telegram to President Truman on April 9, stating "The choice for our people, Mr President, is between statehood and extermination," was elected President of the new State of Israel. On May 17, eight more nations recognized the new state: Czechoslovakia, Guatemala, Nicaragua, Poland, South Africa, Soviet Union, Uruguay, and Yugoslavia. But on that momentous Friday night, the Arab attack on the newly formed State of Israel commenced. The next day, six Arab armies — Egypt, Iraq, Lebanon, Saudi Arabia, Syria, and Transjordan — invaded. This was the beginning of the full-blown wars, the wars of attrition, and the *intifadas* that have continued virtually unabated until the time of this writing. Fierce fighting at the outset, with Arab advances, threatened to snuff out the very life of the infant State. Yet despite the odds, and despite Israel's lack of an air force, heavy artillery, or heavy equipment, despite the exhaustion of the *Haganah*

(soon to be called the Israel Defense Forces), the IDF put up fierce resistance, bolstered by the arrival of fighter planes from Czechoslovakia.
After savage fighting, the Arab Legion that had been stopped only
thirty-five kilometers from Tel Aviv managed to capture the stranded
Jewish Quarter in the Old City of Jerusalem, but it was unable to break
through to the New City. The IDF also was unable to rout the Arab Legion from Latrun, which controlled the road to Jerusalem. But in the
dead of night, with remarkable ingenuity, and backbreaking undercover
work on the mountainous cliffs leading to Jerusalem, the IDF built the
so-called "Burma Road"—an alternative route to the besieged city, and
brought in food and military supplies, thus saving it from starvation
and capitulation. When it became clear that the Israeli counterattack
had gained strength and made significant gains, the Security Council
called for a truce, which came into effect on July 18, 1948. It was, however, an edgy truce: one-sixth of the Israeli population, 100,000 citizens, remained in the armed forces; Count Bernadotte of the UN suggested excluding the Negev from the new State; many Arabs did not
accept the truce, and the Arab Legion continued to reject the UN's
recognition of a Jewish State. At the outset of the Partition Plan, the Syrian delegate to the UN had declared that "Arabs and Moslems throughout the world will obstruct it, and all Asia with its thousand million will
oppose it" (Gilbert 39–48). How prescient were those words.

During the critical months between the UN partition plan of November 1947 and the May 14 Declaration of Independence, Marie
Syrkin had remained in the United States. She was, of course, completely consumed with the tumultuous events in Palestine. Friends and
acquaintances who came to America from abroad kept her immediately
up-to-date. In January of 1948, Marie's close friend Golda Meir arrived
in New York to raise desperately needed funds for arms for the embattled *Yishuv*. Marie had last seen her only the year before in Palestine,
but this time she was startled by the change in Golda's appearance. "I
saw Golda two days after her arrival," Marie has written. "She looked
more than a year older, and sad. Perhaps 'sad' is the wrong adjective; it
suggests melancholy, and melancholy suggests passivity—a quality foreign to her" (*Way* 197). However, Marie admiringly notes that in the
two and half months that Golda spent in the United States, she raised
fifty million dollars. Golda then returned to Palestine in April as a member of the Zionist Executive, eager to participate in the debate about the
pros and cons of declaring an independent state. Here, Marie deliber-

ately points out that Meir was among the thirty-seven signatories to Israel's Declaration of Independence — one of only two women, Rachel Kagan of Wizo and Golda Meyerson (*Woman* 209).

Within two days of the Declaration, just after the Sabbath, Golda made her way back to America. "She was being bombarded with cables from the United States, assuring her that if she would fly to America immediately she would be able to translate the excitement about the emergence of Israel into needed millions" (*Woman* 209). But this time she returned to the United States as the emissary from the new State of Israel. Golda's old friend, Marie Syrkin, had celebrated the Declaration of Independence in New York with friends and now eagerly awaited Golda's arrival and a jubilant reunion.

When I saw her shortly after her arrival, she stopped in the middle of a conversation and said with an almost childish delight, "We have a state; imagine, we have a state." This simple, almost naive pleasure was in its way more touching than the historic solemnity with which the event was formally hailed by her and other spokesmen at public celebrations. The joy was personal, intimate. I realized then, as I realized in other contacts with Israelis, how much longer one lifetime of direct involvement was than 2,000 years of abstract longing. For the rest of us it was the fulfillment of the Zionist dream, and great though this was, the feeling was not as vivid or keen as that of the most ordinary citizen of Israel whose life had been lived in the land." (*Valor* 231)

Marie comments as well that on this visit "the Emissary . . . was a very different person from the tense, tight-lipped woman I had seen five months earlier when she had come from the embattled Yishuv. Despite the fact that . . . the situation was even more precarious — the five invading armies had already crossed the borders of the new state — Golda was radiant" (*Valor* 231).

Marie had intended to fly to Israel with Golda soon after the June 11 truce was signed, but that plan had to be scrapped because Golda had experienced complications in the form of blood clots and phlebitis after suffering a leg fracture in an auto accident. The phlebitis would plague Meir for the rest of her life. Despite the fact that Golda had just been appointed Israeli Minister to Moscow, she was now confined to her bed in the Hospital for Joint Diseases and would probably have to remain there for a few weeks. Marie, however, impatient to get back to what was now "Israel," could not be deterred, even by her friend Golda's serious condition.

The Truce and the Arab Exodus

Though the truce had been signed just before Marie Syrkin arrived in late June of 1948, the dangers were still immediately apparent. Nonetheless, despite the threatening facts on the ground, there was the exhilaration that the State of Israel after centuries of exile had actually come into existence. Soon after her arrival, she assessed the mood of the country: "I have heard many attempts to characterize this period. Even the seasoned veterans of the struggle are groping for words to express their sense of wonder at what has come to pass. Indeed the word *ness* [miracle] is the one heard most frequently. A current joke divides the population into three classes: pessimists, optimists, and nessimists, and the latter seem to have won the day" (*State* 81).

Marie Syrkin's presence in the nascent state gave her a bird's eye view of the War of Independence that would continue to rage on for six more months, as Arab irregulars mounted continuous attacks on Jewish settlements; as Egyptian forces fought to seize the Negev; as fighting in the Galilee, on the coast, in the cities, throughout the country persisted; as the IDF resisted and counterattacked. What she experienced and what she learned she reported in a lengthy, detailed article titled "The Siege of Jerusalem" (*Frontier*, December 1948). On January 5, 1949, Egypt, facing mounting losses in manpower, territory, and materiel, agreed to negotiate the Armistice that the UN Security Council had called for in November. A truce was once again imposed on January 7. But there would be long-lasting fallout.

The UN estimated that during the nine months between April and December, three quarters of a million Arabs had fled Palestine. That figure, however, has since been challenged by historians on the left, right, and center; and the cause of the flight has been explained by Arabs and Jews from every political perspective. From the pro-Arab side, the conventional argument was that Israeli aggression forced the exodus; from the pro-Israeli side, the contention was that the Arab leaders and the Mufti of Jerusalem urged the Palestinians to flee. The facts, without question, are far more complex and have been revisited and argued beginning in 1948 and continuing until this day. One thing, however, seems clear: this event is the matrix out of which the current hostilities in the Israeli/Palestinian conflict were born and were nurtured.

When Marie set foot for the first time on what in her absence had be-

come the State of Israel, she could not catch her breath for the powerful emotions that overwhelmed her. Yet she was all too aware of the dangers that were still to be passed. Moreover, the Arab exodus was, as she
has put it, "in full swing." She had returned to Israel with a reputation
as one of the most important journalists in the Jewish world, respected
for her keen intellect and her ability to put her strong polemical stances
into clear but adroit sentences. She immediately was asked to draw up a
report on the Arab exodus and the Israeli treatment of the holy places
for the newly formed Israeli Bureau of Information. For this project,
she was provided with two traveling companions, a driver and a translator. The translator proved to be something of a misogynist who resented having to deal with a woman on the strenuous trip they were to
take through the Galilee. Marie, when recounting this trip, was eager to
insist that she asked for no help, even when walking on rocks or crossing streams. She was, at the time of the trip, forty-nine years old. The
trip was to result in a report of the Israeli government to the United Nations on the subject of Israel's treatment of the Holy places. Marie
Syrkin was charged with writing that report.

By this time, it was clear to Marie that her domestic life with Charles
Reznikoff was over—though neither she nor Charles made any move
toward a divorce. On leave from high school teaching, she accepted a
position for the year in the Ministry of Foreign Affairs in Tel Aviv, in
order to consider the idea of permanent residence. Meanwhile, long
distance, she continued her work at the *Jewish Frontier,* and wrote for
other publications, including a monthly article for *Jewish Affairs,* the
monthly journal for South African Jewry. Marie's work for the Ministry
for Foreign Affairs in the Press and Information Division had made her
a prominent figure in Israeli political journalism; an indispensable member of the Jewish press with close ties to the highest-ranking political
leaders in the Labor Zionist government. Yet, she still was not at all sure
that she wished to make *aliyah.* Her lack of Hebrew was, of course, a
great drawback. Her family was in America, and in those days, commuting between the Middle East and New York was not an everyday journey. At one point, Golda tried to interest her in becoming the editor of
the *Jerusalem Post;* but again, though the *Post* was an English-language
paper, Marie's lack of Hebrew made it impossible. Now, fifty years of
age, she wanted time to figure out what to do with the rest of her years.

By March 1949, Marie Syrkin was back in New York. Abe Herman at
the Foreign Ministry wrote to her at the *Frontier,* "Just a note to inform

you that Walter Eytan has agreed to our request that you be given six
months unpaid leave as from the 14th of March, 1949. Walter added to
his note to us the following proviso: 'but I want to be sure she comes
back.' All I can do is re-echo this remark. Would you please get in touch
with Aubrey [Abba] Eban at the earliest opportunity in order to take
up with him the question of handling the Jerusalem stuff." In April, she
was informed that the Press and Information Division and most of its
staff was to be detached from the Foreign Ministry and to form a special
Division attached to the Prime Minister's Office. In New York, she had
met Moshe Sharrett, the Foreign Minister and requested a few conditions for her future work; she would like to stay in close contact with the
United States and would like to spend a few months a year there as well.
In May, Marie received a letter from Abe Herman on the stationery of
the Office of the Prime Minister, Press and Information Division, informing her that the transfer of office had been made and the new director would be Gershon Agronsky. "The Prime Minister's Office," Herman wrote, "has been informed that you are away on leave and will
be returning. Naturally this means that your job is awaiting you on
return. . . . I hope it does not make you feel too bad if I emphasize how
much we have missed you not only personally but also in relation to
your work. We have been hard put to it to find anyone adequate to replace you and the position now is that we have given up the attempt. We
are, in fact, counting very much on your coming back" (Archives 1 f. 14).

Such a letter had to have produced mixed emotions. On the one
hand, who could refuse such a flattering invitation? On the other, she
was really not certain that she wished to take up permanent residence in
Israel. At her age the prospect of such a total change and commitment
was daunting. But rescue was at hand. As Marie simply put it in her
memoir of her husband Charles, "A *deus ex machina* appeared in 1950
through my appointment to the English Department of newly established Brandeis University in Massachusetts. Two books I had published
were responsible for deliverance from high school drudgery" (*Man and
Poet* 51). The real truth was that Abram L. Sachar was now the President
of Brandeis University. He had followed her career and knew that although Marie Syrkin did not have the standard academic requirement,
the Ph.D., she had a very substantial and unique non-standard vita.

Chapter 14

Academia at Last

The Brandeis Years

MARIE SYRKIN CLAIMED that the president of the newly established Brandeis University, Abram Sachar, had offered her a position in the Humanities Department on the basis of two of her books. With this, she further claimed, President Sachar became the *deus ex machina* who rescued her from the choice of two unsatisfactory courses of action: emigration to Israel or a continuation of her disintegrating domestic situation (*Man and Poet* 51). This, however, was a modestly imprecise description of Sachar's offer and of her own decision to accept it. Ever since Marie's college days at Cornell University, she had longed to have a Ph.D., to be a member of the academic intellectual community as a professor of English Literature. Now, in 1950, at the age of fifty-one, with that dream all but vaporized, Marie's fantasy became fact.

A quarter of a century later, Abram Sachar published his memoir of the beginnings of Brandeis University as it developed from a bankrupt veterinarian-cum-medical school in Waltham, Massachusetts, into the first Jewish-sponsored nonsectarian, privately funded liberal arts college in the United States. Brandeis' first twenty-plus years were the years of Sachar's incumbency as its president. In his account of those years, Dr. Sachar described the criteria by which the earliest faculty was chosen, Marie Syrkin included. His words make it clear that his choice did not rest simply on two of her books.

Marie Syrkin came to us out of the New York high school system with few of the degrees and awards that look impressive in a vita. Apparently she needed none. She was a superb teacher and a prolific writer. Her father, Nahum [*sic*]

Syrkin, one of the world's great Zionist leaders, a contemporary of Herzl and Nordau, had opened to her family extraordinary opportunities to see the world through the shapers of our time and he described them and their contributions in a style that was penetrating and perceptive. Her *Blessed Is the Match,* the moving story of the Jewish resistance movement and the embers plucked from the burning in the holocaust period revealed a talent that was worth watching.[1]

Marie Syrkin arrived on the Brandeis campus in the fall of 1950. She was just in time for the fall semester of incoming students, approximately 225 freshmen and sophomores. There were no senior students, as the school was just entering its third year of classes. At fifty-one years of age, Marie was no longer the young beauty in a striking bonnet as she appears in a photographic portrait of 1917. A bit heavier now, her short black hair showing strands of grey, was pulled back with a few curls resting at the nape; prominent dark eyebrows arched over a perfectly straight, but slightly upturned nose above shapely lipsticked lips. She was older, but still beautiful. Marie liked clothes, but she was never given to *haute couture* and tended toward tailored dresses or suits, nylon stockings, and sensible shoes—the better to stand throughout the day's classes. Perhaps her years in a New York City high school made her too unaccustomed to teaching while seated. She was a mature, middle-aged professor of Humanities who was addressed by her students as Miss Syrkin. She was, moreover, the first (and only, in that year) female professor of an academic subject at Brandeis.

When Marie Syrkin arrived in Waltham, Massachusetts, just before the fall semester began, the first item on her agenda was to find a place to live. She has written that "in 1950 Charles seemed to agree with my decision to move to New England. The $60 a month flat on 18th Street would now be his sole responsibility as I would have to manage on the modest salary of $5500, the going rate for an assistant professor" (*Man and Poet* 52). Since Marie did not drive a car, it was important for her to live as close to the campus as possible. She found an adequate apartment on the second floor of a development of very undistinguished garden apartments that accommodated a few teachers and mostly working people. It was located less than a mile from the university, in an area on the edge of Waltham known as Roberts. The three-room apartment had little to recommend it; true, the rent was not high, it was close enough to the university for Marie to walk there (she was a good walker), and it was very near the Roberts commuter train stop, which went to Porter

Square in Cambridge and to Boston, but it was also quite isolated and lonely. Not surprisingly, she did not last more than a couple of years there. It had not taken Marie long to make a new circle of friends, most of whom lived in Cambridge. She struck up a very close and long-lasting friendship with Denah Lida, who later headed the Spanish program at Brandeis and whose husband was a professor at Harvard. By 1953, Marie had moved to 24 Concord Avenue in Cambridge.

The new apartment was situated close to Harvard Square, on a quiet street with trees, and no trolley or bus lines. After a couple of years of the isolation of Waltham, she was exhilarated by the new intellectually heady Cambridge atmosphere. Her living room was furnished in the then popular style of Danish Modern: light wood with a nubby beige fabric for her sofa. Had she lived into the twenty-first century, Marie would be amused to find that her trendy new furniture had become collectors' items known as "retro" and sold at very high prices. There were reproductions on the walls, a phonograph, and stuffed bookcases — and a kitchen that did not get heavy-duty use. I was once invited to a dinner there that included "virtuous carrots" and canned S.S. Pierce whole chicken. Marie may have had a lifetime relationship with sweets, but she did not love cooking. One of the reproductions on her living room wall was of Chagall's famous green-faced rabbi wearing *tefillin* (phylacteries). Its glass had a crack over the Hebrew word *hai* (life). Charles had written a poem about it, but Marie took it with her when she moved to New England, remarking to visitors, in ironic *sotto voce,* that such is the state of orthodoxy today.

In her very first years at Brandeis, Marie was fortunate to have a few friends living right on campus. She had known Ludwig Lewisohn from her Zionist activities and admired him as a critic and novelist. He had come to Brandeis at postretirement age, though with an international reputation as an eminent man of letters; but it was Louise, Ludwig Lewisohn's fourth wife, with whom Marie developed a friendship that would last long past Ludwig's death in 1955. The Lewisohns had been given an apartment on the ground floor of "the Castle," a replica of a medieval fortress castle — once part of the veterinarian school, now a women's dormitory. The Lewisohns, in fact, became rather unofficial self-appointed hosts who entertained visiting dignitaries, faculty, and students alike in their refurbished Castle apartment.

There were others in the early years who Marie either knew from the past, such as Max Lerner, or some with whom she struck up new friendships, such as Milton and Eva Hindus and Frank and Fritzi Manuel; and there were two members of the English faculty whose arrival in 1953 was something of a coup for President Sachar: Irving Howe, the editor of *Dissent* and well-known literary critic; and Philip Rahv, the literary critic and founder of *Partisan Review*. They were to prove a vexatious pair of colleagues for Marie. Though brilliant in their field — considered linch-pins of the so-called New York Jewish Intellectual cohort — they were rather arrogant in their attitudes towards those who held opposing ideological views or whom they deemed intellectually unworthy. The anti-Stalinist but still Marxist *Partisan Review* group had little in com-mon with the "other" New York Jewish Intellectuals, the editors and readers of the affirmatively Jewish *Jewish Frontier, Menorah Journal,* or *Reconstructionist*. As Irving Howe himself described the "New York In-tellectuals" in *Commentary* in 1968, they have "a common focus of intel-lectual interests; and once you get past politeness — which becomes, these days, easier and easier — a common ethnic origin [Jewish]. They are, or until recently have been anti-Communist; they are, or until some time ago were, radicals; they have a fondness for ideological specula-tion; they write literary criticism with a strong social emphasis; they revel in polemic; they strive self-consciously to be 'brilliant'; and by birth or osmosis, they are Jews." To this last defining clause, Howe added, that they were the "first group of Jewish writers to come out of the immi-grant milieu who did not define themselves through a relationship nos-talgic or hostile to memories of Jewishness."[2] To this, Marie Syrkin might have asked, "How, then, *did* they define themselves Jewishly — simply through the accident of birth? Or perhaps through their alien-ation from their Jewishness?" She also might have reminded Howe that he and his friends came quite late to recognize either the trauma of the Holocaust or the painful birth of the State of Israel; the unfolding of Soviet Russian history was more compelling for many of them than the fate of the Jews. Later, Howe would freely admit to this.

It was thus that the two groups of intellectuals, the New York Jew-ish Intellectuals and the affirmative "other" New York Jewish Intellectu-als came face to face when Abram Sachar caused the twain to meet at Brandeis.[3] In an ironic twist of American Jewish history, Philip Rahv and Irving Howe were employed at the same institution as Marie Syrkin, Ludwig Lewisohn, and a bit later, Syrkin's fellow editor at the *Jewish Frontier,* Ben Halpern. This promised to cause some high anxiety for Marie within a few years.

Marie began her first year at Brandeis teaching the conventional curriculum: Survey of British Literature, Shakespeare, and Introduction to
Poetry; but it would not be long before she would introduce innovative
materials. She was likely the first university professor to offer a course in
American Jewish literature. Some time in the early 1960s Marie scrawled
some ideas for such a course and noted the seriousness of the popular
novelist Edna Ferber; this recognition was well in advance of the much
later feminist rediscovery of Ferber as a politically engaged, Jewish-
American feminist writer. Syrkin's notes became the syllabus for a
course she would offer many times, as well as for her 1964 essay in *The
American Jew,* edited by Oscar Janowsky, entitled "Jewish Awareness in
American Literature." Another "first" for Marie was the course on
Holocaust literature that she introduced in the early 1960s. The material
of her course was condensed into what was to have been a series of essays exploring "The Literature of the Holocaust." The first essay begins
with the following explanation:

Last year I undertook to give a course on the Literature of the Holocaust at
Brandeis University. The attempt to define the scope of the course for the university catalogue and to draw up a book list indicated the peculiar problems
which beset such an endeavor. The difficulty lay not merely in the lack of familiar guide-lines: the absence of well-tried texts, comfortable anthologies with
notes and critical studies of the period. While any course in a fresh field might
present this challenge, its content would be determined by more or less defined
criteria. The literature of the Holocaust, however, eludes the usual classifica-
tions because of the very nature of its theme. The accepted literary categories —
novels, plays, verse, essays — are unsatisfactory because they assume a measure
of formal achievement to warrant consideration; there are minimal standards
for our imagination and too close for critical perspective — for even the smallest
of the Elizabethan or Victorian small fry. But when we deal with the Holocaust —
an event too awful for our imagination and too close for critical perspective —
the whole jargon of literary criticism seems an impertinence.[4]

The literary categories Syrkin suggests are: first, the diaries — on-the-
scene accounts ranging from the innocence of an Anne Frank to the sophisticated "passionate historian" Emannuel Ringelblum or the educa-
tor Chaim Kaplan. Of this genre, Marie points out that "whatever the
degree of foreboding — and the mature men in the Warsaw ghetto have
few illusions or hope — the impact of events is registered without benefit

of hindsight; the reader knows what is hidden from the writer. This tragic irony makes the diaries peculiarly moving and differentiates them from the many circumstantial accounts which will be written by survivors after a lapse of years." Syrkin's first (and only) *Midstream* essay is devoted to this genre. Further issues of the Journal were intended to discuss the Holocaust as reflected in two other genres: "Memoirs written in retrospect and in completed knowledge," and "Works of the imagination which, in fiction and verse, seek to recreate the experience." For some inexplicable reason, Marie never did publish the intended further studies. She did, however, teach her course in 1964 — ten years before Lawrence Langer's 1975 groundbreaking work, *The Holocaust and the Literary Imagination,* a work that Marie herself welcomed and praised as a brilliant analysis. Nonetheless, Marie's course in the Literature of the Holocaust at Brandeis may well be the first of the abundance of courses since then and currently being taught in universities throughout the world.

During her first years as an academic, Marie had to make a slight intellectual adjustment: she would continue in her role at the *Frontier* as editor and commentator on the political scene, and she would remain active in the Zionist movement; but if she wanted to be promoted and granted tenure at Brandeis, she would have to produce traditional scholarship as well. She came to Brandeis in 1950 — this meant that she would be eligible for tenure discussions in six years, and this meant that she had best produce a book. There would be no dearth of articles on a variety of important subjects, one of the best a rejoinder to Arnold Toynbee in *Jewish Frontier* in 1954. Toynbee had written eight volumes of his *Study of History.* In the last volume, he wrote a chapter entitled "The Modern West and the Jews." With little pretense of the erudition one might expect in an attack upon the learned Professor Toynbee's argument, Marie Syrkin began her polemic:

I make no pretense to the scholarship required for an evaluation of Mr. Toynbee's monumental work as a whole, and I approach the Toynbean sweep and erudition as humbly as most of his fascinated readers. But in the chapter on the Jews the author is not discussing Hindu, Babylonic [*sic*] or Andean societies. Here he is on familiar territory and his statements are no longer obscured by the aura of his formidable and mysterious learning. When one has finished this chapter the vision of Toynbee, half mystic, half historian, pointing to God's web on the loom of time, becomes a bit shaky. The robes of the prophet drag all too plainly in the dust of human bias and error.

The bias and error refers to the current situation in the Middle East and Mr. Toynbee's anti-Jewish and pro-Arab prejudices, which appear "most spectacularly in a section of his chapter significantly headed 'The Fate of the European Jews and the Palestinian Arabs, A.D., 1933–1948.' "The equation" Syrkin argues, "between the fate of European Jewry and of the Palestinian Arabs is made in the very title." She admits that Toynbee seems adequately "appalled by the 'maniacal sadism'" of the Nazis, and that he deplores the "moral nadir to which the Germans sank," but she points out that

Toynbee permits himself the following sentiments: "But the Nazi Gentiles' fall from grace was less tragic than the Zionist Jews." On the morrow of a persecution in Europe in which they had been the victims of the worst atrocities ever suffered by Jews or indeed by any other human beings, the Jews immediate reaction to their experience was to become persecutors in their turn for the first time since A.D. 135 — and this at the first opportunity that had arisen for them to inflict on other human beings who had done the Jews no injury, but who happened to be weaker than they were, some of the wrongs and sufferings that had been inflicted on the Jews.

Syrkin adds, "Mr. Toynbee sanctimoniously concludes the indictment with the blasphemous statement that, 'On the Day of Judgement the gravest crime to the German Nationalists' account might not be that they had exterminated a majority of Western Jews but that they had caused the surviving remnant of Jewry to stumble.'" Syrkin's rejoinder to this piece of prophetic interpretation is the barbed understatement, "Such sensitiveness to Jewish virtue can only be explained by a whole-hearted indifference to Jewish survival."

The rest of the Toynbee interpretation of current events regarding the flight of the Arabs from Palestine and their present situation in refugee camps, Syrkin rebuts with facts drawn from available texts, reports, Arab radio broadcasts, the Arab press, and from her own presence on the scene. No wonder she concludes her attack with an "impious question: If this is how the great historian treats a local and contemporary moment, just how erudite is the rest of the vast erudition?"[5] Coincidentally, or perhaps not coincidentally, two years later in 1956, Maurice Samuel published his fine book, *The Professor and the Fossil: Some Observations on Arnold Toynbee's A Study of History.*[6]

Nonetheless, despite Syrkin's stinging essay about the British professor, unless she produced a full-length book in a couple of years, she herself would not be promoted to Associate Professor. Fortunately, she already had begun work on such a book: *Way of Valor: A Biography of Golda Meyerson*. This was a risky project, and Marie knew it. She was certainly aware that her colleagues in the English Department would be dismissive of what would be regarded as a piece of ideological propaganda, and not a serious work of scholarship. Indeed, in a conversation that I personally overheard on the Brandeis campus of those years, Irving Howe, walking and conversing with his colleague, Philip Rahv, mentioned Marie Syrkin's name. Rahv guffawed, and responded, "Marie Syrkin? She's no intellectual — she thinks that *The Great Gatsby* is about bootleggers!"

Had Marie overheard that conversation, she still would not have been deterred. She had encountered other skeptics closer to her ideological home. By this time, Golda Meyerson had become world famous as Israel's first Minister to Moscow (the Soviet recognition of Israel had been immediate and required a positive diplomatic response). When the new minister appeared at the Moscow Synagogue on the Jewish High Holidays of 1948, 40,000 Jews famously congregated in the streets to catch a glimpse of her and to hail her and the State of Israel. Marie included in her biography the historic photograph of Golda Meyerson in the center of the throngs of Soviet Jews nearly crushing her on that momentous day. But at this time, as well known as Meyerson had become in the outside world as a spokesperson for the State of Israel, in the new State itself, she had assumed a less attention-getting role as Labor Minister. Marie's decision to write her friend's biography puzzled her colleagues. Certainly the English department at Brandeis did not regard it as an appropriate work of scholarship; and even in the new State the response was tepid. Why then, I asked her outright, *did* she choose to write this book? Marie answered my question directly and quite simply:

She's everything I'm not. I really admired this kind of person — though I'm much cleverer than she is — but she had virtues that seemed to me so impressive. Were I to write about Golda today I would have to add many elements to my evaluation of her. She retained many of her virtues, but to say that power doesn't go to your head is nonsense. It doesn't corrupt — it did not corrupt her, but it certainly altered her. . . . You become so inured to praise that it doesn't mean anything anymore and you take for granted all these endless compliments and these multitudes chasing you, and it becomes really wearying, but if you lose it you may miss it if it's suddenly not there. But Golda never had a chance to miss it, though she didn't die as Prime Minister. (Personal interview)

The biography appeared in 1955. The following year Marie Syrkin came up for tenure. Not surprisingly, the department was split. She had the support of men like Thomas Savage, Osborne Earle, and her most vigorous advocate, Milton Hindus. Ludwig Lewisohn had died the year before. The main detractors were Irving Howe and Philip Rahv. It was clear that they would find her scholarship wanting. First, they could claim that the subject of her book was inappropriate; that they were not Zionist sympathizers certainly was not in Marie's favor.[7] Even more so, they probably argued that her book had no scholarly apparatus. No footnotes, no bibliography, no index. (The fact that Irving Howe's 1952 critical study of Faulkner had no apparatus either, was beside the point.) Her supporters might contend that Marie was a journalist who was unaccustomed to providing scholarly documentation, but that was hardly a justification, and might only buttress her opponents' accusation that she was no intellectual. Then too, gender bias may have played a role. Rahv and Howe certainly were not opposed to female intellectuals — at least ones that they themselves had chosen as colleagues, such as Mary McCarthy or Hannah Arendt, but Marie Syrkin, they maintained, was *not* an intellectual, and they had *not* chosen to include her in their personal pantheon of cerebral women.

After a tough battle, with her friend, Milton Hindus, in the vanguard as her persevering advocate, Marie Syrkin won her tenure and promotion at Brandeis. This left her free to pursue her own research, writing, and curricula predilections. Nonetheless, Marie may have been not a little unsettled by the tenure fight and by the fact that the biography did not receive nearly the widespread favorable reception of the two preceding books. Disappointment may explain why she did not save as many reviews as she would for her later revisions of the book in 1963 and 1969. But the work (which perhaps too clearly was a labor of love) had been published and she was now Associate Professor Marie Syrkin. Her attention would turn to a project she had had in mind since 1951. Her father Nachman had died on September 6, 1924 and had been buried in New York. He was reburied in Kinnereth, Israel, on September 6, 1951. "The true moment of the memorial," Marie has written, "came twenty seven years . . . [after Nachman Syrkin's death] when Ben-Gurion stepped out of the shadows on the shore of Kinnereth and vowed at the re-interment: 'Syrkin, your vision shall be fulfilled'" (*Memoir* 228). It was at this moment that his daughter vowed to play a part in the fulfillment of that vision; she would write a biographical memoir of her father, the great personality whose life was devoted to a passionate advocacy for socialist Zionism as a solution to the "Jewish problem." In 1960, Marie Syrkin's, *Nachman Syrkin: Socialist Zionist: A Biographical Memoir and Selected Essays,* was published. In the preface, she writes, "Perhaps nothing could better indicate the triumph of the idea [the synthesis of socialism and Zionism] than the fact that most of the surviving friends and comrades of my father, whose recollections I sought, were to be found in the realized Jewish State of which Nachman Syrkin had dreamed. The house in which I stayed while gathering material for this biography, too, had its poignant fitness: I wish to thank Golda Meir, Foreign Minister of Israel, for her friendship and hospitality during the months I spent in her home in Jerusalem" (*Memoir* 7). The dedication reads: "For Zivia, daughter of Nachman, and David, his grandson." This volume was more warmly received than the biography of Golda Meyerson (Meir); accounts of parent-child relationships, particularly when the parent is long dead, permit greater frankness than that of good friends who are living.

On March 2, 1961, Maurice Samuel wrote to Marie Syrkin:

I stayed up most of last night reading your book, and I have been so shaken by it that I have to write you immediately, lest I become paralyzed by reflection. . . . It's a very beautiful book, Marie, because of its honesty, and (am I misled by personal involvement?) The central expression of your personal relationship to the subject is in the passage on page 156. "as I grew into womanhood many personal conflicts were to arise between my father and me. In his relationship to his daughter he was as dramatic, self-willed and sure of his rightness as in all other aspects of his life. But the difficulty of that struggle is as much mine as his and its details, since they involve others still alive, must be omitted." I remember how great I knew your father to be, and how I hated his self righteousness. I remember my occasional conviction that if he had been gentle, kind, "understanding," you and I would have remained together. (There's probably little foundation to the idea). (Archives 1 f. 12)

In this, Samuel may or may not have been right—but at that moment, Marie and Charles Reznikoff, mostly living apart, but getting together in New York "for an occasional weekend and for holidays" (*Man and*

Poet 53) were not divorced and never would be. Samuel, who had been married to Gertrude Kahn for forty years, would at last divorce her and marry Edith Brodsky one year after writing this letter of lost love to Marie.

At the time of Marie's departure to New England, Charles remained in their apartment on 18th Street in New York. She has written that at the time she did not realize the bitterness of his resentment of her leaving. But many years later, after his death, an unpublished "scarcely veiled autobiographical novel" he had written during the period after departure was discovered among his papers. "I was totally unaware of its composition," she confessed,

> though even during the years of our separation he generally showed me what he had been writing. His secrecy in regard to *The Manner Music* was the one exception and with good reason.[8] A major theme of the novel, in addition to its Hollywood ambience, is the dilemma of the creative artist whose work will not earn his keep and who is abandoned to his fate by uncomprehending relatives and friends. The wife of the main character, a composer, is a petulant, pretty, notably unsympathetic female Zionist, a high school teacher who tactlessly keeps complaining about her fatigue and lets her talented, unappreciated husband end his poverty-stricken quest in Bellevue. A *roman a clef* with a vengeance! . . . I read Charles' novel in 1976 in sorrow at the intensity of the suffering revealed. I had not suspected his anguished sense of abandonment because while the fundamental problem depicted in the book was searingly real, the actual facts were far less dramatic than the fiction. I could well understand why, though the novel was the most powerful and accomplished prose work he ever wrote, he never breathed a word of its existence to me even in the years after my return from Brandeis.

To this confession Marie Syrkin adds, "He had been less hesitant in verse" (*Man and Poet* 52).

When the separation discussion first began, there had been a period of mutual worry about how they would manage financially. Yet, contrary to Marie's expectations, Charles soon undertook a number of projects that, as Marie explains, "provided him with a modest, by our standards adequate, livelihood: first, the writing of the history of the Jewish community of Charleston, then a history of the Jewish community of Cleveland (which he never completed), and subsequently, the editing of the papers of Louis Marshall." Marshall was a constitutional lawyer,

president of the American Jewish Committee, and defender of Leo
Frank; his papers were published as *Louis Marshall: Champion of Liberty;
Selected Papers and Addresses* (Philadelphia, JPS 1957). But when this proj-
ect came to an end in 1957, Marie explained, they were both troubled:

My hard hearted announcement that he would have to manage his own affairs
had long shriveled. I was then editor of *Jewish Frontier,* [Hayim Greenberg had
died in 1953] a Labor Zionist monthly with much ideology and little money.
Fortuitously, the only paid employee, the managing editor who ran the magazine in New York, left for richer pastures. My comrades agreed that since the
basic responsibility for the magazine would remain mine, Charles could be entrusted with the post just vacated. . . . Though Charles was relieved that his
economic problem had been settled on a long term basis, he was both resentful
of the chores the job entailed, and needlessly painstaking in their execution.
With no aptitude for journalism he despised the facile generalizations of the
craft and the superficial editorials that would have to be dashed off in response
to a current crisis. (*Man and Poet* 53)

Marie's major complaints about Charles' temptation to apply artistic
standards to the articles of an underfunded political journal notwithstanding, she is quick to point out (somewhat patronizingly) that at the
Frontier office, though no one had an idea of the quality of his work,
"everyone liked him: he seemed gentle and acquiescent. At the printers
he was a favorite. They forgave his slowness in their marvel at the aesthetic results achieved. That he was a 'poet,' a designation privately
equated with shlemiel, explained any failure to fit into a familiar mould"
(*Man and Poet* 54).

Marie's recall of her marital relationship in the 1950s and early 1960s
is, of course, purely subjective. Charles left his own evidence. Unlike the
Reno correspondence of 1930,[9] this time no cache of letters was to be
preserved between them from those years, but there are letters from
Charles to his old friend, Al. A letter written during the Christmas holiday and dated December 28, 1951, hints at strain. "Dear Al and Millie:
Your beautiful gifts came last night just as Marie was about to return to
Brandeis. Their beauty and your generosity touched us deeply. (Marie
will thank you herself from Waltham.) We hope the New Year will bring
you much happiness. Charles" (*Letters* 326). One wonders why Marie
was leaving just before the New Year. In years past, she has fondly recalled, the two of them would spend New Year's Eve reading favorite

poetry aloud to one another. In other letters over the seventeen year semi-separation, Charles' letters to Al always end with some reference to Marie, (e.g., "Love to you and Millie from both of us.") Then, on April 8, 1961, Charles sent the following letter to his wife:

Dear Marie:

Since there is now the possibility that I may actually have some money to leave in case I die, until I have the opportunity of making a formal will, I wish you to know — and everybody else concerned — that I want you to have everything I have, tangible and intangible.

Incidentally, although I do not think the occasion will arise in the immediate future — and I certainly hope not — I want you to know that I want the simplest possible Orthodox Jewish funeral — burial in a plain wooden box and no speeches.

Your husband,
Charles Reznikoff
To Marie Syrkin Reznikoff
24 Concord Avenue
Cambridge, Mass. (*Letters* 329)

This account of the problematic Syrkin/Reznikoff relationship in the Brandeis years is succinctly summarized in Marie's comment: "Nevertheless, despite the lack of a common household, for seventeen years, we maintained a common life" (*Memoir* 54). This remark was written circa 1983, some seven years after Charles' death, regarding events more than thirty years in the past.

By the 1960s, Marie's academic career had hit its stride. Her polemical essays and literary critiques were appearing regularly in a wide range of publications, Jewish and non-Jewish, from *Commentary* to *Dissent*. And by this time, she had made her peace with her colleague Irving Howe.[10] Howe had come to respect Marie's intelligence, but primarily, he had come to value her as a compassionate friend. Milton Hindus' wife, Eva, has remarked that in Marie, Howe had "found a soft shoulder to cry on" in his complicated marital situation at the time. By 1983, when *Jewish Frontier* published its January/February issue with *Marie Syrkin, a Tribute by Her Friends, Colleagues, and Students,* on its front cover, Irving Howe contributed these words:

I believe in Marie Syrkin. I believe in the kind of life she has led, a life of commitment to values beyond the self. . . . Being merely, indeed spectacularly, human, Marie has made mistakes. One pleasure of our friendship has been the readiness we have each shown to correct the other's mistakes. She has had to do more correcting than I have. But it is this which one values most in life — the crisscrossing of persuasions, the interplay of sincere opinion, the complete belief in the good faith of one's friends and comrades. I believe in Marie Syrkin because I value the kind of life she has led, the kind of life she leads. . . . I value her good humor, I value her self-irony, but most of all, I think of a remark someone once made about Thomas Hardy — that the world's slow stain had not rubbed off on him. There can be no greater praise, and I think it is true for Marie. That is all. (*Frontier,* January/February 1983, 8)

Perhaps Marie had played some role in Irving Howe's effort to "reconquer his Jewishness." He writes in his autobiography, *A Margin of Hope,*[11] "The reconquest of Jewishness — more a reconnoiter than a march — had some positive aspects, and one of these was a growth of feeling for the new state of Israel. It didn't happen quickly, or quickly enough; I wasn't one of those who danced in the streets when Ben Gurion made his famous pronouncement that the Jews, like other people, now had a state of their own. I did feel an underglow of satisfaction, but my biases kept me from open joy. . . . And I suppose a little Zionism did creep into one's heart?" (*Margin* 276). Howe then openly confesses that "Memory points a finger: 'You were slow, you were dull in responding to the Holocaust.' I plead guilty" (*Margin* 247). To Howe's confession, Marie Syrkin adds in her admiring 1982 review in the *Jewish Frontier* (December 25) of Howe's memoir, "Of the many who broke away from their Jewish antecedents, Howe was one of the few who would make a return journey, not in a brief spurt of nostalgic memory but consistently and creatively." The reviewer was not one who long held on to a grudge. Nor was the reviewed.

Perhaps the most clarifying episodes on Howe's road to the reconquest of his Jewishness came in the "civil war that broke out among New York intellectuals" (*Margin* 270), after the publication of Hannah Arendt's report on the Eichmann trial. Because of their high regard for her, many American Jewish intellectuals awaited Arendt's account of the trial with great anticipation. But her reports from Jerusalem turned out to be far from what they had expected.[12] Arendt's *New Yorker* reports in 1960, followed by her book, *Eichmann in Jerusalem: A Report on the Banality of Evil*[13] ignited a volcanic eruption in the Jewish intellectual world. Though she had claimed that this was to be a reporter's account

of the events of the trial, it was, in reality, the report of a political jour-
nalist-philosopher, and as such, ranged far beyond the courtroom itself.
By applying to the Eichmann case some of the theories of her book on
totalitarianism (*The Origins of Totalitarianism*), she arrived at two astonishing conclusions: First, she coined the original but puzzling phrase,
the "banality of evil." It was perhaps even more perplexing to those who
knew her book on totalitarianism, for in that work Arendt had characterized the attempt of totalitarianism to "rob man of his nature under
the pretext of changing it" as absolute or "radical" evil. Now, it appeared that she was arguing that Eichmann could not be regarded as a
monster or as demonic because he was merely an ordinary person
caught in a system that "robbed man of his nature;" that is, his human
nature. There was no intentionality to his deeds, for he operated within
a system that dehumanized and reduced man to something closer to animal nature, making him far less capable of individuality, independent
action, and thought. To many readers, it certainly looked as if this was
an attempt to whitewash.

Worse was Arendt's assertion that the Jewish councils were accom-
plices in the fate of the Jews. In the paragraph that forever scandalized
her name, she claimed,

Wherever Jews lived, there were recognized Jewish leaders, and this leadership,
almost without exception, cooperated in one way or another, for one reason or
another, with the Nazis. The whole truth was that if the Jewish people had
really been unorganized and leaderless, there would have been chaos and plenty
of misery, but the total number of victims would hardly have been between
four and a half and six million people.

The sum of these two insights, then, suggested that, whereas the per-
petrators were incapable of action, the victims were quite capable.
Hence, responsibility resides in the behavior of the victim. These mal-
adroit contributions to the analysis of Nazism made her report of the
trial a *cause cèlébre*.

Arendt's articles in *The New Yorker* immediately drew criticism from
most corners of the Jewish world. Perhaps the most disturbing to her
were the private letters of disapproval from German Jews who had been
her friends before the war. Doubtless, the most important attack, because it was a public one, came from the eminent Hebrew University
scholar, Gershom Scholem. In the U.S., public criticism began with a

scathing critique in the *New York Times* by the American prosecutor and witness at the Nuremburg trials, Judge Michael Musmanno.[14] Then, the historian Dr. Jacob Robinson, one of the prosecution team at the trial, revealed the many factual errors in Arendt's report and pointed out that Arendt had no knowledge of the untranslated monographs in Yiddish and Hebrew dealing with the *Judenrate*. A barrage of attacks ensued: Norman Podhoretz, Walter Laqueur, Morris Schappes. Lionel Abel contributed his "The Aesthetics of Evil" to the *Partisan Review*, and Marie Syrkin published her attack in Irving Howe's *Dissent*. Howe, the editor of *Dissent*, has written "What struck one in reading *Eichmann in Jerusalem* — struck one like a blow — was the surging contempt with which she treated almost everyone and everything connected with the trial, the supreme assurance of the intellectual looking down upon those coarse Israelis" (*Margin* 271). He then chose Marie Syrkin to write the response for his journal (*State* 184–197). Syrkin opened her attack with a list of Arendt's credentials:

It looked like a foolproof choice. Who better to report on the trial in depth than Hannah Arendt, scholar, student of totalitarianism and of the human condition, and herself a German Jewish refugee who came to the United States after the rise of Hitler. Consequently it was with more than ordinary anticipation that many readers approached the *New Yorker* issue in which the first of her articles finally appeared. As one plodded through five successive issues, this initial expectation was quickly and thoroughly disappointed. I write this regretfully because of my long admiration for Miss Arendt's great intellectual gifts. But the reader soon discovered that in her alternate roles of Clio, muse of history, and Dike, spirit of Justice, Miss Arendt was as fallible as any mortal. Her air of Olympian detachment only served to make her preconception and tendentious reporting the more distasteful. All-too-human bias and brash manipulation of the evidence are more tolerable when offered less ostentatiously as oracular pronouncements.

Syrkin's concluding remarks adumbrated the sentiments that Gershom Scholem would express in his letter to Hannah Arendt in the January 1964 issue of *Encounter*. Scholem had accused Arendt of having "little trace" of love for the Jewish people. Marie put it this way:

What is at the root of the shortcomings of Miss Arendt's trial of the trial is *her* view of Jewish history, a view held by assimilationists of the Council for Judaism stripe on the one hand, and "radicals" of the old school on the other. In this view every affirmation of Jewish national awareness is culpable and to be strictured either as multiple loyalty or treason to a larger international ideal. That is why a Jewish intellectual of Miss Arendt's caliber is able not only to distort the facts but—more important—*to fail so signally in sympathy and imagination* [Italics mine]. (*State* 1980)[15]

Syrkin's closely argued, stinging attack was quickly followed by a barrage from all positions on the Jewish political spectrum. Arendt, in fact, complained to her friend, the philosopher Karl Jaspers, that "all the non-Jews are on my side now . . . and not a single Jew dares to stand up for me publicly, even if he is completely with me." With what Walter Laqueur has called Arendt's "streak of paranoia" (see the exchange of letters in the *New York Review of Books*, April 12, 2007), she complained that the "criticism was a conspiracy between the Israeli government and the Jewish organizations who dominate it." Arendt's closest friend, Mary McCarthy, now held the opinion that "It is as if *Eichmann in Jerusalem* had required a special pair of Jewish spectacles to make its 'true purport' visible." Perhaps McCarthy wasn't terribly off the mark.

Then in 1964, in response to the raging controversy, the deep divisions in the New York intellectual world, the furious sense of insult and betrayal, Irving Howe's journal, *Dissent,* organized a now legendary public forum in "the seedy Hotel Diplomat of midtown Manhattan" (*Margin* 274). It was an un-book party for *Eichmann in Jerusalem,* for the invited author declined to attend. Yet it was also a *bar mitzvah*—so to speak—a coming of age for the American Jewish intellectuals who until then had neither spoken nor written of the Jewish problems abroad. Since the 1930s their eyes had been on the fate of the Soviet Union and making it in America rather than on the critical issues facing Jews at the hands of the Nazis, the Arabs, and the Communists. But the absent author's ideas had shocked into life a delayed acceptance of their Jewish selves. Her assertions of the banality of the defendant and the complicity of the victims, her attacks on Zionist nationalism, Ben-Gurion, the prosecutors, even the Hebrew language that the trial was conducted in, to say nothing of her imperious tone, galvanized these heretofore reluctant Jews into solidarity with other Jewish intellectuals, whose focus all along had been on their embattled fellow Jews in Europe and Palestine.

"Hundreds of people crowded into the hall," writes Irving Howe,

where Lionel Abel and Marie Syrkin, a veteran Labor Zionist writer, spoke against Arendt's thesis, while Raul Hilberg, an authoritative scholar of the

Holocaust, and Daniel Bell spoke more or less for her. We had asked Hannah herself to come, but she did not answer our letter. The meeting was hectic, with frequent interruptions: Abel furiously pounded the table; Alfred Kazin intervened nervously at the last moment to defend Arendt; Vladka Meed, a heroic survivor of the Warsaw ghetto uprising, passionately attacked Arendt's views in Yiddish; and I as chairman translated rapidly from a Yiddish speech made by a leader of the Jewish Socialist Bund. Sometimes outrageous, the meeting was also urgent and afire. (*Margin* 274)

Between 1964 and the next cataclysmic year in Jewish history, 1967, Marie wound up her last few years at Brandeis University before her retirement in 1966. She returned to New York to resume domestic life with her husband, Charles Reznikoff, continued to write regularly for a variety of publications, published an anthology of the selected writings of Hayim Greenberg with her own introduction, and she was elected to membership in the Executive of the World Zionist Organization/ Jewish Agency. To the dismay of many of the Zionist functionaries in America, Marie Syrkin had been named to the WZO–Jewish Agency Executive in 1966 by the demand of the chairman of the Jewish Agency, Louis Pincus and others in the party in Israel. As Syrkin — with uncharacteristic self-pride — has explained, "I was not a political '*macher*' in any of the organizations, . . . I did not go around making organizational speeches nor was I engaged in any of the organization intricacies, like so many of the good and faithful workers of the various parties. I was a writer — an intellectual. . . . I was thrilled! I realized what it means to be a member of the WZO Executive; it's a very important post; a very small select group. . . . As a member of the WZO Executive *I'm* a powerful figure" (Personal interview).

At the first Congress after the State came into being in 1951, the first to be held in Jerusalem, "the new tasks of Zionism were defined as being 'to strengthen the State of Israel, to gather the exiles in the land of Israel, and to guarantee the unity of the Jewish People'" (*P.D.* 325). The expectation was that all Jews in Israel and in the Diaspora would assist in the building of the State; but these expectations became disappointments as *aliyah* and financial contributions proved far weaker than had been anticipated. There was no unified world Jewry, and by 1965, the Zionist movement had lost its motivating power. The Israeli government lost faith in the WZO and began to seek other ways to connect with American and European Jewry.

Such was the situation as Marie Syrkin understood it when she retired from Brandeis in 1966, at the age of sixty-seven, and took up her
new life in New York. What she did not know at the time was that
within a year the situation would change drastically; the Six Day War
that began on June 5, 1967, was to energize and unify world Jewry and
in effect, save the WZO and make Zionism once more relevant. Jews all
over the world instantly recognized the significance of Israel and what
the defeat of the State would mean. The Twenty-Seventh Zionist Congress of 1968 would produce the Jerusalem Program, which now defined
Zionist goals as: "The unity of the Jewish People and the centrality of
Israel in its life; the ingathering of the Jewish People in its historic
homeland, *Eretz Yisrael,* through aliyah from all lands; the strengthen-
ing of the State of Israel founded on prophetic ideals of justice and
peace; the preservation of the identity of the Jewish People through the
fostering of Jewish and Hebrew education and of spiritual and cultural
values; the protection of Jewish rights everywhere." With these ennobling ideals, the recently elected Marie Syrkin could not disagree. Indeed, she had a hand in writing them.

The years in which Marie served on the Executive would turn out to
be perhaps *the* watershed years for the development of the State: the Six
Day War and—for better and for worse—the conquest of the West
Bank. Still, she confessed that with all its intoxication, her new post on
the Executive also had its disappointments. Syrkin said (with some awe)
that there were various luminaries, such as the President of the WZO,
Nahum Goldmann, the Warsaw ghetto fighter, Zivia Lubetkin; and two
other members from the American Section, one with whom she developed a surprising but great friendship, J. B. Schechtman, and one whom
she spoke of with an admixture of esteem and envy. The friendship with
Schechtman was not a natural one for the Labor Zionist representative,
Marie Syrkin, because he was the representative for the Revisionists and
the biographer of Vladimir Jabotinsky. Marie's friendship with Schechtman began when a resolution calling for a pay increase from $9,000 to
$10,000 was introduced. Marie argued that because she was aware of
the need for financial stringency, she voted against it—even though she
was now living in New York, which was more expensive than Cambridge, and had an office at the Jewish Agency headquarters at 515 Park
Avenue, as editor-in-chief of the Herzl Press. Schechtman also voted
against it. "He was a principled man," she explained; "we were at opposite ends of the political spectrum, but I liked him very much. He was a

very genuine person. I trusted him completely, though I disagreed with him, but he was an honorable soul on his terms. He wasn't a phony" (Personal interview).

Marie's friendly relationship with Schechtman was not matched by her appraisal of Rose Halprin, a General Zionist who alternated with Emanuel Neumann as Chairman of the American Section of the WZO–Jewish Agency. Halprin, a well-to-do New Yorker born in 1895, was four years older than Marie Syrkin. She had been a longtime Zionist leader who had served as president of Hadassah for six years during two separate terms and was Hadassah's first representative to the Zionist General Council and served on the Executive of the Jewish Agency for over twenty years. Having spent a few years living in Palestine as Hadassah's Palestine correspondent, she became fluent in Hebrew. In 1963, the General Zionists had split into two groups: one wing, headed by Rose Halprin and Rabbi Israel Goldstein, represented those who refused to identify with any Israeli Party; the other wing, headed by Emanuel Neumann, held ties to the Liberal Party and the Independent Liberal Party in Israel.

As Marie began to describe Halprin, she declared that "the most brilliant politician there, of course, was Rose Halprin. Ohhh! *She* was a brilliant woman. The implacable battle between her and Emanuel Neumann, the fighting for precedence there — two embattled enemies; their rivalry — the grossest, simplest, coarsest rivalry." It is true that Marie admired Halprin's "cleverness," but Halprin also seemed to pose a bit of a threat, especially because as Marie put it, "She was impeccable: what would be the harmony of her costume and her hat? — Rose Halprin's hats were known as a joke of the time." Apologetically Syrkin added, "But she was a *remarkable* politician, remarkably astute, and sharp — and she had all the honors. That comes with such a position. She was not ignored. She was a very powerful figure. She was fought by Emanuel Neumann, who also was no slouch." In what appeared to be a nonsequitur, Marie added flatly, "His book is very interesting."

At this point, Marie interrupted her narrative to search for a book hidden in her overstuffed bookcase. "This is Emanuel Neumann's recollections" she said, handing me the book. "It's an autobiographical recollection [*In the Arena: An Autobiographical Memoir*], published by the Herzl Press, in which there's a very interesting photograph. . . . He gives a very interesting account of his life and his activities and all his *hochmas* [wise statements]. . . . Now look at this picture," Marie, smiling, quietly instructed me. "A meeting of *Midstream*. . . . This is me," she said, pointing to herself. "This is Shlomo Katz, that marvelous guy." And, pointing to another figure she asks me, "Do you recognize him? Samuel," she answers herself sotto voce. Louder, she continues, "He was invited to the meeting; he said he would participate in the editorial board at that time, but nothing came of it." Next, she identifies the others in the photograph, "Left to right: Professor Marie Syrkin, Consul General Arnon, Neumann, and Shlomo Katz." When I asked Marie whether or not she felt discomfited by constantly meeting up with Maurice Samuel this late in the game, she quickly responded, "No, no. It was so buried by then — and besides, superseded. . . . I mean, so much had happened to me afterwards." That, perhaps was true. But the fact was that in a discussion of her appointment to the Executive that included naming some of her colleagues, the mention of Neumann reminded her of the photograph in his memoir — which she seemed to have remembered because of Maurice Samuel's picture. Free association?

Marie's tenure on the Executive Committee came at a time of great national angst in Israel. In the aftermath of the War of Independence, Israel seemed to believe that the existing postwar conditions could be maintained indefinitely; that the refugee problem, that Arab political intransigence and continued armed attacks could be managed. But the refugee issue did not disappear and instead intensified as the population multiplied and clamored for the right of return. In the light of these conditions Marie wrote an article in which she expressed sympathy for the refugees, but argued for the justice of Israel's cause. Her opening statement are words that would resonate with a steady crescendo for decades to come. "If there is anything that can be said to trouble Americans sympathetic to Israel, Jewish and non-Jewish alike, it is the problem of Arab refugees." She quotes the Commissioner-General of UNRWA, who reported that the situation had not become "less complex or less dangerous to the peace and stability of the region" and added that the refugees have not become any less intense about their desire to return to their homes. "From their standpoint" [the Commissioner] recently told the current session of the General Assembly, "a nation has been obliterated and a population arbitrarily deprived of its birthright. This injustice still festers in their minds." Marie's answer to this charge, while acknowledging its validity, puts forward her argument on ethical grounds. The following long quotation constitutes the heart of Marie Syrkin's politics before, during, and after the wars of 1967 and 1973. If she were alive today, these words surely would be at the center of her argument against the contemporary claim of "progressive" or "post-Zionist" Jews who call for a binational State or for the dismantling of the Jewish State altogether.[16]

Though it is obvious that the Arab refugees are being used by the Arab states as pawns in a political game, such exploitation does not necessarily invalidate claims put forward on their behalf. The Arabs continue to call for "repatriation," Israel continues to refuse, and people whose scruples can only be those of conscience and not of *Realpolitik,* continue to wonder how Jews, themselves such recent refugees, can bear to add to the sum of human suffering by declining to admit refugees into Israel. Even committed Zionists are disturbed by this question. Exile and longing for return — key words in Jewish national experience — carry powerful echoes. Am I as a Zionist insensitive to these echoes? Do I ignore them, hoping solely for the success of Israeli arms? Despite the hazard of self-righteous protestations by a partisan, let me address myself to the ethical issue.

I write, of course, on the premise that the establishment of Israel was an act of historic justice and that its continued existence is to be desired. On the Arab postulate that Israel must be obliterated and its inhabitants driven into the sea, there is no room for discussion. On the assumption, however, of Israel's right to survival, is the Jewish state facing in the Arab refugees a reverse Zionism whose impulse it should be the first to meet with sympathy? The comparison, superficially intriguing, is essentially false. Jews were driven to the "national home" granted by the Balfour Declaration by homelessness, necessity, a centuries-old historic attachment, and a search for a national identity. They purchased and reclaimed its deserts and swamps, acre by acre, and finally defended a shrunken area of it against the attack of the combined Arab armies. None of these elements, physical or emotional, lies behind the Arab will to return.

The very origin of the Arab refugee problem indicates the difference. The tragedy of the Jewish refugee lay in his absence of choice. He was driven out by force or by decree and he fled from a real, not a mythical, terror. His only refuge was the remote "homeland" which the Arab refugee left of his own will; the Arab was free to remain. There is a crucial difference between fleeing *to* a land because of desperate need, and fleeing *from* the same land without need. But perhaps the simple historical record makes the point best. (*State* 119–120)

Following these introductory arguments, Syrkin presents what she insists is the historical record. The items on her agenda are: (1) Why the

Arabs fled; (2) a comparison between Jewish survivors and Arab refugees; (3)Palestinian nationalism versus village patriotism; (4) the true number of refugees. The bulk of her argument concerns the Arab flight. She tells the reader that she arrived in Palestine in 1948 when the Arab exodus was in full swing, and that she was given the task of drawing up a report on the subject for the Israeli Bureau of Information. Her travels through the Galilee were at a time when there were no documents — only the "fresh reactions of Jews and Arabs [who had chosen to stay], as yet undoctored by policy." Her personal interviews and eyewitness experiences led her to the conclusion that most of the flight occurred in response to instructions from the Arabs' own leaders who told them that the war would quickly be over and they could then return to their homes. With quotations from personal interviews, Arab newspapers, British newspapers, Arab radio broadcasts, Syrkin insists that the exodus was certainly not Israeli policy, but a result of Arab instruction, propaganda, and fear.

Having presented her case, Marie Syrkin sums it up with this last statement: "I do remain troubled by the moralists, Jewish and non-Jewish, who blandly, and I think sanctimoniously, fail to weigh the Arab and Israeli case in the same scale" (*State* 132).

Meantime, events in the Middle East began to assume a menacing look. Syria intensified its attacks on Israeli settlements in the north; on the eastern border, Egypt stepped up the mobilization of its armed forces; Lebanon, Iraq, Jordan, and Saudi Arabia moved their troops to the rest of Israel's borders; on Egypt's insistence, the UN forces withdrew from the Sinai and Gaza, and Egypt blockaded the Straits of Tiran, Israel's outlet to the Red Sea. On May 27, 1967, President Nasser announced his intentions: "Our basic objective will be the destruction of Israel. The Arab people want to fight. . . . The mining of Sharm el Sheikh is a confrontation with Israel. Adopting this measure obligates us to be ready to embark on a general war with Israel" (Gilbert 68). It was impossible to conclude anything other than that war was inevitable. The Israelis took him at his word. Pace Tom Segev who sees the events differently.[17]

By May 31, there were 100,000 Egyptian troops, 1,000 tanks, and 500 guns in the Sinai poised for attack. Israel's existential fear was intensified by the silence of the international community. Did the world *not* hear Nasser's blatant threat? Did the nations *not* understand the meaning of the abrogation of international guarantees of navigation rights? And what of the betrayal of the Security Council, whose members said not a word about the obvious meaning of all the posturing, threats, and massing of the combined Arab troops against a fellow member of the United Nations? Abba Eban expressed the despair and terror of the Israelis as they lived these angst-ridden days: "As we looked around us we saw the world divided between those who were seeking our destruction and those who would do nothing to prevent it."[18] Once more, the Israelis were left to their own adroitness: on June 4, they were outnumbered three to one by the enemy forces on their borders; on June 5, they launched a pre-emptive strike on the airfields throughout Egypt, destroying the Egyptian air force. Six days later, the war was over and the enemy forces vanquished. In what the religious community saw as nothing less than a miracle—the work of God—others saw as the magnificent courage of the Israeli armed forces under the brilliant command of Yitzhak Rabin, but nonetheless "miraculous." Battles were won in places with Biblical significance: Judea and Samaria; Mount Scopus; Rachel's tomb; the Machpelah (tomb of the patriarchs); the Old City of Jerusalem; the Western Wall. These were, for the religious, events of messianic implication. And for the nonreligious, they were days of euphoria; but such days were not to be seen very soon again.

Describing the Six Day War as an ideological watershed, Amnon Rubenstein has written,

The ideological and practical ramifications of the Six Day War were so all-encompassing in Israeli thinking and politics that there is justification for regarding it as a turning point in Zionist and Israeli history. [When the war was over] anxiety gave way to exhilaration. . . . [B]eyond the barbed wire lay the enchanted lands to which no Israeli could be indifferent. Within Israel the war unleashed a national debate as to the aims and goals of Zionism and its relationship with Judaism. A new sense of history began to permeate the public debate. (Rubinstein 76–77)

When the lightning-quick war was ended, the Israelis and much of the world had a new adjective to attach to the young State: "invincible." The Israelis had proven their military might and their ability to overcome the combined power of the Arab States. But it would not last for very long. On November 22, 1967, the UN Security Council unanimously passed the now famous "land for peace" Resolution 242, which calls for the "withdrawal of Israeli armed forces from territories occupied in the recent conflict," (after much negotiation the word "all" was eliminated from the phrase "all territories") and the "termination of all claims or states of belligerency." Resolution 242 also calls for the mutual recognition by the belligerents of all established states (i.e., Egypt, Syria, Jordan, Israel) and the establishment of peace, with secure and recognized boundaries. The Israelis insisted on omitting the phrase in the Arab-Soviet motion that calls for "total withdrawal to prewar lines." The Arabs responded with the infamous words: "no peace, no negotiations, no recognition." And so, Resolution 242 remains unimplemented to this day.

True, the war had established Israel as a mighty military force, turning the stereotype of the Jew as a powerless victim into the stereotype of the invincible. But it also left Israel in control of the Sinai, the West Bank, the Golan Heights, and Gaza; a combined area that more than tripled Israel's size and put about one million Arabs under its control, adding to the 500,000 that lived in Israel proper. It also united a Jerusalem that had been divided since 1948. Moreover, the control of the territories emboldened both the Religious Right and the security hawks, who together began to speak of annexation of the occupied areas — an idea that had not been in the minds of the Israeli leadership who had set up a military administration in the expectation of negotiating a peace agreement that would cost some land compromise. Ideas of annexation, however, were the origin of *Gush Emunim* (bloc of the faithful), a new religious Zionist movement that wedded theology to politics; they held that in order to complete the Zionist purpose, there must be Israeli sovereignty over the biblical lands of Judea, Samaria, and Gaza — though Gaza was a major Philistine city in biblical times.

Perhaps it was Israel's new-found self-confidence that began to erode the West's support. Or perhaps it was the gradual growth of Jewish settlements on the West Bank that began to change public opinion. Or perhaps it was the West's increasing dependence on Arab oil. As the years passed, and within Israel ideas of "Greater Eretz Israel" garnered greater political support, Israel met with harsher criticism from the rest of the world. The security council, Amnon Rubinstein reports, "adopted an almost Pavlovian reaction to anything concerning Israel and habitually issued one-sided condemnation. Public criticism in the western press grew. Third World countries became restless" (Rubinstein 79–80). The western political left — particularly the academic New Left — turned away from Israel and toward the Arabs as the conquered territories began to be called the "occupied territories."

Marie Syrkin's years on the Zionist Executive were exciting, but not as untroubled as one might wish for one's retirement years. True, there was the short-lived euphoria of the Six Day War victory. Equally true, as she has said, her domestic life with Charles now was peaceful, pleasant, and "happy." Family life was — as she might have put it — bringing her "*naches*" in the form of filial achievement. Marie's son, David, was now a highly successful nuclear physicist. He had received his Ph.D. in physics from Harvard University in 1948 and married Beverly Bronstein. In 1954, he had taken a position in the physics department at the University of Washington in Seattle, where he served as chair from 1976 to 1984. He retired in 1994 after an eminently distinguished career. David Bodansky, grandson of Nachman Syrkin, son of Marie Syrkin and Aaron Bodansky, had inherited a powerful combination of genes. A gentle, soft-spoken research scientist, neither literary nor a political activist, his own extraordinarily successful career as a nuclear physicist — specializing in the hazards of nuclear energy — does, in fact, reflect familial social concerns. That he was a scientist and not a writer of poetry or politics may be explained by the following personal anecdote: Once in my student days, while Marie was traveling by car to New York with me, I innocently asked her what her son did. "He's a nuclear physicist," she answered. "Oh," I replied in a tone of great surprise. "*Your* son?" I asked with incredulity, knowing that Marie was not aware that the automobile she was riding in was a bottom-of-the-line Chevrolet; she had innocently asked if it was a Cadillac. But she responded to my question immediately and sharply: "He was not an immaculate conception [*sic*], you know!"

Marie Syrkin's adolescence had been a lonely one, her household consisting only of her father and herself; but at the time of her retirement, her family had increased by two grandsons, Daniel and Joel Bodansky, one niece, and one nephew, Eve and Jonathan, the children of Marie's sister and brother-in-law, Zivia and Morton Wurtele. Marie Syrkin's tribe would later increase by the addition of five great-grandchildren and several grandnieces and nephews.

Though her personal life was a comfort in her "retirement," Marie's political life was anything but soothing. Having been appointed to the Zionist Executive in 1966, she was in the catbird seat with regard to the events in Israel. Marie's biography of Golda Meir had been written in 1955 when Golda was minister of labor; the revised edition was published in 1963, after she had become foreign minister; a new revised edition would appear in 1969 after the death of Prime Minister Levi Eshkol and Golda Meir's election to the office of prime minister. Just after Eshkol's death, Marie appeared on American Public Television with Simcha Dinitz, who was then Israel's minister of information in Washington, D.C. It was an appearance that I clearly recall in vivid black and white. At the close of the program, the moderator asked Simcha Dinitz who he thought would become the next prime minister. Dinitz named a few likely candidates. But just as the program was about to close, from the right hand corner of the screen, in barely above a whisper, came Marie Syrkin's voice: "What about Golda?" The answer was very soon to come, when Golda Meir was elected in 1969 to be the fourth prime minister of the State of Israel.

In 1969 Marie Syrkin published the third edition of her biography of *Golda Meir,* subtitled *Israel's Leader.* It ends with Meir becoming prime minister and goes no further than that. Perhaps that was for the best. The 1955 edition, titled *Way of Valor,* had received only a mild positive critical response. Though Golda had been in the world's eye during her year's experience as minister to Moscow, Syrkin's book ended with Golda Meir as Labor Minister—which did not have much resonance in the world outside of Israel. Nonetheless, in 1963, when Golda came to the world's attention as Foreign Minister, Marie revised her book, changed the title to *Golda Meir: Woman with a Cause* and brought it up-to-date. This time there were many more reviews in the Jewish, American, and foreign press. Probably 90 percent of them were favorable, but the ones that really counted were not. The *Commentary* reviewer claimed that the subtitle "an Authorized Biography" was misleading because "Mrs. Meir has in conversation disclaimed any responsibility for the work." It is designed, the reviewer argues, "to draw attention to the fact that the author has been close to her subject for many years." The reviewer in the *New York Times* is kinder, but says, "It can be no surprise that Miss Syrkin, who reveres [Meir] (but without idolatry) occasionally commits some of the deadly sins of "authorized" biography. Miss Syrkin notes a few minor weaknesses in her subject, but nothing major." The most wounding criticism came from Walter Laqueur in an Anglo-Jewish paper. Commenting that "Miss Syrkin's biography is not on a sufficiently wide scale" and "that there is not enough depth and detail," Laqueur goes on to say that since Syrkin is tied to Meir by "bonds of friendship, she could not write candidly and critically in these circumstances." Too many questions, he argues, are left unanswered both politically and personally. Laqueur damns with faint praise when he says that the book provides a "good sketch for a portrait. As such it is no doubt of value, but one has the feeling Miss Syrkin could have written a far more substantial biography, and one regrets that she did not aim her sights high enough." In a mostly positive review, the *Times Literary Supplement* added the critique that sometimes Syrkin "seems too eulogistic" and in some places "rather sentimental." In 1969, when Golda Meir became prime minister, Marie again changed the title and the publisher to *Golda Meir: Israel's Leader,* and brought it up-to-date. One obvious motivation was that there was more material, for Golda had done more and achieved much as the elected fourth prime minister of the State of Israel, and was recognized even in the outside world as a rare female head of State. Moreover, in this edition, Marie removed the subtitle "An Authorized Biography." Was this because one reviewer implied that Golda had not authorized it? Or was it to distance herself from her subject. This time the reviews were better, but some still complained of too much personal involvement. Curiously, Syrkin's file contained folders of reviews and letters for each of her books, but only those for the 1964 edition of the biography were saved.

Despite the euphoria after the Six Day War victory, events on the ground were far from salubrious. The war had resulted in Israel's occupation of the West Bank and the Gaza Strip, bringing a million and a half resentful Arabs (including the 500,000 in Israel) under the control of the Israelis. In the north, the Israeli conquest of the Golan Heights, it is true, brought Syrian bombardment of the settlements below virtually to an end, making it possible for Israel to found a few Golan settlements; but 70,000 Syrians had fled the Golan and became part of the edgy refugee population. The Gaza Strip became a prime base for terrorists to attack Israeli settlements just over the southern border; and on the West Bank, over a half-million Arabs came under an Israeli military administration. Nonetheless, Israel did try to encourage and fund economic development. By the end of 1970, the unemployment rate had dropped from 12 percent to 3 percent, as each day tens of thousands of Arabs freely crossed the Green Line (the Israel-Jordan border from 1949–1967) to work in Israel, attend schools, and get treatment in hospitals. Arabs in Israel also crossed the border in the opposite direction for a variety of reasons. But, according to Martin Gilbert, "between June 1967 and December 1968 there were 159 terrorist raids deep inside Israel from the West Bank, mostly against busy civilian centers and markets." The Arab terrorists, in an effort to turn sporadic acts of terrorism into full-scale guerilla war, launched 1,029 raids on border areas as well, aided and encouraged by Syria, Jordan, Iraq, Egypt, and Algeria (Gilbert 74). In the meanwhile, Israeli counterterrorist activity on the West Bank included reprisals in which the military blew up more than 5,000 houses, expelled several hundred Arabs, and established 16 Israeli settlements on the West Bank. Lebanon too became a base for terrorism; northern Israel became a target for Lebanon's Palestinian refugees' shelling, crop-burning, and raids. In Jordan, too, 20,000 *fedayeen*, recruited and trained by the P.L.O., which had been established in 1964, had found haven and grew in influence and power, until King Hussein turned against them and expelled them for fear of being overthrown. Inside Israel itself, hundreds of Israeli civilians and soldiers were killed and many more wounded. This period of border and interior terrorist activity was referred to as the "War of Attrition," after the statement of the Egyptian President, Gamal Nasser, on June 23, 1969: "I cannot conquer the Sinai, but I can wear Israel out and break its spirit by attrition" (*P.D.* 312). To make matters even worse for Israel, after the 1967 War, the Soviet Union, in its intention to bring the Middle East into its sphere of influence, severed diplomatic relations with Israel and supplied arms to Egypt and Syria, and economic aid to Sudan, Iraq, and Yemen. This was indeed a war of attrition.

Just after Golda Meir became prime minister in 1969, Marie Syrkin published an article titled "Who are the Palestinians" (*Midstream*, January 1970). Much of this article appeared in the 1969 revised version of her biography of the newly elected prime minister, along with her assertion that Golda had come to the Middle East when the entire area was known as Palestine and both Jews and Arabs were called Palestinians. Golda, Marie argued in defense of her subject, had referred to herself as a Palestinian for decades, and found it difficult after the State to regard only the Arabs as the Palestinians. Marie's essay begins with her report that on November 2, 1969, the fifty-second anniversary of the Balfour Declaration, an advertisement appeared in the *New York Times* under Arab sponsorship that urged President Nixon to "assume the role of 'peacemaker' and reverse the process begun by the Balfour Declaration by undoing the 'dismemberment and mutilation of Palestine, its mutilation from a land sacred to and inhabited by Moslem, Christian, and Jew, to a land which is the exclusive domain of a few.'" That this apparent offer of moderation, however, was "contingent on the dissolution

of the Jewish state may not have immediately struck the casual reader"
Marie contended. "Instead of the usual call for driving the Israelis
into the sea, they would be permitted to dwell as a minority in a hypo-
thetical Palestinian state where they would presumably be as safe and
happy as the Jews of Egypt, Iraq, or Syria. . . . Obviously, Israel is unlikely to accede to a formula for its extinction no matter how graciously
phrased."

Syrkin's argument next examines the origin of "Palestinian" nationalism; she maintains that classic Arab sources never referred to Palestine
as anything but south Syria, and instead concentrated on the unity of
Syria. She points out that "so rabid a figure as the first head of the Palestine Liberation Organization, Ahmed Shukairy, had no hesitation in announcing to the Security Council on May 31, 1956, that 'it is common
knowledge that Palestine is nothing but southern Syria.'" Syrkin further
maintains that "The concept of Palestine as a separate national entity
that arose among Arabs was a purely negative reaction to Zionism after
the Balfour Declaration." Moreover, she argues that whatever the many
explanations for the flight of Arabs from Israel in 1948, believed or
dismissed,

none makes adequate allowance for the swiftness and readiness with which the
flight took place. People picked themselves up as though they were going from
the Bronx to Brooklyn, not as though they were abandoning a homeland. Part
of the speed was due to irrational panic, part to the assurance of return after victory, but it was undoubtedly abetted by the subconscious or conscious feeling
that flight to a village on the West Bank or across the Jordan was no exile. The
Arab who moved a few miles was in the land he had always known though not
in the same house. . . . Only in the case of the Arabs has village-patriotism been
raised to a sacred cause.

Syrkin's position was to cause considerable controversy, but though
she firmly held to these views, she also was pragmatic in the world of
realpolitik. She reminds her readers that the Israeli Government has repeatedly announced its readiness to negotiate "secure and agreed" borders whenever the Arabs were ready to discuss peace. Her choice among
many solutions to the ongoing problem is the "proposal to set up a
Palestinian entity on the West Bank. . . . Such a Palestinian state could
serve to satisfy newborn Palestinian nationalism and in conditions of
peace, prosper economically in partnership with Israel. The emergence

of such a state would mean compromises for both parties to the conflict. Israel, regardless of victory, would have to accept the narrow confines of its much amputated state, and the Arabs would have to come to terms with the reality of Israel" (*Midstream*, January 1970, 13–14). This had been her position since her 1946 article in favor of Partition.

During her years on the World Zionist Executive, Marie remained extremely busy with writing, editorial work, Zionist activism, as well as speech-writing for her friend Golda. In 1971, Syrkin wrote a review of the best-selling book in America, *The Israelis: Founders and Sons,* by Amos Elon, in which he contrasts the values of the founders with that of the sons. Her review, titled "Low-Down on the Israelis: An Answer to Amos Elon," was not favorable. But Elon took the trouble to write to Marie after reading her critique: "I read with great interest your review of my recent book. Its interest for me was enhanced not merely by the high esteem with which I have read your work in the past two decades, but also by the fact that it was one of the few, if not the only, review which was sharply critical of what I had written" (Archives 2 f. 1). Elon can probably be regarded as one of the founders, among the sons of the founders, of the new revisionist historians.

During Golda Meir's years as prime minister, Marie continued to write speeches and articles for her, including Golda's essay in *Foreign Affairs* of April, 1973, "Israel in Search of Lasting Peace," which covers much of the same ground as the 1970 *Midstream* essay. Marie's rhetorical hand in this article is easy to identify; it is not likely that Golda would have quoted Voltaire.

The months after the appearance of the Meir-Syrkin essay in *Foreign Affairs* were punctuated by increased Palestinian-Arab terrorism, including hijackings, attempted bomb attacks on planes outside of Israel, and stepped-up bellicose rhetoric, all leading to the Yom Kippur War. The war began shortly after noon on Saturday, October 6, 1973, when Egypt and Syria launched a surprise attack against Israel on two fronts: the Egyptians attacked across the Bar Lev Line along the Suez Canal; the Syrians attacked along the Golan Heights. Israeli intelligence was aware that there had been a buildup of forces along the Egyptian and Syrian fronts, which had been chalked up to routine military exercises. "This assessment reconciled with an Israeli intelligence conception that Egypt would not launch a war against Israel without superior air power and Syria would not go to war alone. It was fortified by a highly deceptive plan mounted by the Egyptians and Syrians parallel to their actual military preparations" (*P.D.* 337). They attacked with their full complement of forces, but made one miscalculation: the attack took place on Yom Kippur, the holiest day of the Jewish calendar, when the armed forces were either in the synagogue or at home, making it possible to save valuable time by mobilizing very quickly. This time the war did not end in six days. It lasted from October 6 to October 24. The fighting was fierce, and although the Israelis overcame the setbacks of the first few days by the stunning maneuver of crossing the Suez Canal, occupying a strip of land on the western bank and thereby cutting off the retreat of the Egyptian Third Army, the cost in Israeli lives — almost 3,000 dead and untold numbers of horribly wounded — was enormous, as were the psychological wounds and the political consequences.

For Marie, despite Israel's final victory in the war, perhaps one of the most unsettling consequences came in the form of the bitter attacks on her friend Golda Meir, who was held responsible for the Yom Kippur War and for Israel's lack of preparedness for the surprise attack. After the war, Meir was assailed not only for her part in it, but also for her entire resumé and political personality. Moreover, she was accused of dismissing Anwar Sadat's peace overture in 1971 and thereby missing the greatest opportunity to prevent war.[19] Whatever the ultimate historical assessment of her career may be, Golda was often referred to as a "legend in her own time," celebrated internationally as one of the very few women to hold so high an office, yet she was unfortunate in that it fell to her to preside over Israel during the disastrous Yom Kippur War. Chaim Herzog, who was a Major-General in the Yom Kippur War, a military analyst, head of Israeli military intelligence, and later, the sixth president of Israel, has written in his book, *The War of Atonement,* that Moshe Dayan, a controversial hero of the Six Day War and defense minister at the time of the Yom Kippur War, bore much of the responsibility for the outbreak of the war. Calling Dayan indecisive, Herzog writes that despite his May directive "to prepare for war in late 1973 and in the light of all the intelligence in the first week of October and on Yom Kippur morning," Dayan opposed the chief of staff's demand for total mobilization. "He told Mrs. Meir that he was 'against total mobilization but he would not resign'; he left the decision about the attack into Syria on Wednesday 10 October, to her; he declared that he would 'not make a *jihad*' against the crossing of the Suez Canal by the Israeli forces although he opposed it" (Herzog 281). He had, in other words, given Meir very bad advice.

Herzog, however, goes on to say that "after the war Dayan went out of his way to praise Mrs. Meir, and justifiably so, because it was to a great degree her strength of character and ability to remain composed in the most difficult circumstances which counteracted Dayan's pessimistic nature and his jeremiads." Herzog, however, is no worshiper before Golda Meir's reputation; not blind to her failings, he makes the following assessment:

Mrs. Meir's method of government brought about a system whereby there were no checks and balances and no alternative evaluations. Her doctrinaire, inflexible approach to problems and to government was to contribute to the failings of the government before the war. She was very much the overbearing mother who ruled the roost with an iron hand. She had little idea of orderly administration and preferred to work closely with her cronies, creating an *ad hoc* system of government based on what was known as her "kitchen." But once war broke out these very traits proved to be an asset. She was strong and adamant and gave the country the powerful leadership it required both in time of war and in the involved post-war political negotiations. On many occasions she, a woman who had reached seventy-five, found herself thrust into a position where she had to decide between military options proposed by professionals. She decided, and invariably decided well, drawing on a large measure of common sense which had stood her in good stead." (Herzog 281, 282)

Marie's revision of her biography of Golda had been published in the year that Golda became prime minister. Much had happened between the first and third editions. Yet, if Marie were to make a further revision, what indeed would she have said? Surely the nine years between Syrkin's last revision and Golda's death would have necessitated some changes in assessment—political and personal. It would have to account for the downward trajectory of Meir's career. Still, despite the losses of the Labor Party in the elections after the Yom Kippur War, Meir did succeed in forming a new coalition government. But the demobilized reserve army's protest movement and the first report of the Agranat Commission criticizing the failures of the IDF and its intelligence and military leaders, with recommendations for a number of dismissals, were devastating. Though the report said nothing about Moshe Dayan, it did praise Golda Meir; but there were public demands for Dayan's resignation—for that matter, demands for the resignation of the entire government. Meir, under these circumstances, decided to hand in her resignation to

the president, bringing down the whole government. She led the caretaker government until Yitzhak Rabin took over two months later. She
resigned from the Knesset and retired to private life; but now at seventy-
five, she was old, exhausted, and very ill. The last two years of her life
were unrelievedly sad as she faced criticisms that she held to outworn
politics that were unable to understand the newer realities of Israel
and that she did not come to terms with the mood of the younger *sabra*
society.

As early as January 1974, Marie Syrkin had written a letter of advice
to her friend. On February 5, Lou Kaddar, Golda's personal aide wrote
back to Marie: "Our common friend has read—without too much pleasure—your letter of January 14, 1974, telling her to retire (I put it
bluntly). She thinks about it, off and on, and doesn't like a bit of it." By
the end of April, Golda had become convinced of the need to step
down. Perhaps Marie's letter of April 22 was a contributing factor.
"Dearest Golda," writes Marie, who certainly understood the political
circumstances, but whose personal friendship remained steadfast:

My first impulse was to congratulate you on your decision to retire, but "congratulate" is the wrong word. I have no doubt whatever that this decision is the
best possible course for you personally. But I am also aware that the loss of your
leadership is an added blow to Israel's stability at this time. . . . The friends who
love you wanted you to enter history, unscathed, at the hour of your highest
glory. But that was probably an unworthy wish. Your life and that of Israel have
been one, and there was no way in which you could have failed to share Israel's
current trial. But now you can at last be the elder statesman minus the political
hurly-burly, and you can work on your great book. And you will have time to
"loaf and invite your soul"—not to mention grandchildren and good books.
Perhaps I will even have a chance to see you perform your wonders with
blintzes and gefilte fish not in a "kitchen cabinet" but in an unpartisan kitchen—
as I once did shortly after you retired from the Foreign Ministry.

                                                    With all my love, Marie

Golda did not reply directly, but on May 7, Lou Kaddar sent a reply. "I
gave her your note, she read it and said there was no need for her to
answer. . . . Of course her decision to quit was the only one left to her.
As a matter of fact, she didn't take it, it was pushed down her throat, and
not too gently either."

If Marie Syrkin ever thought about writing another update of her biography, it became unnecessary when Golda Meir decided to write her autobiography. Quite naturally, assuming that Golda would ask her to help "write" her autobiography, Marie was rudely surprised when Golda chose an Israeli journalist, Rinna Samuel, for the job. Perhaps the publisher made the decision on the grounds that there were serious criticisms of Marie's biography, or perhaps Golda thought that Marie knew *too* much. In her own biography, at Golda's request, Marie had left out personal details about her friend's several affairs (now known) with such well-known figures as David Remez and the president of Israel, Zalman Shazar. In letters from Golda's close personal assistant, Lou Kaddar, as well as from letters from Rinna Samuel herself, it was clear to Marie that Golda was not being cooperative at all. Meantime, Rinna Samuel wrote to Marie for some assistance:

in addition to your own familiarity with the people, family, friends, places and times — and to what I gather was quite a lot of interviewing in various parts of this country as well as abroad — did you also by any chance accumulate a file? If you did, have you kept this file (letters, clippings, excerpts from diaries, etc.) or have you, perhaps, deposited them somewhere? Or (a horrendous thought!) Have you destroyed it? . . . I don't need to tell you how grateful I would be for some guidance from you, but I suppose that will have to wait until you come back to Israel. (Archives 2 f. 1)

Marie's reply was both gracious and noncommittal:

I was delighted to hear from you after all this time. First of all, congratulations on your assignment. I think there is a great book in the making. . . . I'm sorry to tell you that, unfortunately, immediately upon the publication of my biography, I threw away all the elaborate notes, etc., that I made. Living in a small apartment as I do keeps me from accumulating much material whose loss I susequently mourn. However, I doubt whether my notes would have been of much use. Your problem, as I know from experience, will be to get G. to talk. . . . I will be most happy to assist you in any way I can and I am glad that you wrote to me. Good luck.

In late October of 1974, Marie received a letter from another dear friend, one she shared with Golda — Sulamit Schwartz Nardi, who had been an advisor to Abba Hillel Silver, and then to five Israeli presidents. Her letter was written just after President Zalman Shazar's death. Both

Sulamit and Marie were privy to Golda's long-term affair with Shazar. "Dearest Marie," she begins: "Our world shrinks and loses the best and is at the same time terrifying. At least that's how *we* feel. As I stood at Zalman's grave on Mount Herzl on a hamsin day with Meyer Weisgal behind me and Golda, bowed, not far away, I kept thinking of you. He was a phenomenal person and there really can't be his like again." By now, at the age of seventy-five, Marie was watching her circle of friends dwindle: Hayim Greenberg had died in 1953, Maurice Samuel, in 1972, and Ben-Gurion, in 1973.

Though Marie took regular trips to Israel in these years, in April 1975, she was in New York, where she received chapters of Golda's book as they were completed. Lou Kaddar wrote on April 1, "All the chapters you have not seen will be sent to you from London [from the publisher] and G. will be very grateful if you read them and let her have your remarks. On April 27, Kaddar thanked her: "Your comments arrived together with Rinna so that the timing was wonderful. Everybody was happy with them and they have been acted upon. . . . The book is being completed this week" (Archives 2 f. 1). *My Life,* by Golda Meir, was published in 1975. It did not mention Rinna Samuel's participation, nor anybody else's.

In New York, Marie's life with Charles continued in its contentments. By the 1960s and early 1970s Charles was finally receiving recognition. New Directions — *San Francisco Review* published a volume of his selected poetry with an introduction by C. P. Snow. Younger poets such as Harvey Shapiro, David Ignatow, and Allen Ginsburg began to discover him; his old friend, Al Lewin, had moved to New York in the 1960s and frequently invited Charles to meet famous film and theater people in his Fifth Avenue home. The most unexpected event of all, however, came in 1971, when Reznikoff was awarded the Morton Darwin Zabel literary prize of $2,500 by the National Institute of Arts and Letters. Marie recalls, "On this occasion *he* was on the dais. At the age of 76 he was being honored by his peers. A younger friend said to me, 'It comes too late.' My feeling was, thank God, it came in time."[20]

In 1975, Marie retired from editorial work and began to think about the future. She was seventy-five and Charles was eighty. New York had always been home base to them, but at their age, weather began to make a difference. Too cold in the winter, too hot in the summer. "I thought it might be pleasant," Marie has written, "for us to live on the West Coast in Santa Monica, the charming sea-coast town I remembered from Charles' Hollywood venture and from subsequent trips. The climate was kindly and there were the Palisades along the ocean for long walks. 'Not long enough,' Charles objected. But on the whole he did not reject the notion." Charles was at peace at this point in his life. As they sat together talking of the projected move, he told Marie "You know, I never made money but I have done everything that I most wanted to do." She has said of their talk that afternoon,

I have always been glad to remember that on the day he did not know would be his last he spoke with such deep satisfaction of his eighty years. He had won the battle not for success as it is generally measured but for the greatest luxury of all—to write what he wanted at his own pace in his own way. With no premonition of illness—he had walked his customary six miles that morning—we sat down to an early supper. I had just turned on the six o'clock news when he complained of indigestion. The doctor summoned from his ground floor office in Lincoln Towers diagnosed a massive heart attack. He died in nearby St. Vincent's hospital shortly before dawn on January 22, 1976. On admission the attending physician had told me that I would be allowed to see him shortly as his condition was stable, but the hours stretched while I waited. By the time I was summoned he was dead. There had been no farewell. A few lines I wrote describe how it was:

Finality
Death, the great kidnapper,
Snatched you suddenly
Asking no ransom.

We were at dinner chatting.
He broke in with two gentle, black attendants
And a noisy ambulance.

When I came back before dawn
The cups were still on the table
And I was alone.
(*Man and Poet* 65–66)

This intensely personal poem says more about the relationship between Charles and Marie than almost anything else. It is her finest tribute to her husband in terms of the matter that held them together throughout the on- and off-years of their marriage: Poetry. It speaks, in its spare statement, of that aching moment when one becomes aware of the finality, the reality of loss and loneliness. It is a fitting tribute to her husband, Charles Reznikoff, written in the simple style he had taught her to love. It should also be noted that the image of Death as the great kidnapper appears here for the second time in Marie Syrkin's poetry. The first was in the memorial poem for the death of her child:

> They should not have done what they did:
> The two men with gloves
> and faces I cannot remember
> Who came to carry you off
> Before my eyes. Silently they seized you,
> Kidnappers.

With this word, Marie linked her two great losses.

Charles was buried in a plain pine coffin in a traditional Jewish funeral. The poets, Harvey Shapiro, and David Ignatow, and a close friend, Milton Hindus, spoke at the chapel. The following day, a two-column obituary appeared in the *New York Times*. And to the astonishment of family members who had been skeptical about Charles' career, the room was filled to overflowing with distinguished guests, young people, and readers and admirers of his poetry. Marie regretfully admits, "To the last I had underestimated everything." Yet, she always knew the value of his poetry; for the headstone of his grave, rather than the ordinary headings, such as "Father, Husband, or Son" above the names and dates, she chose the archaic English word for poet, "Maker." "That's what he had been, unswervingly, unpretentiously, a maker of poems. To be engraved on the tombstone I selected a line of his that I particularly loved, 'And the day's brightness dwindles into stars.' Throughout his life Charles saw unblinkingly that the brightness dwindles: He also saw the stars" (*Man and Poet* 67).

Epilogue

SOON AFTER CHARLES' DEATH, Marie decided to go ahead with their plans to leave New York for Santa Monica. It was a logical move, for her closest family lived on the West Coast. Her sister, Zivia, lived in Santa Monica, and her son David lived in Seattle. At the age of seventy-seven, it was best not to be alone. She did not seem "elderly" to those who knew her — Marie Syrkin's mind and wit were still super sharp, and she retained the beauty that age can sometimes still reveal; but age as a subject began to occupy a larger part of her creative imagination. She complained, "Today I can write with as much passion about old age as I once could about love." I recall our conversation, in the year that she retired, when she took me to lunch at Serendipity, a trendy restaurant around the corner from Bloomingdale's, near her office. I did not think her old; but she lamented, "Oh, I can't bear it. All the beautiful lines of poems that I had by heart that I can no longer retrieve." Trying to spread balm on her obvious pain, I naively replied, "But, oh, Marie — it doesn't matter. You can always look it up," to which she snapped back: "Yes, but what if you can't remember where to look it up!" Later, she put the pain into verse. "The lovely lines are departing, / They glide away piecemeal, / Whom I held by heart." (*Gleanings,* "Forgetting," 15).

Yes, she would leave New York for what she knew would be the de-nouement of "The Long and Active Life of Marie Syrkin." To be sure, there was yet more to come. More recognition, more concerns about the world, more pleasures in family life; but also more awareness of one's powers passing.

It would be amusing
To write a love poem again.

I know all the rhymes
But my false teeth
Not my cold heart
Shame me. (*Gleanings,* "Inhibition," 27)

The encounter with the long past and short future became a major subject of the poetry of her late years. Friends, foes, mentors, lovers, and
husbands were gone: Hayim Greenberg had died in 1953; Aaron Bodansky, in 1960; Maurice Samuel, in 1972; David Ben-Gurion, in 1973;
Charles Reznikoff, in 1976. In her prefatory words to her collected
poems, *Gleanings: A Diary in Verse,* Marie explains that "these poems
were written over a period of sixty years — from the age of eighteen to
the present and are presented in reverse chronology." The preface is
signed "Marie Syrkin, Santa Monica 1978." She was nearing eighty and
very conscious of it. The first poems are numbered and collected under
the rubric "Of Age"; poem number two is a witty, wry, retrospective
comment on both love and age. She knew both intimately.

Women live longer than men:
The few that I loved are dead.
Had I the power to summon
Whom would I bring to my bed?

Had three Eurydices waited
In the flitting world underneath
No Orpheus would have descended
To make his bargain with Death.

I envy his pure assurance:
He had only one shade to name.
How memory mixes the moments
And makes of all choosing, shame.
(*Gleanings* 13)

The poet sidesteps an answer to her own question, but more to the
point is the fact that since Marie did live longer than most of her male
colleagues, it left her, in the last decade of her life, having to justify her
past as an idealistic polemicist for the Labor Zionist movement, as an
apologist for the words and actions of her dear friend Golda Meir, as an

antagonist of the New Left, as a bewildered but vocal adversary of the ascension of Likud, as an unshaken believer in her own interpretation of history in the face of the new revisionist historiographers, and as an unapologetic pre-postmodern feminist who in 1985, at the age of eighty-six, would write a piece entitled "Does Feminism Clash with Jewish National Need?" (*Midstream,* June/July 1985) that would ignite controversy in the Jewish feminist arena and a year later would inspire a "Symposium: Does Judaism Need Feminism?" in *Midstream.* In the 1985 article, Syrkin reports on a conference on Jewish feminism that was held in August 1984 in which leading American feminists participated and during which "intriguing questions" arose. She reports that religious feminists "added a surprising angle — surprising because it came from avowed feminists. They suggested that there may be a conflict not only between feminism and Orthodox Judaism but between feminism and the national survival of the Jewish people." Another issue was raised by a secular Israeli feminist who asked a different question bearing on Jewish national need: "Since Israel urgently requires educators for the integration of newcomers why is it more 'advanced' for a woman to be a lawyer than a school teacher — an occupation resented by many who viewed it as a device to relegate them to lesser spheres" (April 1986). Marie undoubtedly knew from experience whereof that question arose. Thus Syrkin concludes that

Both the religious and the secular feminists face a basic dilemma — the clash between national need and the desire for personal fulfillment. The question of national responsibility is peculiar to Jewish feminism. American women have no worries about the vanishing American when shaping their personal lives. Countries other than the Western democracies are endangered by overpopulation rather than a diminishing birthrate. In the Diaspora, feminists who stress their Jewish allegiance cannot escape examining the nature of their commitment.

In Israel however, "the nexus between national redemption and the emancipation of women was recognized from the start of Jewish settlement in Palestine. *The Plough Woman,*[1] a fascinating collection of memoirs written by women pioneers who came to Palestine in the early decades of the twentieth century, reveals how early the problems surfaced."

Marie's new home at 1008 Second Street was a sunny two-bedroom apartment with a balcony overlooking a tree-lined street, in a white stucco low-rise just a couple of blocks from the Pacific Ocean with its long promenade for walking. Charles may have been the Olympic walker, but Marie too loved to walk—especially along the shore in the shade of the palisades. What she felt and thought when she took those walks is there for all to see in her bittersweet poem titled "On the Palisades."

> I do not envy the hot young embracing
> Or lying in the grass or bounding by.
> But when two old folk, arm in arm, stroll slowly
> I think of you—not dead before your time
> But old like me.
>
> It was not always good between us two—
> Yet, you, familiar, sometimes loved and loving,
> How well we would have walked in this bright air,
> Beside this blue, grey, glittering sea,
> Despite the halting canes, the fallen faces,
> Sometimes in quarrel and sometimes content.
> (*Gleanings* 17)

The tone of Marie Syrkin's poetry may have turned elegaic in these late years, but her prose remained as polemical as ever and her opinions were still capable of flexibility though, she would argue, always with fidelity to principle. Her last decade was lived in what is sometimes ironically termed "interesting times," giving her ample subject matter for her wit, wisdom, and often comic take on serious subjects. Several major events had happened since Golda Meir had stepped down as prime minister. Meir had been replaced by Yitzhak Rabin, who had defeated Shimon Peres by just a few votes. Peres was Syrkin's first choice, for she admired him and regarded him as a "true intellectual." Rabin, the first *sabra* to become prime minister, a war hero of the 1948 War for Independence, and IDF Chief of Staff in the Six Day War, had been ambassador to the United States and then minister of labor in the Meir government and succeeded Meir after she stepped down. Less skeptical and more open to negotiations with Anwar Sadat than Meir had been, in 1975 Rabin signed interim agreements with Sadat regarding Israel and Egypt as well as a "Memorandum of Understanding" between the two States. Sadat, who was more of a pragmatist and less ideological than Nasser, had made a decision to end the presence of Soviet military consultants in Egypt, to step up the process of de-Nasserization, and to establish a stronger relationship with the United States, the better to court American intervention in breaking the Middle East deadlock. It was a clever strategy that opened the way for the relationship he formed with Nixon's Secretary of State Henry Kissinger during Kissinger's famous shuttle diplomacy. Meanwhile, in Israel revelation of corruption in the Labor Party, of increasing inflation, and the disclosure of the fact that Rabin's wife had failed to close her illegal bank account in the United States forced Rabin and his government to resign in March 1977. New elections were held, and to the utter dismay of Marie Syrkin and her Labor Zionist friends, for the first time a right-wing Likud government came to power with the former Revisionist — Irgunist Menachem Begin as the new Prime Minister. In the United States there was also a change of power: In 1974 Richard Nixon had resigned over the Watergate scandal and was succeeded by Gerald Ford who lost the next election in 1976 in an extremely close vote (probably because he had issued a pre-emptive pardon to Nixon). Ford was succeeded by Jimmy Carter who then orchestrated the Camp David accords — a framework for peace in the Middle East — signed after months of negotiations and deadlock that were followed by a thirteen-day meeting at Camp David and finally signed on September 17, 1978, by Anwar Sadat, Menachem Begin, and President Jimmy Carter. The Accords agreed that Security Council Resolution 242 was to be the basis on which a peace agreement would be implemented. Menachem Begin had begun the process the year before by inviting Sadat to visit Jerusalem as the first stage in negotiating a comprehensive peace treaty with Egypt, which included recognizing the rights of the Palestinian people for a homeland. Sadat accepted the invitation and was given a jubilant reception when he addressed the Knesset.

But not everybody was ecstatic over the events. Marie Syrkin was highly skeptical, and in an article entitled "The Revisionist in Power" (*State* 155–162) she laid out her demurral: "Old Labor Zionists like myself cannot pretend to enthusiasm for either the domestic or the foreign policies of Begin. At the same time I am repelled by the cynical pro-Arab tilt of the Carter administration and the readiness of Israel's active foes to shed crocodile tears over her intransigence." In this quintessentially Labor Zionist appraisal Syrkin commented on Sadat's visit to Jerusalem: "I find the hosannas that greeted Sadat as a messenger of peace excessive, especially since the frequent repeated public offers by

Israeli leaders to travel to Cairo or Damascus for face-to-face negotiations evoked no such genuflections." Marie Syrkin was also capable of error.

In the end, Begin, too, proved unexpectedly flexible in the area of territorial concessions; indeed he made an even trade which Syrkin summed up as the following: 100 percent of the Sinai for 100 percent of the West Bank. Marie Syrkin thought it a very bad deal. The flowers of the Sinai *kibbutz* in Yamit and elsewhere, she held, as well as Sinai oil, were not worth a settlement policy that would threaten the democratic and Jewish character of the State by the "incorporation of the West Bank with its million Arabs into the Jewish State. . . . If there is to be any hope for peace," Syrkin argued, "then Begin's fixation on the sacred historic right of the Jewish people to Judea and Samaria, the biblical names for the West Bank, should be removed. Paradoxically, Begin is much readier for territorial concessions in other areas." Syrkin contended that the effort would be better spent on new settlements in the underpopulated areas of the Galilee, the Negev, and the Dead Sea area.

During these distressing months, Marie received a stream of upsetting reports from Lou Kaddar about Golda Meir's multiple physical ailments (*Archives* 2 f. 1). Marie had known that Golda had been suffering in silence about her cancer condition for the last decade; more recently it was two eye operations, shingles, arthritis among other ailments. Moreover, her "mood was bad," reported Kaddar. Perhaps the bad mood was psychological as well as physical, for Kaddar writes that Marie's corrections were made to Rinna Samuels chapter in Golda Meir's autobiography on the Yom Kippur War about which "Rinna had no official papers. . . . G's memory was especially hazy about it and sees that this particular piece is just no good. It is Golda who asked me to write to you and ask you whether you would be able — and willing — to come to Ramat-Aviv, at about middle of April, maybe for a few weeks, so that you could rewrite this whole chapter. . . . G. is expecting your answer soon."[2] Marie, however, declined the invitation. It is not difficult to imagine Marie's emotions at being asked to ghostwrite for the ghostwriter. Still, Marie was deeply saddened by the state of her old friend's health. Forty-three years of friendship are not to be brushed aside.

My Life, by Golda Meir, was published in Israel, France, Germany, England, and America in 1975. The copy that Golda gave to Marie was intimately inscribed:

Dear dear Marie:
Our deep friendship for so many years was one of my greatest treasures. Our friendship and love was mutual. But I am indebted to you for so much that I cannot reciprocate. You know and I know.

> With all my love,
> Golda
> January 12, 1976.

The last sentence most probably refers to Marie's decision to leave Golda's love affairs out of her biography. It was, one remembers, before the age of "tell-all" biography.

Golda's health continued its steady decline as she went in and out of the hospital with assorted ailments. Cancer was having its piecemeal repast. But Golda's will was adamantine. At this moment, the American playwright William Gibson informed Meir that he planned to write a play about her; he gave her his outline for the drama, which she then sent on to Marie Syrkin who wrote a positive response. "Your letter clinched the matter and I was given permission to give Golda's O.K. to Gibson" wrote Lou Kaddar to Marie. When the play was finished, Marie was told that it would open in New York starring Anne Bancroft. Despite her abysmally declining health, Golda made plans to attend the opening and invited Marie to stay with the family at the Americana Hotel. "Of course, it would be lovely if the play is a success. Otherwise a general suicide might be contemplated," Lou Kaddar wrote. The play was not a success, the reviews were bad, and Golda decided to pack up and go back to Israel. This was the last time Marie saw her friend alive.

Golda Meir returned to Israel just in time for the visit of the Egyptian president and, as Lou Kaddar put it in her letter of December 14, 1977, she "was a tremendous success with him. . . . She won't admit that she was impressed by him but I can assure you that she was. The Israeli people was at its very best and it was wonderful to live through it all. We can't believe nothing will come out. We all pray that Sadat and Begin stay alive and well. . . . G. is deeply hurt, of course. She does not yet believe in Sadat's honest intentions, nor in Begin's wisdom. I hope she is proved wrong—whatever pain it causes her."

A quarter of a century later, William Gibson would revise his play several times, finally renaming it *Golda's Balcony;* it would be billed as a new play, it would be produced on Broadway by the Manhattan Ensemble Theater starring Tovah Feldshuh as Golda; it would have a long run, and it would tour America. But, between the time it was first produced and its incarnation twenty-five years later, not only the play underwent revision, but so did Golda herself as the new historians began to chip away at Golda's image, reducing it in size, and arguing that all her American biographers, beginning with Marie Syrkin, were hagiographers who did not tell the truth about their subject. Marie Syrkin, one revisionist historian argues, "played a major role in publicizing the facts of Meir's life and in helping to keep her memory alive" (Schmidt 157). Marie's first biography was written in 1955; the next two updates were published as Golda became prime minister. Thus, Syrkin could hardly be trying to keep her friend's memory alive. And whatever revision of Golda she herself might make, Marie would always believe that Golda had remained true to and acted upon her belief in the values of socialism and the just cause of Zionism. Golda Meir died of lymphoma at 4:30 P.M. Friday afternoon, December 8, 1978. Perhaps it was when Marie Syrkin received this news that she was moved to write her poem entitled "For Golda" which she did not publish until 1984.

> Because you became a great woman
> With strong features
> Big nose
> And heavy legs,
> None will believe how beautiful you were,
> Gray-eyed and slim ankled.
>
> The men who loved you are dead,
> So I speak for the record.
> Indeed you were lovely among maidens
> Once
> In Milwaukee and Merhavia,
> And sometimes in Jerusalem.[3]

Or it could have been the leave-taking in Israel that inspired Marie to write her poem after she returned home from Golda's funeral. Syrkin had been invited by President Carter to be a member of the United States Presidential Delegation to fly to Israel aboard Air Force One to the funeral of Golda Meir. The party was comprised of Senators, Congressmen, the Secretary of State, labor leaders, Jewish community leaders, the president's mother, and a "few old friends." Carter himself did not attend, but his mother Lillian, the head of the delegation, greatly impressed Marie not only with the fact that she "could sincerely voice her admiration of a contemporary she had never met" (*State* 163), but also by her outspoken, somewhat indecorous, folksy speech. She was "quite a character," Marie explained. But in a remembrance written about a month later, Syrkin described her own experience as a member of a "prestigious delegation — and not oblivious of its glamor — to attend the funeral of the woman I had held in love and honor for over 40 years."

I had known for some weeks that Golda was dying, so that the news, when it came, had only the shock of finality, not surprise. Now in the midst of State Department officials, political notables, and distractions of this particular flight, she kept eluding me. Even in the throng on Mount Herzl, where we stood in a driving rain huddled under umbrellas, she was remote. The prayers at the grave site could not be heard by most of us, nor could we see the ceremony. Only the immediate family and the chief dignitaries stood close enough to view the austere proceedings. I wondered if Golda would have wanted this huge state funeral from which, because of the number of foreign delegations and government officials, the plain folk of Jerusalem had to be excluded. In endless processions the men and women of Israel had circled around the bier where the body lay in state, and they lined the streets as the cortege wound its way up to Mount Herzl. But the ordinary citizens were neither in the limited hall of the Knesset at the services nor at the burial, for compelling reasons of space and security. Nevertheless I could not help thinking that just as Golda had forbidden the reading of eulogies at her funeral, had she known how large and distinguished an array of personages from all parts of the world would preempt the ranks of the mourners she would have left word that room be found for the kibbutzniks and comrades she had cherished. But her simple instructions had been written before she became Prime Minister and she had failed to anticipate the pomp that would attend her passing. Not that she would have been indifferent to the magnitude of the tribute; she was human enough to appreciate recognition, but an even stronger impulse of her nature was an abiding loyalty to those who had shared her struggle and who had been her fellows for over a half a century. I had witnessed too many poignant meetings between her and comrades from the distant days of Merhavia to the present to doubt that such would have been her feeling. (*State* 163–164)

After the funeral, Marie returned to Santa Monica, saddened indeed, but not ready to quit the world herself. There would be ten more years of activity and life in Israel, New York, and California.

One of Marie's great gifts was the capacity to maintain strong family ties and to make and keep friends. Now that she lived in Santa Monica she was nearer to Zivia, the sister she loved with all her heart (and the feeling was mutual). Because of the age difference — a full generation — Zivia, who was only two years older than Marie's son David, was as much a daughter as a sister. Their professional lives, however, had taken somewhat different paths; Zivia had become a Ph.D. in mathematics, and she and her husband, the distinguished atmospheric scientist Morton Wurtele, had taught at UCLA since 1958. Despite Zivia's interest in mathematics and Marie's self-deprecatory claim to ignorance of science and technology, the two shared interests central to their lives, most especially, Israel, where Zivia maintained an apartment and became friends with many of Marie's comrades — including Golda, Lou Kaddar, Shulamit Nardi, and the Labor Zionists who pioneered the land and founded the northern *kibbutz* Kfar Blum located just at the base of the Golan Heights. Zivia and Morton's children Jonathan and Eve were deeply loved by Marie — though they too pursued fields mysterious to their aunt. Jonathan, a professor of physics at UC Berkeley, became a member of the *kibbutz* Kfar Blum and as Lou Kaddar reported in a letter to Marie, "Jonny is in the army and is . . . driving a tank!" Eve was to become a highly regarded, much published professor of genetics and cell biology.

Meantime, Marie now was geographically closer to her son and his family. Visits to and from Seattle were somewhat easier and more frequent than from New York: only two and a half hours by air and considerably cheaper. By the time Marie moved to Santa Monica her grandchildren had grown into young men. She had a very loving relationship with the whole family, and it even gave her a chance to practice the kind of clever rhymed verse she had always enjoyed writing. When her twelve-year-old grandson won a swimming meet, she rewarded him with a comic tribute in verse in which she gave him some cautious advice. The poem "For Joel" ends:

> If you should think this counsel erring,
> Consider, Grandma's not a herring.
> Nevertheless, felicitation!
> But, grandson, swim in moderation.[4]

During one of Marie's trips to Seattle in the early 1970s, David introduced her to a fellow faculty member, a Victorianist in the English department who was Jewish, religiously observant, and Zionist. No doubt David, who was not especially involved in any Jewish organizational groups either on or off campus, thought that his mother might enjoy the company of Professor Edward Alexander as he showed her the Jewish sights and sounds of Seattle. It was a successful match, and Ed Alexander and Marie Syrkin became friends and correspondents, writing letters to one another over a period of a fifteen years. They were indeed an odd pair. Their politics were opposed: Marie, on the left and Ed, on the right. This, however, did not stand in the way of their friendship, for that was based on absolute respect for one another's intellectual capabilities and commitment to Israel. The letters are filled with comments about Israel and the Begin government, (on which they did not exactly agree), despair about the poor quality of the Zionist journal *Midstream* under the editorship of Joel Carmichael. Alexander's admiration for Marie was demonstrated in two interviews with her that he arranged and conducted for the University of Washington television channel.

The last ten years of Marie Syrkin's life showed only a slight decline of activity, words, and accomplishment. On May 27, 1979, Brandeis University awarded Marie Syrkin an Honorary Doctor of Humane Letters. The Citation read: "Pioneer at Brandeis, Biographer of the Mighty and the Martyred, Activist and Archivist, Wherever Modern Jewish History Was Being Made, There you made your Home." Marie now had the doctoral degree that she had always yearned for, but her immediate incredulous response to me after the ceremony that I had attended was "Did you see who I was marching with? Eudora Welty! Can you imagine, Eudora Welty! I love her writing—and she got an honorary degree too!"

The next year, in October 1980, the Labor Zionist Movement held a celebration in honor of Marie Syrkin's eightieth birthday and the seventy-fifth anniversary of the movement. Then on February 6, 1980, Marie received a letter from Teddy Kollek, the mayor of Jerusalem inviting her to be the guest of the State of Israel at *Mishkenot Sha'anim* (Peaceful dwelling) that had been built in 1860 by Sir Moses Montefiore as the first building outside the walls of the Old City, thus making it the first building in the modern city of Jerusalem. The compound had been restored in its original style and had nine furnished modern apartments with breathtaking views of the Old City walls and Mount Zion. Intended for use by visiting artists and scholars, *Mishkenot* was meant to contribute to the intellectual and artistic life of Jerusalem. Marie, accompanied by her friend Ruth Kunzer, professor of literature at UCLA, stayed at *Mishkenot* from June 3 to June 25, 1980. The visit was sponsored by Martin Peretz, a former student and longtime admirer who had acquired *The New Republic* in 1974 and was its editor-in-chief; Peretz had commissioned her to write an article about Jerusalem that appeared in the November 1980 issue. But in a letter to Ed Alexander she wrote, in a P.S., "I was invited for *2 weeks* (emphasis Marie's) to *Mishkenot Sha'ananim.*" Was her nose a bit out of joint at the short stay? Marie also remarked that a "fellow Dweller" was Lucy Dawidowicz, whom she had known since their days in Munich in 1946 when Marie was working for the Hillel Foundation and Dawidowicz was with the JDC. Later, the two women would not entirely share a political or religious perspective. In 1988, however, I received a letter from Lucy Dawidowicz who told me that she always felt a "sense of kinship" with Marie. Indeed, in the years when Marie was living in Santa Monica and would make periodic trips to New York, she would get together with Dawidowicz. On one occasion in 1988, just a few months before Marie's death, Lucy Dawidowicz held a luncheon for Marie at her apartment on West 86th Street. Among the invited guests were the editor of *Commentary,* Neil Kozodoy and his then wife Ruth, the novelist Norma Rosen and her husband Bob, and Cynthia Ozick and her husband Bernard. Norma Rosen remembers that event clearly. She recalls that she had expected Marie to be a gritty, chunky, plain-looking, unstylish woman, somewhat in the Golda Meir mold, and was more than surprised to meet a slight, still pretty, somewhat "flirty" woman in a flowing flowered summer dress. During the luncheon chitchat, someone mentioned the Beatles musician John *Lennon.* Marie's hearing however, had become a victim of age; she had heard *Lenin* and said, "Lenin! Don't tell me you are still arguing about Communism!" But Ozick, remembering that moment as a glorious though hilarious one, remarked that it showed that Marie's ear was "always attuned to history — to the grand sweep of things" (Private conversation April 2007).

The year after her stay at *Mishkenot,* Marie returned to Jerusalem in July 1981 to receive a prestigious award. The citation of it read "In admiration and appreciation for the person she is and the work she has done and continues to do on behalf of the Jewish people and the Jewish State, the Hebrew University of Jerusalem has named Marie Syrkin its Solomon Bublick Prize Laureate for 1981." She wrote to Ed Alexander about this, but in a typically Marie remark she scrawled this P.S., "The Bublick Prize carries with it 'the very small sum' according to [Avram] Harmon of $1,000. What some people call 'small.'"

The awards, prizes, and degrees increased by yearly degrees: She had been honored by the State of Israel Bonds in 1972; in 1980 a celebration was held in honor of her eightieth birthday and the seventy-fifth anniversary of the Labor Zionist Movement; in 1983 the *Jewish Frontier* published a "special double issue" entirely devoted to tributes to her by her friends, colleagues, and students; the Hebrew Union College–Jewish Institute of Religion in Los Angeles awarded Marie Syrkin the degree of Honorary Doctor of Humane Letters in 1984; in 1987 the City of Los Angeles at the thirtieth biennial convention of *Na'Amat* USA awarded Marie Syrkin the Golda Meir Human Relations Award. And on October 4, 1987, in Los Angeles, the National Committee for Labor Israel-Histadrut bestowed the Histadrut Menorah Award. Then, in June of 1988, the Reconstructionist Rabbinical College granted her an honorary degree known as the *Keter Shem Tov,* (Crown of the Good Name). I had the great privilege of reading out her accomplishments and bestowing the honor upon her. It was an especially tender moment for us both, for she had been the most important teacher in my life and I, a most willing student.

Nonetheless, I also wanted to instruct Marie — the most ardent secularist I knew in those early days at Brandeis. She had almost convinced me. But I had soon after discovered the philosophy of Mordecai Kaplan and had become a willing student again under the tutelage of Ira Eisenstein, Kaplan's son-in-law. Thus, once in about 1983 when Ira Eisenstein and I were attending a convention in Los Angeles, he asked to join me when I visited Marie. The meeting was unforgettable. Totally ignored, I listened as he answered her query about whether or not there really were two sets of ten commandments in the Bible. He said yes, asked for a text, and proceeded to give her a one-hour Bible lesson (Exodus 20 and 34) as she, dazzled, listened attentively to his lesson. It was an amazing and amusing moment as I observed my first teacher take a lesson from my second teacher.

A few years later, when Ira Eisenstein published his autobiography, I sent it to Marie. She wrote to Eisenstein to tell him that she read it "with absorption and pleasure." Her letter is an example of her lasting capacity for connections, of her sentimentality, in the good sense, for a rich past, and for the still sharp critical faculty of a woman nearing ninety. "Dear Ira," wrote Marie Syrkin:

First there was the thrill, not shock, of recognition. I had known so many of the people you mention in similar connections. . . . But this coziness is only one, and more limited, aspect of my appreciation of your book. I admire the simplicity and candor with which you describe not only your personal *sturm und drang* but the whole tangle of being a rabbi and starting an organization and a journal. In the woes of the latter I am well versed. One rarely reads a personal account that is so honest, not in sensational revelations, but in regard to the actual problems human beings face professionally and intellectually. (Archives 1 f. 14)

In her last years in Santa Monica, Marie Syrkin continued to lecture, sometimes appearing on double bills and in a double interview in *Moment* with her neighbor Trude Weiss Rosmarin, the founder of the *Spectator;* she kept up with current events and ideas, including a book on contemporary literary critical theory; she published a collection of her essays *The State of the Jews;* and she published a volume of her own poems called *Gleanings: A Diary in Verse.* Her articles continued to appear in a variety of publications. She wrote essays and editorials on Jews and Blacks, on Nellie Sachs, Philip Roth,[5] Henry Roth, Jesse Jackson, Jews for Jesus, Zionism, America, literature, and anything about which she felt compelled to speak her mind. And she went on writing poetry.

Marie Syrkin's long and brilliant life came to an end when she died within weeks from pancreatic cancer in a Santa Monica Hospital on February 1, 1989. She was buried in the Westwood Village Cemetery in Los Angeles.

On May 16, 1989, a memorial service was held at the New York Historical Society. The speakers came from a variety of aspects of her life and all were her friends. Martin Peretz had been her student; Irving Howe had been her colleague at Brandeis; Ben Halpern had been her colleague at the *Jewish Frontier* as well as at Brandeis; Naomi Replansky was a poet who read from Marie's and Charles' poetry; Peter Osnos, her nephew; Lucy Dawidowicz, an old friend; and Leon Wieseltier, a younger friend and admirer. The music was the slow movements of two Beethoven sonatas for violin and piano. The memorial ended fittingly with *Hatikvah.*

Notes

Introduction *(pages 1–7)*

1. This unpublished poem appears in a group of poems written from 1979 on, after the publication of *Gleanings*. They were collected by Naomi Replansky from various sources.

2. "Marie Syrkin and Trude Weiss Rosmarin: A *Moment* Interview," *Moment* Sept. 1983: 37–44 (Hereafter cited parenthetically in text as *Moment*).

Chapter 1. *Marie's Birthright (pages 11–48)*

1. Marie Syrkin, *Nachman Syrkin, Socialist Zionist: A Biographical Memoir and Selected Essays* (New York: Herzl Press, 1960) 61, 62. (hereafter cited parenthetically in text as *Memoir*).

2. Howard Sachar, *The Course of Modern Jewish History* (New York: Vintage, 1990) 80–92 (hereafter cited parenthetically in text as Sachar).

3. "Mogilev," *Encyclopedia Judaica*. CD-ROM (Israel: Keter, 2002) (hereafter cited parenthetically in text as *Judaica*).

4. qtd. in S. Ettinger, *A History of the Jewish People,* ed. H. H. Ben Sasson (Cambridge: Harvard U Press, 1976) 882 (hereafter cited parenthetically in text as Sasson).

5. The May Laws stated that no Jew could move his or her place of residence to any rural area of Russia, including the Pale of Settlement. Thus, the crowded cities were immediately sealed off and Jews were prevented from moving to the villages. Those already in the rural or village areas also had stringent new restrictions. See Sachar, 282–283.

6. Shmarya Levin, *Forward from Exile* trans. and ed. Maurice Samuel (Philadelphia: Jewish Publication Society, 1967) 252–253. (hereafter cited parenthetically in text as Levin).

7. Hayim Nachman Bialik, "The City of Slaughter," trans. Robert Michael in *Menorah Review* 57 (Winter 2003): 2.

8. qtd. in David Vital, "The Afflictions of the Jews and the Afflictions of Zionism: The Meaning and Consequences of the 'Uganda' Controversy," *Essen-*

tial Papers on Zionism eds. Jehuda Reinharz and Anita Shapira (New York: a NYU, 1996) 126 (hereafter cited parenthetically in text as Vital).

9. Amos Elon, *Herzl: A Biography* (New York: Holt, Rhinehart and Winston, 1975) 401–420.

10. Lucy S. Dawidowicz, *From That Place and Time: A Memoir 1938–1947* (New York: W. W. Norton, 1989) xiii.

11. Marie Syrkin, *The State of the Jews* (Washington, D.C.: New Republic, 1980) 1 (hereafter cited parenthetically in text as *State*).

Chapter 2. A Bronx Adolescence (pages 49–70)

1. Emanuel S. Goldsmith, *Architects of Yiddishism at the Beginning of the Twentieth Century* (New Jersey: Fairleigh Dickinson, 1976) 180.

2. In 1901, the historian Simon Dubnow presented his theory of autonomism, which conceives of a Jewish national and cultural autonomy in the Diaspora.

3. Marie Syrkin, "Morris High School, Class of '16," *The New Republic* November 7, 1983: 22–27 (hereafter cited parenthetically in text as Morris High).

4. Marie Syrkin, personal interview with Carole Kessner, January, 1989. I had many conversations and correspondence over the years with Syrkin and can date only one *official* taped interview, which occurred for a week in January 1989 (hereafter cited parenthetically in text as Personal interview).

5. Actually, Marie did distinguish herself; she was the editor of her high school yearbook.

Chapter 3. That Fabulous Summer: Maurice (pages 71–90)

1. Marie Syrkin, Diary: Age 16. March 28–June 4, 1915. Personal copy, given to me by Marie Syrkin (hereafter cited parenthetically in text as *Diary*).

2. Marie Syrkin's sister, Zivia Wurtele, gave me a box of letters that she found after Marie's death. Zivia knew that the box had been given to Marie by Eugenia Shafran many decades before, when Eugenia had just been married and her husband asked her to break with her old friends and to dispose of her old letters. Thus, she gave the box to Marie and asked her to hold them for her—which Marie did for the rest of her life. The box contained letters from Eugenia's father, from a group of women friends, but most importantly, there were letters from Marie and to Marie and from Maurice Samuel and to Maurice Samuel, who was their mutual friend at the time. A few letters were quite surprising as well as revealing (hereafter referred to parenthetically in the text as private collection).

3. Marie Syrkin, letter to Eugenia Shafran, undated, Marie Syrkin Papers, American Jewish Archives, Cincinnati. Most of Marie Syrkin's letters to Eugenia are held in this collection, but a few are in the box in my possession noted above (hereafter cited parenthetically in text as Shafran, Archives).

4. Maurice Samuel, letter to Marie Syrkin dated September 22, 1915, Marie Syrkin Papers, American Jewish Archives, Cincinnati (hereafter cited parenthetically in text as Samuel, Archives).

5. In 2007, *The New Republic* published an advertisement, which ran for many months, celebrating the fiftieth anniversary of the Roth Statute and promoting a new book on the subject.

6. Samuel Roth, letter to Marie Syrkin dated August 23, 1916, Marie Syrkin Papers, American Jewish Archives, Cincinnati (hereafter cited parenthetically in text as Roth, Archives).

Chapter 4: Elopement and Annulment (pages 91–120)

1. Maurice Samuel, *Little Did I Know: Recollections and Reflections* (New York: Knopf, 1963), 267. (hereafter cited parenthetically in the text as *Little Did I Know.*

2. This is an undated letter. The internal evidence points to 1916 or 1917. The letter was found in the box that Marie Syrkin had held for Eugenia Shafran.

3. Eugenia Shafran married a man named Ganzbarg; he was a painter and a Communist who opposed Eugenia's relationships with her Zionist friends. After her marriage, Eugenia severed her connections with Marie and Maurice Samuel, etc. She lived in the Bronx and had a home in upstate New York. She spent her last years in a Jehovah's Witness retirement home in Pennsylvania.

4. See Stephen Duncombe and Andrew Mattson, *The Bobbed Haired Bandit: A True Story of Crime and Celebrity in 1920's New York,* (New York: NYU Press, 2006).

5. During the summer Maurice Samuel wrote frequently to Marie Syrkin. She kept the letters, and most of them are held in the American Jewish Archives in Cincinnati, Ohio. These letters are undated, but internal evidence shows that they were written in the summer of 1917. They will be referred to parenthetically in the text as Archives, Summer 1917.

6. Marie had finished one year at Hunter and would continue for another. But she planned to apply to Cornell for the Fall 1918 semester.

7. In 1919 Pinhas Rutenberg settled in Palestine where in 1923 he founded the Palestine Electric Corporation which built several large hydroelectric dams on the Jordan River. This brought considerable progress—illumination and refrigeration—to the pioneering population of the country and greatly improved the standard of living and the growth of industry in the Yishuv (Sachar 457).

8. Maurice Samuel Papers, American Jewish Archives, Cincinnati, Ohio Collection 89, Box 30, Folder 7 Diaries, Notebooks 1913–1922, n.d. (hereafter cited parenthetically in the text as Samuel, *Diary*).

9. Marital Annulment Documents, Brandeis University Library, Marie Syrkin Papers, Special Collections (hereafter cited parenthetically in text as Annulment Documents).

10. From September 28, 1917 through January 1919 the letters from Maurice Samuel to Marie Syrkin, held at the American Jewish Archives, are only sporadically dated. The approximate dates of the undated letters are determined by internal evidence. I will quote from them without individual documentation, except where I am able to supply the accurate date in the text.

Chapter 5. Marriage, Motherhood, and Tragedy (pages 121–158)

1. Anzia Yezierska describes the same experience in her 1925 novel, *Bread Givers,* when she writes about arriving at an out-of-town college: "Before this, New York was all of America to me. But now I came to a town of quiet streets, shaded with green trees. No crowds, no tenements. No hurrying noise to beat the race of the hours."

2. "Cornell University," *Encylopaedia Brittanica,* 1942 ed.

3. Brandeis University Library, Marie Syrkin Papers, Special Collections. Letters from Maurice Samuel to Marie Syrkin, Dec. 7, 1918 (hereafter referred to in text as Brandeis, Letters). During her life, Syrkin gave a small group of her letters from Maurice Samuel to the Brandeis University Library, though the bulk was deposited after her death in the American Jewish Archives.

4. Copy of the letter from Maurice Samuel to Marie Syrkin, dated February 26, 1919 was given to me by Marie Syrkin.

5. Gerald Sorin, *A Time for Building: The Third Migration, The Jewish People in America* ed. Henry Feingold, vol. III, (Baltimore: Johns Hopkins UP) 212.

6. Ben Halpern, "The Americanization of Zionism 1880–1930," *Essential Papers on Zionism,* eds. Jehuda Reinharz and Anita Shapira (New York: NYU Press, 1996) 318–336 (hereafter cited parenthetically in text as *Essential Papers*).

7. This letter was contained in the box of Eugenia's letters that Marie Syrkin held for safekeeping.

8. Series H, Box 1, Folder 14 contains the Secretary's book of the Zionist Society of Cornell University (1919).

9. This letter from Eugenia to Marie was found in the box held by Marie Syrkin.

10. Marie Syrkin, *Gleanings: A Diary in Verse* (Santa Barbara: Rhythms Press, 1979) (hereafter cited parenthetically in text as *Gleanings*).

11. Marie Syrkin, "Avuka." *New Palestine* August 4, 1923: 140. (hereafter cited parenthetically in text as Avuka).

Chapter 6. David, Divorce, and the Death of Nachman (pages 159–182)

1. David Bodansky in an E-mail dated May 17, 2005 (hereafter E-mail will be cited parenthetically in the text as E-mail). The personal interviews and telephone conversations that I had with David Bodansky and his wife, Beverly, during the time that I was preparing this book will be cited hereafter parenthetically in text as personal conversation.

2. In my search for Eugenia Shafran, who disappeared from Marie's life in the late 1920s, I determined that she had lived in the Bronx, married a Communist who was a painter named Marc Peter Ganbarg, and had a home in upstate New York. Her obituary appeared in the *Gospel Herald*, Volume LXIV, Number 17, April 27, 1971, page 338. Surprisingly, it reads, "Ganbarg Eugenia, daughter of Nathaniel and Bertha (Ostromogilsky) Shafran, was born at Kiev, Russia,

January 31, 1897; died of a heart attack at Landis Homes, Lititz, Pa., Apr. 2 1971; aged 74y.2 m.2 d. She was married to Marc Peter Ganbarg who preceded her in death Oct. 20th, 1963. She was a member of Hernley Mennonite Church. Funeral Services were held at the Buch Funeral Home Manheim, Pa. Interment in Hernley Cemetery." I also received an E-mail from John Kraybill, a fellow member of the Landis Home whom I tracked down, who wrote

My wife Thelma and I live at Landis Homes, which is the Mennonite Retirement Village where Eugenia Ganbarg lived for about a year in 1970–71. Thelma and I lived in New York City from 1953 to 1966 where I served part time as pastor of the Seventh Avenue Mennonite Church, located at 146th Street and Seventh Avenue . . . in upper Manhattan. During our years in New York City I worked part time driving a taxi to supplement my income. I also had a friend . . . who owned the Fordham Private Car Service. . . . In 1964 [he] asked me to take Eugenia Ganbarg from her apartment in the south Bronx to her house that she owned in Worcester, New York, which is west of Albany. I have kept a diary for the past 45 years and my diary indicates that between November 5, 1964 and June 28, 1966 I made ten trips back and forth to take Eugenia to her upstate home or to bring her back to the Bronx. . . . Attending the Fox Street Mennonite Church 1960's was a young woman by the name of Lillian Bruckhart who was from the Lancaster County, Pennsylvania area and her home church was Hernleys Mennonite, the church that Eugenia later joined while she was here at Landis Homes. Lillian married Bernie Spanier, a jewish christian that she met while living in the Bronx. Bernie and Lillian lived among jewish people in the Bronx and often visited their neighbors, especially persons that were alone, as was the case with Eugenia Ganbarg. . . . Thelma and I believe that it was through the influence of Bernie and Lillian Spanier that Eugenia converted from her jewish background to the Christian faith in the early 1960's. The fact that Eugenia joined Lillian's former church, Hernleys Mennonite, when she moved to Landis Homes, makes us fairly sure that this was how it took place.

3. Personal conversation with wife of Maurice Samuel's son Gershom, in Jerusalem, July 2005.

4. Much of the correspondence from Maurice Samuel to Eugenia Shafran was found in the box that Marie Syrkin had held (hereafter cited parenthetically in text as Samuel, Box).

5. Louis Kaplan, "On Maurice Samuel's Twenty-Fifth *Yahrzeit*," *Judaism*, September 22, 1997.

6. Charles Madison, *Jewish Publishing in America* (New York: Sanhedrin Press, 1976) 226.

7. Vladimir Jabotinsky, *Political Dictionary of the State of Israel* (Jerusalem: Jerusalem Publishing House, 1993). (Hereafter cited parenthetically in text as *P.D.*)

8. Marie Syrkin, "Charles: A Memoir," *Charles Reznikoff: Man and Poet*, ed. Milton Hindus (Maine: National Poetry Foundation Inc. Univ. of Maine at Orono, 1984) 37 (hereafter cited parenthetically in text as *Man and Poet*).

9. The friend might have been Samuel Roth. In a curious irony, in 1920

Reznikoff's first volume of modest but commercially published poems appeared. The publisher was Roth himself, who also owned The Poetry Bookshop in Greenwich Village. Roth was a great admirer of Reznikoff's poetry.

Chapter 7. A New Life: Charles (pages 183–213)

1. Reno <http://www.jour.unr.edu/outpost/specials/wedding%20Pkgx./div2 .reno.html>
2. Milton Hindus, ed., *Selected Letters of Charles Reznikoff 1917–1976* (Santa Rosa: Black Sparrow Press, 1997) 11 (hereafter cited parenthetically in text as *Letters*).
3. Ira Eisenstein, "Henry Hurwitz: Editor, Gadfly, Dreamer," *The "Other" New York Jewish Intellectuals*, ed. Carole S. Kessner (New York: NYU Press, 1994) 191–205 (hereafter cited parenthetically in text as *Other*).

Chapter 8. An Unorthodox Marriage: Palestine and Hollywood (pages 217–240)

1. Charles Reznikoff, *Poems 1918–1936*, vol. I (Santa Barbara: Black Sparrow Press, 1976) (hereafter cited parenthetically in text as *Poems* I).
2. Irving Howe, "For Marie," *Jewish Frontier* January/February (1983):8 (hereafter cited parenthetically in text as "For Marie").
3. Lucy Dawidowicz, *The War Against the Jews* (New York: Holt, Rinehart & Winston, 1975) 47 (hereafter cited parenthetically in text as *War v. Jews*).
4. MideastWeb.orgpalpop.htm (hereafter cited parenthetically in text as Mideast Web).
5. "Jewish Agency" *Political Dictionary of the State of Israel* (Jerusalem: Jerusalem Publishing House, 1993) (hereafter cited parenthetically in text as *P.D.*).
6. Golda Meir, *My Life* (New York: G.P. Putnam's, 1975) 55–56 (hereafter cited parenthetically in text as Meir).
7. Marie Syrkin, *Golda Meir: Woman with a Cause* (New York: G.P. Putnam's, 1969) 95 (hereafter cited parenthetically in text as Syrkin, *Woman*).
8. Marie Syrkin, *State of the Jews* (Washington, D.C.: New Republic, 1980) 164–165.

Chapter 9. At the Nexus of the "Jewish Problem" (pages 241–261)

1. Walter Laqueur, *A History of Zionism* (New York: Schocken, 1976) 319 (hereafter cited parenthetically in text as Laqueur).
2. Shabtai Teveth, *Ben-Gurion and the Holocaust* (New York: Harcourt Brace, 1996) xliii (hereafter cited parenthetically in text as Teveth).
3. These were terms that became familiar words in Max Lerner's course on American Civilization in the early years of Brandeis University. The lectures

would later appear in his book, *America as a Civilization* 2 vols. (New York: Simon and Schuster, 1964, 1967).

4. Marie Syrkin gave me a carbon copy of her typescript of this poem, which was written in 1934.

5. Mark A. Raider, *The Emergence of American Zionism* (New York: NYU Press, 1998) 33–34 (hereafter cited parenthetically in text as Raider).

6. Marie Syrkin ed., *Hayim Greenberg Anthology* (Detroit: Wayne State, 1968) 10–11 (hereafter cited parenthetically in text as *Greenberg*).

7. Marie Syrkin, "That First Decade," *Jewish Frontier* January–February 1983: 41. Reprinted from December 1979) (hereafter cited parenthetically in text as *Frontier*).

8. Irving Howe, "The New York Intellectuals: A Chronicle and A Critique," *Commentary* 46, no. 4 (October 1968) 29 (hereafter cited parenthetically in text as "Intellectuals").

9. Adam Kirsch, "Subject and Object," *The New Republic Online*, (Feb. 16, 2006).

10. Amnon Rubenstein, *The Zionist Dream Revisited* (New York: Schocken, 1984) 55–56. (hereafter cited parenthetically in text as *Zionist Dream*).

11. Michael Brown, *The Israeli-American Connection: Its Roots in the Yishuv, 1914–1945.* (Detroit: Wayne State, 1996) 224.

12. In 1965, Marie Syrkin wrote a letter to the editor in the *Jerusalem Post*, dated January 12. In it she attacked David Ben-Gurion for his current campaign to discredit the Eshkol government in the Lavon affair, which concerned a 1954 intelligence fiasco when an Israeli spy ring was caught in Egypt during Pinhas Lavon's tenure as Israel's Minister of Defense. Lavon was dismissed from his post. The controversy was about who was responsible and whether or not Lavon should be rehabilitated. The issue festered for over ten years, and in her 1965 letter, Syrkin writes, "Were this campaign by Mr. Ben-Gurion against his former comrades cast in the form of respectable political opposition, there would be no reason for adverse comment. But when Mr. Ben-Gurion characterizes ministers of the Government of Israel as 'liars,' and casts aspersions not only on their competence but also on their integrity, he goes beyond the bounds of permissible polemic." Syrkin also expresses her concern that Ben-Gurion's style is harmful to Israel at home and in the Diaspora. But she also praises him and recounts his "secure" and "glorious" place in modern Jewish history. Ben-Gurion's reply follows. He argues his own case and refers to his 1965 pamphlet, "Things As they Are," in which he says that he examines the facts as he knows them, which led to his conclusion that Levi Eshkol should not be Prime Minister and Minister of Defense. Though he opened his letter saying, "Since I know and admire Marie Syrkin as a lover of Israel, I shall try and give her a correct version of things as they really are, and hope that when she returns to the U.S. she will no longer be a party to this slander." He ends his account as follows: "I am almost certain that Marie Syrkin did not read the pamphlet, and has no idea of what I contended there out of concern for the honour and standing of the State of Israel — for these are no less dear to me than they are to Marie Syrkin. As one who was a friend of her esteemed father, the late Labor Zionist ideologist Nachman Syrkin, I suggest that she study the problem fully before

she expresses her opinion on it." The whole affair ended in 1965 with a temporary split in the Mapai Party when Ben-Gurion created the Rafi Party.

Chapter 10. On the Jewish Frontier: The Twenty-First Zionist Congress (pages 262–289)

1. Zeev Sternhell, *The Founding Myths of Israel* (Princeton: Princeton University Press, 1998) ix.

2. Maurice Samuel, letter to Marie Syrkin dated July 27, 1936, special collections, Brandeis University Library (hereafter cited parenthetically in text as Brandeis Library).

3. H. H. Ben-Sasson, ed. *A History of the Jewish People* (Cambridge: Harvard University Press, 1976) 986 (hereafter cited parenthetically in text as Ben-Sasson).

4. Martin Gilbert, *The Arab-Israeli Conflict: Its History in Maps* (London: Weidenfeld and Nicolson, 1976) 20–23 (hereafter cited parenthetically in text as Gilbert).

5. William M. Brinner and Moses Rischin, eds., *Like All the Nations? The Life and Legacy of Judah L. Magnes* (Albany: SUNY Press, 1987) 119 (hereafter cited parenthetically in text as Magnes).

6. Michael Berenbaum, *The World Must Know* (Boston: Little Brown, 1993) 22 (hereafter cited parenthetically in text as Berenbaum).

Chapter 11. The War, the White Paper, and the Rescue of Jews (pages 290–319)

1. Saul Bellow, *Seize the Day: The Portable Saul Bellow* (New York: Viking, 1974) 105.

2. William L. Shirer, *The Rise and Fall of the Third Reich* (New York: Simon and Schuster, 1960) 383 (hereafter cited parenthetically in text as Shirer).

3. Henry Feingold, *A Time for Searching: Entering the Mainstream 1920–1945,* The Jewish People in America IV (Baltimore: Johns Hopkins, 1992) 229–230 (hereafter cited parenthetically in text as Feingold).

4. Irving Howe, "For Marie," *Jewish Frontier* January/February 1983, 8.

5. "World War 2 Timeline 1939–1945" <http://www.worldwar-2.net/prelude-to-war/prelude-to-war-index.html> (hereafter cited parenthetically in text as worldwar-2).

6. The affidavit was for the purpose of emigration to the United States.

7. Charles Reznikoff, *The Manner Music* (Santa Barbara: Black Sparrow, 1977).

Chapter 12. Wartime Horrors: Personal Unhappiness (pages 320–352)

1. Charles Reznikoff, *Family Chronicle* (Princeton: Markus Weiner, 1988).

2. Charles Reznikoff, *Inscriptions: 1944–1956* (Santa Barbara: Black Sparrow Press, 1959) 39 (hereafter cited parenthetically in text as *Inscriptions*).

3. *Common Ground*. VIII, I (Autumn 1947): 1 (hereafter cited parenthetically in text as *Common*).

4. Marie Syrkin, *Your Schools, Your Children* (New York: L. B. Fischer, 1944) (hereafter cited parenthetically in text as *Schools*).

5. Charles Reznikoff, "Passover," *The Poems of Charles Reznikoff: 1918–1975* (New York: David R. Godine, 2006) 242.

6. Ira Eisenstein, *Reconstructing Judaism: An Autobiography* (New York: Reconstructionist Press, 1986) 162–164.

7. <http://www.ibiblio.org/pha/policy1942420101a.html>.

8. Yehuda Bauer, *A History of the Holocaust* (New York: Franklin Watts, 1982) 200–207 (hereafter cited parenthetically in text as Bauer).

9. Marie Syrkin, "What American Jews Did During the Holocaust," *Midstream* October 1982: 6–12 (hereafter cited parenthetically in text as *Mid.* October 1982).

Chapter 13. Postwar Projects: DP Camps, Blessed Is the Match, *Israel (pages 353–394)*

1. Marie Syrkin, *Blessed Is the Match* Rev. ed. (Philadelphia: Jewish Publication Society, 1980) 13 (hereafter cited parenthetically in text as *Blessed*).

2. Ben Halpern, "The Human story of 6,000,000 dead," rev. of *Blessed Is the Match,* by Marie Syrkin. Copy of unknown newspaper article given to me by David Bodansky.

3. Marie Syrkin, *Way of Valor: A Biography of Golda Meyerson* (New York: Sharon Books, 1955) 114 (hereafter cited parenthetically in text as *Valor*).

4. Michael Cohen, *Truman and Israel* (Berkeley: Univ. Of California Press, 1990) 111 (hereafter cited parenthetically in text as *Truman*).

5. In her October 1982 article in *Midstream*, "What American Jews Did During the Holocaust," Syrkin writes the following:

An indefatigable exponent of militancy, Peter Bergson, member of the Revisionist Irgun and organizer of an Emergency Committee to Save the Jews in 1943, is presently offering the unvarnished truth about the Jewish "establishment." A film devoted to his achievements, *Who Shall Live and Who Shall Die,* peddles a simple thesis: only the Irgun group tried to save Jews from extermination. Jewish leaders, among whom non-Begin Zionists were the chief malefactors, cared more about "getting into the Harvard club" than about rescue; they deliberately thwarted Bergson's valiant efforts. From the screen, an aging Bergson admonishes a shocked audience: "Wise should have torn his coat; Jews should have stoned the White House. If not for Jewish obstruction, he, Bergson, might have saved a million Jews."

In 2006, an off-Broadway play once again revived his story.

6. Moshe Halbertal, "Morality and Strategy in the War on Terror: The Israel Experience," lecture, YIVO, October 10, 2006.

7. Sara Schmidt, "Hagiography in the Diaspora," *American Jewish History* June 2004: 157–188 (hereafter cited in text as Schmidt).

8. David Grossman, "Memorial for Yitzhak Rabin," *Forward* 10 Nov. 2006, A13.

9. *B'nai Brith Hillel Foundations Foreign Student Program*. Report about Hillel's program to bring foreign students to study in the U.S. after World War II. Letter and report sent to Marie Syrkin on August 3, 1982, by Rabbi Oscar Groner, International Director.

10. Cynthia Ozick, "Remembering Maurice Samuel," *Art and Ardor* (New York: Alfred A. Knopf, 1983) 214.

11. Irving Howe, "Maurice Samuel, 1895–1972," *New York Times Book Review*, (May 21, 1972) 55.

12. Marie Syrkin, ed. "The S.S. Exodus," *Golda Meir Speaks Out* (London: Weidenfeld and Nicolson, 1973) 66–72.

13. Amos Oz, *A Tale of Love and Darkness* (London: Chatto & Windus, 2003) 344 (hereafter cited parenthetically in text as *Tale*).

14. David Ben-Gurion, *Israel: A Personal History* (New York: Funk & Wagnalls, 1971) 92 (hereafter cited parenthetically in text as Ben-Gurion).

Chapter 14. Academia at Last: The Brandeis Years (pages 395–432)

1. Abram L. Sachar, *A Host at Last* Spec. ed. (Boston: Little, Brown, 1976) 217.

2. Irving Howe, "The New York Intellectuals: A Chronicle and a Critique," *Commentary* Oct. 1968: 29.

3. Carole Kessner, *The "Other" New York Jewish Intellectuals* (New York: NYU Press, 1994).

4. Marie Syrkin, "The Literature of the Holocaust: I. The Diaries," *Midstream* May 1966: 3–20.

5. Marie Syrkin, "Toynbee and the Jews" reprinted in *State of the Jews*, with a response by Arnold Toynbee and a reply by Marie Syrkin.

6. Maurice Samuel, *The Professor and the Fossil* (New York: Alfred A. Knopf, 1956).

7. Irving Howe would revise his position to a more positive one at a later time. And Philip Rahv would leave his estate to the State of Israel.

8. Charles Reznikoff, *The Manner Music* (Santa Barbara: Black Sparrow Press, 1977).

9. Charles Reznikoff's letters to Marie Syrkin between 1928 and 1939 became available in 1989 when they were added to the Register of Charles Reznikoff Papers 1912–1976 (MSS 0009) held in the Mandeville Special Collections Library of the Geisel Library, University of California, San Diego. There are no later letters except for a letter of will dated 1961.

10. On April 10, 1977, Irving Howe wrote to his friend Marie Syrkin, "I'm very well. I have formed an attachment with a lovely Israeli woman — which perhaps rounds out my return . . . I expect to be going to Israel in August. . . . Any chance of seeing you there?" (Archives 1 f. 5).

11. Irving Howe, *A Margin of Hope: An Intellectual Autobiography* (San

Diego: Harcourt Brace Janovich, 1982) (hereafter cited parenthetically in text as *Margin*).

12. In a letter to Marie Syrkin of April 10, 1977, Irving Howe recalled the furor that had surrounded the Arendt report about the Eichmann trial: "I've read the new introduction to Blessed with pleasure. It stirred up memories of the old debates after Arendt's book came out. That was really quite a fight, wasn't it?"

13. Hannah Arendt, *Eichmann in Jerusalem: A Report on the Banality of Evil* (New York: Viking Press, 1965).

14. Michael Musmanno, "Man with an Unspoiled Conscience," *The New York Times Book Review,* May 19, 1963.

15. In the January issue of the *New York Review* Hannah Arendt had written an article titled "The Formidable Dr. Robinson," who had attacked her book on Eichmann pointing out that she had not read among other reports, the Yiddish language accounts of the tragedy. On March 17, 1966, in an article titled "The Jewish Establishment," Marie Syrkin responded to Arendt's article. A reply by Hannah Arendt followed Syrkin's piece.

16. For a counter-argument to those suggesting a One-State Solution, see Alvin Rosenfeld, "'Progressive' Jewish Thought and the New Anti-Semitism," American Jewish Committee <http://www.ajc.org/>, file format PDF/Adobe Acrobat.

17. Tom Segev, *1967: Israel, the War and the Year That Transformed the Middle East* (New York: Henry Holt, 2007).

18. Amnon Rubinstein, *The Zionist Dream Revisited* (New York: Schocken, 1984) 76 (hereafter cited parenthetically in text as Rubinstein).

19. Chaim Herzog, *The War of Atonement: October 1973* (Boston: Little Brown, 1975) 18 (hereafter cited parenthetically in text as Herzog).

20. This was not his first prize: In 1963, he had been awarded the Kovner Prize by the Jewish Book Council of America.

Epilogue (pages 433–446)

1. Mark A. Raider and Miriam B. Raider-Roth, eds., *The Plough Woman: Records of the Pioneer Women of Palestine* (1932; Waltham: Brandeis University Press, 2002).

2. Lou Kaddar, Golda Meir's personal assistant, gave me a packet of letters that Marie Syrkin wrote to her during the period from 1972 to 1981. The letters from Kaddar to Marie are held in the American Jewish Archives in the Marie Syrkin Papers.

3. Titled "For G.M.," the poem is included in a typewritten group of poems gleaned by Marie Syrkin's longtime friend, the poet Naomi Replansky, from various sources. Replansky notes at the top of the first page, "written from 1979 on, after publication of *Gleanings."* The collection was given to me by Marie Syrkin's sister, Zivia Wurtele.

4. The poem was sent to me by Marie Syrkin's son, David Bodansky.

5. A letter from Marie Syrkin to Irving Howe (June 9, 1985) shows that Syrkin had not changed her views about Roth. Having just read *Zuckerman Bound,* in which Roth has created in the character of Milton Appel a thinly disguised Irving Howe, Syrkin writes, "Roth is apparently incapable of intellectual controversy or debate and can only flail out, reduced to shabby ad hominen cracks. Apparently you wounded him beyond all expectation (even my letter rankled). By now his obesession with the Jews has become an apologia for his whole life as well as an implicit plea for rehabilitation. . . . I can't understand why his 'best-seller' audience is not bored into refusal to buy this unrelenting exhibition of narcissism and nastiness. Even the verve that carried 'Portnoy' has deserted him." Of course, when she wrote this, Marie Syrkin had not read Roth's brilliant novel *American Pastoral,* which would be published twelve years later.

Index

Plates, located in the plate section following page 242, are indicated with the abbreviation "pl." in **bold**.

berg, 250; health scare of, 207–209; as high school English teacher, 165–166, 173, 218, 229, 244, 246, 265, 268, 276, 287, 289, 291; as Hillel Foreign Student Program screener, 379–380, 383; impact of traumas upon, 156–158, 164–165, 172, 174–175; interviews given by, 5, 448n4; as Israeli Foreign Affairs officer, 393; last days of, 4–5, 6–7; as literary critic, 332–334; literary critical faculty of, 128; love affairs of (see Roth, Samuel; Samuel, Maurice); love of walking, 436; marriages of (see Bodansky, Aaron; Reznikoff, Charles; Samuel, Maurice); Meir's influence on, 231; "moratorium" period in life of, 2–3, 174–175; as mother, 153–154, 156–157, 160; moves to United States, 50–51; as multilingual, 32, 49–50, 52, 393; musical talent of, 58; in Palestine, 233–240, 268–270; patriotism of, 325; as polemicist, 382–383, 400–401, 410–411; pregnancies of, 150, 152–153, 159; prose style of, 61, 154, 155, 235, 248, 271, 349; religious views of, 15–16, 201–202, 329–334; retirement of, 67, 430–431; roles played by, 2; romantic sentimentality of, 72–73, 94, 361–362; self-assertiveness of, 101; separate travels from Reznikoff, 232, 264; sexual mores of, 77–78, 81, 87, 96, 103, 179; social temperament of, 219; university education of (see Cornell University [Ithaca, N.Y.]); U.S. public education critiqued by, 348–349; writing habits of, 353; WWI war effort and, 123–124; Yiddish poetry translations of, 155, 174, 188–189, 245
——nonfiction writings: *Blessed Is the Match*, 357–363, 375; *Golda Meir: Israel's Leader*, 421–422, **pl.**; *Golda Meir: Woman with a Cause*, 421–422; *Man and Poet*, 286–287; *Nachman Syrkin: Socialist Zionist*, 45–46, 61, 404; *The State of the Jews*, 46, 262–263, 327, 369, 446; *Way of Valor*, 370, 402–403, 404, 420–421; *Your School, Your Children*, 348–349. See also *Jewish*

Frontier, MS as journalist at; *specific journals*
——poetry, 212, 245; "Aryan Love Song," 247–248; during college years, 152–153, 224–225; early efforts at, 72, 75, 83, 84, 89, 94–95; "Forgetting," 433; "For G.M.," 457n3; "For Golda," 440; "For Joel," 442; *Gleanings: A Diary in Verse*, 149–150, 353–354, 362, 434, 446; "Inhibitions," 433–434; "Maternity," 150; memorial poem for first son, 359, 432; "My Uncle in Treblinka," 372–373; "Old Letters," 149–150; "On the Palisades," 436; "On the Record," 254–255; "Quotations," 163; on Reznikoff's death, 431–432; Reznikoff's influence on, 219; "Saint Joan," 362; "Second Chance," 1; "Shirley," 166; "To a Christian Friend," 353–354
——as Zionist activist/journalist, 167; American awareness of Holocaust and, 340–343; *Avuka* and, 154–155; awards received by, 443–445, **pl.**; Biltmore Manifesto and, 346–347; during college years, 145, 173; DP camps investigated by, 373–374, **pl.**; eye-witness reports/commentary, 245; growing reputation, 175–180, 224; Jewish refugee problem and, 327–328; on *Kol Israel* radio station, 363–365; on Palestinian nationalism, 423–425; on Sadat visit to Jerusalem, 437–438; Samuel and, 173–174; TV appearances of, 421, 443; U.S. pro-Nazi elements and, 324–327; at World Jewish Congress, 272–274; as WZO/Jewish Agency Executive member, 412–415, 420, 425; as Zionist Congress delegate, 307, 308–314, 374

Syrkin, Masha (aunt; stepmother), 38, 103; child born to, 150–151; marries Nachman Syrkin, 138–140, 145, 159; MS moves in with, 165, 180; as MS's stepmother, 159

Syrkin, Nachman (father): appearance of, 22, 65, 145, **pl.**; Bassya's illness/death and, 66–67, 71–72; birth of, 12–13; Bodansky and, 141–144, 147, 160;